Instructional Models
Strategies for Teaching in a Diverse Society

Second Edition

Thomas J. Lasley II
University of Dayton

Thomas J. Matczynski
University of Dayton

James B. Rowley
University of Dayton

WADSWORTH

THOMSON LEARNING ™

Australia • Canada • Mexico • Singapore • Spain • United Kingdom • United States

WADSWORTH

THOMSON LEARNING

Education Editor: Dan Alpert
Development Editor: Tangelique Williams
Editorial Assistant: Lilah Johnson
Technology Project Manager: Jeanette Wiseman
Marketing Manager: Becky Tollerson
Advertising Project Manager: Bryan Vann
Project Manager, Editorial Production: Trudy Brown
Print/Media Buyer: Barbara Britton

Permissions Editor: Stephanie Keough-Hedges
Production Service: Forbes Mill Press
Text Designer: Cloyce J. Wall
Copy Editor: Ardella Crawford
Cover Designer: Stephen Rapley
Cover Image: PhotoDisc
Compositor: Wolf Creek Press
Text and Cover Printer: Phoenix Color

Printed in the United States of America
1 2 3 4 5 6 7 06 05 04 03 02

For more information about our products, contact us at:
Thomson Learning Academic Resource Center
1-800-423-0563
For permission to use material from this text, contact
us by:
Phone: 1-800-730-2214
Fax: 1-800-730-2215
Web: http://www.thomsonrights.com

Library of Congress Cataloging-in-Publication Data

Lasley, Thomas J.
    Instructional models : strategies for teaching in a
diverse society / Thomas J. Lasley II, Thomas J.
Matczynski, James Rowley.—2nd ed.
        p.   cm
    Includes bibliographical references and index.
    ISBN: 0-534-52840-6
    1. Teaching—United States. 2. Multicultural
education—United States. 3. Instructional systems—
United States—Design. 4. Minorities—Education—
United States. 5. Educational change—United States.
I. Title: Instructional models. II. Matczynski,
Thomas J. III. Rowley, James B. IV. Title.

LB 1025.3 .L37 2002
371.102—dc21   2001043526

Wadsworth/Thomson Learning
10 Davis Drive
Belmont, CA 94002-3098
USA

Asia
Thomson Learning
60 Albert Street, #15-01
Albert Complex
Singapore 189969

Australia
Nelson Thomson Learning
102 Dodds Street
South Melbourne, Victoria 3205
Australia

Canada
Nelson Thomson Learning
1120 Birchmount Road
Toronto, Ontario M1K 5G4
Canada

Europe/Middle East/Africa
Thomson Learning
Berkshire House
168-173 High Holborn
London WC1 V7AA
United Kingdom

Latin America
Thomson Learning
Seneca, 53
Colonia Polanco
11560 Mexico D.F.
Mexico

Spain
Paraninfo Thomson Learning
Calle/Magallanes, 25
28015 Madrid, Spain

There is no need to add to the criticism
of our public schools. The critique is extensive
and can hardly be improved on.
The processes of learning and teaching,
too, have been exhaustively studied.
One thinks of the books of…Jonathan Kozol,
Herbert Kohl. . . . The question now is what to do.

GEORGE DENNISON

In memory of
Thomas J. Matczynski

T. J. L.

For my sons,
Joseph and Jonathan . . .
May learning be the greatest adventure
of your lives

J. B. R.

Brief Contents

Contents

Ⓢ ECTION B: EFFECTING INSTRUCTIONAL MODEL USAGE

UNIT 1: MODELS THAT FOSTER REASONING SKILLS

UNIT 4: MODELS THAT FOSTER RELATING SKILLS

SECTION C: REFLECTING ON INSTRUCTIONAL MODEL USAGE

Preface

Teachers often bemoan their teacher-preparation experiences with horror stories concerning the lack of involvement with the "real world of teaching," instructors who were not aware of the technological advances available for classroom use, programs and instruction that did not expose them to the numerous culturally diverse groups in our society, programs where courses and experiences were fragmented and splintered, and a curriculum that rarely focused on the repertoire of instructional models and the corresponding academic and social skills needed by tomorrow's citizens. Although many teacher education programs have begun to address selected structural and curricular problems, the profession must do something about the current teacher workforce in terms of valid criticisms about teacher instructional intransigence and about the impact that teachers make on student learning. Far too many teachers teach just as they were taught. This text is a partial response to this circumstance. It provides a means to identify, describe, apply, and explore various instructional models and their subset of pedagogical skills.

When I heard a schoolteacher warn the other night about the invasion of the American educational system by foreign curriculums, I wanted to yell at the television set, "Lady, they're already here." It has already begun because the world is here. The world has been arriving at these shores for at least ten thousand years from Europe, Africa, and Asia.

ISHMAIL REED

Instructional Models: Strategies for Teaching in a Diverse Society is designed for preservice and inservice teachers of any subject area who are interested in exploring more fully the instructional options that students in America's classrooms need in order to achieve learning goals. The culturally diverse context of this text is limited to an examination of how the cognitive processing skills of learners, based upon gender and racial characteristics, can be enhanced or diminished by the instructional models used by teachers.

The intended audience is preservice and inservice teachers who are in the process of expanding their repertoire of instructional models and teaching skills and who have not been exposed, in a practical way, to the expanding body of research findings concerning the teaching-learning process. Teachers play a central role in defining the teaching-learning process; they are the central players in reforming education; and, they must acquire a repertoire of teaching abilities and skills and the knowledge of how to work with culturally diverse populations of students in order to be successful in working with the students now populating American schools.

Instructional Models takes a broad approach to the multiple teaching models, skills, and techniques that are so necessary in working with culturally diverse student populations. American communities are becoming more pluralistic each year. This nation includes large numbers of people from many different cultures, ethnic and racial backgrounds, and lifestyles. We are increasingly becoming aware of these differences through our experiences in schools, in the workplace, and in our everyday lives. In Chapter 2, we describe the influence that culture exerts in determining an individual's learning style and the positions and values each individual holds concerning the various issues confronting our society. Throughout this text, we will offer ideas, activities, and directions that can be utilized in teaching culturally diverse populations of students—the suggestions relate to issues surrounding our becoming a more diverse nation that celebrates and values the diversity of America's people.

Further, *Instructional Models* provides teachers with practical applications of the models presented from both fictional and "real-world" classroom settings. Whether the reader is an undergraduate student, a graduate student, or a staff-development participant, the lessons and activities found within this text will provide assistance in using the various instructional models. Furthermore, teachers will find valuable implementation suggestions, applicational examples, and evaluation criteria for each instructional model presented in this text. One disclaimer must be mentioned, however, before we proceed: Given the numerous variables that go into instructional decision-making, we can honestly say that no one instructional model can or does address all student cognitive skills or styles within a given lesson. Curricular demands, student motivation, and student cognitive styles are among some of the considerations teachers must take into account when designing lessons. These considerations are identified and discussed within each chapter.

We have divided the text into three sections. Section A, "Contextualizing Instructional Model Usage," presents the conceptual framework for the text. In Chapter 1, "The Educational Context for Diversity," we document why the study of instructional models is necessary in the context of the changing demographic categories of race and gender in the United States and the effects of these demographic changes upon classroom instruction. We also describe how to foster student growth that is more responsive to the demands for greater teacher accountability. A critical component of this text is promoting and managing diversity in the classroom in order to develop individual student knowledge and skill. In Chapter 2, "Culturally Diverse Learners," we provide information concerning cognitive styles of learning; we present the major research findings concerning the relationship of gender, race, and cognitive styles; and we describe the implications of the research on cognitive styles for teacher use of alternative instructional models. Section B, "Effecting Instructional Model Usage," provides a thorough description of the planning process for instruction. In Chapter 3, "Instructional Alignment," a brief description of the various instructional models and families presented in subsequent chapters is presented. In addition, this chapter focuses upon the need for teachers to plan instructional lessons; the role of goals and objectives in planning; and how to develop performance objectives in the cognitive, affective, and psychomotor domains. Finally, ideas on how to evaluate student achievement of the performance objectives are presented.

In Chapters 4 through 11, we describe the characteristics of different models for presenting skills, content, and ideas to students. The chapters are divided into 11 components:

1. *Introduction.* Each chapter begins with a brief anticipatory set relative to the model. The introductory ideas suggest how the model creates a richer environment for student learning.

2. *Case Study.* Each chapter begins with a classroom episode demonstrating the usage of the model. This consists of a set of classroom interactions with the teacher implementing the instructional model.

3. *Theoretical Perspective.* Each instructional model is described in detail along with supporting research data. This description provides the philosophical and psychological underpinnings behind each model, and the learning skills that are being developed and learned by students.

4. *Teaching Phases.* Each chapter provides a detailed description of how to plan lessons and units utilizing the model. Examples of lessons including goals, objectives, and sample activities are provided. Once planning is complete, the reader encounters selected instructional alternatives. Useful and practical ideas on how to implement each model discussed are provided. Elementary and secondary school examples are presented so that the reader is aware of how each instructional model is implemented for each level of schooling.

5. *Applications to Diverse Classrooms.* Each chapter provides a description of how the instructional model relates to the learning needs of diverse populations of students. The learning skills taught by using the instructional model are identified through the use of cognitive style strengths based upon gender and cultural group. Examples of the use of alternative cognitive styles are made available to the reader, especially regarding the use of relational and analytical cognitive skills.

6. *Prevalent Issues in Diverse Classrooms.* Each chapter includes a discussion of those common issues that classroom teachers have experienced in implementing each instructional model. Particular attention is given to how the instructional model enhances the inclusiveness of the classroom teacher in embracing the ideas of all students.

7. *Evaluation Criteria.* Each chapter includes evaluation processes and examples for the reader to use in assessing instructional model usage. A brief description of evaluation procedures is based upon the model underpinnings and skills to be developed by teachers.

8. *Sample Lessons.* Each chapter includes two case studies that should help readers understand how to implement the instructional model. The second case study includes reflections by the teacher who actually taught the lesson. The teacher reflects on both the effectiveness and problems associated with the model.

9. *Lesson Preparation.* Each chapter offers suggestions on how to prepare lessons.

10. *Technology.* Each chapter includes a discussion of how technology can be used to both enhance and extend teacher use of the model and student engagement with ideas.

11. *Summary.* Each chapter concludes with a summary of the major components of the model and a brief discussion of the model's strengths and usage with diverse populations.

Section C, "Reflecting on Instructional Model Usage," consists of Chapter 12, "Developing Teachers for the Culturally Diverse." In this chapter, emphasis is on teachers as leaders of the instructional process, Fuller (1969) and Fuller and Bown's (1975) research on teacher career stages, the application of these stages to teacher decision making in terms of the purpose of schooling, inclusive and noninclusive teacher behaviors that determine student opportunity to learn, coaching as a vehicle for self-improvement, and the kind of society for which children are being prepared to live.

The text concludes by emphasizing the importance of encouraging and supporting continuous improvement and the growth of school staffs through the use of an action planning format. Individually, the chapters provide glimpses of both the complexity and intricacies of effective teaching. Though some "scripting" in teaching is now being encouraged through programs such as Success for All, truly professional teachers understand that no silver bullets for enhancing students learning exist. Good teaching is hard work: It requires thought, reflection and creativity. The models outlined in this text are not the answer, but they can be, if used correctly, part of the solution.

REFERENCES

Fuller, F. 1969. "Concerns of Teachers: A Developmental Perspective." *American Educational Research Journal* 6: 207–226.

————, **and O. H. Bown.** 1975. "Becoming a Teacher." Pp. 25–52 in K. Ryan (ed.), *Teacher Education.* 74th Yearbook of the National Society for the Study of Education. Chicago: University of Chicago Press.

Reed, I. 1988. "America: The Multinational Society." *Multi-Cultural Literacy.* St. Paul, MN: Graywolf Press.

Tyson, H. 1994. *Who Will Teach the Children?: Progress and Resistance in Teacher Education.* San Francisco: Jossey-Bass.

Acknowledgments

The first edition of this book included an acknowledgment written by Dr. Thomas Matczynski. As we were preparing to revise the text, Dr. Matczynski took ill and subsequently died in February 2000. This book meant a great deal to him. In the first edition of the text, Tom reflected on those who most influenced him with the following thoughts:

> There are many individuals who have played a large part in the development and completion of this text. I would like to thank Bruce Joyce and Marsha Weil, who in the 1970s piqued my initial interest in the study and teaching of instructional models. Library research, proofreading, and checking reference accuracy are tedious and thankless jobs—thanks so much to Fr. Joe Massucci, Beverly Tillman, Carolyn Talbert-Johnson, Bickley Lucas, Jane Rafal, Dale Frederick, and Kristin Ross for their work, patience, and ideas.
>
> Mentors, colleagues, and friends are rare! Joe Rogus has been all of these for approximately 30 years. Thanks for reacquainting me, after 15 years as an administrator, with the instructional models used in working with teachers. Ellis Joseph, our former dean, has provided me with the opportunities and resources to continue growing and learning personally and professionally. What a great leader he is—he enables and empowers individuals to achieve, to create, and to be critics of society.
>
> In addition to editing, proofreading, indexing, and critiquing my work, my office colleague, Suzette Pico, impressively coordinated word processing, library research, and managing the work between two writers and innumerable draft versions that made this book possible. She rightfully earns accolades from all of our clients for her positive personality, caring and competent manner, and sharp administrative mind. Besides this book, she

has managed and organized my teaching schedule, consulting practice, and work with the Dayton Public Schools. Thank you so much, Suzette—you are without peer!

T. J. M.

These words resonate with me because they suggest that no book emerges without the thoughtful input of lots of personal and professional mentors and friends. For example, I, too, want to acknowledge the work of Bruce Joyce and Marsha Weil. Their book *Models of Teaching* fostered my initial interest in the topic of teaching models. My own students' struggles with the Joyce and Weil text was also the impetus for my desire to write this one. My hope is that this book will speak to some who are not able to connect with the ideas presented in the *Models of Teaching* text.

My greatest debt of gratitude goes to the hundreds of students who have used the models, taped their lessons, and allowed me to have a glimpse of their classroom life. I learned a lot by watching others teach—most of the classroom episodes described in Chapters 4 through11 are based on, either directly or indirectly, lessons presented by my graduate students. To all, thank you.

A number of professional colleagues made this book possible. I especially want to thank Patricia Hart, Carolyn Talbert-Johnson, Beverly Tillman, Joe Rogus, Joe Massucci, Jan Rafal, Dale Frederick, Bickley Lucas, and Kristin Ross.

This is the first major writing project of this type I have undertaken with Jim Rowley. Jim has been a professional friend for years and his contributions for this text, especially the technology focus of each chapter, really strengthen the text. Ms. Mary Kate Sableski was instrumental in doing much of the detail work for this revision. She is a good thinker and excellent problem solver.

Mea Maio, my office colleague, typed all of my portions of this text. No person I know evidences her patience and warmth in dealing with obsessive-compulsive behavior. She can also read my writing—although she has had to start wearing glasses. I hope the former was not the cause of the latter. For Mea's friendship, thoughtfulness, and caring support, I am most indebted!

Finally, I want to thank my family. Janet, my wife, is a teacher in an urban school. She caused me to see the need for the book, and she made me realize that many of the theoretical ideas had practical applications. My daughters, Elizabeth and Julianne, have spent a lot of time talking about their teachers— the good, the really good, and the "others." Their best teachers made them want to read when they came home and to seek knowledge even when outside the classroom. Janet, Elizabeth, and Julianne all influenced the way I thought about this book and helped shaped the ideas.

T. J. L.

Special Acknowledgment

The authors wish to express special thanks to the following teachers whose teaching episodes are the basis for many of the teaching episodes included in this book: Elaine Bennett, Judy Cox, Anne Futrell, Kerri Gayheart, Joyce Hayes, Stephanie Kortyna, Sarah Lloyd, David Morgan, Robin Root, Belinda

Seagraves, Cheryl Skamfer, Debbie Tauber, Abby Taylor, Melissa Webb, Lori Yowler, and Mindy Cline. Special thanks go to the teachers who put together the reflections in each of the model chapters: Tracy Roman, Chad Raisch, Janet Lasley, Mavis Franklin, Nonie Chick, Tina Buckmaster, and Emilie Greenwald. Though their lessons were "abbreviated" to make them readily readable, we hope we still maintained the clear structure of each lesson.

The authors wish to express gratitude to the following colleagues for their thoughtful critiques of the text: Jo Alexander, Auburn University at Montgomery; Ann Anzalone, Educational Consultant, Dayton, Ohio; Jan E. Goings Covington, Gonzaga University; Katharine Cummings, North Dakota State University at Fargo; Judy Lehr Guarino, Furman University; John McIntyre, Southern Illinois University; Alice K. Mikovch, Western Kentucky University; Karen Cachevki Williams, University of Wyoming; and Donna Wiseman, Northern Illinois University.

We are also grateful to the following reviewers and revision survey respondents who played an important role in our manuscript development process for the second edition: Donal Ambrose, Rider University; Sylven Beck, George Washington University; Thomas Bibler, University of Tennessee-Chattanooga; Sally Bing, University of Maryland–Eastern Shore; Clifford Edwards, Brigham Young University; Antonio Eppolito, LeMoyne College; Sharon Feaster, Augusta St. University; Bruce Larson, Western Washington University; Gretchen Lockett, Harris Stowe State University; Eveleen Lorton, University of Miami; Kelton Lustig, Christian University; Virginia McCormack, Ohio Dominican College; Clyde Paul, Southwest Missouri State University; Priscilla Salem, Friends University; and Susan Thompson, University of Memphis.

A Final Note

The teaching episodes in this text are in some instances fictional and in other instances variations on real classroom lessons. Pseudonyms are used for some of the classroom teachers involved; those teachers acknowledged provided the essential ideas for the narratives presented to the readers in the numerous teaching cases. The Case Study II and Teacher Reflections in Chapters 4 through 11 are real teachers and their own reflections.

One additional acknowledgment goes to Pat Kelleher. Pat helped immeasurably in revising the first couple chapters of this book. Her daughter then became quite ill and died in early 2001. We owe Pat a special debt of gratitude.

- *Contextualizing
Instructional Model Usage*

ONE

• *The Educational Context for Diversity*

Chapter Objectives

At the end of this chapter, readers will be able to

1. *Describe the demographic characteristics of the dominant racial and ethnic groups that populate American schools.*
2. *Describe how educational reform has evolved in American schools.*
3. *Outline strategies that have been and are being used to reform American schools.*

PURPOSE OF THE **T**EXT

Instructional Models focuses upon the culture of the classroom and the behaviors that teachers and all those who have instructional leadership roles exhibit in working with youngsters. *Instructional Models* is based upon the belief that teachers want to be a part of the solution, not a part of the problem. It is also based on the notion that students need to engage content in different ways in order to fully understand the complexity of ideas.

And a pervasive spiritual impoverishment grows. The collapse of meaning in life—the eclipse of hope and absence of love of self and others, the breakdown of family and neighborhood bonds—leads to the social deracination and cultural denudement of urban dwellers, especially children. We have created rootless, dangling people with little link to the supportive networks—family, friends, and school—that sustain some sense of purpose in life. We have witnessed the collapse of the spiritual communities that in the past helped America face despair, disease, and death and that transmit through the generations dignity and decency, excellence and elegance.

CORNEL WEST

CASE **S**TUDY

Today has not been a good day for Eduardo. His ear hurts, and his stomach feels upset; but his mom is running late for work, and he has to eat breakfast before she leaves. There is cold cereal to eat, but no milk to put on the cereal. Marguerite, his single mom, cannot take any more time off from work unless Eduardo is really sick, so he prepares to go to school alone. Before Marguerite leaves for work, she reminds Eduardo to return his library book; but by the time he leaves for school 45 minutes later, he has forgotten it. Eduardo, who is a 2nd grader, arrives too late for the school breakfast program and can't get anything else to eat until lunchtime. It is very hard for Eduardo to concentrate, to listen to his teacher, and to become involved with group activities, because his ear hurts so badly, and his stomach aches for some good food.

Eduardo's mom isn't having a good day herself! She can't concentrate on her work because she is constantly worrying about Eduardo. She wonders if he's gotten to school on time, if he's remembered his library book, and if he is concentrating on what the teacher is teaching. She is raising Eduardo alone. She is not receiving any support from his father and is having trouble making ends meet. She wants to be more involved in Eduardo's schooling, meet with his teacher, help with his homework, and get ideas on how best to help Eduardo, but she can't take time from work without losing the pay they both so badly need. Marguerite is working two minimum-wage jobs just to pay for food, clothing, and their apartment. No matter what she tries to do to help, she never seems to get ahead. Bills keep piling up, and no end is in sight! Marguerite knows Eduardo isn't doing his best in school and wonders about how much of what they are going through as a family affects his school progress. She doesn't know what to do and doesn't know where to go for help. ▪

Eduardo is not alone in today's world. More families need at least two incomes in order to make ends meet, but more children are a part of single-parent families than ever before in the history of this nation. Presently, mothers of two-thirds of America's preschool children and three-fourths of all school-age children work outside of the home. Of the homes where there is only a single parent, 42 percent are at the poverty level compared with only 8 percent of two-parent families.

Even more troubling is that in the fall of 1998, nearly half of all entering kindergartners came to school with one or more risk factors evident in their home environments. No data suggest that this situation has changed over the past couple of years. America's children are at risk (Thomas and Bainbridge, 2001).

And those risks are evident in both what happens at home and with what occurs at school. Sadker (2001) documents the reality of America's high risk environment—see Figure 1-1. As we begin the twenty-first century, we do need to focus on how schools can enhance life for students who come from a variety of families, racial and ethnic groups, economic situations, and multilingual environments. They are America's future.

❶HE CULTURALLY DIVERSE SCHOOL: A STATUS REPORT

Our nation's changing cultural demographics are playing a critical role in conversations concerning school success. The public school students of the future will be even more socially, economically, and educationally diverse than ever before; more students will come from backgrounds in which English is a second language, a circumstance that accounts for "15 percent of all children in urban schools" (Roberts, 1993, p. 60); and more will have a cultural and racial membership that is African, Hispanic (Latino), or Asian.

If the diverse characteristics of America's children were merged into one classroom, of thirty students . . .

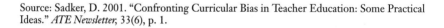

18 would be white.	5 would be African-American.
15 will live in a single-parent family at some point in childhood.	5 have a foreign-born mother.
15 will never complete a single year of college.	5 have no health insurance.
	5 live with a working relative but are poor nonetheless.
10 were born to unmarried parents.	4 were born to a teenage mother.
10 will be poor at some point in childhood.	4 speak a language at home other than English.
10 are a year or more behind in school.	
7 were born poor.	3 will never graduate from high school.
7 were born to a mother who did not graduate from high school.	3 live at less than half the poverty level.
	2 have a disability.
7 live with only one parent.	2 have difficulty speaking English.
6 would be Hispanic.	1 would be an Asian American.
6 live in a family receiving food stamps.	1 might be a Native American.
6 are poor today.	1 lives with neither parent.

Several are likely to be bi-racial or bi-cultural. And for every 22 classrooms . . . 1 student will be killed by gunfire before age 20.

FIGURE 1-1   Diversity of America's Children

Source: Sadker, D. 2001. "Confronting Curricular Bias in Teacher Education: Some Practical Ideas." *ATE Newsletter*, 33(6), p. 1.

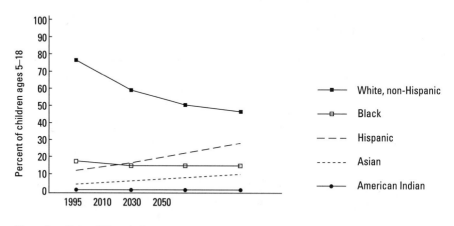

FIGURE 1-2   Changing School Population

Note: Percents do not add to 100 because the Hispanic population includes members of several races, including Blacks and Whites.

Source: Shade, B., C. Kelly, and M. Oberg. 1997. *Creating Culturally Responsive Classrooms*. Washington, DC: American Psychological Association, p. 76.

Figure 1-2 clearly illustrates that as the percentage of white students has gradually dropped (and will continue), minority student enrollments have grown, especially for Hispanics. Unfortunately, these "diverse" students tend to be most affected by the directions and consequences of societal change because they have limited voice in the content and direction of educational practice and social policy.

Chineworth (1996) notes that "Schools are powerful institutions. Schools are sources of learning, socialization, and indoctrination. . . . Schools can dispel myths and/or perpetuate them" (p. 16). She continues, "Individuals learn their community cultures at an early age. However, when they enter a learning environment, their cultures are displaced so that the hegemonic culture may be known" (p. 17). Chineworth suggests that introducing "the scholarship of 'multiculturalism' would help to initiate a new thrust for other cultures to view their own history" (p. 17).

The racial groups in this country have increased at vastly different rates. The sheer volume of new immigrants may demand that if inclusion is the goal of citizenship, then it will require much more tolerance by our present citizenry than has ever occurred in the past. Promoting and managing diverse populations is the next great challenge facing American society and its schools.

With the arrival of a new immigrant population, a corresponding group of immigrant children—approximately two million—has entered our nation's classrooms. Research from ETS suggests:

> In the three decades between 1950 and 1980, about 450,000 immigrants came to the United States legally each year. By 1980, that number had soared to 800,000 annually. One team of researchers has projected that about 22 percent of U.S. school-age youth in 2010 will be children of immigrants . . . compared to only 15 percent in 1990. (Carnevale and Fry, 2000, p. 17)

New immigrants to a country "typically arrive at the beginning of their prime childbearing years" (Riche, 1991, p. 28). Interestingly, that same group of immigrants tends to raise children who outperform American students in United States classrooms. Indeed, Steinberg (1996) reports in one of the largest studies of its kind:

> Foreign-born students—who, incidentally, report more discrimination than American-born youngsters and significantly more difficulty with the English language—nevertheless earn higher grades in school than their American-born counterparts. . . . It is not simply that immigrants are outperforming nonimmigrants on measures of school achievement. On virtually every factor we know to be *correlated* with school success, students who were not born in this country outscore those who were born here. And, when we look only at American-born students, we find that youngsters whose parents are foreign-born outscore those whose parents are native Americans. (p. 97)

According to all population projections, the face of America will become even more diverse in the decades ahead. As Figure 1-2 suggests, the United States population will look quite different by 2050. Indeed, some projections even indicate that European Americans will become a "minority" group by the year 2050. Educators must make every effort to understand the diverse students who are coming to schools, and they must be able to accept and value the gifts, talents, and background each child brings to the educational enterprise, and to help each youngster become a contributing and successful citizen of America's new future. Those youngsters are America's future leaders.

The data listed on the following pages are categorized according to the cultural groups described in this text. Clearly each of these groups can be divided into multiple subgroups. All the data are taken from different U.S. Census Bureau reports published during the past several years. Our point in making these observations is not as demographers to empirically document population facts but, rather, to illustrate the inherent and emerging diversity of American society. The key is to view the patterns and trends and not specific population facts.

Native Americans

- The Native American or Indian population grew from 0.8 percent of the total population in 1990 to 0.9 of the total population in the United States in 2000. This increase probably cannot be attributed to birthrate increases alone. For example, there is now a greater likelihood for individuals to report themselves as Native Americans.

- There were about 2 million American Indians, Eskimos, and Aleuts living in the United States in 1990, with a great majority living on 314 reservations. There are about 2.5 million people of Native American heritage living in the United States currently. Of that number 533,000 were students in elementary and secondary high schools.

- The educational achievement levels of Native Americans improved significantly during the 1980's but remained considerably below the national average: 66 percent of Native Americans over 25 years old were high school graduates. Only 9 percent of Native Americans completed a bachelor's degree, as compared with 20 percent of the total population. Table 1-1 describes the ten states where American Indians are most evidenced and provides the percentage of the total state population that Indians represent.

African Americans

- African Americans now represent 12.8 percent of the United States population. As reported for the 1998–99 school year, 7,932,000 black students attended public elementary and secondary schools.

- African American populations are largely located in urban cities, with the following cities having the largest proportion: Baltimore, Chicago, Detroit, Houston, Philadelphia, Los Angeles, Memphis, New Orleans, New York, and Washington, DC. African Americans represent 50 percent or more of the population in Baltimore, Detroit, Memphis, New Orleans, and Washington, D.C.—see Table 1-2 for descriptions of states in which the highest percentage of African Americans reside.

TABLE 1-1 States Ranked by American Indian and Alaska Native Population, July 1, 1999

State	Percent of Total Population
1. Alaska	16.4
2. New Mexico	9.5
3. South Dakota	8.2
4. Oklahoma	7.8
5. Montana	6.5
6. Arizona	5.5
7. North Dakota	4.8
8. Wyoming	2.3
9. Washington	1.8
10. Nevada	1.8

Source: Population Estimates Program, Population Division, U.S. Census Bureau, Washington, DC. Internet Release: August 30, 2000

TABLE 1-2 States Ranked by Black Population, July 1, 1999

State	Percent of Total Population
1. District of Columbia	64.4
2. Mississippi	36.5
3. Louisiana	32.4
4. South Carolina	29.8
5. Georgia	28.7
6. Maryland	28.1
7. Alabama	26.1
8. North Carolina	28.1
9. Virginia	20.1
10. Delaware	19.8

Source: Population Estimates Program, Population Division, U.S. Census Bureau, Washington, DC. Internet Release: August 30, 2000

Hispanic Americans

- The Hispanic American population grew more than all other cultural groups. It has expanded to a total of 32.4 million individuals, or 11.9 percent of the total United States population. In the 1998–99 school year there were 6,939,000 Hispanic students in the elementary and secondary public schools. The number of Hispanic Americans will surpass African, Asian, and Native Americans by the year 2020. They will represent 14 percent of the population in 2010, and 23 percent in 2050.

- Nearly 9 out of 10 Hispanic Americans live in just 10 states, and the largest proportion resides in just four states: California, Texas, New York, and Florida. Other states with significant numbers of Hispanic Americans in their population are: Illinois, New Jersey, Arizona, New Mexico, Colorado, and Massachusetts—see also Table 1-3.

Asian Americans

- In 2000, Asian Americans numbered over 10 million individuals, a rise from 8.5 million in 1990. The total Asian American population is 8 percent of the entire United States population. The increases in population are a result of immigration from China, Korea, the Philippines, and other Asian and Pacific Island areas.

- Education is highly valued in Asian communities, yet the educational achievement of various ethnic groups varies widely. For example, the proportion of Japanese completing high school in 1990 was 88 percent; the figure for the Hmong was only 30 percent. Table 1-4 describes where Asian Americans are living and the percent of the total population they represent.

TABLE 1-3 States Ranked by Hispanic Population, July 1, 1999

State	Percent of Total Population
1. New Mexico	40.7
2. California	31.6
3. Texas	30.2
4. Arizona	22.7
5. Nevada	16.8
6. Florida	15.4
7. Colorado	14.9
8. New York	14.6
9. New Jersey	12.6
10. Illinois	10.5

Source: Population Estimates Program, Population Division, U.S. Census Bureau, Washington, DC. Internet Release: August 30, 2000

TABLE 1-4   States Ranked by Asian and Pacific Islander Population, July 1, 1999

State	Percent of Total Population
1. Hawaii	63.6
2. California	12.2
3. Washington	6.8
4. New Jersey	5.8
5. New York	5.6
6. Nevada	4.9
7. Alaska	4.5
8. Maryland	4.0
9. Massachusetts	3.8
10. Virginia	3.8

Source: Population Estimates Program, Population Division, U.S. Census Bureau, Washington, DC. Internet Release: August 30, 2000

STATE OF EDUCATIONAL REFORM

While the schools' customers (that is, youngsters, parents, and employers) are changing dramatically in a demographic sense, many schools and school districts in this nation remain basically the same as they were well over 100 years ago. Our world is changing—into a world increasingly based upon a global economy strongly undergirded by the need for citizens who are scientifically, mathematically, and technologically literate. Workers for tomorrow's world will be those who are able to think and solve complex problems, make decisions based upon consensus techniques, engage in a process of lifelong learning, tolerate ambiguity and uncertainty in a fast-paced global society, acknowledge cultural diversity and its value to the total community, and work cooperatively in teams to create and implement new ideas. Writers rightfully have noted that the issue of "global competitiveness" will involve the educational sector (Barker, 1992; Osborne and Gaebler, 1992). While school administrators worry about comparative test scores with neighboring school districts, policymakers and business leaders are focusing upon comparative performances with students, nationally and internationally (Finn, Kanstoroom, and Petrilli, 1999; Stevenson and Stigler, 1992). Though the solutions proffered differ according to political disposition or personal ideology, all agree that the need for a new workforce to educate America's youngsters in a more diverse and global society is critical.

Unfortunately, far too many American schools and classrooms look just like they did in the early 1900s. For the most part, the following conditions still exist in schools today as they did a century ago:

1. School calendars are organized around the assumption of agrarian lifestyles.

2. Schools operate based upon conditions that were more prevalent during the industrial age—mass production and employee conformity. American schools look and function like factories, which likely explains why the factory metaphor is so frequently used in describing schools.

3. Students follow a lockstep structure of 12 years of "schooling"; they "collect" a certain number of Carnegie units.

4. School schedules are structured as if mothers were home to greet their children in the mid-afternoon and as if nuclear families were still the norm.

5. Student progress is measured through Carnegie unit accumulation, a practice designed at the beginning of the twentieth century. The number of units varies state by state, but the practice is almost universal.

6. School curricula are sequenced or articulated from one grade level to another, but teachers determine what to teach and how to teach it.

7. Instruction occurs predominantly through the model of deductive pedagogy (lecturing)—a higher education anomaly. Rarely do teachers utilize instruction that draws upon what Gardner (1985, 1991) calls students' multiple intelligences.

As a result of these conditions, students are still not realizing their full potential as learners. They have constricted perceptions of both their own potential and their own abilities; they see education as something that happens *at school*; and they measure their performance by rather narrow criteria of success (knowing answers), rather than on a broader understanding of what it means to be a learner (knowing how to ask questions and then find the answers to those questions). Botstein (1997) is more penetrating in his analysis. He writes: "The challenge . . . is to find ways to engage the early onset of adolescence and its attendant freedoms and habits. How can we harness the ages thirteen to eighteen effectively for learning?" (p. 85). Our answer is by creating new school structures (which goes beyond the scope of this book) and by developing new strategies for teaching content, which is our focus.

Adam Urbanski, a prominent voice in the American Federation of Teachers, stated it well when he reflected several years ago upon the nature of teaching and learning in American schools (Ribadeneira, 1990): "We know, based on research, that people remember about 10 percent of what they hear, 20 percent of what they see, 40 percent of what they discuss, and 90 percent of what they do. But we still largely use one teaching style: I talk, you listen, and you learn" (p. 1). Unfortunately, talking and teaching are considered synonymous by far too many teachers. As a result, too many active students who are physically and psychologically mature are treated like passive learners—the result is that they either psychologically withdraw or physically dropout.

The problem with schools is not that educators don't know what works. An abundance of research data exists concerning how the teaching-learning process works and what teachers can and should do that will stimulate motivation and learning in students. The problem is that many schools and teachers won't do what they should in terms of using the current research findings. As an example, many companies in the corporate world have software applications that teach reading, writing, and mathematics, yet only a small percentage of this nation's schools teach with sensitivity to what is known relative to computer applications. In fact, too few schools have computer hardware available for students to use such software effectively in classrooms. In the meantime, over the past 20 years, the corporate sector has not only drastically changed the way it does business (because of the computer), but also it has radically changed its training methods based upon technology and alternative instructional models.

What have schools done to adopt the advances in the workforce and the corresponding technology? Very little! Despite an information-rich, biotechnology-oriented world, outmoded instructional approaches and conditions persist. Educators must begin addressing how the current educational paradigm influences students and how they function in an academic environment. The current educational paradigm is based upon three antiquated beliefs:

Old Belief 1: Academic achievement is derived from innate ability,

Old Belief 2: Innate ability in youngsters is unevenly distributed among the population of students, and

Old Belief 3: The above two beliefs are unalterable.

Instructional Models directly challenges these beliefs. Educators must begin basing their instructional repertoire upon three fundamental new world views about schools and young people.

New Belief 1: All youngsters can learn at significantly higher levels if teacher instructional practice changes to accommodate the diverse learning styles of students. This is true *if* teachers understand that not all students can learn exactly the same thing, in the same amount of time, and at the same level of performance and that students need to have certain "conditions" met if they are to be ready to learn (Thomas and Bainbridge, 2001).

New Belief 2: Teachers can learn how to teach more successfully if they are provided with proper preparation. This is true *if* teachers are given appropriate opportunities to practice their teaching skills and are coached on their performance.

New Belief 3: Teachers must emphasize considerably higher expectations for students. This is true *if* teachers understand that high expectations do not mean high uniform performances. Not all students can achieve the same goals, but all students can experience a value-added measure if appropriate educational opportunities are provided.

Substantial research has been conducted concerning the teaching-learning process and teacher expectations (see Brophy, 1983; Dusek, 1985; Good and Brophy, 1997; Marshall and Weinstein, 1984; Rosenthal and Jacobson, 1968). That research provides historical context for why larger research entities such as the Educational Testing Service and the Milken Family Foundation have affirmed (a) that teachers do make a difference and (b) that what they do in classrooms makes that difference (see Wenglinsky, 2000). Wenglinsky found that classroom practices that engage students actively in learning do influence student achievement. Specifically:

The largest effects on student achievement came from classroom practices. Students whose teachers conduct hands-on learning activities outperform their peers by about 70% of grade level in math and 40% of grade level in science. Students whose teachers emphasize higher-order thinking skills out perform their peers by about 40% of a grade level in math. (p. 7)

Educators must begin applying these research findings to instructional and curricular practices in a way that maximizes the learning of every student regardless of age, gender, racial and ethnic background, or physical ability. When students walk into classrooms, they need to be confronted with a teacher who sees their potential and helps them achieve their potential as learners. Rose (1995) describes one such teacher (Yvonne); she sees the possibilities in learners and the active nature of the teaching process:

> Yvonne continued, "Teachers will say either 'We can't lower our standards' or 'This poor child is reading below grade level, so I'll need a third- or fourth-grade book.' But what you need is to find a way to make that eighth grade book *accessible*. You have to respect the child. . . . I used to give a speech to new teachers in which I began by enumerating all the adjectives used to describe our kids: *slow, poor, impoverished, deprived, oppressed*. We get so busy looking at children in terms of labels that we fail to look for the *potential*—and to demand that kids live up to that potential. I tell these teachers, 'Do not think that because a child cannot read a text, he cannot read *you*.' Children can tell right off those people who believe in them and those who patronize them. They can tell once they come into the room—as if there's a smell in the air—they can tell right away if this teacher means business or if this teacher is, as they say, *jive*. They rise to whatever expectations are set. They rise or fail to rise. And when they rise, they can sometimes rise to great heights." (p. 17)

RATIONALE FOR INSTRUCTIONAL REFORM

In 1983, the nation sounded the educational alarm with the now-famous report *A Nation at Risk* (National Commission on Excellence in Education, 1983). Since that report was released, over 300 national and state reports have been presented; most states have increased graduation requirements; and 700 state statutes have been enacted stipulating what should be taught and how it should be presented (Sadker and Sadker, 2000). Most reports focus upon concepts such as lengthening of the school day; increasing the standards for high school graduation, including emphasis on the academic core and the "educational basics"; emphasizing mathematics, science, and technology; developing business and industrial partnerships; improving pay and working conditions of teachers; emphasizing the use of technology, including computers, in the education of youngsters; and implementing state legislative exit examinations for high school graduation. Many of these recommendations have been implemented at the state level though a regulatory process to mandate reforms. The authors of the reports, the state legislative bodies, and various local boards of education hold a set of assumptions concerning how schools should function given the current organizational structure. That structure, all too often, is a bureaucratic model in which management decides what is to be accomplished, directs employees to accomplish what has been dictated, and monitors the work that is to be implemented. The accountability mania currently sweeping the United States is understandable, but will likely only exacerbate this situation. The notion that regulatory agencies and their mandates can "change" what schools do and how these ends are accomplished is highly problematic. True, enhanced accountability will change (and is changing) school cultures, but only teachers can effect the kinds of change that will truly make a long-term difference in students' lives, and teachers can effect such changes only if they know how to work with parents and to build on the culture of the students.

Given the recommendations, mandates, and large sums of money that have been invested in reform, just what has been the progress to date? Some suggest the impact of reform initiatives upon youngsters in America's schools has been minimal and characterized by a myriad of "movements" that have resulted in more confusion than answers (Ravitch, 2000). There have been lots of innovations, but a limited number of meaningful changes. Ravitch writes: "If there is a lesson to be learned from the river of ink that was spilled in the education disputes of the twentieth century, it is that anything in education that is labeled a 'movement' should be avoided like the plague" (p. 435). Cuban (1988) notes that "innovation after innovation has been introduced into school after school, but the overwhelming number of them disappear without a finger-print" (p. 86). In essence, the critics claim, America has educational innovation without educational change. The school dropout rate in this country remains high, and concerns about the preparedness of American students remains strong. But not all news is bad. In 2000, ACT and SAT scores were up (see Figures 1-3 and 1-4). More important, high school students appear to be taking tougher courses. Further, Americans are attempting to educate a much broader segment of the population than was evidenced decades ago. Botstein (1997) observes:

> Many critics of American schools are fond of comparing today's results with those from the past, forgetting that during the first half of this century only a quite narrow and more privileged part of society received the chance to finish high school. If one eliminated the lower third of today's high school graduates—defined not by race or ethnicity, but by family income—and tested the remainder, American schools might not look so bad when compared with those of other countries. (p. 87)

More and more school, business, and community leaders recognize that school reform has not worked, and they believe they know why: Reform efforts have been piecemeal, and the emphasis upon what occurs in the classroom with regard to teaching practices and behavior has not been highlighted. Teachers do make a difference, a fact that is highly advertised as part of Sanders' Tennessee value-added studies that illustrate how an individual teacher can impact the learning of a student (Sanders, 2001). The basic problem with school structures is a failure to create at individual school sites a collaborative culture between the community, which includes parents and student peer cultures, and the school. The hierarchical school structures are efficient but ineffective in engendering educational programs that address the needs of the diverse student communities. Noncollaborative structures cannot adjust to groups or individuals with needs different from the goals that the traditional organization defines. For this and other reasons that will be described

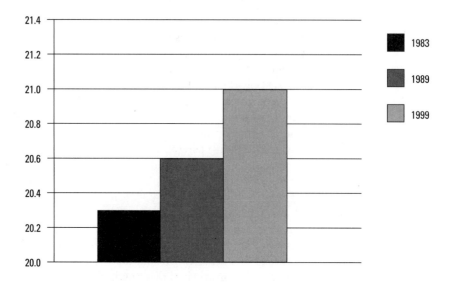

FIGURE 1-3   ACT National Average Composite Scores, 1983, 1989, and 1999

Note: The ACT uses a scale of 0–36.

Source: *Do You Know the Good News About American Education?* 1997. Center on Educational Policy and American Youth Policy Forum. p.17.

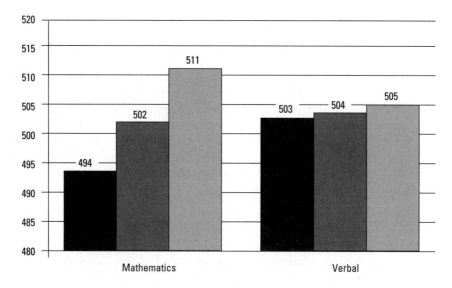

FIGURE 1-4   Mean SAT Scores for College-Bound Seniors, 1983, 1989, and 1999

Note: The SAT uses a scale of 200–800.

Source: *Do You Know the Good News About American Education?* 1997. Center on Educational Policy and American Youth Policy Forum. p.16.

later, there is an urgent need to reconceptualize how schools function collaboratively with a variety of significant others (for example, parents) and how teachers can work collegially to use and implement new instructional models. The focus of this text is on the latter, but the significance of the former cannot be dismissed. Stevenson, Chen, and Lee (1993) cogently note:

> We attribute the early superiority of American children to the greater cognitive stimulation provided by their parents, who indicated that they read more frequently to their young children, took them on more excursions, and accompanied them to more cultural events than did the Chinese or Japanese parents. . . . As American children grow older, parents appear to be less likely to provide the kinds of enriched out-of-school experiences that they did before the children entered first grade. (p. 55)

Much of the Japanese success has been attributed to the collegial nature of the teachers' lives within schools (Stevenson and Stigler, 1992; Stigler and Hiebert, 1999). Something similar can and must occur in American schools. In essence, American teachers need to work more collaboratively with both parents and their teacher colleagues. Almost 20 years have passed since *A Nation at Risk* (National Commission on Excellence in Education, 1983); thousands of meetings have been held; and the mass media has covered reform with forums, special news editions, and television specials. Significant numbers of people are involved in the reform juggernaut, including the President of the United States, members of Congress, governors, state school officials, legislatures across the country, school boards, and executives from almost every large organization in the country. The need has been so pressing to the perceived survival of American society that the President and the nation's governors established a presidential commission to examine the problem and make recommendations. An outcome of their activities has been the establishment of an educational "Marshall Plan," with a concomitant set of national educational goals. The goals are both ambitious and comprehensive:

1. All children in America will start school ready to learn.

2. High school graduation rates will increase to at least 90 percent.

3. American students will leave grades four, eight, and twelve having demonstrated competency over challenging subject matter including English, mathematics, science, history, and geography. All students will learn to use their minds well, so that they may be prepared for responsible citizenship, future learning, and productive employment in our modern economy.

4. The nation's teaching force will have access to programs for the continued improvement of their professional skills and the opportunity to acquire the knowledge and skills needed for instructing students for the next century.

5. United States students will be first in the world in mathematics and science achievement.

6. Every adult American will be literate and will possess the knowledge and skills necessary to compete in a global economy and exercise the rights and responsibilities of citizenship.

7. Every school will be free of drugs and violence and offer a disciplined environment conducive to learning.

8. Every school will promote partnerships that will increase parental involvement and participation in promoting the social, emotional, and academic growth of children. (U.S. Department of Education, 1994)

Governors and chief state school officials now have the challenge to develop strategies to reach these national goals. Some data suggest that progress is being made (see Table 1-5). Almost everyone believes these goals are critical to the survival of our nation; they also believe we need to reform schools. What they disagree about is how to achieve these goals. How can overall progress toward goal achievement be made more positive? We emphasize the need to reinvent teaching practices and the culture of teachers' classrooms because of the complex, changing demographics occurring in American society. American culture is dynamic and diverse. There is not a prototypical American! And the diversity is most evident when considering facts about cultural groups and women, the welfare and prison systems, America's standard of living, school dropouts, and innovative technology.

TABLE 1-5 Progress Report on National Educational Goals

Since 1989, the nation has been working toward the achievement of national education goals crafted by Presidents Bush and Clinton and the nation's governors. Following are measures of those goals that schools, students, educators, and policymakers were expected to meet by 2000. As indicated, the nation has made progress in some areas, but no measurable headway in others.

	Baseline	**Update**	**Progress**
Goal 1: Ready to Learn			
All children in America will start school ready to learn.			
Children's Health Index: *Has the U.S. reduced the percentage of infants born with 1 or more health risks? (1990 vs. 1996)*	37%	34%	Better
Immunizations: *Has the U.S. increased the percentage of 2-year-olds who have been fully immunized against preventable childhood diseases? (1994 vs. 1997)*	75%	78%	Better
Family-Child Reading and Storytelling: *Has the U.S. increased the percentage of 3- to 5-year-olds whose parents read to them to tell them stories regularly? (1993 vs. 1996)*	66%	72%	Better
Preschool Participation: *Has the U.S. reduced the gap (in percentage points) in preschool participation between 3- to 5-year-olds from high- and low-income families? (1991 vs. 1996)*	28 points	29 points*	No change
Goal 2: School Completion			
The high school graduation rate will increase to at least 90 percent.			
High School Completion: *Has the U.S. increased the percentage of 18- to 24-year-olds who have a high school credential? (1990 vs. 1997)*	86%	86%	No change

TABLE 1-5 Progress Report on National Educational Goals *(continued)*

	Baseline	Update	Progress

Goal 3: Student Achievement and Citizenship

All students will leave grades 4, 8, and 12, having demonstrated competency over challenging subject matter including English, mathematics, science, foreign languages, civics and government, economics, arts, history, and geography.

Reading Achievement: *Has the U.S. increased the percentage of students who meet the goals panel's performance standard in reading? (1992 vs. 1994)*

	Baseline	Update	Progress
Grade 4	29%	30%*	No change
Grade 8	29%	30%*	No change
Grade 12	40%	36%	Worse

Writing Achievement: *Has the U.S. increased the percentage of students who can produce basic, extended, developed, or elaborated responses to narrative writing tasks? (1992 vs. 1994)*

	Baseline	Update	Progress
Grade 4	55%	—	
Grade 8	78%	—	
Grade 12	—	—	

Mathematics Achievement: *Has the U.S. increased the percentage of students who meet the goals panel's performance standard in mathematics? (1990 vs. 1996)*

	Baseline	Update	Progress
Grade 4	13%	21%	Better
Grade 8	15%	24%	Better
Grade 12	12%	16%	Better

Science Achievement: *Has the U.S. increased the percentage of students who meet the goals panel's performance standard in science? (1996)*

	Baseline	Update	Progress
Grade 4	29%	—	
Grade 8	29%	—	
Grade 12	21%	—	

History Achievement: *Has the U.S. increased the percentage of students who meet the goals panel's performance standard in history? (1994)*

	Baseline	Update	Progress
Grade 4	17%	—	
Grade 8	14%	—	
Grade 12	11%	—	

Geography Achievement: *Has the U.S. increased the percentage of students who meet the goals panel's performance standard in geography? (1994)*

	Baseline	Update	Progress
Grade 4	22%	—	
Grade 8	28%	—	
Grade 12	27%	—	

(continued)

— Data not available
* Change considered not statistically significant

TABLE 1-5 Progress Report on National Educational Goals *(continued)*

	Baseline	*Update*	*Progress*

Goal 4: Teacher Education and Professional Development

The nation's teaching force will have access to programs for the continued improvement of their professional skills and the opportunity to acquire the knowledge and skills needed to instruct and prepare all American students for the next century.

	Baseline	*Update*	*Progress*
Teacher Preparation: *Has the U.S. increased the percentage of secondary school teachers who hold an undergraduate or graduate degree in their main teaching assignment? (1991 vs. 1994)*	*66%*	*63%*	*Worse*
Teacher Professional Development: *Has the U.S. increased the percentage of those reporting that they participated in professional-development programs on one or more topics since the end of the previous school year? (1994)*	*85%*	*—*	

Goal 5: Mathematics and Science

United States students will be first in the world in mathematics and science achievement.

International Mathematics Achievement: *Has the U.S. improved its standing on international mathematics assessments? (1996)*

Grade 4	*7 out of 25 countries scored above the U.S.*
Grade 8	*20 out of 40 countries scored above the U.S.*
Grade 12	*14 out of 20 countries scored above the U.S.*

International Science Achievement: *Has the U.S. improved its standing on international science assessments? (1996)*

Grade 4	*1 out of 25 countries scored above the U.S.*
Grade 8	*9 out of 40 countries scored above the U.S.*
Grade 12	*11 out of 20 countries scored above the U.S.*

Mathematics and Science Degrees: *Has the U.S. increased mathematics and science degrees (as a percentage of all degrees) awarded to*

	Baseline	*Update*	*Progress*
• all students? (1991 vs. 1995)	*39%*	*42%*	*Better*
• minorities (Blacks, Hispanics, American Indians/Alaskan Natives)? (1991 vs. 1995)	*39%*	*40%*	*Better*
• females? (1991 vs. 1995)	*35%*	*37%*	*Better*

Goal 6: Adult Literacy and Lifelong Learning

Every adult will be literate and possess the knowledge to compete in a global economy and exercise the responsibilities of citizenship.

	Baseline	*Update*	*Progress*
Adult Literacy: *Has the U.S. increased the percentage of adults who score at or above Level 3 in prose literacy? (1992)*	*52%*	*—*	
Participation in Adult Education: *Has the U.S. reduced the gap (in percentage points) in adult-education participation between adults who have a high school diploma or less and those who have additional postsecondary education or technical training? (1991 vs. 1995)*	*27 points*	*32 points*	*Worse*

TABLE 1-5 Progress Report on National Educational Goals *(continued)*

	Baseline	Update	Progress
Participation in Higher Education: *Has the U.S. reduced the gap (in percentage points) between white and black high school graduates who*			
• enroll in college (1990 vs. 1996)	14 points	11 points*	No change
• complete a college degree (1992 vs. 1997)	15 points	17 points*	No change
Has the U.S. reduced the gap (in percentage points) between white and Hispanic high school graduates who:			
• enroll in college? (1990 vs. 1996)	11 points	9 points*	No change
• complete a college degree? (1992 vs. 1997)	15 points	17 points*	No change

Goal 7: Safe, Disciplined, and Alcohol- and Drug-Free Schools

Every U.S. school will be free of drugs, violence, and the unauthorized presence of firearms and alcohol.

	Baseline	Update	Progress
Overall Student Drug and Alcohol Use: *Has the U.S. reduced the percentage of 10th graders reporting doing the following during the previous year:*			
• using any illicit drug? (1991 vs. 1997)	24%	40%	Worse
• using alcohol? (1993 vs. 1997)	63%	65%*	No change
Sale of Drugs at School: *Has the U.S. reduced the percentage of 10th graders reporting that someone offered to sell or give them an illegal drug at school during the previous year? (1992 vs. 1997)*	18%	33%	Worse
Student and Teacher Victimization: *Has the U.S. reduced the percentage of students and teachers reporting that they were threatened or injured at school during the previous year?*			
• 10th grade students? (1991 vs. 1997)	40%	33%	Better
• public school teachers? (1991 vs. 1994)	10%	15%	Worse
Disruptions in Class by Students: *Has the U.S. reduced the percentage of students and teachers reporting that student disruptions interfere with teaching and learning?*			
• 10th grade students? (1991 vs. 1997)	17%	18%*	No change
• public school teachers? (1991 vs. 1994)	37%	46%	Worse

Goal 8: Parental Participation

Every school will promote partnerships that will increase parental involvement and participation in promoting the growth of children.

	Baseline	Update	Progress
Schools' Reports of Parent Attendance at Parent-Teacher Conferences: *Has the U.S. increased the percentage of K–12 public schools which reported that more than half of their parents attended parent-teacher conferences during the school year? (1996)*	78%	—	

(continued)

TABLE 1-5   Progress Report on National Educational Goals *(continued)*

	Baseline	Update	Progress
Schools' Reports of Parent Involvement in School Policy Decision: Has the U.S. increased the percentage of K–12 public schools which reported that parent input is considered when making policy decisions in three or more areas? (1996)	41%	—	
Parents' Reports of Their Involvement in School Activities: Has the U.S. increased the percentage of students in grades 3–12 whose parents reported that they participated in two or more activities in their child's school during the current year? (1993 vs. 1996)	63%	62%*	No change

Source: National Education Goals Panel. 1999. "Progress Report on National Education Goals." *Education Week.* January 13, 1999. p. 29.

The Need for Reform

Given that America is becoming more diverse and given that reform is a clear part of the landscape, some realities are beginning to emerge that suggest just how significant the diversity issue is for Americans. Let's consider some selected but powerful challenges. Once again, all the data are from U.S. Census Bureau reports.

Challenge 1: The Changing "Face" of America

- Thirty-six percent of students enrolled in public elementary and secondary schools were considered part of a minority group in 1996, an increase from the 1970s. This increase is largely due to the growth in the percentage of Hispanic students.
- Since 1970, black students have accounted for approximately one out of every three students who lived in central cities and attended public schools. In 1996, 10 percent of the students who lived in a metropolitan area outside of a central city and who attended public schools were black, up from 6 percent in 1970.
- In 1996, approximately one out of every four students who lived in a central city and who attended public schools was Hispanic, up from approximately 1 out of every 10 students in 1972.
- The percentage of black and Hispanic students enrolled in private schools increased between 1972 and 1996, rising from 5 percent each for black and Hispanic students in 1972 to 9 percent for black students and 8 percent for Hispanic students in 1996.
- In the school year 1998–1999, there were 46.5 million students enrolled in public elementary and secondary schools in the 50 states and the District of Columbia. Of these students, 533,000 were American Indian; 1,898,000 were Asian/Pacific Islanders; 6,939,000 were Hispanics; 7,923,000 were black, non-Hispanics; and 29,142,000 were white, non-Hispanics.

Challenge 2: The Number of Persons Left Out of the Educational Process

- One of every 10 individuals aged 16 to 19 was neither enrolled in school nor graduated from high school. The percentage was the highest among Hispanics (22 percent) compared with 14 percent among African American, 10 percent of European Americans, and 5 percent of Asian Americans. Among adult Hispanics, only 49.8 percent have a high school diploma (Roberts, 1993).

- America is evolving toward two classes of citizens—one that is literate and relatively productive, and one that is illiterate, dependent upon social services, and a physical and moral threat to the other (Browsher, 1993).

- African Americans will constitute 14.5 percent of all 18–24-year-olds, but they will only account for 11.9 percent of the 18–24-year-old undergraduates (Blair, 2000).

Challenge 3: The Achievement Gap Between Blacks and Whites

- The achievement gap between blacks and whites in the United States has its roots in the history of racial struggle in the United States. Slaves were denied any type of education because it would cause unrest. Some slave owners did not abide by these laws as was the case with Frederick Douglas when the wife of his slave owner taught him to read. "The ignorance did not concern the instruction itself; rather, as long as Douglas was ignorant of the motive behind the denial of access, he could not fashion a strategy to overcome the obstacle of illiteracy" (Chineworth, 1996, p. 32).

- The issue of IQ differences between blacks and whites has been discussed for hundreds of years. Nesbitt (in Jencks and Phillips, 1998) states in *The Black and White Test Score Gap*, that in the early nineteenth century most Europeans may have "believed that their intellectual skills were congenitally superior to those of Africans" (p. 86). He goes on to say that in the early twentieth century the IQ test seemed to reinforce that. Nesbitt concludes by saying that recent studies do not show a genetic difference on test scores, but do indicate "strong evidence for a substantial environmental contribution to the IQ gap between blacks and whites" (p. 101).

- Jencks and Phillips (1998) cite that even though the gap has narrowed since 1970, "the typical American black still scores below 75 percent of American whites on most standardized tests. On some tests the typical American black scores below more than 85 percent of whites" (p. 1). The authors also note that no genetic evidence has been found "indicating that blacks have less innate intellectual ability than whites" (p. 2).

- In recent studies the question of the test score gap's widening after beginning school has been raised. Phillips, Crouse, and Ralph (1998) assert that "our results imply that we could eliminate at least half, and probably more, of the black-white test score gap at the end of the twelfth grade by eliminating the differences that exist before the children enter first grade" (p. 257). At the same time, the Council of Great City Schools is actively seeking to identify ways of closing the achievement gap. Based on experiments in a number of cities (e.g., Houston), the Council identified some promising practices—see Table 1-6—for closing the achievement gap.

Challenge 4: The Capacity of Students to Become Technology-Literate

- Exploring the access Americans have to information technology is important to evaluate where the schools fit into the picture. Thornburg (1997) refers to data from the U.S. Census Bureau showing that about 45 percent of homes have computers in them, many of those connected to the Internet. However, the acquisition of computers is closely related to family income. He states, "that 70% of homes with a combined income of $70,000 or higher have computers in them; 10% of homes with a combined income of $10,000 have computers in them, and the numbers follow a nearly linear progression for intermediate income levels" (p. 13). This holds true regardless of whether the homes are rural, suburban, or urban.

TABLE 1-6   Common Strategies for Closing Achievement Gaps

The following are some of the most common strategies for closing achievement gaps that are being used by urban school districts. These strategies, although not exhaustive, are intended to provide examples of the strategies being implemented in urban districts.

- *Extended professional development for staff*
- *Reduced class size*
- *Early identification of at-risk students*
- *Clear expectations for students and staff*
- *Establishing and reviewing annual achievement goals*
- *Increased parental involvement*
- *Extended learning time: longer school-day, longer school year, summer school, after-school tutorials, and Saturday enrichment opportunities*
- *Increased emphasis on reading in early grades*
- *Additional use of instruction and curriculum specialists*
- *Increased community partnerships and minority mentoring programs*
- *Disaggregating and monitoring student achievement data*
- *Using multiple assessments*
- *Increased extracurricular activities*
- *Developing and implementing content and performance standards*
- *Implementing school based improvement planning and accountability*

Source: "Closing the Achievement Gap in Urban Schools," Washington, DC: Council of Great City Schools, 1999, p. 37.

- Thornburg (1997) argues that unless schools have the latest in technology equipment and trained teachers, the gap between those who have technology in their homes and those that do not will seriously affect the ability of students to meet the demands of the communication age, as well as their incomes.

- Educators have the responsibility of providing students with the skills to meet the changing times in business. School technology plans are expensive. Setting up partnerships with the business community is one way to help as well as providing the community with citizens who can meet the demands of the ever changing technology (Morse, 1997).

- A digital divide is emerging in America. Public schools with high poverty levels have less Internet access than do those with low poverty levels.

- The capacity for students to become technology literate is complicated by the way a variety of resource needs are evidenced in schools and the specific technology skills of the teachers in those schools. If educators have any hope of ensuring that students become technology literate, it is imperative that the challenge of building schools' technology capacity be addressed. If it is not, there is little hope that high school graduates will evidence the types of competencies outlined by the International Society for Technology in Education (2000), which are sampled below:

  Prior to completion of Grade 12 students will:

  1. Identify capabilities and limitations of contemporary and emerging technology resources and assess the potential of these systems and services to address personal, lifelong learning, and workplace needs.

  2. Make informed choices among technology systems, resources, and services.

  3. Analyze advantages and disadvantages of widespread use and reliance on technology in the workplace and in society as a whole.

  4. Demonstrate and advocate for legal and ethical behaviors among peers, family, and community regarding the use of technology and information.

  5. Use technology tools and resources for managing and communicating personal/professional information (e.g., finances, schedules, addresses, purchases, correspondence).

  6. Evaluate technology-based options, including distance and distributed education, for lifelong learning.

  7. Routinely and efficiently use online information resources to meet needs for collaboration, research, publications, communications, and productivity.

  8. Select and apply technology tools for research, information analysis, problem-solving, and decision-making in content learning.

  9. Investigate and apply expert systems, intelligent agents, and simulations in real-world situations.

  10. Collaborate with peers, experts, and others to contribute to a content-related knowledge base by using technology to compile, synthesize, produce, and disseminate information, models, and other creative works. (p. 5)

Ⓕactors Beyond Teacher Control

Clearly some of the problems evidenced in schools relate to factors beyond teacher control. Indeed, Steinberg (1996) found that one of the primary reasons for the failure of school reform efforts was the diminution of adult involvement to reinforce the values and ideas taught at school. Because American parents become less involved as children get older, the burden on schools to counter the student culture of indifference becomes even more onerous. In Steinberg's words:

> National studies of American families show that parental involvement drops off precipitously between elementary and secondary school—precisely at a time when youngsters' susceptibility to peer influence is rapidly rising. Moreover, . . . evidence indicates that this sort of parental disengagement is not limited to school matters, but affects a whole range of issues, including monitoring and regulating the child's relationships with friends, the child's use of leisure time, and the child's choice of activities. To the extent that diminished involvement in their children's lives renders parents' influence less powerful, the door is opened for peers to step in and exert a significant impact on each other's behavior—including their behavior in school. And this is precisely what happens between the sixth and tenth grades. At this point, in fact, children's achievement is more easily influenced by their peers than at any other time in their school career. (p. 142)

But many of the problems confronting schools are classroom based. Even if parents were supportive, schools would struggle to transmit effectively the requisite knowledge needed for students to succeed. As researchers gather classroom data, it has become increasingly apparent that teachers have very limited instructional repertoires (Goodlad, 1990) and have limited knowledge about the kind of new world that is emerging, the kind of knowledge and skills needed in an international economy, and the way human resources—diverse groups of individuals not normally part of a traditional organizational culture—can help fashion a new and better environment for all of us. It has also become apparent that teachers' teaching methods do link to student achievement gains (Blair, 2000).

The current classroom paradigm of teacher-centered instruction has reached its limits of pedagogical usefulness—it has a place in terms of teaching specific skills and content, but it is a model that is either misused or overused and far too infrequently properly used. Branson (1988) argues that the 100-year-old paradigm cannot be improved with programs such as "adopting-a-school," lengthening the school day, increasing teacher pay, offering leadership-development courses, or providing strategic-planning workshops. Different instructional strategies are required if teachers are to educate effectively those diverse student populations who are enrolling in our nation's schools.

To make substantial and significant change in schools, educators must dramatically change the way students are taught. Americans cannot tolerate, nor can this nation afford, a society in which some children become fully educated and others do not. We must avoid creating a society of informational "haves" and "have nots." In a world of advanced technology, new ways of communicating will inform as well as entertain. Such communication vehicles will educate and increase productivity levels; they will also pose real problems if young people are unable to assimilate in a critical fashion all the new knowledge they have available.

Giroux (1992) describes what he sees as the demise of democracy in the United States. He bases his claim upon three trends: the downward movement in voting patterns of the public, the polarization of the haves and have nots, and the vested interest groups (lobbyists) who tend to steer the government in ways that are highly individualistic. Such assertions are very interesting in the light of increasing democratization of countries and regions around the world. These regions look to America as a beacon of democracy to emulate, yet Giroux is pessimistic about our own country's future. The pessimism he describes stems from the notion that the basic purpose of schools is to prepare students as citizens in a democracy. Democracy demands full participation, and the latter is only possible if all students are fully educated to their potential, which means that they can think critically about the content they learn in schools. Democracies require educated citizens in order to maintain themselves, and educated citizens are those individuals who can explore, critique, and create ideas.

Ⓢchools: Progressive and Traditional

The Goals 2000 is an outgrowth of *A Nation at Risk* (National Commission on Excellence in Education, 1983). Some would suggest that those goals, however well intentioned, have placed education at risk because they are being used by politicians and the business community to leverage educational policies that potentially compromise the ability of teachers (Ohanian, 2000). Such policies will likely shape the way teachers teach because Goals 2000 tacitly narrows instructional and curriculum options. In Ohanian's words:

> The noisy alliance of politicians, CEO's, think tank entrepreneurs, and media camp followers remains intent on standardizing education, proclaiming that every kid in America should march in lockstep through the same curriculum. These advocates of a one-size-fits-all curriculum send out a message of school failure that has been rebutted . . . by Gerald Bracey and by, among others, David Berliner and Bruce Biddle, Clinton Boutwell, and Richard Rothstein.
>
> The rhetoric is important. Ever since Hillary Rodham Clinton was first lady of Arkansas and helped negotiate President Bush's American 2000 scheme, the rhetoric has pushed for standardization of national curriculum, with the goal of shoving out kids who don't fit so that those who are left can do their duty to the "Fortune 500." In the name of America's triumph in the global knowledge economy, corporate chiefs and their allies want to end kindergarten as we know it, to deny children's diversity in every grade, and to install a rigid system of tests and measures that will force a national curriculum onto the schools. Once that curriculum is in place, politicians can claim that every student has an equal opportunity to become a global worker. The mantra of the market-place education is "Algebra or elimination."

When students fail, members of the ruling elite can send them to their rightful place on the minimum-wage dunghill with the admonition, "Well, we gave you an equal opportunity to meet the goals." Few people in corporate/politico/infotainment circles are asking how much sense it makes to institute tougher academic standards for the students who are failing the current standards. (pp. 352–353)

Goals 2000 and the emerging high stakes environment of American schools are causing some teachers to think in instructionally constricted terms. It is also causing ideological debates between traditionalists and progressivists (see Chall, 2000). Our intention is to have teachers broaden their pedagogical options; professional teachers possess a repertoire of skills that are used selectively in ways that serve the best interests of the clients—students. Professional teachers know how and when to use direct instruction or cooperative learning. That is, we believe that good teachers are progressivists and traditionalists. Though some might argue that this is pedagogically impossible, we assert that if educators possess a "long view" of educational practice, it is imperative to think in both progressivist and traditionalist terms because who one teaches and what they need to learn dictates how instruction occurs.

Unfortunately, many teachers and reformers assume that student-centered, culturally relevant teaching is universally good, while teacher-centered, content-focused teaching is inherently negative. We contend that good schools and effective teachers encompass both views. Too many "culturally relevant" teachers forget to teach the basics; on the other hand, the likely outcome of a teacher-dominated, culturally irrelevant classroom can be student psychological and physical withdrawal, which may partially explain the alarming dropout rates in urban schools.

Some successful urban schools—public and private—have highly teacher-dominated classrooms. They also are likely supported by stronger family and community structures that emphasize the communal organization of schools (Lee, 1997), especially evidenced in Catholic schools. Specifically, these schools provide myriad opportunities for face-to-face contact between and among all those who are responsible for shaping a child's education.

Schools must teach the basics and the joys of learning. In that regard, traditionalists and progressivists must create a tenuous but genuine working relationship. Teachers who use culturally relevant materials in the classroom are bringing the familiar environment of the child into the unfamiliar world of the classroom. They are communicating that they value students' cultural environment, developing a culturally affirming and responsive atmosphere within the classroom. Regrettably, many teachers focus so exclusively on cultural relevance that they fail to see that students do not understand essential content. Urban schools must embrace both traditional and progressivist ideas, emphasizing the former in the elementary grades and the latter as students establish a solid knowledge base. Interestingly, support for this position even comes from some critics of traditional approaches. Chall (2000) writes:

The major conclusion of my study in this book is that a traditional, teacher-centered approach to education generally results in higher academic achievement than a progressive, student-centered approach. This is particularly so among students who are less well prepared for academic learning—poor children and those with learning difficulties at all social and economic levels.

Are these conclusions also applicable to students of all ages and grade levels and for all subjects—reading, math, science, and social studies? These questions are more difficult to answer from the research evidence. Although there are quantitative studies at both the elementary and high school levels, the great majority are at the elementary grades. However, in spite of the differences in numbers, the outcomes are generally the same—an advantage for achievement of the traditional approach in both elementary and high school. But there are a few signs in the research that the advantage of the traditional, teacher-centered approach is less in high school than in elementary school. This is suggested by the Eight-Year-Study of high school students, which found no significant differences between a progressive or a traditional approach. But the small differences that were found seemed to favor the progressive, student-centered approach.

As research evidence becomes available, we may well find that each approach has some advantage for academic achievement at different levels of education and proficiency. We may find that the traditional approach is more effective for beginners who first acquire knowledge and skills. Then, as they move beyond the basics, a progressive approach may prove more effective. . . . (pp. 182–183)

ⓕ OCUS OF INSTRUCTIONAL MODELS

As previously stated, this text focuses upon the culture of the classroom and the behaviors that teachers exhibit in working with youngsters. If teachers acquire and use a wider repertoire of instructional models, many of the problems confronting schools (as previously described) will be mitigated because students will be more active participants in the cultural realities of schools. This text will focus on the acquisition of the information and the application of appropriate teaching skills and styles that enable a teacher to be progressive and traditional with the diverse set of learners in American classrooms. Teachers will learn:

- How diverse groups of students learn to use their different learning dispositions and intelligences (parts to wholes, wholes to parts, visual, auditory, kinesthetic/tactile) to make sense out of a complex social world.

- How using different instructional models draws upon the learning dispositions of diverse students and utilizes the natural power and skills that such students possess. This, in turn, helps motivate them to learn.

- How most of what students encounter in society involves an active engagement with ideas or people. It is only proper to utilize these same active processes in formal teaching/learning encounters. Such activity results in both the increased acquisition of knowledge, the enhanced retention of information, and the improved application and use of academic and social skills.

- How utilizing alternative instructional models will allow students to acquire and apply various thinking skills and problem-solving processes. Such skills are crucial to an informed citizenry in a democratic society.

- How students who are challenged to learn in ways that are foreign to their natural dispositions will have an increased capacity to learn more easily as they encounter complex phenomena. As Hunter (1985) stated, almost two decades ago, "The more skilled the teacher is in using [an instructional] model, the more independent and successful learners can become and the greater the variety of teaching and learning styles that can be used" (p. 59). Students will acquire an increased capacity to learn by acquiring the various critical-thinking skills embedded within the different instructional models.

- How students will change in terms of their enthusiasm for learning, acquisition of information, and application of academic and social skills as their repertoire of learning strategies is enhanced. They will be able to accomplish more types of learning in various types of settings through the engagement of different phenomena.

ⓣEXT PURPOSES

Because *Instructional Models* is based upon the belief that teachers want to be part of the solution in educational reform, the text attempts to provide a means for the teachers to cultivate their talents. Most teachers simply lack the opportunities, awareness, and/or skills to be critical players in the myriad solutions of educational reform. The need for new types of teacher preparation, both in teaching strategies and awareness of traditions and cultural behaviors, should now be a basic element of teacher education. Teachers can actively engage in using the ideas and activities of this text; through this engagement they will gain the knowledge, skills, and attitudes required to join in the *re*-invention of schools and the *re*-creation of classroom learning cultures. To this end, the following goals are identified for development throughout the remainder of this text:

1. To describe why the use of varied instructional models in the classroom is important in working with all students in America's schools. In essence, teachers should know when and how to be both traditional and progressive.

2. To plan and organize instruction utilizing an appropriate instructional model—learning goals dictate teaching strategies.

3. To design lessons applying various instructional models and that involve use of different technologies.

4. To become skilled practitioners in utilizing alternative instructional models in grades K-12.

5. To match a specific instructional model with specific learning skills and styles of students.

6. To provide experiences in developing problem-solving and critical-thinking skills.

7. To provide sample lessons that demonstrate the use and implementation of each instructional model.

8. To provide opportunities to practice and develop the skills necessary for living in a diverse, global society.

Instructional Models: Strategies for Teaching in a Diverse Society provides numerous practical examples from various subject areas in order to demonstrate all of the instructional models. The context of this text is pedagogical and cultural—our diversity as a nation must be recognized, appreciated, and utilized if we as a nation are going to continue to sustain a world leadership position in this millennium. This text has been written because educators can no longer ignore a vital, untapped resource—student and cultural diversity. Ideas concerning how the classroom culture might be changed to be more flexible, hospitable, and supportive of diverse groups in our society will be described. One means to promote such a cultural change is to look critically, yet supportively, at what we do as educators, and to begin developing professional growth activities that can lead to new teaching approaches. This text provides a venue to help facilitate the instructional change that is so needed in our nation's schools.

ⓡEFERENCES

Aldrich, H. E. 1979. *Organizations and Environment.* Englewood Cliffs, NJ: Prentice Hall.

Barker, J. A. 1992. *Future Edge: Discovering the New Paradigms of Success.* New York: William Morrow.

Blair, J. 2000. "Study Links Effective Teaching Methods and Test Score Gains." *Education Week.* October 25, 2000. pp. 24–25.

Botstein, L. 1997. *Jefferson's Children.* New York: Doubleday.

Branson, R. K. 1988. "Why Schools Can't Improve: The Upper Limit Hypothesis." *Journal of Instructional Development* 10(4): 15–26.

Brophy, J. 1983. "Research on the Self-Fulfilling Prophecy and Teacher Expectation." *Journal of Educational Psychology* 75:631–661.

Browsher, J. E. 1993. "Why and How to Restructure Education Systems." Paper presented at the meeting of the Association for Supervision and Curriculum Development, Washington, DC (March).

Carnevale, A. P., and R. A. Fry. 2000. *Crossing the Great Divide: Can We Achieve Equity When Generation Y Goes to College?* Princeton, NJ: Educational Testing Service.

Chall, J. S. 2000. *The Academic Achievement Challenge.* New York: Guilford Press.

Chineworth, M. A. (ed.). 1996. *Rise 'N' Shine: Catholic Education and the African-American Community.* Washington, DC: National Catholic Educational Association.

Cuban, L. 1988. "Constancy and Change in Schools." Pp. 85–103 in P. W. Jackson (ed.), *Contributing to Educational Change: Perspectives on Research and Practice.* Berkeley: McCutchan.

Do You Know the Good News About American Education? 1997. Center on Educational Policy and American Youth Policy Forum.

Dusek, J. (ed.). 1985. *Teacher Expectations.* Hillsdale, NJ: Erlbaum.

Finn, C. E. Jr., M. Kanstoroom, and M. J. Petrilli. 1999. *The Quest for Better Teachers: Grading the States.* Washington, DC: The Thomas B. Fordham Foundation.

Gardner, H. 1985. *Frames of Mind* (rev. ed.) New York: Basis Books.

———. 1991. *The Unschooled Mind: How Children Think and How Schools Should Teach.* New York: Basic Books.

Giroux, H. A. 1992. "Educational Leadership and the Crisis of Democratic Government." *Educational Researcher* 21(4): 4–11.

Good, T., and J. E. Brophy. 1997. *Looking in Classrooms* (7th ed.). New York: Longman.

Goodlad, J. I. 1990. *Teachers for Our Nation's Schools.* San Francisco: Jossey-Bass.

Hunter, M. 1985. "What's Wrong with Madeline Hunter?" *Educational Leadership* 42(5): 57–60.

International Society for Technology in Education. 2000. Eugene, Oregon.

Jencks, C., and M. Phillips (eds.). 1998. *The Black and White Test Score Gap.* Washington, DC: Brookings Institution.

Lee, V. 1997. "Catholic Lessons for Public Schools." Pp. 147–163 in D. Ravitch and J. Viteritti (eds.), *New Schools for a New Century: Redesign of Urban Education.* New Haven, CT: Yale University Press.

Marshall, H., and R. Weinstein. 1984. "Classrooms Where Students Perceive High and Low Amounts of Differential Teacher Treatment." Paper presented at the annual meeting of the American Educational Research Association, New Orleans, LA.

Morse, G. 1997. "Technology Partnerships." Pp. 45–48 in A.A. Zukowski, MHSH, and R. Haney (eds.), *New Frontiers: Navigational Strategies for Integrating Technology into the School.* Washington, DC: National Catholic Educational Association.

National Commission on Excellence in Education. 1983. *A Nation at Risk: The Imperative for Educational Reform.* Washington, DC: U.S. Department of Education.

National Education Goals Panel. 1999. "Progress Report on National Education Goals." *Education Week.* January 13, 1999, p. 29.

Ohanian, S. 2000. "Goals 2000: What's in a Name?" *Phi Delta Kappan* 81(5): 345–355.

Osborne, D., and T. Gaebler. 1992. *Reinventing Government.* Reading, MA: Addison-Wesley.

Phillips, M., J. Crouse, and J. Ralph. 1998. "Does the Black and White Test Score Gap Widen after Children Enter School?" Pp. 229–272 in C. Jencks and M. Phillips (eds.), *The Black and White Test Score Gap.* Washington, DC: The Brookings Institution.

Ravitch, D. 2000. *Left Black.* New York: Simon & Schuster.

Ribadeneira, D. 1990. "Educators Say School Reform Is Not Enough." Boston Globe (1) (November 13): 1.

Riche, M. F. 1991. "We're All Minorities Now." *American Demographics* (October): 26–34.

Roberts, S. 1993. *Who We Are.* New York: Houghton-Mifflin.

Rose, M. 1995. *Possible Lives: The Promise of Public Education in America.* New York: Houghton-Mifflin.

Rosenthal, R., and L. Jacobson. 1968. *Pygmalion in the Classroom: Teacher Expectation and Pupils' Intellectual Development.* New York: Holt, Rinehart, & Winston.

Sadker, D. 2001. "Confronting Curricular Bias in Teacher Education: Some Practical Ideas." *ATE Newsletter* 33(6).

Sadker, M., and D. Sadker. 2000. *Teachers, Schools, and Society* (5th ed.). Boston: McGraw-Hill.

Sanders, W. 2001. "Measurement and Analysis to Facilitate Academic Growth of Student Populations." Presentation to American Association of Colleges for Teacher Education, Dallas, Texas.

Shade, B., C. Kelly, and M. Oberg. 1997. *Creating Culturally Responsive Classrooms.* Washington, DC: American Psychological Association.

Steinberg, L. D. 1996. *Beyond the Classroom: Why School Reform Has Failed and What Parents Need to Do.* New York: Simon & Schuster.

Stevenson, H. W., and J. Stigler. 1992. *The Learning Gap.* New York: Summit.

Stevenson, H. W., C. Chen, and S. Lee. 1993. "Mathematics Achievement of Chinese, Japanese, and American Children: Ten Years Later." *Science* 259: 53–58.

Stigler, J., and J. Hiebert. 1999. *The Teaching Gap.* New York: Free Press.

Thomas, M. D., and W. L. Bainbridge. 2001. "'All Children Can Learn': Facts and Fallacies." *ERS Spectrum* (Winter).

Thornburg, D. 1997. "2020 Visions for the Future of Education." Pp. 13–18 in A. A. Zukowski, MHSH, and R. Haney (eds.), *New Frontiers: Navigational Strategies for Integrating Technology into the School.* Washington, DC: National Catholic Educational Association.

U. S. Department of Education, National Education Goals Report. 1994. *Building a Nation of Learners.* Washington, DC: U.S. Printing Office.

———. The NCES Common Core of Data (CCD), "State Nonfiscal Survey of Public Elementary/Secondary Education," 1994–95, 1997–98, and 1998–99.

Wenglinsky, H. 2000. *How Teaching Matters: Bringing the Classroom Back into Discussions of Teacher Quality.* Princeton, N.J.: Educational Testing Service.

Zehr, M. A. 2000. "Un Dia Nuevo for Schools." *Education Week,* November 8, 2000, 20(10): 43–45.

Culturally Diverse Learners

Chapter Objectives

At the end of this chapter, readers will be able to

1. *Describe what is meant by cognitive styles of learning and the constructs that have implications for improving the learning process.*

2. *Identify and describe the major research findings concerning cognitive style in terms of gender and the cultural groups examined in this book.*

3. *Identify and describe the implications of the research on cognitive styles for teacher use of alternative instructional models.*

DIVERSITY AND LEARNING

As we discussed in the first chapter, if we look at classrooms across America—whether in urban centers of the East Los Angeles, East Harlem, or East Cleveland; or the rural areas of Arkansas, Tennessee, or Kansas; or the suburbs of Atlanta, Miami, Phoenix, or Washington, D.C.—we can find students who represent all levels of diversity. In any one of these geographical locations, a visitor to a typical classroom has a better than 50-50 chance of encountering an almost equal split of students by gender (though females have the majority); students who bring various ability levels to the classroom including those with physical, emotional, and mental exceptionalities; students who come from various socioeconomic backgrounds, with their corresponding advantages and disadvantages; students who represent different religious preferences; students who evidence a wide range of racial and ethnic backgrounds, including those whose primary language is not English; students who do not come from traditional family environments; and an increasing number of students who resent what the school has to offer and how it is delivered to them by teachers. Given the diversity found within individual classrooms, is it any wonder that teachers throw up their arms and rhetorically plea: "What am I going to do with all of these kids?"

In addition to the primary characteristics of diversity (that is, gender, age, race, ethnicity, and physical disabilities), classrooms also have students who learn in various ways, at various paces, and through various instructional approaches. The learning needs of students are varied and are based upon many factors such as past

All our children ought to be allowed a stake in the enormous richness of America. Whether they were born to poor white Appalachians or to wealthy Texans, to poor black people in the Bronx or to rich people in Manhasset or Winnetka, they are all quite wonderful and innocent when they are small. We soil them needlessly.

JONATHAN KOZOL

background and experiential development, as well as upon present and future opportunities to grow and excel.

Students have different styles and preferences for learning. Some students learn best by taking the whole of an issue and breaking it into parts; others learn by taking the parts and creating a new whole. Some students work best in a very highly structured and teacher-directed manner; others learn best in a more open, nondirective classroom climate. Some students learn best through deductive processes; others learn primarily through inductive processes. Some students learn visually; others rely heavily on an auditory mode; still others acquire essential skills through kinesthetic/tactile (hands-on) experiences. Finally, some students learn best through independent activities. These diverse characteristics and corresponding cognitive styles require an answer to three questions:

- Should all students and all groups of students (by race, age, gender, and so on) be taught in the same manner?
- Do students have learning-style preferences that correspond to specific instructional models?
- Do student needs and past experiential development affect how students learn and, thus, how teachers teach?

In the following pages we offer our answers to these questions. Let us start by talking about the most critical elements in a student's ability to learn: the teacher. Mamchur (1996) relates that being a teacher now assumes that one takes on roles that were once expected of the family. Because of the added responsibilities these roles demand, she feels that if "teachers understand natural learning style patterns and behaviors" (p. 1), they will be better teachers and will reach more students. Mamchur cites four ways that understanding learning differences can help teachers:

> First, teachers have a method to teach that is diverse and adaptive enough to meet the various learning style needs of students who are not necessarily oriented toward schooling. Second, teachers can indicate to students that they care about the individuality and integrity of each learner. Third, because learning style is related to teaching style, teachers can better understand their own teaching styles and strengths and weaknesses. And fourth, teachers can gain insight into how they work together in this particular world we call school. (p. 1)

Only teachers who utilize a variety of instructional models will be successful in maximizing the achievements of all students. Through the use of a variety of teaching models, not only will students be more inclined to achieve the diverse goals established by teachers, but students will also acquire a variety of skills and approaches to personal learning that transcend their natural learning dispositions.

No one best approach exists for teaching all students in all situations. Using an effective instrument to determine student (and teacher) learning style patterns is one tool that teachers can use in lesson planning and organization (Mamchur, 1996). Individual exceptions within cultural groups must be considered in an analysis of cultural group cognitive styles. The teacher's responsibility is to be knowledgeable about the disposition of students, and to vary instruction to accommodate different student needs. But as much as learning-style instruments help in giving teachers information, they usually fail in providing answers. Our solution is simple: address the diversity of student learning needs by using a variety of teaching approaches.

Recognizing that learning styles may be linked to individual learning preferences within ethnic and cultural groups is significant for teachers' professional education (Irvine and York, 1995). It is equally important to guard against stereotyping learning styles to a particular ethnic group as there are many cultural differences within each major cultural group (Hispanic-Mexican, Puerto Rican, Central American, South American, Haitian) and to be clear that the relationship between learning styles and student achievement is, at best, tenuous. Irvine and York (1995) assert:

> The applicability of the leaning-styles research is limited. Understanding this limitation is particularly important in the education of children of color. One core assumption inherent in the learning-styles research is that children outside of mainstream culture learn better when teaching matches their preferred style. However, research on learning styles using culturally diverse students fails to support the premise that members of a given cultural group exhibit a distinctive style. Hence, the issue is not the identification of a style for a particular ethnic or gender group, but rather how instruction should be arranged to meet the instructional needs of culturally diverse students. Teachers who understand the preferred style of a student can use that knowledge to design and plan instruction and to encourage students to experiment with a wider repertoire of learning approaches. (p. 494)

ⒸOGNITIVE STYLE

There are three major types of learning domains: cognitive, affective, and psychomotor. (We will discuss these more fully in Chapter 3.) The school, through its curriculum, instruction, testing, and physical resources, tends to emphasize almost exclusively the cognitive domain, and within that domain, the development of verbal and mathematical skills. The process of thought and its product—the acquisition of information and knowledge—is what is meant by *cognition*. The manner in which a student acquires and processes information characterizes a "cognitive style." Most research on the development of cognitive style (learning styles) indicates that family socialization practices and social class play a salient role in determining learning preferences in youngsters (Ramirez and Castaneda, 1974; Witkin, Moore, Goodenough, and Cox, 1962).

Nieto (1996) writes:

> Social class . . . has been proposed as equally or more important than ethnicity in influencing learning style. Because membership within a particular social grouping is based on both economic variables and values, the working class may differ from the middle class not only in economic resources but also in particular values and practices. The reasoning behind the hypothesis

that social class is a more important influence on learning style than is ethnicity is that the intellectual environment and socialization of children in the home may be due more to economic resources than to cultural resources. (p. 139)

The significant role models in a child's life, the "teaching" styles of families, the types of learning encouraged, and the ways in which these learnings are encouraged, seem to contribute to the development of specific learning styles in children. A study by Ramirez (1991) introduced the term "flex." Flex is the "ability to switch styles to conform to environmental demands" (p. 18). Ramirez refers to this as bicognition where those of different ethnic groups "shuttle between different cognitive and cultural styles" (p. 21).

Three constructs that relate to cognitive style and have implications for improving the learning process have been identified by Keefe (1979): (a) field independence vs. field dependence, (b) perceptual modality preferences, (c) conceptual tempo. The first two are especially germane to our discussion of how students learn and will be the only ones discussed in this chapter. Though the research linking these to student achievement is very limited, the key point we draw is to understand how the differences in how students process information suggests a real need for teachers to accommodate those differences in how they organize the learning environment.

Table 2-1 illustrates the general dispositional differences between those who are *field-dependent* and those who are *field-independent* (see also Witkin, Moore, Goodenough, and Cox, 1977). The former evidence a great deal of social sensitivity and are easily influenced by peers and those who are around them as learners. Field-dependent learners are also more easily influenced by social reinforcement. Finally, field-dependent learners are less able to structure and assimilate unstructured material that would be readily assimilated by field-independent learners. That may explain why strategies such as direct instruction appear to have so much power with urban youngsters who come to school with less mainstream cultural and intellectual capital (but with just as much ability) than their suburban counterparts. Direct instruction (Chapter 9), as you will see clearly, structures the learning process for the learner—the lessons are highly scripted. Field-independent learners, on the other hand, can more readily embrace abstract, impersonal ideas and they are less influenced by social dynamics. Provide a field-independent learner with unstructured ideas, and he or she can more comfortably organize the material and create a meaningful structure.

It is imperative that readers know that field-independent learners are not smarter than field-dependent learners. Quite simply, they are just different learners and depending on the circumstances, field-dependent or field-independent students may be advantaged. That is why instructional variation is important. A reliance on one approach advantages a particular type of student.

Perceptual modalities refer to the senses (kinesthetic, visual, and auditory) that are used for organizing information and making sense out of the external environment. Students utilize these three senses in understanding the school environment and in learning new information within the school setting. Because this construct to learning is not absolute, many students also learn through a variety of other approaches (Dunn and Dunn, 1979). However, most

TABLE 2-1 Cognitive Style Differences

Field-Dependent	Field-Independent
Disposition to be:	Disposition to be:
■ Relationship-oriented	■ Task-oriented
■ A processor of information using kinetic/ tactile and/or aural senses	■ A processor of information using the auditory senses
■ Person-oriented	■ Object-oriented
■ Interested in viewing reality or phenomena in a global manner	■ Interested in viewing reality or phenomena in parts or components of a whole
■ Group-oriented in behavior	■ Individually oriented in behavior
■ Effective in collaborative relationships	■ Effective in competitive relationships
■ Socially oriented	■ Not as socially oriented
■ Motivated by holistic approaches to learning	■ Motivated by linear, sequential approaches to learning
■ Effective at oral learning experiences	■ Effective at visual-spatial learning experiences

Source: J. A. Anderson. 1988. Cognitive Styles and Multicultural Populations. *Journal of Teacher Education* 39:2–9, A. G. Hilliard, III. 1976. *Alternatives to IQ Testing: An Approach to the Identification of Gifted Minority Children Final report to the California State Department of Education;* M. Ramirez, III, and A. Castaneda. 1974. *Cultural Democracy, Bicognitive Development and Education.* New York: Academic Press.

educators rarely use the kinesthetic approach. Regrettably, the predominant style in schools is auditory because teachers do so much talking in school classrooms. Teachers talk, students listen.

The two approaches described above provide a "rich" conceptual structure concerning the learning processes that individuals use in acquiring and understanding information. Such learning styles are sometimes cultural and sometimes biological, but they all refer to individual dispositions. In the next section, we examine cultural dispositions—that is, how various gender and racial groups approach learning tasks.

Before leaving our discussion of cognitive style, a short discussion of Howard Gardner's (1985) multiple intelligences is needed. The notion of what it means to be smart changed throughout the twentieth century. At some points, intelligence was viewed as a fixed, specific ability. Those with a high IQ were thought to be smart regardless of circumstance. Gardner's contribution to education was to ask not, How smart are you? but rather, How are you smart? As Table 2-2 suggests there are many different ways in which an individual might evidence intelligence, and those different ways suggest how readily one can and will learn content material.

Unfortunately, schools are oriented to just two of the intelligences (logical-mathematical and linguistic). Regrettably, the national reform agenda that emphasizes math and reading achievement is likely to further reinforce this focus in just two intelligences.

TABLE 2-2 Gardner's Multiple Intelligences

- Logical-mathematical. *Skills related to mathematical manipulations and discerning and solving logical problems* (related careers: *scientist, mathematician*)

- Linguistic. *Sensitivity to the meanings, sounds, and rhythms of words, as well as to the function of language as a whole* (related careers: *poet, journalist, author*)

- Bodily-kinesthetic. *Ability to excel physically and to handle objects skillfully* (related careers: *athlete, dancer, surgeon*)

- Musical. *Ability to produce pitch and rhythm, as well as to appreciate various forms of musical expression* (related careers: *musician, composer*)

- Spatial. *Ability to form a mental model of the spatial world and to maneuver and operate using that model* (related careers: *sculptor, navigator, engineer, painter*)

- Interpersonal. *Ability to analyze and respond to the motivations, moods, and desires of other people* (related careers: *psychology, sales, teaching*)

- Intrapersonal. *Knowledge of one's feelings, needs, strengths, and weaknesses; ability to use this knowledge to guide behavior* (related benefit: *accurate self-awareness*)

- Naturalist. *(Gardner's most recently defined intelligence.) Ability to discriminate among living things, to classify plants, animals, and minerals; a sensitivity to the natural world* (related careers: *botanist, environmentalist, chef, other science- and even consumer-related careers.*)

Source: Sadker, M. P. and D. M. Sadker (2000). *Teachers, Schools, and Society.* Boston: McGraw-Hill, p. 88.

The key for effective teachers is to find ways of varying the approach to learning so that students approach ideas from lots of perspectives. The beauty of inquiry (Chapter 5) or concept formation (Chapter 6) is that a learner can use two or three intelligences as part of a single lesson to explore, for example, why leaves fall from trees. The teacher can still use direct instruction to teach content but can also encourage spatial intelligence (examine different shapes of leaves) and naturalist intelligence (knowing where to find different types of tree leaves) in order to explore a topic central to the curriculum. Again, the key is variation—changing the way ideas are explored and investigated.

REVIEW OF RELATED RESEARCH

Any discussion of racial or ethnic dispositions is fraught with social and political complications. It is all too easy to move from an observation to a prescription. For example, to assume that cooperative learning is a model of choice for Native American students just because Native Americans rely heavily on interpersonal cooperation would be ludicrous.

Caine and Caine (1995) demonstrate that the mental models of teaching need to be changed for effective teaching: "The traditional mental model of learning is being challenged in many quarters, but alternative theories are still fragmented and limited to supporting specific approaches, such as thematic instruction, cooperative learning. . . . By contrast, brain-based teaching and learning takes a holistic approach, looking at teaching developmentally, socioculturally, and in other broad ways" (p. 44). Caine and Caine reflect on the issue of a diverse society and how it fits with educational policy and practice. Their research focuses on "community building, based on small process groups that embody the spirit of dialogue. . . . Understanding other cultures and ethnic groups happens when we experience each other in dialogue as learners" (pp. 145–146). Teachers who work with diverse populations must learn to communicate with those students and their parents.

As educators, the goal is to create instructional programs that advantage all students. That objective can be accomplished only if teachers know how to vary their instructional approach to help students learn disciplinary concepts.

In this section, we identify and describe the research findings on learning styles for four cultural groups: Native Americans, African Americans, Hispanic Americans, and Asian Americans. Findings within any one of these groups may indicate that 55 to 70 percent of the cultural group learn in a specific manner. However, as noted earlier, the reader cannot generalize from these findings that all individuals within that cultural group learn in the same manner. Some patterns have emerged for various cultural groups (Vernon et al., 1988), and we shall identify and describe these in this literature review. However, individual differences within each cultural group require cautious interpretation. There are no monolithic cultural approaches to learning, no universal generalizations. Indeed, there are just as many learning-style exceptions within European American groups as there are among and between other cultural groups in society (Dunn et al., 1990).

In the following sections, we provide general descriptions about learning dispositions for selected cultural groups. The reader needs to be aware of what the research says concerning how different cultural groups learn, and to understand the ways in which the various instructional models can enhance the overall performance of individual students. With such understandings, the reader can then use the extant research as a pedagogical tool for *thinking* about the learning potential of different students. This information should never be used as an instructional weapon with which to intellectually force all students to conform to some stereotypic image of how an African American or Hispanic American learns. As Sternberg (1994) notes: "There are different ways of capturing [or thinking about] children's learning styles. The important thing is to take them into account—to teach in a way that meets the needs of each child. In practice, I often teach the very same concept in different ways, and then assess that concept in various ways" (p. 565).

The purpose of these learning disposition sections is to explore the different ways students learn, with particular attention to the four cultural traditions (Native Americans, African Americans, Hispanic Americans, and Asian Americans) and to gender. The latter, of course, has received considerable attention because of research highlighting the inequitable participation of females in classrooms (Sadker and Sadker, 2000). The purpose of Chapters 4–11 is to equip the reader with a better knowledge of the different instructional models that might be used to enhance the learning potential of students who exhibit different dispositions for learning. Significantly, teachers who use different instructional models will

TABLE 2-3   Racial and Ethnic Distribution of U.S. Population and Public School Enrollment: 1990, 2000, and 2010.

Group	Percentage of U.S. Population			Percentage of Public School Enrollment		
	1990	2000	2010	1990	2000	2010
White American*	76	72	68	69	64	59
African American*	12	12	13	16	17	17
Hispanic American	9	11	14	11	14	18
Asian American	3	4	5	3	4	5
Native American	1	1	1	1	1	1

*Excludes persons of Hispanic origin

Note: Some columns do not total 100 due to rounding.

Sources: Estimates and projections based on U.S. Department of Commerce, Bureau of the Census, *Statistical Abstract of the United States*, 1996 (Washington, DC: U.S. Government Printing Office, 1996), pp. 24-26; U.S. Department of Education, National Center for Education Statistics, *The Condition of Education*, 1995 (Washington, DC: U.S. Government Printing Office, 1995), p. 336; U.S. Department of Education, National Center for Education Statistics, *Digest of Education Statistics*, 1995 (Washington, DC: U.S. Government Printing Office, 1995), p. 60.

address the different learning needs of students. We contend that good teachers vary instruction even when they are using a prescriptive strategy such as direct instruction. Unfortunately, some teachers lack the skill and knowledge to vary how they teach content. Chapters 4–11 provide a variety of models that teachers can use.

The great variations among individuals within groups lend credence to the need for educators to begin using diverse instructional models with and for culturally diverse student populations. Two types of knowledge, one cultural and the other pedagogical, form a basis for achieving Sternberg's (1994) ideal result: "Children with different learning and thinking styles . . . [being] given the opportunity to show what they can learn and how they use it" (p. 565).

America's population is changing. That is clearly evidenced by the data in Table 2-3. As we begin this discussion of different learning styles, keep in mind that the demographic landscape of America is changing just as the ideological orientations are becoming more polarized. The diversity and range of views will make for interesting times, but knowledge will better prepare you as you confront the realities of classrooms that are much more diverse than they were thirty years ago.

Native American Learners

One of the great difficulties in studying Native American learning styles has to do with the diversity among the various tribes within the Native American culture. For example, the Sauk Fox, Navajo, Cherokee, and Seminole tribes are very different. However, Native American tribes share some similar cultural orientations: "A Native American identifies first with his clan, then with his tribe, and then as an Indian" (Bert and Bert, 1992, p. 4). For a Native American, culture and religion are powerful entities; they cannot be separated. They are interrelated systems that are conceptually integrated (Herring, 1989; Loftin, 1989). There are similar rites and traditions that most if not all Native Americans have in common:

- The belief in a harmonious universe where everything has a sacred life. Religious symbols and rites are common across most tribes.
- The belief that human beings are part of and not superior to nature.
- The belief that every individual has rights and deserves dignity and respect.
- The belief that individuals are a part of the whole group and are subjugative to the good of the group.
- The belief that leadership is based on ability and earned respect (Loftin, 1989; Tooker, 1983).

Soldier (1985, 1989), using similar core values to those listed above, describes how the Native American youngster may need to interact with a teacher within the traditional classroom. One of the first values that Soldier describes is the emphasis upon the **dignity of the individual**—specifically, children are afforded the same respect as adults. Children are taught to seek the wisdom and counsel of their elders; at the same time, they are encouraged to be independent and to make their own decisions. The locus of control is more internal in Native American culture. Native American youngsters may respond, therefore, to a teacher (who represents external authority) with confusion and/or passivity when confronted with demands to recognize external control.

Philips (1972,1993) sought to determine why Native American youngsters appeared more silent during classroom discussions than mainstream cultural students. She discovered, at the Warm Springs Indian Reservation in Central Oregon, that Native American youngsters were in cultures that valued **internal locus of control;** that they carefully observed adults who were involved in completing daily tasks, especially how they performed ordinary tasks; and that Native American children are often taken care of by older siblings to whom they turned for help. Such approaches to learning placed Native American youngsters at a distinct disadvantage in the traditional American classroom: Traditional classroom teachers function in an authoritarian manner; they closely monitor student activities; and they rely heavily upon lecture and recitation as the dominant forms of instruction.

For the Native American student, teachers are not always considered leaders simply because of their position or authority. An individual in Native American culture is a leader when others choose that individual because of his or her perceived abilities and/or knowledge. The teacher must learn to earn the student's respect before a student will follow and obey instructions from the teacher. Additionally, in traditional classrooms, youngsters are expected to display their knowledge in front of peers, and most classroom interactions are closely controlled by the teacher. For the Native American student, such classrooms are foreign to their cultural background and the manner in which they learned how to learn.

Native Americans value and develop acute **visual discrimination.** One of the common generalizations about Native American cultures is that information processing is conducted through the use of the visual mode—visual-spatial strength (Swisher and Deyhle, 1989). Native American children are taught to learn through careful observational techniques: For example, the nonverbal expressions of adults, changing weather conditions, the ecological alterations of earth, the behavioral changes and expressions of adults, and so on. Native American students approach learning through visual activity; they prefer to learn by observation before performance, and they seem to learn in their natural settings through experimentation (Swisher and Deyhle, 1987). Because of their visual perceptual strength, Native Americans demonstrate a high level of field independence. Studies by Dinges and Hollenbeck (1978), Halverson (1976), McShane (1980), and Utley (1983)—conducted with many different Native American tribes—suggest that Native Americans can be just as field-independent, if not more so, as European Americans. Another strength for Native Americans is the use of imagery as a tool for understanding complex concepts (Tafoya, 1982). Anyone who doubts the rich imagery of Native American traditions should read popular fiction such as Leslie Silko's *Ceremony* or James Welch's *Fool's Crow.*

Further descriptions of Native American students emphasize the use of **global processing skills** over behavioral, sequential processes (Bryant, 1986; More, 1990). Global processing emphasizes the whole of phenomena; it makes use of overviews and placing phenomena within the context studied. Isolated skill instruction emphasizes the "parts" and seeks to have learners divide phenomena into specific substructures without consideration to broader meaning. As a consequence, whole-language type learning may be more efficacious for a global learner than an exclusive reliance on the phonetic approaches found in some schools (More, 1990). Indeed, the whole-language movement is an outgrowth, in part at least, of the work of Sylvia Ashton Warner, who worked with the Maori tribe in New Zealand. Global processing allows learners to "own" the content in ways not engendered through behavioral approaches (Flippo, 2001).

Another core value for Native Americans is **cooperation.** Because the extended (clan or tribal) family is so important in the Native American culture (consider, for example, the Indian Child Welfare Act of 1978), youngsters tend to be group-oriented rather than self-centered. Personal property is not a familiar concept to many young Native Americans because of their cultural experience that emphasizes sharing what they have with others. Sharing behavior often conflicts with the ethos created by a traditional teacher, who accents respecting personal property, labeling possessions, taking care of one's own belongings, and being the best in the class (for example, a spelling bee champion). According to Soldier (1985), Native American children are "far more advanced than their non-Indian counterparts in such social behaviors as getting along with others, working in groups, taking turns, and sharing" (p. 187). The Native American student's culture traditionally teaches helping relationships rather than interpersonal competition.

It is very clear that the cognitive style of many Native Americans is often different from what is valued and taught in most schools. Because of this difference, the learning of American Indian children is adversely affected. Nieto (1996) writes:

Core Indian values of respect and value for the dignity of the individual, harmony, internal locus of control, and cooperation and sharing inevitably influence students' reactions to their educational experiences. That a teacher's best intentions may be ineffective if students' cultural differences are neglected in curriculum and instruction is seen by . . . ethnographic work among Indian school children on the Warm Springs Reservation. Students performed poorly in classroom contexts that demanded individualized performance and emphasized competition. Their performance improved greatly when the context did not require students to perform in public and when cooperation was valued over competition. Cooperative learning, which is compatible with many values of Indian families, is an approach worth exploring. It may be helpful in other settings as well. That is, cultural compatibility is only one criterion for using particular strategies; another is exposing all children to a variety of ways of learning. Nevertheless, research of this kind is important if we are to grasp how children from different cultural backgrounds respond to teachers' behaviors and what teachers can do to change how they teach. (p. 145)

Philips (1972, 1983) indicates that Native American adults teach youngsters to listen, observe, pay close attention, and practice on their own (independently)—to learn by observing and watching adults, and to learn through listening to and observing those who are respected as elders. The only occasion when a public display would take place is when a new skill or knowledge is to be demonstrated or performed for others. This notion of "private learning" (Swisher and Deyhle, 1989) has been verified by other researchers for the Oglala Sioux children (Brewer, 1977), Navajo youngsters (Longstreet, 1978), and Yanqui youngsters (Appleton, 1983).

Current research concerning Native Americans has moved from an examination of student deficiencies related to language ability, cultural background, and cognitive development to studies focusing upon social and economic discrimination (Ogbu, 1983, 1987, 1989), which strongly criticizes the school as a central player of discriminatory practices. The latest research identifies the cognitive skills of Native Americans as strengths, not weaknesses (Benjamin, Chambers, and Reiterman, 1993; Grantham-Campbell, 1992; Macias, 1989; Shutiva, 1991). Thus, it is the responsibility of the school to alter its instructional practices and structure to utilize fully the cognitive skills and intellectual strengths of Native American children.

For those readers who doubt the power of cultural and individual genetic dispositions for Native Americans in terms of how they negotiate the world, consider the words of Linda Hodges (1996), a woman who adopted an Apache child in 1969 (prior to the Indian Child Welfare Act). At the age of 26, her adopted son returned to his tribe. She writes:

Andrew learned that both his parents died years ago in alcohol-related incidents, but found a brother, grandmother, great-grandmother and dozens of aunts, uncles, and cousins. They gave him a welcome-home party and showered him with gifts. He felt comfortable with them. Only the language they usually spoke set him apart. He enrolled in the tribe, is thinking of moving to the reservation and wants to be buried in the cemetery where his birth parents rest.

He learned that his family never wanted his mother to sign him away. He was told that her decision to relinquish two of her three children for placement in non-Indian homes caused such a rift with her family that, while under the influence of alcohol, she took an overdose of sleeping pills and died. The family never stopped searching for the missing children.

Although Andrew grew up in our happy home, the positive change in my son once he touched his roots, and the ease into which he entered the lives of his large family, makes me think that the pull of the ingrained cultural memory is stronger than even the most loving adoptive bonds. (p. A15)

Table 2-4 provides a description of the learning dispositions of Native American students. Notice in the following description, though, how those dispositions are warranted by a teacher sensitive to how Native American students learn. Rose (1995) poignantly writes:

One of the stories Michelle told was of Arachne, the proud Greek maiden whom Athena turned into a spider. Both the Navajo and the Hopi have spider women in their lore—though each is a very different kind of figure from Arachne—and Michelle used this link to set out on the story. "Arachne was a maiden, beautiful, young, just about your age . . ." And she stopped and turned, feigning mild puzzlement. She reached out to the girl closest to her. "Uh, Hana, how old are you?" "Sixteen," Hana said. "Ah, sixteen," repeated Michelle, not missing a beat. "That was *ex-actly* her age. So, anyway, here's the lovely Arachne at her loom . . ." And having drawn Hana—and, through Hana, all the girls—into the story, she continued telling us of Arachne's pride in her tapestries and her bold challenge to Athena, the best of the weavers among the goddesses. "So, of course, they had a contest," she exclaimed, her fingers picking at the air as though she were weaving the figures herself. "They spun and spun, and these beautiful gods and goddesses appeared in the fabric. Why, Hana, you could even see the expressions on the faces of the gods! And they spun and spun. And when they were done, whose tapestry do you think was better?" Murmurs here: Athena's . . . no, Arachne's . . . Whose? "It was hard to tell," said Michelle, dropping her hands to her side. But Athena, indignant, shredded Arachne's tapestry (Michelle slashed the air) and turned her into a spider. "She shriveled up and her arms got skinny and crooked, like this." The storyteller hooked her right arm and let it quiver. "And today this spider woman continues to weave her web. We see her all over . . . everywhere . . . all around us." The students were smiling; a few applauded. Michelle turned her head slightly, closing her eyes momentarily, dramatically, and raised a hand. She had more to say.

She talked about the spider woman in Leslie Silko's *Ceremony* and about Navajo tales in which pride and retribution are the central themes. She shifted between the ancient Greek and the Native American, not looking for neat parallels, but suggesting correspondences. The myths and tales, she said, were "compelling and beautiful because they're so invested with power." But, though powerful, they were also present, kind of everyday. They were real for Michelle, not an artifact, not sealed away. I had read *Oedipus* a number of times in the past—had taught it, in fact—and had

TABLE 2-4   Capitalizing on Native American Dispositions

Teachers need to:

■ *Establish a conceptual context for new academic content.*

■ *Provide time and space for thinking and personal reflection.*

■ *Emphasize visual stimuli within the learning environment.*

■ *Develop a warm and supportive classroom environment through the use of cooperative learning.*

■ *Utilize imagery as a tool for understanding complex concepts.*

■ *Provide an overview and rationale to help place academic content within a context to be studied.*

never understood, no, *felt*, the spiritual dimension of the play as I did sitting in that little room. I was suddenly curious to reread a classic that I figured I knew, that I had wrapped up in its historical gloss, nicely under control. But looking at Misrach's photographs and listening to Michelle made the world of the Greeks real and disturbing. (pp. 374–375)

African American Learners

For African American students the opportunity to use **oral modes of expression** (Goldstein, 1971; Kochman, 1972) to engage in **kinesthetic/tactile activities** and to **strengthen interpersonal relationships** are central to their intellectual growth (Hale-Benson, 1986; Hilliard, 1989; Shade, 1989). African Americans share a unique cultural heritage, and their learning styles are integrally linked with their historical culture (Hale-Benson, 1982). The influence of culture must be viewed by educators as a preferential or stylistic choice; it is not suggestive of intellectual inferiority or superiority. Hale-Benson (1986) believes that, as a result of their cultural heritage, African Americans are more **affective, relational,** and **holistic** in their orientation to learning than European American students. The issue of African American cultural heritage, however, has become problematic given the increasing cultural diversity present in African American communities (Slaughter-DeFoe, Nakagawa, Takanishi, and Johnson, 1990). Children of color attending America's schools are now coming from Caribbean, South American, African, and, of course, African American families. While these individuals struggle with different social and economic circumstances, all are designing their own means of maintaining a personal and cultural identity.

Anderson (1988), like Hale-Benson (1986), noted that the African Americans' psychological orientation is more affective than that of European Americans: "The most characteristic feature of the African system is its focus on unity and connection" (p. 6). Cooper (1987) takes a similar position in her examination of language in the African American culture: "Black language is anchored in an aesthetic and a world view that are different from those of the Western tradition. . . . [It] reflects a holistic cognitive style and right-brain hemispheric dominance that is in diametric opposition to the Western ideal of analytic style and left hemispheric dominance" (p. 61).

Matthews (as cited in Cooper, 1987) elaborates:

> The Black mind sees a thing as a connected whole, as against the view of the things as a [set] of isolated particulars. . . . The wholeness approach is a habit of seeing things whole before they are seen as broken apart. Instead of seeing 10 things as 10 separate units, the Black perspective tends to see 10 things as 10 parts of a single whole. . . . One wants to envision the ecology rather than the cell because the cell behaves one way outside of the ecology—and in a totally different way when put back into the ecology. (p. 19)

Gilbert and Gay (1985) found that some African American students grow up within a context that integrates the intellectual, physical, and emotional abilities and skills. African American students often respond to a teacher's question using voice, emotion, and nonverbal characteristics. African American students often respond orally, in unison, and in a choral manner based upon traditional modes of verbal expression—oral communication and group participation. If teachers are unaware of these cultural characteristics and historical antecedents, they may interpret this student responsiveness as unruly, disruptive, and unacceptable to the traditional decorum of the classroom. On the other hand, part of the success of (scripted) direct instruction in some school settings with African American populations may be that the technique, which requires choral responding, often mirrors salient cultural characteristics that emphasize high verbal involvement. As partial evidence of this phenomenon, consider this description of one (scripted) direct instruction classroom by Traub (1999). Even though Hamstead Hill has a substantial white student population, the example illustrates the active verbal involvement of students in response to teacher questions within the context of a direct instruction lesson.

> A teacher slowly circles her second-grade class, which is grouped in five rows of five children. Reading from a spiral notebook, she barks, "What word?" And the children, their eyes locked on a vocabulary list in their workbooks, cry out in unison, "Taste!" The teacher sharply snaps her fingers at the side of her head. "Next word! What word?" "Ankle!"
>
> Snap. "Next word! What word?"
>
> "Tasted!"
>
> Snap. And so on, down to the bottom of the column. "Great job! Touch on the first word of Column 4. Good touching! What word? . . ."
>
> You can hear the shouted call-and-response echoing up and down the hallways of Hamstead Hill, a school close to Baltimore's Inner Harbor that serves a predominantly working-class population. The shouting isn't absolutely necessary; Janet Mahoney, a third-grade teacher, says that she winces when she hears it. But since the DI script is mostly written in the imperative mode, and students generally respond in unison, and communication on both sides is speedy and short, the classroom often descends into earsplitting *obbligato*. At the same time, the transaction is anything but chaotic. One bit of information is separated from another by unmistakable punctuation—a fingersnap, a clicker, a clap. (pp. 39-40)

Students of color tend to be more field dependent (Olstad, Juarez, Davenport, and Haury, 1981; Ramirez, 1982)—that is, they contextualize knowledge and look for conceptual relationships. Shade (1984) noted that African Americans develop unique cultural patterns and have specific methods for organizing and processing information. The African American child is also more likely to be field-sensitive (for example, to have the need for a warm and positive classroom setting, to use collaborative and cooperative instructional styles, to utilize kinesthetic activities, and to use people-oriented examples and role models) and less able to perceptually differentiate visual-spatial tasks than other groups (Kelly, 1984; Shade, 1981). Boykin (1994) and Tuck and Boykin (1989) have reinforced the research of Slavin (1977) and Slavin and Oickle (1981) concerning the use of cooperative learning strategies with African American youngsters. The youngsters in these studies achieved at a much higher level using cooperative learning strategies when compared with traditional classroom techniques. Boykin, in fact, asserts that African American students achieve at a higher level using cooperative learning strategies because of their cultural dispositions concerning relational learning (Boykin, 1994; Tuck and Boykin, 1989). Boykin consistently found that African American youngsters preferred to work cooperatively in groups even when external rewards were removed. He argues that this learning preference is an African American cultural norm; an argument that is consistent with Ladson-Billings's (1990, 1992) research concerning socialization and the distinctive ways of learning in African American communities.

The African American orientation to field sensitivity may also play a part in student abilities to interpret facial expressions (for example, how the student interprets the eye contact of a teacher). In studies concerning the gazing behavior of various cultural groups, LaFrance and Mayo (1976) found that European Americans tended to look away from conversants when speaking, but to look at them when listening to the speaker. On the other hand, African Americans tended to look away when listening to someone but looked directly at the individual when speaking. This may help explain the frustrations of European American teachers who often view African American children as belligerent or inattentive based upon student-to-teacher eye contact.

Further, while the preferred modality for receiving information by European Americans is visual, many African Americans process information utilizing kinetic and tactile senses (Guttentag, 1972; Morgan, 1981). From studies focusing on the kinesthetic mode, it seems apparent that many African Americans are much more skilled at utilizing kinesthetic processes as compared with European American children. Regrettably, the high degree of kinetic skill, especially for African American males, has led to negative perceptions by educators (Hale-Benson, 1986), as well as an inordinate amount of failing grades and special education placements (Harry, 1992; Obiakor, 1992). Ironically, just as some disdain learning approaches that use kinesthetic elements, Harriett Ball (described later in this book) uses a learning approach at the KIPP academy in Houston to help urban youngsters achieve their full potential and memorize information.

African Americans are socialized to be person-oriented rather than object/thing-oriented (Prom, 1982; Shade, 1984; Young, 1970, 1974). Shade and Edwards (1987) found that African American households tended to have pictures or statues of people; European American families tended to have pictures or

TABLE 2-5 Capitalizing on African American Dispositions

Teachers need to:

- *Develop a classroom climate characterized by warmth and encouragement.*

- *Utilize oral modes of expression within the classroom.*

- *Structure the classroom in formal rather than informal ways.*

- *Utilize collaborative work environments that promote social interaction.*

- *Provide overviews and rationale to help place academic content within a context to be studied.*

- *Provide concept learning that moves from the concrete to the abstract.*

- *Design learning activities that promote kinesthetic/tactile modalities.*

- *Be aware of the affective dimension of the classroom environment as well as how the teacher relates to all students.*

- *Utilize people-oriented examples and situations in the learning activities presented.*

- *Utilize as many positive role models as possible in the lessons presented to students.*

statues representing nature and/or abstract art. Damico (1983), in a comparison of black and white 6th grade youngsters, used photography as a vehicle of analysis and concluded that African American children chose to include people in their photos, while European American children were more inclined to depict objects or physical settings in their photos. The learning preference for African Americans tended to focus more on people and events as opposed to ideas and objects. This does not mean that ideas and objects are ignored, but rather that they are merged into lessons that focus on people and events.

In the following classroom example, Rose (1995) describes how Stephanie Terry works with her African American students to build their language and learning skills. The short vignette illustrates how wide the teacher "casts her net" to ensure the involvement of all students. After reading the vignette, review Table 2-5 and compare Ms. Terry's approach with the ways in which teachers can capitalize on African American learning dispositions.

> "It's all part of it," Stephanie had said to me. "Everything contributes to the writing. The animals, the books, the music, the things on the wall, the African themes and images—it all feeds into their journals. And the activities. They need lots of opportunities to talk, to hear good books, to ask questions, to share experiences with classmates, to help each other, to read the things they've written." So any given reading at the Author's Chair may grow from a number of sources, all part of the classroom environment. . . .
>
> There were, of course, the books. Each day, Stephanie read at least one book to the class: fairy tale or folktale, a story about children, biography, history, an account of other cultures, an explanation of the biology or ecology of the creatures living along the wall of the classroom. In any given month, then, the children might hear a tale set in the African rain forest, a linguistic romp by Dr. Seuss, an explanation of the Navajo cosmology, information on

the newt or hermit crab, the life of Harriet Tubman or Rosa Parks, a story about a magic fish or a spirited girl or a trickster spider. (p. 114)

Hispanic American Learners

Classifying all people of Spanish descent as Hispanic Americans (also called Latinos) is fraught with difficulties, especially when one considers the myriad of potential ethnic groups—Columbian, Cuban, Mexican, Puerto Rican, and so on. Roberts (1993), in his review of 1990 U.S. Census data, found that among all people who identified themselves as of Hispanic origin, 61 percent were Mexican, 12 percent were Puerto Rican, 5 percent were Cuban, with the remaining 22 percent from the various countries in Central and South America. Additionally, there is the problem of labeling the racial/ethnic group—*Hispanic* is favored in Florida and Texas and by Cubans; *Latino* is preferred in California. Most of the research cited below has been conducted with children who are described by the researchers as Mexican American. Because most multicultural education texts and the U.S. Census Bureau utilize the term *Hispanic Americans*, we will use this descriptor.

There are considerable differences between and among Puerto Ricans, Cubans, Mexicans, Columbians, and other ethnic groups who are referred to as Hispanic Americans. Because this descriptor embraces so many ethnic groups, there is little appreciation for the characteristics of diversity within and among the groups. Within each group there are differences related to language (dialect differences), social class, acculturation, and educational background. Newly arrived immigrants differ greatly from individuals who may be third- or fourth-generation U.S. citizens. Older-generation Hispanic Americans may call themselves Spanish Americans, speak a different form of Spanish, and differ in their customs and the foods they eat (Keefe and Padilla, 1987). The early Cuban immigrants to the United States after Castro took power came from a highly educated and socially mobile economic class compared with the more recent Cuban immigrants (Suarez, 1993). Furthermore, there are black Cubans and Puerto Ricans who have a common culture with white Cubans and Puerto Ricans even though they are often misnamed as *African Americans.*

Compared with African Americans and European Americans, Hispanic Americans enter school later, leave school earlier, and are less likely to complete a high school education (Howe, 1994). Hispanic Americans remain the most undereducated racial group in the United States (De La Rosa and Maw, 1990; Tienda, 2000).

Hispanic American students regard family and personal relationships as important and are comfortable with cognitive generalities and patterns (Cox and Ramirez, 1981; Vasquez, 1991). These qualities help explain why Hispanic American students often seek a personal relationship with a teacher and are more comfortable with broad concepts rather than component facts and specific information.

Ramirez (1973) reports that European American students do better in competitive situations; Hispanic American students perform better when members of the family are in a position to benefit from their performance. Further, "the traditional Mexican American is encouraged to always view themselves as an integral part of the family. The child is reared in an atmosphere which emphasizes the importance of interpersonal relationships. Consequently, the child develops greater sensitivity to social cues, and to the human environment in general" (p. 902).

Ramirez (1982) further reported that Hispanic American youngsters are much more **group-oriented** than European Americans, flourish at academic tasks when cooperative learning is the instructional strategy, and are much more sensitive to the social environment of the classroom. He found that Hispanic American students tended to be much more responsive to adult role models, less comfortable with trial-and-error instructional strategies, and less interested in the details of academic, abstract tasks.

An interesting pair of studies focusing upon child-rearing practices was conducted by Ramirez and Castaneda (1974) and Cox and Ramirez (1981). Each study utilized both observations of students and interviews with mothers and the observation of their mothering skills. The authors compared Hispanic American and non-Hispanic American elementary students and collected data around two child-rearing practices—"traditional" and "modern." Traditional child-rearing practices were oriented toward encouraging children to work cooperatively and learn by modeling; traditional parents motivated children through the use of social rewards. Modern child-rearing practices, on the other hand, utilized trial-and-error learning, encouraged children to work individually, and focused on motivation through nonsocial rewards. Both studies noted that youngsters reared in families using *both* traditional and modern child-rearing practices were more flexible in learning disciplinary concepts, social skills, and academic content than those children raised with a single approach. Such "dual" children, regardless of ethnicity, could work either individually or in groups, cooperate or compete, function in field-sensitive or field-independent situations, and were motivated by both social and nonsocial rewards. The more flexible children in the study were labeled *bicognitive*, because they could function in both field-independent and field-sensitive cognitive styles. In other words, "dual" children could adapt to different situations and teaching styles. The educational strengths of these children emerged because of their bicognitive abilities.

In research conducted on cognitive style, Cohen (1969), Messick (1970), and Ramirez (1973, 1982) found that most Hispanic American children tended to be field dependent and to do their best work on **verbal tasks.** The children in these studies also learned material more easily when it included the use of humor, social content (for example, the use of issues that affected the community), and some fantasy and the opportunity for creative expression. The children were also extremely sensitive to the opinions of others. European American children, on the other hand, did best on analytical tasks; they were able to learn material that was inanimate and impersonal more easily; and their performance was not greatly affected by the opinion of others. These data are reinforced by Kagan and Buriel (1977), Keogh, Welles, and Weiss (1972), and Ramirez and Castaneda (1974), who indicated that Hispanic American children were more group-oriented, more field-sensitive to the outside environment, and more positively responsive to role modeling than European American students. Such data support similar conclusions found in studies dealing with

Native Americans and African Americans. Hispanic American youngsters tend to be less competitive; and less interested in details, isolated factual information, and nonsocial academic situations.

Kagan and Madsen (1971) studied the motivational styles of Hispanic American children. They found that Hispanic American children were **less competitive** than European American children, and that Hispanic American children are also more highly motivated in the cooperative setting than in the competitive setting. Ramirez and Price-Williams (1974) demonstrated that Hispanic American children scored higher than European American children on need affiliation and the need to be comforted.

This research was further confirmed by a number of other research studies. Kagan and Zahn (1976), in a study comparing Mexican American and Anglo American (as labeled by Kagan) youngsters on reading and mathematics achievement, found that Mexican Americans were more **field-sensitive/dependent,** which is quite different from the way schools tend to be structured. Knight and Kagan (1977), in an analysis of Anglo American and Mexican American 5- to 9-year-old children, found that Anglo American children tended to be much more competitive, made fewer choices related to equality, and exhibited superiority behaviors. Prosocial, altruistic, and group involvement behavior tended to be exhibited by Mexican American youngsters. Finally, in a study by Kagan and Knight (1981), confirmation was made with all of the previous studies—Anglo American children were more competitive than Mexican American children and exhibited higher levels of achievement motivation than Mexican American youngsters.

The final aspect of analysis we shall consider about Hispanic Americans—language issues—also applies in the next section to Asian Americans. There are schools in this nation where a myriad of different languages are spoken daily by students. If the schools and teachers do not help students maintain and utilize their first language, educators are, for all intents and purposes, indicating to youngsters that they are not valued. The language a person speaks is part of who that person really is. If schools try to strip youngsters of their primary language, educators are telling these youngsters that the school does not respect them as whole individuals. As America's student population grows more diverse, the question of how to address non-English student learning needs becomes more complicated and political. Good teachers in a multicultural context are, of necessity, bicultural—they know how to mediate between a student's experiential development and the school's current behavioral expectations. Good teachers are language sensitive; indeed, even those who are English-first advocates must be sensitive to how words in English might better be understood by non-English-speaking students. Teachers need to remember that students are not just learning academic skills at school; they are learning the value of education. Clayton (1996) writes:

> The process of acculturation is not just learning a language; it is also learning the values that underlie the culture or the behaviors that make sense in the culture. As such, it can involve a profound change in a person, particularly in children who want so much to be accepted by their peers. Value systems come into conflict, and the cross-cultural student and family are often the battleground. (p. 62)

TABLE 2-6 Capitalizing on Hispanic American Dispositions

Teachers need to:

■ *Emphasize the use of social interaction within the classroom.*

■ *Utilize collaborative work environments that promote verbal tasks.*

■ *Provide overviews and rationale to help place academic content within a context to be studied.*

■ *Utilize the family, its role, and its importance in the lives of youngsters.*

■ *Develop a more personal relationship with students.*

■ *Utilize positive role models in all classroom activities.*

Throughout the past several decades even those focused on researching and studying Hispanic Americans have been conflicted on what constitutes educational "best practice." Davis (2001) reports on the different ideological views regarding educating Hispanic students, with approaches ranging from Emory Stephen Bogardus' "anglo conformity" and full assimilation and Americanization to Herschel Thurman Manuel's pluralistic views emphasizing the importance of schools helping students retain and elaborate their language. What does not differ among those with different ideologies is that all Hispanic students must be well educated to ensure full integration in the American economy.

Research findings support the notion that if teachers are cognizant of the cognitive dispositions of their students, capitalize on the students' dispositions (see Table 2-6), and utilize culturally congruent content and instruction (including, where possible, the use of the student's native language), students and their families will respond in a very positive manner. As Clayton (1996) observes:

> Learning styles are influenced by culture in the socialization process within the family and community and by ecological adaptations, and as such, are somewhat a reflection of the larger culture. . . . One or another learning style is not better; there is no value judgment involved. It is simply a fact of difference. A continuous clash of styles between teacher and student can mean frustration for both. Identification, recognition, and understanding of the difference can help both cross-cultural student and teacher. (p. 54)

No teacher in America has received more publicity for his work with Hispanic students than Jaime Escalante. Examine this classroom segment (as described by Mathews, 1988) and see how he creates a personal connection for the impersonal concept of "absolute value," and then relate Escalante's approach with the ideas in Table 2-6.

> "You guys play basketball? You know the give and go?" He bounced an imaginary ball in front of him . . . He crouched with his back to an imaginary basket, passing the ball to an imaginary guard crossing on his right. He repeated the routine, this time passing to the left.
> "The absolute value function is the give and go. I have two possibilities. If this fellow on this side is open, it is going to be from the left." He wrote $x < 0$ on the board. "If it is from the right, then $x > 0$."

"So my little ball is going to be the absolute value. I don't know which ball I'm going to use. This guy has two options, come from the left, he's gonna make it, or come from the right. Every time you see a number between two bars"—he wrote $|x|$ on the board—"you have to, you have to, you have to say, well, all right, it's coming from the left or from the right. You have to break it down into two parts. I can do that."

He wrote:

$|a| = a$ if $a > 0$
$|a| = a$ if $a < 0$

"But you must take into consideration three positions, I call, the three-second violation. Now. I don't really understand what is the three-second violation. Can somebody explain to me?"

". . . I use the three-second violation my own way. The three-second violation is, this is one ball: $|x| < a$; this is the second ball: $|x| = a$; and the third ball: $|x| > a$. That right?"

"Yeah, right."

"How many you see?"

"Three."

"You know, you gonna be in bad shape if you don't know how to solve these three things." He thumped the board next to each expression. "When the *absolute value* is greater than a, when the *absolute value* is equal to it, when the *absolute value* is less than a. You have to *know* this three-second violation. Look."

He wrote, with sweeping gestures, the meaning of each expression in turn:

$-a < x < a$ $\qquad$ $x = a$ $\qquad$ $x < -a$ or $x > a$
$\qquad\qquad\qquad\qquad$ $x = -a$

"As soon as you see that, absolute value of x is more than a, be able to say, immediately, minus a is more than x, or x is more than a." (p. 118–119)

Asian American Learners

The Asian American population in the United States represents about 4 percent of the total population (Sadker and Sadker, 2000) or approximately 9 million people. This increase in population has been due primarily to the enactment of the Immigration Act of 1965. Though a majority of Asian Americans live in just three states—California, Hawaii, and New York—they are less isolated geographically than ever before. Asian Americans are also very diverse—Chinese, Filipinos, Japanese—with the remainder coming from various other Asian countries (Roberts, 1993). Koreans are also increasing as a percentage of the American population, as are Vietnamese, Asian Indians, and the Hmong.

Because of the relaxation of immigration laws, there are two groups of Asian Americans commonly found in the United States: Those born in the United States some 200 years ago, and those who are recent immigrants (Cordova, 1983). Asian Americans born in the United States are much more likely to be assimilated into the mainstream culture (Cabezas, 1981), speak English fluently, live in middle-class neighborhoods, and tend not to identify themselves along ethnic lines. Immigrant Asian Americans clearly demonstrate a wide range of backgrounds. In search of political and economic stability, these individuals tend to identify along ethnic lines, have a limited English speaking ability, and bring with them to this country the concomitant characteristics of poverty and despair.

Research findings concerning Asian American students' cognitive styles are relatively sparse. This is partly because until only recently there were so few Asian Americans in American schools that researchers had not taken seriously any need to study this group of students. The research that does exist has indicated that many Asian Americans are extremely hard working, high achieving, and non-verbal, and seek careers in science and mathematics (Yoshiwara, 1983). That may partially explain their high performance as evidenced by the following:

- Asian Americans/Pacific Islanders have a college graduation rate of 42 percent. One year after graduation, they have the highest starting salary of any racial and ethnic group.

- Typically, Asian Americans score approximately 50 points higher than the national average on the math portion of the SAT. Their combined verbal and math SAT scores rank them higher than whites, American Indians, Latinos, and blacks.

- Although they are just 4 percent of the total population, Asian Americans have a much higher percentage representation at prestigious universities, such as Harvard and Stanford. (Sadker and Sadker, 2000, p. 433)

New studies are needed in order to understand and help Asian American students, especially those recent immigrants who have entered our nation's schools. Whatever the reason for the dearth of research, the data thus far lean in the direction of field-independent styles for Asian Americans (Dunn, 1993). This may be one reason why Asian American students do so well in American schools—the structure, the instructional approaches, and the adherence to authoritarian methods (high teacher control) are congruent with Asian American teaching-learning approaches. There is also growing evidence that the more assimilated the Asian American students are, the more their performance mirrors that of other American cultural groups (Steinberg, 1996). For example, Shanker (1996) indicates that "the more Asian-American students become Americanized, the less well they perform—which, incidentally, disposes of the idea that their success is based on genetic superiority. Assimilated, Asian-American students are no more successful than anyone else" (p.17).

Yu and Bain (1985) studied the cognitive styles of Chinese and Chinese-English 8- to 11-year-old students in Hong Kong and Alberta, Canada. They found that the Chinese and Chinese-English students in both Hong Kong and Canada performed much more in a field-independent manner than did Anglo students; recall that Anglo students tend to be more field independent than other racial and ethnic groups.

The results of Enright (1987) and Hansen (1984) also confirm the results of Yu and Bain (1985). Chinese students in both Hong Kong and North America perform in a field-independent manner. One reason for this finding may be the **strong visual-spatial skill development** of Chinese students as reported by Flaugher and Roch (1977) and Vernon (1984).

Two studies, one by Hansen (1984) and the other by Hansen-Strain (1987), are worth examining. Hansen (1984) compared Filipino and South Pacific Island students. She found that the Filipino students functioned in a field-independent manner as compared with South Pacific Island students, and that the males were more field-independent than the female students.

Hansen-Strain (1987) compared Hawaiian with South Pacific Island students. She, too, found that the Hawaiian students were more field-independent; and, once again, the males of all groups were more field-independent than the females.

Relative to the socialization of Asian American (Chinese, Japanese, Korean, and Vietnamese) children, Cabezas (1981) found that the mothers utilized a variety of question-asking behaviors in their child-rearing practices that appear to positively influence the **analytical skills** of Asian students, especially in comparison with the direct commands, modeling, or cuing found in more traditional homes. Because of these child-rearing practices, the youngsters in this study interacted positively with and sought verbal approval from their mothers. This research is in direct opposition to the view held by many American teachers that many Asian American youngsters are shy and withdrawn, and that they do not possess the requisite verbal skills necessary to be successful in school. In actuality, Asian American students' reluctance to interact in class discussions probably has more to do with the lack of teacher encouragement to engage in verbal interactions than to any innate lack of verbal ability (Pang, 1990).

Au and Kawakami (1985) also identified the importance of verbal interactions in their research with Hawaiian American students. They found that by structuring reading lessons around culturally affirming and compatible learning styles, students would concentrate on reading lessons twice as much as they would with traditional teaching approaches. The approach used in the Au and Kawakami study used a culturally familiar interactional pattern labeled "talk story"—a process in which the children tell a story together. Group, rather than individual, performance is the emphasis of this culturally congruent form of communication. As the story is told, teachers allowed their students to break in when they wanted to, rather than calling upon individual students to participate and contribute to the discussion. This culturally affirming teaching approach creates a style of teaching and learning that engenders a sense of caring, a family atmosphere, and the sharing of reading responses.

Because so few research studies concerning Asian American students have been conducted, educators tend to stereotype all members of this cultural group. Suzuki (1983) reinforces this observation by stating:

> Many teachers stereotype Asian and Pacific American students as quiet, hardworking, and docile, which tends to reinforce conformity and stifle creativity. Asian and Pacific American students, therefore, frequently do not develop the ability to assert and express themselves verbally and are channeled in disproportionate numbers into the technical/scientific fields. As a consequence, many Asian and Pacific American students undergo traumatic family/school discontinuities, suffer from low self-esteem, are overly conforming, and have their academic and social development narrowly circumscribed. (p. 23)

TABLE 2-7   Capitalizing on Asian American Dispositions

Teachers need to:

- *Emphasize visual-spatial skills within classroom lessons.*

- *Utilize analytic skills in the tasks designed for students.*

- *Provide learning activities that provide opportunities for students to take parts and/or components and design new wholes and/or solutions.*

- *Provide time and space for thinking and personal reflection.*

The current literature base needs to be expanded to include more recent research on immigrants from Southeast Asia and how their performance fares in our nation's schools. Very little data on the cognitive dispositions of these immigrants are currently available (see Worthley, 1987). As Pang (1990) has cautioned, researchers must be cognizant of the limited research findings concerning Asian Americans in explaining the behavior of all Asian Americans. Still, in working with Asian American students, teachers should consider the dispositions as outlined in Table 2-7.

Gender

The notion that males and females process information differently raises serious and controversial questions, just as it has for most non-European American groups. Whether a hierarchy of male and female learning characteristics exists is an issue that sparks a heated debate. Whether girls and boys receive differential treatments in classrooms, though, is questioned by few. Sadker and Sadker (2000) note:

> Research tells us that teachers talk differently to female than to male students. Boys are reprimanded more often (one study shows that they receive eight to ten times as many control messages as girls do) and are punished more harshly. Not only do teachers punish boys more, but they also talk to them more, listen to them more, and give them more active teaching attention.
>
> When teachers learn that in many classrooms boys get more than their fair share of questions, they often express disbelief. "This certainly doesn't apply to me" is a common reaction. "I direct questions to all of my students. I interact with them equally."
>
> Of course, not all teachers interact more with boys. But, for most teachers, who are immersed in a dizzying number of interactions with students— as many as one thousand a day—it is impossible to track questioning patterns accurately. Frequently, when the teachers are shown videotapes or an objective tally of the number of questions directed at girls and boys, they are surprised at the disparities in interaction. Awareness and appropriate training can promote change to fair and effective instruction. (pp. 443–444)

The consequences of that differential behavior are questioned by some researchers (Center on Educational Policy, 2000). A growing body of research even suggests that the gender gap in terms of participation in rigorous high school courses may be closing (if it is not already closed). The notion of whether hierarchical cognitive differences exist is bothersome to many women's groups and to us because it implies national differences that some use as justification for prejudicial practice. This discussion of gender cognitive style is presented similar to those provided for the other cultural groups presented in this chapter. The research findings are provided to help teachers consider the possibilities for how to organize instruction, identify and utilize student cognitive dispositions, and enhance student cognition by providing experience in alternative styles of learning.

McCaulley, MacDaid, and Kainz (1985) classified learners as either "thinkers" or "feelers." In their research, those learners who utilized the thinking mode—approximately three-fourths of whom were male—preferred instruction that was objective (more field-independent), and utilized the skills of analysis, evaluation, and discourse. Individuals who preferred the feeling mode—approximately two-thirds of whom were female—learned best through instruction that was personal and caring, focused on issues of human values, utilized collaboration and cooperative learning, and was designed around academic material that stressed the improvement of people's lives and the relevance of ideas to the real world. The findings of McCaulley et al. ring true to previous research cited in other sections of this chapter that classified learners as feelers (field-sensitive learners) or thinkers (field-independent learners).

Kolb (1984) and Smith and Kolb (1986) reinforce the McCaulley et al. findings by critiquing how males and females process information. Although the two groups were equally distributed, the researchers found that 59 percent of females preferred the processing of information through concrete, hands-on experiences (field-dependent). Of the males in the study, 59 percent preferred processing information through abstract conceptualization (field-independent).

Belenky, Clinchy, Goldberger, and Tarule (1986) extended the research further through a lucid description of women's ways of knowing. Belenky's "ways of knowing" classification is of two types. The first type is preferred predominantly by women and is classified as "connected knowing." Through this knowing type, information is processed in an integrative, involved, empathetic, and subjective manner. The focus is upon understanding in the sense that the learner has a personal acquaintance with the thing (idea) or person being studied. It requires that the learner place herself/himself in the other person's place or context. The second type of knowing is preferred mostly by men and is classified as "separated knowing." This knowing type is conducted through an abstract, objective, and removed process. In other words, it requires a separation between the thing or person studied and the knower/information processor. This way of knowing follows strict rules by which data or an issue are evaluated. Belenky et al. (1986) state that neither way of knowing is necessarily better or worse than the alternative, but in understanding how children learn (whether male or female), teachers are in a better position to help youngsters reach their full potential.

The cognitive style differences among European American women are not unique. There are also cognitive style differences among women of non-European American cultures. The research findings indicate that educational environments tend to be biased by gender as well as by culture (Howard, 1987). As we found previously in our analyses of several selected cultural groups,

TABLE 2-8   Capitalizing on Female Dispositions

Teachers need to:

- *Develop a warm and supportive classroom environment through the use of cooperative learning.*

- *Provide an overview and rationale to help place academic content within a context to be studied.*

- *Relate what is to be studied to a context in the "real world."*

- *Develop a classroom climate characterized by caring and personal environments.*

- *Facilitate classroom discussions and interactions.*

women also tend to value cooperation rather than competition, working together in teams, and helping others achieve tasks and fulfill responsibilities.

Belenky et al. (1986) and other research findings are very similar to a recent report released by the National Foundation for Women Business Owners (1994) concerning women's leadership behavior. The report identifies a number of characteristics that women tend to exhibit in their interactions with others— for example, an **emphasis upon intuition,** upon values and feelings in dealing with others, and **upon relationships** with others built over time. Women tend to see success through building relationships with people, developing strong team-oriented groups, reaching decisions through the use of consensus techniques, and accomplishing something worthwhile for themselves and others. Men, on the other hand, tend to rely on logic and rational thinking processes, and find success by achieving goals and tasks for their own sake.

Gilligan (1982) and Baker Miller (1986) found similar and recurrent differences between men and women in terms of field independence—field sensitivity. Women who tend to be classified as field-sensitive in cognitive style were found to value affiliation with their coworkers, tended to develop a personality or style oriented toward relationships rather than autonomy, and exhibited a preference for cooperative interaction or collaboration rather than competition. Similarly, Baxter Magolda (1989) found the same type of difference when college-age men and women were studied. The most important finding identified was women's preference for cooperative, relationship-oriented interaction with themselves, peers, and their college instructors (Baxter Magolda, 1989).

Teachers need to be aware of the learning preferences evidenced by men and women, but many educators quite rightly express frustration with what to do with that knowledge. How does the teacher act on it? Table 2-8 provides modest direction, but gender equity, similar to racial or ethnic equity, requires thoughtful awareness and careful action (Bailey, 1996). By being aware of the fact that people are different, regardless of their racial, ethnic, or gender affiliation, teachers can accommodate those differences by varying instructional strategies so that students have opportunities to use their strengths. The teacher's responsibility is also related to modifying the curriculum to ensure that the materials used and content covered are reflective of the richness of the human family. History is not simply a white, male experience; it is something that all people, regardless of race or gender, have experienced. As a consequence, teachers need to provide a curriculum that embraces that richness and helps students see their "face" in our country's past and its future.

Ⓢ UMMARY OF THE FINDINGS

We have examined and presented the salient research findings concerning cognitive styles by gender and by selected cultural groups. We will now identify some broader cognitive characteristics among those various groups. Reliance on broader categories is fraught with difficulties, especially if teachers use the knowledge to narrowly define how to teach each child. But such categories can help immeasurably if they are used as a way of considering the importance of variability in instructional approach. We are going to take all the diverse ideas about how different cultural groups learn and fit them into the notions of field independence and field dependence, which we described earlier in this chapter. This approach will enable the reader to think through the complexities of teaching in a way that is more instructionally manageable. Our approach is not without conceptual support. Educational anthropologist Edward Hall (1989) argues: "Over thirty years of teaching students and learning from them have convinced me that no two people learn in exactly the same way. I am also convinced that there are major categories into which learning styles can be fitted" (p. 32). The approach is not without support. It is also not without problems.

Focusing just on field dependence-independence is reductionistic and oversimplifies the complexity of the learning process because it represents just one cognitive style dimension. Still, our goal is for you as a teacher to think about how different learners can be and to appreciate that the only way to deal with those differences is to be able to use a variety of teaching strategies. Because students possess different preferences, teachers necessarily must offer a range of options in order to connect with a whole class. True, a teacher may "play" to a preference, but in doing so he or she cannot totally ignore students whose preferences are quite different from the teacher's.

It is important to note that we are not saying that if a teacher works predominantly with African American students that the teacher should use only teaching strategies that foster field-dependent student dispositions, though it may explain the apparent efficacy of direct instruction practices with African American students. Our point is that by knowing that students are different, the teacher purposefully varies instruction to draw upon student strengths and develop student weaknesses in ways that reflect intentionality—the teacher knows the purpose of the instructional strategy and how that strategy will work to the benefit of all students.

Table 2-9 presents our classification of the cultural groups analyzed in this chapter and their cognitive style dispositions—field-sensitive/dependent or field-independent. Recall that in Table 2-1 we presented the research findings of field-dependent and field-independent learners. In actuality, learners seldom

TABLE 2-9 Cultural Group Classification by Cognitive Style

Field-Dependent	Field-Independent
■ Hispanic Americans	■ European American males
■ African Americans	■ Asian Americans
■ European American females	■ Native Americans
■ Recent Asian American immigrants	■ Other cultural groups with a high degree of assimilation

fall neatly into a category. Almost all are somewhere on a continuum. Hence, individuals often fall on a continuum between the two extremes of field sensitivity-field independent or global-analytical. Once again, all learners, regardless of their racial or gender affiliation, have acquired, through cultural experiences and role demands, cognitive style characteristics and utilize these characteristics throughout the continuum of field dependence–field independence.

Table 2-10 describes the teaching style characteristics reflected based on the disposition of the teacher. Thus, a field-dependent teacher is likely to prefer instructional situations that stimulate lots of interactions among students (cooperative learning), whereas a field-independent oriented teacher may prefer lecture formats where classrooms are more impersonal in tone. We all have preferences and inclinations to think that how I like to teach is how all should teach. Our dispositions influence personal pedagogical inclinations. The problem emerges if our students have dispositions at variance with ours, and yet we offer little variability in how content is presented. The likelihood that teacher and student styles will differ is reasonably great. America's teaching force in the mid-1990s was approximately 85 percent non-Hispanic White and only about 15 percent were minorities. Yet America's student population is increasingly economically and racially diverse (Newman, 1998).

Table 2-11 outlines the applications for using the field-dependent and independent construct for understanding how to motivate students. Taken together the three tables suggest how teachers might look at students, how teachers might exhibit pedagogical preferences, and how teachers can motivate students. In the next section we extend this thinking and consider implications for classroom practice.

IMPLICATIONS FOR CLASSROOM PRACTICE

In the previous sections of this chapter, we provided the reader with a synopsis of selected research findings for women and cultural groups. This synopsis provided data that were both unique to and common among the various groups examined. We found that women and many cultural groups tend to be more field dependent in their cognitive styles, more group rather than individually oriented, more sensitive to the social environment around them, and more responsive to adult role models. Additionally, these same cultural groups tended

TABLE 2-10   Field-Dependent and Field-Independent Teaching Styles

Field-Dependent	**Field-Independent**
■ Prefers teaching situations that allow interaction and discussion with students	■ Prefers impersonal teaching situations such as lectures; emphasizes cognitive aspect of instruction
■ Uses questions to check on student learning following instruction	■ Uses questions to introduce topics and following student answers
■ Uses student-centered activities	■ Uses a teacher-organized learning situation
■ Viewed by students as one who teaches facts	■ Viewed by students as encouraging them to apply principles
■ Provides less feedback; avoids negative evaluation	■ Gives corrective feedback; uses negative evaluation
■ Strong in establishing a warm and personal learning environment	■ Strong in organizing and guiding student learning

Source: Good, T., and J. Brophy (1990). *Educational Psychology*. New York: Longman, p. 616.

TABLE 2-11   How to Motivate Students

Field-Dependent	**Field Independent**
■ Through verbal praise	■ Through grades
■ Through helping the teacher	■ Through competition
■ Through external rewards (stars, stickers, prizes)	■ Through choice of activities, personal goal chart
■ Through showing the task's value to other people	■ Through showing how the task is useful to them
■ Through providing outlines and structure	■ Through freedom to design their own structure

Source: Good, T., and J. Brophy (1990). *Educational Psychology*. New York: Longman, p. 617.

to be less competitive, less sensitive to spatial incursions by others, less comfortable in trial-and-error situations, and less interested in the details of nonsocial tasks (Ramirez, 1982). The question that most classroom teachers may now ask would be: "What do all of these findings mean to me in working with diverse student populations?" The question is appropriate in terms of how these findings affect classroom practice.

The first implication that can be drawn from our previous discussion relates to the attitudes and expectations teachers may have toward culturally diverse learners. When teachers misunderstand (or fail to understand!) the cultural behaviors, nonverbal cues, and verbal interactions of culturally diverse students, they sell such students short. This underestimation of intellectual power and potential, failure to challenge young people's minds, and the ridiculous placement of labels upon students do irreparable harm. Teachers who are unaware or unappreciative of the rich cultural and cognitive backgrounds that diverse students bring to the classroom underestimate students' cognitive potential, academic achievement, and complex language abilities. Through his research contrasting African and African American cultures with European and European American cultures, Hilliard (1992) found that teachers who had low expectations for students would slow the pace of instruction, fragment instruction, and fail to offer conceptually oriented instruction. Hilliard (1992) elaborates: "Thus, we see that it is not the learning style of the child that prevents the child from learning; it is the perception by the teacher of the child's style as a sign of incapacity that causes the teacher to reduce the quality of instruction offered" (p. 373).

The second implication we can draw from the research relates to the need for teachers to acquire a repertoire of instructional models for use in their classrooms. To identify an instructional model for use in teaching a lesson is of little value unless that model is specifically appropriate in achieving lesson objectives. Teachers must have a repertoire of models to draw from rather than rely solely on one teaching approach—which is often the way they were taught. The teacher of the future must be skilled in using several instructional models in order to accommodate the diverse student cognitive styles in a classroom. By varying the instructional model, the teacher can be more assured the students will have an opportunity to "play to" their learning strengths and to develop skills in areas of "weakness." Further, future teachers must provide students with opportunities to learn through the use of alternative cognitive styles—some with which students have had much practical experience, and other approaches with which students have had little or no practical experience.

As educators, our responsibility is not only to help youngsters experience and learn about new phenomena, but also to help fashion new ideas and to assist youngsters in discovering their own intellectual abilities. Through the use of alternative instructional models (which are used effectively and appropriately) and different learning modalities students will have access to experiences that provide them with new learning approaches and the corresponding intellectual skills. Sherrie Moss and Millie Fuller (2000), two middle school teachers, describe this "sensitivity" in their work with middle grade students.

> Only small percentages of any group of learners respond best to purely auditory stimuli. Therefore, every lesson should include a kinesthetic component. Kinesthetic learners make up the largest category of middle school students, and brief moments of activity can help imprint a lesson. Here are a few examples. In learning the marks of punctuation, a class can move in a line as it reads a text. When students come to a comma, they execute a hula movement. As the reading continues, the students perform other preassigned actions for each mark of punctuation. Or in learning the states of matter in a science class, the students can create a "dance of the molecules." Or the Cartesian coordinate system can be illustrated by particular arm and leg movements when students refer to each quadrant. Social studies provides rich material for kinesthetic activities. Each student can be assigned to a particular historical character and given a movement to execute or a line of dialogue to speak when his or her character is mentioned. Both

animate and inanimate objects may have such dialogue and movements. For example, the Rosetta Stone might say, "I am the key, read me." (p. 274)

The consideration of various student learning styles leads to another implication that calls for new ways to organize and implement learning for youngsters. Alternative teaching approaches, which this text emphasizes, foster the cognitive learning, interpersonal situations and relationships, hands-on learning, laboratory work, and projects that involve individuals and/or groups more directly in their own learning. Education is not something teachers *do to* students; it is, instead, something teachers do *with them*. Good teachers learn as they teach because they become intellectually engaged with the students.

A final implication that arises from the research findings emphasizes learning within a natural, rich environment. When students learn in ways that are natural for them, a number of positive outcomes result—increased academic achievement, increased social acceptance by others, improved self-concept, an enhanced (and more positive) feeling toward the notion of learning, increased creative energy, increased self-direction, and improved basic skill development (Dunn and Dunn, 1979; Moss and Fuller, 2000; Olstad et al., 1981; Saracho and Spodek, 1984; Shade, 1984). When teachers (1) utilize a combination of visual, auditory, and kinesthetic modes, (2) consider field dependence/field independence and (3) use understandings of conceptual tempo to understand how students might solve problems, all students will be educated in an environment that more nearly matches their learning needs. Although each of us exhibits a preferred learning style, students who learn through more than one learning modality develop richer understandings of new concepts and acquire a larger repertoire of academic and social skills. When any one of us is in the process of acquiring either new information or new skills, we learn by using alternative learning modalities.

Care must be taken by the reader to utilize critically the concepts and ideas discussed in this chapter. That is, the ideas are tools to help in the creation of individualized classroom environments—not facile labels to classify whole groups of people. No cognitive style is better or worse than any other style. The only judgment that can be made is that different cognitive styles exist because of the multiplicity of cultural influences and personal dispositions. Cultural groups and male and female students do learn differently from one another (the research supports this). However, individuals within each group learn differently mainly because of either their involvement within the mainstream culture or the complex child-rearing practices they experience within the "home" culture in which they grow up.

All youngsters can learn, but they need to be taught in ways that warrant them as learners so they can more fully achieve their potential. By varying their instruction and recognizing the intellectual gifts of the learners, teachers can be more assured that each student's needs are being met. An important educational initiative for the classroom teacher is to recognize and implement what is known from the research, acquire a repertoire of instructional alternatives to be used with youngsters, and organize and implement a system of individualization in order to better serve America's culturally diverse student populations. That is, effective teachers in culturally diverse settings not only think about the learner as a learner but also strive to create conditions in which that learner's "voice" can be heard so that it is clear that student views have significance. Mike Rose (1995), in his description of successful teachers in diverse cultural settings, powerfully reinforces this perspective:

> But two things seemed to hold across classrooms [in multicultural settings]. First, a teacher's authority came from multiple sources—knowledge, care, the construction of safe and respectful space, solidarity with students' background—rather than solely from age or role. Though there were times when our teachers asserted authority in a direct and unilateral way, in general, authority was not expressed or experienced as a blunt exercise of power. As one of Stephanie Terry's first-graders put it, "She doesn't fuss a lot."
>
> The second thing to note was that even in classrooms that were run in a relatively traditional manner, authority was distributed. In various ways, students contributed to the flow of events, shaped the direction of discussion, became authorities on their own experience and on the work they were doing. Think of Stephanie Terry's students reporting on their observations of the tree frog and hermit crab and Michelle Taigue's Navajo and Hopi students explaining slang and dialect on the reservation. There were multiple pathways of authority, multiple opportunities for members of the class to assume authority. And since authority and the generation of knowledge are intimately connected—those who can speak affect what is known—there were multiple opportunities to shape the knowledge emerging in the classroom. (pp. 414–415)

CONCLUSION

Most of the current literature in leadership and in organizational theory emphasizes a new type of worldview. Every few hundred years the world begins a transformation wherein society rearranges its values; its views of reality; its social, political, and economic structures; its incorporation of peoples, and its manner of conducting business. We are in the midst of such a process—a transformation of the world's scientific, educational, and political paradigms. One of the most noticeable of these transformations is that historically disenfranchised groups (that is, women, Native Americans, Africans, Asians, and Hispanics) are now seeking to play a more active role in setting a direction for the global, economic society. They want to be included, not excluded! And, yet, in many contexts throughout the country, especially urban situations, students are excluded (Hill, Campbell, and Harvey, 2000). Charters and choice are efforts to foster inclusion at the school district level. Instructional variability is the means of accomplishing it at the classroom level.

As a consequence, a new set of demands is being placed upon schools to provide and produce a workforce that meets the demands of an international society (Drucker, 1993; Kanter, 1989; Toffler, 1990). In discussions at national and international conferences, and in the literature of sociology, management, and political science, critical characteristics are identified as being required by this new workforce. Individuals in this society will need to

- Value diversity in the workplace, both in terms of the primary characteristics of diversity (for example, age, gender, race, physically challenged) and in terms of diversity of thought.
- Exhibit a willingness to continue learning and growing throughout their lives.
- Value collaborative, team-oriented work relationships.
- Function in consensus-reaching structures rather than hierarchical, bureaucratic structures.
- Exhibit a willingness to focus on relationship-oriented behavior by which individuals are empowered in the decision-making process.
- Think globally in the use of knowledge, skills, and attitudes.
- Exhibit knowledge and the use of the various forms of technology (that is, computers, videotapes, distance learning, and so on) to communicate, learn, and work.
- Function in a more personal rather than formal manner in interactions with others.
- Energize others through charisma, knowledge, and conviction.
- Empower others to function in creative and innovative ways to perform work and/or discover new ways of working.

Ironically, many of these same traits are similar to the qualities attributed to women and the various cultural groups in our society. Clearly, new skills are going to be needed for success in our emerging society: the ability to accept and appreciate cultural and gender diversity; the ability to conceptualize problems in both a whole and linear, sequential manner; the ability to function in cooperative work teams that value interaction and alternatives; and the ability to utilize kinesthetic/tactile, hands-on learning and experimentation. Such skills, dispositions, and capacities need to not only be developed and enhanced among women and the disenfranchised cultural groups of society, but be promoted and developed within our total society.

If our citizens are to be contributing members in this information-based society, educators will need to encourage full student participation, share information and power, enhance student self-worth, and energize student excitement in learning and being a critical player in this global society. These characteristics can be developed in our schools if we begin looking critically at what we do in schools and how we function with youngsters in their preparation for world participation. Interestingly, research suggests that when teachers can accurately assess student cognitive styles and then structure some learning experiences accordingly, the impact on student self concepts and school is both real and substantial (Good and Brophy, 1995).

Prominent psychologist and educator Mihaly Csikszentmihalyi (2000) captures what is needed for adolescents. His recommendations relate to the real needs of America's high school students who all too often are disengaged from education—a situation documented by lots of researchers including Hill,

Campbell, and Harvey (2000). Csikszentmihalyi is pointed in his recommendations and they relate both to the content of this chapter and to the models in the following chapters.

- *Develop high school curricula in academic subjects that stress creativity, flexibility, and emotional intelligence.* In the future it will be essential to establish more links between disciplines, to see commonalities among different subjects, and to master synthetic as well as analytic approaches to learning. . . .

- *Encourage high schools to provide more instructional time in academic subjects and to use that time in ways that are intellectually engaging for the students.* Compared to other societies, ours spends much less time exposing students to academic subjects . . . Schools should place less reliance on passive instructional formats such as lectures and audiovisual presentations. Group projects should be utilized more widely, taking advantage of teenagers' natural inclination to work together with peers. Other instructional formats that engage students' attention are individual work and testing. . . .

- *Encourage intrinsic motivation and teach children to enjoy what they do for its own sake, not just for the sake of getting good grades.* Children who enjoy overcoming challenges will seek out challenging situations in their adult lives. They will be more likely to seize new opportunities, to seek new ways of doing things, to work on tasks that have unclear solutions, and to inspire others to work on difficult problems. . . .

- *Find situations that are more play-like for disadvantaged youth.* Students who perceived their life in more play-like terms were more likely to matriculate in selective postsecondary schools. The importance of play in the lives of young people as well adults is well established, and it will become even more important in the rapidly changing labor market of the future. (pp. 234–236)

Teachers who know their content and how to teach it are teachers who create an engaging curriculum that makes the learning process enjoyable. Learning is work, but teachers who can think beyond ordinary instruction are going to find more rewards for themselves and their students than they ever imagined possible. Significantly, teachers who vary the instructional environment for students are creating a vital learning environment for themselves.

ⓇEFERENCES

Anderson, J. A. 1988. "Cognitive Styles and Multicultural Populations." *Journal of Teacher Education* 39: 2–9.

Appleton, N. 1983. *Cultural Pluralism in Education: Theoretical Foundations.* New York: Longman.

Au, K., and A. Kawakami. 1985. "Research Currents: Talk Story and Learning to Read." *Language Arts* 62(4): 406–411.

Bailey, S. M. 1996. "Shortchanging Girls and Boys." *Educational Leadership* 53(8): 75–79.

Baker Miller, J. 1986. *Toward a New Psychology of Women* (2nd ed.). Boston: Beacon.

Baxter Magolda, M. B. 1989. "Gender Differences in Cognitive Development: An Analysis of Cognitive Complexity and Learning Styles." *Journal of College Student Development* 30(3): 213–220.

Belenky, M. F., B. M. Clinchy, M. R. Goldberger, and J. M. Tarule. 1986. *Women's Ways of Knowing: the Development of Self, Voice, and Mind.* New York: Basic Books.

Benjamin, D. P., S. Chambers, and G. Reiterman. 1993. "A Focus on American Indian College Persistence." *Journal of American Indian Education* 32(2): 24–40.

Bert, C. R. G., and M. Bert. 1992. *The Native American: An Exceptionality in Education and Counseling.* ERIC Document Reproduction Service No. ED 351 168.

Boykin, A. W. 1994. "Harvesting Culture and Talent: African-American Children." Pp. 324–371 in J. Spencer (ed.), *Achievement and Achievement Motives.* Boston: W. H. Freeman.

Brewer, A. 1977. "An Indian Education." *Integrated Education* 15: 21–23.

Bryant, H. W. 1986. *An Investigation into the Effectiveness of Two Strategy Training Approaches on the Reading Achievement of Grade One Native Indian Children.* Unpublished doctoral dissertation. Vancouver: University of British Columbia.

Cabezas, A. 1981. *Early Childhood Development in Asian and Pacific American Families: Families in Transition.* San Francisco: Asian.

Caine, R. N., and G. Caine. 1995. "Reinventing Schools Through Brain-Based Learning." *Education Leadership* 52(7): 43–47.

Center on Educational Policy and American Youth Policy Forum. 2000. *Do You Know the Good News About American Education?* Washington, DC: Author.

Clayton, J. B. 1996. *Your Land, My Land: Children in the Process of Acculturation.* Portsmouth, NH: Heinemann.

Cohen, R. A. 1969. "Conceptual Styles, Culture Conflict, and Nonverbal Tests of Intelligence." *American Anthropologist* 71: 838–856.

Cooper, G. C. 1987. "Right Hemispheric Dominance, Holistic Cognitive Style, and Black Language." Pp. 61–86 in J. A. Anderson (ed.), *Benjamin E. Mays Monograph Series* 1(1).

Cordova, F. 1983. *Filipinos: Forgotten Asian Americans.* Dubuque, IA: Kendell and Hunt.

Cox, B., and M. Ramirez III. 1981. "Cognitive Styles: Implications for Multiethnic Education." Pp. 61–71 in J. Banks et al. (eds.), *Education in the 80s: Multiethnic Education.* Washington, DC: National Education Association.

Csikszentmihalyi, M. 2000. *Becoming Adult.* New York: Basic Books.

Damico, S. B. 1983. "The Two Worlds of School: Differences in the Photographs of Black and White Adolescents." Paper presented at annual meeting of American Educational Research Association, Montreal.

Davis, M. 2001. "No Simple Americanizers: Three Early Anglo Researchers of Mexican American Education." *The Educational Forum* 65(2): 136–143.

De La Rosa, D., and C. E. Maw. 1990. *Hispanic Education: A Statistical Portrait 1990.* Washington, DC: National Council of La Rosa.

Dinges, N.C., and A. R. Hollenbeck. 1978. "Field-Dependence-Independence in Navajo Children." *International Journal of Psychology* 13: 215–220.

Drucker, Peter F. 1993. *Post-Capitalist Society.* New York: HarperCollins.

Dunn, R. 1993. "Learning Styles of the Multiculturally Diverse." *Emergency Librarian* 20(4): 24–30.

———, **and K. Dunn.** 1979. "Using Learning Style Data to Develop Student Prescriptions." Pp. 109–122 in National Association of Secondary School Principals, *Student Learning Styles: Diagnosing and Prescribing Programs.* Reston, VA: NASSP.

Dunn, R., J. Gemake, F. Jalali, R. Zenhausern, P. Quinn, and J. Spiridakis. 1990. "Cross-Cultural Differences in Learning Styles of Elementary-Age Students from Four Ethnic Backgrounds." *Journal of Multicultural Counseling and Development* 18(2): 68–93.

Enright, D. S. 1987. "Cognitive Style and First Language Background in Second Language Test Performance." *TESOL Quarterly* 21: 565–569.

Flaugher, R. L., and D. A. Roch. 1977. "Patterns of Ability Factors Among Four Ethnic Groups." Research Memorandum No. 7. Princeton, NJ: Educational Testing Service.

Flippo, R. F. (ed.) 2001. *Reading Researchers in Search of Common Ground.* Newark, DE: International Reading Association.

Gardner, H. 1985. *The Mind's New Science.* New York: Basic Books.

Gilbert, S., and G. Gay. 1985. "Improving the Success in School of Poor Black Children." *Phi Delta Kappan* 67(2): 133–137.

Gilligan, C. 1982. *In a Different Voice: Psychological Theory and Women's Development.* Cambridge, MA: Harvard University Press.

Goldstein, R. 1971. *Black Life and Culture in the United States*. New York: Thomas Crowell.

Good, T. L., and J. Brophy. 1995. *Educational Psychology*. New York: Longman.

Grantham-Campbell, M. 1992. "Successful Alaska Native Students: Implications 500 Years After Columbus." Paper presented at the meeting of the American Anthropological Association, San Francisco (December).

Guttentag, M. 1972. "Negro-White Differences in Children's Movement." *Perceptual and Motor Skills* 35: 435–436.

Hale-Benson, J. 1982. *Black Children: Their Roots, Culture, and Learning Styles*. Baltimore: Johns Hopkins University Press.

———. 1986. *Black Children: Their Roots, Culture, and Learning Styles* (rev. ed.). Baltimore, MD: Johns Hopkins University Press.

Hall, E. 1989. "Unstated Features of the Cultural Context of Learning." *Educational Forum* 54(1): 21–34.

Halverson, B. 1976. *Cognitive Style of Preschool Seminole Indian Children.*Unpublished doctoral dissertation, Florida State University, Tallahassee.

Hansen, L. 1984. "Field Dependence-Independence and Language Testing: Evidence from Six Pacific Island Cultures." *TESOL Quarterly* 18: 311–324.

Hansen-Strain, L. 1987. "Cognitive Style and First Language Background in Second Language Test Performance." *TESOL Quarterly* 21: 565–569.

Harry, B. 1992. *Cultural Diversity, Families, and the Special Education System*. New York: Teachers College Press.

Herring, R. D. 1989. "Counseling Native American Children." *Implications for Elementary School Guidance and Counseling* 23 (April): 272–281.

Hill, P., C. Campbell, and P. Harvey. 2000. *It Takes a City: Getting Serious About Urban Reform*. Washington, DC: Brookings Institute.

Hilliard, A. G. III. 1976. *Alternatives to IQ Testing: An Approach to the Identification of Gifted Minority Children*. Final report to the California State Department of Education.

———. 1989. "Teachers and Cultural Styles in a Pluralistic Society." *NEA Today* 1: 65–69.

———. 1992. "Behavioral Style, Culture, and Teaching and Learning." *Journal of Negro Education* 61(3): 370–373.

Hodges, L. 1996. "Blood Ties." *New York Times* (July 19): A15.

Howard, B. C. 1987. *Learning to Persist/Persisting to Learn*. Washington, DC: Mid-Atlantic Center for Race Equity, American University.

Howe, C. 1994. "Improving the Achievement of Hispanic Students." *Educational Leadership* 51(8): 42–44.

Irvine, J. J., and D. E. York. 1995. "Learning Styles and Culturally Diverse Students: A Literature Review." Pp. 484–492 in J. H. Banks (ed.), *Handbook of Research on Multicultural Education*. New York: Macmillan.

Kagan, S., and R. Buriel. 1977. "Field Dependence-Independence and Mexican-American Culture and Education." Pp. 279–328 in J. L. Martinez, Jr. (ed.), *Chicano Psychology*. Orlando, FL: Academic Press.

Kagan, S., and G. P. Knight. 1981. "Social Motives Among Anglo American and Mexican American Children: Experimental and Projective Measures." *Journal of Research in Personality* 15(1): 93–106.

Kagan, S., and M. C. Madsen. 1971. "Cooperation and Competition of Mexican, Mexican-American, and Anglo-American Children of Two Ages Under Four Instruction Sets." *Developmental Psychology* 5: 32–39.

Kagan, S., and G. L. Zahn. 1976. "Field Dependence and the School Achievement Gap Between Anglo-American and Mexican-American Children." *Journal of Educational Psychology* 67: 643–650.

Kanter, R. M. 1989. *When Giants Learn to Dance*. New York: Simon & Schuster.

Keefe, J. W. 1979. "Learning Styles: An Overview." Pp. 1–17 in *Student Learning Styles: Diagnosing and Prescribing Programs*. Reston, VA: National Association of Secondary School Principals.

Keefe, S. E., and A. M. Padilla. 1987. *Chicano Ethnicity*. Albuquerque, NM: University of New Mexico Press.

Kelly, J. A. 1984. *Influence of Culture, Gender and Academic Experience on Cognitive Style*. Unpublished dissertation, Vanderbilt University, Memphis, TN.

Keogh, B. K., M. F. Welles, and A. Weiss. 1972. "Field Dependence-Independence and Problem-Solving Styles of Preschool Children." Technical Report. Los Angeles: University of California.

Knight, G. P., and S. Kagan. 1977. "Development of Prosocial and Competitive Behaviors in Anglo-American and Mexican-American Children." *Child Development* 48(4): 1385-1394.

Kochman, T. 1972. *Rappin' and Stylin' Out: Communication in Urban Black America*. Urbana, IL: University of Illinois Press.

Kolb, D. 1984. *Experiential Learning*. Englewood Cliffs, NJ: Prentice-Hall.

Ladson-Billings, G. 1990. "Like Lightning in a Bottle: Attempting to Capture the Pedagogical Excellence of Successful Teachers of Black Students." *International Journal of Qualitative Studies in Education* 3(4): 335–344.

———. 1992. "Liberatory Consequences of Literacy: A Case of Culturally Relevant Instruction for African American Students." *Journal of Negro Education* 61(3): 378–391.

LaFrance, M., and C. Mayo. 1976. "Racial Differences in Gaze Behavior During Conversation." *Journal of Personality and Social Psychology* 33: 258–285.

Loftin, J. D. 1989. "Anglo American Jurisprudence and the Native American Tribal Quest for Religious Freedom." *American Indian Culture and Research Journal* 13(1): 1–52.

Longstreet, W. S. 1978. *Aspects of Ethnicity*. New York: Teachers College Press.

Macias, C. J. 1989. "American Indian Academic Success: The Role of Indigenous Learning Strategies." *Journal of American Indian Education* (August, special issue): 43–52.

Mamchur, C. M. 1996. *A Teacher's Guide to Cognitive Type Theory and Learning Style*. Alexandria, VA: Association for Supervision and Curriculum Development.

Mathews, J. 1988. *Escalante: The Best Teacher in America*. New York: Henry Holt.

McCaulley, M. H., G. P. MacDaid, and R. E. Kainz. 1985. "Estimated Frequencies of the MBTI Types." *Journal of Psychological Type* 9: 3–8.

McShane, D. 1980. "A Review of Scores of American Indian Children on the Seschler Intelligence Scales." *White Cloud Journal* 1: 3–10.

Messick, S. 1970. "The Criterion Problem in the Evaluation of Instruction: Assessing Possible, Not Just Intended, Outcomes." Pp. 183–202 in M. C. Wittrock and G. D. E. Wiley (eds.), *The Evaluation of Instruction: Issues and Problems*. New York: Holt.

More, A. J. 1990. "Learning Styles of Native Americans and Asians." Paper presented at the annual meeting of the American Psychological Association, Boston. ERIC Document Reproduction Service No. ED 330 535.

Morgan, H. 1981. "Factors Concerning Cognitive Development and Learning Differentiation Among Black Children." In A. E. Harrison (ed.), *Conference on Empirical Research in Black Psychology* 6: 14–22.

Moss, S., and M. Fuller. 2000. "Implementing Effective Practices." *Phi Delta Kappan*, 82(4): 273–276.

National Foundation for Women Business Owners. 1994. *Styles of Success: The Thinking and Management Styles of Women and Men Entrepreneurs*. Washington, DC: National Foundation for Women Business Owners (July).

Newman, J. W. 1998. *America's Teachers*. New York: Longman.

Nieto, S. 1996. *Affirming Diversity*. White Plains, NY: Longman.

Obiakor, F. E. 1992. "A Cultural Ecology of Competence Among Inner-City Blacks." Pp. 45-60 in M. Spencer, G. Brookins, and W. Allen (eds.), *Beginnings: The Social and Affective Development of Black Children*. Hillsdale, NJ: Lawrence Erlbaum Associates.

Obgu, J. U. 1983. "Cultural Discontinuities and Schooling." *Anthropology and Education Quarterly* 13: 290–307.

———. 1987. "Variability in Minority School Performance: A Problem in Search of an Explanation." *Anthropology and Education Quarterly* 18(4): 312–334.

———. 1989. "The Individual in Collective Adaptation: A Framework for Focusing on Academic Underperformance and Dropping Out Among Involuntary Minorities." Pp. 181–204 in L. Weis, E. Farran, and H. Petrie (eds.), *Dropouts from School: Issues, Dilemmas, and Solutions*. Albany: State University of New York Press.

Olstad, R., J. Juarez, L. Davenport, and D. Haury. 1981. *Inhibitors to Achievement in Science and Mathematics by Ethnic Minorities*. Bethesda, MD: ERIC Document Reproduction Service No. ED 223 404.

Pang, V. 1990. "Asian-American Children: A Diverse Population." *Educational Forum* 55(1): 49–66.

Pease-Alvarez, L., E. Garcia, and P. Espinoza. 1991. "Effective Instruction for Language Minority Students: An Early Childhood Case Study." *Early Childhood Research Quarterly* 6(3): 347–363.

Philips, S. 1972. "Participant Structures and Communicative Competence: Warm Springs Children in Community and Classroom." Pp. 370–394 in C. Cazden, V. John, and D. Hymes (eds.), *Functions of Language in the Classroom.* New York: Teachers College Press.

———. 1983. *The Invisible Culture: Communication in Classroom and Community on the Warm Springs Indian Reservation.* New York: Longman.

———. 1993. *The Invisible Culture.* Prospect Heights, IL: Waveland Press.

Prom, S. E. 1982. "Salient Content and Cognitive Performance of Person- and Thing-Oriented Low Income Afro-American Children in Kindergarten and Second Grade." Doctoral dissertation, Howard University, Washington, DC.

Ramirez, M., III. 1973. "Cognitive Styles and Cultural Democracy in Education." *Social Science Quarterly* 53: 895–904.

———. 1982. "Cognitive Styles and Cultural Diversity." Paper presented at the annual meeting of the American Educational Research Association, New York City (May).

———. 1991. *Psychotherapy and Counseling with Minorities: A Cognitive Approach to Individual and Cultural Differences.* New York: Allyn and Bacon.

———, and A. Castaneda. 1974. *Cultural Democracy, Bicognitive Development and Education.* New York: Academic Press.

Ramirez, M., III, and D. R. Price-Williams. 1974. "Cognitive Style of Three Ethnic Groups in the U.S." *Journal of Cross-Cultural Psychology* 5(2): 212–219.

Roberts, S. 1993. *Who We Are.* New York: Times Books.

Rollman, S. A. 1978. "The Sensitivity of Black and White Americans to Nonverbal Cues of Prejudice." *Journal of Social Psychology* 105: 73–77.

Rose, M. 1995. *Possible Lives: The Promise of Public Education in America.* New York: Houghton-Mifflin.

Sadker, M., and D. Sadker. 2000. *Teachers, Schools, and Society* (5th ed.). Boston: McGraw-Hill.

Saracho, O. N., and B. Spodek. 1984. *Cognitive Style and Children's Learning: Individual Variation in Cognitive Processes.* ERIC Document Reproduction Service No. ED 247 037.

Shade, B. J. 1981. "Racial Variation in Perceptual Differentiation." *Perceptual and Motor Skills* 52: 243–248.

———. 1984. "Afro-American Patterns of Cognition: A Review of the Research." Paper presented at annual meeting of American Educational Research Association, New Orleans, LA.

———. 1989. "The Influence of Perceptual Development on Cognitive Style: Cross Ethnic Comparisons." *Early Child Development and Care* 51: 137–155.

———, and P. A. Edwards. 1987. "Ecological Correlates of the Educative Style of Afro-American Children." *Journal of Negro Education* 86: 88–99.

Shanker, A. 1996. "Succeeding in School." *New Republic* (July 1): 17.

Shutiva, C. 1991. "Creativity Difference Between Reservation and Urban American Indians." *Journal of American Indian Education* 31(1): 33–52.

Slaughter-DeFoe, D. T., K. Nakagawa, R. Takanishi, and D. J. Johnson. 1990. "Toward Cultural/Ecological Perspectives on Schooling and Achievement in African- and Asian-American Children." *Child Development* 61: 363–383.

Slavin, R. E. 1977. *Student Team Learning Techniques: Narrowing the Achievement Gap Between the Races.* Report No. 228. Baltimore, MD: Johns Hopkins University, Center for the Study of Social Organization of Schools.

———, and E. Oickle. 1981. "Effects of Cooperative Learning Teams on Student Achievement and Race Relations: Treatment by Race Interactions." *Sociology of Education* 54: 174–180.

Smith, D. M., and D. Kolb. 1986. *Users Guide for the Learning Style Inventory: A Manual for Teachers and Trainers.* Boston: McBer.

Soldier, L. 1985. "To Soar with Eagles: Enculturation and Acculturation of Indian Children." *Childhood Education* 61: 185–191.

———. 1989. "Cooperative Learning and the Native American Student." *Phi Delta Kappan* 71(2): 161–163.

Steinberg, L. 1996. *Beyond the Classroom: Why School Reform Has Failed and What Parents Need to Do*. New York: Simon and Schuster.

Sternberg, R. J. 1994. "Commentary: Reforming School Reform: Comments on Multiple Intelligences: The Theory in Practice." *Teachers College Record* 95(4): 561–568.

Suarez, Z. E. 1993. "Cuban Americans: From Golden Exiles to Social Undersirables." Pp. 164–176 in H. P. McAdoo (ed.), *Family Ethnicity: Strength in Diversity*. Newbury Park, CA: Sage.

Suzuki, B. H. 1983. "The Education of Asian and Pacific Americans: An Introductory Overview." In D. T. Nakanishi and M. Hirano-Nakanishi (eds.), *Education of Asian and Pacific Americans: Historical Perspectives and Prescriptions for the Future*. Phoenix, AZ: Oryx Press.

Swisher, K., and D. Deyhle. 1987. "Styles of Learning and Learning Styles: Educational Conflicts for American Indian/Alaskan Native Youth." *Journal of Multilingual and Multicultural Development* 8(4): 350.

———. 1989. "The Styles of Learning Are Different, but the Teaching Is Just the Same: Suggestions for Teachers of American Indian Youth." *Journal of American Indian Education* (August, special issue): 1–14.

Tafoya, T. 1982. "Coyote Eyes: Native Cognition Styles." *Journal of American Indian Education* 21(2): 21–33.

Tienda, M. 2000. "Minorities in Higher Education: Troubling Trends and Promising Prospects." Speech presented at the Annual Convention of the University Council for Educational Administration. Albuquerque, NM.

Toffler, A. 1990. *Powershift*. New York: Bantam Books.

Tooker, E. 1983. *The Development of Political Organization in Native North America*. Washington, DC: American Ethnological Society.

Traub, J. 1999. *Better By Design? A Consumer's Guide to Schoolwide Reform*. Washington, DC: Thomas B. Fordham Foundation.

Tuck, K., and A. Boykin. 1989. "Verve Effects: The Relationship of Task Performance to Stimulus Preference and Variability in Low-Income Black and White Children." Pp. 84–85 in A. Harrison (ed.), *The Eleventh Conference on Empirical Research in Black Psychology*. Washington, DC: NIMH.

U.S. Department of Commerce, Bureau of the Census. 1996. *Statistical Abstract of the United States*. Washington, DC: U.S. Government Printing Office.

U.S. Department of Education, National Center for Education Statistics. 1995. *The Condition of Education*. Washington, DC: U.S. Government Printing Office.

U.S. Department of Education, National Center for Education Statistics. 1995. *Digest of Educational Statistics*. Washington, DC: U.S. Government Printing Office.

Utley, C. A. 1983. "A Cross-Cultural Investigation of Field-Independent/Field Dependent as a Psychological Variable in Menominees Native American and Euro-American Grade School Children." Madison, WI: Wisconsin Center for Education and Research.

Vasquez, J. A. 1991. "Cognitive Style and Academic Attainment." Pp. 163–179 in J. Lynch, C. Modgil, and S. Modgil (eds.), *Cultural Diversity and the Schools: Consensus and Controversy*, London: Falconer Press.

Vernon, P. A., D. N. Jackson, and S. Messick. 1988. "Cultural Influences on Patterns of Abilities in North America." Pp. 208–231 in S.H. Irvine and J.W. Berry (eds.), *Human Abilities in Cultural Context*. Cambridge, MA: Cambridge University Press.

Vernon, P. E. 1984. "Abilities and Achievements of Ethnic Groups in Canada with Special Reference to Canadian Natives and Orientals." Pp. 382–395 in R. Samuda. J. Berry, and M. Laferriere (eds.), *Multiculturalism in Canada: Social and Educational Perspectives*. Toronto: Allyn & Bacon.

Witkin, H. A., R. B. Dyk, H. F. Faterson, D. R. Goodenough, and S. A. Karp. 1962. *Psychological Differentiation*. New York: Wiley.

Witkin, H. A., C. A. Moore, D. R. Goodenough, and P. W. Cox. 1977. "Field-Dependent and Field-Independent Cognitive Style and Their Educational Implications." *Review of Educational Research* 47: 1–64.

Worthley, K. M. 1987. "Learning Style Factor of Field Dependence/Independence and Refugee Students." Master's Thesis, University of Wisconsin, Stout (July).

Yoshiwara, F. M. 1983. "Shattering Myths: Japanese American Educational Issues." P. 23 in D. T. Nakanishi and M. Hirano-Nakanishi (eds.), *Education of Asian and Pacific Americans: Historical Perspectives and Prescriptions for the Future*. Phoenix, AZ: Oryx.

Young, V. H. 1970. "Family and Childhood in a Southern Negro Community." *American Anthropologist* 72: 269–288.

————. 1974. "A Black American Socialization Pattern." *American Ethnologist* 1: 405–413.

Yu, A., and B. Bain. 1985. Language, Social Class and Cognitive Style: A Comparative Study of Unilingual and Bilingual Education in Hong Kong and Alberta. Hong Kong: Hong Kong Teachers' Association.

B

Effecting Instructional Model Usage

Instructional Alignment

Chapter Objectives

At the end of this chapter, readers will be able to

1. *Identify and describe what an instructional model is and how it can be used by teachers.*
2. *Identify and briefly describe eight different instructional models.*
3. *Describe the purpose of instructional planning.*
4. *Differentiate between goals and objectives.*
5. *Differentiate between the cognitive, affective, and psychomotor learning domains.*
6. *Design objectives utilizing the different taxonomical learning levels.*
7. *Design lesson plans for the instructional models that are enhanced by the integration of technology.*

INTRODUCTION

Do you recall when you first learned how to play golf, made an afghan for a family member, used a computer to be more productive at work, or played backgammon as a leisure-time activity? In each case, some critical information was necessary to understand the new skills; you had to learn specific cognitive and psychomotor skills in order to apply the information previously learned; feelings were elicited from applying the cognitive and psychomotor learning; and certain activities helped you acquire a satisfactory level of proficiency. New tasks or skills are difficult to acquire because there is so much information to deal with, so many subskills to learn and apply, and so much practice required for satisfactory performance.

Two examples illustrate our point. Many years ago, the authors of this text began learning to play golf. We say "began learning" because after all of these years, countless rounds of golf, and many thousands of dollars, we each continue to look for and seek the "perfect" round of golf. On our golfing odyssey, we learned some basic information about the game: its terminology, its rules and regulations, its means of scoring, and even a little about its history. In addition, we practiced how to hold a golf club, how either to prevent a slice or to promote a fade, how to prevent a hook or promote a draw, how to position the body and feet depending upon the club used, how to chip—getting the golf ball up and down to the hole—and how to putt, perhaps the most critical activity in lowering one's score.

The way to real growth is not to become more powerful or more famous, but to become more human and more tolerant.

HELEN STEINER RICE

The information and skills needed to play the game effectively are complex—from head position, to keeping the left arm straight (if a right-handed golfer), to the follow-through. We learned that applying appropriate rules and skills is situational; the game requires constant learning, practice, and coaching.

Let's look at another example of acquiring information and skills to illustrate our point about the connection between learning, practice, and coaching—making an afghan. To make an afghan, the apprentice needs to know how to read and follow a pattern, how to differentiate the various types of pattern styles and yarn textures available, how to determine the different types of yarn (baby vs. wool vs. acrylic yarn), and how to choose between the different weights of yarn (3 oz. vs. 4 oz.). The information needed to make an afghan depends upon the type of afghan being made. In addition, there are various types of stitches that the apprentice needs to know and practice (for example, the chain stitch, the double or triple crochet stitch, and the shell stitch). Each pattern chosen calls for specific stitches to be used and thus the need for higher levels of proficiency. As a side note, if you have ever made an afghan, whether for a twin- or king-size bed, you know from experience that the information and crocheting skills needed for success take much time, practice, patience, perseverance, and coaching. With information, skill, practice, and help from others, the results are astounding! Whether you play golf or make an afghan effectively, each task calls for the acquisition of information and skill, the use of logical thinking, some understanding of mathematical probability, and the application of all of this in some form of guided practice.

Similarly, information, practice, and coaching are absolutely requisite to learning alternative instructional models. The learner must acquire basic information about each model in order to understand how it operates; specific instructional skills relative to each model must be practiced in order to implement the model effectively. Once the various subskills are acquired, the learner must engage in a cycle of practice, coaching, and more practice before the knowledge and skills acquired previously can be used comfortably. Only through the application of this knowledge and the corresponding skills and steps inherent in each instructional model will each learner achieve some level of proficiency and make the model a part of an instructional repertoire. Quite simply, reading about the models is not sufficient. In order to use the models effectively, you need to practice, and as you practice them you need to both reflect on what you think about students' responses to the model and, directly, to receive feedback from a knowledgeable mentor who knows the model.

Instructional Models: Strategies for Teaching in a Diverse Society presents eight teaching models that expand the instructional repertoire of teachers and enable teachers to create more culturally relevant instruction. To use the models, a teacher will need basic theoretical information about each model, technical skills relative to the effective use of each model, and opportunities to apply the knowledge and skills to everyday practice. The teacher also needs a substantial level of subject matter mastery. Good teachers know a lot about what they teach. For teachers of diverse student populations, this requirement is especially essential because they have to know how to adjust instruction to the unique learning needs and conceptual understandings of students (Irvine and

Armento, 2001). Consider Ladson-Billings's (1994) account of one successful teacher of African American students:

> On one particular day, when the students had finished reading a Greek myth about a princess, Devereaux asked, "How would you describe the princess?" Her question was designed to elicit responses about the princess's character, but the first student to respond began with a physical description. "She was beautiful, with long blond hair," said the student. Nowhere in the story was there a description that matched this response. "What makes you say that?" Devereaux asked. "Because that's the way princesses always are," the student replied. "I don't have long blond hair and neither does anyone else in here. Does that mean that none of us could be a princess?" Devereaux asked. The student and several others seemed resigned to the fact that was the case. Devereaux feigned disbelief that they were unaware of black princesses.
>
> Slowly, without fanfare, Devereaux walked to her bookshelf and selected a book, John Steptoe's *Mufaro's Beautiful Daughters* (1987), about two African sisters, one good and one evil. After reading the fourth graders the book, Devereaux asked how many students still believed that a princess had to have long blond hair. No one raised a hand. (p. 92)

Knowing about the availability of additional resources or the applicability of ancillary concepts requires that teachers possess more than a superficial understanding of curriculum materials and disciplinary ideas. Teachers need depth in their content background in order to help ground the learning process for the students they teach. Ms. Devereaux exhibits such depth in the previous example. Irvine and Armento (2001) make it even clearer that culturally responsive teaching focuses on both content depth and an instructional repertoire that enables all students to explore the content in-depth. Indeed, they actually provide lesson plans for teachers to use. Though we appreciate the approach, we disagree with the implication: teachers need a step-by-step presentation of the content and how to teach it. We value teachers as thinkers and decision makers and, as such, we argue for their designing their own lessons.

❶NSTRUCTIONAL MODELS AND FAMILIES

Learning an instructional model is, in many respects, very similar to learning to play golf or make an afghan. If you recall, one of the critical components of making an afghan was the utilization of patterns, whether commercially prepared or created by the afghan-maker. Without a pattern, blueprint, or outline, neither the afghan-maker nor the teacher will be able to achieve the desired ends. Similarly, the selection of an instructional model is critical because it is based upon the desired objective(s) of the teacher. Thus, the instructional procedures (the instructional model) for teaching a concept, academic content, and/or an academic or social skill will depend upon what the students are expected to learn as a result of the instructional model chosen by the teacher (see Figure 3-1).

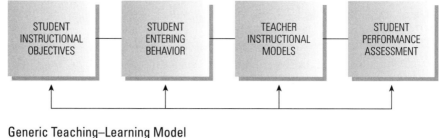

FIGURE 3-1   Generic Teaching–Learning Model

When planning to cook lobster bouillabaisse, a chef does not use a recipe for sourdough bread; a blueprint for a log cabin home will not result in a brick colonial; and neither will use of an 18-foot runabout be appropriate to cross one of America's Great Lakes, even though a pilot has appropriate nautical maps. So, too, instructional models have varying purposes. Some are designed to organize information, others to develop critical thinking skills, and still others to help students work in a collaborative manner. The appropriate teacher instructional model will be determined based upon the student instructional objectives the teacher seeks to develop. The approach that teachers take in working with students is dependent upon the teachers' thinking regarding the process of teaching, not just the content of lessons.

Content issues are receiving much more attention today because of the poor performance of American students on international comparative tests and because of the national emphasis on standards. Content, as Ladson-Billings (1994) and Irvine and Armento (2001) poignantly illustrate, is extremely important, but how teachers present and organize content also has significant implications for how students learn. If the American public—specifically corporate America—wants students to engage in critical thinking, not just recite facts, then they need students who have been engaged in solving problems and thinking through the complex nature of ideas.

The critical-thinking skills that teachers seek to foster will develop only if they have identified what is expected from students (for example, the recall of facts, creative thinking, organization of information, team-generated solutions, problem-solving, critical thinking, collaboration, and so on). As Figure 3-1 illustrates, once instructional objectives are identified, a corresponding teacher instructional model is matched to develop the intended student instructional objectives. A teacher who wants to develop skills might use direct instruction. A teacher who is concerned with fostering critical thinking might consider inquiry. The instructional models presented in this book cover a wide range of potential instructional goals (for example, recalling and organizing information, utilizing critical thinking, identifying and describing concepts and generalizations, or experiencing collaborative work environments). These models have been chosen not only to help teachers recognize how to use new teaching approaches, but also to help them determine when to use such models as they relate to specific learner outcomes.

Drawing on the work of Hanson, Silver, and Strong (1986), Joyce and Weil (1986, 1992), and Joyce, Weil, and Calhoun (2000), and building on the growing body of research on diversity (see Irvine and Armento, 2001), we attempt to

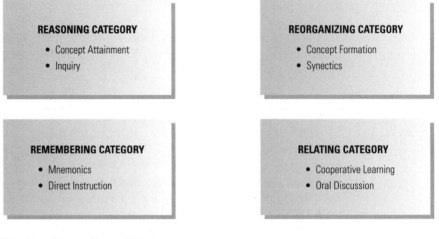

REASONING CATEGORY
- Concept Attainment
- Inquiry

REORGANIZING CATEGORY
- Concept Formation
- Synectics

REMEMBERING CATEGORY
- Mnemonics
- Direct Instruction

RELATING CATEGORY
- Cooperative Learning
- Oral Discussion

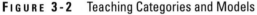

FIGURE 3-2   Teaching Categories and Models

classify the instructional models presented in this text around four broad categories. The four categories (*reasoning, reorganizing, remembering,* and *relating*) deal with the range of intellectual skills students must exhibit in order to experience success in schools composed of diverse student populations. Two instructional models are discussed within each of the four categories. The two instructional models are not the only examples for each instructional category, but they do represent models that best achieve the student learning goals for each category. Figure 3-2 presents a graphic representation of the four model categories and the corresponding instructional models we shall describe within each of the categories. A brief description of the instructional categories and the eight instructional models follows:

Category I: Models That Foster Reasoning Skills

Models that foster reasoning skills provide students with opportunities to acquire concepts from various disciplines and the skills involved in critical thinking and problem-solving. Such models expose students to strategies that elicit the styles of thinking necessary to process information, formulate conclusions, identify hypotheses, and test alternative solutions. The focus of reasoning models is not only acquiring thinking skills, but also enabling students to defend their choices when they use data.

Concept Attainment   Based on the work of Jerome Bruner et al. (1959), concept attainment was designed to teach concepts to students and the corresponding thinking skills of categorizing concepts. Through the use of positive and negative examples, students are able to define a concept and determine the concept's essential attributes. The model is very useful in teaching the skills of comparison and contrast, differentiation, and interpretation.

Inquiry   Based on the work of Richard Suchman (1962), inquiry was designed to teach students to form questions, create hypotheses, and test theories. Using a discrepant event or puzzling situation as a basis for discussion with students, this model helps students become more skilled at problem-solving. Students generate hypotheses as they collect and analyze data. Through the use of this model, students acquire the skills of hypothesizing, evaluating, and problem-solving.

Category II: Models That Foster Reorganizing Skills

Models that foster reorganizing skills help students reexamine what they have learned or have understood, and to apply this knowledge to new situations. Further, these models help develop intellectual skills such as inquisitiveness and metaphorical thinking; and they also foster the student's imagination, personal insight, and inductive processes.

Concept Formation   Created by Hilda Taba (1971), concept formation (some describe it as concept development) was designed to help students organize information, make connections among data, and create and test hypotheses. Through the use of this model, students will learn how to group data on the basis of similarities, and form categories and labels based on those data. The model is useful in teaching the skills of comparing and contrasting, categorizing, applying, analyzing, and synthesizing data.

Synectics   Created by William Gordon (1961), synectics was designed to use analogies, metaphors, and the power of personal imagination as tools for problem-solving. The model develops creativity in learners and is very useful in fostering collaboration, exploration, analogies, and creative thinking.

Category III: Models That Foster Remembering Skills

Models that foster remembering skills help students acquire information and skills through practice, drill, and memorization. In this category the teacher determines what is important for students to learn and designs instruction that helps students learn and remember discrete facts and skills. The emphasis is upon the retention of information and the performance appraisal of students in determining the retention of knowledge.

Mnemonics   Based on the work of Pressley, Levin, and Delaney (1982) and Lorayne and Lucas (1966), mnemonics was designed to help students memorize and acquire information. Mnemonics can be used to help students learn both low-level information (facts) as well as more complex concepts from different disciplines.

Direct Instruction   Based on the work of Anderson, Evertson, and Brophy (1979), Good and Grouws (1979), Hunter (1984), and Rosenshine (1983), direct instruction was designed to help students learn basic skills and/or discrete pieces of information. The model is especially effective in mathematics, reading, and language arts. Further, this model is useful in learning not only cognitive skills/information but also selected psychomotor skills. Direct instruction utilizes a step-by-step sequence of teaching to help students recall and recognize facts and data.

Category IV: Models That Foster Relating Skills

Models that foster relating skills provide students with an opportunity to understand others and themselves through enhanced interpersonal communication and group process approaches. The purposes of these models are the development of a positive self-concept, an increase in communication skills, the development of team-oriented skills, and the acquisition of knowledge.

Cooperative Learning Created by Slavin (1980, 1987) and Johnson, Johnson, Holubec, and Roy (1984), cooperative learning was designed to help students develop team-building skills by the experience of working with others in cognitive task situations. Through formal cooperative learning strategies such as STAD and JIGSAW, and informal strategies such as think-pair-share, students are able to experience different leadership roles, learn the skills necessary in building collaborative cultures in the classroom, and acquire the communication skills needed to work effectively with other group members.

Oral Discussion Originally made famous by Socrates, oral discussion utilizes a questioning format to enhance classroom discussions. Teacher questions are used to check student understanding. Classroom interactions that enhance higher-order thinking processes (factual, interpretative, and evaluative) in students are encouraged and directed by the teacher.

Ⓢ UMMARY OF MODELS

These eight instructional models are neither specific to any particular age group, student ability level, or student grade level, nor are they subject-matter specific. Each instructional model can be utilized, within reason, with any age youngster and within the framework of teaching any academic discipline. Each model has been used with a variety of K-12 students and with various types of student ability groups. In presenting each instructional model, we provide examples of both elementary and secondary education case studies and lesson plans from a variety of academic disciplines (that is, mathematics, language arts, science, art, and social studies). Additionally, a section entitled "Applications to Diverse Classrooms" will be used to describe the appropriateness of each model for culturally diverse students.

The instructional models presented in this text are predicated on the idea that there is no "best" way to teach all youngsters in all situations, though there may be a best way to teach some content based on a teacher's instructional goal. As we described in the teaching-learning model depicted in Figure 3-1, there are many learning goals: recalling facts, forming generalizations, working in teams, identifying concepts, and solving problems through various thinking processes. The choice of an instructional model is based upon the complex educational goal(s) established by the teacher for students and *by the depth of understanding that teachers have of the students in their classrooms*. Further, these goal choices are based not only upon a knowledge of how to use a specific instructional model, but also upon an understanding of what cognitive skills each model will engender in students. Teachers of diverse student populations understand that knowledge is dynamic and evolving, and that students are complex. Teachers who are instructionally limited commit a form of pedagogical malpractice—they teach in ways that mitigate student growth and "academically damage" students in succeeding subsequently in school. A first step toward eliminating this circumstance would be for a teacher to reflect upon the following types of "self-directed" questions in designing culturally relevant instruction for students:

1. What specific knowledge and skills (academic and social) do I want students to achieve at the completion of a lesson or unit?

2. What specific interests, prior experiences, and cognitive styles do my students bring to the classroom learning environment?

3. Which instructional models best help me explore the concepts and teach the skills I want my students to learn?

4. Which instructional models are most appropriate given my students' interests, prior experiences, and learning styles?

This last point is critical in implementing, adapting, and evaluating instructional models. To choose culturally relevant instructional models, teachers must know the students they teach, know how to instructionally approach culturally diverse student populations, and know how to utilize various instructional models. This needs to occur in order both to match teaching and learning styles, and to provide all students with the opportunities to learn and experience phenomena in varying educational contexts. As we will describe in the following chapters, such knowledge of instructional models and the concomitant skills necessary to implement these models are critical in opening the minds and souls of culturally diverse learners to be contributing members of American democracy and the new global economic society. They also create more culturally responsive classrooms, which create significant benefits for students—see Table 3-1.

❶HE PLANNING PROCESS

The place to begin anything—whether it is reading a book, watching a movie, or teaching youngsters about the world in general—is at the beginning. In the teaching-learning process this means that teachers need to decide what their students must accomplish, what their students need to do, and what is expected of students once instruction by teachers is completed. Successful people in society have a game plan for their personal and professional lives. Such people know where they are going on a day-to-day basis. They set goals! The human

TABLE 3-1 Basic Beliefs of Culturally Responsive Educators

Culturally Responsive Educators

1. *Hold high academic and personal expectations for each child.*

2. *Provide for each child equitable access to the necessary learning resources and sufficient opportunities to learn.*

3. *Ensure that learning outcomes are meaningful, relevant, useful, and important to each child.*

4. *Nurture learning-support communities for each child (families, peers, homework hotlines, community centers).*

5. *Facilitate the maximum growth of each learner by making informed academic adaptations that match and build upon the learner's prior knowledge, experiences, skills, and beliefs.*

6. *Build positive and supportive school and classroom learning environments that are grounded in mutual and genuine respect for cultural diversity.*

7. *Promote classroom climates built on social justice, democracy, and equity.*

8. *Promote individual empowerment, self-efficacy, positive self-regard, and a belief in societal reform.*

9. *Value diversity as well as human commonalities.*

10. *Believe that it is their role and responsibility to provide effective and empowering instruction for each child.*

Source: Irvine, J. J., and B. J. Armento (2001). *Culturally Responsive Teaching*. New York: McGraw-Hill, p. 23.

system is goal seeking by design and may be compared with an airplane's autopilot. Once the target (goal) is locked on, all efforts are focused on the target in order to attain the desired end (goal). Winners have definite purposes in life—losers wander aimlessly and generally self-destruct! Even when goal-directed individuals are not actively pursuing a set of goals, they are thinking about them. *Purpose* (a goal) is the motivator that powers a winner's life. In fact, as winners are about to achieve goals, they begin identifying other goals to pursue. They are never satisfied with achieving one set of goals as an end—they continually redefine new goals that motivate them even further in life.

Successful people can describe where they are going and why, approximately how long it will take, what they plan to do on the way, and who will share the journey with them. They have a plan for their lives! Similarly, effective teachers have game plans—plans that indicate what they expect from students, how they plan to help students reach these expectations, and what students are expected to do after the instructional process is completed. Such plans turn teacher thoughts and goals into new opportunities for students. The planning process is a key factor in successful teaching, whether that teaching requires students to recall information, perform specific skills, formulate new concepts and use them with phenomena, utilize problem-solving practices in addressing community issues, or apply collaborative skills in working with other human beings. In order to be successful in utilizing the instructional models, effective teachers plan their strategies by identifying student goals and objectives. The focus for successful teachers is on an instructional plan and the accomplishment of goals and objectives.

The intent of the planning process is to decide what is expected of students—goals and objectives—and to identify what the teacher will do—instructional activities, strategies, and materials—that will help teachers facilitate student achievement, and to decide how to assess what students have learned. The result of planning either a lesson or unit of instruction consists of a series of instructional strategies that have a common purpose or focus. The chapters in this text will provide these strategies in the form of instructional models. Sometimes the instructional model revolves around a series of questions to promote student inquiry, others focus upon formulating concepts and generalizations, while still other models teach social or academic skills.

One of the more illustrative examples we have come across concerning goals, destinations, and directions is the fabled sea horse story created by Mager (1984). Its theme is simple: If you don't know where you are going, how will you know if you've arrived there?

The Fable of the Sea Horse

Once upon a time a Sea Horse gathered up his seven pieces of eight and cantered out to find his fortune. Before he had traveled very far he met an Eel, who said, "Psst. Hey, bud. Where 'ya goin'?"

"I'm going to find my fortune," replied the Sea Horse proudly.

"You're in luck," said the Eel. "For four pieces of eight you can have this speedy flipper, and then you'll be able to get there a lot faster."

"Gee, that's swell," said the Sea Horse, and paid the money and put on the flipper, and slithered off at twice the speed. Soon he came upon a Sponge, who said,

"Psst. Hey, bud. Where 'ya goin'?"

"I'm going to find my fortune," replied the Sea Horse.

"You're in luck," said the Sponge. "For a small fee I will let you have this jet-propelled scooter so that you will be able to travel a lot faster."

So the Sea Horse bought the scooter with his remaining money and he went zooming through the sea five times as fast. Soon he came upon a Shark, who said, "Psst. Hey, bud. Where 'ya goin'?"

"I'm going out to find my fortune," replied the Sea Horse.

"You're in luck. If you'll take this short cut," said the Shark, pointing to his open mouth, "you'll save yourself a lot of time."

"Gee, thanks," said the Sea Horse, and zoomed off into the interior of the Shark, there to be devoured. (p. vii)

The problem with some classrooms today is that all too often neither teachers nor students know where they are going. This situation is changing, some would suggest, thanks to a national reform agenda that emphasizes a focus on clear academic standards. Further, more and more states are matching assessment practices to these standards, and President Bush is calling for grade 3–8 assessments of all students to ensure academic growth. Still, for many teachers, just getting through the day is their goal. As a result, they generate just enough energy and just enough motivation from their students to get through that day.

Fuller and Bown (1975) called these "survival" teachers. Effective teachers (or expert teachers) know where they are going and where they are leading their students, and that's why they are successful! Such teachers seem to have a game plan for the classroom—they know where they are going on a day-to-day basis. Someone unknown once said, "Whatever the mind can conceive—and truly believe—can be achieved." We can make amazing things happen for ourselves and for students if we let ourselves dream (develop a plan) and make it come true (develop a set of strategies).

Because we tend to move in the direction of our dominant thoughts—whatever we are thinking about—we unconsciously move toward the achievement of those thoughts. Another way of putting it is: One must have a dream if one is going to make dreams come true. And your dreams, your directions, and your destinations need to be translated into a plan in the form of goals and objectives—goals for life, goals for the day, and goals for instruction. Let's now take a look at what we mean through the examination of a definition for and examples of *instructional goals*.

ⓌHAT IS AN INSTRUCTIONAL GOAL?

In most classrooms across America, youngsters are expected to know something about academic content—facts, concepts, and generalizations. A youngster in an E. D. Hirsch Core Knowledge school may be expected to know things at a different level or point in time than other students, but with the emergence of academic standards, the content emphasis is increasing for all students. Further, youngsters are expected to acquire and apply skills unique to an academic subject by applying these skills in the study of academic information. Youngsters are also expected to adopt various attitudes and values that American society considers important in terms of our culture, and that are a derivation of the knowledge and skills acquired in the examination and utilization of the academic content.

Determining an instructional purpose is an initial step in the instructional planning process. This takes the form of identifying instructional goals and objectives. This step of the planning model (Figure 3-3) emphasizes what the students will be expected to do after the teacher has implemented an instructional model. Once the teacher has identified instructional goals and has converted these into performance objectives, there is no prescribed sequence in implementing the planning model. The process becomes interactive in that different steps or elements of the model interact with one another.

The instructional planning process model in Figure 3-3 involves three general steps that all teachers need to take in planning lessons or units of instruction:

1. Identifying what students will achieve or accomplish after the lesson or unit is completed. This will involve the first two steps of the model: identifying student goals and identifying student performance objectives. (Both of these will be discussed in the next section of this chapter.)

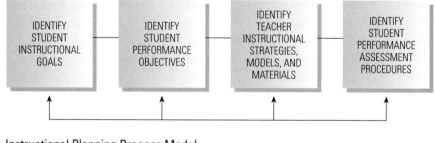

FIGURE 3-3   Instructional Planning Process Model

2. Identifying how the teacher will help students achieve the goals and objectives of the instructional lesson or unit. (This will be described in Chapters 4 and 11 of this text.)

3. Identifying how well the students have achieved or accomplished the instructional performance objectives identified in the second step of the planning model. (This will be discussed in the remaining sections of this chapter.)

All steps in the instructional planning process model are important and interact with one another. Curriculum evaluators call this interaction the concept of *internal consistency or alignment*: Objectives, instructional strategies, and performance assessment must all relate to one another and be congruent based upon what has been developed previously in the model. However, the essential step in implementing the planning process is the first: identifying instructional goals and converting them into student performance objectives. Without these, instructional models and strategies will not provide you the means to arrive at your pedagogical destinations.

Knowledge, skills, and attitudes are what we expect students to acquire and apply in their academic studies. In order for teachers to design plans for students to accomplish these expectations, a variety of directional statements need to be written by teachers. Some of these statements are written very broadly with verbs such as *understand, appreciate, aware, or believe*. Other statements are more performance-oriented and utilize such verbs as *list, differentiate, share, or defend*.

Instructional goals, especially as we will define them here, are broad statements of direction that identify what is expected of students. Goals serve as initial organizers and provide direction for educational participants, including teachers, who plan and write curricular programs, guides, or courses. They are written broadly and in general terms because they cover a breadth of content over longer periods of time. Examples of broad goal statements are as follows:

To understand the causes of the Civil War.

To appreciate the works of Edgar Allan Poe.

To use effective personal health practices.

To understand and appreciate the human experience.

TABLE 3-2	Verbs Associated with Goals: Words and Phrases Open to Many Interpretations

To understand

To appreciate

To grasp the significance of

To have faith in

To realize

To enjoy

To believe in

To recognize

To fully sense

To take satisfaction in

To understand how human resources are influenced by social and political systems.

To describe how the multicultural composition of American society enhances the quality of life for all Americans.

To know the primary colors.

In the planning process, goals provide a general direction for instruction. However, goals such as "producing effective consumers" or "appreciating the literary works of Walter Mosley" or "being sensitive to the dignity of all human beings" are so general that they leave the teacher and the student wondering where to begin instructionally, and what is expected in terms of accountability and achievement (see Table 3-2). Because of this, the next step in the planning process is to take each goal and convert it into specific student performance terminology. In other words, the teacher needs to determine what is expected of students in specific ways that can be assessed in terms of performance.

Ⓦ HAT ARE PERFORMANCE OR INSTRUCTIONAL OBJECTIVES?

The intent of instructional planning is to determine what students should accomplish, and then to plot a course of action (instructional models and strategies) that facilitates student accomplishment of objectives. Instructional objectives are an outgrowth of the goals discussed in the previous section. They are written in order to provide specific direction and meaning for what is expected from students. Objectives are important in teacher planning because they help facilitate: (1) an identification of what is expected of students at the conclusion of the study; (2) a basis for organizing instructional activities and materials; (3) a means for determining ways to assess student performance; and (4) a performance level of accountability for students. For purposes of this text, performance objectives are defined in terms of student outcomes—what the *student* will be able to do. They are written in terms that clearly delineate the student behavior that will be evaluated. Examples of broadly defined performance objectives are as follows:

- To list three statements of fact and three statements of opinion.
- To solve at least seven radical equations.
- To run the 100-yard dash.
- To convert data on hunger in selected developing countries to a bar graph.
- To identify Maya Angelou's primary life choices in *Gather Together in My Name* and to identify how she resolved each decision situation.
- To predict the height of a plant on the 21st day of growth, given appropriate light and water.

For many teachers, such broadly defined objectives are more than adequate, especially if the teacher knows the specific indicators of success. But for novice teachers, more precision may be necessary initially to ensure that the teacher and students know precisely the goal to be attained. Generally speaking, the more specific learning experiences are intended to lead to particular learning outcomes, the more well-defined performance objectives should be (Anderson and Krathwohl, 2001).

Readers who take time to examine the performance objectives just outlined will notice that these statements seem reasonably clear, but they are not specific. These performance objectives provide direction to teachers for what instructional models to employ in helping students achieve these outcomes, but they don't provide some essential information. For example, what type of plant will the students grow? What will be the source of the facts and opinions—the students' imagination or a teacher resource? Also apparent with this examination of objectives is the notion that assessment is not as clearly defined as it might be. Performance objectives utilize precise verbs in identifying what is expected of students after instruction has been completed (see Table 3-3 for a list of such verbs).

Performance objectives written to communicate the student outcomes and the means of goal assessment exhibit three essential characteristics—the instructional conditions under which the student performance will occur; the student behavior expected after instruction is completed; and the standard, criterion, or performance level that each student is expected to demonstrate (Mager, 1984).

■ *Instructional conditions under which the student performance will occur.*

The instructional conditions are strategies that the teacher will employ in helping students exhibit the performance expected. The following examples are conditions that could be components of a performance objective:

- Given a three-place subtraction problem with regrouping, . . .
- Given a standard set of tools, . . .
- Without the aid of a calculator or computer, . . .
- When the student is describing a poem by Langston Hughes, . . .

Each condition is written after consideration of the appropriate instructional strategies necessary to achieve the outcome.

TABLE 3-3   Verbs Associated with More-Defined Objectives

To list

To compare and contrast

To construct

To differentiate

To identify

To write

To speak

To assemble

To describe verbally

To describe in writing

To float

■ *Student behavior expected after instruction is completed.*

The student behavior is identified in performance terms that will be acceptable as evidence that the student has achieved the objective. Further, this student behavior is written in specific language so that few, if any, interpretations are apparent in terms of what is expected to be performed. This student behavior is then attached to the instructional conditions as described in the previous step. The following are examples of the two characteristics of performance objectives—conditions and student behavior—put together in proper form:

• Given a linear algebraic equation with one unknown, the student will be able to solve for the unknown without the aid of tables, references, or calculating devices.

• Given a list and discussion of factors leading to significant historical events, the student will be able to select and justify at least three economic factors contributing to the influx of immigrants to the United States since 1980.

• Given a description and demonstration of the first 10 numbers of the numerical system, the student will be able to print these 10 numbers in order.

■ *A standard, criterion, or performance level that each student is expected to demonstrate.*

The performance level provides the teacher with a standard by which to assess instructional effectiveness as well as student achievement. This characteristic defines for the student what is expected and what level of performance is required. Through standards, the teacher will have a measure to determine the depth, breadth, and complexity by which to judge students and to judge the teacher's instructional effectiveness. The following examples are provided to demonstrate this final characteristic of performance objectives:

• Given linear algebraic equations with one unknown, the student will be able to solve 8 out of 10 of these equations without the aid of tables, references, or calculating devices.

- Given the knowledge of how to run a dash, the student will be able to run the 100-yard dash within a period of 14 seconds.
- Given both a description of how to float on water and a viewing of videotapes concerning floating positions, students will be able to float on their backs for at least 1 minute.
- Given knowledge of measurement and weights, the student must be able to use the chemical balance well enough to weigh materials accurately to the nearest milligram.

In summary, performance objectives should consist of an instructional condition, an expected student behavior, and a standard by which to judge achievement. After a teacher has completed a listing of all performance objectives for a lesson or unit of instruction, the teacher can evaluate each planned objective based upon the following three questions:

1. Does the performance objective describe what students will be doing when they demonstrate that they have achieved the objective?
2. Does the performance objective describe the conditions under which students will be expected to demonstrate achievement?
3. Does the performance objective indicate how the students will be evaluated?

If the reader will take into consideration these three questions when designing performance objectives, then students will know and teachers will be very clear in terms of the performance expected and of how evaluation will occur.

Though we have spent time describing the characteristics of performance objectives, we believe that the most important component is the identification of the behavior expected from the students. Remember that performance objectives are written for students and for what is expected of students. Our point is not that teachers must write precise instructional objectives but, rather, that they must know precisely what behavior or cognitive processes they want students to exhibit.

Thus far, we have described how classroom teachers can use performance objectives in a very mechanistic manner. Many of the examples provided previously in this discussion have elicited low-level, convergent thinking processes—right or wrong/correct or incorrect responses. Schooling in America, especially in its best forms, provides youngsters with more than just correct or incorrect responses! As you will recognize in the following chapters, a good number of instructional models (that is, concept attainment, synectics, inquiry, oral discussion) facilitate the development of youngsters' minds through the use of thinking skill development and the application of these skills to culturally relevant curricula and materials.

One system that can be used to write performance objectives and develop higher-order thinking skills was originally created by Bloom et al. (1956) and is referred to as the Taxonomy of Educational Objectives. There are three types of learning objectives (cognitive, affective, and psychomotor) that teachers need to utilize and students need to develop; Bloom has become best known for his work in the cognitive domain.

1. Cognitive Objectives—those that use academic knowledge to develop the intellectual abilities of youngsters.

2. Affective Objectives—those that help youngsters develop values, attitudes, and feelings.

3. Psychomotor Objectives—those that help youngsters develop large and small muscle coordination and manipulative skills.

COGNITIVE DOMAIN

Cognitive objectives deal with academic information and knowledge. Objectives in this domain focus upon what students will accomplish intellectually from the following perspectives: recalling facts, concepts, and generalizations; applying information and concepts; synthesizing various concepts and generalizations; and making judgments according to standards and criteria. Originally designed by Bloom et al. (1956), this taxonomical domain is a system for classifying cognitive educational objectives into a hierarchy of thinking levels. Significantly, Bloom's construct has been revised recently (see Anderson and Krathwohl, 2001) so that it addresses both cognitive and knowledge dimensions. Given, however, that most readers of this text know the "old" construct, that is the one we will use in this discussion. The Bloom categorical taxonomy has been designed from the most simple form of thinking to the most complex—convergent to divergent thinking processes. Therefore, the importance of using this taxonomy, or one of the other cognitive schemas developed by Sanders (1966) or Hunkins (1972), is to promote higher levels of thinking and development for America's students. Research by Henry (1955) first documented that most teachers in schools tend to utilize convergent thinking (that is, correct or incorrect responses, one way of answering questions) rather than divergent thinking (that is, many possible responses, problems that are not immediately solvable). Recent discussion of the problem suggests that the tendency toward low-level objectives and convergent questions is still evident in schools and the emphasis on standards may exacerbate this tendency even though many of the assessment processes used by students encompasses more advanced critical thinking skills.

In order for students to utilize higher-order thinking skills (divergent thinking levels), they must be taught the skills needed in using each taxonomical level. As we shall point out in a later chapter, fostering critical thinking requires that teachers become more subversive in their thinking—teaching students to question more and accept less. Teacher use of different cognitive levels should be evidenced in the types of questions used in class discussions, the types of tests given to students, and the types of performance assessments utilized to assess student knowledge. Each cognitive level is described below along with sample performance objectives for each level in the taxonomy. The sample performance objectives focus only upon expected student behaviors in order to emphasize what students will be doing at each level of the taxonomy.

Knowledge

This level of the cognitive taxonomy requires students to acquire knowledge of factual information. It seeks to have students recall facts, concepts, and generalizations from an academic discipline.

Examples:

- The student will be able to cite at least three causes of the Civil War.
- The student will be able to identify the earth's distance from the sun.
- The student will be able to list three essential criteria for describing a surrealistic painting.
- The student will define, based upon the class lecture, what is meant by the term *electricity*.

Comprehension

The comprehension level checks whether students understand the information learned at the knowledge level. This is demonstrated by one or more of the following processes: translating material from one form of communication to another (that is, using one's own words, role playing, simulations, charting and graphing), interpreting material (that is, comparing and contrasting, drawing relationships), and estimating and extrapolating (that is, predicting effects, drawing implications).

Examples:

- The student will be able to paraphrase the Gettysburg Address in six sentences or less.
- The student will be able to paraphrase Martin Luther King, Jr.'s "I Have a Dream" speech in six sentences or less.
- The student will be able to compare and contrast the economic system of the South in 1860 with the economic system of the South in 2000.
- After a study of Edgar Allan Poe's poem "The Raven," students will describe in their own words the symbolism of the phrase "Quoth the Raven, 'Nevermore.'"
- Given a graph of the growth of a plant over 10 days, the student will predict the growth of the plant on the 25th day, assuming a steady rate of growth. The student will further predict growth rates given different light and water applications.

If you examine the objectives listed above, you should be able to recognize that the knowledge and comprehension levels of the taxonomy elicit only convergent thinking by students. The behavior expected from these levels asks students to perform tasks that lead to correct or incorrect responses. From those teachers using these taxonomical levels, students will acquire information concerning a topic or concept and perform the task required (that is, recall information, translate information or ideas into another form of communication, compare and contrast information, and/or draw relationships or implications). Each of these tasks calls for the use of convergent thinking processes. Though information and the understanding of ideas and concepts are important, it is also necessary to develop higher-order thinking skills in youngsters. The taxonomical levels described below promote student learning through the use of more divergent thinking processes.

Application

The application level deals with taking information that has been studied and understood at the previous levels (knowledge and comprehension) and applying concepts or generalizations to new situations. Application objectives and thinking involve the solving of problems through the identification of issues, and the selection and use of skills and generalizations.

Examples:

- The student will be able to describe three ways in which the Civil War could have been averted.
- After a lesson on the preservation of food, the student will be able to demonstrate a procedure for retarding or preventing the growth of mold on bread.
- Mr. Jones is going to locate a new steel plant in a Midwestern state. The student will identify three possible locations where steel can be produced and transported economically.

As you will recognize, these objectives promote divergent thinking because the tasks presented are not immediately solvable. They take much more student reflection, and they require that students use facts, concepts, and generalizations to draw their conclusions.

Analysis

Analysis objectives are used when the teacher wants students to systematically examine factual content in order to solve problems. For this taxonomical level, students are required to take whole issues (that is, conclusions or generalizations) and to divide these wholes into their component parts (that is, examine whether factual information supports conclusions). Analysis tasks require students to utilize inductive and deductive thinking, recognize assumptions, and identify common mistakes in the reasoning process.

Examples:

- The student will be able to analyze the following assumption: "If the South had successfully seceded from the Union, the United States would never have become a world power."
- The student will identify and describe some of the significant reasons why blacks in South Africa, who comprised a majority, lacked the power to vote prior to 1993.

- The student will be able to either accept or reject the following statements and conclusion:
  a. "Ms. Cortez uses X detergent to wash her clothes."
  b. "Ms. Cortez has found that X detergent gets her clothes whiter than new."
  c. "Therefore, X detergent is the best detergent made!"

Synthesis

Synthesis objectives require students to put together discrete elements (that is, factual material) into a pattern or structure that the elements did not previously form. This taxonomical level offers more freedom of thought (that is, original and creative thinking) than any of the previous levels and truly requires divergent thinking on the part of students.

Examples:

- Given the idea that conflicts in ideologies still exist between the North and South, the student will be able to devise ways of resolving these conflicts.
- Given various information concerning the types and structures of poetic compositions, the student will create a poem using one of these types and structures.
- The student will devise a set of standards that would be useful in defining the proper division of decision-making power between automobile workers and management.
- Because drug abuse is a widespread and growing problem today, the student will write and orally present a plan to decrease the use of drugs by teenagers.

Evaluation

The evaluation level elicits from students a judgment regarding the value of procedures and the imposition of criteria by either the teacher or students. With synthesis, the student creatively puts together different elements or ideas in order to create a new pattern; in evaluation, the student uses decision-making skills and must make decisions that are grounded on sound facts or ideas.

Examples:

- The student will be able to write an essay on the following question: Do you think the Civil War was justified? Why or why not?
- Given newspaper and scientific articles for or against the fluoridation of water, the student will be able to take a position (pro or con) on fluoridation and write three scientific reasons in defense of the position.
- The student will write a short essay defending or opposing the use of Standard English in all American classrooms.

The major purpose of describing and providing examples of each of the levels of the cognitive taxonomy is to provide the reader with a systematic process for

TABLE 3-4   English Literature

Knowledge:

The student will be able to list five distinguishing physical characteristics of the monster Grendel.

Comprehension:

The student will be able to compare and contrast the physical characteristics of the monster Grendel in the poem "Beowulf" and the film Grendel, Grendel, Grendel.

Application:

Based upon the viewing of the film Grendel, Grendel, Grendel, the student will suggest three ways that King Hrothgar and his people might have changed Grendel's attitude toward them.

Analysis:

The student will analyze the following assumption:

"If Cain had not killed Abel, Grendel would not have terrorized King Hrothgar's kingdom."

The student will critique this statement based upon the reading of the heroic poem "Beowulf" and the viewing of the film Grendel, Grendel, Grendel.

Synthesis:

The student will write a modern heroic epic poem that relates the heroic activities of at least one character, and reflects at least two values of modern society.

Evaluation:

The student will write a short essay on the following: "Which character do you believe to be more heroic, Beowulf or Grendel? Why?"

designing objectives according to the levels of thinking. As you will recognize from the descriptions and examples for each taxonomical level, a hierarchy of thinking processes and levels moves from the most simple—knowledge—to the most complex—evaluation. The teacher who utilizes the cognitive taxonomy requires students to acquire information and skills and to apply these to problem situations utilizing both convergent and divergent thinking processes. It is certainly possible, and perhaps even ideal, to use the same academic content and have students move through all the thinking levels, as in the Civil War examples. Tables 3-4 and 3-5 provide additional examples of applying the same content/concept through the cognitive levels. As you analyze these examples, you will notice that each performance objective, similar to the previous examples, emphasizes the resulting student behavior. This is done to emphasize that the student behavior is what the teacher must clearly delimit in terms of what is expected. The conditions under which the behavior will occur and the performance level that the student will evidence are important in the planning process.

TABLE 3-5   Biology—Cells

Knowledge:

The student will identify three components of red blood cells and their specific functions.

Comprehension:

The student will compare and contrast a red blood cell and its various functions with a bone marrow cell and its various functions.

Application:

Given a list of chemicals and the cellular components they interact with, the student will identify which chemicals will clot blood and which will break up or dissolve clots in the least amount of time.

Analysis:

Given a medical procedure and the knowledge that it did not work, the student will determine what steps in the procedure were probably responsible for its failure and describe why.

Synthesis:

The student will be able to construct a model cell containing all necessary components of a cell, eliminating all wasted space and materials, and determine what specific function this cell might fulfill.

Evaluation:

Dr. Jeffrey Geiger of Chicago Hope has one heart donor and two candidates for the heart. He has one-half hour to decide who will receive the heart: a 12-year-old child or an otherwise healthy 55-year-old Nobel Prize winner (for solar engine designs) renowned for her scientific achievements. The student will choose who will receive the heart and describe how and why the choice was made.

However, in this discussion of writing performance objectives, our emphasis is upon writing objectives that are clear and specific in terms of what behavior is expected of students. Readers will note that the levels are, in the words of Orlich et al. (1985), "cumulative and inclusive." As students develop understandings at one taxonomical level, these understandings can subsequently be used for tasks involved in more complex levels of cognitive processing.

We also readily acknowledge that many expert teachers do not have a need for defining specific objectives they hope to achieve, but they do plan. Expert teachers engage in complex planning (which includes thinking through what objectives will be achieved and how they will be accomplished) and in anticipating the events that might mitigate lesson effectiveness (Carter, 1990). They also have the benefit of past experience. Expert teachers design future lessons based on past experiences; novice teachers have few or no past classroom experiences, so the level and depth of their planning (including stating the conditions of objectives) become more important for success.

ⒶFFECTIVE DOMAIN

The cognitive domain, as just discussed, dealt with intellectual abilities—the use of the mind in understanding and using knowledge from the different disciplines. The affective domain involves one's feelings, emotions, interests, attitudes, and values. Developed by Krathwohl, Bloom, and Masis (1964), the affective domain was a natural follow-up to the design of the cognitive taxonomy of educational objectives.

The affective domain deals with how students are affected by their learning, as well as how their feelings and interests affect their learning. In addition, the teacher's attitude toward an academic subject or topic—like or dislike—affects the student's disposition toward what is to be learned. In other words, the teacher's feelings toward what is to be taught or learned has an affective relationship upon the student. The implication for teachers is that students receive/pick up feelings of interest or lack of interest for the subject and then model these same attitudes or interests. Thus, the more teachers are enthusiastic and love what it is that they teach youngsters, the more positively students will react to the teacher and the subject under discussion.

For purposes of describing these taxonomies, it may be necessary to analyze and plan lessons in which the cognitive (knowledge) and the affective (feelings) domains are separated. In fact, many teachers, because of their fear of evaluation in the affective domain (to be addressed later), frequently disregard planning or teaching within this taxonomy. However, in practice—both consciously and unconsciously—the cognitive and affective domains tend to merge together. Think of a youngster who is learning how to use a pencil for the first time. Some specific cognitive understandings that should occur—how to hold the pencil, where to position the fingers, or how to make either letters or numbers. Affective learning also occurs—feelings of comfort or discomfort, interest in being like mommy or daddy in learning how to write, or feelings of success or failure in either holding the pencil or making letters or numbers. The knowledge of what is worth knowing and the feelings that emanate from this pursuit of knowledge consistently commingle in phenomena that students explore. Most learning occurs in this manner!

Krathwohl et al.'s (1964) taxonomy offers a system for planning and organizing objectives in the affective domain. Recall that the cognitive domain is based upon a hierarchy of objectives from the least complex form of thinking—knowledge—to the most complex form of thinking—evaluation. Further, as phenomena are explored, the hierarchy is utilized so that the thinking skills involved in each of the previous levels of the taxonomy are considered—there is a logical progression of the students' thinking. This is not necessarily the case in using the affective domain. The affective domain is based upon the degree to which an individual has internalized and organized attitudes and values. The affective domain is structured around how strongly individuals feel about and are willing to stand up for and defend their attitudes and values. The "lowest" taxonomical level is receiving—the willingness to listen to varying views, whereas the "highest" level is characterization of a value—the willingness to profess their attitudes or values openly. The following descriptions of the five levels of the affective taxonomy of educational objectives provide a clearer explanation of this idea.

Receiving

This level of the taxonomy refers to an individual's willingness to attend to particular classroom stimuli or phenomena. It involves a teacher's acquiring, holding, and directing the student's attention, but it requires that a student willingly and consciously consider some phenomenon or idea.

Examples:

- The student will listen attentively to the pros and cons of capital punishment.
- The student will develop an awareness of the impact of homelessness upon young children.
- The student will demonstrate an awareness of the five classroom rules listed on the chalkboard.
- The student will be able to differentiate nonverbally the sounds of the major instruments in a classical orchestra.

Responding

This level requires active participation on the part of students. The student does something (performs, participates, reacts, speaks, and so on) based upon the stimuli that were presented at the previous level. In essence, the student must act on some new awareness. Real internalization requires that students take action on what they know.

Examples:

- The student will understand the causes of hunger and identify two ways to become personally involved with helping the hungry.
- The student will appreciate the causes of homelessness so that the student can identify social policies that need to be changed to reduce homelessness.
- The student will demonstrate an interest in reading poetry.
- The student will follow simple verbal requests.

Valuing

Valuing emphasizes the worth an individual attaches to phenomena, things, or behaviors. It is based upon an internal set of values but is operationalized by the open behavior of individuals. With valuing, the student is not just acquiescing to some feeling, but rather is intentionally deciding to make a personal commitment to some idea (value).

Examples:

- The student will demonstrate a belief in housing for the poor and homeless by helping construct homes through Habitat for Humanity.

- The student will demonstrate an acceptance of individuals of other races by joining groups that are racially mixed.
- The student will demonstrate an appreciation for the role that science plays in our everyday lives.
- The student will attempt to interest peers that conflict-resolution strategies have value as methods to deal with interpersonal conflict.

Organization

Organization is the process by which individuals begin to formulate value systems. This level is concerned with synthesizing different values, resolving conflicts between values, and constructing an internally congruent value system. This is the level where individuals begin developing a philosophy to live by and determining what it is that they will be committed to as individuals.

Examples:

- The student will learn about personal responsibility and consistently accept responsibility for personal behavior and the consequences derived from that behavior.
- The student will acquire an understanding of ecological issues and will demonstrate this by describing the effects of industrial pollution in urban environments.
- The student will appreciate the importance of long-range plans and will formulate a 5-year plan for life after high school based upon interests, abilities, and beliefs.

Characterization by a Value or Value Complex

Within this level of the taxonomy, an individual internalizes and personalizes a value system. Because this individual has lived by this value system for a long time, a lifestyle of behavior is practiced. Value systems are actualized by individuals at this level through persuasive, consistent, and predictable behavior. In essence, the individual is able to "walk the talk" and to reconcile personal actions with personal convictions.

Examples:

- The student will display safety-conscious behaviors when working in a science laboratory.
- The student will practice cooperation and collaboration when involved in group and team activities.
- The student will demonstrate good health habits through a balanced diet and a regimen of exercise.

The affective taxonomy is based upon how individuals feel about or are willing to defend the values and beliefs that they hold dear. Though it is possible to write affective objectives for all levels of the taxonomy, it is difficult to write them with the same precision of cognitive objectives. Teachers can also write affective objectives from the simplest level—receiving—to the most complex level—characterization—using the same content or concept. However, as one

TABLE 3-6   Harrow's Taxonomy of the Psychomotor Domain

Level	Example
1. Reflex movement	*Knee-jerk and other reflex movements innate at birth*
2. Basic fundamental movements	*Visual tracking of an object, crawling, walking, grasping an object*
3. Perceptual abilities	*Body awareness, figure-ground differentiation, auditory awareness, memory*
4. Physical abilities	*Muscular endurance, agility, strength*
5. Skilled movement	*Simple behaviors such as sawing wood and complex behaviors such as playing tennis*
6. Nondiscursive communication	*Moving interpretatively and using the body creatively to express ideas or emotions*

Reprinted from D. C. Orlich et al. 1985. *Teaching Strategies: A Guide to Better Instruction* (2nd ed.). Toronto, Canada: D. C. Heath.

uses this taxonomy, it becomes more difficult to evaluate student progress because of the time it takes to make a determination of progress and the imprecision that occurs in writing and assessing these objectives. This statement is not an excuse to disregard the use of the affective taxonomy. Affective domain objectives will take more time to develop and evaluate, and attitudinal changes call for even more time and development by teachers and students.

PSYCHOMOTOR DOMAIN

Psychomotor domain objectives emphasize the development of muscular or motor skills. Further, such objectives can be used in the manipulation of instructional materials most often used in hands-on science or mathematics programs. Psychomotor learning can take the form of learning how to hold and use a pencil, throwing or catching a football, climbing a rope, playing a musical instrument, or using scientific laboratory equipment.

Bloom and his colleagues (1956) did not prepare a taxonomy for the psychomotor domain; however, others like Harrow (1972) and Moore (1972) have provided their versions of a psychomotor taxonomy. Though the psychomotor domain is important in the overall learning of youngsters, especially in activity-oriented courses (for example, physical education, human ecology, industrial technology), this text and the instructional models focus more on the cognitive domain than the affective or psychomotor, though obviously student involvement in cognitive tasks influences affective responses. Teachers in activity-oriented courses are able to use the various models, but they tend to do so when teaching specific cognitive skills and understandings. Readers should examine the taxonomical references by Harrow (1972) and Moore (1972) to fully explore the psychomotor domain. Table 3-6 illustrates Harrow's six levels.

Ⓟ LANNING FOR TECHNOLOGY INTEGRATION

Today's teachers have increasing access to various forms of technology that can be used to support teaching and learning, regardless of the type of learning objectives being emphasized. Depending on their local context, teachers find themselves in classrooms or schools that are technology-rich, technology-poor, or somewhere in between. In similar fashion, teachers experience varying degrees of support, or even pressure, to integrate technology into their professional practice. Understandably, the reaction of teachers to the availability of new technologies, and to the demand to use them, differs widely as well. This text seeks to support teachers at varying levels of personal readiness and from diverse technology contexts in planning to use technology to enhance the instructional models.

Technology, when thoughtfully applied, can add significant value to each of the eight models of teaching presented in the upcoming chapters. Ultimately, it is up to teachers to plan for the integration of technology and to articulate the specific ways in which it represents additional value for themselves and their students. The authors believe that this is most likely to occur when teachers view different forms of technology as authentic tools that students will likely need in their current and future lives, inside and outside of school. It is also most likely to happen when teachers have a clear conceptual understanding of the diverse purposes for which technology can be used to enhance the teaching and learning process.

A Technology-Enhanced Learning Framework

One of the authors has a special interest in technology-enhanced learning and has recently developed a conceptual framework to help teachers and school administrators plan for and reflect on the various purposes for using technology to enhance teaching and learning. Known as the ADISC Framework (see Figure 3-4), it identifies five purposes for the use of technology in teaching and learning.

In an effort to support teachers in using technology to enhance the instructional models described in Chapters 4 through 11, each of those chapters includes a description of a specific technology enhancement appropriate for the model being discussed. Each of those technology enhancements is anchored to one or more of the five elements of the ADISC Framework, which is another type of taxonomy. As teachers become more familiar with each of the instructional models, especially with their respective purposes and phases, they can begin to plan their own technology enhancements consistent with those purposes and phases.

In addition to describing a technology enhancement for each model, each of the following chapters describes how to modify the recommended technology enhancement for different grade levels, as well as how to make high-tech and low-tech applications of that enhancement. In addition, the recommended en-

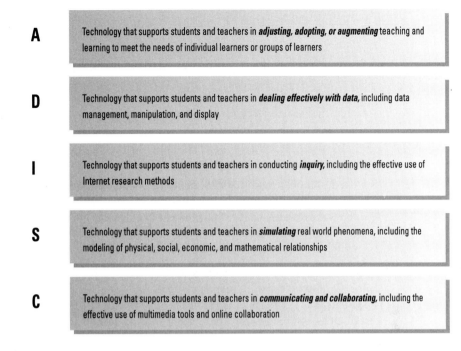

A — Technology that supports students and teachers in *adjusting, adopting, or augmenting* teaching and learning to meet the needs of individual learners or groups of learners

D — Technology that supports students and teachers in *dealing effectively with data,* including data management, manipulation, and display

I — Technology that supports students and teachers in conducting *inquiry,* including the effective use of Internet research methods

S — Technology that supports students and teachers in *simulating* real world phenomena, including the modeling of physical, social, economic, and mathematical relationships

C — Technology that supports students and teachers in *communicating and collaborating,* including the effective use of multimedia tools and online collaboration

FIGURE 3-4 The ADISC Framework

hancement is discussed in terms of its implications for diverse learners. Finally, Web-based resources available to support the enhancement are identified and discussed.

ASSESSMENT

Most of the content in this chapter focuses on establishing clear goals for instruction and on knowing what students are expected to achieve and how they are expected to achieve it. Most of the rest of this book examines the different means for achieving those defined goals. The only missing element is knowing if a goal has been achieved—assessment. Assessment entails the ways in which teachers gather information about student learning. Evaluation is the judgments reached as a result of those assessments.

The following ideas are presented to help teachers better assess and evaluate student performance. Some teacher-defined goals will be relatively easy to assess because they call for simpler forms of thinking—convergent processes (in a direct instruction lesson). Divergent thinking objectives, however, are more difficult to evaluate because students are required to think through problems; such objectives (that are part of concept formation or inquiry lessons) take more time to develop in students and more time to evaluate by teachers. Teachers use a number of different means to assess student performance. Some teachers use multiple choice tests; others rely on true-false or fill-in-the-blank exams; and still others advocate essays. Teachers tend to fall into patterns with regard to student assessment. All methods of assessment can be useful, especially when used appropriately. The problem emerges for students when the teacher-designated assessment strategies fail to provide students with ample opportunities to "show their stuff," to demonstrate what they know, which is why the use of varied teaching strategies helps—students have different ways to show what they know. As Krumboltz and Yeh (1996) observe,

> In developing examinations, many teachers tend to focus on objective information that cannot be disputed. By emphasizing the memorization of facts, however, such teachers discourage debate, inhibit the expression of opinion, minimize teamwork and cooperation, and force students to listen passively—the very worst way to learn. (p. 324)

Of course, finding the best ways for students to demonstrate what they know places a unique set of demands on teachers. Much of what currently passes as assessment is neither well structured nor logically developed. Teachers tend to think of assessment as an "end" rather than as "means to an end." It is, in fact, a bit of both.

It is imperative to consider why so many teachers are limited in their attempts to more effectively assess youngsters. That is, even if teachers decided to become much better assessors of student learning, what problems or limitations would inhibit teacher use of innovative assessment strategies and concomitantly, varied teaching strategies?

Limitation 1—Too Little Time for Planning

Time to plan is almost nonexistent for most American teachers. Even though new scheduling structures (e.g., block scheduling) are being put into place that provide teachers with more time to plan, teachers still find themselves in a position where they have too little time to reflect with others about what students should be able to achieve. Collective thinking (when teachers can share and reflect on teaching practice) among teachers is important, for it is during such times that teachers determine what students must know and how they can better learn. Unfortunately, American teachers have little time for common planning—indeed most have a paucity of time for any planning at all. Stevenson and Stigler (1992) powerfully describe the problem.

> When we informed the Chinese teachers that American elementary school teachers are responsible for their classes all day long, with only an hour or less outside the classroom each day, they looked incredulous. How could any teacher be expected to do a good job when there is no time outside of class to prepare and correct lessons, work with individual children, consult

with other teachers, and attend to all matters that arise in a typical day at school! (p. 164)

There are two ways to solve this time problem within the school. One is to restructure American school calendars so that the school year is longer but that the actual time students spend in school each day is shortened. A longer school year (perhaps 200 to 210 days) is a problem if current class schedules are maintained, but it is a real possibility if teachers actually teach for a shorter time each day. In many countries that have longer school years, the teachers teach no more than 3 or 4 hours a day (e.g., China). They spend the rest of the school day planning and working with individual students.

A second way to allocate more time for teachers is to have them actually spend more time at school. The average American teacher spends 7.3 hours per day at school. True, they often go home and do more school work (i.e., grade papers, etc.), but at home there can be no interactions with colleagues relative to curricular decisions or instructional designs. Once again, Stevenson and Stigler (1992) cogently observe the reality of the American teachers' school day.

Most American teachers . . . arrive at school shortly before classes begin and leave not long after they end. This does not necessarily result in a shorter work week for American teachers. What it does mean is that they must devote their evenings and weekends to schoolwork. (p. 164)

Effective teaching and assessment strategies require planning time. Our suggestions regarding the school year and school day may seem outrageous on the surface, but they make conceptual sense when one considers the need to improve the quality of teachers' lives at school and, we would assert, to enhance, concomitantly, the educational achievement of students. Recall that these radical suggestions for a longer school year and longer school day (coupled with a shorter teaching day), are established practices in countries that regularly outperform American students on standardized tests.

Limitation 2—No Clearly Defined Set of Goals Exists for What Students Must Achieve

The absence of a clearly defined set of core knowledge is one of the biggest impediments to effective assessment. So much attention has been given to local control and classroom teacher autonomy that the skills students must be able to evidence are not well defined. True, the presence of state-adopted texts in some states has created a pseudo core curriculum for students to learn and teachers to teach. But these two truths do not result in quality experiences for most students. Most teachers continue to do their "own thing," and the lack of a common definition of what students should know disadvantages all students to a certain degree, and in particular a growing subset of American students. That segment, incidentally, is perhaps the most vulnerable of America's diverse population of students—America's urban students, the ones who tend to move the most and who evidence lower levels of family and social stability.

E. D. Hirsch (1996) is one of the most ardent and articulate spokespersons for nationalizing the curriculum. His argument is forceful and clear: Provide all students (rich and poor) with a common core experience so that regardless of ethnic or socioeconomic background the public can be assured that what a child has experienced at School A is not substantially different from what would be proffered at School B. Hirsch (1996) writes:

> The public schools of a democracy have a duty to educate all students to their potential. A child's initial lack of intellectual capital is not an immutable given that our schools are powerless to change; rather, it is a challenge that schools can meet by overcoming their academic incoherence. Throughout the world, just one way has been devised to meet the double challenge of educational excellence and fairness: to teach definite skills and a solid core of content appropriate in an effective manner in each year of preschool and grade-school education. (p. 47)

With a common curriculum, teachers can begin to share ideas about assessment that enable them to explore ways to help demonstrate what they know, and what they must know will be similar from teacher to teacher. The idea is not revolutionary; many countries that have high performing educational systems already adhere to such a practice, and organizations such as the National Science Teachers Association and National Council of Teachers of Mathematics argue for some common core knowledge for all students. Regrettably, America's love affair with local control has mitigated its capacity to operationalize educational practices that meet the myriad social demands being placed on schools and the multiple academic expectations being held for students. Somewhere between total local control and a set nationalized curriculum is likely the desired "end." Given the mobility of America's population, some common understandings are essential.

Limitation 3—A Desire of Teachers to Seek "New Age" Solutions to "Old Age" Problems

If it is new, it must be good. Most certainly that statement is true for some things (e.g., a newly prepared meal is better than one that was prepared several days previously), but for many other areas of life, newness does not equate with high quality. Educators, though, are disposed to think of new and good as conceptually and practically equivalent. When portfolios emerged, many educators quickly moved toward the promised land of portfolio assessment. When authentic assessment was proffered as "the answer," there was a rush by many teachers to eliminate objective tests and move toward authentic (performance) assessment. And, when some critics argued against the use of letter grades (i.e., they are demeaning), a new genre of report cards emerged that assessed students in new, albeit ludicrous, ways. Shanker (1995), in his weekly op-ed column, describes one of the new age reporting systems—Shanker's description is based on the comments of a grandfather who has just received his granddaughter's "latest" report card.

> Today's modern report cards are neither reports nor cards. The Spokane Board of Education apparently has joined thousands of other school districts and has morphed (to use a trendy expression) the once familiar report into psycho-social evaluation babble, in which NO CHILD FAILS! This keeps the parents and teachers and school board and taxpayers HAPPY!
>
> I looked at Katy's New Age report, which is now called The Academic Social Growth and Effort Indicator—TASGEI for short—and counted 54 attributes subsumed under a variety of curriculum areas. For each area the students are ranked on a scale of 1 to 5, with 1 being the best.
>
> For example, a 1 means that the pupil is meeting the objectives and is performing skills independently in reading or in math or in work habits. A 4 (formerly called a D) indicates that the pupil needs more time to develop. A 5 (formerly an F) means that the "student chooses NOT to perform skills or activities!"
>
> Had any of us brought home a report card in the good old days with a comment by the teacher that so-and-so ". . . did not choose to participate in arithmetic or in reading," he would have received direct instruction on parts of his anatomy! . . . (p. 15)

Our point here is simply that for far too many teachers, new ideas are used to replace old ones rather than to complement them. When whole language emerged, many teachers mistakenly disdained phonics and relied almost exclusively on literature-based reading instruction. Similarly, when portfolios emerged or when exhibitions were advocated, teachers interpreted that these "new" approaches should be substitutes for objective testing. Suddenly, multiple choice tests were depicted as inherently evil. Hirsch (1996) writes:

> [P]erformance tests are only one of many monitoring devices in classroom teaching. . . . They are not appropriate for large-scale, high-stakes testing because no one has been able, even in theory, to make such tests fair and accurate at reasonable cost in money and time. To serve democratic ends, American educators have pioneered the creation of fair and accurate multiple-choice tests that probe a wide variety of knowledge and skills. The consensus among psychometricians is that these objective tests, rather than performance tests, are the fairest and most accurate achievement tests available. Performance tests, while important as one tool for classroom use, should not play a decisive role in high-stakes testing, where fairness and accuracy are of paramount importance. (p. 243)

Good assessment and evaluation requires thoughtful planning and attention to a variety of elements. Above we described assessment and instructional issues. We now offer some prescriptions for making certain that you know what students must learn.

1. *Write performance objectives in a precise manner*. Avoid writing objectives that are vague, general, or nebulous. Utilize the verbs and examples presented

for each level of the cognitive and affective taxonomies. Write objectives in performance terms that are specific and can be assessed.

2. *Decide upon the content, materials, instructional strategies, and evaluation procedures.* The content, materials, and instructional strategies will be used to help students achieve the performance objectives. The assessment procedures are important in helping assess the degree of achievement.

3. *Select a variety of assessment procedures.* Choose from many sources and types of assessment, depending upon the performance objective and the taxonomical level being implemented. Avoid an overreliance on a few procedures (for example, paper and pencil tests). Besides the typical objective tests found in most classrooms, include such assessment devices as short-answer essays, case studies, student self-evaluation, simulations, role playing, observational analysis, journals and logs, oral and group discussion, portfolios, and others.

4. *Be sure your procedures assess what is taught.* Assess only those skills, concepts, and factual information that students were taught or can be expected to know. Too often educators assess ideas that are not fully examined and explored in the lesson.

5. *Assess frequently.* Students should be assessed often because these experiences can lessen anxiety and fear. The frequency of assessment should be based upon instructional decisions instead of punishment, and this concept should be communicated to students. Testing is one form of diagnosing learning—not the goal of instruction. Teacher evaluation should be objective and subjective, and as teachers get to know students better, more attention should be given to how (and what) students learn than to testing everything they learn. The beauty of using varied teaching strategies is that you get to see students learning in different ways and showing you what they learn.

6. *Assessment demonstrates what you value.* Testing of students is very revealing to observers—by looking at the form of tests and the items on tests, an observer can begin to determine what teachers value in the learning process. Through such observations a determination can be made whether a teacher stresses recall of information or higher-level cognitive and affective thinking. Teacher assessments communicate to outside observers and to students what the teacher believes is worth knowing!

Ⓢ UMMARY

This chapter has provided readers with a description of the instructional planning process and of why planning is so very critical in presenting instructional lessons and units to youngsters. One important aspect of the planning process is the use of goals and objectives. Performance objectives become the teacher's targets toward which instruction aims. The objectives become the focal point of lessons because these objectives are the behaviors that students are expected to perform. Instructional strategies and technology usage are the means to an end.

We now are ready to move on to an examination and description of the eight instructional models. These models are organized around four categories for classification purposes. The models enable students to use facts and concepts in different ways, and those variations result in enhanced cognitive achievement. Students learn best what they use and what they acquire in different ways. In our presentation of these models, we provide a theoretical description of each model, the phases of planning and implementing each model, at least two case studies and a lesson plan to demonstrate how each model is implemented, and evaluative criteria to assess the degree of proficiency in implementing each model. Each chapter that follows also has a discussion of how the instructional model is implemented with culturally diverse students. Applications of cognitive-style research are utilized within each of the instructional model chapters. The emphasis of this text is on the instructional models, but as clearly articulated in this chapter, the models cannot be separated from the instructional goals and student evaluation. If the teacher does not recognize how goals suggest instructional possibilities and how instructional practices dictate evaluative techniques, the teacher will not have an impact on student learning, but instead will be either entertaining students or keeping them busy. Process without content is meaningless, and content is unlearned when teachers are not sufficiently attentive to process.

℞ EFERENCES

Anderson, L. M., C. M. Evertson, and J. E. Brophy. 1979. "An Experimental Study of Effective Teaching in First Grade Reading Groups." *Elementary School Journal* 79: 193–223.

Anderson, L. W., and D. R. Krathwohl. 2001. *A Taxonomy for Learning, Teaching, and Assessing*. New York: Longman.

Bloom, B., M. Englehart, E. Furst, W. Hill, and D. Krathwohl. 1956. *Taxonomy of Educational Objectives: The Classification of Educational Goals, Handbook I: Cognitive Domain*. New York: McKay.

Bruner, J. S., J. J. Goodnow, and G. A. Austin. 1959. *A Study of Thinking*. New York: Wiley.

Carter, K. 1990. "Teachers' Knowledge and Learning to Teach." Pp. 291–310 in W. R. Houston (ed.), *Handbook of Research on Teacher Education*. New York: Macmillan.

Fuller, F., and O. Bown. 1975. "Becoming a Teacher." Pp. 25–52 in K. Ryan (ed.), *Teacher Education* (74th Yearbook for the National Society for the Study of Education). Chicago: University of Chicago Press.

Good, T., and D. Grouws. 1979. "The Missouri Mathematics Effectiveness Project: An Experimental Study in Fourth-Grade Classrooms." *Journal of Educational Psychology* 71: 355–362.

Gordon, W. 1961. *Synectics: The Development of Creative Capacity*. New York: Harper & Row.

Hanson, H., H. Silver, and R. Strong. 1986. *Teaching Styles and Strategies*. Moorestown, NJ: Hanson, Silver, Strong and Associates.

Harrow, A. J. 1972. *A Taxonomy of the Psychomotor Domain*. New York: McKay.

Henry, J. 1955. "Docility, or Giving Teacher What She Wants." *Journal of Social Issues* 11(1): 33–41.

Hirsch, Jr., E. D. 1996. *The Schools We Need*. New York: Doubleday.

Hunkins, F. P. 1972. *Questioning Strategies and Techniques*. Boston: Allyn & Bacon.

Hunter, M. 1984. "Knowing, Teaching, and Supervising." Pp. 169–192 in P. L. Hosford (ed.), *Using What We Know About Teaching*. Alexandria, VA: Association for Supervision and Curriculum Development.

Irvine, J. J., and B. J. Armento. 2001. *Culturally Responsive Teaching*. Boston: McGraw-Hill.

Johnson, D. W., R. T. Johnson, E. J. Holubec, and P. Roy. 1984. *Circles of Learning*. Alexandria, VA: Association for Supervision and Curriculum Development.

Joyce, B., and M. Weil. 1986. *Models of Teaching* (3rd ed.). Englewood Cliffs, NJ: Prentice-Hall.

———. 1992. *Models of Teaching* (4th ed.). Boston: Allyn & Bacon.

Joyce, B., M. Weil, and E. Calhoun. 2000. *Models of Teaching* (6th ed.) Boston: Allyn & Bacon.

Krathwohl, D., B. Bloom, and B. Masis. 1964. *Taxonomy of Educational Objectives, Handbook II: Affective Domain*. New York: McKay.

Krumboltz, J. D., and C. J. Yeh. (1996). Competitive Grading Sabotages Good Teaching. *Phi Delta Kappan*, 78(4): 324–326.

Ladson-Billings, G. 1994. *The Dreamkeepers*. San Francisco: Jossey-Bass.

Lorayne, H., and J. Lucas. 1966. *The Memory Book*. New York: Briercliff Manor.

Mager, R. 1984. *Preparing Instructional Objectives* (3rd ed.). Palo Alto, CA: Fearon.

Moore, M. R. 1972. "Consideration of the Perceptual Process in the Evaluation of Musical Performance." *Journal of Research on Music Education* 20: 273–279.

Orlich, D. C., R. J. Harder, R. C. Callahan, C. H. Kravas, D. P. Kauchak, R. A. Pendergrass, and A. J. Keogh. 1985. *Teaching Strategies: A Guide to Better Instruction* (2nd ed.). Toronto, Canada: D. C. Heath.

Pressley, M., J. R. Levin, and H. Delaney. 1982. "The Mnemonic Keyword Method." *Review of Educational Research* 52: 61–91.

Rosenshine, B. 1983. "Teaching Functions in Instructional Programs." *Elementary School Journal* 83(4): 335–350.

Sanders, N. M. 1966. *Classroom Questions: What Kinds?* New York: Harper & Row.

Shanker, A. 1995. "What's New?" *New Republic*, December 15, p. 15.

Slavin, R. E. 1980. *Using Student Team Learning* (rev. ed.). Baltimore: Johns Hopkins

University, Center for Social Organization of Schools.

————. 1987. "Cooperative Learning and Cooperative School." *Educational Leadership* 45(3): 7–13.

Stevenson, H. W., and J. W. Stigler. 1992. *The Learning Gap.* San Francisco: Jossey Bass.

Suchman, R. J. 1962. *The Elementary School Training Program in Scientific Inquiry.* Report to the U.S. Office of Education, Project Title VII. Project no. 216. Project of the Illinois Studies of Inquiry. Urbana, IL: University of Illinois Press.

Taba, H. 1971. *Hilda Taba Teaching Strategies Program.* Miami, FL: Institute for Staff Development.

Many states are now requiring proficiency exams for students seeking to graduate from high school. Whether such tests are good for education is arguable, but that they are an emerging reality is without doubt. A review of selected tests in one state revealed that many of the items required students to think through a problem and discern an answer. The answer was not something stored in short-term memory; rather it was derived only after students used what they knew in order to make sense out of some "new" problem. In essence, the test item required the student to use reasoning skills.

The two chapters in this section focus on two instructional strategies for students to think through a problem. The first, concept attainment, focuses on teaching significant concepts to students, but the students must use their personal powers of reasoning in order to define the concept's salient attributes. In the second model, inquiry, the students use their observational skills to analyze a phenomenon in a way that enables them to induce a logical explanation for events.

These strategies are not gimmicks for teachers to use. Instead, they represent part of what should constitute the instructional repertoire of every teacher. How and when to use them is a matter of personal preference. But why one would use these instructional models is clear—to make students *think!* ∎

Models That Foster Reasoning Skills

1

FOUR

• *Concept Attainment*

Chapter Objectives

At the end of this chapter, readers will be able to

1. *Identify the specific phases of the concept attainment model.*
2. *Identify strengths and weaknesses of the model.*
3. *Understand the theoretical basis for the model.*
4. *Evaluate sample lessons that utilize the concept attainment strategy.*
5. *Identify ways in which concept attainment enhances the learning abilities of culturally diverse students.*
6. *Create a plan for a personally developed concept attainment lesson.*

❶ NTRODUCTION

The model presented in this chapter is an inductive approach to help students critically think through the meaning of a particular concept (for example, symmetry, parts of speech, balance of power, gravity). Perhaps in an "ideal" world teachers would not need to seriously consider and plan for the types of instruction that may occur in classrooms—students would learn, in essence, despite the instructional model that the teacher uses. Indeed, Rousseau once observed that for a child who wanted to learn to read, any teaching technique would work; the child's natural interests would lead him or her to find a way to decode the written word. If absolutely every student in a classroom exhibited an insatiable desire for knowledge or came from similar cultural (and family) circumstances, then using alternative instructional models might not be an absolute necessity. But because each student is different, because classrooms—regardless of context—are inherently diverse, and because proficiency testing in most states focuses on critical thinking skills and content concepts, it is imperative that teachers create lessons that tap the natural interests and inquisitiveness of students.

It is the consensus of virtually all the men and women who have been working on curriculum projects that making material interesting is in no way incompatible with presenting it soundly.

JEROME S. BRUNER

Several instructional dynamics frame the way in which the teaching process occurs in the classroom (Ornstein and Lasley, 2000)—understanding student differences, determining the length of instruction, identifying how to foster student participation, and evaluating student understanding. These dynamics focus not only on how high ability students learn, but also on how every student can be engaged to think through ideas.

Concept attainment creates an environment where the teacher has frequent access to student knowledge (a necessary precursor for quality instruction), where teachers visibly see the ways in which students are thinking through ideas, where the natural interests and cognitive styles of culturally diverse students are the incentive for student involvement, and where the teacher decides which concepts are significant to warrant in-depth attention and analysis.

One of the prominent concerns of educational reformers is that classroom instruction is too traditional—teacher controlled and teacher centered. Lessons all too often are organized around specific correct and incorrect responses, and students, especially students from culturally diverse backgrounds, have too few opportunities to use their cognitive style dispositions and to explore their own thinking skills. As a consequence, many students, especially those who lack the necessary "academic skills," begin to exit the system psychologically. Such students subsequently become a part of the great mosaic that makes up America— a mosaic that now includes millions of adults who are functionally illiterate but that also has approximately 40 percent of the school-aged population imperiled because of reading deficiencies (Snow, Burns, and Griffin, 1998).

Riley (1997) states in *Design as a Catalyst for Learning* that because of rapid changes taking place in today's business, the need for educating students in other than the traditional methodology is critical. He cites, "it (creative problem solving) is a creative counterpart to the scientific method and presumes there is more than one right solution to any problem and many paths to each alternative" (p. 2). His comments support and encourage the methodology of concept attainment because they suggest that students must both learn content and learn how to analyze that content.

The concept attainment model enables each student to construct and justify an answer to questions that make personal sense. The teacher begins to "shape" the students' thinking by adding new data. Concept attainment is grounded on how students view the world and construct ideas, or in the language of Cajete (1994), a Tewa Indian educator and writer, it is learning that focuses on "seeing the whole through the parts" (p. 31). This instructional model also enhances motivation because students are required to search for ideas that make conceptual sense to them; they can personally invest themselves in the ideas. Because all inductive models have "the search" element in common, they build effectively on the natural curiosity of children regardless of their cultural or social background.

CASE STUDY

Maria Sanchez is preparing to teach the concept of mixed numbers to her 5th grade students. The students already possess a good understanding of proper and improper fractions. Typically Maria uses direct instruction when teaching new skills to students. Today she wants to use a strategy that engenders more active hypothesizing and critical thinking. She starts the lesson by emphasizing the game-like nature of a concept attainment lesson.

"Today, class, we are going to play a game. It's not a complicated game or even a competitive game. Rather, it's a type of guessing game. I want to see if you can guess what idea I am thinking about when you see some examples I place on the board. Over here you see a smiling face—that face represents 'yes' examples. The 'yes' examples all have the characteristics or attributes of the concept I am thinking of. You will also notice a frowning face. The examples under that face do not have the required attributes—they are 'no' examples." Maria then places one "yes" and one "no" example on the board:

$$1\tfrac{1}{2} \qquad\qquad 55$$

"Now, based on the 'yes' example and 'no' example I provided, can you guess or hypothesize my idea? Lupe."

"Small numbers?" Lupe's guess is written down under a third category, labeled "student hypotheses."

"Any other ideas? Jose, what do you think?"

"I think you want numbers that have a whole number and a fraction."

"Good. I'll write that down along with Lupe's.

Mrs. Sanchez looks around for other responses and then continues. "My next examples are 22½, which is a 'yes,' and ⅘, which is a 'no.' Now, what additional ideas do you have?"

LaShanda's hand goes up quickly. "I think the 'yes' examples have to have either a number 1 or 2 in them."

Mrs. Sanchez writes LaShanda's hypothesis on the board.

Mike responds, "I agree with Jose's hypothesis. The 'yes' examples are terms with a whole number and a fraction."

Mrs. Sanchez looks around for other volunteers. Several students respond by agreeing with one of the first three hypotheses. Some suggest even other ideas that make sense given the examples provided by Mrs. Sanchez.

"OK. Let me give you another 'yes' and 'no' example. The 'yes' is 131⅓ and the 'no' is ⅘."

"Based on these, can I eliminate any of the hypotheses that you generated? Mia?"

"Yes, we can eliminate LaShanda's hypothesis. The 'yes' you just gave us has a 3, not just a 1 and 2."

"Good. Does everyone agree?" The students all nod affirmatively.

The lesson proceeds with additional "yes" and "no" examples until approximately eight positive and negative exemplars are on the board. The students have now eliminated all the hypotheses except "numbers that have a whole number and a proper fraction."

As the lesson concludes, Mrs. Sanchez confirms that the attribute identified by the students is in fact essential to defining the concept.

She then adds, "Does anyone know the technical name for what we call numbers with this attribute? That is, what do we call numbers that have a whole number and a proper fraction? Tonya?"

"Mixed numbers?"

"Excellent. That's right. Mixed numbers are numbers that have a whole number and a proper fraction. Now I want you to generate 10 more 'yes' and 'no' examples that we can add to our list. Do that on your own, then I will ask for volunteers to share their 'yes' and 'no' examples with the class, and we will see if everyone agrees with your classification." ■

The preceding case is an example of a concept attainment lesson.

⊕ THEORETICAL PERSPECTIVE

The concept attainment model has deep, rich historical and philosophical roots. Aristotle, over 2,000 years ago, was concerned with how humans discern or "make sense of" the world in which they live. Within the context of that discerning process, people begin to classify the objects and ideas that they perceive. Indeed, Aristotle was the quintessential scientific organizer; his goal was to clarify concepts and order the world he experienced. He did this by creating his own broad categories (living and nonliving things) and then showing how these categories could be further subdivided. Aristotle used characteristics of an object to make the categorization. As Gaardner (1996) notes:

> When Aristotle divides natural phenomena into various categories, his criterion is the object's characteristics, or more specifically, what it can do or what it does.
>
> All living things (plants, animals, humans) have the ability to absorb nourishment, to grow, and to propagate. All living creatures (animals and humans) have in addition the ability to perceive the world around them and to move about. Moreover, all humans have the ability to think—or otherwise to order their perceptions into various categories and classes. (p. 114)

The twentieth-century version of the model is based largely on the research of Bruner, Goodnow, and Austin (1967), and it has been subsequently popularized and identified as a teaching strategy by a number of different authors, most especially Eggen and Kauchak (2001), Joyce and Weil (1972, 1992, 1996) and Joyce, Weil, and Calhoun (2000). The learning of concepts from various academic disciplines is important to understanding the world. Concepts help make the complex and often abstract nature of diverse ideas much more understandable to students. Without concepts, people would have no way of categorizing new ideas efficiently and effectively; they would have to engage in constant learning and could not use past experience to frame new experiences.

At the most basic level, concepts can be either concrete (simple) or abstract (complex). The level of complexity is dictated by the number of inherent attributes within the concept. Concrete concepts (see Figure 4-1) are those things that can be seen, felt, heard, smelled, or tasted on some direct, experiential level; they can be evidenced by the senses and observed in reality. A car, horse, or whole number can be identified using direct experience—the teacher can point to a Ford, or a stallion, or the number 5. On the other hand, abstract concepts (see Figure 4-1) represent nonobservable instances of a larger,

Concrete Concepts		Abstract Concepts
Voting	←——→	Democracy
Reading	←——→	Literary Criticism
Friends	←——→	Interdependence
Fight	←——→	Revolution
Man	←——→	Humankind
Embryo	←——→	Genetic Engineering

FIGURE 4-1   Types of Concepts

complex idea; they are a collection of meanings that cannot be adequately defined by a single or sometimes even several examples or attributes. The concept of *democracy* is one such abstract concept that is often taught in school. Other examples include ecology, literary criticism, or interdependence.

The concept attainment model can be used by elementary school teachers to teach concrete concepts such as mixed numbers, which is the focus of Maria Sanchez's lesson. With high school teachers, the concepts taught will often be more abstract, and in many instances the appropriateness of the concept attainment model must be carefully assessed before teachers consider using it.

In general, concept attainment (CA) is used most effectively by teachers who are teaching concrete concepts; but as a teacher's skills grow in using the CA model, so, too, can the teacher manifest an ability to transform the model's usage to include a greater variety of complex and abstract concepts.

Concepts are characterized by three elements: a concept name, the essential and nonessential concept attributes, and the attribute value within a concept (Joyce and Weil, 1996). The *concept name* is its common identifier—the term given to the myriad examples within a concept category. Hence, the common identifier for a word that represents a person, place, or thing is *noun*. The term *noun*, in turn, has selected essential and nonessential attributes.

An *attribute* is, according to Bruner, Goodnow, and Austin (1990), "any discriminable feature of an event that is susceptible to some discriminable variation from event to event. . . . When some discriminable feature of the environment is used as a basis for 'going beyond' by inference, it serves as a signal. When such a discriminable feature is used as a means of inferring the identity of something, . . . it is a criterial attribute" (p. 26). In essence, a criterial attribute parallels Joyce and Weil's (1996) notion of essential attribute. If an attribute is changed in value and that change makes it impossible to classify the object, the attribute is essential or criterial for categorizing the object. Changing the color of apples is not criterial; changing their shape would be. Quite literally, what students do during a concept attainment lesson is list in their hypotheses the attributes of the concept.

Essential attributes are those characteristics that enable a person to make specific classifications within particular categories. Any term that is a person (Thomas Jefferson), a place (Chicago), or a thing (chair) is labeled a noun. Of course, it can also be labeled a particular type of noun (proper or common), but the type of noun is nonessential to its classification as a noun. *Nonessential at-*

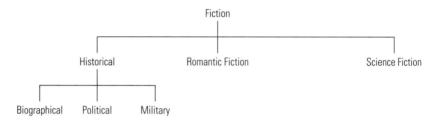

FIGURE 4-2 The Hierarchical Structure of Fiction (Superordinate to Subordinate Concepts)

tributes are those characteristics that are evident in a concept but are not needed for accurate concept identification. Hence, crayons are nouns, but the actual color of the crayons is not needed (color is a nonessential attribute) to make an appropriate designation as a noun. Chicago is a city and is classified as a (proper) noun—where it is located and its size are nonessential to its identification as a noun.

Attribute value is the degree to which some characteristic is manifested in order to categorize a concept accurately (Joyce, Weil, and Calhoun, 2000). Attribute value is typically less pedagogically evident with concrete concepts than it is with abstract concepts. The presence of seeds (not the number of seeds) represents one essential attribute of fruit. The presence of four wooden legs and a seat (not the quality of the wooden materials) characterizes a chair. For abstract concepts, attribute value plays a more prominent role in the categorization process. As an example, for the concept of democracy, the type of participation of the citizens and the choices they have available are important definitional qualities. A citizen in one country may be able to participate in the political process (when the government dictates) and make choices (for candidates the government specifies) yet live in a dictatorship. In another country, the type of participation and choices may be sufficiently different to qualify as a democracy (that is, citizens have full participation in the political process; they can vote for a range of candidates; and political candidates do not require governmental approval in order to appear on a ballot). Attribute value—the degree to which an attribute is manifested in teacher-identified exemplars—is critical to the identification of abstract concepts.

Concepts can also be *superordinate, subordinate,* or *coordinate.* Indeed, one concept can represent or fit definitionally within all of these descriptors. In Figure 4-2, historical fiction is superordinate to political fiction, subordinate to fiction, and coordinate with romantic fiction. The different levels become important as teachers begin to select examples of concepts for concept attainment lessons. In Figure 4-3, apples are subordinate (in a subcategory) to fruit but coordinate (within the same category) with bananas and oranges. Finally, apples are superordinate to the apple types of Macintosh or Granny Smith.

Providing examples to students is critical in teaching concept attainment lessons. Equally important, especially as the concept attainment lessons are implemented, is the use of nonexamples. It is through the use of both examples and nonexamples that students learn to fully explore the attributes of concepts.

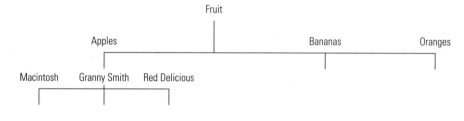

FIGURE 4-3   The Hierarchical Structure of Fruit (Superordinate to Subordinate Concepts)

Examples must possess the essential attributes of a concept, while nonexamples will not have one or more of the essential attributes. Concept attainment lessons require the use of both examples and nonexamples, though how the examples are actually presented to students may vary significantly depending on the type of hypothesizing desired by the teacher.

Concept attainment strategies are intended to frame the essential attributes of a concept while expanding the thinking skills of students. Students in schools are expected to acquire content information and to think actively about that content. Most schools place students in the position of learning content information without critically thinking about how that content is organized or structured—the teacher provides the schema rather than requiring students to independently generate their own conceptual organization.

Concept attainment requires that the teacher identify a significant concept and then structure a lesson so that students identify the salient attributes of that concept. Students must engage in higher-order thinking to determine the concept name and the specific attributes that the teacher predetermines as focal points of a concept attainment lesson.

Teachers usually teach by identifying in lessons a salient concept, providing a definition of the concept (with the appropriate attributes), and then providing examples of the concept (see Figure 4-4). Such a deductive approach is an efficacious one, especially for teaching certain types of functional skills (for example, how to divide or add fractions). But such an approach to teaching also has limitations because it fails to create within students the type of critical thinking skills students need once they enter the world of work. As examples, doctors work from symptoms to diagnosis; lawyers work from a client's problem to an understanding of applicable legal codes; and students retain more when they work from observing and classifying data to defining and articulating concepts. Tennyson and Cocchiarella (1986) compared the effectiveness of treatments in which students induce attributes and definitions as compared with deductive instances where definitions are presented by the teacher and then followed by exemplars. They found that students consistently developed better concept understandings and retained concepts longer when inductive rather than deductive instructional approaches were used.

Concept attainment is an instructional model that utilizes inductive thinking strategies. The teacher moves from specific instances and examples to general ideas and concepts. This instructional process requires that students think through what the student or teacher-generated examples have in common (how

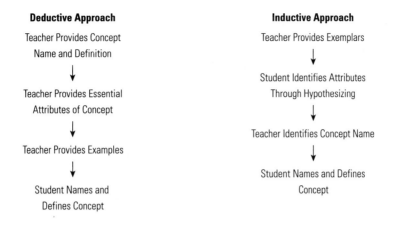

Deductive Approach	Inductive Approach
Teacher Provides Concept Name and Definition	Teacher Provides Exemplars
↓	↓
Teacher Provides Essential Attributes of Concept	Student Identifies Attributes Through Hypothesizing
↓	↓
Teacher Provides Examples	Teacher Identifies Concept Name
↓	↓
Student Names and Defines Concept	Student Names and Defines Concept

FIGURE 4-4 A Comparison of Deductive and Inductive Pedagogical Structures

the exemplars are alike) and how to synthesize those attributes (consider them in combination) to determine a specific concept name.

CONCEPT ATTAINMENT: TEACHING PHASES

Phase I: Concept Identification

Not every concept can or should be taught using the concept attainment approach. Concepts taught using the concept attainment model should be significant and have relatively clear and specific attributes, especially when the teacher is first utilizing this instructional model. Teachers who first use the model should probably start with simple, concrete concepts and then move to more complex, abstract concepts after they have some understanding and comfort level in using this instructional model.

The beauty of the concept attainment model is that although a teacher has a clear concept in mind, the students must identify the essential attributes by thinking about the exemplars the teacher provides. Students become active participants in the knowledge construction of the lesson. They must carefully think about what the positive examples have in common (how they are the same) and eventually determine a concept name that has been predetermined by the teacher. The model works best when a concept has several different defining attributes (for example, a fruit or a part of speech) because student thinking can be expanded upon as the lesson progresses. Once the teacher identifies the concept for the lesson—by examining a textbook, by following a district prescribed course of study, or by assessing a need for students to acquire the concept—students then actually participate in the concept attainment instructional model. Students, in essence, become active participants in constructing their own understandings.

Phase II: Exemplar Identification

Providing exemplars to students is at the heart of the concept attainment model. Exemplars consist of positive and negative examples of a concept. Positive exemplars contain all the necessary critical attributes of a concept. In Maria Sanchez's lesson, the positive example (1½) has all the requisite attributes of a mixed number (that is, a whole number and a fraction). Negative exemplars do not contain a necessary critical attribute—Mrs. Sanchez's example of 55 has a whole number but not a fraction.

The positive and negative exemplars can be presented in several different ways to students. In a later section of this chapter, we will describe an alternative concept attainment strategy that can be used to help students acquire the necessary understandings of the critical attributes.

The first set of positive exemplars provided in the lesson should be relatively clear and specific. The emphasis should not be on tricking students but rather on helping students identify the requisite essential attributes. Eggen and Kauchak (1988) suggest that "examples [should be] selected so that each contains the combination of essential characteristics and none of the nonexamples contain the same combination" (p. 136). Tennyson and Park (1980) suggest that a set of exemplars should contain at least "three examples and five nonexamples which . . . [reflect] the number of critical and variable attributes of the concept" (p. 57).

In selecting positive exemplars, each should illustrate the requisite characteristics. In providing negative exemplars, care should be taken to ensure that nonessential attributes are varied and substantially represent *what the concept is not*. Tennyson and Park (1980) argue that "nonexamples help the student concentrate on critical attributes [especially] when presented in a matched set of examples and nonexamples . . . [but] nonexamples may not facilitate concept learning unless they are matched to examples having similar variable attributes" (p. 59). For Mrs. Sanchez's lesson the nonexamples might include the following: 55 (a whole number), ⅘ (a proper fraction), ⁴⁄₃ (an improper fraction), and .33 (a decimal). The positive examples for her lesson are all mixed numbers: 1½, 22½, 131⅓, but they are not the same type of mixed numbers (that is, 1½, 2⅓, 3¼, and so on). Correct classification occurs most readily when the examples are ordered from easy to difficult (simple to complex), when they differ in essential attributes, and when nonexamples differ from examples in a minimum number of critical attributes. Still, there is no absolute right way to order the exemplars. The goal of the teacher, not the technical structure of a concept attainment lesson, dictates the exemplar order.

Some teachers attempt to "match" examples and nonexamples. Matched exemplars contain similar elements, except each nonexample lacks an essential attribute necessary for accurate concept identification. McKinney (1985) writes, "As an illustration, when teaching the concept of 'domesticated animal,' a teacher may show a picture of a house cat (example) and a tiger (nonexample). They are matched because both are types of cats" (p. 66). Eggen and Kauchak (2001) also suggest that the nonexamples should be varied to ensure that all examples of what the concept "is not" are listed. Further, they suggest that the positive examples include coordinate concepts to the concept being taught.

They use an illustration of metaphor (as the concept being taught) and coordinate concepts of hyperbole, simile, and personification as the nonexamples.

After the students see a variety of positive and negative exemplars (whether matched or unmatched), they can begin to differentiate the exemplars and to engage in the third phase of the concept attainment model: hypothesizing.

Phase III: Hypothesizing

With the concept attainment model, the student is asked to identify the common attributes and eventually identify a label (or name) for the examples provided by the teacher. Phases II and III are cyclical, with the student observing some examples and then hypothesizing. The teacher then shares some additional positive and negative examples, which are followed by additional hypothesizing. At some point in the class discussion, the students will have all the critical attributes identified and all the false hypotheses eliminated. False hypotheses occur early in the process when a limited number of exemplars are available for student review. They are eliminated as a result of the cyclical process, with students identifying those hypotheses that remain valid after all exemplars are available for review. In the case study provided above, recall that after the third set of exemplars is provided by Mrs. Sanchez, she asks: *"Based on these, can I eliminate any of the hypotheses that you generated?"* And Mia responds, *"Yes, we can eliminate LaShanda's hypothesis. The 'yes' you just gave us has a 3, not just a 1 and 2."*

The cyclical process helps students compare items and see how the various exemplars are both similar and different. One problem that some teachers encounter at the early stages of this phase is that a student will guess the correct concept very quickly—"I think it's mixed numbers." If students accurately identify the concept, the teacher should avoid immediately confirming the guess as correct with "Right! You have it!" Instead, the teacher should treat each guess (hypothesis) as equally valid until most or all of the exemplars are identified. Remember the purpose is to foster thinking and to learn the teacher-defined concept. In concept attainment, the thinking process is just as important as the correct identification of the concept, and requiring students to defend their hypotheses is critical. Teachers can do this by simply asking lots of "why" questions. Eggen and Kauchak (2001) observe:

> There are two reasons for asking students to explain why they accept or reject a hypothesis. First, articulating their reasoning helps them develop their thinking. Second, other students benefit from hearing their reasoning described in words. If one student decides that a hypothesis must be rejected, for instance, others may not understand why, or may disagree. Explaining helps keep understanding among the students as uniform as possible. . . . (p. 165)

In essence, the cyclical process entails the following steps:

1. Teacher presents (matched or unmatched) exemplars.
2. Students analyze exemplars, generate hypotheses, and defend responses.
3. Teacher presents additional exemplars.

4. Students add additional hypotheses and eliminate invalid hypotheses.

5. Teacher and students confirm all valid hypotheses and eliminate all invalid hypotheses.

One final note: The actual level or amount of hypothesizing will be dictated by the number of attributes and the concomitant discriminable values of the examples or instances presented by the teacher. Bruner, Goodnow, and Austin (1990) observe:

> The larger the number of attributes exhibited by instances and the larger the number of discriminable values they exhibit, the greater will be the number of hypotheses to be entertained. This is the first constraining factor imposed on problem-solving by the nature of instances encountered. (p. 61)

Once all valid hypotheses have been confirmed and all invalid hypotheses eliminated, the teacher then prepares for closure.

Phase IV: Closure

The closure phase often requires the least amount of teaching time. In this phase of the lesson the teacher reviews the hypotheses that remain after all the exemplars have been presented, and helps the students isolate a working concept name. Recall that Mrs. Sanchez asks, *"What do we call numbers that have a whole number and a proper fraction?"* Some students may recognize the term *mixed number.* If so, the teacher accepts the response: *"That's right. Mixed numbers are numbers that have a whole number and a proper fraction."* However, the teacher also reviews and demonstrates why the concept attributes define whether an item is a positive example or a negative example. For example: *"Let's review the examples. The number $1\frac{1}{2}$ is a mixed number because 1 is a whole number and $\frac{1}{2}$ is a proper fraction, the two together ($1\frac{1}{2}$) create a mixed number. The number 55 is not a mixed number because there is no fraction with the whole number 55."* If students cannot identify the correct concept name, the teacher should provide it: *"You have identified the essential attributes of a number in mathematics we call a 'mixed number.'"* This response is perfectly acceptable, especially with elementary-age youngsters who do not have a prior history with concepts being presented by the teacher through the use of concept attainment.

Many teachers prematurely stop lessons once students identify the concept. They fail to review with students the reasons for the positive and negative exemplar labels. This is a mistake! Even if the very first student guesses the concept name, keep the lesson going until the students begin to home in on the critical attributes and the specific concept. The reinforcement of having students recognize why each exemplar is either positive or negative is extremely important in fostering enhanced student understanding. Further, such reinforcement enables students to proceed more easily to the application phase of the model. Some teachers have students write down the concept name and critical attributes (valid hypotheses) before proceeding. Other teachers just leave the concept name and attributes displayed on an overhead projector or on a chalkboard. Either way, it is important to make certain that the critical attributes are clearly identified before students proceed to the application phase.

Phase V: Application

The application phase enables students to explore fully their understanding of the concept. Students demonstrate an understanding of the concept by creating their own exemplars. Actually, students may be asked to generate their own positive and negative examples. This process allows the teacher to explore the ability of students to define the concept's essential attributes. Mrs. Sanchez said to her students, "*Now I want you to generate 10 more 'yes' and 'no' examples that we can add to our list.*" The students then generate their own examples and must be prepared to describe each exemplar accurately based on the critical attributes. One student may respond that 4½ is a positive example because it has a whole number and fraction and that .46 is not an example because it is a decimal number. The teacher at this point can more fully explore the difference between essential attributes and nonessential attributes. For example, it is essential that mixed numbers have a whole number and a proper fraction. A nonessential attribute is the actual value of the different numbers (for example, for a mixed number the actual value of a whole number or proper fraction is irrelevant to making an accurate classification; or, for a car, a nonessential attribute is the car's color).

INSTRUCTIONAL VARIATIONS

Teachers who introduce concept attainment approaches in the classroom may find students initially confused by the use of exemplars (especially nonexamples) as a way of inducing definitions. We suggest that when teachers first start to use the model they play a simple concept attainment game to help students understand the teaching strategy that will be used. One that we have used and found to be successful follows:

> "Class, in preparing for today's lesson I need to have you play a little game with me. This game focuses on your ability to identify the physical attribute I am thinking of when I call on one of you to stand. For instance, Nguyen [a brown-haired boy with glasses], I want you to stand. Nguyen is a positive example of my idea. Stephanie [a redheaded girl without glasses], I want you to stand. Stephanie is a nonexample of my idea. Based on these two examples, what idea do you think I have in mind?"

The students now begin to hypothesize. Some students think the teacher's idea is "boys." Others think it has something to do with hair color. And still others guess glasses. After all the hypothesizing is completed, the teacher proceeds with more positive and negative examples.

> "Marion is an example of my idea [a brown-haired girl with glasses] and Bob is a nonexample [a blond-haired boy without glasses]."

As the lesson progresses, the students eliminate all hypotheses except "students with glasses."

The high school teacher we originally saw who used this "introduction" then proceeded to teach a lesson on parts of speech. He complimented the students on identifying the correct physical characteristic (students with glasses) and then asked them to see if they could do the same thing with a more abstract concept.

Teachers might use such introductory activities as a way of orienting students to the nature of concept attainment procedures. Such a preparation activity can help students begin to understand the structure of the concept attainment model.

Variations on concept attainment mainly focus on how phases II and III are implemented. Teachers who use concept attainment at different times in the school year may want to alter the manner in which the positive and negative examples are provided and the hypothesizing is conducted. The following variation is provided so that teachers, utilizing this instructional model, can more effectively vary their approaches throughout the school year.

Concept Attainment I

In Concept Attainment I (CAI) the teacher provides one or two positive and negative examples and then asks the student to begin hypothesizing. By limiting the number of initial exemplars, the teacher maximizes the number of hypotheses that will be generated by the students. After the students create a tentative set of hypotheses, the teacher continues by placing another set of positive and negative examples on the board. After each set is provided, the students add or delete hypotheses based on their analyses of the new exemplars. The following is a listing of the example and hypothesizing steps with which students will be involved within a concept attainment lesson:

Concept: Natural Resources

Step I: Teacher presents first set of exemplars
trees—yes
paper—no
animals—yes
gasoline—no

Step II: Students generate hypotheses
- things that are living
- things that are abundant
- things that end in the letter *s*
- things you can touch

Step III: Teacher presents second set of exemplars
sunlight—yes
electricity–no
limestone—yes
cars—no

Step IV: Students add and delete hypotheses
- ~~things that are living~~
- things that are abundant
- things that can be used by humans to do work
- ~~things that end in the letter *s*~~
- ~~things you can touch~~

Step V: Teacher presents third set of exemplars
  crude oil—yes
  kerosene—no
  rivers—yes
  paper bags—no

Step VI: Students refine hypotheses until all invalid ideas are eliminated

The teacher provides as many exemplars as is necessary to identify the appropriate concept attributes (valid hypotheses). The actual number of desired exemplars will vary according to the concept taught, but the positive examples should contain all the essential attributes necessary for fully defining the concept. As a result, Tennyson and Park (1980) note: "The optimal number of examples is probably not an absolute number. It will vary depending upon the characteristics of the concept such as the number of attributes" (p. 61). In the previous example the teacher is teaching the concept of natural resources and completes the lesson once the students identify the salient attributes of the positive examples (for example, occur naturally, are used to make products for humans, have value, and so on). The invalid hypotheses (for example, things that end in s, and things you can touch) are eliminated.

Concept Attainment II

In Concept Attainment II (CAII) the students are provided with all positive and negative examples before the lesson begins. The teacher starts with one positive and one negative example of the concept to be taught, and then lists the other exemplars, without classifying them as either positive or negative, that will be used as part of the lesson. Hypothesizing starts once students recognize the range of available exemplars. The following is an example of how Concept Attainment II is implemented:

Concept: Natural Resources

Step I: Teacher presents one positive and one negative example of the concept
  trees—yes
  paper—no

Step II: Teacher presents a variety of other exemplars
  animal   kerosene
  gasoline   cars
  sunlight   rivers
  electricity   limestone
  crude oil   paper bags

Step III: Students select items to pair with "yes"
  Student 1: "I think electricity will pair with trees."

Step IV: Students hypothesize
  Student 1: "I think your idea is things needed to make paper. To make paper
      you need trees, electricity, and probably gasoline [to run machines]."
  Student 2: "I think your idea is things that grow in a forest.
  Student 3: "I think your idea is things that are living.

The teacher listens to different student ideas and methodically classifies the other exemplars based on each hypothesis presented. For example, after the first student hypothesis, the teacher should ask why? and may even respond: *"If you are right about things needed to make paper, which of the other exemplars would you group with trees?"* Allow students time to think through the category (concept) that they are proposing. Once a student is done, then indicate whether the pairing is correct given the concept you as the teacher are presenting. As students provide exemplars (positive and negative) for each proposed hypothesis, only those that fit the category as the teacher defines it should be listed. As a result of this process, each student begins to rethink the validity of his or her original hypothesis (for example, things needed to make paper) as the teacher reveals which items are in fact "yes" and "no" examples. A student may include electricity under "things to make paper," but needs to eliminate the proposed hypothesis once the teacher labels electricity as a "no." (In this instance the teacher is teaching the concept of natural resources.) Once the students identify the correct hypothesis (or attributes), and all teacher-generated exemplars are labeled, the teacher then asks students to generate their own additional exemplars.

Eggen and Kauchak (2001) propose another variation, which they suggest fosters even more critical thinking. They suggest that teachers provide the first two exemplars (one positive and one negative) and then ask the students to generate a concept name and then their own exemplars (and appropriate hypotheses) that they would classify under the original two exemplars. Students must defend each example based on either an implied or a defined hypothesis. Students would then provide additional examples and defend them. At this stage of the instructional variation, the teacher indicates whether the student's example (as a "yes" or "no") is accurate. Hypotheses are added, refined, or eliminated as a result of this iterative process on the part of the students. As students add more and more examples, the valid hypotheses or attributes are more clearly identified. This technique places the cognitive load on students to defend an idea; it places students in the position of having to think critically about ideas and create their own schema relative to the concepts being taught by the teacher. Further, Eggen and Kauchak note:

> One additional advantage of CA III is the opportunity it affords learners to gather data. CA III is more authentic or realistic than the other two Concept-Attainment formats because students more actively investigate a concept they don't fully understand. Because students are not limited to the examples the teacher provides, they can use more of their own background knowledge and initiative in investigating hypotheses. This increases their control of the learning activity, which has been identified by researchers as a factor increasing learners' intrinsic motivation. . . . In addition, critical thinking is best developed with practice in which students share and explain the thinking processes they use in arriving at their answers. (p. 171)

Concept Attainment I is more appropriate for younger students or for students who are just learning how to use this approach. *Concept Attainment II* may be more effective with older students who have the verbal and critical thinking skills necessary to analyze concepts from several different perspectives. Thus, the efficacy of the different approaches is often dictated by the developmental abilities and needs of the students and the pedagogical proficiency of the teacher in dealing with these needs.

Ⓐ PPLICATIONS TO DIVERSE CLASSROOMS

As the student population in American schools becomes more diverse, it is increasingly important that teachers vary the instructional approaches they use to teach essential content. The use of alternative instructional models is important for several reasons. Such variation enables teachers to match appropriate instructional models with corresponding student cognitive styles and learning modalities. This matching is critical in order to teach students other forms of learning so that they may draw upon alternative styles of information processing when confronted with unfamiliar phenomena, and to vary instructional approaches to teaching and learning in order to sustain the interest and motivation of today's multimedia/sensory students.

As we noted in Chapter 2, American schools tend to favor field-independent forms of thinking in which concepts are often disconnected or decontextualized from examples. This type of schooling for the most part is teacher-centered and is oriented toward deductive thinking processes (deductive teaching requires linear, sequential thinking on the part of students). Indeed, Hale-Benson (1982) contends that "not only does the school reward the development of the analytic style of processing information, but its overall ideology and environment reinforces behaviors associated with . . . [such a] style" (p. 34). Clayton (1996), in her work with cross-cultural students (students from other cultures who enter U.S. schools), reinforces Hale-Benson's point: "In the United States, there is emphasis, for example, on the task to be accomplished, on linear thinking, on decontextualized information, on 'the facts' rather than feelings, on details rather than the whole, on ways of presenting the self to others, on ways of asking questions, and on the attention given to activities" (p. 7).

Hilliard (1976) and others suggest that many culturally diverse students approach cognitive tasks through the use of more field-sensitive modes. That is, their cognitive style is one that is oriented toward divergent thinking, inductive learning, and creative processing. Concept attainment fosters divergent thinking (through hypothesizing), engenders inductive thinking (through student examination of specific instances before a general definition is provided), and enhances creative processing (through the ability of students to create their own patterns for the specific exemplars provided by the teacher). Because the concept attainment model utilizes relational processes to teach concepts, it plays to the cognitive strengths of many students of color and female students. The model seeks to develop the skills of comparing and contrasting phenomena. Students are not told the answer in CA approaches; rather they are expected to create and defend their own hypotheses based upon the exemplars presented to them by the teacher.

All students, and especially culturally diverse students, need opportunities to demonstrate their conceptualizations rather than simply recite back to the teacher what the teacher defines as correct. With concept attainment the teacher "sees" the thinking of the students—how they organize ideas and how they define concepts prior to seeing the teacher's cognitive structure. In Maria Sanchez's lesson, readers should assess the number of different ways in which divergent thinking was fostered and how an evolving definition of the concept occurred. Mrs. Sanchez required, for example, the students to look for patterns (she does not tell them the pattern), and she fostered meaning by having the students justify their answers.

Concept attainment is also a normal way for teachers to draw on the cultural knowledge of students by using examples that they know rather than to use examples that are unknown or possibly personally irrelevant. Some of the more popular instructional programs for students of color are those that rely heavily on the entire knowledge base of the students being taught. That does not mean that the curriculum is compromised. Rather, it enables the teacher to enrich what students experience in the classroom. The following illustration, though not specifically concept attainment in nature, suggests how culturally embedded examples can enhance a traditional concept. It is taken from Sainte-Marie's (1999) description of the "Cradleboard Teaching Project":

> The Cradleboard project is . . . providing a core curriculum "though Native American eyes" to all learners. Then we create cross-cultural partnerships of widely distant classes, and the two classes study Native American culture together.
>
> We create core curriculum in geography, history, social studies, music, and science that matches national content standards for elementary, middle school, and high school levels, and we present it through a Native American perspective. For instance, in their examination of the principles of sound, middle school students learn about frequency and amplitude and wavelengths and changing lengths of a column of air by studying flutes, as well as drums and rattles and mouthbows and Apache violins. In our first interactive multimedia CD-ROM, "Science: Through Native American Eyes," we use video, spoken word, animation, text, and music to present principles and constraints of building materials used in various styles of Native American lodges. The trick to all of this, of course, is to do it in such a way that the culture doesn't get in the way of science, and vice versa. Science itself has no ethnicity. We all use and are affected by scientific principles regardless of our ethnic backgrounds. So this CD-ROM study of wavelengths, in which we give children virtual hands-on access to interactive sliders like those used in recording studios, seems most appropriate. We could be using piano or trumpet sounds; but instead, we use Native American musical instruments, adding a cultural component without compromising the core subject. (p. 37)

Concept attainment enables the teacher to create a more instructionally differentiated classroom. Such a classroom provides learners with a different avenue to learning the requisite content material deemed essential for students to learn. The most recent Turning Points 2000 (Jackson and Davis, 2000) text issued by the Carnegie Corporation highlights that differentiated instruction does not mean that a teacher uses 25 different strategies to reach 25 different students. It means, instead, that with diverse learners (and almost all American classrooms are diverse), it is imperative for teachers to approach content learning in different ways. Concept attainment should be one of those ways.

ⓟREVALENT ISSUES IN DIVERSE CLASSROOMS

Several issues preclude teachers from using concept attainment effectively. The following section focuses on a set of common issues that teachers confront when they use concept attainment for the first time. After each question, we have highlighted some possible responses that may prove useful to those attempting to use the technique effectively, especially with the diverse learners that constitute a growing part of America's classrooms.

Q: *How do I deal with those students who do not want to participate in a lesson?*

A: It is quite common for some students to be apprehensive about participating in and to think creatively about generating hypotheses—especially students who are part of cultural groups where competition is not encouraged (see Chapter 2; Cooper, Johnson, Johnson, and Wilderson, 1980; Cox and Ramirez, 1981; Hale-Benson, 1986; Ramirez and Castaneda, 1974; Shade, 1984; Shade and Edwards, 1987; Soldier, 1989; Vasquez, 1991). Inductive strategies have an implicitly open quality. As students use the inductive approach, they will learn to appreciate the inherent ambiguity of ideas; however, initially the teacher may need to call on a variety of nonvolunteers to offer answers. Teachers should call on students who may, at times, be reticent to respond—but teachers must be comfortable in waiting for student responses. One cooperative learning technique (numbered heads together, NHT, to be described in Chapter 10) may be especially useful in helping reticent students generate ideas. In this approach, the teacher forms the students into groups of three and then has the students in each group count off by threes (that is, one student is assigned the number 1, another 2, and another 3). The teacher then asks the different groups to generate ideas in response to specific teacher questions. For instance, in the example at the beginning of this chapter, Mrs. Sanchez could have asked students to do the hypothesizing in NHT groups instead of just calling out individual ideas. Once the NHT students have completed their group hypothesizing in response to a question, the teacher calls for all number "2s" to raise their hands, and then calls on one of the 2s to share the group's ideas. NHT lowers the personal risks associated with each student generating ideas. In essence, the ideas are more representative of the group's thinking.

Q: *How do I deal with students who dominate and have a need to be right all of the time?*

A: One of the biggest problems with inductive strategies emerges when some "gifted" students try to dominate the lesson. These students "know" the answers, and all too often teachers inadvertently play into their hands. The purpose of inductive teaching is to expand student thinking—everyone's thinking. As a consequence, it is absolutely imperative that teachers do not intentionally acknowledge some responses as better than others. Explore all the students' ideas. Instead of praising each response with a "great" or "wonderful," spend more time examining why the response makes sense to the student or how the student sees the response as relevant. Ask quite a few "how," "what," and "why" questions as students think through the possibilities of a hypothesis. The beauty of inductive strategies is that teachers "see" more of the students' thinking. The problem with traditional approaches (for example, lecture) is that teachers expect students to assimilate ideas in precisely the same way as the teacher, and then the teacher has a tendency to call on a narrow range of students to respond (Sadker and Sadker, 1994). There are times when such an approach is essential, but at other points the teacher's goal is focused more on critical thinking, and in those instances concept attainment is appropriate for teaching a curricular concept.

Q: *Do my exemplars really make that much difference in who participates?*

A: Yes! Some teachers create exemplars for each lesson that require just one representation of an idea. That is, they consistently use words or pictures to represent an idea. For students who come from cultural backgrounds where linguistic intelligence is valued and fostered, such narrowness may seem efficacious—the approach plays to their strengths. Unfortunately, many students have other types of intelligence that teachers fail to tap in a way that allows for individual expression of creativity and cognitive exploration. Teachers at all grade levels who use concept attainment need to utilize a variety of exemplars to communicate ideas—objects, pictures, words, music, metaphorical expressions, and even the students themselves (for example, recall the sample activity earlier in this chapter where the students with and without glasses were asked to stand). Concept attainment fosters what Cajete (1994) describes as a type of indigenous teaching (that is, teaching that builds on the natural dispositions of children) because the teacher can use larger ideas and because students are required "to listen, to look, to create, and to reflect . . . [in a way that enables them] to see things deeply" (p. 227).

One of the greatest stimuli to enhanced student self-esteem is success; and one of the best ways to foster success is to vary how ideas are presented so that students from different social, cultural, and personal backgrounds can, at times, play to their cognitive style dispositions.

Q: *Is it important to vary learning modalities when using the concept attainment model?*

A: Very definitely yes! Teachers at all grade levels and content areas who use this instructional model need to vary choices of modalities—visual, auditory, kinesthetic—within a concept attainment lesson. The more alternative modalities presented within the lesson, the more likely it is that the teacher will reach all youngsters in the learning process. Recall from Chapter 2 that a number of unique attributes were discussed regarding how individuals within cultural groups process information; these attributes have implications for designing instruction for students. The research conducted by Damico (1983) and by Shade and Edwards (1987) concerning the use of people-oriented pictures and statues has use in planning concept attainment lessons. Their research findings indicate that when working with African American youngsters, as opposed to European American youngsters, people-oriented examples tended to have a greater impact on student learning. African American, and Hispanic American youngsters as well, tended to relate positively when people-oriented examples were used within classroom lessons. The learning principle is clear: whenever possible, especially when teaching concrete concepts, use both animate and inanimate examples in concept attainment lessons. Teacher use of nonverbal expressions, the use of imagery in understanding complex concepts, changing environmental conditions, and the use of warm, cooperative environments can play an important role in the success of implementing this model (Loftin, 1989; Soldier, 1985; Swisher and Deyhle, 1989). The use of a wide variety of examples that utilize alternative styles of modality (visual, kinesthetic, and auditory) in the form of objects, pictures, words, music analogies and metaphors, and role playing will have a profoundly positive effect upon the development of student thinking.

❸ EVALUATION CRITERIA   ☒

Teachers who first use the concept attainment strategy will struggle to make certain they include all the phases of the lesson, and they may need to refer to notes or other resources to keep the direction and flow of the lesson on target. As instructional proficiency with the model increases, so, too, will the teacher's flexibility in organizing the lesson. In general, the following types of questions need to be asked in understanding whether a lesson has been properly developed and sequenced.

Phase I: Concept Identification

1. Is the concept a significant frame of reference for additional student learning?   ☐ Yes   ☐ No

   Is the concept important?   ☐ Yes   ☐ No

2. What type of concept (concrete or abstract) has the teacher decided to emphasize?

   Concept name: _____

   What are the superordinate, subordinate, and coordinate concepts that students may need to know?

   Superordinate: _____
   Subordinate: _____
   Coordinate: _____

Phase II: Exemplar Identification

1. What type of concept attainment strategy did the teacher choose to use (CAI, CAII)?

   CAI ____   CAII ____

2. Are the positive examples clear prototypes for the concept?   ☐ Yes   ☐ No

3. Does the teacher allow for substantial amounts of student hypothesizing (that is, attempt to explore a broad range of possibilities)? □ Yes □ No

4. Does the teacher eliminate invalid student hypotheses as the lesson progresses? □ Yes □ No

5. Are equal numbers of positive and negative examples provided? □ Yes □ No

6. Are a sufficient number of exemplars provided (approximately 8 to 10 exemplar pairs)? □ Yes □ No

7. Are students asked to defend their hypotheses? (Students often guess without thinking—teachers need to focus the students' thoughts on the validity of proposed ideas.) □ Yes □ No

Phase III: Hypothesizing

1. Does the teacher clearly define the concept so that identified attributes are presented? □ Yes □ No

2. Does the teacher review why "yes" and "no" examples received the classification they were given? □ Yes □ No

3. Do the students know the technical name for the concept? □ Yes □ No

Phase IV: Closure

1. Do the students have an opportunity to generate their own exemplars? □ Yes □ No

2. Are students required to defend their exemplars? □ Yes □ No

3. What types of relational and analytical skills are emphasized in the lesson? List: _____
_____
_____

◈ SAMPLE LESSONS

The following classroom episode is intended to help readers fully understand the concept attainment model. The first scenario is a concept attainment lesson that focuses on object weight; the second lesson plan utilizes the concept attainment approach with high school pupils and is followed by personal reflections of the high school teacher who taught the lesson.

CASE STUDY I

Joyce Sampson is preparing her 1st grade students to understand the concepts of big and little for a science lesson. She teaches in an inner-city elementary school in a Midwestern city. Today she wants to focus on the concept of heavy objects.

She begins by placing a 5-pound bag of sugar in front of a big sign labeled "yes" and putting a cotton ball in front of a sign that reads "no."

"Class, you know the game we sometimes play where you attempt to guess the idea I am thinking of? Well, today we are going to play that game again. The 5-pound bag of sugar is an example of my idea. The cotton ball is not an example. What do you think my idea is? Aoki?"

"I think it is stuff you can eat. I eat sugar. I don't eat cotton."

Ms. Sampson places the phrase "things you eat" on the board under the label "student guesses."

"OK, who is next? Jeremy."

"I think it's stuff you use in cooking. My mom uses a lot of sugar when she makes cookies."

"Great. I'll write 'things needed for cooking' right under Aoki's guess. What else? Rosetta?"

"I think it's something that has lots of little parts. The bag has lots of tiny pieces of sugar."

Ms. Sampson looks at the bag and the cotton, and before she writes down "things made up of lots of small pieces," she asks Rosetta to take a small magnifying lens and look at the cotton ball.

"Doesn't the cotton have a lot of little parts?"

"Yes, but they are connected," responds Rosetta. "I am thinking of things that are tiny but not connected."

"OK, you've convinced me." Ms. Sampson writes Rosetta's guess on the board.

The students generate about four more ideas before Ms. Sampson says, "Let's look at a second set of 'yes' and 'no' examples. This gallon of water is a 'yes' and this little pillow is a 'no.' The two new exemplars are placed in front of the signs.

"Now what new guesses do you have? And does the water eliminate any of our previous guesses?"

Almost all of the first set of guesses still stand. The students argue a bit about whether to keep "things that are tiny and not connected" on the board. One or two students believe that it should stay. Most believe that water is *one* substance and therefore Rosetta's guess should be eliminated. Jack raises his hand and says, "I think your 'yeses' are all heavy."

The students now have six guesses on the board. They include:

- things you eat
- things used in cooking

- things that are heavy
- things that you use with food
- things that you find in a kitchen
- things that are good for you

"Let me give you one more set of examples. This [unabridged] dictionary is a 'yes.' And this paperback book is a 'no.'

The students all raise their hands.

"Before you respond," says Ms. Sampson, "I want you to think about your current guesses. If this [unabridged dictionary] is a 'yes,' then can we keep 'things you eat'?"

The students respond in unison, "No."

"How about 'things used in cooking'?"

Again, "No!"

"How about 'things that are heavy'?"

"Yes!" (Though a couple of students yell "Not for me.")

Ms. Sampson proceeds until only "things that are heavy" is left. She then asks students to look at four more examples that she has available: a slipper, a big boot, a puzzle piece, and a big, framed picture.

"Tell me which of these is a 'yes' and which is a 'no.'" The students correctly label each item.

"Now work with your partner and develop your own list of 'yes' and 'no' examples. I will have each one of you share your examples with the class. Let's see if your friends can indicate whether your examples are 'yes' or 'no' examples." ■

Follow-Up Questions

1. Is the concept "heavy"—an appropriate one for concept attainment?

2. What type of concept attainment strategy (CAI or CAII) did the teacher use in presenting the lesson?

3. Are the examples and nonexamples clear and appropriate for the students' age level?

4. Identify how you might have taught the concept "heavy" using concept attainment. What other instructional strategy might be used to teach this concept?

5. Identify other examples and nonexamples you might provide to the students. What other examples would you include to ensure that all students' needs would be met?

6. What should Ms. Sampson have done differently in teaching the concept to the class?

⊙ASE STUDY II

Tracy Roman is studying symmetries of graphs with her high school advanced algebra students. A relatively traditional teacher, Tracy attempts to teach the concept of even and odd functions using a nontraditional approach—concept attainment. Notice that she uses a variation of Concept Attainment II. She lists all additional examples and labels them and then asks for hypotheses.

"Class, today, we are going to study a concept, but I am asking you to see if you can discover what it is yourselves. The graph I am going to give you here has the concept." Tracy then draws a "yes" example on the board.

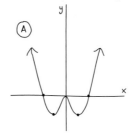

"Now, class, here is a second example, and it is a "no."

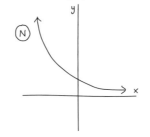

"Who can hypothesize what concept I might have in mind?"

Several students raise their hands and respond. After some brief hypothesizing, the four students generate hypotheses on the board.

- Functions
- Go through the origin
- Both arrows pointing upwards
- Symmetric

Tracy then lists the following examples on the board.

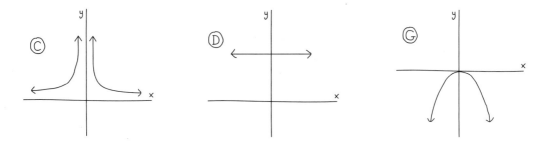

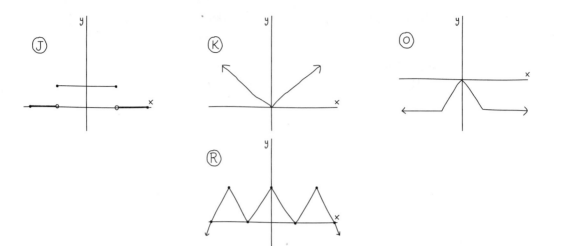

(And about 10 additional examples)

"By looking at all of these, class, can anyone either eliminate a hypothesis or generate a new hypothesis? Josh?"

"I think you can eliminate functions because you have some functions in the 'no' column."

"Does everyone agree?" The students almost unanimously concur with Josh's assertion.

"Mary? What do you think?"

"Well, because of examples C, D, J, and R, I think you can eliminate passes through the origin."

"Sue, do you agree with Mary?"

"Yes."

"Class?" The students nod their heads affirmingly.

The lesson progressed but the students struggled a bit because some of the "no's" represented the concept, but just not in the same way.

Tracy finished the lesson by placing a transparency on the overhead that contained many additional examples. With the added exemplars, students were able to come up with the concept "symmetric" over the y-axis. She then marked an ordered pair (x,y) on the graphs and asked the students to name another point on each graph.

She asked students to compare the values of F(x) and F(–x) and students reached the conclusion that F(–x)=F(x).

At the end of the lesson she formally labeled the concept "Even Functions" and then placed on the overhead all the "odd functions."

The students then generated three conclusions about odd functions, one of which was that odd functions are symmetric over the origin. Further, she asked students to sketch three more even and three more odd functions.

Teacher Reflections

To say I am a traditional math teacher is a major understatement. I thrive on lecture and teacher-directed instruction. I could give class notes and example problems bell-to-bell every day of the school year and never run out of material. So as I reflected upon setting goals during my thirteenth year of teaching, I decided to step outside of my comfort zone. I proposed trying five different teaching methods throughout the year, the first being concept attainment.

I thought I had created three times as many exemplars as I needed, but since I presented the concept attainment to three different classes, I used different exemplars each period based upon the hypotheses they formed. Sometimes I chose my next example to reinforce a hypothesis, and sometimes I chose one that challenged a hypothesis. Though I was very nervous about not being able to control the outcome of the lesson, I was thrilled with the results of the entire exercise. My students actively engaged in mathematical debate, all the while using proper terminology. I watched students who typically said less than five words per week participate voluntarily. I saw other students thinking creatively, a necessary problem-solving skill, for the first time all year. It was easy to achieve 100 percent participation by asking those who did not volunteer their own hypotheses whether they agreed or disagreed with others' statements.

This is a fairly easy model to try first, as there are only a few well-defined steps. Also, I found the lesson moved quickly. It was possible to complete the exemplar/hypothesizing cycle, reach closure, and ask students to apply the concept within a 47-minute class period.

It is important to think about how you will respond to students' hypotheses. Specifically, make sure to answer the following questions:

1. How will I respond if a student guesses the correct concept after just one set of exemplars?

2. How will I respond if someone offers a hypothesis that doesn't make any sense at all?

I found it extremely important to treat all statements as valid until eliminated by the class and to treat no statement as "correct" until the closure phase. In addition to preparing ample examples, it is well worth your time to really think about your responses and nonverbal cues, as well as about leading and guiding questions, before presenting a concept attainment lesson. ∎

⑤ UGGESTED LESSON DEVELOPMENT: QUESTIONS FOR REFLECTION ✔

Once teachers have a reasonably good understanding of how and when to use the model, they need to develop their own lesson plan as follows:

1. Determine the concept to be taught.

2. Identify the essential concept attributes that students need to learn and make certain that all those attributes are represented in the examples.

3. Select positive and negative concept exemplars—be especially concerned with using a variety of perspectives (visual, kinesthetic) to represent the idea or concept.

4. Determine whether CAI or CAII approach will be used.

5. Identify follow-up activities for students once they identify the concept.

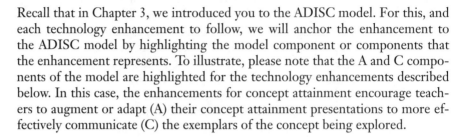

Recall that in Chapter 3, we introduced you to the ADISC model. For this, and each technology enhancement to follow, we will anchor the enhancement to the ADISC model by highlighting the model component or components that the enhancement represents. To illustrate, please note that the A and C components of the model are highlighted for the technology enhancements described below. In this case, the enhancements for concept attainment encourage teachers to augment or adapt (A) their concept attainment presentations to more effectively communicate (C) the exemplars of the concept being explored.

Creating a Concept Attainment Presentation

Teachers employing concept attainment strategies typically do so after carefully preparing the lesson. After identifying the concept to be explored, they thoughtfully generate the *positive and negative exemplars* to be presented to the students and select Concept Attainment I or Concept Attainment II as the strategy of choice. Using a presentation software program in conjunction with a computer projector or classroom monitor offers a technology-enhanced method of presenting exemplars to the students.

The selection of the presentation software to be employed will depend on what is available to teachers in their respective classrooms, schools and districts. Typically, teachers have access to and familiarity with HyperStudio, Power-Point, ClarisWorks, KidPix, or other similar programs. Teachers unfamiliar with such programs or those who have not acquired skill in their use will want to consult a media consultant, computer teacher, or technology proficient colleague for technical assistance. This same person will likely be able to provide support in acquiring and using the necessary presentation hardware.

In the case of Concept Attainment I, each *set* of positive and negative exemplars can be recorded on a separate *slide* and then advanced at the teacher's discretion. Teachers desiring to keep all exemplar pairs in the students' view may prefer to place all positive and negative exemplars on a single slide and use the software's *build function* to reveal each set of exemplars progressively. In the case of Concept Attainment II, the first slide in the presentation reveals the initial positive and negative examples. The second slide would then add a variety of other exemplars without a yes or no classification.

In either of the previous cases, teachers can prepare a *concept identification* slide that follows the exemplar slides. This slide contains the *concept name* and is shown after the students have correctly identified the concept. Additional slides can then be presented to further expand on the concept that has just been introduced. The content of such slides is limited only by the creativity of the teacher. They might, for example, include a definition of the concept, a schematic that presents the concept in the context of other related concepts, a famous quote about the concept, a related cartoon or picture, or perhaps a significant question to extend students' thinking about the concept. Figure 4-5 illustrates a simple four-slide presentation created in PowerPoint to deliver the Concept Attainment II lesson presented earlier in the chapter in the section on

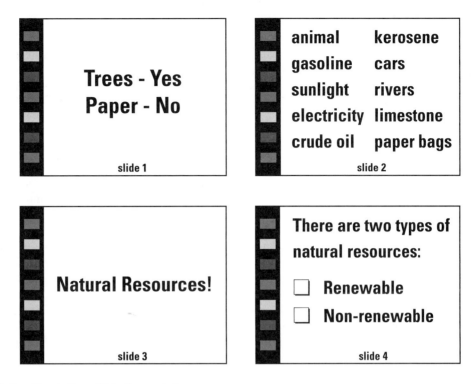

FIGURE 4-5   Simple Four-Slide Presentation

natural resources. Notice that the fourth slide in the show extends the concept by introducing two new concepts for students to explore.

Using presentation software to develop a concept attainment lesson becomes an especially creative endeavor when teachers choose to use pictures or photographs as their exemplars. Artwork and photographs can be scanned from print materials, taken from a CD-ROM of clipart or downloaded from a clip gallery on the Web, and then imported to the electronic slide. Once a concept attainment *slide show* has been created, backed up, and filed, it stands ready to be used time and time again. Teachers who have a classroom computer connected to a classroom monitor or projector can then access the show spontaneously when a teachable moment presents itself that calls for the use of the saved presentation.

Grade Level Modifications

Primary and elementary grade teachers may want to give special consideration to using pictures as positive and negative exemplars as a way of addressing the needs of children functioning at varying levels of reading ability. It may be especially helpful, for example, to develop exemplars that include both pictures and words.

Intermediate and secondary teachers often have students in their classrooms with sophisticated technology skills. Such teachers may consider asking such students to produce a concept attainment presentation. In such a scenario, a teacher might provide the student with the content of the presentation or allow groups of students to develop the content. Allowing groups of students to create such a presentation has the multiple advantages of testing their understanding of the concept being explored as well as deepening their understanding of the concept attainment strategy.

Low Tech/High Tech Applications

Teachers with limited access to, or knowledge of, presentation hardware and software may prefer a low-tech approach to producing a concept attainment presentation. In this method, teachers can develop their exemplars in any word processing program, using font sizes appropriate for classroom presentation. Hard copies of the printed pages can then be converted to traditional transparencies for use on a standard overhead projector. This low-tech approach retains the high-tech advantage of saving teachers from using a black or white board to present the exemplars each time the lesson is presented. It also allows for the presentations to be saved for future use.

Teachers with experience in the use of presentation software may consider the high-tech option of creating two slide shows, one for the presentation of exemplars, and one for the recording and monitoring of students' hypotheses. Such teachers can then run the two shows simultaneously, switching from exemplars to hypotheses as needed.

Value Added for Diverse Learners

Integrating technology into concept attainment lessons can prove valuable to students with various learning styles. Using pictures and or photographs as exemplars can provide students the visual stimuli and imagery that facilitates their understanding of complex concepts. When possible, given the concept being explored, teachers can also facilitate student engagement and understanding by purposefully selecting visual images that are culturally representative. Using sound clips to enhance the exemplars will support auditory learners. Finally, providing students with hard copies of the presentation helps meet the needs of those learners who prefer to interact personally with the lesson by having their hands on a physical artifact or who need more time to review the lesson at their own pace. Most presentation software programs have a feature that allows for printing of a hard copy of the presentation.

Web-Based Resources

Teachers who are inexperienced with developing electronic presentations will generally find it easy to master the process of creating simple slides. With experience and growing confidence they will likely enjoy learning to use many of the more sophisticated functions available. User-friendly help programs that provide clear directions on how to perform many tasks support most all presentation software programs. In addition, teachers using Microsoft PowerPoint can take advantage of an online tutorial for the software by going to http://www.dowslane.org/techresources.htm. Finally, for teachers interested in enhancing their concept attainment presentations with pictures or photographs, the Microsoft Clip Art Web site (http://dgl.microsoft.com/) is an excellent resource. A library of digital pictures can also be searched and downloaded through AltaVista (http://www.altavista.com).

ⓈUMMARY

Concept attainment is a strategy that teachers can use periodically to enhance the motivation of students to learn and to engage students in different types of critical thinking activities while teaching specific concepts and concept attributes. Because the strategy has a gamelike quality, students actively participate in the hypothesizing phase. Teachers who use the model note that one of its distinct advantages is that students who fail to participate within traditional classroom structures are much more readily involved in the hypothesizing phase. The reason for this circumstance is simple: Every hypothesis that can be defended is acceptable. Many of the students' ideas will be creative—they will look at the phenomena presented by the teacher in very different ways. Such creativity is a positive possibility for all students, but especially for culturally diverse students. Notice, though, that alternative explanations are encouraged, but in concept attainment, a specific concept is taught and must be learned.

Students in schools are generally very aware that they must make certain they have the correct answer before they respond. For many students, this fact becomes the primary reason they choose not to participate—they either do not want to be wrong, or they do not want to be right at the expense of a fellow student.

Arriving at the correct concept attributes and concept name are important in concept attainment. But the hypothesizing process of CAI and CAII are sufficiently open so that students will feel more willing to participate and to take the chance of proffering their ideas. Indeed, some of the best hypotheses will often be offered by "nonparticipant" students who have learned not to be actively engaged—they have learned that teachers want "correct" answers, not defensible hypotheses. One strength of concept attainment is its ability as an instructional model to help students fully explore and develop their own thinking skills—to take intellectual risks.

ⓇEFERENCES

Bruner, J. S., J. J. Goodnow, and G. A. Austin. 1967. *A Study of Thinking.* New York: Science Editions.

———. 1990. *A Study of Thinking.* New Brunswick, NJ: Transaction.

Cajete, G. 1994. *Look to the Mountain: An Ecology of Indigenous Education.* Durango, CO: Kivaki Press.

Clayton, J. B. 1996. *Your Land, My Land: Children in the Process of Acculturation.* Portsmouth, NH: Heinemann.

Cooper, L., D. Johnson, R. Johnson, and F. Wilderson. 1980. "Effects of Cooperative, Competitive, and Individualistic Experiences of Interpersonal Attraction Among Heterogeneous Peers." *Journal of Social Psychology* 111(2): 243–252.

Cox, B., and M. Ramirez III. 1981. "Cognitive Styles: Implications for Multiethnic Education." Pp. 61–71 in J. Banks et al. (eds.), *Education in the 80s: Multiethnic Education.* Washington, DC: National Education Association.

Damico, S. B. 1983. "The Two Worlds of School: Differences in the Photographs of Black and White Adolescents." Paper presented at annual meeting of American Educational Research Association, Montreal.

Eggen, P. D., and D. P. Kauchak. 1988. *Strategies for Teachers.* Englewood Cliffs, NJ: Prentice-Hall.

———. 2001. *Strategies for Teachers.* (4th ed.) Needham Heights, MA: Allyn and Bacon.

Gaardner, J. 1996. *Sophie's World.* New York: Berkeley.

Hale-Benson, J. 1982. *Black Children: Their Roots, Culture, and Learning Styles.* Baltimore: Johns Hopkins University Press.

———. 1986. *Black Children: Their Roots, Culture, and Learning Styles* (rev. ed.). Baltimore: Johns Hopkins University Press.

Hilliard, A. G., III. 1976. *Alternatives to IQ Testing: An Approach to the Identification of Gifted Minority Children.* Final report to the California State Department of Education.

Jackson, A. W., and G. A. Davis. 2000. *Turning Points 2000.* New York: Teachers College Press.

Joyce, B., and M. Weil. 1972. *Models of Teaching.* Boston: Allyn & Bacon.

———. 1992. *Models of Teaching* (4th ed.). Boston: Allyn & Bacon.

———. 1996. *Models of Teaching* (5th ed.). Boston: Allyn & Bacon.

Joyce, B., M. Weil, and E. Calhoun. 2000. *Models of Teaching* (6th ed.). Boston: Allyn & Bacon.

Loftin, J. D. 1989. "Anglo American Jurisprudence and the Native American Tribal Quest for Religious Freedom." *American Indian Culture and Research Journal* 13(1): 1–52.

McKinney, C. W. 1985. "A Comparison of the Effects of a Definition, Examples, and Nonexamples on Student Acquisition of the Concept of 'Teacher Propaganda.'" *Social Education* 49: 66–70.

Ornstein, A. C., and T. J. Lasley. 2000. *Effective Teaching* (3rd ed.) Boston, MA: McGraw-Hill.

Ramirez, M., III, and A. Castaneda. 1974. *Cultural Democracy, Bicognitive Development and Education.* New York: Academic Press.

Riley, R. 1997. "Learning through Design." Pp. 1–18 in M. Davis, P. Hawley, B. McMullan, and G. Spilka (eds.), *Design as a Catalyst for Learning.* Alexandria, VA: Association for Supervision and Curriculum Development.

Sadker, M., and D. Sadker. 1994. *Failing at Fairness.* New York: Charles Scribner's Sons.

Sainte-Marie, B. 1999. "Beyond Autumns Stereotypes." *Education Week*, October 27, 1999. p. 37, 39.

Shade, B. J. 1984. "Afro-American Patterns of Cognition: A Review of the Research." Paper presented at the annual meeting of the American Educational Research Association, New Orleans, LA.

———, **and P. A. Edwards.** 1987. "Ecological Correlates of the Educative Style of Afro-American Children." *Journal of Negro Education* 86: 88–99.

Snow, C., M. S. Burns, and P. Griffin (eds.). 1998. *Preventing Reading Difficulties in Young Children.* Washington, DC: National Academy Press.

Soldier, L. 1985. "To Soar with Eagles: Enculturation and Acculturation of Indian Children." *Childhood Education* 61: 185–191.

———. 1989. "Cooperative Learning and the Native American Student." *Phi Delta Kappan* 71(2): 161–163.

Swisher, K., and D. Deyhle. 1989. "The Styles of Learning Are Different, But the Teaching Is Just the Same: Suggestions for Teachers of American Indian Youth." *Journal of American Indian Education* (special issue, August): 1–14.

Tennyson, R. D., and M. Cocchiarella. 1986. "An Empirically Based Instructional Design Theory for Teaching Concepts." *Review of Educational Research* 56: 40–71.

Tennyson, R. D., and O. Park. 1980. "The Teaching of Concepts: A Review of Instructional Design Research Literature." *Review of Educational Research* 50(1): 55–70.

Vasquez, J. A. 1991. "Cognitive Style and Academic Attainment." Pp. 163–179 in J. Lynch, C. Modgil, and S. Modgil (eds.), *Cultural Diversity and the Schools: Consensus and Controversy.* London: Falconer Press.

Inquiry

Chapter Objectives

At the end of this chapter, readers will be able to

1. *Understand the theoretical basis for the model.*
2. *Identify the essential phases of the inquiry model.*
3. *Identify the strengths and weaknesses of the model.*
4. *Describe ways in which the inquiry model enhances the learning opportunities for culturally diverse student populations.*
5. *Create an inquiry lesson for personal use in a classroom.*

INTRODUCTION

American schools are instructionally organized more for the transmission of discrete knowledge than they are for student construction of personal knowledge. The former assumes that knowledge is fixed and that the teacher is the source of that knowledge. Students, as a consequence, work independently to acquire necessary, teacher-defined information. Because of this orientation, students exit the school environment often knowing lots of disconnected facts but not fully understanding what they have acquired. An example illustrates the point. Most readers of this text know how to divide ¼ by ½. The division of fractions (learning how to invert and multiply) is rather standard fare in the intermediate grades. If you know how to divide these numbers, let's now look at the question: "Why does one invert the ½ to derive the correct answer?" If you don't know the reason for inverting, perhaps you can tackle a "simpler" problem: "Think up a story problem for ¼ divided by ½." If you are struggling with the examples, don't feel as though you are alone. Borko and her colleagues (1990) found that almost 70 percent of all elementary education majors were unable to develop a story problem for this simple algorithm.

> *Inquiry is a method of teaching; nothing more, nothing less. It is an approach to learning which is based on sound and established concepts, and it is directed toward achievement in content areas as well as toward development of the rational powers.*
>
> ROBERT F. BIBENS

Some of the reasons for the above circumstance are related to the fact that prospective teachers do not have the academic background knowledge required to fully understand requisite mathematical concepts. Tyson (1994) writes that "many subjects that teachers are expected to teach in public school aren't taught in college. . . . [For example] mathematics majors are rarely exposed to fractions, at least not as students in the mathematics department . . ." (p. 11). Another reason for this lack of conceptual understanding is that elementary and secondary school students are rarely required to think, to question, and to explore ideas. Most questions asked in a classroom are teacher-initiated. Those that do originate with students typically deal with procedural issues (that is, how should an assignment be accomplished?). Hyman (1980) described two research studies, one involving 43,531 classroom behavior incidents, of which only 728 included student questions; the other involved an ethnographic study in which student initiated questions accounted for only 4 percent of the classroom instructional time. Is it any wonder that American students lack depth in what they have studied? Teachers are performing most of the intellectual work; they are doing the thinking for the students.

Inquiry requires that the teacher engage students with content in a way that fosters exploration, discovery, and critical thought (Good and Brophy, 1994). Students become active participants in the learning process because they can use what they already know to explore the reasons for what they sense. As a consequence, the inquiry instructional model utilizes student past experiences (cultural and intellectual) to become a part of the teaching-learning process. Inquiry also has two inherent advantages over more didactic approaches. First, it builds on the natural curiosity of students and, hence, is more motivational, especially for students who feel disenfranchised within classrooms because they seldom are the first to know the *right* answer. With inquiry, student success is based on good questions, not right answers. Second, because the assumptions of inquiry methods are different from those of more traditional, teacher-directed approaches, many students can experience success who were unable to achieve at a higher level using more traditional instructional approaches. Formulating a question is far different from knowing an answer. Ironically, many high-achieving students are very good at the latter, but quite weak with respect to the former. On the other hand, many students from dysfunctional family environments who are suspicious of the school as an advocate for their learning have learned how to ask difficult, and at times contentious, questions; these same students have spent much less time memorizing correct answers. Even though inquiry builds upon the natural curiosity of students, the teacher's role is to channel the students' interests and ideas in ways that develop their critical reasoning abilities.

ⒸASE STUDY

Sarah Lange teaches 5th grade in a midwestern school district. She wants her students to engage in critical thinking about vertebrates. Her lesson today focuses on the interrelationship of animals—how they often work together to secure food.

"Class, today we are going to act like scientists. I want you to observe a phenomenon (an event) and then hypothesize (or guess) what you think is happening. Because you are scientists your role is to ask me a lot of questions. The only unique thing about this approach is that I can respond to your questions

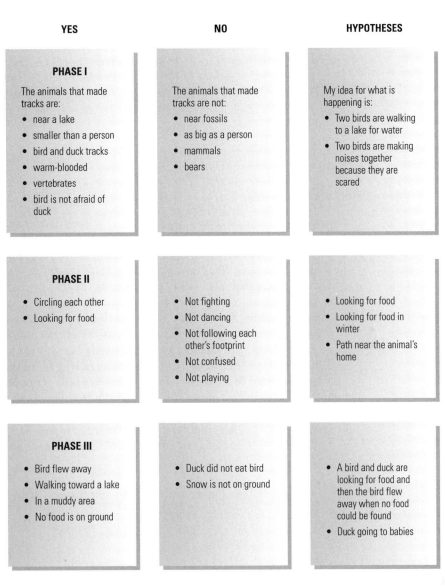

YES	NO	HYPOTHESES
PHASE I		
The animals that made tracks are:	The animals that made tracks are not:	My idea for what is happening is:
• near a lake • smaller than a person • bird and duck tracks • warm-blooded • vertebrates • bird is not afraid of duck	• near fossils • as big as a person • mammals • bears	• Two birds are walking to a lake for water • Two birds are making noises together because they are scared
PHASE II		
• Circling each other • Looking for food	• Not fighting • Not dancing • Not following each other's footprint • Not confused • Not playing	• Looking for food • Looking for food in winter • Path near the animal's home
PHASE III		
• Bird flew away • Walking toward a lake • In a muddy area • No food is on ground	• Duck did not eat bird • Snow is not on ground	• A bird and duck are looking for food and then the bird flew away when no food could be found • Duck going to babies

FIGURE 5-1   Data for Inquiry Lesson on Animal Tracks

only with either a 'yes' or a 'no' response. So your questions must be designed so that you only get a 'yes' or 'no' response from me."

"I'm going to show you many pictures, and your job is to ask me questions about what you see. If my answer is positive, I'll put the information in the 'yes' column [Ms. Lange points to a column on the board with a 'yes' in the heading. See Figure 5-1.] If my response is negative, I'll put the information in the 'no' column. Once we have enough information, I'll ask you to start making some hypotheses or guesses. I'll put that in the third column labeled 'hypotheses.' Everyone ready?"

The students respond with a choral "Yes."

"I want you to know that the first set of questions you ask should focus specifically on what you see in this picture (see phase I of Figure 5-2). Basically, class, I want your questions to focus on what is obvious—on facts about what you see rather than on a theory about what is happening. The tracks you see in this figure were left in the mud, and scientists have found them. Now, what questions do you have? Nick?"

"Is there a lake nearby?"

"Yes, Nick, there is." Ms. Lange walks to the board and in the 'yes' column writes the phrase "near a lake." (See Figure 5-1.)

Ms. Lange turns to the class, and Reuben asks whether fossils are nearby. Ms. Lange says "No" and writes "near fossils" in the "no" column right under her lead sentence that reads "The animals that made tracks are not: . . ."

The next student asks whether one of the animals that made the tracks was as big as a human, and Ms. Lange writes that it is not. This question is followed by a query regarding whether one of the animals is smaller than a person and Ms. Lange notes that it is. Ms. Lange then has the students ask a series of questions on the size of the animals that made the tracks.

Then a student, Suzette, asks, "Are they bird and duck tracks?"

Ms. Lange responds, "Yes, they are. That's excellent! Some of you probably assumed they were bird and duck tracks. Suzette has verified that they are."

The students continue to ask questions, all of which can be answered with a "yes" or "no," and Ms. Lange writes the information on the board as it is gathered. At the end of this phase of the lesson, Ms. Lange asks the students to begin forming hypotheses. How would they make sense out of what they see? One student, Javier, suggests, "Two birds are walking to a lake to get water," and a second student, Milagros, offers "Two birds are making noises together." A third student hypothesizes about the duck.

"Class, before I accept more hypotheses, I want you to look at my next picture." (See phase II of Figure 5-2.) The students express various forms of excitement as they look at the second picture.

"OK, now that you see this picture, what new questions do you have? Seong."

"Are the birds fighting?"

"No," responds Ms. Lange. "That's an excellent question. However, the answer is in the negative." She writes "not fighting" in the "no" column.

Another student asks, "Are they dancing?"

Again Ms. Lange responds with a "No." She turns and writes "not dancing" in the "no" column.

Almost all student hands are raised in the class. Students ask a variety of questions, but all have the common feature of allowing Ms. Lange to respond with a "yes" or "no." After several minutes of questioning, Ms. Lange says, "Class, let's stop again and do some more hypothesizing about what you think is happening in the picture. Your 'yes' responses are going to be the best clues for you to consider." She then calls on Fumiko.

"I think that the birds are really looking for food."

Ms. Lange writes Fumiko's hypothesis on the board and then calls on Esther.

Esther adds that she thinks Fumiko's hypothesis is correct except she believes that it's wintertime. Ms. Lange writes Esther's idea on the board.

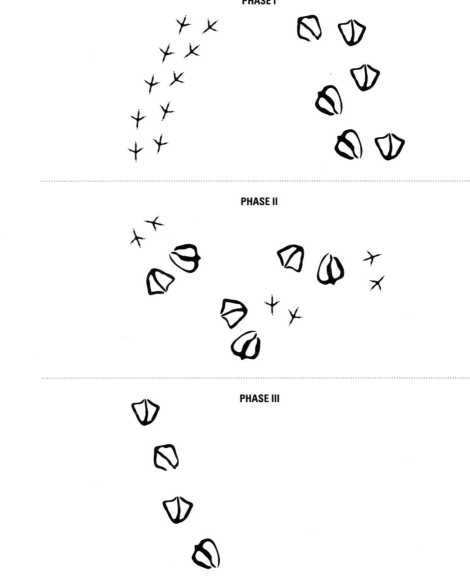

FIGURE 5-2   Phases of Animal Tracks

A couple of students create hypotheses that are not at all related to the data generated in the "yes" or "no" column. Ms. Lange listens to their comments and then asks them to identify the existing data that supports their conclusions. When they are unable to provide support, she comments, "We need to make certain that our hypotheses are related to our data."

"Let's look at a third picture, class, and see if that provides you with some other ideas." Ms. Lange then unfolds the poster paper and reveals another picture (see phase III of Figure 5-2). The students excitedly gasp and raise their hands.

"Class, quiet. I need to be able to hear. OK, Jean, what question do you have?"

"Did the duck eat the bird?"

"No.' Ms. Lange then writes "Duck did not eat bird" on the board and turns to the class and asks, "What other ideas do you have?"

Jonathan asks, "Did the bird fly away?"

"Yes," says Ms. Lange. She then writes "Bird flew away" on the poster paper.

The students continue asking questions. Some ask questions about the duck, and others inquire about the feelings of the bird ("Is the bird afraid of the duck?"). Ms. Lange writes down information and then reviews all the 'yes" and "no" responses.

"Let's do some additional hypothesizing, class. I want you to create one or two more hypotheses, and then let's consider which hypothesis makes the most sense."

The students do some additional hypothesizing, and then Ms. Lange has the students begin a discussion to determine which hypothesis makes the most sense. The students begin the final phase of this lesson by eliminating invalid hypotheses that make little sense given the data in the "no" column. Ms. Lange draws a line through the invalid hypotheses.

The students consider each of the remaining hypotheses and decide on what they view as the most logical hypothesis: "A bird and duck are looking for food, and the bird flew away when no food could be found." This hypothesis, according to the students, seems to make the most sense given the known data. Ms. Lange then confirms that, in fact, that is what occurred.

Ms. Lange asks, "Class, what data from the 'yes' and 'no' columns were the most helpful to you in reaching your conclusion?" The students share their ideas and complete the lesson by doing research on the feeding behavior of different birds and on how animals often compete for food sources. ▪

Ms. Lange's lesson is an example of guided inquiry instruction. The students are asking questions to identify data that subsequently will be used to create workable hypotheses. The model is an inductive one, but its real power is associated with requiring students to critically think about data—data that they generate themselves.

❶HEORETICAL PERSPECTIVE

In Chapter 6 of this text (Concept Formation) we will argue, as did Hilda Taba (1966), that thinking can be taught, but that students need to follow a careful sequence of steps in order to maximize the power of a learning experience. The inquiry model is one structured method of helping students learn to think. The technique is not new; it is, in fact, as old as Western culture. Socrates used inquiry to enable his pupils to reach thoughtful conclusions. Although he did not provide the type of guided ("yes' and "no" question) approach used by Ms. Lange, he did work with his students as they made observations, synthesized information, generated hypotheses, and explored ideas. Socrates attempted to shape students' thinking as they searched for *truth*. Indeed, he was so good at using questions that he ultimately was perceived as impious and paid the price with his life.

Inquiry requires many more intellectual skills of a student than merely knowing content; the student must also be able to understand the dynamics that ground that academic content. Schools place tremendous emphasis on knowing content (a situation that is likely to be even more evident given America's current high-stakes approach to education) and far too little on developing thinking skills. The consequence is that students leave schools with much misinformation. Thinking skills are used to change and refine content understandings. Tyson (1994) describes, for example, a study conducted in the early 1990s when students at Harvard University were asked about the phases of the moon—Harvard students clearly understood that there were phases, but they were unable to explain correctly what caused those phases. Tyson writes: "When asked to explain the phases, virtually everyone cheerfully [explained] that a partial moon occurs when the earth gets between the sun and the moon and casts a shadow" (p. 6). Such misunderstandings are not unusual. Teachers frequently reach the conclusion of a lesson only to discover through some student question or explanation that the students have an erroneous cognitive structure for the facts that were presented.

Inquiry, whether guided or unguided, has three general stages: exploration, invention, and discovery (Bibens, 1980). In the exploration phase, students attempt to clearly understand the pertinent information related to a specific topic. Ms. Lange does not begin by having students offer hypotheses; rather, she initiates the activity by having students identify, through "yes" or "no" questions, the pertinent information that subsequently can be used to generate hypotheses. Bibens writes:

> They [students] are asked to locate pertinent information which has a bearing on the topic. They may draw on what has been found in earlier investigations . . . or even presentations made by the teacher. Once they are satisfied that they have the necessary data, they are asked to arrange their findings in some kind of reasonable pattern. (p. 89)

In the second stage, invention, students are expected to begin to make sense out of the data they generated in the first phase. Students look for patterns and attempt to pull together those ideas that represent reasonable explanations for whatever phenomenon they have observed. They use the pertinent information to form synthesized conceptual representations (or hypotheses). Those hypotheses set the stage for a very important third stage in the inquiry process—discovery.

Bibens notes that it is during the discovery process that students "discover the inadequacies of what they have invented" (p. 90). The discovery stage occurs as the students explore whether the hypotheses really make sense given the array of pertinent data available to them. Once Ms. Lange, for example, had students generate some hypotheses, she had the students examine whether their ideas (hypotheses) could accurately describe the data (in the "yes" column).

The inquiry instructional model presented in this chapter is inductive. The structure given to the inquiry lesson, however, can be either guided or unguided. Most of the attention in this chapter will be on guided inquiry, which is a more defined pedagogical structure for having students generate and analyze data. Guided inquiry moves the students from observations to inferences and then to formulating an explanation (Joyce, Weil, and Calhoun, 2000; Orlich et al., 1985), but the teacher controls the way in which questions are worded (that is, they must be answerable with a "yes" or "no") and the way hypotheses are generated. The teacher controls what the students observe, but the students are free to explore any ideas that they feel relate to the phenomenon they are observing. Many different models of guided inquiry exist in the literature (Joyce, Weil and Calhoun, 2000; Orlich et al., 1985; Shulman and Tamir, 1973). How we use the inquiry model relates specifically to a teacher-controlled process (the requirement of convergent student questions) for having students make observations, and then proceed from those observations to the stage of hypothesizing.

Unguided inquiry, on the other hand, enables students to be more creative. The teacher still controls the overall dynamics of the classroom situation, but the students are given much more latitude in the types of questions they ask during the lesson. In addition, the teacher is not attempting to position students toward a specific hypothesis to explain a phenomenon. Ms. Lange, using guided inquiry, knew which hypothesis was correct. Ms. Lange clarified students' ideas in an effort to position them toward a logical explanation. (Sometimes there is no one correct explanation, and the teacher fosters student thinking regarding the *most workable* hypothesis.) Similar closure is not required for unguided inquiry. If a teacher has students read a Pat Conroy novel (for example, *Beach Music*) and then asks, "What observations about the South do you have that might explain the protagonist's relationship with his parents?" the teacher is not attempting to derive one specific set of ideas. Rather, the teacher is looking at how the students use their observations of characters in *Beach Music* to support generalizations about how Conroy grew up in the South.

Orlich and his colleagues (1985) argue that unguided inquiry works best once students understand the guided inquiry process. Though he uses a slightly different definition of guided inquiry than the one we use, we believe his assertions are still essentially true. Students need practice in the process of making careful observations. Such practice is probably monitored best through guided inquiry approaches in which teachers subtly influence the direction of student thought.

GUIDED INQUIRY: TEACHING PHASES

Phase I: Discrepant Event and Confronting the Problem

Guided inquiry lessons begin by having the teacher create an event or present a problem that cannot be easily explained or immediately solved. Wright (1981) provides one of the best definitions of a discrepant event—"a phenomenon which occurs that seems to run contrary to our first line of reasoning" (p. 575).

The students in Ms. Lange's class were asked to look at the various duck and bird tracks and make some sort of sense out of what they observed. The third phase of the discrepant event created particular excitement because it was at this point that students saw duck tracks, but no bird tracks.

The key to a good inquiry lesson is an effective discrepant event. Teachers who have experimented with the inquiry model will quickly note that the more powerful the discrepant event, the better the student participation in a lesson. A weak discrepant event is one that can be explained quickly and that has very few competing ideas that represent possible explanations for the event. A powerful discrepant event is one that engenders a tremendous number of student questions and can potentially be explained in several different ways. The following examples are from three classroom lessons the authors have observed, and Table 5-1 is an example of several others identified by Wright and Govindarajan (1992).

1st grade: The teacher takes two eggs (one soft-boiled and the other hard-boiled) and asks the students to explain why one egg will spin for a long time and the other just a couple of times.

7th grade: The teacher uses tongs and takes an empty pop can that has been heated on a hot plate and places it in cold water. Once in the cold water, the pop can implodes. Students are asked to explain why the implosion occurs.

11th grade: The teacher takes raisins and places them in a jar of carbonated water. Once in the water, the raisins begin to "dance" or move up and down in the jar. Students are asked to describe why this movement occurs.

All three of these discrepant events focus on science, but a discrepant event is possible in every disciplinary area. The only disciplinary area that often proves problematic for teachers is mathematics. Because of the very nature of traditional mathematics (that is, mathematicians describe behavior in order to predict behavior, and they use mathematical theory to accomplish this), mathematics teachers, especially high school mathematics teachers, often express frustration when attempting to generate good discrepant events. However, teachers should be able to identify axiomatic paradoxes for use with students of all ages. The mathematics evidenced in the social sciences (e.g., voting strategies in elections) provide one place where discrepant events are evidenced. The most natural areas for using the inquiry technique are social studies, science, and language arts. In general, the more content depth a teacher has acquired in the academic discipline, the easier it is to recognize complex relationships and to determine what discrepant events are embedded within the content of a discipline.

One additional note regarding discrepant events is needed. It is imperative, especially for guided inquiry, that teachers have some reasonable knowledge of the phenomenon the students are observing. Several years ago, one of the authors watched a dry ice lesson for an intermediate-level class. The teacher uncovered the dry ice, and the vapor that emerged looked like smoke; the students were, to say the least, very engaged. Her discrepant event was, "How can something so cold create something that looks so hot?" There was only

TABLE 5-1   Sample Discrepant Events

Phenomenon, Event, or Question	Probable Student Response	Conceptual Discrepancy	Scientific Principle or Concept Illustrated by Conceptual Discrepancy
1. An amoeba could theoretically become as large as an elephant if it were in a liquid medium of suitable temperature and nutrients.	True	False	In general, volume increases by the power of three, while surface area increases by the power of two. The area/volume ratio decreases as size increases. Eventually, the surface area would become too small to accommodate the needs of the organism.
2. Can two individuals who are both brown-eyed, whose forefathers all had brown eyes, become the biological parents of a child with blue eyes?	No	Possible	The possibility exists when a mutation of the dominant brown-eyed gene takes place in both the sperm and the egg that produced the zygote with the recessive trait of blue eyes.
3. Girls are physically more flexible than boys.	False, at least as indicated by boys.	True. Have both sexes face a wall and pace back three steps. Place a chair between each student and the wall. Ask students to bend over with their head against the wall, take hold of the chair, and in one motion stand up straight. Girls can do this easily. Boys will find it impossible.	The superior aperture of the pelvis is greater and wider in females, allowing greater flexibility. Also, the pubic arch in females forms an angle greater than 90 degrees, causing the female to have a greater freedom of movement. In males, both the above features are not as prominent.
4. It is not possible to light sugar cubes with a match. What will happen if you sprinkle burnt cigarette ash on a cube before lighting it with a match?	Nothing	It will burn.	Cigarette ash acts as a catalyst. The scientific concepts of catalyst and catalytic functions in biochemical systems should be stressed. An interdisciplinary extension into the study of physiological chemistry of glucose (in sugar cubes) and its metabolism in the body will interest students.

(continued)

TABLE 5-1   Sample Discrepant Events *(continued)*

Phenomenon, Event, or Question	Probable Student Response	Conceptual Discrepancy	Scientific Principle or Concept Illustrated by Conceptual Discrepancy
5. A man's weight went from 190 lbs. to 0 lbs. and back to 190 lbs. in one day and he lived. Is this biologically possible?	No	Yes	Introduce concepts of mass and weight in antigravity conditions by informing students about the phenomenon; also, this serves as an excellent interdisciplinary focus when aspects of physics and biology are discussed. If the man traveled to and returned from space in one day, his mass would remain constant but he would be weightless in space.

Adapted and reprinted from E. L. Wright and G. Govindarajan. 1992. "Stirring the Biology Teaching Pot with Discrepant Events." *American Biology Teacher* 54(4) (April): 205–210.

one difficulty. As the students asked questions (and they were truly excited about what they saw!), the teacher repeatedly had to answer, "I don't know." After several minutes, the frustration of the students became apparent. The teacher does not need to know everything about a phenomenon, but the teacher must possess sufficient knowledge to sustain the momentum of an inquiry lesson and enough knowledge to "guide" the inquiry of the students. There are exceptions to this observation, but they really are exceptions. Teachers really need to be educated in the content areas in order to know how to use questions to enhance student learning.

Phase II: Questioning and Data Gathering

Once students have observed a discrepant event, the next step is to have students ask questions about what they have observed so that they can verify the nature of the "objects" and gather more data. The questions that the students ask should be structured so that the teacher can answer with either a "yes" or a "no" response. The teacher first asks students to identify pertinent information. Students have a tendency to jump ahead and identify possible hypotheses—they attempt to develop theories before they fully understand the facts. Students should generate hypotheses (phase III of the inquiry process) only after all available pertinent information (facts) are identified. Ms. Lange, for example, should have tried to elicit some specific data about the types of animal tracks students saw in the picture. (*"Class, ask me questions about the types of animals who made these tracks, and then ask questions about the patterns of the tracks."*) There is absolutely nothing wrong with focusing students' attention on what types of questions to ask.

If a student asks a question and if it cannot be answered with a "yes" or "no" response, then ask the student to reword the question: "Please reword that so I can answer it with a 'yes' or 'no.'" This is a very common problem! Some teachers try to help students understand how to engage in inquiry by playing 20 Questions with the students. The "20 Questions" game enables the students to practice the "yes" and "no" questioning skills and to understand the guided inquiry process.

Teachers who have used this strategy also have found it useful to record data generated by the students as the students ask the questions. Ms. Lange created a chart for the students (see Figure 5-1). Other teachers have found it useful to use a handout similar to the one in Figure 5-3. As students generate questions that can be answered with a "yes," they place the appropriate information in the "yes" column. If a "no," then they use the "no" column.

Such a strategy is especially useful with young children, but it is potentially helpful for all students, especially when a substantial amount of data is to be generated and when the students are not accustomed to this type of critical-thinking experience.

After the students have generated many basic "yes" and "no" pieces of information, the teacher can then ask the students to move on to the next stage, which requires student hypothesizing.

Phase III: Experimenting and Generating Hypotheses

In the hypothesizing phase, the teacher attempts to have students synthesize the "yes" column information in a way that will enable them to create a logical explanation of what they see. As the students provide their guesses or hypotheses, it is imperative that the teacher continue to ask clarifying questions such as the following: *"What facts in the 'yes' column were most useful in forming your hypothesis? Are there any 'no' facts that would eliminate or contradict your hypothesis?"* In essence, the teacher writes down all student ideas but also challenges students to defend their ideas and conceptually ground their hypotheses. Teachers should attempt to solicit as many hypotheses as possible. The goal during this phase is to see how each student is synthesizing the information in order to formulate a hypothesis that can be defended with the use of data.

Phase IV: Closure and Formulating a Hypothesis

Once all hypotheses have been generated and tested, the teacher begins to focus the students' attention on eliminating invalid hypotheses. At this point some teachers find it very useful to analyze each hypothesis relative to the "yes"

My "Yes" Information Is   My "No" Information Is

My guess is: _____

Explain why this is your guess: _____

_____

_____

_____

_____

_____

FIGURE 5-3   Record Data Chart

column data. Ms. Lange did not do this in her "bird track" lesson. If she had, she would have taken the first hypothesis and asked something like, *"Class, let's look at each fact we have and see if it supports the various hypotheses you have generated. Our first hypothesis is, 'Two birds are walking to a lake.' Given what we know at this point (our 'yes' data), is this hypothesis valid? First, is there a lake nearby? [Students are directed to the chart (Figure 5-1) and to notice that 'lake' is, in fact, listed.] Second, are the tracks smaller than those that might be made by humans? . . ."* The teacher would then continue through the "yes" column data and either retain a hypothesis (if all the "yes" data applies) or eliminate it (if the pieces of "yes" data conflict with a hypothesis). Such systematic checking of the data is particularly important for students who are experiencing the technique for the first time. It forces students to consider closely each piece of data.

A common scenario in implementing the inquiry model is for students to conclude the lesson with several workable hypotheses. If the hypotheses are variations on the same idea, then the teacher can work with the class to synthesize the wording and to create one workable hypothesis. If, however, the hypotheses represent very different explanations of the same phenomenon, the teacher should have students return to the previous discussion and gather more data. More "yes" and "no" questions need to be asked until the students can either validate or reject each one of the hypotheses.

Phase V: Analysis

At the completion of the inquiry lesson, once a valid hypothesis is agreed upon by the class, the teacher asks the students to evaluate which data helped them determine the valid hypothesis. The teacher, through phase V, is attempting to focus the students' attention in a way that makes them more critical consumers of information. Recall that Ms. Lange asked, *"Class, what data from the 'yes' and 'no' columns were the most helpful to you in reaching your conclusion?"* Students generally will identify two or three key prior questions that really helped them understand the phenomenon. A common student response might be something like, *"Nick's question was the one that really did it for me. When you answered 'yes' to his question about the lake, that's when I knew what was occurring."*

Phase VI: Extension

Once students have a working hypothesis and know the relevant data that support that hypothesis, the teacher then needs to identify ways of extending the students' thinking. Ms. Lange had students do research on the feeding behavior of birds, but other variations might also be considered. As we will discuss in the next section, it is at this point that the natural interests of the students can be nurtured and the teacher can foster a more culturally responsive classroom atmosphere.

Unguided Inquiry: Teaching Phases

Unguided inquiry, at least the way we present the model, involves many of the same cognitive tasks as Taba's (1966) "interpretation of data." That is, in unguided inquiry the students are looking at raw data and then evolving personal theories to explain how that data can be logically connected.

Phase I: Provide Data

The teacher begins an unguided inquiry lesson similar to a guided inquiry lesson, by providing some type of discrepant event or unstructured data. As an example, Orlich and his colleagues (1985) describe how some teachers use discarded phone directories from different cities and then ask students to discuss what they see in the directory. In unguided inquiry, the teacher is not look-

TABLE 5-2 Cost of Garbage Collection and Disposal in Selected Ohio Cities

CITY	YEAR	TOTAL NET COST	COST PER CAPITA	COST PER TON
Cincinnati	1909	$90,000	$.25	$2.59
Cleveland	1909	38,989	.07	0.87
Columbus	1909	40,706	.23	2.46
Dayton	1908	21,000	.19	2.11
Zanesville	1909	5,695	.21	4.71

Source: *Investigating Solid Waste Issues,* Ohio Department of Natural Resources, 1994.

Observations: What do you notice? (Write down facts.)

1. _____

2. _____

3. _____

Questions: What additional information do you need? (Write down your additional questions.)

1. _____

2. _____

3. _____

Generalizations: What significant relationships are evident?

1. _____

2. _____

3. _____

ing for a particular explanation, a single workable hypothesis. Rather, the teacher is attempting to see how students synthesize information and make sense out of what they observe. Other types of data that might be provided include charts or graphs that require students to analyze and then ask questions about the data provided. Table 5-2 provides data on garbage disposal and collection for several Ohio cities.

Based on the data provided, the students would then be asked to generate observations (possible questions and/or hypotheses) that they perceive as relevant given the data in the chart. The observations could be declarative statements (*"Cincinnati's costs were greater than Cleveland's"*) or questions that require them to collect more information (for example, what was the population of each city in 1908 or 1909?). Another example can be found in Table 5-3. In this instance, students would make observations about the way in which two households spend money and consume resources.

TABLE 5-3   Household Resource Uses: Two Cases
Annual Income and Expense Figures

Case: Wesley and Wilma

Wesley and Wilma enjoy the benefits of having two children and two incomes. If they monitor their spending carefully, they have a few dollars left over for emergencies or special occasions. Working leaves Wilma with little free time. It also requires that everyone in the family contribute to housework to make sure all the necessary chores are accomplished.

Average trash disposal per week: 20 pounds

Income before taxes:	$38,262
Total expenditures:	32,753
Food at home:	3,066
Food away from home:	1,987
Shelter:	7,951
Clothing:	1,985
Transportation:	6,384
Health care and pension:	3,959
Personal taxes:	3,761
Other expenses:	5,004
Utilities including sanitation and waste collection:	2,114

Case: Horace

Horace is a college graduate with a degree in business. He was recently hired for his first job as assistant manager at Big's Warehouse. Horace leads an active single life. He spends little time at home in his small apartment, except to eat microwave dinners and watch TV. His active single lifestyle leaves him with little cash. He uses credit to finance his independent lifestyle and to make sure his telephone answering machine is in good working order.

Average trash disposal per week: 3.5 pounds

Income before taxes:	$18,551
Total expenditures:	18,726
Food at home:	1,794
Food away from home:	1,288
Shelter:	5,875
Clothing:	1,353
Transportation:	5,623
Health care and pension:	3,291
Personal taxes:	2,980
Other expenses:	4,232
Utilities including sanitation and waste collection:	1,749

Source: *Investigating Solid Waste Issues,* Ohio Department of Natural Resources, 1994.

Observations: What do you notice? (Write down facts.)

1. _____

2. _____

3. _____

Questions: What additional information do you need? (Write down your additional questions.)

1. _____

2. _____

3. _____

Generalizations: What significant relationships are evident?

1. _____

2. _____

3. _____

Phase II: Make Observations and Ask Questions

Once the students have had an opportunity to examine the data, the next phase in unguided inquiry is to make relevant observations. Some of the students may make declarative, factual statements about the data: "*Cincinnati spent more per capita in 1909 for garbage disposal than did Cleveland.*" With declarative statements the teacher attempts to focus students' attention on why this might have been the case. The teacher may or may not know the answer—that is relatively unimportant. The key issue is to enable students to make thoughtful observations and to determine what other data they might need in order to answer specific questions. Indeed, as a follow-up, students might be asked to do research on some of the unanswered questions.

As the students make observations, the teacher keeps track of what observations have validity and what questions need answers. As with guided inquiry, it is probably best to write the information on the board (or on notepaper) as the students generate ideas. In some cases the teacher might find it useful to place sections on the data sheet for students to make their observations, write questions, and prepare generalizations.

Phase III: Create Generalizations

After a substantial amount of data are generated, the next step is to determine what generalizations make sense relative to the ideas the students have enumerated. A generalization is nothing more than the relationship between two or more concepts. One generalization might be "*The size of a city influences directly the costs of collecting and disposing of garbage.*" Any generalization is acceptable as long as students can show what data they used to formulate and support their ideas. The teacher at this phase in the lesson is literally teaching the students how to learn, to be critical consumers of ideas, and to recognize how to support an argument with data. In this phase of the lesson, the teacher needs to ask plenty of questions such as, *"What ideas that we have on the board support your generalization?"* or *"What additional data would you need to make your generalization even stronger?"* All student generalizations should be written on the board so that students can clearly identify the conceptual relationships. It may be useful then to review each generalization and to assess the degree to which students perceive that data are available to support each of their statements.

Phase IV: Follow-Up

In the final phase of the lesson, the teacher can ask students to engage in several different types of activities. Each of these activities (for example, defending generalizations and predicting alternatives) is intended to enable students to refine their thinking and to consider what additional information might be required.

Defending a Generalization Ask students to select the generalization they like the best and then to describe (in one or two paragraphs) why that statement is the best representation for their ideas.

Predicting Alternatives Ask students to make "what if" predictions based on the generalizations and data they have available. For example, one generalization for Table 5-1 might be "Cities on lakes have lower disposal costs than do cities that are situated on rivers." As a consequence, a prediction the students might make is "Chicago had lower disposal costs in 1909 than did Indianapolis." The students can then do research on their hypotheses to determine the level of support for their ideas.

Of course, not all the predictions can be analyzed. But unguided inquiry lessons are enhanced when some of the predictions are examined to determine if the students' ideas can be verified.

APPLICATIONS TO DIVERSE CLASSROOMS

Inquiry approaches play to the natural interests and curiosity of students; and in terms of dealing with diverse learners, there is no better academic equalizer than the intrinsic interests of students. Teachers who know how to engender student involvement based on intrinsic interests create, according to Wlodkowski and Ginsberg (1995), "culturally responsive" classrooms. In essence, culturally responsive teaching does not create circumstances in which the teacher imposes knowledge on students, but rather it is teaching that enables students to deepen their understanding of and enthusiasm for ideas that have personal meaning and relevance.

Inquiry fosters substantial intragroup student cooperation to solve an intellectual problem. The students work together as a group to determine what data are relevant and which hypotheses are most viable. Intrinsic motivation is not an idea that is oriented toward only African American or Hispanic American students—it is a disposition that helps all students regardless of their cultural backgrounds.

Wlodkowski and Ginsberg (1995) describe four conditions that are essential for culturally responsive teaching: establishing inclusion, developing attitude, enhancing meaning, and engendering competence. We'll examine how two of these interplay within the context of an inquiry lesson. First, inquiry as an instructional model fosters inclusion—it is an inclusionary process. Every student question has inherent worth—inquiry reveals something about how a student is understanding content material. Even a "no" response by the teacher helps in the inquiry process. American children are oriented toward knowing the correct answers, and certainly in most situations correct answers have fundamental importance. But many students get turned off to learning when they discover they cannot always give the answer that the teacher wants on demand. With inquiry, all questions have merit and all answers have importance! All student contributions have significance! More important, when the teacher creates lessons that are inclusionary and meaningful, the lesson embraces students' cultural differences (Wlodkowski and Ginsberg, 1995). It is a culturally inclusive process because it values and accepts all student observations, ideas, and generalizations.

Second, by observing phenomena and attempting to make sense out of the ideas, students experience enhanced meaning and enhanced motivation. That is, they can construct their own questions and their own meaning about the discrepant event they observed. Their ideas are then combined with the thinking of the other students in the classroom. The teacher constructs inquiry in order for students to ask "why" something is true. The "why" becomes the motivating force according to Wlodkowski and Jaynes (1990) because the

> students feel a little perplexed and wondering. This will cause them to think harder and reflect more deeply. Ask questions like "Why is it that the world can produce enough food to feed everyone, yet starvation runs rampant even in countries with the highest standards of living?" or "If you look at a mirror your image reverses from left to right; why not from top to bottom?" Introducing contradictions, using experiments, and playing the devil's advocate are instructional processes that bring unusual and different information to students in an exciting way. (p. 92)

The inquiry model places much more emphasis on the students' abilities to think through problems. Students examine an event or phenomenon and inductively attempt to determine a plausible explanation. That inductive process fosters substantial levels of creative thought and forces students to examine ideas from a holistic perspective. Ms. Lange's teaching is especially powerful in this regard because she continued to expand the complexity of the phenomenon. As a consequence, new meanings emerge based on new facts that the teacher presents.

Not only does the relational nature of inquiry enable culturally diverse learners to participate, but it also enables a type of co-learning (between teachers and students) that enhances learning possibilities for female students; students have an opportunity to see the thinking of the teacher. Indeed, Polling (1995) notes that alternative assessment strategies "that do work well for girls include *embedded assessments*—activities in which students, usually in groups, perform experiments, discover patterns, and arrive at hypotheses" (p. 32).

Female students benefit when the teacher structures lessons to maximize student thinking and creativity; but all students, regardless of their gender or cultural background, benefit when the teacher structures lessons that build on students' intrinsic interests and when the teacher recognizes the worth of each student's contributions.

PREVALENT ISSUES IN DIVERSE CLASSROOMS

The inquiry approach requires real teacher skill and lots of teacher "on-the-spot" thinking. Because students are controlling the questions, the teacher becomes much more vulnerable to the feeling of losing instructional control. The questions that follow are typical of the issues teachers have confronted when they first use the inquiry strategy.

Q: *What happens when students ask questions that are "yes" or "no" oriented, but that require a more descriptive response by the teacher?*

A: It is not at all uncommon for students to ask a question that is worded to elicit a "yes" or "no" response but that, if answered with a "yes" or "no," would create conceptual confusion. In essence, a clear "yes" or clear "no" would communicate misinformation about what happens in the discrepant event. When this occurs, the teacher has two choices. First, the teacher can request that students either rephrase the question or ask another question that is narrower in scope. One of the weaknesses of Ms. Lange's lesson, in fact, is that she does not provide enough clarifying information to the students. When one of the students asks about the bird flying away, Ms. Lange responds "Yes." She might have said something like, "Yes, but ask me specific questions about why the bird flew away." With inquiry, it is perfectly legitimate for the teacher to encourage students to focus on a specific aspect of an event. Quite obviously, the teacher needs to limit the degree to which this occurs. If the teacher's descriptive responses and requests for rephrasing questions are done too much, the open-ended, creative aspect of inquiry is destroyed. But if teachers provide no direction, it is also possible that students will fail to develop a clear picture of all the variables evident in a discrepant event.

A second option available is for the teacher to respond with a "yes" or "no" and then provide additional information to make certain that students clearly understand what the "yes" or "no" means. At times it is just too difficult to move the students toward the questions the teacher believes need to be asked, especially when the questions are intended to clarify an idea. The authors have seen teachers literally destroy the flow of a lesson because the teacher spends 5 minutes trying to get students to ask a particular question. A good inquiry lesson demands that teachers know when to ask clarifying questions and when to simply provide information that students need.

Q: *How can I make certain that all students participate? Some students just want to dominate the process; others do not want to be involved at all!*

A: The so-called "bright" students immediately want to provide the "right" answer. Darling-Hammond (1995) writes, "Today's schools were designed when the goal of education was not to educate all students well but [rather] to process a great many efficiently, selecting and supporting only a few for 'thinking work'" (p. 153). The objective of inquiry is to enable all students to think and perform in an inquiring mode. Strategies for accomplishing maximum student participation include the following:

1. Begin the lesson by having all students jot down three questions, and then have each student in the class ask one question of the teacher. Students need to have three questions available in order to ensure that they have alternatives to questions that might be asked by peers.

2. Use a "numbered heads together" technique (see Chapters 4 and 10) that enables students to work in groups of three to generate ideas. This technique enables everyone to participate, even if some students are having difficulty thinking of good questions.

Teachers need to understand that some students have learned *not* to participate. Such learned behavior may occur for a variety of reasons but often is evidenced because the students fear failure. A couple of suggestions: First, realize that some students so fear failure that they don't even want to try new tasks. For such students, inquiry can be a positive way of helping them see that anyone can ask a question and that almost all questions have merit. Second, if the discrepant event is especially perplexing, let students know that the task of discovering a valid hypothesis will not be easy. In this way, you are implicitly letting students know that failure is OK. Stipek (1993) writes:

> There is evidence that simply describing a task as highly difficult can improve the performance of those who chronically worry about failure. . . . Presumably, their performance is less debilitated by anxiety because if they fail, they can attribute the failure to the extreme difficulty of the task rather than to their own incompetence.
>
> [One researcher] . . . provides a compelling demonstration of how describing a task as difficult can alleviate students' anxiety and enhance effort. He gave sixth-grade children a series of matching tasks that were constructed in such a way as to assure failure. Following this failure experience, children were given an anagram task to work on and their behavior was carefully observed. Children who were told that the subsequent task was moderately difficult completed fewer anagrams than children who were told that the anagram task was very difficult. Thus, the concerns about competence that were created by the failure experience on the matching tasks, and the performance deficits associated with such concerns, were alleviated by simply telling children that the next task was very difficult. Presumably this message allowed children to try hard without risking demonstrating low competence on yet another task. . . . The effect was especially prominent for boys, suggesting that boys may be more concerned about their public image than girls. (p. 153)

Q: *You indicated that elements of cooperative learning can be used in implementing the inquiry model. Will cooperative learning work in all cases using this model?*

A: Cooperative learning strategies are effective as an instructional model for all students, but particularly with those students from African American and

Hispanic American communities and cross-gender groups (Hale-Benson, 1986; Hilliard, 1989; Shade, 1989). This model must also be gauged by knowledge of the students served by the teacher. Caution should be exercised based upon the students' cultural affiliation. Not all Asian American or Hispanic American ethnic groups are necessarily receptive to working with one another (Pang, 1995). Historical animosities continue to be resurrected and promulgated within some Asian American or Hispanic American communities. In those cultures that perpetuate male dominant roles or nationalistic attitudes, cooperative learning strategies may cause strong feelings of concern, animosity, and even anger. This source of conflict emanates from historical antagonisms. Pang (1995) describes how a teacher had a Vietnamese American and Cambodian American student working in cooperative group strategies. The teacher asked the Vietnamese student to work with the Cambodian student, assuming that each would be happy with this arrangement because they had similar immigrant experiences. Pang describes that the Vietnamese student "explained diplomatically that he did not think the other student would accept his help. This greatly surprised the teacher, but the prediction of the student was confirmed when the Cambodian student said, 'I do not want to accept help from a Vietnamese'" (p. 414). We mention this in order to make teachers aware of the sensitivities needed in designing group work situations (see Chapter 10) for culturally diverse student populations.

At this point, some who are reading this book will question the efficacy of this approach. It seems too loose and open, too student centered. Our advocacy for using selected and appropriate student-centered approaches as a complement to traditional instruction is a result of America's current educational realities. (Notice that we say complement, not substitute.) Quite simply, huge numbers of students are psychologically and physically dropping out of school, and many are doing so because they feel disconnected. They are exiting because what schools offer simply does not engage them personally and intellectually. Table 5-4 illustrates how time is allocated in American school activities. But Csikszentmihaly and Schneider (2000) are even more direct in their indictment of schools and teaching practices. They use the concept of "flow," which is a description of optimal experiences in which there is a "close match between high levels of challenge and the skills that are appropriate to the task at hand" (p. 97). Too little challenge or too little skill, and "flow" is disrupted. Many students never experience flow at school because of the sameness of school instruction and the limited ways in which students can demonstrate their skills. Most urban students and many students of color have real facility with language but have too few appropriate ways of verbalizing their ideas in school. Inquiry is a method conducive to fostering flow, and that, in turn, will enhance student engagement.

Q: *Don't inquiry lessons take more time, and how can those time issues be accommodated?*

A: Another issue is time. This is especially true at the secondary level. Good inquiry lessons take more time than a typical class period that is allocated at a high school level. New scheduling structures accommodating block approaches are enabling some teachers to use a wider range of instructional models. Queen (2000) discusses the utility of block structures, especially as they relate to using

TABLE 5-4 Percentage of Time for Common Activities in School Subjects

Lecture

1. Vocational education	40.0[a]
2. History	33.5
3. Art	30.1
4. English	28.6
5. Math	27.6
6. Science	26.9
7. Social science/studies	21.3
8. Foreign language	20.0
9. Computer science	8.0

Audiovisuals

1. Social science/studies	17.4
2. History	15.8
3. Art	14.4
4. English	13.8
5. Foreign language	11.1
6. Science	8.6
7. Vocational education	8.3
8. Computer science	4.1
9. Math	1.8

Group Activities

1. Science	8.6
2. Art	4.8
3. Foreign language	3.3
4. Social science/studies	2.9
5. Math	2.1
6. English	2.0
7. Vocational education	1.6
8. History	1.3
9. Computer science	0.0

Tests/Quizzes

1. Math	26.3
2. Foreign language	23.3
3. History	18.3
4. Social science/studies	14.6
5. Science	14.0
6. English	12.7
7. Computer science	8.3
8. Vocational education	5.0
9. Art	4.8

Individual Work

1. Computer science	62.5
2. Vocational education	35.0
3. Art	30.1
4. Math	27.6
5. Foreign Language	23.3
6. English	21.5
7. Science	18.7
8. Social science/studies	17.5
9. History	14.5

[a] The total percentage of time spent on various classroom activities for each school subject does not here total to 100 because not every kind of activity is here reported, but rather four of the most common ones and group activities.

Source: Mihaly Czikszentmihaly and Barbara Schneider, *Becoming Adult* (New York: Basic Books, 2000), p. 151.

inquiry type models. Teachers who are in block structures will find inquiry especially useful. Queen (2000) and others describe how the extended time periods make it imperative that teachers utilize new and different models of presenting content. A ninety-minute lecture to high school students (or any students!) is just not appropriate. Queen observes that "teachers should change activities every 10 to 15 minutes" (p. 219) and that a variety of instructional strategies could and should be used during broader "blocked" times. Inquiry is one of those approaches that makes great sense.

Ⓔ VALUATION CRITERIA ❌

The inquiry instructional model is often very difficult for teachers to use because they are unaccustomed to allowing students to ask questions. Because the students have more control of an inquiry lesson, teachers often feel as though the lesson lacks structure and definition. That sense of not having control is one of the most difficult aspects of using this instructional model. Teachers must be comfortable with allowing students to dictate how the content is sequenced (after all, the order of their questions will determine the sequence with which different concepts are addressed). The teacher's responsibility is to enable students to structure and synthesize the ideas meaningfully. The following questions are presented so that teachers (and perhaps a peer coach) can design and critique inquiry lessons presented to students.

Phase I: Discrepant Event

1. Does the discrepant event present students with a problem that is not immediately solvable? ☐ Yes ☐ No

2. Are students intrigued and interested by the problem/discrepant event? ☐ Yes ☐ No

3. Does the teacher clearly present the discrepant event in a way that enables students to see all dimensions of the phenomenon? ☐ Yes ☐ No

Phase II: Question Sequence

1. Does the teacher begin the questioning phase by having students identify all the pertinent data (that is, verify the nature of the objects involved in the event)? ☐ Yes ☐ No

2. Are all student questions worded to elicit a "yes" or "no" teacher response? ☐ Yes ☐ No

3. Does the teacher distinguish the difference between fact-oriented questions (questions oriented toward specific data) and theory-oriented questions (questions focused more on a defined hypothesis)? (Recall that the first set of questions should focus on eliciting factual information.) □ Yes □ No

4. Does the teacher help students keep track of what data are being generated (that is, the teacher uses some system like a grid or matrix)? □ Yes □ No

5. Are all students participating in the data-generation process? (Teachers should call on volunteers and non-volunteers to ensure full student participation.) □ Yes □ No

Phase III: Generating Hypotheses

1. Do the students have ample opportunities to create workable hypotheses? □ Yes □ No

2. Are students required to identify what data support their proposed hypothesis? □ Yes □ No

3. Are students required to critically discuss the viability of the different hypotheses? □ Yes □ No

Phase IV: Closure

1. Are students able to eliminate invalid hypotheses by specifically describing why a particular hypothesis is unworkable? □ Yes □ No

2. Are students able to generate more "yes"/ "no" questions that enable them to narrow the number of possible hypotheses? □ Yes □ No

3. Are students able to refine existing hypotheses so that each statement (hypothesis) is conceptually clear? □ Yes □ No

Phase V: Analysis

1. Are students able to identify the best working hypothesis? □ Yes □ No

2. Are students required to make predictions based on each hypothesis? □ Yes □ No

Phase VI: Extension

1. Is there a logical follow-up activity that
   extends the students' thinking regarding
   the event?   ☐ Yes   ☐ No

SAMPLE **L**ESSONS

The following sample lessons illustrate the variety that is possible with regard to
inquiry teaching. In the first lesson, a whole-language teacher demonstrates how
it is possible to use inquiry in a language arts lesson. The second case (lesson) is
one of the most creative inquiry lessons that the authors ever observed.

CASE **S**TUDY **I**

Ms. Kline teaches 1st grade at Wilson Elementary School. She begins the class by
talking to the students about what it means to be an author. She also reviews with
them the names of some of their favorite authors and illustrators. At this point she
tells them that she has written a book that she wants them to read along with her.
The teacher-made picture book is titled "A Day in the Barnyard." She begins
reading the book and has the students read (as they are able) the text with her:

> "Cockadoodle-doo," said the rooster. It was a beautiful, sunny morning on
> the farm. Daffney Duck had an early start as she bathed in the cool lake.
> Benny Bluebird went out to catch his breakfast. A plump red bird said,
> "Chirp, Chirp," as he enjoyed this glorious morning.
> "Oink, Oink," said Penny Pig. She slowly left the barn in search of some
> sticky mud.
> "Oink, Oink, Oink," she said as she slipped deep into the brown muck.
> Suddenly Linda Lamb stuck her head out the barn door. "Stop all that
> racket," she yelled. Benny dropped his breakfast. Daffney stopped in mid-
> stroke, but Penny continued to play. "Oink, Oink," Penny snorted as she
> continued sloshing in the mud. She got so carried away that her back feet
> slipped out from under her and she fell with a splat! Mud sprayed up and
> hit Linda square in the face! Linda came storming out of the barn and went
> right up to Penny.
> "Let's go," Linda said.
> "Where?" asked Penny.
> "We're going out to the forest alone," she answered.
> Penny reluctantly followed Linda into the muddy, shady forest. Penny
> thought Linda must have gotten up on the wrong side of the bed.
> Back in the barnyard, hours had passed and the animals were worried
> about Penny and Linda. They decided to go into the forest and look for
> them. When they reached the edge of the forest, they stopped suddenly.
> "What's this?" asked Daffney. "What happened here?" asked Benny.

When Ms. Kline turns to the last page, she drops her voice and asks, "What happens here?" (It appears that Penny Pig has disappeared.) The students are hushed by her voice change, but they are also excited as they look at Linda Lamb's footprints and see that Penny's have disappeared.

"To find out what occurs, we are going to play 20 Questions." She then turns to a large piece of poster paper and tells the students to ask questions so that they can discover what really happens in the story. Because Ms. Kline has played 20 Questions with the students several times in the past, she tells them to ask questions in exactly the same way as they have when they played the game before.

"Before we start, I'm going to ask someone to tally the number of questions that we ask. We'll keep track of that as well as the information that you are able to generate. OK, let's begin. Who wants to ask the first question? Gregory."

"Were they fighting?"

Ms. Kline responds "Yes" and writes on the poster board, "They were fighting." She turns to Melissa and asks, "What's your question?"

Melissa asks, "Did one of them die?"

Ms. Kline responds with a "No" and shares with the students that because the answer is "no" she will not put any information on the board. She is only putting "yes" information on the board.

Another student asks, "Are those bear footprints that I see?" Ms. Kline indicates that they are and writes, "The footprints were made by a bear" on the poster paper. (See Table 5-5.)

The lesson progresses for another 10 or 15 minutes, and the chart paper is full of "yes" ideas. At several points in the lesson, the students respond with "ohs" or "ahs" as they think they understand what happened at the end of the story. The students ask almost 30 questions in their search for an answer to the story's ending.

She then says, "Based on the information we have, what do you think happened?" The first student says, "I think they became friends." Another responds, "I think the pig jumped on the lamb's back and got out." A third student gives a long explanation but draws on ideas that have no support from the "yes" data board. Ms. Kline reminds the students that their ideas must support the conclusions that appear on the "yes" board.

A total of five hypotheses (or guesses) are offered (see Table 5-5). Ms. Kline takes several minutes to review each hypothesis and asks all the students to critically think about whether each "hypothesis" has support from the "yes" data. The students eliminate a couple of the hypotheses. A lot of discussion ensues as students explore the viability of each hypothesis. Ms. Kline carefully reviews each piece of data to determine if each hypothesis works. The students end up with two possible hypotheses.

Ms. Kline says, "You have done a great job. Now let's finish the story and find out whose explanation is correct." She turns back to her picture book and reads the conclusion to the story.

As Benny and Daffney puzzled over this question, they saw Linda and Penny slowly coming out of the woods. What! Penny is on Linda's back.

Linda sat down to let Penny off her back. Then she explained, "Penny and I were off to a mud fight when she got completely stuck in the mud. She couldn't even move, so I offered her a Piggy-back ride."

TABLE 5-5 Chart from Ms. Kline's Lesson

Yes	*Guesses*
■ *They were fighting*	■ *They became friends*
■ *One walked out*	■ *The pig jumped on the lamb's back and snuck out*
■ *The footprints were made by a bear*	■ *The lamb got lost*
■ *The lamb walked out*	■ *The pig went back to the barn*
■ *The lamb ran at the pig*	■ *The lamb stayed in the woods*
■ *Penny got on the lamb's back*	

Benny and Daffney were so glad that their friends were all right that they hurried back to the barnyard to eat.

Ms. Kline completes the lesson by analyzing what data were most useful and identifying which hypothesis was the best explanation.   ■

Follow-Up Questions

1. What type of inquiry lesson is this—guided or unguided?
2. Is the question "What happened to Penny?" an appropriate discrepant event?
3. What might Ms. Kline have done at the end of the lesson to foster additional critical thought?

CASE STUDY II

Chad Raisch teaches sixth grade social studies. He is interested in teaching his middle grade students how the growing of rice is determined by supply and demand.

He begins his lesson by briefly reviewing the concepts of supply and demand. He shows the students a Furby, which is an interactive pet introduced in 1998 and sold for $30. At the time it was the hottest item on children's holiday gift lists, and auction bids for it online reached four figures. Students in his class are shown the Furby, which responds to sound, music, talking, and light—it also says some simple words and phrases. The students observe the Furby and then are asked, "Why would customers spend so much for something so simple?"

He continues, "In fact some people paid almost 100 times what the Furby is worth! What I'd like for you to do is explore the answer to this question by asking me questions, but all must be answerable with a 'yes' or 'no.'" (Students in his class have been schooled in the "yes"/"no" format through exposure to weekly riddles.)

Jonathan asks, "Did a lot of children really want the Furby?"

Mr. Raisch responds, "Yes, it was really in tremendous demand."

"Was it easy to find places that had the Furby even though it was expensive?" Elizabeth queries.

"No, unfortunately, few stores were able to keep it in stock."

The students question Mr. Raisch for several minutes, asking questions such as, "Was it originally expensive? Did children think the Furby was cool? Was the Furby originally scheduled to be sold during the holiday season?"

After students collected some data through the questioning, Mr. Raisch asked, "What ideas or generalization might explain the Furby phenomenon?"

Students proffer a wide variety of explanations, which Mr. Raisch explores individually as each student suggests what would logically explain the behavior of customers. Several students generate hypotheses that are finally shaped into, "If demand is high and supply is low, the price for purchasing an item will dramatically increase."

Once students have a firm grasp on that idea, Mr. Raisch asks, "Class, what do you think that the producers did once they realized the Furby was a hit?" The students are very engaged now and offer lots of alternative theories.

As the lesson closes, Mr. Raisch asks the students to generate their own examples of the supply/demand phenomenon and how prices are ultimately affected.

Teacher Reflections

I vaguely remember my first few introductions to the relationship between supply, demand, and price. I think I know why. These concepts were not built on my prior knowledge or my past experiences. Instead, I "learned" these concepts by reading about them in a textbook accompanied by graphs detailing how price was affected by consumer demand and seller supply. Maybe I was dense, but I don't think so.

One of the great benefits of the inquiry method, as I have observed, is that it builds on the natural curiosity of learners and helps them become better thinkers. In the particular case of the Furby lesson, my students are asked to make sense out of something that at first might not make much sense. Through the course of gathering information through question asking, generating hypotheses, and analyzing hypotheses, students are able not only to build on and critique the ideas of others, but also to see that asking good questions is, in many respects, just as important as knowing the right answers. For in "solving" the discrepant event, you can't have one without the other.

The inquiry method can offer the teacher and learner a real opportunity for active and "personalized" learning. Because students can identify with the value of a Furby, or the latest Beanie Baby, or a mint Mickey Mantle baseball card, they can better understand how limited supply and consumer demand help determine the price of a good in a market economy. ∎

⑤UGGESTED LESSON DEVELOPMENT: QUESTIONS FOR REFLECTION ✔

Once teachers understand the theoretical basis of inquiry and know how to foster student questioning in the classroom, they should develop their own classroom lesson. The following suggestions are offered as a guide:

1. Identify a phenomenon or idea that students should explore and would interest them.
2. Identify an appropriate discrepant event that is related to the phenomenon.
3. Determine whether guided or unguided inquiry should be used.
4. Create a data-collection device for keeping track of the information that students generate.
5. Identify a process for collecting hypotheses.
6. Determine an appropriate follow-up or closure activity for helping students synthesize material.

TECHNOLOGY ENHANCEMENT A D I S C

In this section, we will discuss through the ADISC model how technology can be used to enhance the inquiry process (I) and foster communication and collaboration through an effective use of multimedia tools and online collaboration (C).

USING MULTIMEDIA RESOURCES TO PRESENT A DISCREPANT EVENT

A strong inquiry lesson begins with an engaging and not easily resolved discrepant event. Today's teachers have unprecedented access to an increasingly rich and diverse source of multimedia resources that can be used to create dynamic and compelling discrepant events. In preparing this section of the text, one of the authors identified four topics that he believed had potential for the application of the inquiry strategy. The four topics and their related disciplines were mitosis (biology), strip mining (earth science, geography), the trail of tears (American history), and Shakespeare (English literature). Using www.ask.com and spending just five minutes on each search resulted in the discovery of the following Web-based resources that could be quickly downloaded and transformed into intriguing discrepant events. The respective discoveries included a video modeling the phases of mitosis; an aerial photo of a Kentucky strip mine; a diary entry written by an observer after witnessing a mother bury her child and then compelled to rejoin the forced march; a one paragraph description of the life of the man from Stratford implying that he was likely illiterate.

Importantly, all of the just described media presented themselves in forms that could be easily adapted as discrepant events with little effort. The key, of course, is having the creative insight to recognize what, if any, modifications would be necessary to turn the media resource into a discrepant event. Similarly, the trail of tears memoir once excerpted from its Web site context contains no reference to the trail of tears and could be interpreted as occurring at almost any time, and in almost any culture.

Teachers desiring to use multimedia resources to create discrepant events are, of course, not limited to finding and adopting Web-based resources. Today, most teachers have access to technologies they can employ to create their own multimedia artifacts. Digital cameras and camcorders, for example, can be used to capture still or moving images that can then be presented as discrepant events. In addition, scanners—common in many schools—allow teachers to scan images from books and magazines that hold the potential as starting points for inquiry lessons. Once a photograph or drawing has been scanned into a computer, software such as Photoshop, Microsoft Word, CorelDraw, or any typical scanning software can be used to modify the image in whatever ways are necessary to create or heighten the discrepancy. For example, *cropping* a photo can often provide the starting point. One teacher the authors observed used this technique to begin an inquiry lesson on child labor abuses in nineteenth century America. Working with a single, scanned photo of children at work in a coal mine, she created a series of five photos that gradually revealed more and more clues about the context in which the children were portrayed.

Grade Level Modifications

The various multimedia methods described on the above pages have application to teachers at all grade levels. Teachers should, of course, be mindful of the developmental needs of their students. For example, some primary and elementary children may prefer to develop their *"yes" and "no" questions* based on relatively simple still images that can be examined more closely for a longer period of time. Conversely, some middle grade and secondary students are more likely to be engaged by moving images and more complex media or data. Experimentation with different forms of media, including print, still images, and moving images, should help teachers better understand the relative power of each for individual children.

Low Tech/High Tech Applications

In addition to relatively high-tech approaches, such as capitalizing on Web-based multimedia resources, teachers should not overlook the numerous low-tech opportunities for creating and presenting a discrepant event. For example, carefully selecting a short section of videotape can provide an easy and effective method of presenting a discrepant event. Likewise, commercially produced laser disks or CD-ROMs typically contain a plethora of print documents, photographs and video artifacts that, when viewed in isolation, can serve as wonderful points of departure for an inquiry lesson.

In contrast, teachers interested in creating their own multimedia-based discrepant events may want to explore the use of a video editing system such as a Casablanca or Avid, which will support them in creating personalized videos that facilitate the use of a mix of media sources.

Value Added for Diverse Learners

Teachers should consider the needs of their students in determining the way to present their discrepant event. Visual, auditory, and kinesthetic modalities can all be incorporated through the variety of medias that are available. Additionally, incorporating discrepant events can allow teachers to represent issues related to cultural diversity within their lesson.

Web-Based Resources

The Web is filled with resources to locate a video clip, digital picture, written accounts and much more. As mentioned previously, www.ask.com is one such resource. Search engines like AltaVista (www.altavista.com) and Google (www.google.com) will allow an individual to search specifically for a digital picture, video clip, and other such multimedia files. Teachers can search and find the resource for their exact need.

Ⓢ UMMARY

Gunter, Estes, and Schwab (1995) observe that "good questions are more important than right answers" (p. 135). Although many educators may embrace the spirit of this phrase, few structure their classroom practice in ways that validate the statement. Through the exams given, the assessments provided, and the dialogue fostered, teachers tend to communicate to students that deriving right answers is the goal of the educational enterprise. Good schools are often defined as those that enable students to learn factual knowledge. Conservative syndicated columnist Thomas Sowell wrote about one "good" school—Hillsdale Academy. According to Sowell, this school is one where students learn the facts. They know who Julius Caesar, Constantine, and Augustus were, and they can describe in some detail the legacy of the Roman Empire. Clearly, facts are important. But the putative ignorance of American students is vastly overemphasized, especially when students in today's schools are compared with earlier generations of Americans—those who claim that after they walked 10 miles to school in the snow, they had to learn much more than today's students. Indeed, considerable research exists that suggests that, if anything, current student populations are more knowledgeable than were those in the past (Whittington, 1991). Whittington observes:

> Advocates for reform of education and excellence in public schooling should refrain from harkening to a halcyon past (or allowing the perception of a halcyon past) to garner support for their views. Such action, or inaction, is dishonest and unnecessary. Indeed, excellence is a goal that should be advocated on its own merits, as should the advocacy for higher standards than those of the past. (p. 778)

What is missing in far too many classrooms is instruction that requires students both to *think* and *know*. The inquiry instructional model fosters both of these dimensions! A good question requires knowledge, just as a correct answer requires understanding. A student who is going to be successful in school and in life must possess both abilities. As Gunter, Estes, and Schwab (1995) comment: "Although it is true that those who succeed in school are often those who can remember the 'correct' answer, those who succeed in life are usually those who are willing to ask questions and search for solutions" (p. 165).

®EFERENCES

Bibens, R. F. 1980. "Using Inquiry Effectively." *Theory Into Practice* 19(2): 87–92.

Borko, H., C. Brown, R. Underhill, M. Eisenhart, P. Jones, and P. Agard. 1990. *Learning to Teach Mathematics for Understanding.* College Park: University of Maryland.

Csikszentmihaly, M., and B. Schneider. 2000. *Becoming Adult.* New York: Basic Books.

Darling-Hammond, L. 1995. "Restructuring Schools for Student Success." *Daedalus* 124(4): 153–162.

Good, T., and J. E. Brophy. 1994. *Looking in Classrooms* (6th ed.). New York: HarperCollins.

Gunter, M. A., T. H. Estes, and J. Schwab. 1995. *Instruction: A Models Approach* (2nd ed.). Boston: Allyn & Bacon.

Hale-Benson, J. 1986. *Black Children: Their Roots, Culture, and Learning Styles* (rev. ed.). Baltimore: Johns Hopkins University Press.

Hilliard, A. G., III. 1989. "Teachers and Cultural Styles in a Pluralistic Society." *NEA Today* 1: 65–69.

Hyman, R. T. 1980. "Fielding Student Questions." *Theory Into Practice* 19(1): 38–44.

Investigating Solid Waste Issues. 1994. Columbus, OH: Ohio Department of Natural Resources.

Joyce, B., M. Weil, and J. Calhoun. 2000. *Models of Teaching.* Boston: Allyn & Bacon.

Orlich, D. C., R. J. Harder, R. C. Callahan, C. H. Kravas, D. P. Kauchak, R. A. Pendergrass, and A. J. Keogh. 1985. *Teaching Strategies: A Guide to Better Instruction* (2nd ed.). Lexington, MA: D. C. Heath.

Pang, V. 1995. "Asian Pacific American Students: A Diverse and Complex Population." Pp. 412–424 in J. Banks and C. Banks (eds.), *Handbook of Research on Multicultural Education.* New York: Macmillan.

Polling, A. 1995. "Gender Balance: Lessons from Girls in Science and Mathematics." *Educational Leadership* 53(1): 30–33.

Queen, J. A. 2000. "One School Tackles the Change to Block Scheduling." *Phi Delta Kappan* 82(3), 214–222.

Shade, B. J. 1989. "The Influence of Perceptual Development on Cognitive Style: Cross Ethnic Comparisons." *Early Child Development and Care* 51: 137–155.

Shulman, L., and P. Tamir. 1973. "Research on Teaching in the Natural Sciences." Pp. 1098–1148 in R. M. W. Travers (ed.), *Second Handbook of Research on Teaching.* Chicago: Rand McNally.

Stipek, D. J. 1993. *Motivation to Learn* (2nd ed.). Boston: Allyn & Bacon.

Taba, H. 1966. *Teaching Strategies and Cognitive Functioning in Elementary School Children.* Cooperative Research Project 2404. San Francisco: San Francisco State College.

Tyson, H. 1994. *Who Will Teach the Children? Progress and Resistance in Teacher Education.* San Francisco: Jossey-Bass.

Whittington, D. 1991. "What Have 17-Year-Olds Known in the Past?" *American Educational Research Journal* 28(4): 759–780.

Wlodkowski, R. J., and M. B. Ginsberg. 1995. "A Framework for Culturally Responsive Teaching." *Educational Leadership* 53(1): 17–21.

Wlodkowski, R. J., and J. H. Jaynes. 1990. *Eager to Learn.* San Francisco: Jossey-Bass.

Wright, E. L. 1981. "Fifteen Simple Discrepant Events that Teach Science Principles and Concepts." *School Science and Mathematics* 81: 575–580.

———, and G. Govindarajan. 1992. "Stirring the Biology Teaching Pot with Discrepant Events." *American Biology Teacher* 54(4) (April): 205–210.

The history of ideas is replete with examples of how people constructed and then reshaped ideas. For example, in the early 1800s, the earth was thought to be 6,000 years old. The generations from Adam and Eve to the present were meticulously documented by theologians. Then along came Charles Darwin, who in 1859, with his publication of *The Origin of Species*, caused people to rethink how humankind came to inhabit the earth. Darwin was trained as a theologian (indeed he graduated from Cambridge, with a degree in theology in 1831), but he challenged the thinking of the clergy. Darwin built on the ideas of other scientists, such as Sir Charles Lyell and Jean Baptiste de Lamarck, both of whom had created their own organizational schema about animal behavior and geologic phenomena—Lyell was a biologist and Lamarck was a zoologist. Darwin's work revolutionized how people thought about the evolution of human beings—he "reordered" scientific ideas. Subsequently, of course, Darwin's work itself has been reordered and challenged—to the point, in fact, that many have intellectually cycled back to the original creationist perspectives that dominated in the 1800s.

The beauty of the human experience is the ability to look at the complexity of the universe in ways that make multiple interpretations possible. The evolution of ideas is really a reordering and reorganizing of what others, who lived earlier, have accomplished. Socrates, who was concerned with man's place in society, juxtaposed his ideas with those of the sophists and the natural philosophers. Plato relied heavily on Socrates; and Aristotle, the master scientific organizer, evolved the ideas of his predecessors even further. Over the past couple thousand years, people have been creating new frontiers of knowledge using what is known—the boundaries of the unknown have been pushed back, and the area that constitutes the "known" is constantly being restructured.

In the next two chapters, two techniques are provided that make it possible for students within classrooms to engage in their own forms of intellectual reordering. Both models require that students actively engage themselves with data, and both enable the creative capacities of students to be extended. Students can see, therefore, that they have a capacity to generate their own meanings and that some of those meanings might even make more sense than what they have learned previously. ▪

Models That Foster Reorganizing Skills

SIX

• *Concept Formation*

Chapter Objectives

At the end of this chapter, readers will be able to

1. *Understand the theoretical basis for the model.*
2. *Identify the essential phases of a concept formation lesson.*
3. *Identify the strengths and weaknesses of the model.*
4. *Evaluate the lessons that use the concept formation model.*
5. *Describe ways in which concept formation enhances learning opportunities for students from culturally diverse backgrounds.*
6. *Create a concept formation lesson for classroom use and understand how technology can be used to enhance the lesson.*

❶NTRODUCTION

The purpose of concept formation is to "see" the thinking processes and conceptual schema of students. In far too many classrooms, what students experience is the reality of the teacher's thinking. That is, the teacher does the thinking for the students. The teacher determines what concept is going to be taught, provides the students with a definition of that concept, gives a variety of examples that illustrate the definition, and then provides practice activities (homework) to ensure that students learn the material. Some might describe this approach as traditional. Parker (1987) described this as the content mastery approach. Such an approach is disadvantageous when it occurs with such regularity that students have no opportunity to critique what they are learning or fully understand why they are learning the material.

The traditional content approach is not educationally unsound. Indeed, in many instances, such a strategy has real efficacy, as the reader will recognize in Chapter 9 when we will discuss direct instruction. However, the teacher-controlled approach to learning becomes a barrier to student growth when students are not provided with instructional alternatives. The ideal instructional system eliminates the use of one model exclusively; the ideal system utilizes many different instructional strategies as a means of tapping the full intellectual potential of students. Wiggins and McTighte (2000) capture this idea effectively: "Given the complexity of all instructional methods, there is no one best or

> *So you might say that the challenge of education is, on the one hand, to preserve the imagination and the questioning and the theoretical stance of a 5-year-old, but on the other hand—gradually but decisively—to replace those ideas that are not well-founded with theories, ideas, conceptions, stories, which are more accurate.*
>
> HOWARD GARDNER

preferred approach to teaching for understanding. No single method of teaching will work all the time. Particular instructional methods and techniques follow from the specific types of learning needed to achieve the desired results (evidence of understanding) in the unit or course" (p. 162).

Concept formation is an instructional model that places the *emphasis on student thinking, not teacher thinking.* This focus upon who is thinking is a very important distinction and must be kept in mind when using this instructional model. In order for this model to have maximum impact, teachers need to sequence and plan the way in which students approach prescribed learning activities. In essence, teachers create the conditions (set the stage), but the students are given latitude in terms of how to respond and think (create their own "play"). Whimbey (1977) asserts that to teach students how to think, teachers must carefully demonstrate to students how to process information, and then provide students with an opportunity to practice what they have learned.

Concept formation, according to Parker (1987), enables students to systematically examine data in a way that (1) fosters an understanding of how a label for a concept is just that, a "label"; (2) engenders more complex thinking "about the content, [and creates] further sense making as learners try to capture with a single term [determined by them] the similarities' essence" (p. 52); and (3) enables students to connect their experiences with the available data. As Parker notes, "Student generated labels are more likely to be connected meaningfully to students' present experiences than are conventional [teacher provided] labels . . ." (p. 52).

This last characteristic of concept formation is perhaps most important for teachers of culturally diverse youngsters. Because students come to school with such varied backgrounds from varied child-rearing practices, the concept formation model enables teachers to build on the existing cognitive schema and life experiences of students. It also fosters a respect for what students know. Rather than having students sit in classrooms where they are *"being done to,"* students are in a position to *create their own meaning,* to warrant their own backgrounds, and to compare what they know with what is already known (Haberman and Post, 1995).

ⒸASE STUDY

Lou Tripodi is preparing to teach a 4th grade earth science unit on the different types of resources that human beings use. Lou typically uses the direct instruction model in introducing concepts and ideas, but because he believes his students have a reasonable understanding of the available resources, he decides to use a different instructional model to explore the concept. He wants to see how his students have organized ideas associated with the way resources are used by people to lead a quality life.

"Today, class, we are going to begin a unit on resources that people use to sustain and enhance the quality of their lives. I'm going to list some resources on the board as examples. I then want you to add additional terms of your own."

Mr. Tripodi proceeds by listing on the board the following terms:

1. crude oil	9. forests
2. paper	10. water
3. rain	11. fish
4. trains	12. coal
5. chemicals	13. factories
6. minerals	14. electricity
7. trucks	15. atomic energy
8. gasoline	16. natural gas

After he completes the listing, he asks the students to add other resources that they feel are important to people's quality of life. The students provide additional examples such as trees, wildlife, soil, lakes, rivers, plants . . . When the list grows to approximately 50 terms, he asks them to stop.

"Well, we have a nice listing of items here. Are there any terms you don't understand? For example, does everyone know what crude oil is? Robin, let's make sure we all know what that term means."

Robin responds, "Crude oil is the stuff in the ground that oil companies pump out and use to make gasoline."

"That's right," responds Mr. Tripodi. "Actually, there are many more by-products than gasoline, but gasoline is most likely what you would think of first. Now, are there any other terms that you want to discuss before we start?"

The students nonverbally respond that they understand all the terms, and Mr. Tripodi checks by questioning them on some of the terms listed.

Mr. Tripodi continues the lesson. "I am going to provide each one of you with a sheet of paper that has three circles on it. I want you to work in your peer pairs [he has each student paired with a fellow student] and group these terms in a way that makes the most sense to each of you. For example, if I select one term, such as 'paper,' what item(s) or term(s) would you put with it?"

"I would select trees," reacts Huan-Kun.

"Why?" questions Mr. Tripodi.

"Because you make paper from tree pulp. I learned that a while ago when I had Ms. Kunjufu in social studies."

"Excellent. Now, let's see how many other items we can put with the two terms, paper and trees."

The students expand the category to eight items—some of which are from the original listing of 50 terms. Others are new items that the students believe fit and that they thought of as the lesson progressed. After about five minutes Mr. Tripodi stops further categorization and labels the grouping, "Things needed to make paper."

He states: "Using the same process we used here, I now want you to create your own groups of items. Select one item, any item, and then see what other terms fit with the one you selected. Then after you have as many terms placed together in the circle as you can think of, label the group. Think of a name that is appropriate for all the items you have grouped together."

The students work for 15 minutes creating their own word groupings. Mr. Tripodi walks around the room, checks on the students' progress, and then draws three large circles on the board.

"Let's see how you did," states Mr. Tripodi. "Lucinda, give me one of your groupings."

Lucinda lists all the items from one category, and Mr. Tripodi writes them down in a circle as follows:

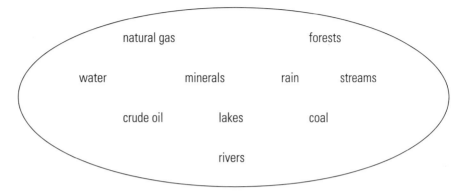

"Lucinda, what descriptor do you have for this group?"

Lucinda responds, "Natural resources that people use."

"Good," responds Mr. Tripodi. "Now, class, what other items might we put into this grouping that Lucinda's group left out? You may even be able to identify some that were not on our original list."

The students add six additional terms before Mr. Tripodi stops the process and goes to the next peer group and asks them for one of their word groups.

The students create 10 different groupings before Mr. Tripodi stops the lesson. Many of the groupings focus on natural resources. Mr. Tripodi has the students regroup the terms into large concept groupings and some into smaller groupings.

"Class, let's go back to Lucinda's grouping. What I want to do now is look more carefully at the interrelationship of the natural resources we've identified and the actual products that result from those resources. I want you to read Chapter 4 in your text and then select two resources from Lucinda's grouping and identify some products that result from each resource. I also want you to write a generalization about why resources are important to people." ∎

The preceding case is one type of inductive lesson titled "concept formation"—the students are forming major concepts from a smaller subset of concrete and abstract items. In this chapter, we will explore the concept formation model, and focus on how and when this model can be used to expand student critical thinking.

ⓣHEORETICAL PERSPECTIVE

The concept formation model is one of several teaching strategies first popularized by Hilda Taba (1966). Actually, Taba identified several different strategies (or cognitive tasks) that teachers could use to enhance the thinking skills of students. Concept formation is one approach in the use of inductive models, and in some respects it represents one of the most uncomplicated strategies for classroom teachers.

The purpose of concept formation is to enable students to differentiate a set of ideas presented by the teacher. Students move from a specific set of exemplars to broader conceptual categories that have the characteristics of those exemplars. Students engage in more higher-order thinking when they are required "to manipulate information or ideas in ways that transform their meaning and implications . . . [and] arrive at some conclusion or interpretation" (Newmann and Wehlage, 1993, p. 9). The manipulation of concept exemplars enables students to compare and contrast different interpretations of the ideas that are available for categorization and classification.

In traditional classrooms that emphasize teacher-centered pedagogy, teachers identify the categorizations for students, and students become relatively passive learners who are expected to learn the teachers' categorizations. That is, the teacher starts by stating something like, *"Today we are going to study natural resources. A natural resource is something that is not made by humans but is used by people to enhance the quality of their lives. An example would be crude oil. . . ."* In essence, the teacher tells the student the idea and then defines that idea for students. The question is: Does telling students an idea, teach an idea? Parker (1987) asserts that it does not: "[Telling an idea does not teach an idea] except of course for the few students in the room who will do the necessary thinking whether or not the teacher encourages it; they also tend to be the field-independent learners who require less context in order to assimilate information. That makes it [teacher telling] a very weak strategy. . . . Teachers have often heard themselves say, 'I told them and told them and told them, and they still didn't learn it!'" (p. 52).

In utilizing the concept formation model, students become active participants in the learning process because they construct their own intellectual meanings for their own categorizations. The students make a series of decisions that influence how the ideas (or exemplars) will be organized, and the teacher is positioned to monitor how students are thinking about selected concepts. In essence, both teachers and students become active participants in the learning process. Teachers become active participants because they must continually monitor the students' thinking, and the students are actively engaged because they create their own schema from the available data (the exemplars provided).

The concept formation model uses a very active instructional pattern between individual students and the data. That pattern is important because it requires students to use information-processing skills in observing and interpreting data (examples) provided by the teacher. If it is true, as Taba (1966) postulated, that there "is a sequence in the development of abstract and symbolically mediated thought" (p. ii), then students need to be provided with opportunities to explore how to structure ideas on their own rather than to have that structure created for them by the teacher. The concept formation model requires that students make observations, compare and contrast data, and then draw conclusions about the interrelationships of that data. As Borich (1988) asserts, the approach is used when "students are asked to draw a conclusion, make a generalization, or develop a pattern of relationship from data. It is a process in which students observe specific facts and then generalize to other circumstances to which the facts apply" (p. 174). Most important, though, concept formation should help students build concepts and become critical thinkers because it forces students to interpret data (Sparks-Langer, Pasch, Starko, Moody, and Gardner, 2000).

CONCEPT FORMATION: TEACHING PHASES

Phase I: Data Generation

The first phase of concept formation requires that students examine a data set. That data set can be either teacher- or student-generated. With teacher-generated data, the teacher makes a determination regarding what ideas to present to students, and each student in turn categorizes the data into "concept groupings." For example, a teacher of social studies may use a set of terms associated with the continent of Africa (for example, *Nile River, Zulu, Sahara, nomads,* and so on). The students would take these terms and inductively create categories such as *landforms* or *tribes* or *cultural groups.* An English teacher might give the students an extensive set of words such as *yellow, beautiful, fire, store, box,* and so on. The students would then be asked to create groupings that might include the various parts of speech—*adjectives, nouns, verbs.* The actual labels of noun, verb, and so on would not be imposed on the students by the teacher. Rather, the labels would emerge from the students' understandings of the concept—parts of speech. The students, however, may or may not use the actual terms *noun, verb, adjective.* With an inductive strategy such as concept formation, the actual category label that students generate may not be the category label that the teacher expects. The category label is the students' to formulate and appropriately defend, not the teacher's to dictate. However, the teacher can help shape the emergent categories by sharing with the students the focus of a lesson: *"See how many categories you can create that deal with important features of Africa"* or *"Put together groupings that focus on parts of speech."*

Student-generated data occur in response to a rather open-ended question provided by the teacher. As an example of this, we once observed a teacher who had just completed a unit on the Revolutionary War. The teacher asked the students to go to the chalkboard and write down a word or phrase that captured something about the Revolutionary War that was important to them. The process was iterative. After every student listed one term on the board, the teacher asked the students to carefully read what terms were listed and to add any other terms they thought deserved inclusion. After some time passed, a large number of additional terms were added to the board. This process continued until the chalkboard was literally covered with a wide variety of words and phrases. From this point the teacher began the process by having the students sort, categorize, and label the data. Another example we witnessed involved a high school science teacher's conducting a unit on water resources. This teacher asked the students to identify all the items they could think of related to water usage. As each student responded, the teacher wrote the term on the chalkboard. The students created over 100 water-related terms, which formed the basis for a concept formation lesson. And yet another was a 4th grade teacher who had just completed a unit on the Holocaust. She asked students to go to the board and write down terms they associated with the Holocaust. Such lessons enable teachers to literally recognize (to "see") the schema used by students. With such information, the teacher is in a better position to identify student understandings and misunderstandings.

In the teaching scenario that introduced this chapter, the teacher used a combination of student- and teacher-generated data. Mr. Tripodi began by listing 16 resources that he thought students should consider. The students then provided additional items of their own, using the conceptual lead provided by Mr. Tripodi. With younger children, a combination of teacher- and student-generated data may be necessary, especially if the unit material being covered is not well known by students. Teachers should not hesitate to add data to the data set, especially if students are inadvertently leaving out certain critical terms.

Essentially, there are many appropriate alternatives to generate data. The teacher's goals for a lesson, coupled with the background knowledge of the students, will dictate which approach—teacher-generated or student-generated data or some combination of each—is most efficacious for helping students subsequently construct categories that make conceptual sense.

Phase II: Data Grouping

In phase II of the model, students take all the data and begin to create groupings of conceptually similar terms. There are several ways to accomplish this successfully. Before beginning the grouping process, the teacher needs to check carefully and make certain that all of the students understand the meanings associated with each listed term. This can be accomplished by asking students to define selected terms, randomly asking students to define terms, or asking students if they need specific terms defined before the lesson begins. Once all terms are defined and clarified, the teacher can begin the grouping process, usually through the use of a teacher-generated example. That is, the teacher can ask a student to pick any term from the available list and to place that term in a large circle. (Incidentally, there is nothing magical about circles. The circle is nothing more than a symbolic way of "enclosing" or defining a concept.) Recall that Mr. Tripodi began the grouping process as follows: *"I am going to provide each one of you with a sheet of paper that has three circles on it. I want you to work in your peer pairs and group these terms in a way that makes the most sense to each of you. For example, if I select one term, such as 'paper,' what item or term would you put with it?"*

The students construct the groupings based upon their own perceptions of how the terms fit with one another. They place as many terms together in one circle (or group) as they feel logically and conceptually fit. Once they "fill a circle," they then pick another term at random, place it in the next circle, and begin the grouping process again. Remind students that terms can be placed in several different circles. Once a term is used in one circle, it is not excluded from use in other groups.

Some students tend to label the groups before they begin the categorization. This needs to be discouraged by the teacher. Teachers should encourage students to select a "first" item randomly and then conduct the grouping process based on that first selection: What item is similar to the first item? Students should be cautioned, in essence, not to label a group too quickly.

Sparks-Langer et al. (2000) argue that it is important for the teacher to do some anticipating of categories so that the teacher questions can be used to shape the students' thinking. The goal is not to make the students think like the teacher, but the categories (or groupings) formed need to be conceptually sophisticated in order to achieve the objectives of the lesson and to maximize the best use of the model. In essence, carefully observe students as they form their categories and do not hesitate to help them shape those categories with questions. For example, Sparks-Langer et al. (2000) use a "shaping" question relative to heating a home: "If we relied on wood for heat, perhaps we could plan a wooded lot near the home so we would never run out of fuel. Are there any of our other sources for which we could plan for additional fuel?" (p. 214).

Phase III: Labeling

Once students have created their groupings, they then determine the best concept label for that grouping of items. Recall that for Mr. Tripodi's class a 10-item group emerged (*natural gas, forests, water, minerals*, and so on), and one of the students (Lucinda) provided the label, "*Natural resources that people use.*" Parker (1987) notes that "by letting students label the concept . . . we accomplish several things. First, we want students to learn that the name is just that, a name for the idea, not to be confused with the idea itself. . . . Second, the naming act involves further thinking about the content . . ." (p. 52).

The labels should be simple conceptual descriptors that connect and embrace all the terms listed within the circle. The students are the ones who have responsibility for creating the labels, not the teacher. The teacher can have a preconceived concept that needs to be taught, but that concept should not be imposed on the students. Some teachers become very intrusive because they believe they know what labels are best suited for the item groupings (and in many instances this is true). But, in general, the teacher's concept should emerge from the lesson just as naturally as does the students'. Remember, one of the goals of the concept formation model is to provide students with opportunities to create or construct their own meaning relative to the enumerated terms. The teacher also needs to require that students justify the categories. Students should be able to explain why each item is included in a grouping.

Teachers should not hesitate to challenge student thinking by asking plenty of "why" questions. Students should be able to defend each item within each group by describing why and by what criteria they categorized each item.

Phase IV: Expanding the Category

Once students have grouped and labeled the terms, the teacher reviews each grouping to determine how students thought through the categorization process. Some teachers have each student pair describe one of its label groupings for the entire class. Peer pairs may describe the grouping category on a transparency, or they may write the terms and category label on the chalkboard. As each label grouping is described by a peer pair, the teacher and the students have responsibility for determining what additional items could logically be placed in that grouping. The teacher also checks the understandings of the other students in the class. Recall that Mr. Tripodi asked, after the first grouping was presented, *"Now, class, what other items might we put into this grouping that Lucinda's group left out? You may even be able to identify some that were not on our original list."*

Expanding the category is necessary to fully explore the meanings and interrelationships of the identified terms. Some teachers just have students present their categories; they provide no critique of what else makes sense to add to each grouping. One of the salient goals of concept formation is to enhance the thinking skills of students, and for that to occur, teachers need to extend and expand student understanding of concepts by identifying additional terms and by delineating the rationale for including the additional terms within the various groupings.

Phase V: Closure

The final phase of the concept formation model varies depending on the objectives of the unit and/or the purposes of the teacher. For those teachers who use the technique to introduce units of instruction (that is, the teacher wants to see how students are thinking about an idea and to explore their schema before content coverage occurs), the closure process may include nothing more than collecting the groupings and explaining to students that they will reexamine the "groupings" once the unit is completed. Students will then have a "before and after" perspective on a concept—they will be able to see their schema before a unit of instruction is presented and after the unit is completed.

Other teachers use concept formation as a unit review—at the conclusion of a unit. They want to see how students have developed and organized their understandings of the key concepts that the teacher presented during the unit of instruction. Once students present categories in this way, the teacher may have them do one or more of the following: (1) create a generalization relative to each of their categories, (2) describe how different terms within a category relate to one another, or (3) create an assignment from the listed terms that enables students to explore fully the meanings of the different terms in that category. Recall that Mr. Tripodi used the third approach when he stated: *"Class, let's go back to Lucinda's grouping. What I want to do now is look more carefully at the interrelationship of the natural resources we've identified and the actual products that result from those resources. I want you to read Chapter 4 in your text and then select two resources from Lucinda's grouping and identify some products that result from each resource."*

If the generalization (or first) option were to have been selected, Mr. Tripodi might have requested the following: *"Class, for each one of your categories, I want you to create a generalization that indicates the relationship of the items you selected and the title you developed. For example, for Lucinda's grouping I might develop the generalization, 'Resources such as crude oil are found naturally in the earth and are used to make products that we use in our homes.' Then I want you to support that*

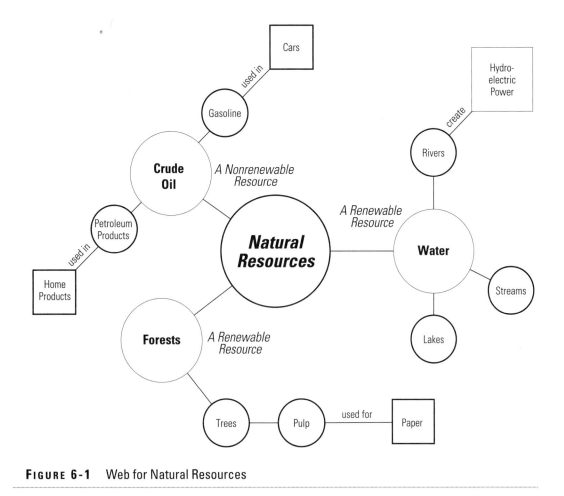

FIGURE 6-1   Web for Natural Resources

generalization by providing an example. In this instance you will actually identify a product that is used in your home."

The second option, showing how terms interrelate, can be accomplished through the creation of "webs." Students would select a conceptually broad item to use as the title for their category and to serve as the conceptual focus; they would then develop a web such as the one in Figure 6-1. The teacher might have the students extend the web in each area until an item appears that is synthetic or manufactured rather than naturally occurring. Hyerle (1996) observes that "practiced with depth, . . . webs offer students the opportunity to break the stiff intellectual molds of the 'behavioralist' classroom and to spin new interpretations and construct new forms of knowledge" (p. 37). Webs help students develop a measure of fluency with the ideas offered by the teacher. As students brainstorm the various conceptual relationships, they develop a better and deeper understanding of requisite content area concepts. Arends (1994) outlines four steps to constructing a web.

Step 1. Create the core; which is the focus of the web. This would be the name of the concept.

Step 2. Construct strands branching out of the core. These strands are critical attributes of the concept.

Step 3. Draw strand supports, which connect the critical attributes to the concept.

Step 4. Identify the strand ties, which show relationships among the various attributes. (p. 295)

APPLICATIONS TO DIVERSE CLASSROOMS

For too many teachers and schools, multicultural issues are addressed through isolated "set-aside" programs: "African-American Studies Week," "Women Heroes," and so on. The problem with the set-aside, or "additive," approach is that students all too often are able to dismiss ideas about African Americans or Hispanic Americans or women because they view them out of any meaningful context.

Because teachers control the curriculum and students have limited opportunities to infuse their own directions and views, the likelihood that set-aside perspectives will occur is even further enhanced. Textbooks and curriculum materials, until very recently, have been very male and very "white"—some teachers attempted to correct this problem by highlighting a few persons of color during Black History Month. Such an approach is well meaning but counterproductive. It tends to isolate, hierarchically, people in history rather than to integrate them in ways that warrant their contributions on an equal basis. Concept formation and other inductive strategies provide some measure of assurance that students can begin to use their own frames of reference (their own cultural schema) to shape personal learning. They can use what they know to enhance what the teacher wants them to know. Teachers who use concept formation are often fascinated by the number of student ideas that they (the teachers) never thought of—or if they thought of them, never perceived their relevance to the larger set of ideas being studied.

Students who engage in inductive (concept formation) activities are able to create a meaningful (personal) context for their ideas, exhibit divergent thinking processes, use their own creative sense of how ideas fit together, and creatively think about how concepts interface with one another. In the words of Irvine and Armento (2001):

> Conceptual learning is demonstrated when learners are able to apply ideas to new examples and when they are able to provide examples from their own experience. It is important to encourage students to construct their own examples of new ideas for a number of reasons. First of all, the student is able to see that the new idea has relevance and does exist in his/her own life and is able to verbally name examples in a range of ways. In addition, the teacher is able to test for understanding of new ideas when students are able to provide examples that match the meaning of the new idea. (pp. 27–28)

TABLE 6-1   Order of Performance for Various Ethnic Groups

African Americans:	verbal ability, reasoning, space conceptualization, number ability
Chinese Americans:	space conceptualization, number ability, reasoning, verbal
Jewish Americans:	verbal, number ability, reasoning, space conceptualization
Puerto Rican Americans:	space conceptualization, number ability, reasoning, verbal

Source: Hale-Benson, J. 1982. *Black Children: Thin Roots, Culture, and Learning Styles.* Baltimore: John Hopkins University Press: 29.

These types of learning opportunities support field-dependent cognitive styles more than field-independent ones. Further, they enable students to use their verbal abilities and refine their reasoning skills to defend ideas that they provide in defense of hypotheses. Variability in classroom instructional approaches is best illustrated through analysis of Table 6-1. As you will notice, verbal and reasoning skills represent significant strengths for African American students but areas of potential weakness for Chinese American students. Teachers who rely heavily on one instructional approach disadvantage subsets of students whose preferred styles are not compatible with a particular teacher's preferred approach. Remember, instructional variability is one of the best palliatives for addressing the needs of diverse student populations in the classroom.

As one begins reflecting upon the alternative learning styles, some readers may be inclined to assume that because they teach in an affluent or suburban setting, the performance characteristics of the students will not be the same as evidenced by students in lower socioeconomic neighborhoods. In other words, they may believe that social class is a significantly more important factor than racial or ethnic affiliation (for example, that poor, at-risk students think alike because of the similar socialization process they experience).

The literature fails to support this view fully. In fact, ethnicity may be more important than social class. That means teachers should know just as much, if not more, about the racial and cultural dimensions of student learning as they do about a student's socioeconomic circumstances. Hale-Benson (1982) notes:

> Each [racial or ethnic] group was markedly different both in the *level* of each mental ability and in the *pattern* of these abilities. The most interesting finding . . . was that social class variation within the ethnic group does not alter the basic organization or pattern of mental abilities peculiar to that group. . . . Social class is a factor; but ethnicity emerged as the primary factor. (pp. 29–30)

Nieto (1996) reinforces Hale-Benson's observation and cites James Banks' work as conceptual grounding for her associates. Nieto writes,

> Social class . . . has been proposed as equally or more important than ethnicity in influencing learning style. Because membership within a particular social grouping is based on both economic variables and values, the working

TABLE 6-2   Question Matrix

WHAT IS?	WHERE/ WHEN IS?	WHICH IS?	WHO IS?	WHY IS?	HOW IS?
WHAT DID?	WHERE/ WHEN DID?	WHICH DID?	WHO DID?	WHY DID?	HOW DID?
WHAT CAN?	WHERE/ WHEN CAN?	WHICH CAN?	WHO CAN?	WHY CAN?	HOW CAN?
WHAT WOULD?	WHERE/ WHEN WOULD?	WHICH WOULD?	WHO WOULD?	WHY WOULD?	HOW WOULD?
WHAT WILL?	WHERE/ WHEN WILL?	WHICH WILL?	WHO WILL?	WHY WILL?	HOW WILL?
WHAT MIGHT?	WHERE/ WHEN MIGHT?	WHICH MIGHT?	WHO MIGHT?	WHY MIGHT?	HOW MIGHT?

Source: Wiederhold, C., and S. Kagan. 1992. "Cooperative Questioning and Critical Thinking." P. 203 in N. Davidson and T. Worsham (eds.), *Enhancing Thinking Through Cooperative Learning*. New York: Teacher's College Press.

class may differ from the middle class not only in economic resources but also in particular values and practices. The reasoning behind the hypothesis that social class is a more important influence on learning style than is ethnicity is that the intellectual environment and socialization of children in the home may be due more to economic resources than to cultural resources. In a comprehensive review of related studies, Banks found in general that ethnicity seemed to have a greater influence on cognitive style than did social class. He also found that ethnic differences persisted in spite of upward mobility. This line of research points out the apparently strong and continuing link between culture and learning. (p. 139)

Some emerging voices are suggesting, however, that at least in terms of attitudes, differences within racial and ethnic groups are just as great as those between groups (Etzioni, 2001). Indeed, the contention is that race does not necessarily determine how one responds to or feels about events. Similarly, race or ethnicity does not dictate how a child learns, though it is certainly a salient factor to be considered.

The key for those working with diverse groups is to find multiple ways to engage students in thinking about ideas. One of those ways is through the use of teacher questions.

Table 6-2 is a question matrix that can be used to help teachers foster enhanced student reasoning. Effective teachers ask a range of questions (what, how, why, and so on). They want to see if students know the material and if they can then defend what they know. "What" questions focus on knowledge; "why" questions foster the reasoning that grounds that knowledge. As the teacher moves beyond the "what is?" question, students are required to use higher-level thinking skills (see Wiederhold and Kagan, 1992). They are also required to consider more complex conceptual relationships. The use of "why," "what," and "how" questions is absolutely essential to enable students to think through their categories and their ideas. Although the matrix questions were originally designed for student use (that is, students in cooperative groups would use the word pairs of "what is?" or "what might?" in cooperative learning settings), we offer them here as a guide for teachers to use as they consider how to facilitate better student thinking during concept development work: "Class, *which* of these terms *might* be grouped together? *Why would* these terms be grouped together?"

CASE STUDY

Stephanie Kovina is an inner-city teacher who uses concept formation as an instructional model in order to provide her students with an opportunity to explore their own reasoning skills. Notice how she uses higher-order questions to explore the students' understanding in the topic of sea creatures in the following lesson.

Stephanie Kovina is presenting a lesson on "Creatures of the Sea" to her 3rd grade students. She is near the end of this unit of instruction. She begins the lesson by gathering the students around a bulletin board that has pictures of 40 or 50 sea creatures—crabs, otters, sea horses, and so on. The students spend several minutes identifying the different creatures the teacher selects. The students call out creatures' names, and Ms. Kovina writes the names as they are identified: penguin, sea horse, dolphin, whale, crab, walrus, fish, otter, shark, starfish, jellyfish, pelican, seagull, and so on.

After the students complete the identification process, Ms. Kovina asks that they turn around and look at the chalkboard where she has drawn two large circles. Next to the circles are individual pictures of the various sea creatures the students have previously identified. She asks the students to look carefully at the pictures, and for a third time, she identifies each sea creature's name.

"Class, HOW COULD I separate these pictures into two groups? Think about what we have been studying and decide on how the different pictures could be divided."

Latoya responds by indicating that she would put two penguins in one circle and a lobster and crab in the other.

"Good answer, Latoya," responds Ms. Kovina. "Now WHAT PICTURES WOULD you put with these? What would go with penguins and what would go with the lobster and crab?"

Another student, Mariko, shares that the whale and dolphin would fit with the penguin.

"Does everyone agree?" asks Ms. Kovina. "WHERE DO YOU think they should go? Leroy?"

Leroy wants them with the lobster and crab.

Ms. Kovina asks why Leroy would make that classification. Rashid provides another reason for the classification.

The students proceed through the classification process until all the sea creatures are categorized. When there is any disagreement, Ms. Kovina asks

WHY THE STUDENTS ARE MAKING the classification. They have to defend their answers. She asks a large number of "why" questions to force the students to think in more depth about the concepts. The students develop two groupings, A and B.

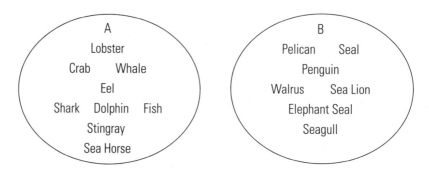

The toughest single item classification occurs for the "turtle." The students are divided regarding whether it should go in group A or group B. Ms. Kovina finally has the students vote, and the sea turtle is placed in group B.

She then asks the students to determine how each category could be labeled. "CLASS, WHAT NAME DO YOU THINK WOULD be appropriate for each of these groupings?"

Takesha responds by saying that if the sea creatures in group A are out of the water for a very long period of time they will die.

"Excellent. WHAT COULD we call this grouping of sea creatures who need water in order to live?"

After some discussion, group A is labeled "Creatures that breathe in the water"; group B is labeled "Creatures that breathe in the air."

Ms. Kovina then gives the students pieces of blue paper (for the sea) and green paper (for the land). Students also receive pictures of all the sea creatures because their task is to glue the different sea creatures on the appropriate color of paper based upon the labeled classifications. ■

This lesson has a very different feel from the one found in most traditional classes. Traditional lessons tend to emphasize "What is?" questions, where students identify the names of animals presented by the teacher. Students must think quickly. In many cases they provide incorrect responses in order to give the teacher some form of response. Other students decide not to respond at all for fear of being wrong. In concept formation, students have an opportunity to explore their own ideas and understandings. Teachers who use this approach will recognize that students are very skilled reasoners, even though they reason differently from the teacher. Some students who never raise their hands in response to "What is the definition of a natural resource?" will more quickly respond when asked "Which resources did you use this morning before you came to school?" or "Why do we need natural resources in order to live?"

The focus of concept formation is to enable students to construct their own understandings about phenomena. One especially positive aspect of concept formation is that both teachers and students become active participants in the teaching-learning process. Teachers must thoughtfully identify ways of helping students examine ideas; in other words, they must ask a variety of questions that help students form categories that can be justified. Students, on the other hand, must be able to see how different ideas (or terms) relate to one another. Student conceptual constructions enable teachers to view students as they put together the different ideas. Teachers can literally see the students' thinking!

The questioning strategies of teachers and the capacity to wait for student responses are critical to the success of this instructional model. Teachers cannot allow students to engage in concept formation on their own. Rather, the teacher must help students fully explore ideas, conceptual interrelationships, and broader understandings about how different ideas fit together. That is why some teachers use the closure phase of this model to have students develop a generalization about the different conceptual categories. In this way, the teacher can readily recognize how students are constructing larger understandings. With that knowledge, the teacher is then prepared to determine how to proceed with future lessons.

PREVALENT ISSUES IN DIVERSE CLASSROOMS

Concept formation fosters student thinking, but it also makes some teachers feel as though they have lost control. Because students are more intimately involved in the data-analysis process, many teachers confront problems directly related to the structure, timing, and use of this instructional model. As indicated earlier, concept formation is not a pedagogically complicated strategy (that is, it does not have lots of steps), but problems do emerge when teachers use the technique.

Q: *Which is preferable, student- or teacher-generated data?*

A: It depends on the goals of the teacher. If the teacher wants the students to explore data relative to a traditional concept (for example, a sentence), then it makes sense for the teacher to provide the data. In such an instance, a teacher might limit the data set in order to limit the labels presented by the students (that is, the teacher wants students to specify a label that is conceptually congruent with one predetermined by the teacher). If, on the other hand, the teacher is reviewing information from a thematic unit, then student-generated data may make more sense. Students might be permitted to generate data as long as the momentum of the lesson is maintained. Wiggins and McTighte (2000) suggest a particular model for thinking about how to choose a teaching model (see Table 6-3). Clearly, the instructional goals defined by the teacher dictate which model is most appropriate to use.

Q: *Don't I waste time with the concept formation model?*

A: Whenever teachers relinquish some control, they will feel as though they are wasting time. One problem associated with the traditional school structure that is now increasingly high stakes oriented is the need to focus only upon basic

TABLE 6-3 Choosing a Teaching Approach

Didactic (Deductive)	Constructivist (Inductive)
Facts	Concepts and principles
Discrete knowledge	Systemic connections
Definitions	Connotations
Obvious	Subtle
Literal	Symbolic
Concrete	Abstract
Self-evident	Counterintuitive
Predictable result	Anomaly
Discrete skills and techniques	Strategy (using repertoire and judgment)
Recipe	Inventions
Algorithms	Heuristics

Source: Wiggins, G., and McTighte, J. (2000). *Understanding by Design.* Washington, DC: Association for Supervision and Curriculum Development; p. 164.

skills, those skills that are easy to measure in a standardized fashion. As discussed earlier in Chapters 2 and 3, one of the most required skills in the global economy is a thinking, informed citizen. Thus, the need to help prepare future citizens with the thinking skills necessary should be a primary goal of schools. Teaching students to think is not a time-efficient process, but it does pay dividends in terms of what they learn. As Parker (1987) notes:

> Thinking takes time. Consequently, the amount of content to be learned needs to be reduced if thinking is to be infused into the curriculum and if, in turn, the curriculum is actually to be learned. The difficulty of this reduction makes it no less necessary. Too much content encourages superficial "coverage." . . . When content is merely covered, even if many important details are included, students have not necessarily been engaged in thinking about it; consequently, whatever measurable, so-called achievement may result from it is not to be taken too seriously. (p. 50)

Reich (2001) argues even more forcefully for educating students who can think in nonstandardized ways. In his words:

> Paradoxically, we're embracing standardized tests just when the new economy is eliminating standardized jobs. If there's one certainty about what today's school children will be doing a decade or two from now, it's that they won't all be doing the same things, and they certainly won't be drawing on the same body of knowledge. The purpose of education is not only to train people to become productive participants in an economy, of course. And yet, the work that people will do after they leave school has a necessary bearing upon what and how they learn. (p. 64)

Q: *How can I use the cognitive style strengths of my students with the concept formation model?*

A: In utilizing the concept formation model, the teacher should be cognizant of the cognitive style strengths of the student population. Applying this model through cooperative learning techniques would be essential for those students who learn best through such collaborative approaches (Shade, 1989; Soldier, 1989; Vasquez, 1991). Using pairs and triads to generate terms, identifying and assessing alternative hypotheses and conclusions, and identifying groupings of terms will play to the strengths of the culturally diverse students described in Chapter 2. Further, the use of manipulatives (for example, in science and mathematics) will utilize the kinesthetic style strengths of many African American and Hispanic American students (Morgan, 1981; Soldier, 1989), but is important for all students regardless of their racial or ethnic backgrounds.

   The use of both animate and inanimate pictures and objects to demonstrate concept groupings and terms helps in the development of concepts as described by the research of Prom (1982), Shade (1984), and Shade and Edwards (1987). Many of the teachers we have observed use objects or pictures and have students manipulate those within their groups. The hands-on nature of the learning really helps students see the conceptual groupings emerge.

Ⓔ VALUATION CRITERIA

The concept formation instructional model is an inductive approach to student learning. School districts often use evaluation methods that are essentially deductive in nature (for example, they expect teachers to proceed from big ideas to exemplars rather than from exemplars to big ideas). This reality complicates the evaluation process and makes it even more imperative that supplemental assessment strategies be used. The following evaluation criteria can be used by teachers to assess a concept formation lesson. Readers might practice using the criteria with the lesson presented by Ms. Kovina.

Phase I: Data Generation

1. What is the purpose of the concept formation activity? Is it used as a way of initiating a unit? Reviewing unit material? Other? Describe.   _____
   _____
   _____

2. How are data generated by students or teachers categorized? Describe.   _____
   _____

3. Is sufficient data generated before the teacher begins the categorization process? Explain.   _____
   _____

4. Does the teacher clarify the meaning of all enumerated data to make certain students know the meanings of the various terms? In what ways?   ☐ Yes   ☐ No

Phase II: Data Grouping

1. Do students have a clear understanding of what they are expected to do in terms of categorizing the data? □ Yes □ No

2. Does the teacher provide students with materials for creating the categories? (For example, sheets of paper with circles.) Evaluate the type of materials utilized. □ Yes □ No

Phase III: Labeling

1. Does the teacher warrant all student groupings as valid? (That is, the teacher avoids using words such as "Right" or "You got it" that suggest there are correct categories.) □ Yes □ No

2. Do the students have logical labels for their groupings? □ Yes □ No

3. Does the teacher require students to defend their categories and explain the rationale for each label grouping they have created? Explain how the teacher exhibits this behavior. □ Yes □ No

Phase IV: Expanding the Category

1. Are students required to expand the categories once the teacher presents each grouping to the class? In what ways does this occur? □ Yes □ No

2. Are students able to add data to each category from different sources (that is, they can even add data that were not initially enumerated in phase I)? Provide examples. □ Yes □ No

Phase V: Closure

1. Does the teacher offer a follow-up activity that builds on student understandings relative to the categories they formed? Describe and provide your impression of the follow-up activity. □ Yes □ No

The following classroom episodes are intended to help readers further understand the concept formation model. Read each scenario and respond to the questions that follow. Notice that for Case Study II, the teacher who actually taught the lesson reflects on her thoughts regarding the effectiveness of the concept formation strategy.

CASE STUDY I

"Class, we have been studying the Middle Ages for several weeks. You now understand that *Middle Ages* and *Medieval Times* are two terms that represent the same time period. I want you now to write down several terms that best represent the Middle Ages to you."

"I am now going to ask that each of you go up to the board and write down at least three terms that you associate with that time period."

The students then begin to go to the board and list words such as *squire, serf, noble, knight, manor,* and so on.

After the students finish enumerating the data (approximately 50 terms), the teacher has the students get into groups (four students to a group) and create categories for the data.

"For all the data we have, class, see if you can group these terms together in a way that makes sense to you. Place items together that fit together. You can use any definition you want to create the fit."

The teacher gives the students sheets of paper with several large circles and has the students begin the categorization process. After 10 minutes, the students finish and the teacher requests that one group present its first set of data for the class to examine.

Shaneca's peer group provides the first set of data—*Sir Lancelot, King Arthur, King William*—and labels the group "People of the Middle Ages." The second group offers the group "Castle Parts." All the student groups provide their concept groupings until the board is literally full of terms.

At that point the teacher asks the students to review the work that they have put on the board and see if they can add anything to any of the concept groups that have been formed. She also reviews and refines the concept group names to determine if better language could be used to explore the meaning for a group of terms. ∎

Follow-Up Questions

1. In what ways would a teacher-generated set of data be more useful than a student-generated set of data for a unit?

2. How many terms should teachers allow students to generate (this teacher allowed 50) before proceeding to phase II?

3. What approaches should teachers use to help students form the categories? That is, should the teacher select one term and ask students to form a sample group around that term, or should students be free to create their own groups from the beginning of the lesson?

4. How can concept categories be expanded to explore student understandings of the ideas presented by the teacher?

5. What other types of closure activities could be used to help students use the categories they create?

CASE STUDY II

Tracy Roman has been teaching a lesson on angles in her high school geometry class. The students are developing a reasonably good grasp of the concepts, but she now wants to see how they organize the different terms.

"Class, over the past week or so we have covered a lot of conceptual ground. I now want to see how you are organizing and defining that content."

She then hands out a worksheet that contains the following terms:

amplitude	periodic
angle	periodicity theorem
angle measure	phase shift
circular arc length	Pythagorean identity
circular functions	radian
circular sector area	revolution
complements theorem	sector
cosine	sides of an angle
cosine function	sine
cycle	sine function
degree	sine wave
disk	supplements theorem
identity	tangent
initial side	tangent function
measure of an arc	unit circle
opposites theorem	vertex of an angle
period	vertical shift

"Now, first, let's see if there are any of these terms that you do not understand." For the next several minutes the students clarify the meanings of all the terms.

Tracy calls on some students to offer definitions, and in other instances she simply states a definition herself. Once she is convinced everyone has a good understanding of the terms, she hands them a piece of paper with three circles on it, with each labeled Concept 1 or Concept 2 or Concept 3.

"Now, class, I want you to create some groupings for me. Pick a term, say 'measure of an arc,' and decide which of the other terms closely goes with that one. Group those together and then label the group with a new term that you think fits all the different terms." The students work in groups for 10–15 minutes and then Tracy brings them back together where they discuss the various groupings and show that they really understand the terms.

Her goal was to extend the students' understandings of geometric concepts. Indeed as she walked around the room she checked their understanding by giving lots of examples to individual students. She then had the students take a short quiz. The first five questions on the quiz were:

1. Define an angle. _____.

2. The measure of an angle represents _____and _____.

3. Explain the difference between an angle with a measure of 65 and one with a measure of -65 .

4. List three units of measure used with angles.

   _____   _____   _____

5. Define *unit circle*. _____.

Teacher Reflections

My ideas for this concept formation lesson actually emerged from a previous concept attainment lesson. After studying a chapter on properties of functions, I thought I could use the same examples I generated for the concept attainment lesson to form a concept formation chapter review. This ended up being a powerful review of vocabulary and concepts, though at first I was concerned that it would not be rigorous enough to challenge students.

The amount of time involved in preparing materials and gathering supplies was slightly greater than my typical review preparation time. However, the results were extremely rewarding. There was very little, if any, down time and a high engagement level using groups of four students each. Every student in each group had an assigned, non-threatening duty, so complete participation was achieved in all classes. As group dynamics evolved, I saw personalities blossom that I didn't know existed. Students who were leaders in our classroom setting were not necessarily the emerging leaders in small group settings. Understanding that there were no incorrect labels as long as they could be justified, students had spirited discussions about defending the groupings they formed.

You must be careful that time doesn't get away from you during the labeling and expanding phases and that you leave appropriate time for closure. I also found that presenting categories to the class one group at a time became tedious in large classes, and I lost some students' attention before the closure phase. In the future, I may ask students to rotate a copy of their categories around the room, so that groups can individually make corrections and/or additions to the other groups' categories. This approach may keep more students active in the review and revision process. ∎

Teachers who are developing a concept formation lesson plan need to consider the following questions.

1. Will the reorganizing approach of concept formation be used to introduce or review a set of concepts?

2. What type of data-generation approach (student or teacher) makes the most sense, given the students who will use the approach?

3. How many groupings will the students create and how many terms (at a minimum level) must be in each group?

4. How will the concept groupings be reviewed? Will students work individually or in groups?

5. What closure activity will be used to extend the students' understandings of the concepts?

ⓉECHNOLOGY ENHANCEMENT   A D I Ⓢ Ⓒ   ◆

Readers should now be familiar with how were are using the ADISC model to illustrate ways in which technology can be used to enhance classroom lessons. Far too many teachers fail to see that technology should create a value-added for a lesson—it should help make content more accessible or understandable for students. Technology is not used for its own sake; it is used to help students better assimilate content.

Using Graphic Organizer Software to Model Student Thinking

The concept formation strategy engages students in generating, categorizing, labeling, and visually representing their ideas. All of these thought processes can be enhanced when teachers employ computer software specifically developed to support such an approach to teaching and learning. One popular piece of such software available to teachers is *Inspiration*. This visual learning tool can support teachers and students in each of the five phases of the concept formation model. In *diagram view* the software enables teachers or students to create and modify a wide variety of concept maps, webs, idea maps, and other graphical organizers. When in *outline view*, the software allows users to prioritize or rearrange ideas quickly, a function especially helpful during Phases IV and V of the concept formation strategy.

Figure 6-2 illustrates a sample concept map (or web) created by a sixth-grade physical education student in response to a list of sports given by his teacher. While some students chose to categorize by type of sport (individual vs. team or "normal" vs. extreme) or by its popularity, this student chose to categorize by whether the sport was old or new.

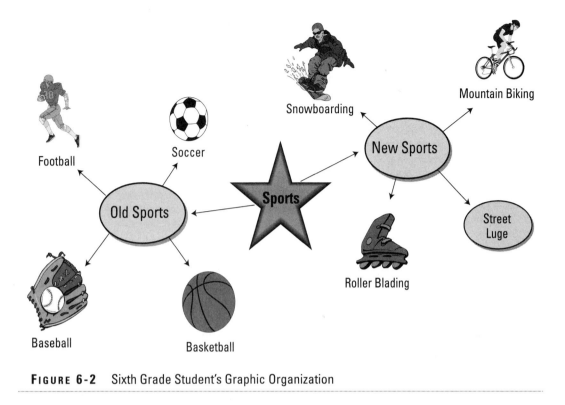

Football

Soccer

Snowboarding

Mountain Biking

New Sports

Old Sports

Sports

Street Luge

Roller Blading

Baseball

Basketball

FIGURE 6-2 Sixth Grade Student's Graphic Organization

The use of graphic organizer software such as *Inspiration* is, of course, influenced by a variety of factors including the goals of the teacher, the number of computers in the classroom, and the availability of classroom presentation hardware, to name a few. Another important variable is whether the software is being used by the teacher, the students, or by both teacher and students. For example, in one application a teacher with a single computer in her classroom and no access to presentation hardware might use the software to create and reproduce blank *concept maps* for students to complete. The teacher could then take the hard copies of the students' work and employ the software to create finished handouts to be used by the students as they continue their study, write a paper, or prepare for a quiz or test.

In contrast, a teacher working in a classroom with four computers all running the desired software might engage cooperative learning groups in using the software to classify and label their own data sets. With the availability of presentation hardware, each group could then make a whole class presentation of their work providing the rationale for how and why they classified the terms. Finally, while interacting with the students and their maps the teacher could use the software to edit or expand the students' work.

Grade Level Modifications

Teachers at all grade levels could use Inspiration to develop concept formation lessons. The software is user friendly for students in the upper elementary, intermediate and secondary grades. Kindergarten through 3rd grade teachers desiring to engage their students in using a similar tool specifically tailored for the primary grades will want to explore Kidspiration. This program, developed by the same company that created Inspiration, provides younger children with ways to express and organize their thinking.

Low Tech/High Tech Applications

Using graphic organizer software to generate and manipulate concept maps or webs can be a low- or high-tech application, depending on how it is integrated into lesson design and on what functions of the software are employed. With any software program, teachers and students need to acquire the essential knowledge and skills prerequisite to effective use. Once the fundamentals are grasped, however, users can produce basic maps and other graphics while experimenting with the software's more sophisticated tools.

One intriguing high-tech application now possible with *Inspiration* involves embedding live hyperlinks in a graphic organizer. Utilizing this feature, teachers or students can create seamless connections to the resources of the World Wide Web, opening a whole new range of teaching and learning possibilities.

Value Added for Diverse Learners

Utilizing graphic organizer software to support the concept formation strategy represents a technology enhancement that offers the following benefits for diverse learners. Kinesthetic/tactile learners are likely to be more engaged when provided the opportunity to interact with a computer keyboard to manipulate the software. Such software also supports students in expressing their aesthetic dispositions by providing a wide variety of pictures and graphics to accentuate their maps and webs. Students motivated by visual stimuli and imagery will especially profit by seeing their thinking portrayed in such an attractive and formalized way. *Inspiration* allows teachers to print posters of student maps or webs so they can be displayed in the classroom and school community. Finally, using computer-based graphic organizers should especially stimulate students who possess visual-spatial skills or those who prefer part-to-whole approaches to problem solving.

Web-Based Resources

Teachers working in school buildings or districts that have not purchased *Inspiration* or *Kidspiration* may download thirty-day trial versions of the software by going to http://www.inspiration.com. The Web site also provides a free tutorial to help teachers quickly use the sample program they download. This is a rich Web site that in addition to providing the free downloads offers many examples of how teachers from diverse grade levels and disciplines have used the software in their classes. The website also provides information on two books teachers may find particularly helpful: *Classroom Ideas Using Inspiration* and *Meeting Standards with Inspiration* are practical guides designed to help teachers integrate visual learning strategies at various grade levels and across academic disciplines.

⑤UMMARY

Concept formation is one of three different instructional strategies (or cognitive tasks) that Hilda Taba (1966) identifies as useful in enhancing the thinking skills of students. The other two strategies are interpretation of data, which we allude to in Chapter 5, "Inquiry," and application of principle, which Taba suggests has a very specialized function:

> The essence of this task [application of principle] is using information already possessed to explain something new, to predict consequences of events, or to hypothesize about causes and effects. For example, if one knows what a desert is, the way of life a desert permits and how water affects agricultural production, one can predict what might happen to the desert way of life if water became available. While interpreting and generalizing from raw data [concept formation] is an inductive process, applying known facts and generalizations is a deductive process. (p. 41)

We emphasize the concept formation strategy because it fosters requisite inductive thinking skills and because teachers generally find it quite easy to learn and use. Concept formation is also motivational for students because it enables them to explore their own understandings about an idea or topic. Students pursue personal questions and create their own constructs; as a consequence, the teacher is able to see how students are "putting together" an idea. In Piagetian terms, the teacher actually views the schema of the students.

Teachers who use concept formation note that the type and level of student participation is very different from what is found in a traditional lesson. Because there are no necessarily correct responses, students are much freer to explore personal ideas and perspectives. Some "nonparticipation" students seem more willing to take a risk once they know that their constructed concept is just as valid as the ideas created by other students, especially if they can effectively and appropriately defend their answers.

ⓇEFERENCES

Arends, R. 1994. *Learning to Teach*. Boston: McGraw Hill.

Borich, G. 1988. *Effective Teaching Methods*. Columbus, OH: Merrill.

Brown, R. 1973. "Taba Rediscovered." *Science Teacher* 40(8): 30–33.

Etzioni, A. 2001. *The Monochrome Society*. Princeton, NJ: Princeton University Press.

Haberman, M., and L. Post. 1995. "Multicultural Teaching in the Real World." Pp. 337–353 in A. C. Ornstein (ed.), *Teaching: Theory and Practice*. Boston: Allyn & Bacon.

Hale-Benson, J. 1982. *Black Children: Their Roots, Culture, and Learning Styles.* Baltimore: Johns Hopkins University Press.

Hyerle, D. 1996. *Visual Tools.* Washington, DC: Association for Supervision and Curriculum Development.

Irvine, J. J., and B. J. Armento. 2001. *Culturally Responsive Teaching.* Boston: McGraw Hill.

Morgan, H. 1981. "Factors Concerning Cognitive Development and Learning Differentiation Among Black Children." Pp. 14–22 in A. E. Harrison (ed.), *Conference on Empirical Research in Black Psychology 6.*

Newmann, F. M., and G. G. Wehlage. 1993. "Five Standards of Authentic Instruction." *Educational Leadership* 50(7): 8–12.

Nieto, S. 1996. *Affirming Diversity* (2nd ed.). New York: Congman.

Parker, W. C. 1987. "Teaching Thinking: The Pervasive Approach." *Journal of Teacher Education* 38(3): 50–56.

Prom, S. E. 1982. "Salient Content and Cognitive Performance of Person- and Thing-Oriented Low Income Afro-American Children in Kindergarten and Second Grade." Doctoral dissertation, Howard University, Washington, DC.

Reich, R. 2001. "Standards for What?" *Education Week* 20(41), June 20, p. 64.

Shade, B. J. 1984. "Afro-American Patterns of Cognition: A Review of the Research." Paper presented at annual meeting of American Educational Research Association, New Orleans, LA.

———. 1989. "The Influence of Perceptual Development on Cognitive Style: Cross Ethnic Comparisons." *Early Child Development and Care* 51: 137–155.

———, and P. A. Edwards. 1987. "Ecological Correlates of the Educative Style of Afro-American Children." *Journal of Negro Education* 86: 88–99.

Soldier, L. 1989. "Cooperative Learning and the Native American Student." *Phi Delta Kappan* 71(2): 161–163.

Sparks-Langer, G. M., M. Pasch, A. J. Starko, C. D. Moody, and T. G. Gardner. 2000. *Teaching as Decisionmaking.* Upper Saddle River, NJ: Merrill Prentice Hall.

Taba, H. 1966. *Teaching Strategies and Cognitive Functioning in Elementary School Children.* Cooperative Research Project 2404. San Francisco: San Francisco State College.

Vasquez, J. A. 1991. "Cognitive Style and Academic Attainment." Pp. 163–179 in J. Lynch, C. Modgil, and S. Modgil (eds.), *Cultural Diversity and the Schools: Consensus and Controversy.* London: Falconer Press.

Whimbey, A. 1977. "Teaching Sequential Thought: The Cognitive Skills Approach." *Phi Delta Kappan* 58: 255–259.

Wiederhold, C., and S. Kagan. 1992. "Cooperative Questioning and Critical Thinking." P. 203 in N. Davidson and T. Worsham (eds.), *Enhancing Thinking Through Cooperative Learning.* New York: Teacher's College Press.

Wiggins, G., and J. McTighte. 2000. *Understanding By Design.* Washington D.C: Association of Supervision and Curriculum Development.

Synectics

Chapter Objectives

At the end of this chapter, readers will be able to

1. *Identify the basic phases associated with the synectics model.*
2. *Identify the strengths and weaknesses of synectics.*
3. *Understand the theoretical and empirical grounding for the synectics model.*
4. *Evaluate lessons that use synectics strategies.*
5. *Create a lesson using synectics to help students creatively think through content material.*

❶NTRODUCTION

No cultural group holds the patent on creativity. A quick perusal of eminent individuals who have evidenced excellence in their personal performance and who have been creative in their exploration of ideas illustrates that regardless of personal or cultural background, creative ideas are possible. In literature the names range from Toni Morrison (African American) to Amy Tan (Asian American) to Gerald Viznor (Native American) to Jose Antonio Villarreal (Hispanic American). With regard to mathematical reasoning the names include Benjamin Bannecker (African American), Yuan Lee (Asian American), Luis Alverez (Hispanic American), and Robert Whitman (Native American). In essence, cultural background neither advantages nor disadvantages the capacity for creative thought. Some individuals may be more creative than others, but a genetic cultural advantage cannot be claimed by any group.

Creative thinking is a by-product of how students learn to explore ideas. Although some argue that creative problem-solving cannot be taught (see Torrance, 1986), many others assert that students can learn how to think creatively if they use "disciplined" techniques for thinking through problems. Synectics is one such step-by-step technique. It is a technique that can be used by all students, not just those who claim the status of "gifted" or "talented." Indeed, one of the real advantages of synectics is that all students can participate in the creative process because creativity is more broadly defined as "everyday thinking that results in something new, either to the person doing the thing or to the world" (Weaver and Prince, 1990, p. 379). A definition such as this suggests that everyone has an ability to think about old ideas in new ways. The

Every human being has this creative urge as his or her birthright. It can be squelched and corrupted, but it cannot be completely extinguished.

MIHALY CSIKSZENTMIHALYI

203

essence of the creative process is for each individual to make new connections that make personal sense and enhance personal perspective.

Teachers tend to make conceptual connections for students. They create the conceptual structures; students are expected to memorize those structures and, on demand (through tests), give back what has previously been given to them by the teacher. The intellectual "cost" of this approach for many students is substantial. As Weaver and Prince (1990) argue, it tends to "foreclose on many promising lines of thought. [Students in these types of classrooms have] . . . a way of thinking that seems to be reinforced by an emphasis on precision, on right and wrong answers, and on punishment for mistakes" (p. 379). Many suggest that high stakes testing is exacerbating the conformist thinking of students. Ovando (2001) writes:

> Unfortunately, high-stakes testing, such as TAAS [the Texas proficiency test] often forces administrators to sacrifice creativity and inspiration in teaching and learning for the top-down pressure to coach students to do well on these tests. Schools that meet or exceed established test criteria are rewarded monetarily and with kudos in the Rio Grande Valley. Students who do well on the TAAS, and thus make the schools look good, are given favorable press in the local and state media and sometimes receive personal awards. Conversely, teachers and administrators whose schools underperform on the TAAS exams jeopardize their careers—and in extreme cases the future of their schools. (p. 30)

Whether TAAS compromises student creativity is debatable but that creativity is important for future American citizens is not. As the following simulated 4th grade classroom example illustrates, creative problem-solving can occur in lots of different contexts and does not mean an absence of intellectual rigor. Rather, it is a way of enabling students to see (and reinforce) the familiar in new and more intellectually demanding ways.

CASE STUDY

"Class, we have been studying the earth for the past week, and you are developing some good understandings about the structure of our planet. Today I want you to look at the earth in a slightly different way. Specifically, I'm going to suggest that the earth is like a peach." At this point the teacher, Mr. Rodriguez, gives a peach to each of the student pairs (students are working in groups of two) and asks them to cut open the peach and look at its various parts.

"Before you explore my idea, my analogy, I want you to list all the things that you know about the earth on the left side of the paper I'm providing you, and all the things you know about peaches on the right side." The students fill in the chart (the final product of one student group looks like the one provided in Figure 7-1). Mr. Rodriguez then has students review their charts, and several additional items are added that students think make sense but that go beyond obvious ideas (see Figure 7-1 below the dashed lines).

The Earth	The Peach
mantle	fuzz
outer (liquid) core	pit
inner (solid) core	juice
crust	pulp
Mohorovic boundary	bruise
faults	----------
rocks	stem
----------	
seismograph	
primary waves	
secondary waves	
epicenter	

FIGURE 7-1   Synectics Brainstorming Chart

Mr. Rodriguez then continues the lesson. "Excellent! You have really generated a tremendous number of good ideas. Now let's go back to my original idea. I asked you to consider that the earth is a lot like a peach. How is that true? In what ways is the earth like a peach? With your peer partner, identify three ways that the earth is like a peach." The students work together in pairs for a couple of minutes, and then Mr. Rodriguez asks them to share their ideas.

"Roberto, why don't you share one of your ideas?"

"The earth is like a peach because they both have hard centers. The peach has a pit, and the earth has a solid core."

"Good," responds Mr. Rodriguez. "In fact, the core makes up about 15 percent of the earth's total volume, and the pit looks like it is about the same volume for the peach. Another idea, Portia?"

"The earth has a mantle, and the peach is made up of pulp. The mantle is very thick for the earth, and the pulp is most of the peach."

"Do you recall what the mantle is made up of?"

"Yes, rocks," replies Portia. The students continue to make several comparisons before Mr. Rodriguez stops them. He puts each comparison on the board as students suggest other ideas.

"You have really developed some terrific ideas. Now I want you all to close your eyes. Think with me for a few minutes about what it must be like to be the earth. Picture yourself as the earth, a living thing. People are drilling holes in you. They are building big buildings on you. They are polluting you with pesticides. Tell me now how you feel. And when you make your statement, be sure to start with the words, 'I feel.'. . . In other words, say something like 'I feel happy because people need my resources in order to live.' OK? (The teacher then pauses for a moment.) Ernesto, why don't you start us off."

Ernesto responds, "I feel hurt because the people keep drilling more and more holes in me. They take out my crude oil and then create pollution."

"Sarah?"

"I feel bruised because of the strip mining that occurs. They keep scraping away more and more of my surface. It's painful."

"Minda. What do you feel?"

"I feel used. People appear to have no concern for who I am."

Mr. Rodriguez allows the students to develop their ideas for almost 10 minutes and then says, "Now I want you to think what it must be like to be a peach. Share your ideas with me. Aurora?"

"I feel hurt when they pick me off the tree. It feels so good to grow on the tree and have the wind blow against me. Then some guy puts his big hand on me and pulls me off." (Several students laugh and poke fun at Aurora.)

"Luis."

"I feel . . . "

The lesson continues with the students articulating how they feel to be a peach.

"Now that you've shared how it feels to be a peach and the earth, I want you to think about the differences between a peach and the earth. In what ways are peaches and the earth different? We agreed that in some ways they are similar. Now consider ways in which they are different. Work with your partners to generate three differences."

The students work for several minutes, and the teacher then asks them to share their ideas.

The first student, Tara, suggests that the peach grows on a tree but that the earth doesn't grow on anything.

Another student, Javier, shares that a peach can be used in preparing meals, but the earth (the dirt) cannot be eaten.

The students share lots of ideas. On occasion, some students argue points—one student points out that the earth is part of the solar system, and that's like the peach being part of the tree.

After much sharing, the teacher asks the students to think of other objects to compare to the earth that they like better than a peach. Students work in their groups and generate an example that they like better, including an explanation of why their analogy is a good one. Many students use other fruits. Some, though, use other objects. One asserts that the earth is like a baseball because the surface is rough and has seams (like mountains), has an inner substance that is hard (like rocks in the mantle), and so on.

At the end of the lesson, the students are asked to read a section from the text on plate tectonics and to create a chart regarding the volume, density, and mass of the earth's different components. The students must also draw a diagram of the earth and of their analog. (See Figure 7-2 for a student example.)

Finally they are asked to prepare a short essay that describes why they agree with or disagree with strip mining as a way of extracting valuable ores from the earth.

Mr. Rodriguez uses synectics to help students understand the structure of the earth in a new and unique way. The teacher and students possess a substantial content knowledge base, but they are examining the concepts and facts in unique ways. ■

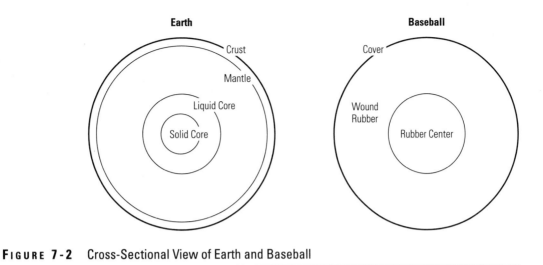

FIGURE 7-2   Cross-Sectional View of Earth and Baseball

THEORETICAL PERSPECTIVE

The basis of synectics is helping students see old ideas in new ways. Synectics creates within the students an excitement about concepts that are both familiar and unfamiliar. Students may not, and hopefully would not, be as excited as Archimedes was when he discovered the principle of fluid displacement (supposedly he jumped out of his bathtub and ran down the street, *naked*, yelling "Eureka!"), but they can begin to attach new meanings to familiar ideas. And those new meanings can foster a new enthusiasm for ideas.

The etymology of synectics traces to its Greek roots: *syn* means to bring together and *ectics* refers to diverse elements (Weaver and Prince, 1990). At the heart of a synectics lesson is the teacher's ability to use various forms of metaphoric thinking such as similes, metaphors, personification, and oxymorons. Metaphorical thinking causes students to look at reality in different ways—it shatters conventional views. This shattering process is perhaps the weakest aspect of the American educational system. American schools foster at least three different types of thinking: appositional, divergent, and generative. Unfortunately, too much emphasis is placed on the first type (appositional), and too little emphasis is placed on generative. *Appositional thinking* occurs, according to Weaver and Prince (1990), when students "limit their trial connections to material that is close to the problem" (p. 380). American students are seemingly preoccupied with relevance issues—How does this fact help me? When will I use this? It is not that appositional thinkers lack content understandings, they just censor their thinking in ways that limit their full exploration of ideas. They have, in essence, a very "low tolerance for anything that does not seem pertinent" (Weaver and Prince, 1990, p. 380).

Divergent thinking often creates instructional problems for teachers. When students think divergently, they develop a wide variety of ideas, but their intellectual leaps frequently fail to pay positive cognitive dividends because they do not see the conceptual connections between ideas. Of course, in some instances this is quite acceptable, especially when the teacher wants to involve all students in a lesson but is not particularly concerned that they reach a specific conclusion or analyze data in a distinctive manner.

Synectics fosters *generative thinking*. The generative thinker "is open to divergent beginnings but eagerly searches for connections to make ideas more workable" (Weaver and Prince, 1990, p. 380). Certainly synectics is not the only way to foster generative thinking, but because of its step-by-step nature (its almost linear, sequential structure), it is one of the best ways to enable students to see how ideas connect.

Synectics was first introduced by William Gordon (1961). Gordon's notion was that creativity was and is a fundamental part of everyday activity. It is not a special ability, but if fostered properly by the teacher, it can be extremely useful in enhancing the problem-solving potential of students, indeed of all people regardless of their role. In addition, Gordon argued that "students" (or all learners) need to know that the creative process is not the exclusive domain of a "privileged" few. All students have an ability to be creative if they understand the process of creative thought and if they learn some strategies for engaging in creative problem-solving. Finally, because creative exploration is not necessarily the "right" of one student, it is possible for students to learn how to be creative both individually and cooperatively. Indeed, both individuals and groups can learn to create ideas in very similar ways if they understand how to make conceptual "excursions." An excursion is nothing more than a process of seeing problems in new ways. Weaver and Prince (1990) provide a more detailed description:

> There are three simple steps in using excursions. First, put the problem temporarily out of mind. This enables one to get distance from the problem he or she is working on. Second, deliberately focus on apparent irrelevancy. This can generate surprising or unusual connections. Third, force-fit the irrelevant material together with the problem and allow your mind to invent a way of connecting them. Force-fitting is a trick of the mind. Our mind automatically struggles to fit new connections into an existing pattern or, failing that, to create a new pattern. Being open to that new pattern or line of thought will enable us to produce ideas that are both useful and original. (p. 384)

This description provides the reader with a general framework for creative excursions. The following description (Synectics I), which is structured similarly to that of Mr. Rodriguez's lesson on the earth's structure, is a simplification of the synectics process and also parallels the one proffered by the Association for Supervision and Curriculum Development ("Teaching Strategies Library: Part Two"). A second description (Synectics II) is also provided; it more closely matches a conceptualization of Gordon's (1961) work as represented by Joyce, Weil and Calhoun (2000) and Gunter, Estes, and Schwab (1995).

⑤YNECTICS I: TEACHING PHASES

Phase I: Identification of Topic Area

The synectics lesson begins once the teacher determines what concept the students should fully explore. Typically, the teacher will want students to develop a fuller, richer understanding of some big idea. If the class has been studying the respiratory system, the teacher might want students to focus on respiration and to understand in new ways how respiratory functions parallel what happens in other types of complex systems. In essence, the first step in synectics is to identify what concept, ideas, or knowledge structures require fuller exploration and development by the class.

How will the teacher know what ideas require such exploration? Through intuition and experience! Teachers who use synectics see it as a way of helping students see "*old*" ideas in new ways. The history of ideas is filled with examples of people who evidenced this ability for creative insight, except they seemed to do it almost naturally: Copernicus thought about the earth's relationship to the sun in ways that contradicted other astronomers; Freud thought about dreams in ways quite different from those who preceded him (that is, he describes manifest dreams, the actual imagery of a dream, latent dreams, and the hidden meaning of the imagery). Students, in synectics, begin to think about the earth or cells or respiration in new ways, and their revelations represent new understandings.

Phase II: Direct Analogy

Once the teacher identifies what concept to extend and explore, the teacher then creates a direct analogy. A direct analogy is nothing more than a metaphoric comparison between two ideas (one the concept and the other an analog). For the respiratory system, a direct analogy might be "How are a train and train track like the respiratory system?" Recall that Mr. Rodriguez offered the direct analogy of "*The earth is like a peach.*"

Many teachers find it difficult to identify *perfect* direct analogies. That's because few, if any, perfect analogies exist. All objects differ in some ways; as a result, all efforts to create comparisons that reveal objects as identical in every way will fall short of the ideal. As Joyce, Weil and Calhoun (2000) note, "the real purpose of a direct analogy is to transpose the condition of the real topic or problem situation to another situation in order to present a new view of an idea or problem" (p. 224).

The teacher poses the direct analogy and asks students to think of (1) all the characteristics of the conceptual object, (2) all the characteristics of the analog, and (3) all the ways that they are analogous. A simple example follows for "An opera is like a football game" (see Table 7-1), which incidentally, is a direct analogy that one of the authors used while teaching a synectics lesson on opera to adults in Vienna, Austria—the goal was to enable the students to think about operas in a different way.

TABLE 7-1   Analogical Comparison for Opera and Football Game

Characteristics of Opera	Characteristics of Football Game	Comparison
Costumes	Uniforms	An opera is like a football game because in an opera the performers wear costumes, and in a football game the players wear uniforms.
Acts	Quarters	An opera is like a football game because in an opera there are acts, and in a football game there are quarters.
Diva	Quarterback	An opera is like a football game because both have "stars"—in an opera the soprano who sings the lead role is called a diva; in a football game the star is called the quarterback.

Students are expected to make a list of the characteristics of the object and the analog. Once exhaustive lists of individual characteristics are developed, they then make the comparisons. Some teachers find it useful actually to write out the comparisons; others rely on verbal representations.

Phase III: Personal Analogy

Once students have an understanding of the direct analogy, they then attempt to "lose themselves" in the concept. This is both an exciting and a challenging step for students—though much depends on how the teacher organizes and orchestrates the experience. The teacher needs to be able to sell this idea to the students by asking them to become the conceptual object and the analog. Recall that Mr. Rodriguez started this phase by stating, *"You have really developed some terrific ideas. Now I want you all to close your eyes. Think with me for a few minutes about what it must be like to be the earth. Picture yourself as the earth, a living thing . . ."* The students then go on to share their ideas. One student, Ernesto, responds that "I feel hurt because the people keep drilling more and more holes in me." Ernesto's response is a first-person description of an emotion—he feels hurt. But students can, according to Gordon (1961), describe other first-person sentiments as well. They may provide factual descriptions, like the student, Sarah, who felt bruised because of all the strip mining that occurs on her "surface." Or the student might have an empathic response similar to Minda's. Minda shared that she felt exploited and that she identified with the earth as an organic object. Personal analogies release the creative impulses and enhance the intellectual vitality of the individual. Gordon (1961) writes, "Personal identification with the elements of a problem releases the individual from viewing the problem in terms of its previously analyzed elements" (p. 37).

The teacher should encourage students to become both the analog and the object. As students express their ideas, the teacher lists the description, emotions, facts, or empathic feelings on poster board or on the chalkboard. This helps students see the commonalities associated with their feelings; it also is essential if teachers decide to use a compressed conflict strategy, which we will describe in the alternative model Synectics II section.

Phase IV: Analog Contrast

In the fourth phase, the student begins to contrast the analog and the conceptual object. As we shared earlier, no metaphoric comparison is perfect. All comparisons fall short in some ways! Thus, in the fourth phase, students begin to examine differences between the analog and the concept. Mr. Rodriguez offers the following as a transition to phase IV: "Now that you've shared how it feels to be a peach and the earth, I want you to think about the differences between a peach and the earth. In what ways are peaches and the earth different? We agreed that in some ways they are similar. Now consider ways in which they are different. Work with your partners to generate three differences."

One problematic statement that teachers use (and it is especially noticeable on the Association for Supervision and Curriculum Development Teaching Strategies tapes) is to say something similar to this: "Class, we have been studying how the earth is like a peach. But is the earth really like a peach? No. I don't think so. Let's look at all the differences." Such a statement ("No. I don't think so.") implicitly says to the students: "I lied to you earlier. I said the earth was like a peach. Now I'm telling you that it's not." The teacher can create the contrast without being so pedagogically duplicitous. Teachers should simply share with students that conceptual objects and analogs are both alike and different. In the previous two phases the similarities are emphasized. In phase IV the students examine and list the differences. Encourage the students to write down statements that describe these differences and then have them share those with the class. Recall that Tara (from Mr. Rodriguez's class) noted that a peach grows on a tree, but that the earth does not grow on anything.

Phase V: New Analogy

Once students have examined both similarities (phases II and III) and differences (phase IV) between the conceptual objects and the analog, they are ready to create their own direct analogy, which is hopefully conceptually stronger than the original direct analogy. Most teachers who have conducted a synectics lesson observe that at some point during the implementation of a synectics lesson either they or the students think of metaphoric ideas that they like better than the one originally presented. Phase V provides an opportunity to explore new metaphoric possibilities. In phase V, the teacher asks the students to generate their own analogs. Mr. Rodriguez has the students work in groups in this phase as a way of stimulating more ideas. This is a good way to proceed, especially if students are using the model for the first time. As students develop more comfort with this instructional model, it will become more possible to have them work either independently or in cooperative learning groups to think of analogies that make sense.

Phase VI: Topic Refocus

Once students have finished the activity, the teacher should return to the original theme or conceptual topic and have students provide their reflections. Mr. Rodriguez had his students write a short essay that described their support for or opposition to strip mining. Synectics lessons should immeasurably enhance the type of language used by students to express their ideas and attitudes. Essay responses, of course, are not the only refocusing tasks a teacher might use (for example, the students might watch a movie on strip mining and orally discuss their reactions or go on a field trip to a rock quarry and take pictures of the effects of mining). The critical dimension is to make certain that students return to the original topic in order to "play with" the concept in a different way.

ⓈYNECTICS II: TEACHING PHASES

The Synectics I lesson structure just outlined is a relatively simple form of the creative process encouraged by Gordon (1961). Many teachers find Synectics I a good one to start with when they first begin to use creative-thinking activities in the classroom. A second form of synectics, which some teachers we have worked with describe as more complex, requires the use of a compressed conflict. In this approach the teacher intentionally fosters contradictory ideas, but this is done in such a way that it enables students to formulate familiar ideas in new and creative ways. Many of the phases are similar to those outlined in Synectics I. However, some significant differences do exist, and these, in particular, will be given a more detailed description. The case study in the sample lessons section at the end of this chapter is an example of the compressed conflict approach.

Phase I: The Topic

The teacher begins a compressed conflict synectics lesson in a similar fashion to that described in Synectics I. The students typically have spent some time prior to the synectics lesson trying to understand some specific content material. For example, they may have been studying a topic such as revolutions or cell structure or natural resources. Whatever the topic, the teacher begins by having students share descriptive words or phrases that they associate with the topic. The teacher then writes these terms on the chalkboard as they are being shared.

Phase II: Direct Analogy

Once all the terms are listed, the teacher begins to create a direct analogy. In the Synectics I lesson, Mr. Rodriguez provided the direct analogy. *In this instructional variation, the students are responsible for creating the metaphoric idea.*

The process begins when the teacher asks the students to look at the terms on the board and then think of a *game, plant,* or *machine* that they would associate with those terms. For example, for *opera* the students might begin by generating the descriptive terms in Table 7-2.

TABLE 7-2   Descriptive Terms for Opera

Long	Treachery
Several acts	Expensive
Costumes	Hatred
Music	Lots of people
Singing	

TABLE 7-3   Personal Analogy Statements

Tired because the game is so long.	**Dirty** because I'm muddy after the game.
Beautiful because my costume or uniform is so expensive.	**Protected** because of my equipment.
	Energized because of the cheering audience.

When one of the authors taught a lesson on opera, students were asked to think of a game that had the identified qualities (that is, was long, involved costumes, and so on). They generated a long list of potential analogical ideas that included things like the following:

Baseball because the games are long, the players wear uniforms, and so on.

Hockey because the players seem to hate one another and have to wear cumbersome, expensive uniforms.

Football because of the pageantry and the large number of people who watch in the stadium.

Based on the many game options generated, the students were then asked to identify their favorite possibility among all those generated by the class—in the case of the lesson on opera, the author's class selected football: An opera is like a football game! This analogy was then written on the board and became the foundation for the next phase of the lesson. Incidentally, make certain all the students know the game. On a couple of occasions, teachers have selected a game (for example, chess) for the class to use only to discover that many students did not know how to play. That makes the next phase almost impossible to operationalize.

Phase III: Personal Analogy

This phase parallels what occurs in phase III of the Synectics I variation. Essentially, the students describe what it feels like to be the object and the analog. In the case of the opera and football game analogy, students would describe what it feels like to be a football game, and the teacher writes the terms down as students provide them. The terms in Table 7-3 are provided for the opera and football game analogy. Notice that the students provide a brief explanation justifying the term. The teacher should solicit student responses and require that students defend their responses with a "because" statement.

Phase IV: Compressed Conflict

Teachers who read about using compressed conflict often find the notion of combining words that are in dynamic tension with one another to be an overly complex process. But teachers who have enabled students to use compressed conflict find it to be very effective in fostering creative thought on the part of the students. With compressed conflict, the teacher has the students look at the descriptive terms used during the personal analogy phase (phase III) and then combine those terms that tend to be opposite one another. For example, beautiful and dirty or tired and energized. That is, things are not normally thought of as being both beautiful and dirty, but a football coach would perceive a lineman as "beautiful" if his uniform is dirty at the end of a game.

The students combine words that conceptually (and dynamically) fit together (for example, beautiful and dirty are adjectives describing how one looks), yet are contradictory when found in nature (that is, how can one be both beautiful and dirty?). The teacher has the students generate as many compressed conflicts as they can identify. The students should then vote about which of the compressed conflicts they like the best. In this instance, let us assume that beautiful and dirty are selected.

Phase V: New Analogy

The teacher next asks the students to create a new direct analogy. The teacher takes the compressed conflict (beautiful and dirty) and has students identify some object (animal or machine or food) that has these compressed conflict qualities. The object (animal or machine or food) does nothing more than provide a focus for the students' ideas—it keeps their ideas somewhat together in the pattern of their thinking. The options developed in this case might be:

- An engine in a car (the engine is dirty, but the car is beautiful)
- A "dirt" cake as a dessert (the cake looks messy once eaten, but it is beautiful just before the dessert is cut and distributed)

After students generate a number of new possibilities, the teacher then asks them to select the one they like the best. (Usually students reach some sort of consensus, but the teacher may need to do some modest "directing" to make certain all students understand the selected new analogy.) In this case, the students select "an engine in a car."

Phase VI: Topic Refocus

In this phase, the teacher begins to revisit the original topic. If the original topic was the students' perceptions of the opera, then the teacher asks the students to consider how the opera (the topic) is like an engine in a car (the new analog). The students then generate as many ideas as possible—actually this process usually starts slowly, and then as some students see possibilities (that is, other students create ideas), the rest of the students in the class become more generative in their thinking. For instance,

An opera needs music, and a car requires gasoline.

An opera needs a conductor, and a car requires a driver.

Phase VII: Extension

After students have generated a substantial list of new ideas concerning the concept, the teacher should begin to critically extend some of the students' ideas. The teacher might, for example, have students write a description of what it means to "run" an opera, or to develop a report on all the different elements that need to be in place if an opera is to be "run" effectively.

Some teachers get to phase VI and let the lesson drop. This significantly mitigates the power of this instructional model. The model is intended to stimulate student thinking about a topic, and unless the teacher intentionally extends the students' thoughts about the topic and forces them to reexamine that topic, the full impact of the lesson will not be achieved. Remember synectics is not a gimmick or game. It is, instead, a pedagogical vehicle for enhancing the quality of student thought.

Ⓐ PPLICATIONS TO DIVERSE CLASSROOMS

Synectics embraces the fundamental notion that not all learners are the same, but that all learners are able to think creatively. Students make sense out of their environment in different ways; they construct meaning based on their experiences and their individual, unique interactions with the ideas presented by the teacher. A number of professional organizations (for example, National Science Teacher's Association, National Council for the Social Studies) have presented the notion that schools should espouse and implement a "less is more" philosophy. They implicitly suggest that schools are endeavoring to cover too much material too quickly. The issue for teachers becomes one of understanding how to develop lessons that extend learning opportunities for students. Teachers tacitly ask: How can I extend my lesson once students seem to understand the ideas that I think are important? How can I enable students to "play with" the ideas? Synectics is one way of substantively extending the way in which students experiment with ideas, and it does so in a way that uses the background experiences of each child.

The students in synectics use their own images and ideas to make sense out of the world. The teacher, in turn, uses what he or she knows about the content and the learner to make ideas "come to life." This is what is proposed by Foster (1993), Henry (1990), and Ladson-Billings (1994, 2001), to name a few, when they suggest that the culture of the school should utilize the ideas, resources, and experiences of the local community. Ladson-Billings (2001) writes:

In my conception of culturally relevant pedagogy these components are reflected in the academic achievement proposition of the theory. Certainly, every teacher should know the content. Elementary teachers need to know enough mathematics, English, science, and social studies to provide rigorous intellectual experiences for their students. They also need to know their students and know how their students learn. Finally, they need to know the unique aspects of teaching particular subjects. How one teaches mathematics is different from how one teaches history. Culturally relevant teachers adjust their teaching to meet the demands of both the learners and the subject matter disciplines. (p. 75)

The relationship between the culture of the community and the culture of the school has many powerful positive effects upon learning. This instructional model is one strategy that facilitates such a dynamic relationship. The teacher may begin with a direct analogy, which reflects the teacher's schema, but the students subsequently create their own analogs that evolve out of their own experiences (the students' schema). Metaphoric thinking is intensely personal because students have to transcend impersonal concepts in ways that have personal meaning: How does it feel to be the earth? Gardner (1995) talks about the "personalization of education"; it is education based on such propositions as "we are not all the same; we do not all have the same kind of minds; education works most effectively for most individuals if . . . differences in mentation and strengths are taken into account . . ." (p. 208). Synectics takes such differences into account. Indeed, the model encourages divergent and generative thinking in ways that warrant the uniqueness of each child. Synectics fosters many different types of thinking. Students who are both field-dependent and field-independent can benefit, though field-independent may find they respond better to Synectics II, which allows students to create more of the analogs; field-dependent may respond better to Synectics I, which is structured around a teacher-initiated metaphor. Good and Brophy (1995) write: "More generally, field-independent people are likely to impose their own organization on a perceptual field, but field-dependent people tend to adhere to the existing structure" (p. 529).

Another advantage of synectics is the way teachers can use different intelligences and different learning modalities as part of a synectics lesson. For example, one teacher who taught the circulatory system by using the metaphor that the circulatory system is like a railroad actually had students moving around the room like a train while other students acted as gates (valves). She appeared to want them to "feel" it before they studied it. It is also an interesting way to bring kinesthetic learning into students' understandings of a somewhat abstract concept, the circulatory system.

In synectics, students are expected to be creative, to think divergently, and to express their own ideas. During the past decade, there has been a real movement toward conceptual reductionism, often encouraged by a high stakes testing movement that puts a premium on student test performance. School policymakers attempt to assuage public demands for accountability by focusing on more and more definable and discrete pieces of information (that is, assessing basic skills). Such a circumstance is regrettable because it places students in the vulnerable position of robotically responding to stimuli rather than personally creating meaning and experiencing enjoyment out of what they have learned. Interestingly, the Center for Educational Policy (2001) suggests that part of the achievement gap between black and white students is because of the low expectations placed on far too many minority students. The intent of synectics is to create personal meaning and engage students in more complex problem-solving. The cultural background of the student becomes an asset in such a setting. The goal of the student is not to think like the teacher. Rather, the goal is to look at ideas, whether in relationship to cell structure or revolutions or plate tectonics, in new and different ways, to momentarily suspend the reality of the known with the possibilities of the imagination. When that happens, students see old ideas in new ways and are able to explore the inherent complexity of ideas in ways that reveal more personal meaning. To use Gordon's (1961) terms, they can make either the strange familiar or the familiar strange.

ⓅREVALENT ISSUES IN DIVERSE CLASSROOMS

Teachers who use synectics for the first time are often perplexed by the model—they argue that the steps are difficult to keep track of. Indeed, many teachers we have worked with describe the model as too complicated for students to understand. It is true that synectics can be somewhat complicated, but once teachers have used the model and have understood the inherent structure of the model, they usually feel much more comfortable and confident. The only way to overcome pedagogical discomfort is to practice the model on more than one occasion. Still, even with experience, some problems will emerge. Those problems require that the teacher more fully challenge students by showing them that creativity is an important part of school life.

Q: *How do I deal with students who think that the personal analogy stage is ludicrous?*

A: In our observations of and conversations with teachers, those who have had the most difficulty with the personal analogy stage are teachers who do not see the value in this stage themselves. In essence, it seems that their students embrace the feelings that the teacher projects. Young children and even those in the middle grades seem to have no difficulty with using personal analogies—with becoming the analog and the concept themselves; they can suspend reality and pretend they are something else. Older students, especially those who are very analytical, are often the toughest "sell" because they do not see that using personal analogies represents real learning. For these students, real learning is assimilating new content material, not exploring ideas. Indeed, some "bright" students may not like the model because the teacher is not really "teaching"— telling them facts.

Teachers who work with older students frequently find it useful to have students close their eyes and visualize the metaphoric ideas. Other teachers use concrete objects to facilitate the students' thinking. For example, one teacher who was using the novel *The Pinballs* by Betsy Byars to help students explore their emotions described that emotions are like pinballs. She brought in some handheld pinball machines and then had students engage in personal analogy projections. Concrete objects help students more vitally "feel" the analog and, hopefully, the concept as well.

Much of Gordon's (1961) original work was with older students (that is, adults). Indeed, his book is filled with examples of how individuals in professional roles use personal analogies to explore some old problem in a new way. Gordon writes:

> A chemist makes a problem familiar to himself through equations combining molecules and the mathematics of phenomenological order. On the other hand, to make a problem strange the chemist may personally identify with the molecules in action. Faraday "looked . . . into the very heart of the electrolyte endeavoring to render the play of its atom visible to his mental eyes." The creative technical person can think himself to be a dancing molecule, discarding the detachment of the expert and throwing himself into the activity of the elements involved. He becomes one of the molecules. He permits himself to be pushed and pulled by the molecular forces. He remains a human being but acts as though he were a molecule. For the moment the rigid formulae don't govern, and he feels what happens to a molecule. (p. 37)

Q: *How does the teacher effectively teach a synectics lesson in a standard class lesson period?*

A: The problem in this instance is the teacher's assumption that a lesson should cover one discrete time period of 45 minutes. The reason some schools are embracing block scheduling is because of a need to move beyond the confines of a 45-to-55-minute class period. Longer time periods liberate teachers to use models such as synectics. O'Neil (1995) writes about the block schedule approach:

> The longer class periods liberate teachers whose innovative methods don't fit the traditional schedule. . . . "You cannot just lecture" when classes run past one hour in length. . . ." [As one principal who observed block scheduled teachers noted] "I definitely see a wider variety of cooperative learning, hands-on projects, and other strategies [such as synectics!] aimed at encouraging student involvement [being used by teachers] . . .". (pp. 12–13)

More recently, Queen (2000) describes the mixed results of block scheduling on student achievement, but suggests that as a result of lengthened time periods "teachers used more active instructional strategies [including synectics] and limited their use of lecture" (p. 218).

Of course, not every school embraces block scheduling. High school teachers, as a consequence, may need to use two class periods on some occasions. Elementary school teachers have more flexibility in scheduling and may need to examine how synectics can be used in an interdisciplinary sense—combining language arts with other disciplinary areas. Even in elementary schools, though, more innovative scheduling procedures are being adopted (see Canady and Rettig, 1995). Those procedures are providing teachers with the blocks of time needed to explore ideas in-depth and to extend students' thinking.

The teachers who use synectics for the first time will find that they have to pay close attention to all the steps in the process—many teachers keep a set of notes detailing the phases of the process so that they know what instructional sequence to follow. Although synectics lessons are not necessarily complicated, they are also not easy to conduct unless the teacher has a clear sense of how all the pieces of the lesson fit together. Teachers, therefore, should evaluate their performance using the following questions; but they should be less concerned with whether each step is followed than they are with whether the students are creatively thinking through the ideas by the time a lesson is completed.

Phase I: The Topic

1. Is the concept or "big idea" to be focused on during the synectics lesson sufficiently significant to warrant creative extension? ☐ Yes ☐ No

Phase II: Direct Analogy

Determine whether Synectics I or II will be used. If Synectics I:

1. Does the teacher's direct analogy stimulate student thought? ☐ Yes ☐ No
2. Do the students generate all the characteristics of the object and of the analog? ☐ Yes ☐ No

If Synectics II:

1. Do the students generate an inclusive list of descriptive terms for the concept being taught? ☐ Yes ☐ No
2. What analog category does the teacher use? Game__ Machine__ Plant__
3. Do the students offer and defend analogical ideas? (For example, are the students required to use "because" statements?) ☐ Yes ☐ No
4. Does the class identify one analogy for use in the third phase of the lesson? ☐ Yes ☐ No

Phase III: Personal Analogy

The phase III processes are essentially the same regardless of whether the teacher uses Synectics I or Synectics II.

1. Does the teacher require the students to become both the analog and the concept? ☐ Yes ☐ No

2. Are students required to use "I feel" statements as they express their feelings about being the analog and the concept?   □ Yes   □ No

3. Does the teacher write the terms on the board as the students express their feelings?   □ Yes   □ No

Phase IV: Compressed Conflict

If Synectics I (Contrast):

1. Does the teacher ask students to think of ways in which the analog and the concept are different?   □ Yes   □ No

2. Does the teacher accomplish the contrast between analog and concept in a way that does not diminish the power of the original analogy?   □ Yes   □ No

If Synectics II (Compressed Conflict):

1. Does the teacher ask students to combine words that are in dynamic tension with one another?   □ Yes   □ No

2. Do the students select a compressed conflict that makes a lot of sense to them, and can they defend why they like it?   □ Yes   □ No

Phase V: New Analogy

If Synectics I:

1. Are students able to generate their own new analogies?   □ Yes   □ No

2. Describe how the teacher has students create the new analogies (for example, work in groups, and so on).   □ Yes   □ No

If Synectics II:

1. Are students able to take the compressed conflict and identify an object that exhibits these qualities?   □ Yes   □ No

2. What object does the teacher use as a focus for the new analogy?   __Animal __Food __Machine

Phase VI: Topic Refocus

1. Describe what the students were expected to do after they developed the new analogy and were asked to

reexamine the original topic (for example, write an essay, discuss as a class
new insights about the topic, and so on).

_____

_____

_____

SAMPLE LESSONS

The case provided at the beginning of the chapter was illustrative of Synectics
I. The simulated classroom example provided below is prototypic of Synectics
II. As the reader will note in this lesson, the students are expected to use com-
pressed conflict as part of the analysis and creation of direct analogies.

CASE STUDY I

Ms. Ruth Yellowhawk is preparing to teach her 9th graders a unit on poetry.
The students represent a range of abilities and are heterogeneously grouped for
English class. She knows some of the students enjoy poetry because of previous
work with song lyrics. Still, she wants to get all the students excited about how
poetry can shed new light on their lives and their relationships with others. She
begins by describing how poetry surrounds the students—it's on television, in
songs, on the playground, and in the religious experiences of the various students. She then asks the students to share all the terms they can associate with
poetry. The students generate the following terms: long, confusing, boring,
pretty, interesting, thoughtful, imaginative, complex, and colorful.

After the students list all the terms, Ms. Yellowhawk asks them to think of a
game that has many of the qualities they just listed. One student, Rayford, suggests chess; another, Kalhis, offers the game Jingo; and a third, Jacy, thinks that
a jigsaw puzzle is the most logical.

"Why, Jacy?" asks Ms. Yellowhawk.

"Because jigsaw puzzles take a long time to put together. They can be boring, especially if you do them alone; but they are pretty and interesting to look
at once they are completed."

The students suggest several other games and describe why they fit with the
terms for poetry. But when they are asked to vote for the game they like the
best, the jigsaw puzzle is the class favorite.

"Excellent," responds Ms. Yellowhawk. "Today we are going to look at how
poetry is like a jigsaw puzzle. As we consider this, I want you to close your eyes.
For a few seconds, pretend that you are a jigsaw puzzle. What does it feel like?"
(The teacher lets the students sit quietly for several seconds and then continues
the lesson.)

"Share with me all the feelings that are going through your mind. Joe, what
do you feel like?"

"I feel broken up. There are pieces of me all over the place."

"Great thought. Mindy, how do you feel?"

TABLE 7-4   Feelings About Being a Jigsaw Puzzle

Broken up because I'm all over the place.

Hurt because I'm on the floor and being stepped on.

Tired because it's taking so long to put me together.

Scattered because I'm not together.

Unwanted because as soon as they have me together they take me apart and put me in a box.

Sticky because people have food on their hands and then touch me.

Pretty because when I'm together, I know I look good.

Important because I'm often given as a gift.

Connected because when all my pieces fit together I feel secure.

"I feel hurt because some parts of me are on the floor. The people walk on me and the dog is now sticking part of me in his mouth."

After the students generate a number of feelings and the reasons for the feelings (see Table 7-4), Ms. Yellowhawk asks the students to select the words that go together yet "argue with one another."

One student suggests "unwanted" and "important." Another offers "tired" and "pretty." A third indicates "scattered" and "connected."

Ms. Yellowhawk then asks the students to identify which of the conflicts they like the best. Which one "argues" or conflicts in a way that they really like the tension between the terms?

The students discuss which ones they like the best and then vote to select the conflict: unwanted and important.

"What we now need to do," remarks Ms. Yellowhawk, "is to create a new analogy. Except, in this instance, I want to use your terms, *unwanted* and *important*, as the descriptors for the new direct analogy. Can you think of an animal that is both unwanted and important? Stephen?"

"The snake."

"Why, Stephen?" asks Ms. Yellowhawk.

"Well, a snake is not something most people want around, but snakes do eat some rodents, and they are part of the food chain."

"Shaneca, what do you think?"

"Bees. Bees are a real nuisance, but they pollinate plants and they make honey."

The students go on to identify several other unwanted but very important animals: lion, pigeon, bear, and so on. After several minutes of enumeration, the students are asked to select the one they like the best. They decide on bees. Bees can cause pain and they can be a problem, but their benefits are readily apparent.

"So, students, you have selected bees. Consider bees for a few moments then tell me all that you know about bees." The students list the following:

- They are social (live in colonies).
- They have enemies (bears eat honey).

- They divide the labor (queen bees only lay eggs).
- They make wax.
- They make honey.
- The queen mates with males in flight.
- They are a hobby for some people (beekeepers).

"How can this information about bees help us better understand poetry?" asks Ms. Yellowhawk. "I want you to think of how information about bees can shed more light on poetry. For instance, you said that bees are a hobby for some people. Is it not true that some people make a hobby out of poetry? Some people write it for fun; others read it for enjoyment."

The students share their ideas for several minutes. (For example: Poetry can be like food [honey] because it nourishes your soul. Poetry can be a social experience, especially during poetry readings.)

Ms. Yellowhawk then distributes a set of 10 poems. The students are asked to identify which one "nourishes" them the most and to write a short essay on why that is the case. ■

Follow-Up Questions

1. What other ways might a teacher introduce poetry to students?

2. What other mechanisms might a teacher use to help students think of what it must be like to be a jigsaw puzzle? (This teacher had students close their eyes and visualize themselves as a puzzle. Identify other ways to do this.)

3. What other phrases could be used to describe the compressed conflict? This teacher asked students to select terms that "go together yet argue with one another." Is there a clearer way to describe this to the class?

ⒸASE STUDY II

Mavis Franklin is a 3rd grade teacher and is using synectics to encourage student thinking about selected weather concepts. Interestingly, she wants students to be better prepared to perform well on state proficiency tests that are focusing more on the critical thinking abilities of the students.

"Class, today we are going to explore the topic **weather.** Let's think about weather in new and different ways. One idea is to say that weather is like a person. For example, just like you never know what a person will do next, weather is hard to predict because it changes frequently. Or if friends are feeling 'low,' they are unhappy or feeling 'bad,' just like a low front brings 'bad' weather.

"I'd like for you to think of other ways weather is like a person (she pauses briefly). Now pair with your neighbor and identify three ways that weather and a person are alike." After students work together briefly, the students share their ideas. Ms. Franklin writes the list on a large sheet of paper.

A lot of different ideas emerge and are discussed by the students: "Air pressure is like your emotions because you can feel high or low." After a number of ideas are written down and discussed, Ms. Franklin proceeds.

She praises the students for unique, creative ideas and tells them that they will use their imaginations to pretend they have **actually become weather.** She reminds them of a fantasy they have recently read and has them close their eyes. "Picture yourself as weather; how do you feel? For example, I feel angry, so I will send lightning, thunder, and hail in a storm." Or "I am tired of people always complaining about me; I can never please anyone." The students take several minutes and then share lots of ideas. Ms. Franklin then observes:

"We've explored ways that make the weather like a person and even described how it feels to be the weather. Now I want you to think about the *differences* between a person and the weather. How is the weather NOT like a person? Discuss ideas with your table groups to find three or more differences. Take turns writing them so that you can share." After several minutes, the teacher writes group ideas about weather on a paper cloud and those about people on a paper head. (It is not unusual for teachers to use visuals that provide more imagery in order to stimulate student thinking. Those working with young children may find it especially appropriate.)

This process takes several minutes. Ms. Franklin then hands out chart cards and instructs the groups to write something *different* that weather can be like. The phrase "Weather is like" is placed in the pocket chart and each group puts their best analogy next to it. The students generate a number of ideas, all of which are placed on the board. Ms. Franklin then asks the students to write a haiku about weather using the following structure:

Sample Haiku:

(Where is it happening—5 syllables)	Up among the clouds
(What is happening—7 syllables)	the sun shines its sparkling beams
(When does it happen—5 syllables)	after the dark storm.

The students finish their haikus and share them. In the process they use a lot of the vocabulary she wants them to have in their long-term memory: nanometer, Fahrenheit, humidity . . .

Teacher Reflection

Before teaching, I was concerned about using the Synectics model with younger students, due to its length and the complexity of its parts. I decided to streamline the model as much as possible by making the "feeling" section relate to a person, since personal attributes are often given to weather. This lesson format had not been used previously with my class, so I prepared two examples of each concept to give students a better idea of what was expected. I also had mostly whole class, group, or partner work. Writing materials were prepared ahead of time. Using the haiku for the final topic refocusing would allow creativity in a short amount of time.

Teaching the lesson to my 3rd grade class strengthened my opinion that the synectics model would be more efficiently and appropriately used with older students, particularly middle school and high school age. Although my students were able to think creatively, much extra time had to be spent explaining/

portraying the type of answer needed, especially when working with personification. Perhaps using a more concrete idea than weather might have been easier, but the model still required using all six phases, which made it somewhat lengthy and complex for younger children. During the analog contrast, I suggest that the teacher avoid the statement: "How is _____ **not** like _____?" Instead ask, "How is _____ **different** than _____?" so that the students give positive answers for each comparison.

The Synectics model promoted class participation, creative thinking and group interaction. Students worked well with the similarities and differences, since they were used to working with Venn diagrams. I especially recommend the Synectics model as an occasional instructional change and challenge for students in the middle grades or older. ▪

ⓈUGGESTED LESSON DEVELOPMENT: QUESTIONS FOR REFLECTION ✓

The best strategy for really understanding synectics is to try the model out with a group of students. In preparation for teaching a synectics lesson to a class, the teacher should be attentive to the following steps:

1. Make certain that the concept or focus for a synectics lesson is significant. Synectics lessons take time, and teachers need to make certain that the focus of their efforts is worth the time invested.

2. Determine which synectics approach will be used. (Most teachers we have worked with find Synectics I easier to use than Synectics II, but they find that Synectics II fosters more creative student thinking than Synectics I.)

3. Identify some specific ways of enhancing students' participation in the personal analogy phase.

4. Determine the specific times in the lesson when the teacher will write student responses down on the chalkboard or poster paper.

5. Identify specifically how the students' attention will be refocused on the topic during the final phase of the synectics lesson. What will students be expected to do immediately after they have generated their own new direct analogies?

ⓉECHNOLOGY ENHANCEMENT   A D Ⓘ S C

In this section, we illustrate the ways in which technology can be used to help all students access more content information (I) so that it informs the metaphoric thinking. Much debate currently occurs regarding the digital divide. Such a divide does exist, but its reality is often exacerbated because of teacher failure to show students how to use technology effectively. Teachers can help close the digital divide by enabling students to find new ways of using technology to explore salient concepts.

Creating a Web-Based Treasure Hunt to Enhance a Synectics Lesson

The synectics teaching model deepens students' conceptual understandings by promoting creative and divergent thought processes that foster deep exploration of the content being studied. Teachers desiring to enhance or extend a synectics lesson can do so by creating a Web-based *Treasure Hunt*.

A Treasure Hunt is a teaching and learning tool specifically designed to support focused inquiry utilizing the resources of the World Wide Web. It is an excellent choice for enhancing the synectics strategy because it facilitates students in searching for answers to *big questions*, such as how is the earth like a peach or how is football like opera. It is a particularly valuable enhancement when students do not possess adequate background information about one of the analog concepts, or when teachers want students to go beyond their existing knowledge base when comparing concepts. There are many ways to use a Treasure Hunt in the context of the synectics model. Depending on the goals of the teacher and the availability of internet-connected computers, students can work alone or in cooperative groups; conduct their inquiry in the classroom, in a computer lab, or from home; or conduct the hunt prior to or during class time.

Teachers desiring to create a Treasure Hunt can take advantage of a free, Web-based resource provided by Pacific Bell. *Filamentality* is a fill-in-the-blank, interactive Web site that guides teachers through each step in the process of creating a Treasure Hunt, from picking a topic and constructing the big question, to gathering related Internet sites. Not only does this site support teachers in constructing a hunt, but also it allows them to easily create their own customized Web page so that students, colleagues, and parents can access the hunt from school or home. In preparing this enhancement, one of the authors used *Filamentality* to create a Treasure Hunt focused on the direct analogy "Apollo 11 was like the Lewis and Clark Expedition." As a first time user of this Web site, it took the author approximately one hour to create a Treasure Hunt based on the synectics model. The following three questions were posed: What were the chief characteristics of the Corps of Discovery? What were the chief characteristics of Apollo XI? And finally, how were the Corps of Discovery and Apollo XI analogous? Following the onscreen prompts for creating a Treasure Hunt, ten Web sites providing a wealth of information on both expeditions were identified. Next, specific questions were developed for each site as a guide to student exploration. By carefully selecting sites and preparing targeted questions, teachers can guide students to interesting areas of possible comparison, such as the political forces that influenced Presidents Jefferson and Kennedy to initiate the expeditions.

Grade Level Modifications

The Treasure Hunt strategy can be adapted for students in the upper elementary grades through high school. One aspect of a Treasure Hunt that makes it relatively easy to modify is that teachers select the Web sites they want students to explore. Consequently, teachers can choose sites after considering such factors as reading level, conceptual complexity, print versus visual media, and other factors related to grade-level appropriateness. Teachers in the primary grades may choose to further modify the approach by using image-rich Web sites and facilitating whole-class processing of Phase II. Conversely, teachers in the secondary grades may want to experiment with requiring students to complete their hunt prior to class as an individual or small group project.

Low Tech/High Tech Applications

Creating a Web-based Treasure Hunt and engaging students in a guided Internet research project represents a relatively high-tech enhancement of the synectics model. Teachers with multiple classroom computers and presentation technology might further enhance the model by requiring or inviting students to communicate the results of their hunt in an electronic slide show. As a further enhancement, teachers who have developed a class Web site may ask students to post the results of their hunt to the site so that results can be further analyzed.

Teachers not desiring to use the Treasure Hunt enhancement may want to consider simpler, low-tech tools, such as employing Web-based Venn diagram programs or using the three-column function in a word processing program to create analog comparison tables.

Value Added for Diverse Learners

Using a Treasure Hunt may benefit diverse learners by providing time for students who need more time to process information. It may also help students who need more concrete information or imagery to stimulate the creative thinking process. For example, seeing lists of the equipment and supplies carried by both Apollo XI and the Corps of Discovery might stimulate creative thought in some students who might otherwise have been disengaged. In similar fashion, other students might engage in the process of comparison after seeing pictures of Merriweather Lewis and Neil Armstrong. Finally, teachers sensitive to the cultural and ethnic backgrounds of their students can strategically select Web sites to introduce perspectives representative of those backgrounds.

Web-Based Resources

Teachers interested in exploring the Treasure Hunt as a tool to enhance the synectics model will find a wealth of helpful information at the *Filamentality* Web site (www.pacbell.com/fil). In addition to exploring sample Treasure Hunts and other Web-based learning tools, teachers can use the site to create and post their own hunts.

Graphic organizers can be powerful tools to promote a wide-range of thought processes, including comparative analysis. Teachers wanting to learn more about Venn diagrams and other graphic organizers that support students in comparing and contrasting will find some nice examples at www.graphic .org/goindex.html.

SUMMARY

Synectics is more generative than reactive in character. That is, teachers who structure thoughtful synectics lessons are not trying to elicit a set of student responses to a defined set of teacher questions (reactive instruction). Though reactive instruction is common in schools, it has the most limited potential for eliciting from students the type of generative thinking needed to explore ideas in novel or unique ways, which Ornstein (1995), drawing on the work of Carl Rogers, has described as the very essence of the creative endeavor.

The synectics instructional model fosters generative thinking. Students are not simply reacting to teacher ideas; they are, instead, creating ideas of their own. True, the teacher sets the "stage," but the students determine the direction of the "play." Their ideas and past experiences, not the teacher's, shape how the metaphoric process evolves and how the original topic is examined. This generative process leads to more "ahas" during the instructional sequence. For many veteran teachers, the "aha" feeling has long since been lost! Most teachers experience pedagogical epiphanies at the beginning of their careers because they are teaching content for the first time—and for some, they possess only inchoate understandings of that content themselves. But once planets or revolutions or cell structure have been taught a few times, teachers fall into a pattern of knowing what to teach and how to teach it. The consequence: The "aha" feeling is lost and, concomitantly, some of the excitement of teaching is mitigated. One way to "reconnect" with content is to find new ways of exploring old ideas. The reconnection process does not ensure student achievement gains, though some evidence exists that it does enhance long-term acquisition of content and enhanced student enjoyment of the learning process (Joyce, Weil, and Calhoun, 2000); it also increases the excitement of teachers for ideas and enhances the possible enthusiastic response of students to those ideas. That enthusiasm not only will pay educational dividends in the classroom (some researchers argue that students will achieve more), but it will also be personally beneficial for students because they will have learned a process for creatively exploring ideas and discovering hidden meanings.

REFERENCES

Canady, R. L., and M. D. Rettig. 1995. "The Power of Innovative Scheduling." *Educational Leadership* 54(3): 4–10.

Center for Educational Policy. 2001. *It takes more than testing: Closing the Achievement Gap.* Washington, DC: Center for Educational Policy.

Foster, M. 1993. "Constancy, Change, and Constraints in the Lives of Black Women Teachers: Some Things Change, Most Stay the Same." *NWSA Journal* 3(2): 233–261.

Gardner, H. 1995. "Reflections on Multiple Intelligences: Myths and Messages." *Phi Delta Kappan* 77(3): 200–209.

Good, T., and J. Brophy. 1995. *Contemporary Educational Psychology* (5th ed.) New York: Longman.

Gordon, W. 1961. *Synectics: The Development of Creative Capacity.* New York: Harper & Row.

Gunter, M. A., T. H. Estes, and J. H. Schwab. 1995. *Instruction: A Models Approach* (2nd ed.). Boston: Allyn & Bacon.

Henry, A. 1990. "Black Women, Black Pedagogies: An African-Canadian Context." Paper presented at the American Educational Research Association, Boston.

Joyce, B., M. Weil, and E. Calhoun. 2000. *Models of Teaching* (6th ed.). Boston: Allyn & Bacon.

Ladson-Billings, G. 1994. *The Dreamkeepers*. San Francisco: Jossey-Bass.

Ladson-Billings, G. 2001. *Crossing over to Canaan*. San Francisco: Jossey-Bass.

O'Neil, J. 1995. "Finding Time to Learn." *Educational Leadership* 53(3): 11–15.

Ornstein, A. C. 1995. *Strategies for Effective Teaching* (2nd ed). Madison, WI: Brown and Benchmark.

Ovando, C. 2001. "Beyond Blaming the Victim": Successful Schools for Latino Students." *Educational Researcher* 30(3): 29–31.

Queen, J. A. 2000. "Block Scheduling Revisited." *Phi Delta Kappan*, 82(3): 214–222.

Torrance, E. P. 1986. "Teaching Creative and Gifted Learners." Pp. 630–647 in M. C. Wittrock (ed.), *Handbook of Research on Teaching*. New York: Macmillan.

Weaver, W. T., and G. M. Prince. 1990. "Synectics: Its Potential for Education." *Phi Delta Kappan* 71(5): 378–388.

What content should every student know? And what is the most efficient and effective way to teach that content? With the increased emphasis on student achievement by state education departments and school districts, it is becoming more important for teachers and policymakers to specifically determine what facts, skills, and concepts to teach all students.

Other units in this text emphasize ways in which teachers can foster critical-thinking skills. The two chapters that comprise this unit do not have that as a primary focus. Mnemonics and direct instruction models are efficient means for teaching discrete knowledge, and they are not oriented toward engendering critical perspectives on content. If the teacher is teaching students how to multiply fractions, one strategy for solving $1/4 \times 3/5$ is for the teacher to delineate in a step-by-step fashion the process for deriving the answer of $3/20$. Such a process should not be used when teaching all facts, skills, and concepts, but it most definitely should be a part of the instructional repertoire of every teacher. Teachers who rely too heavily on mnemonics and direct instruction limit the full intellectual potential of students. Those who disdain these instructional models fail to understand that good teachers determine the instructional model based on their instructional goals. Learning to fly an airplane is not something one should learn inductively. And learning to write poetry is not something one assimilates through exclusive reliance on deductive, step-by-step processes. ■

Models That Foster Remembering Skills

EIGHT

• *Mnemonics*

Chapter Objectives

At the end of this chapter, readers will be able to

1. *Identify the essential phases for the effective use of the mnemonic model.*
2. *Identify the strengths and weaknesses of mnemonics.*
3. *Understand the theoretical and empirical grounding for the mnemonic model.*
4. *Evaluate lessons that use mnemonic strategies.*
5. *Create a lesson using the mnemonic instructional model and understand how technology can be used to enhance student learning.*

❶NTRODUCTION

The model presented in this chapter is useful for helping students learn and memorize new information. In ancient times, the memory capacity of individuals was essential to the educational process because books and other printed materials did not exist. Oral traditions were dominant. Salient ideas and stories were remembered and passed down from one generation to the next by those who possessed the gift of imagination and the capacity for memory. Modern American educators still place substantial emphasis on remembering facts, concepts, and generalizations, but they spend very little time showing students how to recall information. Some might argue that memorizing information is antithetical to educational enlightenment. Indeed, many of the recent reform initiatives focus on enabling students to become better problem-solvers and processors of information; students need to know how to access information, but they do not necessarily need to memorize facts. Others view the acquisition of certain facts as essential, if not necessary, to being an educated citizen (Hirsch, 1988, 1996). Our view is that either extreme position represents a potentially negative circumstance. To disdain any need for memorization (why learn facts when you can always look them up?) would be foolhardy. Although it is true that much information can be looked up, imagine the complications of daily life for someone who is so information deficient that the individual could not make change or did not know basic information about how to access necessary services in a community. On the other hand, imagine how ludicrous it would be to memorize mountains of data, some of it remote in relevance, when computer access makes the information instantly retrievable.

All memory, whether trained or untrained, is based on association.

HARRY LORAYNE AND JERRY LUCAS

Sizer (1992) suggests that a balance between the extreme positions can be attained if teachers selectively engage students in what he describes as "exhibitions." In essence, the student in some way must "exhibit the products of his or her learning" (p. 25). Sizer identifies several different types of exhibitions that might be illustrative of the expectations schools have for students to memorize information. Examples include reciting an important speech from history (for example, the Gettysburg Address), drawing a freehand map of the United States, or reciting an important poem (for example, "Mending Wall").

The student memorizes information not only for mental discipline but also to acquire the intellectual habits necessary for leading the good life. One of the essential intellectual habits, argues Sizer (1992), relates to the pleasure "of knowing some things well enough to commit them to memory, and [to the] joy of reciting them" (p. 66).

Teachers need to make conscious decisions about what "exhibits" students need to have in their long-term memory. Such decisions require substantial dialogue about what ideas are so important that they warrant student memorization or, as the following case illustrates, what content knowledge is of sufficient significance that, by memorizing it, students are able to more effectively process other types of relevant data.

Another example of using memorization comes from the KIPP academies that have been featured on *60 Minutes* and hyped by the national media and even President Bush. One of the intellectual leaders of the school is Harriett Ball, who uses mnemonic devices to ensure that students learn essential skills and facts. The following example taken from Ball's work with teachers illustrates how mnemonics can be used to help students learn their multiplication tables.

> With that, she [Ball] says, "Now, let me hear you say your nine-times table."
>
> At first, the voices are confident and in unison: "Nine! Eighteen! Twenty-seven! Thirty-six." But things quickly fall apart, and the teachers [students in the workshop] break out laughing.
>
> "All right, watch this," Ball says. "Lay down your pencils, and don't write anything." She wants the material imprinted in their brains, not scribbled on a piece of paper.
>
> At the blackboard, Ball draws an upside-down T. On the right side of the vertical line, at the bottom, she writes a zero and says, "Remember, zero is your hero!" (If you forget to start with zero, the chart won't work.) Then, moving up the vertical line, she writes the numbers one through nine. On the other side of the vertical line, she writes a nine at the bottom, an eight on top of that, and so on, until she gets to zero. As she writes, she's careful to keep the numbers on the left side lined up with the ones on the right. In fact, she offers a little saying to remind the students to do just that. "Now, I want you to 'keep it lined up,'" she says, writing "KIL U" on the board, "or it will kill you."
>
> The result is a nine-times table, with the number nine (written as 09) on top, 90 on the bottom, and all the other two-digit multiples of nine in between. Ball has similar lessons to help kids learn all the multiplication tables. (Hill, 2001, pp. 32–33)

FIGURE 8-1   The Provinces of Canada

CASE STUDY

Susan Sternberg is preparing to teach a unit on Canada to her 6th grade students. In preparation for the unit activities, Susan expects all the students to know the location of the 11 provinces of Canada and to be able to identify the capitals of each province. Her first lesson today will focus only on the province locations.

"Class, today, in preparation for our unit on Canada, I am going to teach you the locations of each Canadian province. That will be important information for you to know as we work our way through this unit. We will be having discussions that require you to memorize the locations of all Canadian provinces. By the end of our class period, each of you will be able to correctly label the Canadian map I have on the board [see Figure 8-1]. To begin this unit I want you to look at the map of Canada and read each province name silently to yourself." [A couple of minutes pass as the students silently read the province names.]

FIGURE 8-2 Linkword Story about the Provinces of Canada

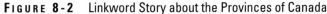

"Now to help you learn the province names, I am going to tell you a story using another map of Canada with linkwords labeled for each province [see Figure 8-2]. The story is about my favorite cartoon character BC and his best buddy Al. You all remember Al! He was the workshop assistant on the television show, *Home Improvement.*

"One day, BC [the teacher points to the location of British Columbia] and his best buddy Al [the teacher points to Alberta] decide to take a trip. The trip is going to be a long one and many supplies will be required, so they will need a strong helper to carry the supplies. To assist them, they pick up *Saskatch* or Big Foot [Ms. Sternberg points to Saskatchewan].

"BC, Al, and Saskatch journey for several days then stumble onto something very unusual—*a tuba man* [or gigantic man sitting in a very tiny tuba— she points to Manitoba]. Can you imagine what this must have looked like? What a strange thing to see! Even weirder to look at is the fact that this tiny tuba is sitting on miles and miles of *tar* [she points to Ontario].

"Let's review what's happened so far: BC and his best friend Al . . . " Ms. Sternberg carefully reviews the first five steps of the story.

"Now, class, something really amazing happens as BC, Al, and Saskatch are watching tuba man on the tar: they are distracted by a Queen who is beckoning them [she points to Quebec]. Jacob, what does it mean to be beckoned?"

"It's when someone motions for you to join them, like this." [Jacob then uses a forefinger to beckon the teacher.]

"Great, Jacob. You're right! What's strange in this instance, though, is that BC, Al, and Saskatch can't figure out what the Queen is using to do the beckoning. Then as they get closer to the Queen, it becomes very clear—the Queen is using a huge new *candlewick* to beckon them [Ms. Sternberg points to New Brunswick]. Wouldn't that be strange to see? A queen using a new candlewick to beckon these three people!

"Well, even stranger is the fact that standing next to the Queen with this candlewick was the candle's owner, *Prince Edward*. [Ms. Sternberg points to Prince Edward Island.] Unfortunately, though, the Prince is not a wealthy prince—he's poor. Very, very poor! That's why he has given the Queen only one candle. Because of that fact, the Prince is forced to drive a rather modest car, a *Nova*." [Ms. Sternberg points to Nova Scotia.]

Ms. Sternberg continues, "At about this same time, the Prince gets tired of standing next to the wick and decides to strike out on his own sightseeing trip. On the way he discovers a brand new land, which he names his *New Found Land*. [The teacher points to Newfoundland.] Wow! Can you imagine his excitement? What a great thing to have happen. Well, the Prince proceeds on his journey and keeps looking for other new places and interesting people [Ms. Sternberg moves her hand across northern Canada], but all the Prince can find are con men [she points to the Yukon].

"Isabelle, what's a *con man*?

"It's someone who pretends to be something he isn't—a fake."

"Right! Class, let's review our whole story." And with that, Ms. Sternberg has the students break up into pairs. They review the substitute words and then review the linkword story. One student tells the story to a student partner and then the peer pair roles are reversed.

Once all the students have the story memorized, Ms. Sternberg carefully describes the substitute term for each province in the story. That is, BC stands for *British Columbia*, and so on.

At the completion of the lesson, she provides the students a blank Canadian map. They fill in the names of each province. Several students have trouble remembering the province of New Brunswick.

"Class, several of you forgot New Brunswick. Can you think of a better image than the one I used, which was *candlewick*?" The students decide on two good possibilities.

Two days later Ms. Sternberg reviews the story again and uses a keyword technique to teach the students the capitals of each Canadian province. ∎

The case study from Ms. Sternberg's class is an example of a teacher-directed mnemonics lesson. The teacher is teaching the students content material they will need for their unit activities. In this chapter, we will more fully explore the mnemonic instructional model and its uses in teaching.

Ⓣ HEORETICAL PERSPECTIVE

As described previously in this chapter, memory systems are not new as learning aids; they date to ancient times. The Greek poet Simonides (circa 500 B.C.) is often considered the originator of the use of trained memory systems (Lorayne and Lucas, 1974). He developed the memory technique because of a rather unusual circumstance. It seems that a banquet hall where Simonides had just eaten collapsed and Simonides was asked to assist with the identification process of the bodies—many were so damaged by the catastrophe that Simonides had to recall where each guest had eaten (Rose, 1985). Rose writes that "in clarifying [Simonides's] . . . method, Cicero explained that you would first visualize a series of places about the house (the Latin for place is locus, from which we get our word location)" (p. 57). The Greeks and Romans used memory systems to help as part of their orations. Oratory was a craft of considerable importance in the days of antiquity, and individuals skilled in its use were expected to deliver long speeches from memory. *Mnemonics* is a term derived from the Greek word *Mnemosyne*, who was the Greek goddess of memory (Higbee, 1996). Lorayne and Lucas (1974) describe how the Greeks associated thoughts with visual images of specific objects:

> What they [the Greeks] did, basically, was associate each thought of a speech to a part of their own homes. These were called "loci," or "places." The opening thought of a speech would, perhaps, be associated to the front door, the second thought to the foyer, the third to a piece of furniture in the foyer, and so on. When the orator wanted to remember his speech, thought for thought, he actually took a mental tour through his own home. Thinking of the front door reminded him of the first thought of his speech. The second "place," the foyer, reminded him of the next thought; and so on to the end of the speech. It is from this "place" or "loci" memory technique that we get the time-worn phrase "in the first place." (pp. 1–2)

Throughout the Middle Ages, the great thinkers (Cicero, St. Thomas Aquinas, and others) used memory aids to help them recall information that would assist them in their quest to master religious and philosophical ideas. Indeed, in the seventeenth century, philosophers (for example, Francis Bacon) explicitly taught memory systems to their students.

The interest in memory systems continues today. Some researchers have been fascinated by the mnemonic abilities of certain individuals. The Russian psychologist Luria (1968), for example, studied a now-famous subject "S," who as a journalist exhibited incredible powers of recall:

> The simplest structure was one S used to recall tables of numbers written on a blackboard. S would study the material on the board, close his eyes, open them again for a moment, turn aside, and, at a signal, reproduce one series

from the board. Then he would fill in the empty squares of the next table, rapidly calling off the numbers. It was a simple matter for him to fill in the numbers for the empty squares of the table either when asked to do this for certain squares I chose at random, or when asked to fill in a series of numbers successively in reverse order. S could easily tell me which numbers formed one or another of the vertical columns in the table and could "read off" to me numbers that formed the diagonals. . . . (p. 16)

Jerry Lucas, Harry Lorayne, and others regularly conduct workshops in which they demonstrate (and help others develop) their powers in memorizing huge amounts of material in short periods of time. These "mnemonists" often appear on talk shows and demonstrate their memory powers by identifying the names of each member of the audience after having met them just prior to the show.

The educational research on the use of mnemonics is increasing, especially with the new emphasis on developing the content knowledge of students (Levin, 1993; Mastropieri, Scruggs, and Levin, 1987; Pressley, Levin, and Delaney, 1982). That research base suggests that mnemonic strategies (or aids to memory) can be useful in developing a student's recall of factual information. However, the results of studies on the topic vary considerably in terms of which methods are most efficacious in fostering student learning. Levin (1993) notes that the best mnemonic strategies are those designed to learn specific content material (for example, a keyword mnemonic for an English vocabulary term), and those that are used with educationally handicapped students. Levin notes that it "is particularly noteworthy [that the keyword and pegword techniques are powerful learning devices with] . . . students with documented learning problems" (p. 238).

Clearly there are variations in how much information different people can remember. Some persons are able to create and use mnemonic devices much better than others—though it does appear that within reasonable limits all people are at least somewhat capable of enhancing their memory capacities. Described below are three such memory-enhancing strategies that researchers suggest have real instructional efficacy.

The *keyword* strategy is a two-stage process of mnemonically transforming an unfamiliar word to something that is familiar. Levin (1993) describes the keyword approach in learning new vocabulary terms:

> Consider a fourth grader challenged to learn the definitions of 20 new vocabulary words by next Monday—words such as *accolades, equestrian, diversion, flatware, persuade,* and *gesture.* Rather than attempting to memorize the vocabulary list through either repeated rote rehearsal or—in the words of one student we tested—"brute force," a student applying [the] . . . *keyword method* would mnemonically transform the unfamiliar vocabulary items into something more meaningful and memorable. Part of the unfamiliar word *accolades,* for example, sounds like the more familiar beverage *Kool Aid* and, thus, the former could be recoded as the latter. Once transformed, the recoded word (or keyword) *Kool Aid* can be meaningfully related to the to-be-remembered definition of accolades (praise for something well done). In this case, one could imagine a group of people raising their glasses of *Kool Aid to toast an accomplished guest of honor.* (p. 236)

FIGURE 8-3   Example of a Mnemonic Illustration: Pegword

Source: M. A. Mastropieri, T. E. Scruggs, and J. R. Levin. 1987. "Learning Disabled Students' Memory for Expository Prose: Mnemonic Versus Nonmnemonic Pictures." *American Educational Research Journal* 24(4): 508.

Keywords are not difficult to learn and have proven useful for enhanced student learning at all levels (Levin, 1993). The keyword strategy may be especially powerful when it is combined with a second mnemonic strategy, the pegword.

Pegwords consist of taking the numbers 1 through 10 and correlating the numbers with rhyming words that the students already know well. Mastropieri, Scruggs, and Levin (1987) write that the "mnemonic 'pegword method' . . . capitalizes on the childhood rhyme, 'one is a bun, two is a shoe, three is a tree . . . ten is a hen" (pp. 506–507). Hence, if a student is learning the three primary reasons for the War of 1812 or the five animal kingdoms, the teacher would create a picture that illustrates the item's number and the pegword. Mastropieri, Scruggs, and Levin (1987) describe how students would learn that the third most plausible reason for the extinction of dinosaurs is the exploding star theory. Figure 8-3 is the pegword illustration for the plausibility of the exploding star theory—notice the tree (three), the star (exploding), and the dinosaur. The third most logical and plausible explanation for the extinction of the dinosaur is the energy created from the explosion of stars—the energy that killed substantial portions of plant life on earth was detrimental to dinosaurs, who needed plant life to sustain their existence. The pegword strategy is not at all new. The strategy can be traced to the mid-1600s and was created to enable people to remember large sets of information (Higbee, 1996).

The *link* strategy is used as a means of connecting ideas. Recall that Ms. Sternberg wanted the students to learn the precise location of each Canadian province as part of her geography lesson. In using the link system, the learner does nothing more than link one item to another—ideally with images that directly interact. To understand the importance of interaction in terms of memory, consider the following observation of Rose (1985):

> We know visual images to be strong. But imagery can itself be strengthened if it is made to be interactive. Psychologist Gordon Bower reported on a test in which subjects were given 12 pairs of words and eight seconds in which to learn them. Only 33 percent of the repeated pairs were remembered, but when the subject was told to create a visual association between the pairs, the correct recall of the pairs shot up to 80 percent.
>
> When the association specifically involved a direct interaction between the images, then the recall went up even further. Thus suppose the pair of words were *dolphin* and *flower.* An acceptable visual image would be a giant daisy floating beside the dolphin. But that brings in no *direct* connection. A better image would be a smiling dolphin blowing a stream of highly colored flowers out of the blowhole on its head. This image has got interaction and movement and color. The more detailed and developed the image, the better. (p. 62)

In the case study, the provinces of British Columbia (BC) and Alberta (Al) were linked as two friends embarking on a trip. To enable the students to remember the location (or the order) of the provinces, Ms. Sternberg created a story that linked the ideas together using substitute words (*BC* for *British Columbia*, and *Al* for *Alberta)*. She accomplished these linkages by using a number of ridiculous associations to help get the students' attention, and to retain their interest and help them acquire the knowledge of the Canadian provinces. For each association the teacher expected students to create visual images and to link one visual image with the next one. Those associations were based on a relatively simple set of rules (Highboy, 1996; Joyce, Weil, and Calhoun, 2000; Lorayne and Lucas, 1974). Specifically, Ms. Sternberg was able to follow these rules:

Rule #1: *Create substitutions.* Essentially, the teacher substitutes or replaces one item that is familiar with another that is unfamiliar. Ms. Sternberg substituted a "*tuba man,*" (or man in tuba), something concrete that students could picture to represent Manitoba, for something that was more abstract (the province's name).

Rule #2: *Create objects that are out of proportion.* The out-of-proportion rule occurs in Ms. Sternberg's lesson by *creating a gigantic man and a tiny tuba.* Part of the effectiveness of good linkages is the use of ridiculous visual images. A gigantic man in a tiny tuba is easier to remember than an average-size man in a normal-size tuba.

Rule #3: *Create exaggeration.* With exaggeration, the teacher literally expands the idea to proportions that extend beyond anything people would normally consider. Notice that for Ontario (*on miles and miles of tar*), the teacher creates an *image of tremendous amounts of tar*, not a more ordinary image that one would normally expect, such as the tuba just sitting on the ground. If you doubt the power of this notion, just consider the fact that what you tend to recall most readily about a day's events are the ridiculous (or unusual) occurrences, not the normal ones.

Rule #4: *Create action.* The characters and images in the link story about Canada are creating action—they all do something: *BC and AL are taking a trip. Quebec is beckoning with the new [Bruns]wick. The Prince is forced to drive a rather modest car, a Nova.* The action helps the learner create stronger linkages.

Using the link strategy takes time and effort on the part of a teacher. The teacher also needs to understand the teaching phases required to help students fully learn the ideas presented as part of the mnemonic model. Those phases are outlined in the next section (see also Joyce, Weil, and Calhoun, 2000).

Ⓜ NEMONICS: TEACHING PHASES

Phase I: Focus Attention

For students to remember anything, they must pay attention to what is important. Anyone who has ever read a book in preparation for a test understands this phenomenon. That individual often takes some type of highlighter and marks passages or ideas that need to be retained for long-term memory. Other devices for recalling information are also used. For example, one of the authors of this book has a daughter who is just starting college. When she prepares for tests, she makes lists of those ideas she needs to remember. Recall that Ms. Sternberg used "focusing" when she said, "*I want you to look at the map of Canada and read each province name silently to yourself.*"

There is no right way to focus students' attention. The key is to make certain that students are really paying attention to what is being taught. Using the author's daughter as an example again, her science grades for one term while she was in middle school were very low. Test after test she received grades lower than her father expected. Then, one day, she showed up at home with a high grade. Her father asked, "Wow, what did you do differently?" She responded somewhat nonplussed, "I paid attention!"

Phase II: Create Connections

Most mnemonic strategies are nothing more than visual or conceptual connections of familiar material with the unfamiliar. Four such connecting strategies can be used in classrooms and have been highlighted directly or indirectly earlier: first-letter mnemonic, keyword, linkword, and pegword.

First-letter mnemonics entail using a series of letters or lines in which certain letters form a name or message when sequenced appropriately. *Acronyms* are the simplest of these mnemonic strategies. When students take art they learn ROY G BIV, which represents the colors of the spectrum (red, orange, yellow . . . indigo, violet); and in geography they learn HOMES, which represents the five Great

Lakes (Huron . . . Superior). A student in one of the authors' classes required her students in English class to memorize the eight parts of speech and used the acronym NAVACIPP (noun, adjective, verb . . . preposition). Acronyms are useful, especially when the number of items to be recalled is relatively limited in number and when the word formed by the first letter makes sense. They have less utility when a large volume of factual material must be remembered or when a meaningful acronym cannot be formed. It is, however, a technique that can be used quickly and efficiently.

There are lots of different uses of acronyms. Hock, Schumaker, and Deshler (2001) even use them to help students recall the steps of the problem solving process:

> The [learning] strategy [using acronyms] might include several steps. The tutor could even create acronyms to help students remember the steps later. For example, the learners first *Map out the problem* by carefully reading it, underlining key words, and determining what to solve. Then, they *Analyze the problem* by identifying the type of problem, looking for similar problems in the textbook, and estimating the answer. Next, they *Take action* by selecting a method or formula. Finally, the students *Have a look back* by comparing the answer with the estimate and by checking their calculations. The students remember the strategy because the first letters spell *MATH.* (p. 50)

Acrostics or superimposed meaningful structures entail using the first letter of words to be remembered, and connecting (or linking) those letters by creating some type of meaningful phrase (Higbee, 1996; Ormrod, 1999). For example, after students learn the five kingdoms in biology, the teacher might say, "*Class, let's think of an acrostic we can use to recall this information. One might be: All (Animal) My (Monera) Pretty (Protista) Ponies (Plants) Fly (Fungi).*" One of the most famous acrostics is the one many people learn relative to the positions of the nine planets: My (Mercury) Very (Venus) Educated (Earth) Mother (Mars) Just (Jupiter) Served (Saturn) Us (Uranus) Nine (Neptune) Pizzas (Pluto). Even some textbooks now use acrostic-like mnemonic devices to help students remember information. The Harcourt Brace Jovanovich (1992) *Mathematics Plus* text encourages students to remember the order of mathematical operations by using Please (Parentheses), Excuse (Exponents) My (Multiplication) Dear (Division) Aunt (Addition) Sally (Subtraction).

In the beginning of this chapter, we showed how Harriett Ball (KIPP) used mnemonics to aid student learning. Now notice a specific example that she used with 6th graders in a Columbus, Ohio, middle school. In this instance, she used a first letter (acrostic) mnemonic device.

> "Good morning. My name is Harriett Ball, and I'm from Houston, Texas. I'm going to do some fun things with math today. All eyes on me. Say, 'Try Big Mac tonight!'"
>
> The kids have no idea who this strange looking lady with the fancy clothes and the long hair and the costume jewelry is, but they quickly get into the groove, repeating her chant: "Try Big Mac tonight!"
>
> "Try Big Mac tonight!"
> "Say it again now!"
> "Try Big Mac tonight!"

"All right," Ball says, "guess what? You just learned how to read a 15-digit number."

The students, baffled, look at each other as if to say, "What's this lady talking about?"

Ball steps up to the blackboard and writes a 15-digit number: 426, 804, 392, 774, 903.

"OK, what's that number?" she asks. "Don't everybody raise your hand up at one time."

One boy makes a half-hearted attempt and then stops.

Ball says, once again, "Try Big Mac tonight," and the kids repeat the phrase. Then Ball writes on the board "TBMT."

"See those letters?" she asks. "That's trillion, billion, million, thousand." Something seems to click inside the students' heads.

"OK," Ball continues, "when you see a number, don't be afraid of it. All you have to do is this: Count your commas and label. Say what?"

"Count your commas and label," the students reply.

"How many commas do you see?" Ball asks.

"Four!"

"So who is this?" she asks, pointing to the first comma.

"Try!"

"Who is this?"

"Big!"

"Who is this?"

"Mac!"

"And this?"

"Tonight!"

Eventually, Ball leads them through the number step by step, showing them how to use the easy-to-remember "Try Big Mac tonight" chant as a tool to figure out the place value of a multi-digit number. The students, mightily impressed with this new information, give Ball—and themselves—a round of applause. (Hill, 2001, p. 36)

Keyword strategies are useful for memorizing social science data (for example, state capitals), scientific data (for example, information about the periodic table), information in the language arts area (for example, the parts of speech), and foreign languages. In fact, the strategy was originally created in the mid-1970s to assist individuals in learning foreign languages (Highboy, 1996). Keywords are useful for recalling facts that need not be remembered in any particular order. With the keyword approach, a familiar term is used to remember an unfamiliar term. Higbee (1996) observes that the keyword mnemonic entails the use of "substitute words and visual associations" (p. 101). The visual associations enhance the memory capacity. For example, when Ms. Sternberg taught the students the province capitals of Canada, she could have created a picture similar to the one in Figure 8-4, where for Winnipeg, Manitoba, you see tuba man (the substitute word for Manitoba), or a giant man in a tiny tuba, holding a Winnie-the-Pooh bear (or Winnipeg). The substitute words are *Winnie-the-Pooh* and *tuba man*, and the visual image is similar to the one in Figure 8-4. In the Bornstein (1983) mnemonic cards for state capitals, the Topeka,

FIGURE 8-4   Example of a Mnemonic Illustration: Winnipeg, Manitoba

Source: Illustrated by Janet Olney Lasley.

Kansas, substitute words are *tapioca* and *can* and the visual association is tapioca in a can. Highboy (1996) observes that keyword mnemonics can be used for learning either abstract or concrete terms:

> The procedure for using imagery to help remember abstract terms is the same as for concrete terms except that you add a step using "substitute words." You substitute a concrete word to represent the abstract word. One way of doing this is to use objects that typify the abstract term: for *liberty*, you might picture the Liberty Bell; for *justice*, a judge; for *happiness*, a smiling face; for *education*, a schoolhouse; for *fashion*, a model; for *depth*, a hole; for *agree*, a nodding head; for *salary*, a paycheck. A second way of substituting a concrete word for an abstract one is to use objects whose names sound like the abstract term: celery for *salary*; fried ham for *freedom*; happy nest for *happiness*. You can even use this technique to remember nonsense syllables: Cage for KAJ; rocks for ROX; seal for ZYL; sack for XAC. . . . Research on the Keyword mnemonic has found that people are quite adept at using the above two approaches to "concretize" abstract materials for effective visual images. However, one study found that for college students who had no

experience with substitute words, the first approach (based on meaning) was more effective than the second approach (based on sound-alikes) but was also more difficult to use. (p. 109)

Link strategies are used to remember ideas and facts that need to be connected. For example, the teacher may want students to remember the names of the original 13 colonies or the sequencing of the different geologic ages of the world. By recalling one link in a sequence, the student is able to create a connection with (and remember) the items (using the substitute words) that are linked with the identified term. If the student recalls the substitute word *tuba man*, then the student will link that with where the tuba sits (on tar, or *Ontario*), and who observed the tuba man sitting on tar, *Saskatch* (or *Saskatchewan*). The "story link" is also a relatively easy mnemonic for teachers to use. We have heard story links used to help students learn the position of colonies, countries, and parts of machinery.

Pegwords are used when the teacher wants students to recall not only the sequence of ideas, but also the specific position of an item. If someone asks who the 16th President of the United States was, the learner should not have to count the "links" to 16, though that is one possibility. Rather, a peg strategy can be used to identify a president quickly.

The pegword strategy is based on the connection of the numbers to rhyming sounds (one is bun, two is shoe, three is tree . . . ten is hen) or to body parts (start with the forehead and work down to the foot). Each noun in the rhyming method (for example, *bun*) rhymes with a corresponding number (for example, one). Once students have learned the pegs, they are ready to peg the word to a specific idea within a sequence. Recall that in Figure 8-3 the major reason that *three (tree)* was used for the dinosaur's extinction was the exploding star theory. Once the student learns the pegword system, that student will visually picture a tree (three) with an exploding star. Or if students use the "body parts" approach, the numbers 1–10 would correspond to body parts: 1 (forehead), 2 (nose), 3 (chin), 4 (shoulder), 5 (elbow), 6 (wrist), 7 (hand), 8 (hip), 9 (knees), 10 (foot). Sprenger (1999) describes how to use the body pegword approach to teach students 10 prepositions.

> When the fly climbed **aboard** my forehead, I noticed that he was **about** two inches from my nose. There was some peanut butter **above** my chin that I was sure he was interested in. I was surprised **after** he flew past my shoulder, **around** my elbow, and landed **beyond** my wrist **on** my hand. Then he buzzed **over** my hip **until** my knee hit him and he rested **under** my foot.

The rhyming pegwords we suggest (and that the students must memorize) are the same as those recommended by Levin (1993) and Sprenger (1999):

one—bun (sun)	six—bricks (sticks)
two—shoe	seven—heaven
three—tree	eight—rake (gate)
four—door	nine—pine (line)
five—(bee)hive	ten—hen

Essentially, the pegs are all concrete images, and these concrete images are used for remembering the order of information. The peg system can also be

FIGURE 8-5   Example of a Mnemonic Illustration: Abraham Lincoln

Source: Illustrated by Janet Olney Lasley.

expanded to help students remember more than 10 objects by simply taking sets of 10 and connecting them to specific seasonal locations (the *loci* system). Hence, 1–10 would be near a house in the spring, 11–20 would be near a lake in the summer, and so on. For example, item 16 (the 16th U.S. President, Abraham Lincoln) could show a Lincoln car with bricks (the peg for six) on its top sitting near a lake in the summer (see Figure 8-5). If the teacher wants to have students also remember certain facts about each president, images can be added to the picture. For example, if the teacher wanted students to remember that Lincoln signed the Emancipation Proclamation and was president during the Civil War, then on one side of the car the teacher could place a man reading a proclamation and on the other side show two men fighting. Highboy (1996) writes about the effectiveness of the combined peg and *loci* strategies:

> Eighth-grade students used the Peg and Loci systems to learn the names of the U.S. presidents. They used the pegwords for the numbers from 1 to 10. Seasonal loci represented decades of numbers; 1–10 was a spring garden scene, 11–20 a summer beach scene, 21–30 a fall football scene, and 31–40 a winter snow scene. Presidents' names were represented by substitute words, and the associations were presented in pictures. Two sample associations are: Tyler (tie) . . . 10 (hen) . . . garden [spring], and Garfield (guard) . . . 20 (hen) . . . beach [summer]. The students also learned biographical information on the presidents. This combined Keyword-Loci-Peg system has been expanded for extreme cases to learn up to 260 items, using alphabet scenes from an *airplane* scene to a *zoo* scene (10 pegwords × 26 alphabet loci = 260 items of ordered information).
>
> Sixth-grade students who were trained over several days in the use of the Peg system used it to learn a list of names and recipe ingredients. In another study, learning-disabled students in the sixth to eighth grades used the Keyword mnemonic (substitute words) and the Peg system to learn information

on dinosaurs. In both studies, students who used the Peg system remembered the information better than those who did not use it. (p. 165)

Use of any of the strategies, first-letter mnemonics, keywords, linkwords, and pegwords, takes practice and requires student attention, as we will discuss more fully in phases III and IV.

Phase III: Create Associations

To remember anything requires effort—learners must pay attention to what they want to learn. Memory capacity is enhanced when the associations that are formed are ridiculous—the more ridiculous, the better! Four rules for creating ridiculous associations were described earlier in this chapter. Those rules, as Joyce, Weil, and Calhoun (2000), Lorayne and Lucas (1974), and Higbee (1996) describe them, are the rule of substitution, the rule of exaggeration, the rule of out-of-proportion, and the rule of action. These four rules are essential for enabling students to fully recall ideas. But even after the students have the visual images clearly in mind, the teacher must create conditions for practice to enable students to recall ideas or facts once they are learned. A teacher may even demonstrate the technique to students similar to what Sprenger (1999) suggests:

> A rhyming peg system works well for me, and it is easy for my students to remember. . . . I always introduce it to my students by first performing a "magic" feat. They are fascinated by this ability and even more pleased when I explain how it is done.
>
> I stand with my back to the chalkboard, and I have one student go to the board and write a list of items suggested at random by the other students. For instance, we might list school supplies. The student compiling the list calls on students one at a time. The students call out both the item and the number on the list where it should be placed. A student might say, "Number four is a ruler." This continues until the list of 10 is complete. The students must give me a moment between items, so I can take the time to "attach" them to my peg. Because my peg for number four is a door, I might imagine a door made out of rulers. The more outrageous I can make my visual image, the easier it will be for me to remember. Therefore, I might imagine opening the door and having thousands of rulers falling on top of me.
>
> When they are finished compiling the list, I give them the list forward or backward. Sometimes they call out random numbers and ask me for the item. I usually get applause for this "miracle." Then I share my peg system with them and give them a list to memorize in 10 minutes or less. Their responses are almost 100 percent accurate. From there we discuss how to use this strategy to study vocabulary by using definitions in their visual images. An example would be the word *pachyderm*. Its definition is "a thick-skinned animal." If it is the first word on the list (remembering that the peg for one is sun), the students may visualize an elephant in the hot sun sweating so much that his thick skin is falling off! In this way the word and the definition are attached to the peg. The students enjoy creating the "pictures" as they use this mnemonic device. (pp. 68–69)

Phase IV: Foster Recall

The only way to remember ideas for a long period of time is to periodically practice or think through what was once learned. Teachers all too often have an implicit philosophy of "once learned, always learned." The spurious nature of this assumption is quickly highlighted once the reader tries to recall the capital of any state not recently visited. If one lives in Maine, try to recall the capital of South Dakota; if South Dakota, try Maine.

The way to enhance recall is to create conditions in which students are forced to think through the ideas several times just after they learn the information (immediate review) and then periodically throughout the schooling experience (delayed review). Both immediate and delayed reviews are essential. Ms. Sternberg (in the case study for Canadian provinces) used immediate review when she had the students break up into pairs and review the story (on the provinces) with a peer partner. She also used delayed review. As you will recall, two days after she presented the lesson on Canadian provinces, she asked the students to review the story in preparation for learning the names of the province capitals. The repetition is important. Hirsch (1996) notes,

> "Once is not enough" should be the motto of long-term memory, though nonmeaningful review and boring repetition are *not* good techniques. The classroom research cited above indicated that the best teachers did not engage in incessant review. Memory studies suggest that the best approach to achieving retention in long-term memory is "distributed practice." Ideally, lessons should spread a topic over several days, with repetitions occurring at moderately distant intervals. (pp. 164–165)

Ⓐ PPLICATIONS TO DIVERSE CLASSROOMS

Twenty to forty years ago, many teachers held higher expectations for students regarding the need to memorize poems, stories, and mathematical facts. A tremendous emphasis was placed on declarative knowledge, or knowledge that focused on "what" questions. Although teachers are now being encouraged to emphasize more procedural knowledge in their classes, some focus on facts and specific content will always be present. Students still memorize their multiplication tables even though the increased use of computers and other quick data-retrieval devices has limited the degree to which teachers feel a need to require students to memorize information.

Some recent educational theories (such as constructivism) implicitly diminish student need for memorization. Constructivist teachers place an emphasis on students' abilities to classify, analyze, predict, and create. As a consequence, some teachers (clearly not all!) may suggest that memorizing facts is antithetical to constructivist thinking. Such an assertion is conceptually erroneous! Students who explore concepts must know certain facts in order to engage in the analysis that is required. The difference is that the facts they use have personal relevance and meaning, rather than having the teacher use a mimetic approach in which students commit to short-term memory information that they subsequently give back to the teacher. The students draw on their own experiences and ideas—they think for themselves. Teachers who attempt to mediate student thinking must possess certain facts in order to help students shape their thoughts effectively. Constructivist teachers ask a lot of questions, but they rely on a tremendous amount of information that will allow them to ask questions that move the students' thinking forward (Brooks and Brooks, 1993). In essence, all students, regardless of their cultural background, and all teachers, regardless of their educational philosophy, need to possess certain facts in order to learn and teach new material. True, constructivist teachers want to see *how* students are learning, not just what they are recalling (Brooks and Brooks, 1999). But, as students are finding their way, they are using facts to develop their big ideas. Some of those facts include ideas for long-term memory—information to be memorized.

Students from some cultural backgrounds readily adjust to the expectation to memorize material. Part of the substantial success of the so-called "model minority" Asian American students is that they are extremely hardworking and high-achieving (Bennett, 1995). (As an aside, it is interesting to note that there is emerging evidence to suggest that the more assimilated the group, even for Asian Americans, the more the performance of that group mirrors the achievement levels of other mainstream groups.) Hard work requires that students pay close attention to what the teacher is teaching—the content of the lesson. Recall that the very first requirement for successful memorization is that a student attend to what the teacher expects the student to learn. Without some level of attentiveness, essential facts and concepts cannot be learned.

The beauty of using a variety of instructional strategies is that teachers are more likely to capture students' interests. A teacher who occasionally uses the mnemonic instructional model, and who helps the students create visual images of the content material, taps the strengths of those students who have high spatial intelligence or who have cultural or personal learning dispositions that favor the visualization process. The teacher does not use this model simply because certain ethnic or racial groups tend to favor visual processes for learning. Rather, the teacher uses a visual strategy because it builds on the strengths of all students (regardless of their cultural background) who learn best by creating visual images, and it enhances the cognitive repertoire of those students who do not rely on visual strategies as a learning device.

Mnemonic strategies are not effortless endeavors. They necessitate work—but they foster a type of work that can be potentially very rewarding. Cajete (1994), in describing the saliency of indigenous educational practice with Native Americans, poignantly points out that "Indigenous teaching revolves around some form of work. Indigenous teachers recognize that work invites concentration and facilitates a quietness of mind" (p. 225). That quietness translates into a capacity of the student to assimilate and construct meaningful learning experiences, and it transcends the learning propensities of any particular cultural group—all students can benefit from such experiences. But for mnemonics to be effective, teachers need to know the cultural backgrounds of their students. Levin (1993) asks and answers a powerful question relative to mnemonic usage with ethnically diverse students:

To maximize mnemonic benefits, must materials incorporating ethnically relevant content be developed by teachers and students from the target populations? Concerning . . . [that] question, it may be assumed that if the specific mnemonic content is not meaningful to a student, then the strategy will not function as intended. In fact, it is bound to complicate the learning process including additional unfamiliar or arbitrary information (e.g., "kool aid" for someone who does not know what that is). In a real mnemonic sense, then, one student's "cool aid" may be another's poison. (p. 241)

In education, far too many people think in polarized terms: One is either a traditionalist (teacher centered) or progressivist (constructivist). That is unfortunate. Mnemonics is a strategy for all teachers. In this regard, we believe the use of mnemonics is appropriate for students who are field-dependent and field-independent. Teachers who work with both types of learners are just providing a device to help them "hold on to" the information they acquire. Perhaps more critical is the way in which mnemonics can move teachers beyond a reliance on auditory approaches to content acquisition. With many different mnemonic devices, the teacher's approach can be much more visual. As a consequence, the teacher identifies what information (or facts) students need to attend to in a picture or word phrase and then carefully directs them in ways to remember that information. Creativity emerges as students create their own mnemonic associations or when they re-create mnemonic strategies that the teacher offers. That is, if students are taught material using mnemonic strategies and then forget some of the material, they need to know how to revise their mental images to make them more ridiculous or vivid so that they will be remembered. Finally, the teacher can foster, through the use of mnemonics, both convergent and divergent thinking. Convergence occurs as the teacher focuses the students' attention on particular ideas (to memorize and attend to). Divergence occurs when students begin to create their own images to replace those of the teacher that "don't work."

PREVALENT ISSUES IN DIVERSE CLASSROOMS

The mnemonics instructional model and its variations were created to help students memorize and acquire factual information. Memorization was once used often by America's teachers. However, with the emphases upon developing thinking skills and applying knowledge and skills to new and complex situations, teachers rarely draw upon this model. This may be due to a shift in instructional goals and priorities or to a lack of training in teacher-preparation institutions. At any rate, the following represent questions that teachers have asked us in our staff development efforts with them:

Q: *How can I create all the required mnemonic devices?*

A: Many teachers look at mnemonics as a difficult pedagogical strategy because of the vast array of pictures and illustrations that are required. Whether students are learning the names and order of the presidents or the location and capitals of the states, teachers perceive the task of creating all the mnemonic strategies as overwhelming. There are a couple of ways in which this problem can be solved. First, some teachers use commercially produced mnemonic materials (see, for example, www.eudesign.com/mnems/). The authors have worked with teachers who have used both the materials created by Rodriguez and Rodriguez (1994) and the Bornstein (1983) illustrations. Bornstein, for example, provides an array of mnemonic aids for learning facts (state capitals, multiplication tables, and so on), remembering names and faces, retaining vocabulary, and recalling numerical data. Illustrations are available for teachers to purchase and use in each of these areas. For learning state capitals, for example, Bornstein provides 50 picture illustrations: Harrisburg, Pennsylvania, is a bird carrying a pencil (in its claws) and preparing to drop it (the pencil) to a man with "Harvey" typed on his chest. For Bornstein's mathematical facts, an illustration, such as 9 x 5, might show Team 9 playing Team 5 on a football field with the ball on the 45-yard line. We are not suggesting that all commercial materials are excellent, just that they represent an option.

Second, classroom teachers can work with specialization teachers (in art, for example) to create their own mnemonic devices. Decide with students what visual pictures represent the best illustration of a fact. Teachers may want to work with students to accomplish this because the students' ideas may make more sense than illustrations conceived of by teachers or commercial publishers. Then have the students in art classes (or during enrichment times) create the illustrations for classroom use. With younger children, teachers may want to solicit the assistance of older students who can help create and design the illustrations.

Third, students can create their own mnemonics for a lesson. One of the ways we have used this is by having either students or teacher groups develop their own mnemonics as a review activity for a lesson. The excitement and enthusiasm this has generated among the groups has been amazing! Students who create their own mnemonics build connections that are more personally meaningful. A teacher's substitute word may not make as much sense to a student as one generated by the student. Highboy (1996) writes:

> There are several possible reasons why you are likely to remember your own mnemonics better. You may put more thought and effort into them than into mnemonics that someone else gives you. Your own mnemonics are likely to be the first associations to come to you at recall time. Another possible reason is that because other people suggest mnemonics different from the ones you would think of yourself, they are not as meaningful to you. (p. 110)

Q: *What facts should the students be expected to learn?*

A: This question will most likely persist as long as America does not adopt a nationalized curriculum. As long as each state and, in many cases, each school district creates its own curriculum, debate will rage regarding what facts are of the most worth. Several years ago, Hirsch (1988) argued that

> Cafeteria-type education, combined with the unwillingness of our schools to place demands on students, has resulted in a steady diminishment of commonly shared information between generations and between young

1066	H_2O
1492	ice age
abolitionism	Iron Curtain
Achilles	Joan of Arc
alienation	Kill two birds with one stone.
baptism	Lennon, John
Bell, Alexander Graham	lesbian
Berkeley, CA	mania
Caesar, Julius	naturalism
capitalism	Practice what you preach.
chivalry	satire
cholesterol	Seuss, Dr.
cross to bear	South Africa
Dark Ages	touché
democracy	visual aid
Dr. Jekyll and Mr. Hyde	Watergate
Every cloud has a silver lining.	War and Peace
Fahrenheit	X-ray
feminism	Yugoslavia
Galileo	zodiac
Golden Rule	

FIGURE 8-6   Examples of Hirsch's Essential Names, Phrases, Dates, and Concepts

Source: E. D. Hirsch. 1988. *Cultural Literacy*. New York: Vantage Books: Appendix.

people themselves. Those who graduate from the same school have often studied different subjects, and those who graduate from different schools have often studied different material even when their courses have carried the same titles. The inevitable consequence of the shopping mall high school is a lack of shared knowledge across and within schools. (pp. 20–21)

Hirsch, of course, offers in his text's appendix a list of terms, dates, and names that every literate person should know (see Figure 8-6). He has also expanded that in his Core Knowledge Series of texts that include books such as *What Your First Grader Needs to Know* and *What Your Second Grader Needs to Know,* and so on through the elementary grades. Whether one agrees or disagrees with Hirsch's essentialist philosophy, and he clearly evidences a Western bias in what he deems to be important information (e.g., Ellis Island is essential for cultural literacy and Angel Island is not), his basic premise holds some merit: Society needs to decide what students need to know and then ensure that a curriculum exists that helps students acquire or learn those ideas. Educators can take a first step toward achieving this if they work together to decide what they perceive as essential ideas—terms, facts, names—that all students should know. This, of course, is being increasingly addressed as states outline clear academic standards. Still, the American propensity is to cover too much material. As teachers, it is imperative that we make clear choices as to what is important and then make certain students learn that material. Even within a constructivist context some measure of consensus can be achieved regarding essential ideas. Recall that Sizer (1992) suggested that teachers identify those "exhibits" that all students should memorize. The teachers in that fictional school were not endeavoring to decide what all students everywhere should know (the Hirsch claim); rather, they were seeking to define in very particularized (school-specific) ways what made sense for their students.

Q: *Are there culturally relevant experiences or techniques that could be used in implementing the mnemonics model?*

A: Certainly! To be responsive, teachers should provide opportunities for students to work with factual information from their personal and cultural frames of reference. The benefits of cultural sources come through sharing of cultures within the group and by conveying to students that teachers are aware of and sensitive to student experiences. Teachers using the mnemonic model might use a choral approach (Gilbert and Gay, 1985), so often found in African American churches. In addition, a very modern technique could involve the use of rap and hip-hop rhymes and rhythms (for example, "Gangsta's Paradise") to teach factual information deemed important for the students to remember. One chemistry teacher, for example, uses songs as a way of teaching chemical formulas. A student who had this teacher recalled that the technique was really great except during exams—it seems that periodically you could hear students humming to themselves as a way of recalling the needed information.

E VALUATION CRITERIA ▪️X▪️

Efforts to evaluate mnemonics lessons require that the assessor first clearly determine the importance of the memorized material. From E. D. Hirsch's (1988) *Cultural Literacy* to Ravitch and Finn's (1987) *What Do Our 17-Year Olds Know?*, to the current focus on high stakes testing and accountability, arguments exist regarding the essential facts and concepts that all students should be able to recite. An important precondition for evaluating any mnemonics lesson is, therefore, what facts or information students should learn, and how essential is that information to the students' overall cognitive development. Considerable debate occurred during the 1990s regarding whether a national curriculum should be in place. Some claim that the academic advantage of countries such as Japan and Germany is caused by the existence of nationalized curricula. While we have some modest concerns with the notion of nationalizing a curriculum, we have no problems with a determination concerning what curriculum concepts (or big ideas) should be taught. Students should not memorize just to memorize! They should purposefully memorize important information from the academic disciplines. Hence, before initiating an evaluation of a lesson, it is important to respond to the following three questions:

1. What are the specific facts and concepts that students need to learn?
2. Is the teacher expecting students to memorize specific isolated facts (for example, capitals) or a specific sequence of facts (for example, the order of the planets)? What are they? List below.

   Specific isolated facts _____

   Specific sequence of facts _____
3. Do these facts or concepts fit within the total curriculum to be implemented?

Phase I: Focus Attention

1. Does the teacher specifically draw the students' attention to the material that they will memorize?   □ Yes   □ No
2. What techniques does the teacher use to focus the students' attention?   _____

Phase II: Create Connections

1. Which of the four mnemonic strategies does the teacher use?

   First-letter mnemonic ___
   Keyword ___
   Linkword ___
   Pegword ___
2. If acronym or acrostic, is the word or phrase clear and understandable?   □ Yes   □ No
3. If keyword, is the teacher using substitute words that make sense and that are vivid in nature?   □ Yes   □ No
4. If linkword, does the teacher have students learn the sequence of facts in ways that are logically interconnected?   □ Yes   □ No
5. If pegword, do the students know the pegs? Are the pegs appropriately connected with the information to be remembered?   □ Yes   □ No

Phase III: Create Associations

1. Which of the four rules does the teacher use to help students expand their senses through the creation of ridiculous associations?
2. Explain how one or more of these strategies is used by the teacher.

   Substitution ___
   Exaggeration ___
   Out of proportion ___
   Action ___
   Peer teaching ___
   Teacher review ___
   Other (explain) _____
   _____

Phase IV: Foster Recall

The final phase requires that the teacher systematically review with students the facts and concepts they have learned.

1. Identify which review strategies the   _____
   teacher uses, and describe whether   _____
   those approaches are effective.   _____

SAMPLE LESSONS

Mnemonic lessons are difficult to structure unless teachers have a very clear sense of the precise information that they want students to understand. Elementary school teachers often find mnemonic lessons easier to develop than do secondary school teachers because of the basic nature of many of the facts emphasized in elementary school. The following case study is for high school students and builds on a research study published by Mastropieri, Scruggs, and Levin (1987).

CASE STUDY I

Ms. Ebony Foxx's 10th graders in advanced-placement (AP) biology are preparing to learn about vascular plants. She wants her students to know the subdivisions of angiosperm and gymnosperm and to know the four classes associated with the two subdivisions (see Figure 8-7). Further, her AP students are expected to memorize the order names as well.

Ms. Foxx has already spent considerable time working with the students to know the definitions of the different terms. The students have learned the division, subdivision, and class labels. What they are having difficulty learning is the order names.

"Class, I know that some of you now have good basic definitions of vascular plants. You understand the differences between angiosperms, or flowering plants, and gymnosperms, which we described as "naked seed plants." As you make progress in your coursework, you need to be able to quickly recognize the various class and order designations. That's where many of you are having difficulty. To assist you in this learning process—to memorize the classes and orders of all the names in the plant classifications—I will show you how to use some mnemonic devices to assist you in learning the names.

"The first mnemonic [see Figure 8-8] is for angiosperms. For you to recall that angiosperms include dicotyledons, look carefully at the picture. Notice that the angel (angiosperm) has a pet dinosaur (dicotyledons). That image should help you connect angiosperm with dicotyledon. Now to remember three of the orders—rubiales, sapindales, and rosales—picture the dinosaur climbing up Rubik's cubes and preparing to lick sap that covers the leaves of a

DIVISION

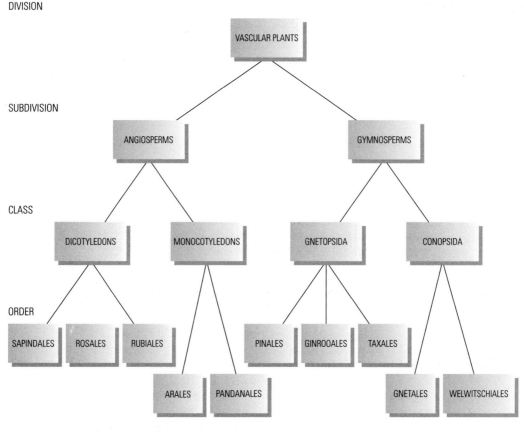

FIGURE 8-7 Plant Classification System

Adapted from M. E. Levin and J. R. Levin. 1990. "Scientific Mnemonomies: Methods for Maximizing More Than Memory." *American Educational Research Journal* 27(2): 304.

huge rose plant. One thing, students, with the advent of molecular biology and the ability to study DNA, the classification of plants is undergoing tremendous revision. As a consequence, many disagreements exist about the specific relationships in the classification system that I am having you memorize.

"Look carefully at the picture and then describe it to your peer partner."

The students all take a moment to look at the picture, then the persons in each pair describe the picture verbally to their partner.

Ms. Foxx continues the lesson. "Let's look now at the other class and order terms for angiosperm. Angiosperms also include monocotyledons, or monocots. Remember that the monocots include such things as wheat, corn, and lilies. Picture an angel—the same one, in fact, that we described earlier—with a pet monkey. And that monkey is very talented, so talented that the monkey can shoot arrows at pandas and successfully hit them [see Figure 8-9]. With this image in mind, you can now remember that angiosperms (angel) includes monocots (monkeys) who shoot arrows at pandas. Once again, class, take a minute to describe the picture to your partner."

FIGURE 8-8 Example of a Mnemonic Illustration: Angiosperm

Illustrated by Janet Olney Lasley. Based on illustration by M. E. Levin and J. R. Levin. 1990. "Scientific Mnemonomies: Methods for Maximizing More Than Memory." *American Educational Research Journal* 27(2): 305.

FIGURE 8-9 Example of a Mnemonic Illustration: Angiosperm

Based on illustration by M. E. Levin and J. R. Levin. 1990. "Scientific Mnemonomies: Methods for Maximizing More Than Memory." *American Educational Research Journal* 27(2): 305.

After a minute or so, Ms. Foxx continues her lesson by reviewing gymnosperms using pictures similar to those for angiosperms, though she shares with the students that the gymnosperm categorical relationships are changing and that the "old" form she is having them memorize may differ from some new forms they will see in college. At the end of the class, Ms. Foxx distributes a blank schematic of vascular plants and asks that the students attempt to complete it keeping in mind the mnemonics she used. The students finish and grade the task. Students who couldn't remember one of the terms (for example, the order names for monocots) are asked to revise their images to make them even more ridiculous. ■

Follow-Up Questions

1. Are the mnemonics that the teacher uses appropriate for teaching the major concepts in this lesson?

2. What other mnemonics might you use to teach the various class and order designations?

3. Identify three alternative strategies teachers might use to help students practice learning the class and order names (for example, peer teaching). Be specific regarding what steps you would have the students follow.

4. What other strategies might Ms. Foxx use for rehearsal and feedback if students are unable to recall one of the terms?

5. Is it appropriate to have students memorize information for which disagreement exists about the specifics of the conceptual relationships? Should dynamic knowledge be committed to memory?

ⒸASE STUDY II

Ms. Chick is a 3rd grade teacher. She is planning to teach a geography lesson to her students and plans to use a mnemonic device to help students learn some essential information.

She begins the lesson by reviewing the number of continents and their names and the number of oceans and their names.

"I am going to teach you a lesson so that you will know the names of the seven continents and the four oceans. When we are done, I will be able to give you a blank map, and you'll be able to label everything."

Ms. Chick turns on the overhead projector and displays a transparency with all the continents and oceans. She carefully has the students look at the map and then reviews all the continents and oceans. The students repeat each term "Africa" and "Asia" as Ms. Chick reviews the globe projection.

"Class, I'm going to share with you a story. It's about a man named Noah. Noah sees a storm coming and he and his friends (NAM and SAM) collect animals in preparation for dealing with the storm. The first things they collect are

Ants and Tics that are huge. They are gigantic, almost scary because they are big, as big as horses. They collect them and then proceed. They get tired and begin to ride the ants and tics. Just then they see a trail, and they discover that it is lined with gold. They are so excited with seeing the gold that they yell, "EUREKA!"

The story continues through a variety of descriptions of animals that Nam and Sam and Noah collect. At some point they put all the animals in an ark. The animals are now warm and cozy.

"Now that they are comfortable, they seem easy to be PACIFIED. *Pacify*, class, means peaceful." The students repeat, "pacify" . . . and the teacher continues through the oceanic terms.

When she finishes, the students clap loudly.

"Now, class, I want to review what all the terms mean. *NAM* means *North America*. What does *NAM* mean, class?"

"North America."

"What does *SAM* mean?"

"South America."

All the terms are reviewed (e.g., *EUREKA = Europe; PACIFIED = Pacific Ocean*).

"Now, class, with your partner, repeat this story. First, you tell the story, and then have your partner repeat it back to you."

All the students break into their partner groups and begin telling the story. Ms. Chick leaves the transparency on to help the students recall the story. As they share the story, Ms. Chick monitors their different versions and corrects the students when they make mistakes. The students repeat the story until they have it "down."

Teacher Reflections

The mnemonics teaching model is an ideal way to foster my 3rd graders' remembering skills for the names and locations of the continents and oceans. It was fun creating the exaggerations and ridiculous associations and then sharing them with teammates as the story evolved. It also gave me several chances to "ham it up," which are opportunities I cherish after 23 years of teaching. Preparing for the link strategy took some time and effort, but the results made it worth the extra time. The students were so engaged with the story and motivated to learn. They were very enthusiastic about repeating it with their partners. I learned how important it is to teach for overlearning so the students can recall the information. This can be accomplished by having them answer in unison when reviewing the names: "Again, class, what are these called . . . ?" This will become easier as a person gains more experience with the mnemonics model. When using a long story link, it works to have a graphic organizer of the substitute words so the students can refer to the visual aid while reviewing. Another important part of this instructional model is the periodic review of the content. It only requires a few minutes each month to review the story. This puts the facts into the students' long-term memory. ∎

SUGGESTED LESSON DEVELOPMENT: QUESTIONS FOR REFLECTION ✔

The use of mnemonics may be appropriate for all classroom lessons. Teachers need to think carefully about how and when to use mnemonics with students. Specific steps to follow are:

1. Determine what facts or concepts students should retain in their long-term memories.
2. Identify specific ways to draw attention to those facts and concepts.
3. Determine what mnemonic strategy (first-letter mnemonics, keyword, peg-word, linkword) is best suited to help students retain the information.
4. Develop strategies to help students practice the use of mnemonics.
5. Identify methods students can use to reinforce their understanding of the memorized information.

TECHNOLOGY ENHANCEMENT A D I S C ◆

The World Wide Web offers teachers an incredible array of resources to support the instructional planning and design process. The technology enhancement for this chapter serves as an excellent example of how teachers willing to search the Web (I) can discover exciting new tools that can augment (A) their efforts to employ the instructional models. In this case, capitalizing on Web-based mnemonic resources enhances the mnemonics model.

Capitalizing on Web-Based Mnemonic Resources

The Mnemonics teaching strategy is popular in many fields of work and study, especially those that require the ability to remember and recall complex data sets. For example, a search of the World Wide Web using the key word "mnemonics" reveals many sites specifically developed by doctors and nurses to help medical and nursing school students remember everything from the bones of the foot to the cranial nerves. Pilots, research scientists, computer programmers and many other professionals have created similar Web sites. Today, numerous sites support teachers and students in finding or developing mnemonic devices for a wide variety of academic disciplines.

Web sites for educators who focus on mnemonics tend to be one of two types. The first type serves as online libraries of mnemonic devices that can be searched by topic. An excellent example of this type of site can be found at www.eudesign.com/mnems/. From this home page, teachers can access and search a database of mnemonic devices in seven academic categories including astronomy, biology and nature, business, chemistry, geography/geology, history, and language/literature. Each of these categories contains many specific topics. One of the strengths of this site is that it catalogues many different types of mnemonics including illustrations, diagrams, linkword stories, as well as

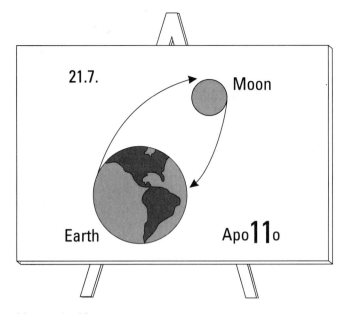

FIGURE 8-10   Men on the Moon

From www.eudesign.com/mnems/

keyword and pegword strategies. For example, one of 24 topics listed in the astronomy category is Man on the Moon. Figure 8-10 illustrates how a mnemonics diagram is used to help students remember the date and time of Neil Armstrong's historic step, as well as the specific Apollo mission on which the historic event occurred.

Another nice feature of this site is that each mnemonic is accompanied with additional information that helps students expand their understanding of the topic of interest. This is a dynamic site that continues to grow and change as teachers contribute favorite mnemonic devices they have found successful in their own classrooms.

In addition to the comprehensive site discussed above, teachers can also take advantage of sites that focus on specific topics. For example, social studies teachers can help their students learn the state capitals by using the mnemonic devices catalogued at www.members.home.net/unknownprogrammer/states. This interesting site provides a mnemonic for each state capital that includes key words as well as a supporting illustration. Similarly, language arts teachers can help students master commonly misspelled words by using the mnemonics strategies found at www.spellingbee.com/lessonplans/lesson2.htm. Finally, science teachers will find a rich collection of mnemonics organized by subject matter at www.cyberbeach.net/~willows/mnemon.htm.

The second type of mnemonics Web site for educators focuses on helping teachers enhance their skill in developing and effectively employing mnemonic strategies. One interesting example of this second type was developed by NASA's Cognition Lab. The site, http://olias.arc.nasa.gov/cognition/tutorials/index.html, was designed to engage students in learning about various aspects of human memory. The site provides links to on-line experiments and learning activities including *The Mnemonicizer*, which helps students create their own *first-letter mnemonics*. Teachers can also find online support for developing and using mnemonics by accessing the University of Toronto's *Learning to Learn* Web site at www.snow.utoronto.ca/Learn2/mod4/mnemonics.html. The site includes tips on the effective design and use of the various mnemonics strategies.

Grade Level Modifications

Modifying the use of the mnemonics model to meet the needs of students at different grade and ability levels is essentially a function of teacher decision-making. In the early elementary grades, teachers should be especially considerate of selecting mnemonic strategies and devices that are developmentally appropriate. In the intermediate grades, teachers should consider encouraging students to create their own mnemonic devices. As described in the following section, this can be a stimulating and creative process as students interact with and learn to manipulate a variety of multimedia resources. Finally, students in the secondary grades can be encouraged to find and utilize the Web-based mnemonic resources that can be found to support practically any field of study.

Low Tech/High Tech Applications

Using an Internet search engine to find mnemonic devices on the World Wide Web constitutes a relatively low-tech enhancement of the mnemonics model. Teachers interested in a more high-tech application might consider having students work together or alone to design and develop mnemonic illustrations and diagrams using multimedia resources such as KidPix, PowerPoint, Hyperstudio, or any word processing software. With the clip art and photographs now available on the Web, students can design mnemonic diagrams or illustrated linkword stories for themselves and their classmates.

Value Added for Diverse Learners

Teachers using technology to enhance the mnemonics model should be mindful of how the various mnemonic strategies might be preferred by students with different learning styles or cultural backgrounds. When selecting mnemonic devices from the Web, teachers should reflect on their personal understanding of the learning preferences of their students. For example, visual learners or Asian American and Native American learners might prefer mnemonic pictures and diagrams as memory devices. In contrast, auditory learners, including many African American and Hispanic students may profit most from hearing culturally grounded linkword stories. Finally, kinesthetic learners may enhance their memory when given the opportunity to physically create mnemonic diagrams or illustrations by manipulating resources such as traditional art supplies or Web-based multimedia materials.

Web-Based Resources

The Web-based resources described above represent only a sampling of the kinds of support that teachers interested in mnemonics can find on the World Wide Web. One excellent way to find mnemonics for specific areas of interest is to conduct your search by entering Booleans that combine the word mnemonics with the specific subject or topic of interest. Using this technique, one of the authors was able to quickly locate mnemonic devices for the parts of speech, photosynthesis, and isosceles triangles.

Finally, teachers desiring to engage students in searching the Web for mnemonic devices should be aware that some sites include mnemonics that employ offensive language or images. Identifying desirable sites and directing students to their specific URLs should prevent this from being a problem for students or their parents.

ⓈUMMARY

Students are confronted with an abundance of new information each day in schools. Teachers frequently assume that students inherently know how to remember all the information that is imparted during a school day. They also forget how much new vocabulary is part of the everyday experience of most students. For example, the amount of new vocabulary introduced in science lessons is often equivalent to that evidenced in foreign language instruction—anyone who has had a son or daughter in a high school biology class of a traditional teacher need look no further than their last chapter quiz to verify this observation.

Mnemonics are a user-friendly way of taking factual information that students need to know and showing them a way that will enable them to remember that information. The technique also draws on the more creative dimensions of a student's intelligence. Because so many mnemonics require visualization (imagination), students can draw on spatial or musical intelligences—they can create pictures or use songs as mnemonic devices.

The critical question, of course, is this: Do mnemonics work? Drawing on the data of a wide variety of researchers, Carney, Levin, and Levin (1993) noted the following:

1. *Content generality*. Mnemonic strategies have been found to improve students' memory for terminology and factual information in a variety of curricular domains, including language arts (English and foreign vocabulary, reading comprehension), social studies, science, mathematics, and art . . .

2. *Student characteristics*. Mnemonic strategies have been used profitably by all types of students, ranging from young children to college-age adults and the elderly, from those with mental disabilities to those with academic gifts, and across a variety of social class groups . . .

3. *Remembering new information*. With particular regard to remembering new vocabulary and technical terminology, of all instructional strategies in current

use or under current scrutiny, mnemonic strategies have proved to be the most effective . . .

4. *Improved retention*. The learning gains associated with mnemonic strategies have been found to last for long periods of time, namely, several weeks and, in some cases, months . . .

5. *Strategy transfer*. Students can be instructed in the effective application of mnemonic strategies so that they are later able to use such strategies on their own in other learning contexts . . .

6. *Strategy flexibility*. Mnemonic strategies can be successfully combined or integrated with alternative instructional strategies as seen fit by either teachers or students . . .

7. *Higher-order thinking*. Critically, and contrary to popular belief, mnemonic strategies do not foster simple rote memory at the expense of comprehension, usage, and problem solving. In fact, the available research evidence suggests that acquiring factual information via mnemonic strategies can often improve students' ability to apply that information . . .

8. *Motivation*. Apart from these performance-based conclusions, feedback received from students indicates that using mnemonic strategies is more enjoyable than traditional methods of study, which in turn increases students' task engagement and persistence. . . . (pp. 26–27)

Clearly, mnemonic strategies have more potential than just helping students retain facts. Used correctly, they motivate some students who within traditional classrooms are permitted to explore only narrow dimensions of their intellectual potential. Lorayne and Lucas (1974) observe that in the "ancient world, a trained memory was of vital importance" (p. 1). In this modern information age, it is even more important! Unfortunately, with the abundance of information access systems now available to students, the expectations for memorizing information are not what they once were. That circumstance is unfortunate! Certainly, an educated person needs to know how to access information, but that person must also know how to retain some of that necessary information once it is accessed.

REFERENCES

Bennett, C. I. 1995. *Comprehensive Multicultural Education: Theory and Practice* (3rd ed.). Boston: Allyn & Bacon.

Bornstein, A. 1983. *Bornstein School of Memory Training*. Los Angeles: Bornstein School of Memory Training.

Brooks, M. G., and J. G. Brooks. 1999. "The Courage to be Constructivist." *Educational Leadership* 57(3): 18–24.

Brooks, J. G., and M. G. Brooks. 1993. *The Case for Constructivist Classrooms*. Washing-ton, DC: Association for Supervision and Curriculum Development.

Cajete, G. 1994. *Look to the Mountain: An Ecology of Indigenous Education*. Durango, CO: Kivaki Press.

Carney, R. N., M. E. Levin, and J. R. Levin. 1993. "Mnemonic Strategies: Instructional Techniques Worth Remembering." *Teaching Exceptional Children* 25(4): 24–30.

Gilbert, S., and G. Gay. 1985. "Improving the Success in School of Poor Black Children." *Phi Delta Kappan* 67(2): 133–137.

Higbee, K. L. 1996. *Your Memory* (2nd ed.). New York: Marlowe.

Hill, D. 2001. "Rays, Rhythm, and Rhyme," *Education Week*, January 17, 2001, 32–36.

Hirsch, E. D. Jr., 1988. *Cultural Literacy*. New York: Vintage Books.

Hirsch, E. D. Jr., 1996. *The Schools We Need*. New York: Doubleday.

Hock, M. F., J. B. Schumaker, and D. D. Deshler. 2001. "The Case for Strategic Tutoring." *Educational Leadership* 58(7): 50–52.

Joyce, B., M. Weil, and E. Calhoun. 2000. *Models of Teaching* (6th ed.). Boston: Allyn & Bacon.

Levin, J. R. 1993. "Mnemonic Strategies and Classroom Learning: A Twenty Year Report Card." *Elementary School Journal* 94(2): 235–244.

Levin, M. E., and J. R. Levin. 1990. "Scientific Mnemonomies: Methods for Maximizing More than Memory." *American Educational Research Journal* 27(2): 301–321.

Lorayne, H., and J. Lucas. 1974. *The Memory Book*. New York: Ballantine.

Luria, A. R. 1968. *The Mind of a Mnemonist*. Chicago: Henry Regnery.

Mastropieri, M. A., T. E. Scruggs, and J. R. Levin. 1987. "Learning Disabled Students' Memory for Expository Prose: Mnemonic Versus Nonmnemonic Pictures." *American Educational Research Journal* 24(4): 505–519.

Mathematics Plus. 1992. Orlando, FL: Harcourt Brace Jovanovich. (See Grade 7 text, p. 169.)

Ormrod, J. E. 1999. *Human Learning* (3rd ed.). Upper Saddle River, NJ: Merrill Prentice Hall.

Pressley, M., J. R. Levin, and H. D. Delaney. 1982. "The Mnemonic Keyword Method." *Review of Educational Research* 52: 61–91.

Pressley, M., J. R. Levin, and G. E. Miller. 1981. "How Does the Keyword Method Affect Vocabulary Comprehension and Usage?" *Reading Research Quarterly* 16: 213–226.

Ravitch, D., and C. E. Finn, Jr. 1987. *What Do Our 17-Year Olds Know?* New York: Harper & Row.

Rodriguez, D., and J. Rodriguez. 1994. *Times Tables the Fun Way*. Sandy, UT: Key.

Rose, C. 1985. *Accelerated Learning*. New York: Dell.

Sizer, T. R. 1992. *Horace's School: Redesigning the American High School*. Boston: Houghton Mifflin.

Sprenger, M. 1999. *Learning and Memory: The Brain in Action*. Washington, DC: Association for Supervision and Curriculum Development.

NINE

• *Direct Instruction*

Chapter Objectives

At the end of this chapter, readers will be able to

1. *Describe the theoretical basis for the direct instruction model.*
2. *Identify the essential phases of the direct instruction model.*
3. *Identify the strengths and weaknesses of the direct instruction model.*
4. *Describe ways in which direct instruction can be used with diverse student populations.*
5. *Create a direct instruction lesson for personal use in a classroom that utilizes various forms of technology.*

❶NTRODUCTION

One of the most misused and least understood models is direct instruction. For as long as schools have existed, "teacher talk" has dominated the way in which students learn information and teachers communicate facts. Indeed, some teachers believe that once they utter the words in the classroom, the students have learned the information. Teacher talk for many teachers has been considered synonymous with student learning. Such a circumstance is regrettable! For although direct instruction does require that teachers make a number of preinstructional decisions, it does not suggest that students are unimportant, passive observers in the teaching-learning process. Direct instruction requires that teachers make explicit instructional decisions, but it also demands that teachers know what they are going to assess and whether students adequately acquire the requisite skills taught by the teacher.

Not all concepts taught by teachers are amenable to direct instruction. Several years ago, the then Secretary of Education, William Bennett, was asked to teach a lesson to high school students on James Madison's *Federalist Paper 10*.

> It would be a mistake to say that this systematic, small-step approach applies to all students or all situations. It is most important for young learners, slow learners, and all learners when the material is new, difficult, or hierarchical.
>
> BARAK ROSENSHINE

Not surprisingly, Mr. Bennett exhibited substantial content knowledge of the James Madison treatise regarding why the Constitution should be ratified. The lesson was taped and a transcript sent to several evaluation experts in the field of education, one of whom had considerable expertise in direct instruction as an instructional model. The expert, Barak Rosenshine, reviewed the tape for instructional effectiveness and suggested that it was difficult to assess the lesson because Mr. Bennett was teaching content concepts, not specific, concrete skills.

What that expert observed is fundamental to understanding how and when to use direct instruction: The model is best used when teachers are teaching skills, not when communicating conceptually complex content ideas. To illustrate this, Rosenshine (1986) describes the difficulty of using some steps of the direct instruction model when teaching content material.

> My main point is that it is difficult to apply some of the major findings we have learnt from studying the teaching of skills to lessons which teach content. Some of these findings include checking for student understanding, providing for active student participation, providing for a high success rate, correcting errors, and providing for guided practice and independent practice. But such findings do not, and will not, transfer easily to the teaching of content. . . .
>
> In this [Bennett's] lesson, the students need practice in explaining the problems and solutions developed in Federalist 10, their relevance for our time, and the view of human nature and human rights embodied in the thought of these founders. The teacher needs to hear how well the students are doing, and the students need feedback on their efforts. All these would occur easily when teaching a skill. Unfortunately, we do not have mechanisms for doing this when teaching content. (p. 306)

In essence, the instructional model a teacher uses is influenced by the instructional goals the teacher establishes. A teacher who wants to teach a specific skill (for example, how to divide fractions, how to diagram a sentence, or how to construct an origami butterfly) is best served by using the direct instruction model. On the other hand, a teacher who wants students to understand social issues or appreciate poetry will be far less pleased, as will the students, with the results of a direct instruction lesson. Rosenshine (1987) writes:

> These findings [about direct instruction] are less applicable for teaching in areas that are less well structured—that is, those in which skills do not follow explicit steps or where concepts are less identifiable and distinct. . . .
> Thus the results of this research are less relevant for teaching composition writing of term papers, reading comprehension, analysis of literature or historical trends, or discussion of social issues or concepts such as liberalism or modernity. (p. 75)

Teachers make decisions about what to teach. If what they plan to teach is a concrete skill, then direct instruction is the most appropriate strategy to ensure maximal student achievement. If the teacher is planning to teach content concepts, then direct instruction still has applicability, though the teacher will need to rely a bit more on the literature regarding lecturing and explaining (see Rosenshine, 1986). That is, for presenting content material the teacher needs to do such things as use questions to maintain student attention, signal transitions between sections, signal those points that are most important, use humor to hold student attention, summarize material within the context of the lecture, give or ask students for relevant examples, and review relevant background knowledge.

Direct instruction requires that teachers proceed in a way that limits information flow but enhances information transfer. The human brain can process only so much information at one time. Some teachers present too much information, and what they do present is covered in a very disjointed fashion. The teacher's obligation is to find ways of clustering and connecting ideas, facts, and information so that students can effectively process what the teacher presents. That means that the teacher must be clear about specifying the goals of a lesson, systematic in identifying how students are to learn material, and vigilant in checking on whether students are actually learning the content. In essence, the teacher must determine what skill to teach and then teach that skill in a step-by-step process. Finally, the teacher must check to see whether students have learned what has been taught. Let us see what this looks like in one 6th grade classroom.

CASE **S**TUDY

Mr. Dale Carthridge begins his mathematics unit with the following statements:

"During the past several weeks we have been studying how to add and subtract fractions. Last week we investigated how to multiply fractions. Let's take a couple of minutes to review the process that we followed in multiplying $\frac{3}{4} \times \frac{1}{2}$." At this point Mr. Carthridge reviews the steps the students should follow in multiplying fractions. Once the class completes the review, Mr. Carthridge begins a new segment of the unit.

"Today, class, we are going to learn how to divide fractions. There will be two purposes for our lesson. First, you will list the specific steps that must be followed in dividing fractions; and second, you will describe why you follow the steps used in the division process."

"Let's begin. First, I want you all to get your slates out and put them on your desks." (Mr. Carthridge has slates and chalk that the students use during math drill and practice exercises.)

"I am going to work three problems on the board. You will see each step labeled clearly, but I want you to perform the work on your slates as I perform the work on the board. The problem we will start with is $\frac{1}{2} \div \frac{3}{8} = ?$"

The teacher then puts the acronym PIRMS on the board: Problem Invert Reduce Multiply Solve. "Let's look at what each of these letters in the acronym mean for $\frac{1}{2} \div \frac{3}{8}$. I call this the PIRMS process."

Mr. Carthridge works the first problem slowly, and next to each of the words he identifies the step the students must follow. When he is finished, the problem on the board looks similar to the one in Table 9-1.

The students have the same problem worked out on their slates. As Mr. Carthridge presents each step, he carefully talks them through the process: "First, class, you state the problem, which in this case is $\frac{1}{2} \div \frac{3}{8}$. Next, class, Step 2: You invert the fraction on the right side. To remember this, just think that it's right to invert on the right. Sharonda, what does invert mean?" (Sharonda correctly describes how to invert.)

Mr. Carthridge meticulously describes the first problem and then erases, at the end, all of the numbers on the right side of Table 9-1 and puts a new

TABLE 9-1 Sequential Organizer for Solving Division Problem

STEP 1: Problem	$1/2 \div 3/8 = ?$
STEP 2: Invert	$1/2 \times 8/3 = ?$
STEP 3: Reduce	$1/2 \times 8/3 = 1/1 \times 4/3$
STEP 4: Multiply	$1/1 \times 4/3 = 4/3$
STEP 5: Solve	$4/3 = 1\,1/3$

problem on the board: $3/4 \div 1/3 = ?$ Once again he very carefully describes the mathematical processes step-by-step. The students follow each step by performing the steps on their personal slates. At the end, Mr. Carthridge erases the problem and all the steps.

"Now, class, I'm going to give you a third problem. But in this case, you will be helping me. Let's begin. I'll start by giving you a problem: $3/5 \div 1/2 = ?$ Joshua, what's the second step that we use?"

"You invert the numbers and multiply."

"Which numbers?"

"The $1/2$."

"Why?" responds Mr. Carthridge.

"Because it's on the right side," says Joshua.

"Yes, and a little later you'll also know the more technical reason for inverting the $1/2$. What's the next step after we have $3/5 \times 2/1$? Jasmine?"

"You simplify."

"And what do you mean by simplify, Jasmine?"

"You see if any of the numbers are factors of the other numbers."

"Excellent. I like how you explained that. Well, are any of the numbers factors and can you simplify? Lanita?"

"No."

"Good. So what's the next step?"

"You multiply."

"Yes. First you multiply the numerators, and then you multiply the denominators. What would you get if you do that? Troy?"

"$6/5$."

"Correct. So $3/5 \times 2/1 = 6/5$. Now the last step is to solve the problem. Remember last week I indicated that this means putting the improper fraction $6/5$ into its lowest terms. And what would that be? Nathan?"

"$1\text{–}1/5$."

"Yes. So $3/5 \times 1/2 = 1\,1/5$."

"Now I want you to do one on your slate. When you finish, please show all your work, and hold your slate up so I can see your work. Now, try $3/7 \times 2/3 = ?$"

The students work the problem and hold up their slates. Mr. Carthridge moves around the room and checks the students' progress. He then gives them three more problems: $1/5 \div 1/3 = ?$; $2/9 \div 4/5 = ?$; and $1/4 \div 1/2 = ?$ After the students complete each problem, Mr. Carthridge reviews each step with the students to make certain everyone understands.

"Tomorrow, class, we are going to look at why you invert to get the answer. Once you know that, you will have an even better sense of why you follow these steps. For homework I want you to do the 20 problems on the worksheet. . . ."

Mr. Carthridge is teaching a concrete skill—dividing fractions—using the direct instruction model. The step-by-step process, coupled with constant efforts to check for understanding, are the foundation upon which this instructional model is grounded. ∎

❶HEORETICAL PERSPECTIVE

Direct instruction is grounded on the fundamental assumption that unless the teacher knows where a lesson is headed, it will be impossible to know whether a goal has been reached. Far too many teachers have an unclear sense of what they want to accomplish during an instructional lesson. They know that they want students to be busy (to work), but they are often less certain of the specific, academic goals they wish to achieve.

Direct instruction is not new! In the 1800s a form of direct instruction was used to teach students how to read. McGuffey (in the 1860s) instituted a system of reading that demanded that teachers repeat and pronounce words in particular ways in order to assist the beginning reader (see Finkelstein, 1989). In fact, M. C. Hippean, who observed American teachers in the 1850s, noted that "teachers were particularly exacting about sounds that were difficult. . . . Teachers explained to the students the position of the teeth and lips, the location of the tongue . . . and then watched carefully to see if students reproduced the sounds properly" (Finkelstein, 1989, pp. 54–55). Reading has always been a focus for direct instruction strategies because reading skills are so fundamental to school success. Bereiter and Engelmann (1966) created the modern "scripted" model as part of the direct instruction program for preschool children to help them acquire basic skills in arithmetic and language. Gagne (1977) conceptualized the basic "nonscripted" model (anticipatory set, statement of objectives, lesson preparation with checks for student understanding, guided practice, and closure) and made it a part of the educational psychology literature. Rosenshine (1983) slightly redefined the technique (see Table 9-2) to a six-step instructional functions model (offer daily review, present new content, initial student practice, provide feedback and corrective assessment, provide independent practice, and offer weekly reviews). Hunter (1976), though, is most notable in popularizing the model. Her model includes a seven-step process that is quite similar to Rosenshine's approach, but clearly it was Hunter's ability to articulate ideas (she was a gifted presenter) that brought life to an otherwise staid model. To Hunter's credit, she never argued that alternative instructional models could not be utilized in her presentation phase, but many teachers who have learned her model use the structure of the lesson in an almost legalistic, linear, sequential fashion. The result has been stilted, uninteresting instruction for many youngsters!

The research on direct instruction suggests that the model has the most power in teaching basic skills. As a consequence, teachers in any academic disci-

TABLE 9-2 Instructional Functions

1. Daily review:

Checking homework

Reteaching areas where there were student errors

2. Presenting new content/skills:

Provide overview

Proceed in small steps (if necessary), but at a rapid pace

If necessary, give detailed or redundant instructions and explanations

New skills are phased in while old skills are being mastered

3. Initial student practice:

High frequency of questions and overt student practice (from teacher and materials)

Prompts are provided during initial learning (when appropriate)

All students have a chance to respond and receive feedback

Teacher checks for understanding by evaluating student responses

Continue practice until students are firm

Success rate of 80 percent or higher during initial learning

4. Feedback and correctives (and recycling of instruction, if necessary):

Feedback to students, particularly when they are correct but hesitant

Student errors provide feedback to the teacher that corrections and/or reteaching is necessary

Corrections by simplifying questions, giving clues, explaining or reviewing steps, or reteaching last steps

5. Independent practice so that students are firm and automatic:

Seatwork

Unitization and automaticity (practice to overlearning)

Need for procedure to ensure student engagement during seatwork (that is, teacher or aide monitoring)

95 percent correct or higher

6. Weekly and monthly reviews:

Reteaching, if necessary

Source: B. Rosenshine. 1983. "Teaching Functions in Instructional Programs." *Elementary School Journal* 83(4): 338.

pline that has a heavy skill base (for example, mathematics) will find the direct instruction model powerful and useful. Rosenshine (1983) reported a series of studies that investigated whether teacher use of direct instruction enhances student academic performance. In several different studies, he found enhanced student academic achievement as a consequence of teacher use of the direct instruction model (Rosenshine also identifies it as "explicit teaching").

Not all studies on direct instruction, however, suggest the "marked" growth described by Rosenshine. In the now-famous Napa Valley studies, researchers collected longitudinal data on the academic growth of students whose teachers were trained using the Hunter model. Stallings and Krasavage (1986) describe the Hunter model as follows:

Basic to the model are five elements of a lesson design. When a new lesson is started, the teacher presents a set activity that involves all of the students. A good set links the students' experience and prior knowledge to the new material to be learned. The set includes a statement of the lesson's purpose and clear, observable objectives. The objectives are stated behaviorally; for example, at the end of the lesson the learner will be able to count by fives to 100. The next element is presenting the new information in small segments. Instruction often takes the form of modeling or demonstration. After each segment of the lesson, all students are checked for understanding. Based on the students' responses, the teacher monitors and adjusts the level of the lesson, reteaching as necessary. The element following instruction is guided practice. Here the teacher provides opportunities for the students to practice the new learning. They are given feedback and assistance until they have mastered the new lesson. When the teacher is assured the students can work independently without errors, a closure activity provides one more practice item. Following closure, students do independent practice to overlearn the material. (p. 118)

The results from the Napa Valley students were disappointing, especially when the long-term effects were measured. Initial gains by students in trained teachers' classrooms were evident, but those gains diminished the longer teachers utilized the direct instruction model. Although a number of researchers offer insights into why that circumstance occurred (see Porter, 1986; Robbins, 1986; Stallings and Krasavage, 1986), their observations do not completely obviate the potential power of the model. One significant observation they made has to do with how teachers use time. For a number of years educators have known that allocated time and student-engaged time were important dynamics for learning success. One of the most important by-products of direct instruction may be how teachers choose to use time and how they work with students to ensure success during the instructional sequence. For teachers who already have high student-engagement rates, the payoffs for direct instruction may be limited; but for those teachers who struggle to maximize student engagement during class lessons, the didactic structure of direct instruction may be efficacious, especially in teaching discrete skills. Porter (1986) confirms this observation based on his investigation of the Napa Valley schools. He writes:

It is interesting to note that the effects of the ITIP [Instructional Theory into Practice] program on student achievement were small, even though fairly substantial changes were produced in engaged time. Even in the disastrous third year, time-off-task was less than half what it had been at the start of the study. Two similar Follow-Through studies conducted at the same time as the Napa project both apparently found that training in classroom management increased time-on-task but did not increase student achievement. . . . A problem cited in . . . [some] studies is that most classes began so high in time-on-task that there was little to be gained. In Napa, six of the 13 classes began above 80% on-task, and 10 were above 70%. Pushing time-on-task above, say, 80% may be of limited value in increasing student achievement. (p. 170)

One other potential negative associated with scripted direct instruction surfaced in work conducted by the High/Scope Educational Foundation. Researchers there compared several methods of fostering academic achievement in young children. They found that scripted direct instruction produced the greatest immediate gains but that as those same children matured, they evidenced more emotional problems. The researchers suggest that the problem is with the highly authoritarian nature of the technique and its lack of emphasis on students' emotional and social needs (Viadero, 1999).

A couple of cautions concerning the criticisms before we present the model. First, most of the research conducted on direct instruction has been with elementary-age students. That fact does not suggest that the model is inappropriate for older students, but it does indicate the limited scope of research to determine the power of the technique with different student populations. Second, direct instruction does suggest specific sequencing of instruction and it does demand that teachers clearly know what skill or content objectives they want to achieve. In essence, teachers provide the conceptual structuring for this model. They create and present the schema that students are expected to learn and assimilate. Teachers who want students to engage in critical thinking will find the model less useful. Direct instruction is a time-efficient way to communicate content, but it does not focus on the complexities and nuances of some disciplinary concepts. Gersten, Taylor, and Graves (1999) observe:

> This brings us directly to a current question in instruction for students with learning disabilities and for students from a variety of linguistic backgrounds: Can principles of direct instruction be merged with more constructivist or open-ended approaches in the areas of language arts, language development, expressive writing, and the teaching of problem solving to culturally and linguistically diverse students?
>
> Traditional direction instruction, as developed to teach basic academic skills to young children, does not make sense for topics and content areas in which the knowledge base is not well defined or well articulated. For example, if the instructional goal is to teach students how to generate questions when they read, then a teacher cannot provide a clear, explicit model. Rather, the teacher can provide and generate a range of models of questions, can encourage students to share the questions they've generated, and can—in an informal but conspicuous fashion—provide students with feedback on the conciseness, relevance, and clarity of the questions they generate. Such an approach has been found to be successful in building reading comprehension and writing abilities. (pp. 91–92)

For example, why does one invert and multiply? Direct instruction avoids some of the mystery, but it can also help ensure that all students know a particular process. Third, much of the research has been conducted by advocates of the technique. That does not invalidate findings, but it does suggest a need for cautious interpretation.

One final observation. Several different forms of direct instruction exist. During the past couple years, direct instruction has been popularized as a result of the heavy emphasis by some high poverty schools on this model (e.g., Success

Ten Schoolwide Reform Approaches at a Glance	Evidence of positive effects on student achievement	Installation cost (1st year)[1]	School support provided by developer	Year introduced in schools	Number of schools	Grade levels
Accelerated Schools	◔ (Marginal)	◑ (Promising)	$27	'86	1,220	K–8
America's Choice	?	● (Strong)	$190	'98	92	K–12
Coalition of Essential Schools	○ (Mixed, Weak)	◔ (Marginal)	NA	'84	1,200	K–12
Core Knowledge	◑ (Promising)	◑ (Promising)	$56	'90	968	K–8
Direct Instruction	● (Strong)	◑ (Promising)	$244	Late '60s	300	K–6
Edison Project	NA	NA	NA	'95	79	K–10
Expeditionary Learning Outward Bound	◑ (Promising)	● (Strong)	$81	'92	60	K–12
Multiple Intelligences	NA	NA	NA	NA	NA	NA
School Development Program	◑ (Promising)	◑ (Promising)	$45	'68	721	K–12
Success for All	● (Strong)	● (Strong)	$270	'87	1,500	PreK–6

● = Strong
◑ = Promising
◔ = Marginal
○ = Mixed, Weak
? = No Research
NA = Not Available

[1] Costs are in thousands of dollars.

FIGURE 9-1 Ten Schoolwide Reform Approaches at a Glance

Source: Traub, J. 1999. *Better by Design.* Washington DC: The Thomas B. Fordham Foundation, p. 12.

for All). Figure 9-1 illustrates the different dominant models and the research base, cost, and number of schools using each model in 1999. As the reader can see, the research support for direct instruction is substantial.

The form of direct instruction represented in the systemic reform framework is "scripted" and parallels what Siegfried Engelmann developed. An example of a scripted lesson is provided in Chapter 2. In scripted direct instruction, the teacher's actions and words are highly prescribed, choreographed, and with lots of feedback. Viadero (1999) describes one teacher:

> Mr. Carpenter's 6th graders . . . were working on their reasoning and writing skills. Their task: Take two sentences and make a new sentence from them that begins with the word "no" and uses the word "only."
>
> "The wolves howled and ate at night," Mr. Carpenter reads. "The wolves did not eat."
>
> Fourteen youngsters bend over the papers, writing the answers as the teacher walks around checking their work . . .
>
> "The answer is . . . ," Mr. Carpenter prompts. The students shout out in unison: "No, the wolves only howled at night." Similar chanting is also audible from classrooms down the hall. (p. 43)

In addition, Engelmann's form of direct instruction emphasized lots of repetition or "recursiveness" of facts and ideas. Traub (1999) writes,

> Another of Engelmann's fundamental pedagogical principles is recursiveness. A teacher in a Direct Instruction classroom may return half a dozen

Direct Teaching

If you wish to teach spelling skills, here is one direct instruction method you can use. Be sure to select words that the students know the meaning of and can read. Then teach spelling.

Teacher:	*Let's spell the word* avalanche. *Watch me. (Teacher writes a word on the board and says letter names.)*
	A-v-a-l-a-n-c-h-e, avalanche. *Everyone say that with me.*
Teacher and students:	A-v-a-l-a-n-c-h-e, avalanche.
Teacher:	*Right.* Avalanche *is spelled* a-v-a-l-a-n-c-h-e. *Now, everyone, write* avalanche *on your paper.*
Students:	*(Students write word.)*
Teacher:	*Did you write* a-v-a-l-a-n-c-h-e, avalanche*? Good! Everyone say it with me.*
Teacher and students:	A-v-a-l-a-n-c-h-e, avalanche.
Teacher:	Avalanche *is spelled* a-v-a-l-a-n-c-h-e. *Now, turn your paper over and write* avalanche.
Students:	*(Students write word.)*
Teacher:	*Did you write* a-v-a-l-a-n-c-h-e, avalanche*? Good spelling.*

This presentation requires only 2 or 3 minutes. In this short time the teacher has modeled the spelling of the word for the class once by writing it and five times orally. Students have spelled the word twice orally, have written it twice, and have been provided with immediate feedback each time. In just a few minutes each student in the class can be provided with several response opportunities.

FIGURE 9-2 Example of Scripted Direct Instruction in Spelling

Source: R. B. Lewis and D. H. Doorlag, 1999. *Teaching Special Students in General Education Classrooms.* Upper Saddle River, NJ: Merrill. p. 96.

times in a given lesson to a definition, a spelling, a mathematical formula; facts learned one day pop up again and again on ensuing days. Engelmann ridicules the "spiral curriculum" advocated by psychologist Jerome Bruner, in which teachers periodically revisit basic ideas, by asking "Don't [cognitive theorists] know that if something is just taught, it will atrophy the fast way, if it is not reinforced, kindled and used?" Indeed, Engelmann makes a telling point about education theory in general when he writes that, "Traditional educators express opinions through metaphysical arguments that revolve around the categories they understand; but the real issues . . . are very picky, precise, technical matters." (pp. 38–39)

Another example of scripted direct instruction is provided in Figure 9-2.

What we describe below is not scripted direct instruction but, rather, more closely matched to Rosenshine's (1983, 1987) notion of explicit teaching. The "nonscripted" approach more easily has adaptability and applicability at all grade levels and in all disciplinary areas and does not require the same degree of procedural prescriptiveness.

Direct Instruction: Teaching Phases

Phase I: Review

The first step in the nonscripted direct instruction model is to review what students already know about the topic to be covered. Although the review process appears self-evident (wouldn't any good teacher conduct a review?), the reality is that many teachers fail to make the conceptual connections necessary for students to see how what is taught one day fits with what was taught on another. Borich (1988) describes several ways that teachers can create meaningful review processes:

1. Students might correct each other's homework at the beginning of a class.
2. Students who represent a range of abilities can be called upon to assess their level of understanding.
3. Teachers can specifically review the material that has been previously taught.

Notice that Mr. Carthridge in the opening case study used the third strategy. He wanted to assess the students' understanding of multiplying fractions so, in a step-by-step fashion, he reviews the steps students must follow when solving a multiplication problem. The second strategy (calling on a range of students) can also be effective. All too often teachers call on top-performing students and exclude input from lower-performing students. The reasons for this circumstance are obvious, but the educational costs are equally evident. For direct instruction to work, students must experience a high degree of success. That success is jeopardized if the teacher ignores an important segment of the student population.

Phase II: Presenting New Material

In the second phase, the teacher begins to frame the ideas and present the new content material. The teacher begins this phase by stating the purpose of the lesson. Some teachers do this in a very explicit way, similar to Mr. Carthridge's approach. Recall that Mr. Carthridge quite specifically noted that there were two purposes for the lesson, and he then discussed those with the class. Some teachers even write TLW (The Learner Will) statements on the board that explicitly describe what students will be able to perform by the end of the class: "*The Learner Will* be able to subtract two-digit numbers" or "*The Learner Will* be able to define what a noun is and correctly identify nouns in a sentence." Teachers who work with older students often resist writing specific objectives. Although this is understandable for some types of lessons that involve substantial brainstorming, we would argue against the practice when teaching students a discrete skill. If you want students to know RNA/DNA translation and transcription, then specifically state that expectation in the form of performance objectives at the beginning of the lesson.

The specificity of the objective also suggests something about assessment. The more generally the objective is worded, the more varied assessment procedures necessarily have to be to ensure that students understand requisite content. Anderson and Krathwohl (2001) cogently make this point:

> Consider the following instructional objective: "The student will learn to add three two-digit numbers with regrouping." This objective can be assessed by many items because of the many possible two-digit combinations from which to select (e.g., 25 + 12 + 65; 15 + 23 + 42; 89 + 96 + 65). Inevitably, teachers select a sample of the possible tasks and use students' performance on that sample to infer how they would do on other similar, but unassessed, tasks. The more general an objective, the larger the universe of possible assessment tasks.
>
> Now compare the relatively narrow range of evidence needed to assess the two-digit addition objective with the broader range of evidence needed to assess learning of the following educational objective: "The student will learn to apply various economic theories." The specificity of the first objective permits inferences to be made about student learning from relatively few assessment tasks. In contrast, the second objective is much broader, thereby allowing for an almost unlimited set of assessment tasks. Because any single assessment can sample only a small portion of the assessment tasks, the more general an objective, the less confident one is about how adequately a student's performance validly represents his or her learning across its full breadth. Again, this concern is particularly salient when objectives emphasize more general knowledge categories or more complex cognitive processes. (p. 22)

In stating performance objectives and describing how various ideas fit (today's lesson with yesterday's), many teachers use advance organizers. An advance organizer, according to Ausubel (1960), is nothing more than a conceptual focus for understanding the context for and meaning of new material (in relationship to old material). Teachers use three types of organizers in presenting content material to students: expository, comparative, and sequential.

Expository organizers are used when a teacher creates a vertical conceptual organization of unfamiliar ideas. That is, the teacher works from a broad conceptual construct and then begins to break down one concept into a number of different subordinate concepts. (Refer also to the discussion in Chapter 4, "Concept Attainment.") The teacher progressively differentiates the disciplinary concepts with students' learning more and more conceptual detail (Joyce and Weil, 1992). If, for example, a teacher has been teaching the parts of speech and plans on covering common nouns, the expository organizer might look something like:

> *"We have been covering the parts of speech. Recall that all sentences are composed of words and each of those words has a function. Some are nouns: a person, place, or*

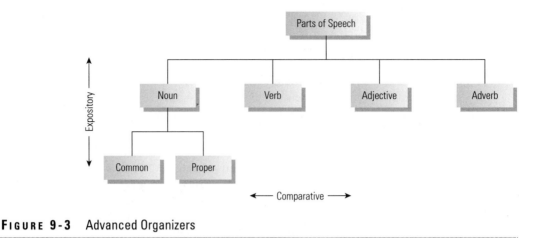

thing. Other words are verbs: they act on the noun. We have also talked about adjectives and adverbs. Today, we are going to begin taking some of these parts of speech and showing how they can be of different types. Today and tomorrow we will be studying common and proper nouns. . . ."

Figure 9-3 shows how the parts of speech would be structured using expository and comparative organizers.

Comparative organizers are used when the teacher utilizes what is known at one level of conceptual thought to make a comparison at the same level (that is, nouns to verbs). Mr. Carthridge uses a comparative organizer when he uses multiplication of fractions to introduce students to division of fractions. Mr. Carthridge uses what the students know about multiplying fractions to help them understand the steps for dividing fractions. Joyce, Weil, and Calhoun (2000) observe that comparative organizers "are typically used with relatively familiar material. They are designed to discriminate between the old and new concepts in order to prevent confusion caused by their similarity" (p. 254).

Sequential organizers are used, particularly in mathematics, to show students the steps that will be followed in performing a skill (Borich, 1988). Mr. Carthridge uses a comparative organizer to help students see the division of fractions in relationship to the multiplication of fractions. But he uses a sequential organizer when he lists the steps on the board for students to follow (see Table 9-1). Although teachers most frequently use advance organizers in deductive (direct instruction) lessons, there is nothing that precludes the use of organizers in other types of lessons. Indeed, teachers who use concept attainment lessons rely on organizers as they decide how to present concepts and identify concept attributes.

Once the students know the purpose of the lesson and understand the conceptual context, the teacher then presents the information. Teachers need to present academic material in a step-by-step fashion by using an abundant number of examples at each step. One of the major weaknesses of many teachers is that they assume too much about what students know. This is especially true of high school teachers, but it is equally true of teachers in general. Japanese teachers tend to teach for overlearning by meticulously taking students through class routines or lessons in a step-by-step fashion (Stevenson and Stigler, 1992). The Japanese also place a premium on understanding the content, and they use problem solving to ensure that students engage the content (Stigler, Gonzales, Kawanaka, Knoll, and Serrano, 1999). American teachers tend to be more focused on keeping students busy and on broad content coverage; teachers seem less concerned with making certain that everyone understands content material before they initiate independent practice. American teachers assume that if they presented the material, students learned it. But they fail to sequence the learning with a sufficient number of step-by-step demonstrations. Rosenshine (1983) notes:

> [R]ecent research in Grades 4–8 has shown that effective teachers of mathematics spend *more time* in demonstration than do less effective teachers. . . . For example, [one researcher] . . . found that the most effective mathematics teachers spent about 23 minutes per day in lecture, demonstration, and discussion, compared with 11 minutes for the least effective teachers. The effective teachers are using this additional presentation time to provide redundant explanations, use many examples, provide sufficient instruction so that the students can do the seatwork with minimal difficulty, check for student understanding, and reteach when necessary. (p. 339)

Notice that the use of repeated explanations (or recursiveness) and numerous examples is essential for student understanding. Educators have long understood that clarity is an important characteristic of good teachers. Clear teachers use different explanations and myriad examples to ensure student understanding. Unclear teachers explain ideas a second time, in the same way, but louder.

Clear teachers also present material in ways that are attentive to the knowledge their students may lack. The efficacy of direct instruction with lower-income students is reasonably well established. Part of what good, clear teachers do with direct instruction is to never assume that students know something that, in fact, they may not know. Gersten, Taylor, and Graves (1999) describe this as teachers who know the "details of curriculum design," and they write,

> Many experimental studies have demonstrated how these details of curriculum design can significantly reduce students' misconceptions. For example, when teaching fractions, traditional curriculum series provide exercises in which students need to discriminate between addition problems and subtraction problems and between division problems and multiplication problems, *but never between addition problems and multiplication problems.*
> Experimental research examined how a conventional sequence for teaching fractions, taken from a major basal series, and a sequence in which students were taught early on to distinguish simple multiplication problems from addition problems affected the learning performance of students with learning disabilities and of remedial high school students. Results indicated that students taught with the conventional sequence *made four times as many errors*

as those taught with the more carefully designed sequence. Most of the misconceptions could be linked to flaws in the curriculum. For example, students explicitly taught to distinguish multiplication problems from addition problems rarely confused them, whereas students never provided with such practice often did. (p. 86)

Phase III: Guided Practice

Once students have been introduced to the skill or content material, teachers proceed by enabling students to practice what they have learned. They can do this by asking a variety of questions, by striving to ensure high levels of student success in answering questions, and by checking for understanding.

The use of questions to assess student understanding is critical to the success of direct instruction. Some questions will be highly specific and demand immediate student recall of a step, process, or piece of information. A quick review of Mr. Carthridge's lesson at the beginning of this chapter illustrates this point. Mr. Carthridge, however, not only asked for informational recall, but he also demanded that students think through why they did what they did. One segment of his lesson illustrates this point:

> "Now, class, I'm going to give you a third problem. But in this case, you will be helping me. Let's begin. I'll start by giving you a problem: $\frac{2}{3} \div \frac{1}{2} = ?$ Joshua, what's the second step that we use?"
>
> "You invert the numbers and multiply."
>
> "Which numbers?"
>
> "The $\frac{1}{2}$."
>
> "Why?" responds Mr. Carthridge.
>
> "Because it's on the right side," says Joshua.
>
> "Yes, and a little later you'll also know the more technical reason for inverting the $\frac{1}{2}$."

One of the most underutilized and misunderstood elements of a direct instruction lesson is guided practice. Most teachers assume that once they have taught material (phase II), they are ready to allow students to engage in independent practice (phase V). This spurious reasoning explains why so many students exit schools with an inadequate understanding of salient skills and content. Rosenshine (1983) observed that the most effective teachers (those who taught students to retain skills or concepts) were those who "spent more time in guided practice, more time asking questions, more time correcting errors, more time repeating the new material that was being taught, and more time working problems under teacher guidance and help" (p. 341).

Asking a lot of questions, though, is only part of the equation for teacher success. Another extremely important ingredient is for students to be able to answer questions correctly—not necessarily 100 percent of the time, but at least at an 80 percent rate. Effective teachers work toward high success rates, and they involve a wide variety of students in the guided practice phase. Anyone who has ever taught knows that it is quite possible to obtain high levels of student success if only certain students are involved. If the teacher calls on only the high-ability students, success rates can be inflated. Effective guided practice requires that the teacher call on a wide range of students, and this can best be accomplished by calling on both volunteers and nonvolunteers. We suggest that guided practice start with involvement by volunteers, and then as the lesson progresses the teacher should call on students who do not have their hands raised (nonvolunteers). Mr. Carthridge used both volunteers and nonvolunteers, but he also relied on a form of group responding—the use of slates on which all students could write their answers. That technique is supported in the research (see W. C. Becker, 1977) and is an excellent way for the teacher to monitor whether students are understanding the content material.

Regardless of what strategy the teacher uses to check for understanding (for example, calling on students to summarize points, calling on students who raise their hands, or students' raising or lowering their thumbs to show agreement or disagreement with the teacher), the important factor is that the teacher assess whether students have really learned the material. Another salient difference between American and Japanese teachers is the emphasis on understanding. Once American teachers provide initial information, they tend to proceed to application. The Japanese spend much more time on ensuring that students understand concepts, a result, perhaps, of a curriculum that is "thinner" than the American curriculum. Stigler et. al. (1999) write,

> [T]here appears to be a clear distinction between the U.S. and German scripts on the one hand and the Japanese on the other. U.S. and German lessons tend to have two phases: an initial acquisition phase and a subsequent application phase. In the acquisition phase, the teacher demonstrates or explains how to solve an example problem. The explanation might be purely procedural (as most often happens in the United States) or may include development of concepts (more often the case in Germany). Yet the goal in both countries is to teach students a method for solving the example problem(s). In the application phase, students practice solving examples on their own while the teacher helps individual students who are experiencing difficulty.
>
> Japanese lessons appear to follow a different script. Whereas in U.S. and German lessons, instruction comes first, followed by application, in Japanese lessons, the order of activity is generally reversed. Problem solving comes first, followed by a time in which students reflect on the problem, share the solution methods they have generated, and jointly work to develop explicit understandings of the underlying mathematical concepts. While students in U.S. and German classrooms must follow their teachers as they lead students through the solution of example problems, Japanese students have a different job: to invent their own solutions then reflect on those solutions in an attempt to increase understanding. (p. 110)

As the reader will note in the next section, student success must also be "read" by the teacher to determine if students really understand ideas in depth.

Phase IV: Feedback and Correctives

Once a student responds to a teacher, the teacher is positioned to see how the student understands the material presented in phase II. A correct response on the part of a student is most desirable, but an incorrect response also communicates important information to a teacher. Incorrect responses reveal something of the conceptual schema of students. Therefore, when students respond to teacher questions, teachers need to assess both the correctness of the response and the nature of their own reaction to students so as to maximize student learning.

If a student responds to a teacher question with a correct, certain answer, *then* the teacher acknowledges the answer ("Yes," "Good," or "Correct") and asks the next question.

If a student responds with hesitancy, then the teacher acknowledges the response ("Yes," "Good," or "Correct") and also provides, according to Rosenshine (1983), some type of "process" feedback. Process feedback is nothing more than a reexplanation of how a student obtained an answer. It might sound something like this:

Teacher: *"What do you do after you invert in dividing fractions? Jerrod?"*

Jerrod: *"You . . . ah . . . you . . . I think you see if it's possible to reduce anything."*

Teacher: *"Right. Remember that the next step is to see if any of the opposite numerators and denominators are factors. So in $\frac{1}{2} \times \frac{8}{3}$, the 2 is a factor of 8. Thus the 2 is reduced to 1. The 2 divides into 2 one time and the 2 divides into the 8 four times."*

If the answer is incorrect, *then* the teacher has three choices:

Choice 1: Match the student's incorrect response with a statement that makes the incorrect response correct. Example:

Teacher: *"What do you do after you invert in dividing fractions? Jerrod?"*

Jerrod: *"You solve the problem."*

Teacher: *"No, you solve the problem after you reduce all numerators and denominators. I asked what you do after you invert."*

Jerrod: *"You reduce."*

Teacher: *"Correct."*

This approach enables students to understand how the relationship of what they say fits with what the teacher expects (this student did know to solve the problem!). It cannot (and should not) be used in every instance, but it does represent an option for the teacher to use.

Choice 2: Reteach the material so that the students see the steps once again. This approach may be especially useful at the beginning of the phase IV process, when students may still have an unclear understanding of the skill or content that is presented by the teacher.

Choice 3: Provide hints or ask an even simpler question. Rosenshine (1983) and Stallings and Kaskowitz (1974) argue for using this technique, but teachers need to be careful when the students do not understand the material well. In essence, hints may be useful when students have a reasonably good grasp of the material just presented by the teacher. But teachers will be ineffectual if students are not able to quickly use the hint to answer a question correctly. We have observed teachers provide so many hints that they both frustrate students and destroy the momentum of a lesson.

Regardless of what strategy the teacher uses, the most important thing to remember is that an incorrect response must not go unrecognized. Further, when a student provides an incorrect answer, the teacher should stay with that student to help elicit a correct response. Such an approach helps teachers see the "process" of how students reason: How did they derive an answer? Most teachers simply call on another student, who provides the correct response. Such a strategy does little to help the first student who responded incorrectly, and it does little to help the teacher understand how a class presentation might have created the incorrect response given by the student.

Phase V: Independent Practice

Perhaps one of the most problematic aspects of direct instruction is independent practice, especially if students do not fully understand a skill or concept. Rosenshine (1983) argues that it is during this time that students go through *unitization* and *automaticity:*

> During unitization the students are putting the skills together. The students make few errors, but they are also slow and expend a good deal of energy toward accomplishing the task. After much practice the students achieve the "automatic" stage where they respond successfully and rapidly and no longer have to "think through" each step. (p. 345)

Independent practice within American schools occurs either during independent seatwork or through homework that is specifically assigned by the teacher. For independent seatwork to be successful, teachers need to spend more time in the guided practice phase to make certain students *know* the skills they are going to practice. American teachers are inclined either to start independent practice before students really know the skills, or fail to review and evaluate the work of students once students spend time working independently (Stevenson and Stigler, 1992). To ensure the maximum impact of independent practice, teachers must make certain students have a reasonable understanding of the skills the teacher has taught.

Work that is assigned to be completed at home requires that students strive for automaticity. Too many teachers assign students skills to practice (for homework) that students simply do not fully understand. Such a circumstance leads to mislearning—students practice skills incorrectly and mislearn how to use a skill. Not only do American children often practice skills at home that they do not fully understand, but when they do have reasonable skill understanding, teachers fail to assign enough practice to ensure automaticity.

Stevenson and Stigler (1992) observed in their cross-cultural study that Asian teachers assign significantly more homework than American teachers; in some cases the rates of assignments were up to seven times as high (these comparisons were for Taipei schools as compared with Minneapolis schools). Homework is not busywork! Homework is intended to ensure that students truly understand the content material presented by the teacher. Some do's and don'ts of assigning homework are provided in Table 9-3.

TABLE 9-3 Some Do's and Don'ts of Homework

1. Do not *ever give homework as punishment.*

2. Do not *make up spur-of-the-moment homework assignments.*

3. Do not *assume that because there are no questions asked about a homework assignment students have no questions about the assignment.*

4. Do not *expect students (even your best students) always to have their homework assignments completed.*

5. Do *understand that not all types of homework assignments are equally valuable for all types of students.*

6. Do *explain the specific purpose of every homework assignment.*

7. Do *listen to what students say about their experiences in completing your homework assignments.*

8. Do *acknowledge and be thankful for efforts students make to complete their homework.*

Source: D. A. England and J. K. Flatley. 1985. *Homework—and Why.* Bloomington, IN: Phi Delta Kappa: 36–37.

In essence, for independent practice to be useful, teachers need to (1) be certain that they have adequately taught material before allowing students to engage in practice, (2) be able to check the students' progress and success in using the skill (by circulating around the room while students work), and (3) be able to provide immediate feedback to students who are having difficulty. That feedback, incidentally, should be of relatively short duration (a quick correction). If a teacher finds that long periods of time are spent explaining material to students, then it is quite likely that the guided practice phase was not sufficient (did not take hold) to ensure full student comprehension of the skill.

APPLICATIONS TO DIVERSE CLASSROOMS

Direct instruction fosters heated debate among educators. Because many teachers equate direct instruction with lecture, there are substantial misunderstandings about the efficacy of this instructional model for culturally diverse students. Direct instruction and lecture are not the same! They have structural similarities, but they are, in fact, different. Direct instruction is skill focused! The goal of the teacher is to teach a specific skill or set of facts in a sequenced, segmented way. Lectures have specific academic content objectives, but the teacher may or may not be interested in teaching specific skills. Typically, in lectures, the teacher is attempting to transmit lots of information (Bligh, 2000), and though lectures may take different forms, they almost always rely exclusively on teacher input without active student responses. Direct instruction requires active student involvement (during guided and independent practice); lecture places students in a more passive role. Indeed, lectures, according to

Bligh (2000) should not be used "to promote thought, change attitudes or develop behavioral skills . . ." (p. 20).

Losey (1995), in an analysis of the learning dispositions of Mexican American students, observed that successful classroom environments were designed around student interests, fostering a level of "belongingness" for students. Direct instruction, when properly implemented, enables both of these circumstances to be evidenced, but to do so requires that the teacher make certain that students recognize the relationship of the skills they are learning to the real-world problems they will face. Relevancy becomes important. Students need to recognize how a skill is relevant for them, and teachers must be able to move beyond the teaching of skills by rote memorization to the teaching of skills or content material within a substantive context. An example of how a teacher contextualized content material will illustrate our point.

A teacher of American government in an urban high school was preparing to teach the amendments of the U.S. Constitution. Such academic material in and of itself is typically not interesting for students. After spending some time discussing the nature of "rights," the teacher shared that the goal for students on this particular day would be to understand which amendment empowered the students to become full participants in the democratic process. The teacher asked all of the students to stand and then told them to listen carefully to the following instructions, and to either sit down or remain standing depending on the way an instruction was worded. The instructions given included:

1. If you are not white, sit down.
2. If you are not male, sit down.
3. If you do not have $2.00 in your pocket, sit down.

After the teacher asked six such questions, one white male student (Josh) remained standing. The teacher then commented something like, "Class, without the amendments to the U.S. Constitution, only Josh would have the right to vote. By the end of today's class, you will know which amendments enable you to remain standing."

This teacher made relevant something that is often perceived by students as arcane. A similar form of relevancy is needed whenever skills or discrete content concepts are taught to all students in general, but to culturally diverse students in particular. That relevancy will affect the teacher's expectations about what students can learn and the students' expectations for their own learning. Relevancy connects the students to the ideas being presented by the teacher. Trueba, Jacobs, and Kirton (1990) observed among the Hmong refugee children that when American teachers refused to adjust their instruction (that is, they would teach skills in isolation, for example), the "children. . . . showed deep frustration and an attitude of hopelessness as they failed to engage meaningfully in learning activities" (pp. 75 & 76). Rothman (1995) is even more pointed in his emphasis on relevancy. He writes,

> Thus teaching abstract concepts, in isolation from the real world, does not help children learn and may in fact keep them from learning. But that is what schools do. Researchers have found, for example, that children in all parts of the world have a highly developed sense of mathematical concepts

such as "number." They know, from observing the world, that if they add something to something else, they will have more of it. (pp. 66–67)

Nonscripted direct instruction limits learning when students cannot connect what they are learning with what they perceive they need to know to be successful in the real world. Hunter (1976) argued for using an anticipatory set—establishing a context for the learning that would occur. Direct instruction is also problematic if the reason for using the technique by the teacher is an assumption that students cannot learn in any other way. Haberman and Post (1995) describe this as a "pedagogy of poverty." Teachers reduce the teaching act to providing information and asking questions, but fail to embrace a personal philosophy that suggests that all students can learn and that requires instructional methods to be adjusted based on what students are expected to learn.

A review of Table 2-9 (in Chapter 2) illustrates how field-dependent the direct instruction teaching approach is. The model is highly interactional (students and teachers), requires teacher usage of questions to check student understanding and is focused on communicating specific content (facts or skills).

Students whose learning is fostered by field-dependent teaching strategies and who need to see connections between what the teacher is teaching and what they are learning will likely respond positively to the technique. More fundamental is what research suggests regarding direct instruction and diverse student populations. In that regard, Gersten, Taylor, and Graves (1999) assert,

> For three decades, research has consistently supported the assertion made by Bereiter and Engelmann in 1966 that many low-income learners, from diverse cultures, enter school with backgrounds highly dissimilar to those of their middle-class peers and need explicit instruction to meet the demands of school. In particular, many lack familiarity with print conventions . . . or the formal language used in schools, or both. Students also may not have sufficient background knowledge and may have difficulty drawing inferences and extrapolating information on their own. Unless instruction is adapted to meet the specific needs of these students . . . many will flounder in classrooms.
>
> In reviewing two decades of research on effective teaching of learners from a variety of cultural backgrounds, [researchers note] . . . that real learning does "not materialize from brief encounters" . . . with new material, but rather develops with the type of systematic guidance and structure provided by a system such as direct instruction. Direct instruction strives to provide a structure or framework so that students can make sense of new concepts, relationships, and learning experiences. With this approach, students are provided with models of reasonable ways to solve problems or follow procedures, are supported amply during the stages of the learning process, and then are provided with adequate practice. (p. 82)

PREVALENT ISSUES IN DIVERSE CLASSROOMS

The direct instruction model is an instructional model that helps students acquire academic skills through practice and drill. The model uses a step-by-step sequence of teacher phases to help students recall and recognize what teachers deem important for students to learn. The model has elicited controversial criticisms from some educational circles. The following questions help address some of these concerns:

Q: *Is it possible to use direct instruction when trying to move students toward analysis or synthesis objectives?*

A: No. One of the reasons so many educators have frustration with direct instruction (in fact, many denigrate the technique) is that it is used inappropriately. A teacher should use direct instruction to teach particular skills or a sequence of actions, not to teach the type of critical thinking required of students through analysis and synthesis activities. One of the recurring themes of this book is that teachers need to know how and when to use different instructional models to achieve particular purposes. Borich (1988) writes,

> Various expressions have been used by different learning theorists to describe these two types of learning [learning to recognize patterns versus learning to carry out a sequence of action], but facts, rules and action sequences are most commonly taught using instructional strategies that emphasize knowledge acquisition, and concepts, patterns, and abstractions are most commonly taught using instructional strategies that emphasize inquiry or problem solving. (p. 143)

Elementary school teachers and those working with low-income students may well find that they use direct instruction more than teachers at the more advanced grade levels or in higher socioeconomic school contexts. Especially in the primary grades, teachers are attempting to teach a large number of facts and skills—they are establishing the groundwork for later learning that students will experience. Direct instruction is not inherently good or bad, and teacher-centered instruction is not necessarily positive or negative. If used properly and purposefully (for teaching of basic skills), direct instruction can have a positive and powerful impact on student growth and development.

Q: *What happens when some students refuse to respond or are afraid to respond to the myriad questions asked by the teacher during guided practice?*

A: There are several ways in which feedback from students can be obtained by the teacher. Much of the original direct instruction work was with young children (Grades K–3) who were from lower-income families. The original direct instruction processes (known as the Follow Through program) required choral (collective) responses from the students in small group situations. The teacher would present a small bit of information, the children would repeat the information, and then the teacher would ask a question focused on that piece of information that required the students to respond as a group (similar to elements of the mnemonic model). The teacher would observe and listen carefully to determine who was and who was not responding to the teacher-directed question.

Recall that Mr. Carthridge required his students to use slates on which to record their answers and show their work. The slates enable the teacher to look around the room and do a quick assessment of whether each student really understands the work.

With older students, some teachers use more peer teaching. With peer teaching the teacher creates pairs and assigns all students as "1s" or "2s." The teacher then teaches the information and when finished asks the "1s" to teach the "2s" the information the teacher just taught the whole class. The teacher listens to the paired explanations, and reteaches material that the students do not fully understand. Once the reteaching is completed, the teacher then asks the "2s" to teach the "1s."

A third strategy that was used by one high school teacher reflects the teacher's need for sensitivity in order to save face for students who do not understand material but who need to know the information being taught to the class. This particular urban high school mathematics teacher asked the students to signal when they were not understanding a step in a mathematical equation by quickly blinking their eyes twice. This enabled a student to say to the teacher, "I don't understand," without having either to utter the words or to be called upon and fail to respond. The teacher reported that the students were extremely good at using the nonverbal device to communicate information to the teacher.

Regardless of what technique a teacher uses, it is imperative that the teacher understand that direct instruction will not work unless information is taught sequentially, in a step-by-step manner, and with vigilant analysis of the students' comprehension of the material. Teachers in the early grades may use "choral" guided practice, while teachers in high school may call on volunteers/nonvolunteers or use peer teaching. All teachers who use this instructional model must constantly assess whether students understand what is being taught.

⊖VALUATION CRITERIA   X

The step-by-step nature of the direct instruction model makes it one of the easier models to assess. Because the information presented is sequenced in such a linear, defined way, observers of direct instruction lessons can typically see the lesson more clearly unfold. Two cautionary notes, though, are needed. First, not every direct instruction lesson requires that every step of the process be followed. Good teachers make decisions about when and how to use an instructional model. Of paramount importance is whether students are learning the material. Of secondary importance is whether the model steps are followed with legalistic precision. Second, direct instruction does not need to be boring. Good demonstrations that excite the students can still be used during phase II of the model to ensure that students understand the content material. It is true that direct instruction is highly structured. It is not true that direct instruction requires teachers to present discrete bits of information in a boring, unenthusiastic manner.

Phase I: Review

1. Does the teacher review ideas from
   the previous day's lesson?   ☐ Yes   ☐ No

2. Does the teacher reteach content
   material that students had difficulty
   understanding?   ☐ Yes   ☐ No

Phase II: Presenting New Material

1. Does the teacher clearly state the objectives for the lesson? □ Yes □ No
2. Does the teacher teach the skill or action sequence in a step-by-step fashion? □ Yes □ No

Phase III: Guided Practice

1. Does the teacher frequently ask questions to assess student understanding? □ Yes □ No
2. Does the teacher call on both volunteers and nonvolunteers? □ Yes □ No
3. Do all students have an opportunity to respond to the teacher's questions? □ Yes □ No
4. Are students successfully responding to most of the teacher's questions (at approximately an 80 percent rate of success)? □ Yes □ No
5. Does the teacher continue to practice the skill until student understanding appears firm? □ Yes □ No

Phase IV: Feedback and Correctives

1. Does the teacher provide specific feedback to students when their responses are hesitant? □ Yes □ No
2. Does the teacher reteach material when student responses are incorrect? □ Yes □ No

Phase V: Independent Practice

1. Does the teacher provide an appropriate number of problems for independent practice? □ Yes □ No
2. Are students assigned homework that is meaningful and appropriate? □ Yes □ No
3. Do students appear to know how to do the homework successfully? □ Yes □ No

SAMPLE LESSONS

Two sample lessons are now provided to illustrate the direct instruction model. In the first lesson, the teacher seeks to have junior high school students understand the difference between common and proper nouns. As you read the case study, identify for yourself when the teacher moves from one phase to the next in her lesson. The second lesson is focused on multiplying two-digit numbers. The first lesson focuses on content concepts and is less skill oriented; the second lesson has more skill elements to it.

CASE STUDY I

Susan Sparks begins her 4th period English class with a brief discussion concerning nouns. The students have already learned that a noun is a person, place, or thing. In today's lesson, Susan wants the 7th graders to describe the difference between common and proper nouns.

"The objective for today's lesson," begins Ms. Sparks, "is to be able to define and identify common and proper nouns. I know some of you have a general idea of the differences, but by the end of our class session today, I want to make certain that each of you can specifically state what a common and proper noun is. John, why don't you help get us started by identifying the nouns in this sentence." (Ms. Sparks points at the following sentence, which she has on the board. "The wealthy brothers were preparing the plantation for the fall harvest when Abraham Lincoln signed the Emancipation Proclamation.")

John responds by listing all the nouns: "I think the nouns are *brothers, plantation, harvest, Abraham Lincoln,* and *Emancipation Proclamation.*"

"Excellent, John. Now what I want us to be able to do is identify the difference between the common nouns and the proper nouns that John has listed. Does anyone know which ones are common and which ones are proper?" Several students offer ideas. Some guess that the capital letters are important in deciding which terms are proper.

"You have some good ideas, class. Now, let's make certain we all understand. A common noun is the general name for a person, place, or thing. So *brothers, plantation,* and *harvest* would be, as some of you suggested, common nouns. A proper noun is the name of a particular person, place or thing. *Abraham Lincoln* is a particular or specific person. The *Emancipation Proclamation* is a particular and very important document.

"I now want to give you some examples of each of these nouns." (Ms. Sparks writes *common noun* and *proper noun* on the board.) "I will provide you with two examples for each, and then I'll ask you to label the rest." Ms. Sparks begins with the following information:

Common Nouns	Proper Nouns
cars	Buick
cities	New York

"Class, as you can see, *cars* and *cities* are general terms for things and places. But *Buick* and *New York* represent a particular thing and a particular place. As I provide you with additional examples, you tell me where to place the terms. All right, where would I place *landmark?* Josiah?"

"It's a common noun."

"Right!"

"And, how about *musician?* Ophelia?"

"Common noun."

"Yes."

"What about *Martin Luther King?* Sarina?"

"Proper noun."

"Great!"

"And, Marcus, what about this object (teacher holds up a baseball)?"

"*Baseball* is a proper noun."

"Why do you think so?"

"Because it's a particular kind of ball."

"True. But *baseball* is a name for a group of objects. There are lots of base-balls. Some have specific names, such as *Rawlings* or *Spaulding,* but when you refer to *ball* as part of a group, it is a common noun. So in this case *baseball* is a common noun."

The class continues until the chart contains the following examples:

Common Nouns	Proper Nouns
cars	Buick
cities	New York
landmark	Statue of Liberty
musician	Michael Jackson
building	Pentagon
street	Main Street
picture	Mona Lisa
pencil	Bic
railroad	Amtrak
baseball	Spaulding

The students accurately label all the terms. Ms. Sparks calls on several non-volunteers. She also matches the examples so that the distinctions are even clearer between common and proper nouns. That is, she matches *cars,* a common noun, with *Buick* (a specific car), a proper noun, *cities* with *New York,* and so on. (In this regard the lesson actually has the "feel" of a concept attainment lesson—see Chapter 4.)

"Class, I now want you to identify with a partner all the proper and common nouns in the following three sentences. Put a line under each common noun and two lines under each proper noun."

The students work in pairs and identify all the appropriate terms. Ms. Sparks checks the students' work as she moves around the room.

"Now, I want you to complete the next three sentences on your own and then show your work to your partner." This time the students work independently, and after completing the three sentences, they show their answers to their partners. Ms. Sparks moves around the room and observes the students as they work. She helps a couple of students, but almost everyone seems to understand.

- *State the purposes of the lesson.*
- *Provide relevant background knowledge for the lesson.*
- *Signal transitions between sections of the lesson.*
- *Use questions to maintain student attention.*
- *Make explicit the internal structure of the content material to be learned.*
- *Identify the most important points.*
- *Use humor to maintain student attention.*
- *Summarize material within the lecture or presentation.*
- *Give or ask for examples to illustrate major concepts.*
- *Avoid vague terms such as "kinda" or "and so forth and so on."*

Adapted from B. Rosenshine. 1986. "Unsolved Issues in Teaching Content: A Critique of a Lesson on Federalist Paper No. 10." *Teaching and Teacher Education* 2(4): 307.

"You can now get your grammar books out and turn to page 73. Do the 10 sentences listed there. Put one line under the common noun and two lines under the proper noun. Please write out the sentences. You can begin." ∎

Follow-Up Questions

1. Describe three other ways this teacher could have introduced the concept of common nouns and proper nouns to the students in the class.

2. Identify other concepts or skills that you might teach that would be appropriate for use with direct instruction.

3. Identify the strategies a teacher can use to deal with an incorrect student response. Which one does Ms. Sparks use? How else might she have responded?

The above lesson focuses on disciplinary content in English—parts of speech. Table 9-4 provides additional information, based on extensive research (see Rosenshine, 1986), that should prove useful to readers who are teaching content concepts rather than skills.

CASE STUDY II

Tina Buckmaster teaches 4th grade. She is preparing to teach a lesson to the students a new way to multiply two digit numbers. She begins the class by clearly outlining the specific objectives for the lesson.

"Today, class, you are going to learn how to multiply two digit numbers, and I am going to show you a specific technique for multiplying two digit numbers."

She then has the students examine a "fact triangle" that can be used to identify products from the multiplication of one digit numbers such as 8×7 and 6×7. As the students give her the facts she asks everyone to chorally give the products. "What is 8×7, class?" And the students then respond "56." She reviews lots of the one digit math facts until the students are quickly providing her with the answers. Occasionally she calls on a specific student, but most are choral responses involving all students.

All the students in the class have mini "white" boards in front of them as Ms. Buckmaster prepares to teach the lesson. The students are asked to do the problems on their boards just as she does them on the "big board."

Ms. Buckmaster has students multiply a one digit number by a second two digit number that ends in zero. She describes these as "extended facts." She gives the students 9×60 and shows in detail the steps for getting 540. She works a couple additional examples and then has the students generate a large number of their own examples. As each example is given she asks the students for choral responses for the answers and then calls on specific students to explain how the answer was obtained. The students exhibit good proficiency.

"Class, that's excellent. You can do all of these extended facts in your head. I'm now going to teach you a more complicated process for multiplying two digit numbers that you'll find just as easy, even though you can't necessarily do the problems in your head like these extended facts."

She then begins to show them a process for multiplying two digit numbers (for example, 75×84) that she describes as "multiplication wrestling." She reviews the "extending facts" process and shows the parallels between that process and the one she is about to teach them. After each step she reviews what she is doing and has the students chorally repeat what she says.

The first numbers that she multiplies are 75×84.

"What is 75 made up of, John?"

"70 and 5."

"Good."

"What is 75 made up of, class?"

"70 and 5," respond all the students in a choral response.

"What is 84 made up of, Sarah?"

"80 and 4."

"Good."

"What is 84 made up of, class?"

"80 and 4," respond the students.

"Now, class, I am going to teach you the four steps for solving this simple problem." She then carefully teaches them steps, using a combination of visuals and auditory cues. She also calls on lots of students (volunteers and nonvolunteers) as well as the whole class in choral response as she reviews the steps.

The students watch her do the steps on the big board and then repeat the processes on their mini boards.

The lesson progresses with lots of examples and lots of active student responses, often with students repeating back to Ms. Buckmaster exactly what she says to them.

At the end of the lesson the students practice problems on their own as Ms. Buckmaster walks around the room and checks their work.

Teacher Reflections

In all the other chapters, we have had the teacher who taught the lesson reflect on the model. For direct instruction, we are going to take a slightly different approach. As this book is being written, there is heated debate about teacher-centered versus student-centered classrooms. Many critics of progressivist educational practices (e.g., hands on learning, discovery approaches) claim that student achievement would be significantly enhanced if more teachers used an approach similar to Tina's. In many respects, we do not disagree. If you are teaching essential facts and skills, teacher directed instruction makes real sense. Review Tina's lesson and reflect on whether what she is teaching is appropriate for direct instruction. Would direct instruction be the model of choice given the objectives she is emphasizing? What other model might be used either in place of direct instruction or as a complement to it? For example, how might the teacher have used collaboration (group work) to help students learn the content?

In essence, for this lesson, we want you to engage in the reflecting process. When you teach facts or skills how closely does your approach match Tina's? Tina's students seem to evidence good comprehension of the content. Does direct instruction help ensure student acquisition of salient facts and concepts?

For us, the teacher-centered versus student-centered debate represents a false dichotomy. Good teaching is not either/or. Good teaching takes into account academic goals and student needs. A 1st grade class attempting to learn a specific mathematics skill is well served by direct instruction. A high school AP English class reading *Hamlet* is not. When would you use an approach like this one in your classroom? ■

SUGGESTED LESSON DEVELOPMENT: QUESTIONS FOR REFLECTION

Once teachers understand the basic elements of the model, they need to carefully design a direct instruction lesson for the students they teach. The steps to follow include,

1. Identify the specific skill or concept that will be taught.
2. Determine the way in which the objective for the lesson will be shared with students (for example, written on the board or verbally presented).
3. Identify the examples that will be used during the presenting new material phase to help students learn the skill or concept.
4. Determine *two* different ways to check for understanding.
5. Identify the problems that will be given to students for independent practice.

TECHNOLOGY ENHANCEMENT ⒶDISC

As the first two chapters made clear, there is, perhaps more than ever before, a compelling need for classroom teachers to meet the individual learning needs of diverse learners. The technology enhancement for this chapter describes how well-designed drill and practice programs, when properly employed, can help classroom teachers significantly augment (A) student learning by adapting

(A) learning experiences that are developmentally appropriate to the needs of individual learners.

Using Drill and Practice Programs to Enhance Direct Instruction

At the start of this chapter, it was pointed out that direct instruction is one of the most misused and misunderstood instructional models. In similar fashion, drill and practice programs are one of the most misused and misunderstood models of computer-assisted instruction. In fact, direct instruction and drill and practice are complementary strategies, that when properly employed, can be powerful teaching and learning tools. Like the direct instruction model, the primary function of computer-based drill and practice programs is to teach students a specific skill or set of skills. They do so by providing students with the opportunity to practice the targeted skill by working on sample problems or items. In addition, such programs provide students with feedback on the accuracy or correctness of their work. Consequently, quality drill and skill programs can enhance the direct instruction process by providing support in the *feedback and correctives* and *independent practice* phases of the direct instruction model.

Drill and practice programs, if properly designed, can have three important benefits. First, they can provide students with *immediate feedback* on the accuracy of their work, making it less likely that they might be memorizing the wrong skills. Second, for many students, working on the computer provides *additional motivation* for practicing their skills. This may be especially true for weaker or less confident students who are alerted to their errors in a more private setting. Finally, drill and practice programs can save teachers considerable time by freeing them from having to grade students' practice work.

Given the above benefits, why are drill and practice programs so frequently maligned and caustically referred to as *drill and kill?* First, it is important to recognize that drill and practice programs are frequently misused in schools, thereby providing ammunition for critics. Such misuse tends to occur when teachers fail to understand the phases of the direct instruction model and assume that computer-assisted drill and practice can substitute for quality teaching in the first three phases of the direct instruction model. While some teachers creatively employ such programs in the first three phases, drill and practice programs, as mentioned earlier, are most appropriately applied in the final two phases of the direct instruction process, *feedback and correctives* and *independent practice*.

Second, critics often argue that computer-based drill and practice programs represent an outdated approach to teaching. The thrust of this argument is that students are taught isolated skills, absent the opportunity to apply them to their own problems or projects. In reality, thoughtful teachers can and do embed computer-assisted drill and practice in the context of authentic problems or situations designed to promote higher order thinking skills or increased levels of student motivation. Take, for example, a 3rd grade teacher who has engaged students in designing and running a classroom store. In this example, having students develop their multiplication skills through drill and practice is anchored to their need to be able to quickly and accurately project profits from selling various items in the store's inventory.

Third, a final criticism of computer-assisted drill and practice often stems from the fact that not all such programs are created equal. Like any instructional software, drill and practice programs can be well or poorly designed. One especially important design feature is a program's capacity for adaptability to various ability levels. Teachers interested in evaluating prospective programs should carefully review them with particular attention to the following questions suggested by Robyler and Edwards (2000):

What control do students have over the presentation rate? In general, better programs provide students with as much time as they need to answer questions and to reflect on feedback before proceeding to the next item. This, of course, does not apply to "timed" reviews or tests which are often included in such programs.

What feedback is provided for correct answers? The quality of a drill and practice program is not necessarily related to the bells and whistles of the software's positive feedback function. Students tend to tire quickly of even the most elaborate displays. Quality programs provide students with feedback that is not overly time-consuming and does not distract students from the purpose of the lesson.

What feedback is provided for incorrect answers? Quality drill and practice programs carefully avoid the classic design error of providing students with more entertaining feedback for incorrect answers, thereby encouraging students to make intentional errors. Ideally, when students make an error they should be promptly informed of their mistake, politely asked to reflect on their work, and encouraged to try a corrective response.

Teachers unfamiliar with computer-assisted drill and practice should consult their building-level or district-wide technology coordinator to determine what programs may be available. In districts with no history of using such programs, interested teachers are advised to conduct an Internet search for information on *computer-assisted learning and elementary mathematics*, or whatever academic discipline is of interest. The other place to begin is by exploring the two Web sites discussed below (see Web-based resources), which provide information from two companies that produce drill and practice and computer-assisted learning programs.

Low Tech/High Tech Applications

Drill and practice programs can be effectively employed in a variety of technology environments including computer labs, multiple computer, or single computer classrooms. A common low-tech application would be to purchase a drill and practice program and use it primarily to provide independent practice for students. This application can be made at the whole-class level by utilizing a computer lab, or at the classroom level, by rotating students to one or more classroom computers.

In contrast, the latest drill and practice programs have an array of features that open up a wide range of new possibilities for teachers interested in capitalizing on the various functions the technology can provide. The latest programs provide teachers with powerful rubrics for assessing individual student performance as well as designing new learning experiences customized to meet the individual needs of students. In addition, the newest Web-based programs include built-in communication tools that support teachers in communicating progress and performance data to parents as well as students. Finally, one of the most exciting features of some Web-based programs is that they allow students to access them from home, providing opportunities for additional time-on-task and potential for parental support and encouragement.

Value-Added for Diverse Learners

Computer-assisted drill and practice programs, when thoughtfully employed, can support diverse learners in the acquisition of important academic skills. All learners, regardless of racial, ethnic, or gender considerations, are most likely to benefit when the teacher first provides an appropriate introduction to the activity by carefully completing the first three phases of the direct instruction model. More specifically, many students from diverse racial and ethnic backgrounds may find drill and practice programs particularly helpful if they are designed to provide the time and space for thinking and personal reflection. Some Native American students may respond favorably to the visual stimuli of many such programs. African American students may be attracted by the kinesthetics provided by computer-assisted instruction. Finally, female students may be motivated when the drill and practice program is embedded in a real world problem or project of personal interest. As we have done in earlier chapters, we caution readers in applying these ideas regarding Native American, African American, or female students in any universal sense. Rather, use the ideas as a means of thinking of the "richness" that needs to be instructionally evident in every classroom if every student's learning needs are to be met.

Web-Based Resources

Today, increasing numbers of companies provide drill and practice programs that can be accessed via the Internet. SuccessMaker (www.successmaker.com), for example, is in the process of moving much of its programming to be delivered via the World Wide Web. Another company, Riverdeep (www.riverdeep.net) provides interested educators with the opportunity to test online demos of a variety of programs. Before making a building- or district-level decision to invest in any drill and practice program, teachers and administrators are well advised to carefully evaluate the program in light of a number of factors including per pupil cost, quality and cost of training available for teachers, and the compatibility of the curricular content with local and state curriculum standards and performance tests.

Ⓢ UMMARY

The direct instruction model is predicated on the fundamental assumption that teachers are responsible for enabling student learning, that all students are capable of learning what teachers present, and that student success requires thoughtful, explicit teacher practice. These assumptions, based on research, are neither new nor revelatory. The now-famous Project Follow Through studies established the initial research base for the technique, and subsequent research by a variety of scholars has confirmed the situational efficacy of the direct instruction model. Direct instruction is not a flashy, innovative strategy, but it is effective, especially when used appropriately in teaching skills or discrete concepts. Many educators disdain the model because they view it as simplistic and reductionistic; it does not problematize disciplinary concepts or cause students to consider why something exists as it does. Direct instruction is a powerful teaching strategy when used appropriately. Its disfavor has occurred largely because it has been either misused or overused. Some teachers and educators have thought that direct instruction means either that the instruction is boring or that it is the only way to teach content. The teaching phase of presenting new material, however, enables teachers to be creative (that is, to use demonstrations). Direct instruction becomes boring when teachers present information in the same way every time they teach or when teacher talk is considered synonymous with student learning. Direct instruction requires that teachers be active in the classroom. As Brophy (1982) argued over two decades ago, "Effective teachers of inner city students actively teach their students in large and small groups demonstrating skills, explaining concepts, conducting participatory and practice activities, and reviewing when necessary" (p. 528). Direct instruction, scripted or nonscripted, is neither a simple nor an easy model to implement; it is a demanding one, largely because it requires teachers to clearly think through how to teach an idea, skill, or fact and then to assess thoughtfully whether students learned what was just taught.

ⓡEFERENCES

Anderson, L. W. and D. R. Krathwohl. 2001. *A Taxonomy for Learning, Teaching, and Assessing.* New York: Longman.

Ausubel, D. P. 1960. "The Use of Advance Organizers in the Learning and Retention of Meaningful Verbal Material." *Journal of Educational Psychology* 17(3): 400–404.

Becker, W. C. 1977. "Teaching Reading and Language to the Disadvantaged—What We Have Learned from Field Research." *Harvard Educational Review* 47: 518–543.

Bereiter, C., and S. Engelmann. 1966. *Teaching Disadvantaged Children in the Preschool.* Englewood Cliffs, NJ: Prentice-Hall.

Bligh, D. A. 2000. *What's the Use of Lecture?* San Francisco: Jossey-Bass.

Borich, G. 1988. *Effective Teaching Methods.* Columbus, OH: Merrill.

Brophy, J. 1982. "Successful Teaching Strategies for the Inner-City Child." *Phi Delta Kappan* 63: 527–530.

England, D. A., and J. K. Flatley. 1985. *Homework—and Why.* Bloomington, IN: Phi Delta Kappa.

Finkelstein, B. 1989. *Governing the Young.* New York: Falmer Press.

Gagne, R. M. 1977. *The Conditions of Learning* (3rd ed.). New York: Holt, Rinehart and Winston.

Gersten, R., R. Taylor, and A. Graves. 1999. In R. R. Stevens (ed.), *Teaching in American Schools.* Upper Saddle River, NJ: Merrill Prentice Hall.

Haberman, M., and L. Post. 1995. "Multicultural Teaching in the Real World." Pp. 337–353 in A. C. Ornstein (ed.), *Teaching: Theory and Practice.* Boston: Allyn & Bacon.

Hunter, M. 1976. *Prescription for Improved Instruction.* El Segundo, CA: TIP.

Joyce, B., and M. Weil. 1992. *Models of Teaching* (4th ed.). Boston: Allyn & Bacon.

Joyce, B., M. Weil, and E. Calhoun. 2000. *Models of Teaching* (6th ed.) Boston: Allyn & Bacon.

Lewis, R. B., and D. H. Doorlag. 1999. *Teaching Special Students in General Education Classrooms.* Upper Saddle River, NJ: Merrill.

Losey, K. M. 1995. "Mexican American Students and Classroom Interaction: An Overview and Critique." *American Educational Research Journal* 65(3): 283–318.

Porter, A C. 1986. "From Research on Teaching to Staff Development: A Difficult Step." *Elementary School Journal* 87(2): 159–164.

Robbins, P. 1986. "The Napa-Vacaville Follow-Through Project: Qualitative Outcomes, Related Procedures, and Implications for Practice." *Elementary School Journal* 87(2): 139–158.

Robyler, M. D. and J. Edwards. 2000. *Integrating Educational Technology into Teaching* (2nd ed.). Upper Saddle River, NJ: Merrill.

Rosenshine, B. 1983. "Teaching Functions in Instructional Programs." *Elementary School Journal* 83(4): 335–352.

———. 1986. "Unsolved Issues in Teaching Content: A Critique of a Lesson on Federalist Paper No. 10." *Teaching and Teacher Education* 2(4): 301–308.

———. 1987. "Explicit Teaching." Pp. 75–92 in D. C. Berliner and B. Rosenshine (eds.), *Talks to Teachers.* New York: Random House.

Rothman, R. 1995. *Measuring Up.* San Francisco: Jossey-Bass.

Stallings, J., and P. Kaskowitz. 1974. *Follow Through Classroom Observation Evaluation, 1972–73.* Menlo Park, CA: Stanford Research Institute.

Stallings, J., and E. M. Krasavage. 1986. "Program Implementation and Student Achievement in a Four-Year Madeline Hunter Follow-Through Project." *Elementary School Journal* 87(2): 117–138.

Stevenson, H. W., and J. W. Stigler. 1992. *The Learning Gap.* New York: Summit.

Stigler, J. W., P. Gonzales, T. Kawanaka, S. Knoll, and A. Serrano. 1999. "The TIMMS Videotape Classroom Study: Methods and Findings from an Exploratory Research Project on Eight Grade Mathematics Instruction in Germany, Japan, and the United States." *Education Statistics Quarterly* 1(2): 109–112.

Traub, J. 1999. *Better by Design.* Washington, DC: The Thomas B. Fordham Foundation.

Trueba, H. J., L. Jacobs, and E. Kirton. 1990. *Cultural Conflict and Adaptation: The Case of Hmong Children in American Society.* New York: Falmer Press.

Viadero, D. 1999. (March 17) "A Direct Challenge." *Education Week* 18(27): 41–43.

American students understand competition. Indeed, many young people are so thoroughly schooled in competition that they believe that helping those around them is inappropriate. Students feel a sense of responsibility for themselves, not for others. School policies and practices consistently reinforce the competitive ethos. High schools rank order students from the top (valedictorian) to the bottom— someone has the distinction of graduating last in the class. Within classrooms, the hand-raising behavior of students reinforces this competitive ethos. Anyone who doubts this should observe what happens when young people are asked a factual question and a student provides the wrong answer— a myriad of other students raise their hands with the correct answer.

Cooperative learning and oral discussion are two strategies that focus on enabling students to connect with one another. These strategies engender a group consciousness and diminish, as a consequence, self-consciousness. Students do not gain an appreciation for the group by chance; they develop such consciousness through experience. And it is the teacher's responsibility to structure such experiences for youngsters.

The two instructional strategies in this unit enable teachers to achieve both cognitive and affective outcomes. Students who learn to work with others not only learn more but also understand more about themselves in relation to others. Developing positive self-esteem, deriving satisfaction from learning, reducing prejudice and bias, and enhancing interpersonal skills are best achieved in learning situations where students work together (and talk together) to achieve a common goal. ■

Models That Foster Relating Skills

TEN

Cooperative Learning

Chapter Objectives

At the end of this chapter, readers will be able to

1. *Describe the theoretical basis of the cooperative learning model.*
2. *Identify the essential characteristics of cooperative learning.*
3. *Identify several different types of cooperative learning strategies that can be used for team building, content mastery, and concept development.*
4. *Identify the strengths and weaknesses of the model.*
5. *Describe ways in which cooperative learning enhances the learning opportunities for culturally diverse populations.*
6. *Create a cooperative learning lesson for personal use in the classroom and understand how to use technology to enhance student cooperation.*

INTRODUCTION

In many American classrooms, the primary learner is the teacher. The teacher decides what content to teach (usually after consulting a district course of study); the teacher determines how to teach the material; and the teacher even creates a conceptual structure for students to follow in learning the material (that is, something quite similar to the discussion on the planning process found in Chapter 3). In essence, the intellectual burden appears to be on the shoulders of the teacher more than it is on students. Some teachers are quite satisfied with this circumstance. They see no reason to instigate change. Others, however, advocate a new direction—one that places more intellectual burden on the student. Roy Smith (1987), a junior high school English teacher, embraces cooperative learning because "it places the responsibility for learning where it belongs: on the students" (p. 663). More recently, Crawford and Witte (1999) note,

> When Ms. Herrera, Mr. Anderson, and Ms. Hayes use student-led groups to complete exercises or hands-on activities, they are using the strategy of *cooperating—learning in the context of sharing, responding, and communicating with other learners.* Working with their peers in small groups, most students feel less self-conscious and can ask questions without a threat of embarrassment. They also will more readily explain their understanding of concepts or recommend a problem-solving approach for the group. By listening to others, students re-evaluate and reformulate their own sense of

The problem with the competitive nature of grading is that it creates a situation in which students hope their classmates will fail.

ROBERT SLAVIN

302

understanding. They learn to value the opinions of others because sometimes a different strategy proves to be a better approach to the problem. (p. 37)

Many teachers experience real discomfort when they do not have complete control over how students process content. Such teachers believe that they have somehow lost control of the teaching-learning process. The irony is that even within the most didactic and structured pedagogical circumstances, the teacher really does not have total control. Teachers cannot make students learn; they cannot force students to assimilate ideas. Teachers experience a false sense of control over what is occurring in the classroom. In essence, they create the environment for learning, but they cannot force students to learn.

The question becomes, then: Under what pedagogical conditions do students learn best? The answer is both simple and complex: They learn best when they have a positive attitude (toward themselves and their classmates) and when they enjoy what they are learning and how they are learning it! These conditions for learning are not easily met, but increasingly advocates suggest that one strategy stands out as an effective vehicle for enabling students to experience enhanced achievement and an improved attitude toward learning. That strategy is cooperative learning! As the reader will recall from the first few chapters of this book, culturally diverse youngsters have demonstrated affective tendencies toward building and maintaining relationships with others. These interactional activities of collaboration and communication by diverse learners are strengths that schools need to capitalize upon in developing the skills of all youngsters. As the following example illustrates, cooperative learning not only focuses on the content knowledge that students need to learn, but also on the social interactions between and among students as they begin to explore ideas together.

ⒸASE STUDY

The students in Ms. Bernardo's 7th grade class have just begun to discuss geologic time. A couple of students share that they watched movies like *Jurassic Park*, and Ms. Bernardo spends a few moments talking about the types of animals the students recalled seeing in the movie—Velociraptors, Tyrannosaurus Rex, and Apatosaurus.

"I'm pleased several of you watched *Jurassic Park*. It's a fun movie though some of it was a bit too violent for my personal taste."

"No, it wasn't," responds Theo. "I loved how those Velociraptors chased after the kids. Those dinosaurs were mean!"

"Well, that's quite true—they were mean! They were, in fact, carnivores. Some believe they were among the fastest and meanest of the meat-eating predators that existed in that time period. But remember that *Jurassic Park* occurred in the present. The animals were just depicted from the past. What I want you to understand is when, in terms of geologic time, the dinosaurs existed in relation to the present. Scientists believe that the earth may be as much as 4.6 billion years old, even though rocks have only been dated to 3.9 billion years. Yesterday I shared with you that there were four major time divisions in

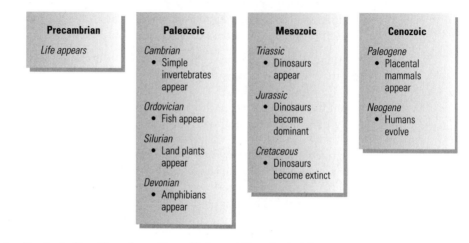

Precambrian	Paleozoic	Mesozoic	Cenozoic

FIGURE 10-1 Geologic Time Descriptor Sheet (Selected Time Periods)

geologic time: Precambrian, Paleozoic, Mesozoic, and Cenozoic. I also indicated that I want you to memorize the order of those divisions, and you used the mnemonic device of Please (Precambrian) pay (Paleozoic) me (Mesozoic) cash (Cenozoic). I hope the device helps."

"Today we are going to look at what animals appeared during the time periods that make up the major geologic time divisions. On the sheet I have provided for you, you will see that I have a brief description of each time period [see Figure 10-1]. What I am going to do today is to use our numbered heads together strategy to enable you to see if you can correctly place each animal in the right time period based on the limited descriptive information I have provided. By the end of the class, I want you to be able to identify when various life forms appeared and to describe how the complexity of life became more noticeable as geologic time progressed. Let's start by having you get into groups of three. Once you're in your group, number off with 1, 2, 3."

Ms. Bernardo places the students in groups with one high, one middle, and one low-ability science student. She predetermined the groupings based on the students' previous test scores in science. The students then get into their groups, number off (1, 2, 3), and prepare for Ms. Bernardo's first example.

"Class, my first example is a rather famous one [she shows the students a picture of a trilobite]. It's the trilobite, the state fossil of Ohio. Discuss among yourselves the time period in which you would place the trilobite."

The students look at the example and begin discussing its characteristics. They share ideas for several minutes, then Ms. Bernardo asks the number 2s in the class to raise their hands. All the 2s put their hands up, and Ms. Bernardo calls on Sonya (a low-ability student).

"Sonya, where would you place the trilobite and why?"

"I would place it in the Precambrian period. Our group thought that these types of animals were common then."

"Good," responds Ms. Bernardo. "Does anyone in that group want to add anything? Kareem [a high-ability student in the same group]?"

"We talked about the fact that the trilobite was an invertebrate and that it lived when marine life was really abundant. I also read stuff about the trilobite, and I know it goes in that time period."

"Excellent! Well, does anyone want to disagree with Sonya's group classification? Have any of you read something different from what Kareem shared?" No students respond.

"You're right, Sonya. It goes in the Precambrian period. Let's look at another animal, the Brontosaurus." Once again an example is shown to the students. This time the excitement is palpable. The students share a few ideas and then look at the teacher, waiting for her to call on someone.

"OK. It looks like you think you know this one. All 3s need to raise their hands." All the 3s raise their hands, and Ms. Bernardo calls on Javier (an average-ability science student). Javier responds, "That's easy. The Jurassic."

"Why are you so certain, Javier?"

"Because the dinosaurs lived during the Jurassic."

"Does everyone agree? Ana?"

"Javier's right about the Jurassic, but they also lived in the Cretaceous period. They became extinct during the Cretaceous. They were abundant during the Jurassic." The students then argue over when the dinosaurs first appeared. The chart says Triassic, but some students disagree.

The class continues to identify classifications, with the groups sharing with one another their ideas, and then responding to teacher questions when Ms. Bernardo asks for a "numbered head" response.

Ms. Bernardo is using one type of cooperative learning approach (numbered heads together) to facilitate enhanced student academic and social achievement. This strategy is one of several relatively simple cooperative learning strategies that teachers can use to foster enhanced student learning and interpersonal cooperation. ■

❶HEORETICAL PERSPECTIVE

Competitive people enjoy competitive situations only when they believe they can *win*. Those persons who love to play "Trivial Pursuit," because they know a lot of trivia, may be the same individuals who do not want to play charades because they are not good at acting out famous phrases, movies, or song titles.

Schools, as presently structured, are competitive places! Students are constantly ranked and compared. They are grouped, sorted, and classified each day, and by the end of every school year all youngsters have a pretty good sense of where they belong. In the early grades, reading achievement appears to be the sorting mechanism. Students who read well have high status; those who read poorly have low status. Cohen (1986) poignantly describes this reality when she observes:

> Rank in reading ability is evidently public knowledge in many elementary classrooms. In most classrooms . . . the students were able to rank each other on reading ability with a high level of agreement. Furthermore, the

teacher's ranking was in agreement with the students' ranking. This means that if you are [a] poor reader, it is not only you who expect to do poorly—all your classmates expect you to do poorly as well! (p. 26)

The move toward heterogeneous grouping has mitigated the effects of some of what Cohen noted; but as students mature, other school practices emerge that replace reading as the salient sorting device. One of those is described by Kagan (1989/1990) as the Whole-Class-Question-Answer:

In this arrangement students vie for the teacher's attention and praise, creating negative interdependence among them. That is, when the teacher calls on one student, the others lose their chance to answer: a failure by one student to give a correct response increases the chances for other students to receive attention and praise. Thus, students are set against each other, creating poor social relations and peer norms against achievement. (pp. 12–13)

In essence, every time a teacher organizes a classroom to achieve some learning goal, students are engaged in more than one type of learning. They learn not only content, but also important information about themselves in relationship to their peers. Certainly some such information can be positive, especially when a student is reasonably secure vis-à-vis varied intellectual abilities. But it is negative when students are uncertain about themselves (and most are!), because it diminishes the students' sense of what they can be.

Johnson and Johnson (1987) would describe the Whole-Class-Question-Answer Strategy as an example of a competitive goal structure. A *goal structure*, simply defined, is how the teacher has students work together to achieve a learning goal. According to the Johnsons, three different types of goal structures exist in classrooms: competitive, cooperative, and individualistic. When students work against one another to achieve a learning goal (Whole-Class-Question-Answer), they are functioning within a *competitive goal structure*. When they work on their own (that is, their peers' performances are of no importance), the goal structure is *individualistic*. And, when they work together to achieve a learning goal, the lesson structure is *cooperative*.

It is important to note that not all lessons need to follow a cooperative structure. There are, indeed, times when competitive and individual goal structures can be used to achieve specific cognitive outcomes (see Table 10-1). In America's classrooms of the past, the teaching strategy of choice has been essentially competitive. For those students who have high mathematical and linguistic abilities (the two skill areas most emphasized in schools), or for those students who come from cultural backgrounds that reward competitive abilities, the school's historical tendencies have been unduly advantageous. Many other students, however, have been disadvantaged by this competitive ethos. For these students (for example, Native American students), to "beat" a friend is the functional equivalent of an act of cultural sabotage!

The pedagogical goal for the teacher should be to achieve an understanding of when and how to use the different goal structures in ways that advantage all students. The focus of this chapter is on cooperative learning, but for those interested in how to utilize competitive and individual goal structures appropriately, we suggest the Johnsons' (1998) *Learning Together and Alone*.

TABLE 10-1 Goal Structures and Cognitive Outcomes

Cognitive Outcome	Cooperative	Competitive	Individualistic
Mastery of factual information			x
Retention, application, and transfer of factual information, concepts, and principles	x		
Mastery of concepts and principles	x		
Verbal abilities	x		
Problem-solving ability and success	x		
Cooperative skills	x		
Creative ability, divergent and risk-taking thinking, productive controversy	x		
Awareness and utilization of one's capabilities	x		
Perspective-(role-)taking abilities	x		
Speed and quantity of work on simple drill activities		x	
Competitive skills		x	
Individualistic skills			x
Simple mechanical skills			x

Source: D. W. Johnson and R. J. Johnson. 1975. *Learning Together and Alone.* Englewood Cliffs, NJ: Prentice-Hall, p. 32.

As Table 10-2 suggests, cooperative learning is useful when (1) the teacher has a defined learning goal that is perceived to be important, (2) the nature of the task is both conceptual and complex (two heads generally do a better job of solving problems), and (3) students can work together in ways that enable all students to be successful—not just the top students. More specifically, there are five components to successful cooperative learning. Using the mnemonic PIGSS, these components can be readily recalled as Positive interdependence (students need to be able to work together); Individual accountability (each student is still assessed on what he or she knows); Group processes (a structure exists for how students will work together); Social skills (particular social skills are emphasized during the group work); and Specific tasks (students work together to achieve a particular goal).

These five components clearly suggest that cooperative learning and group work are not synonymous. Teachers have used groups in classroom situations since the inception of the common school. What is different about cooperative learning is PIGSS. The teacher not only has students work together, but also has them in a structured situation working to achieve a common goal through the use of selected social skills.

TABLE 10-2   Appropriate Cooperative Learning

Interdependence	Positive
Type of Instructional Activity	*Any instructional activity. The more conceptual and complex the task, the greater the superiority of cooperative over competitive or individualistic learning.*
Perception of Goal Importance	*Goal is perceived to be important.*
Teacher–Student Interaction	*Teacher monitors and intervenes in learning groups to teach collaborative skills.*
Student–Materials Interaction	*Materials are arranged according to purpose of lesson.*
Student–Student Interaction	*Prolonged and intense interaction among students, helping and sharing, oral rehearsal of material being studied, peer tutoring, and general support and encouragement.*
Student Expectations	*Group to be successful. All members to contribute to success. Positive interaction among group members. All members master the assigned material.*
Room Arrangement	*Small groups.*
Evaluation Procedures	*Criteria-referenced.*

Source: D. W. Johnson and R. T. Johnson. 1987. *Learning Together and Alone* (2nd ed.). Englewood Cliffs, NJ: Prentice-Hall, p. 44.

For cooperative learning to work properly, the teacher needs to accomplish the following:

1. Specify appropriate instructional objectives.
2. Determine the appropriate group size.
3. Assign students to groups so that groups are heterogeneously configured. Students, in time, need to be assigned specific roles within the groups so that they know how to work with their peers.
4. Arrange the room (and the groups) to facilitate group work.

Students need to work toward some defined group goal, and their success in achieving that goal must be contingent on all other group members' learning the material. Cooperative learning is not one person solving the puzzle while the others watch. Cooperative learning requires that all students have input and that all students participate. As Slavin (1990) notes: "Simply putting students into mixed ability groups and encouraging them to work together are not enough to produce learning gains: students must have a reason to take one another's achievement seriously, to provide one another with elaborated explanations that are critical to the achievement effects of cooperative learning" (p. 138).

The various cooperative learning strategies outlined later in this chapter are examples of strategies that fulfill the conditions for appropriate cooperative learning. Some of the strategies are relatively simple to implement; others require more practice and time. No one strategy is the correct one, and no single strategy should be used exclusively. As teachers use the different strategies, though, the students should begin to see that the teacher is not the only intellectual resource in the classroom. Slavin (1990) reinforces this point with his observation: "Clearly, a cooperative school would have cooperative learning methods in use in most classrooms. . . . Students and teachers should feel that the idea that students can help one another learn is not just applied on occasion, but is a fundamental principle of classroom organization" (p. 142).

A final word. A lot of controversy exists about the efficacy of cooperative learning. Advocates say it's the answer; detractors suggest that it limits learning. A brief summary of both views follows:

A prodigious amount of research now exists regarding cooperative learning. Advocates of the approach argue that the technique enhances student motivation, self-esteem and achievement, especially when compared to the outcomes of competitive or individualistic goal structures. Vermette (1998) notes that the positive effects of cooperative learning on student motivation, self-esteem and achievement are evident across 13 years of schooling; this is true for students of both genders, all ethnicities, and across various disabilities. Cooperative learning provides a healthy, cognitively challenging and supportive environment for all students and will succeed if several conditions are met:

1. Students should be taught why they are being asked to work together.

2. They should be shown how they are expected to interact with each other.

3. The groups should analyze (or process) their own effectiveness. (p. 60)

Vermette outlines the good news. A number of critics offer serious cautions, including the problems of student "free-riders" and "ganging up" effects. Further, Izumi and Coburn (2001) cite the work and ideas of a number of critics in suggesting the following:

According to Hirsch [one educational reformer], parents often complain that, since cooperative learning uses mixed-ability groupings of students, more capable children who want to do more and better work are discouraged on the grounds of not cooperating with the group. Indeed, Adams and Hamm, in their pro-cooperative-learning book, say that, "Groups must try to reach a consensus on a problem." Yet, they say nothing about what happens when that consensus happens to be incorrect, or about students who give in to the incorrect consensus even though they may know and support the correct answer. That higher-ability students may not benefit very much from cooperative learning is one of the downsides of the method, according to Stone and Clements. They note that although there is some evidence that cooperative learning does increase the achievement of low-performing students, "No studies of cooperative learning have found exceptional benefits for high-ability students." Given that cooperative learning produces a disparity in student achievement gains, Stone and Clements ask whether social and motivational outcomes, which are fostered by cooperative learning, should be put on an equal plane with academic outcomes. (p. 27)

The research and ideas of critics offer a mixed view. Nothing too surprising there! If educational practices have demonstrated anything over the past several decades, they have shown that any technique can become a tool or a weapon.

Cooperative learning for us is a tool, one means of achieving certain educational ends. As a professional, your goal must be to determine what you want to achieve, what students need to learn, and how best to merge the two. In many instances, the answer will be cooperative learning.

COOPERATIVE LEARNING: TEACHING PHASES

Because there are so many different types of cooperative learning strategies, it is impossible to outline precisely the specific phases for teachers to follow. In this section, therefore, we will identify some basic phases for teachers to follow in organizing a cooperative learning lesson. In the next section, we will describe different types of cooperative learning strategies that teachers can use. The format for this section is taken from the Association for Supervision and Curriculum Development (1990) Cooperative Learning Series, so readers are encouraged to access the ASCD tapes and manual activities that accompany that series if they desire more detail on the phases. Another resource is the Developing Lifelong Learners series (1996), distributed by Canter and Associates (P.O. Box 2113, Santa Monica, CA 90407–2113).

Phase I: Determine the Lesson to Be Taught

The first phase is to identify whether the lesson to be taught matches the cooperative learning instructional model. If the teacher wants students to increase their speed in solving simple algorithms, cooperative learning would not be the best approach. If, on the other hand, the teacher is interested in enabling students to solve a puzzle or better comprehend academic content, then cooperative learning would be efficacious. In essence, the first task of teachers is to identify what they plan to teach (see Chapter 3, "Instructional Models and the Planning Process") and to determine whether students working in groups represent the best instructional approach to achieving the learning goal.

Phase II: Determine the Appropriate Oorganizational Structure

As the reader will recognize in the next section of this chapter, a myriad of instructional variations can be used to facilitate cooperative (positive) interactions between and among students. In essence, the major decisions relate to group size, group assignment, room arrangement, materials, and roles. Table 10-3 outlines the basic decisions associated with each of the steps. For cooperative learning to work, teachers need to identify the specific objectives they hope to achieve, and students need to know precisely what is expected of them once they start working with their peers. Students need to be in heterogeneous groups that include students of different ability levels in the content area being assigned (that is, math cooperative learning groups may be configured differently from reading cooperative learning groups). The reason for this is quite simple: Different students demonstrate different intellectual strengths, depending on what topic is being investigated. The heterogeneous groups allow students to learn

TABLE 10-3   Decision-Making Information Sheet

Group Size	*When making decisions about group size, the teacher should consider five variables:*
	■ *students' academic and social skills*
	■ *amount of time students have to work*
	■ *nature of the task*
	■ *opportunity for each student to talk and exchange ideas*
	■ *quantity of material to be covered*
Group Assignment	*When deciding how to assign students to groups, the teacher should consider these points:*
	■ *Each student has different strengths and weaknesses.*
	■ *Heterogeneous groups are most powerful.*
	■ *Groups can be heterogeneous on several different variables: ability, sex, ethnic background, perspective, and language.*
	■ *The teacher is responsible for making group assignments and so must consider all these points. Left to form their own groups, students choose to work with friends, and the resulting homogeneous groups limit students' learning experience.*
Room Arrangement	*When arranging the classroom, provide an environment that supports and encourages cooperation:*
	■ *Students in groups need to be close to one another to share materials and exchange ideas quietly.*
	■ *To decrease intergroup distractions, allow space between groups; you can then easily circulate among them.*
Materials	*The distribution of materials can reinforce the message of positive interdependence:*
	■ *With one set of materials per group, students must share and interact frequently.*
	■ *Providing each student with a different part of the materials or information ("jigsawing") requires students to learn specific portions of the lesson content and to reinforce what they have learned with their peers.*
	■ *One set of materials per student allows each to have a copy to review and study.*
Roles	*Role assignments reinforce the message of positive interdependence because success depends on each group member performing his or her role. Also, role assignments can further emphasize the need to use the social skill(s) included in the lesson.*
	■ *The roles must be taught and clearly understood by the students.*
	■ *To give each student a chance to perform different functions, rotate the role assignments.*
	■ *Examples of roles that support social skills are encourager, checker, and observer. Examples of roles that support work skills include recorder, reader, and runner.*

Source: Association for Supervision and Curriculum Development. 1990. *Cooperative Learning Series: Facilitator's Manual.* Copyright © 1990 by ASCD. Used by permission. All rights reserved.

from peers. Altering the groups, depending on the content area (math vs. reading), enables students to understand that not all students are good at all subjects.

Phase III: Define Lesson Objectives and "Role" Tasks

There is an old expression, "If you don't know where you are going, any road will get you there." That's just as true in teaching as it is in life. For teachers to reach a specific destination, they need to know what the destination is and how they will get there—they identify objectives and define and assign the various tasks to the students in the classroom. In cooperative learning lessons, the performance objectives should be both academic and social. Just as not all academic skills are emphasized in a specific lesson, so, too, not all social skills (for example, encouraging, listening) are emphasized in each assignment. Smith (1987), a high school English teacher, noted that he has "students practice only one or two . . . skills during any given lesson" (p. 664). For example, the teacher might have students practice the skills of listening or of accepting the ideas of others. Teachers do not generate a long list of social skills for students to work on if, in fact, they want students to really practice the skills of providing feedback and monitoring the progress of others in the group. In addition, the teacher needs to articulate what roles students will play once they are in their groups. Some teachers will assign one student to be a "checker" (to make certain everyone understands the content material), another student to be a "facilitator" (to make certain everyone participates), and a third person to be a "resourcer" (to make certain all the materials are available). Role assignments are important to ensure that students know what is expected of them. It is also imperative that the roles be rotated. Teachers need to ensure that different students experience different role assignments.

Phase IV: Determine How to Monitor the Students' Work and Process the Lesson

For many teachers, group work is a time for them to relax. Once the students are busy working together, the teacher has time for other endeavors (for example, grading papers, preparing the next lesson). Clearly, teachers need time to do these tasks, especially given the fact that American teachers actually teach longer days and have less time to plan than teachers in many other industrialized countries. Our point is that the time to "catch up" is not during a cooperative learning activity. The teacher's responsibility during this time is to monitor and facilitate how the students are working together. Teachers need to determine what student behaviors will be monitored and to structure specifically how the observations of the students' progress will be made (for example, will the teacher take notes on student interactions or use a check sheet?).

Once the lesson is completed, the students then need to take some time to discuss how the lesson progressed and how well their various groups worked together. Not all teachers complete this phase each time, especially if they are doing a lot of cooperative learning, but this phase is important. It sets a tone that suggests the importance of both the academic and the social skills. Without adequate "processing," students do not have an opportunity to reflect on their actions and their accomplishments. Some teachers have students complete a group self-assessment form. Students are asked to respond (on a 1–5 or 1–10 scale) to questions such as, How do you think your group performed? Did you participate as fully as the other group members in the learning activity?

COOPERATIVE LEARNING: INSTRUCTIONAL VARIATIONS

As indicated earlier, teachers can use a host of cooperative learning strategies to enable students to effectively work together. The more options the teacher knows, the more vital cooperative learning can be as an instructional model. Some of these models are relatively simple to use; others require more practice and attention to detail. It is literally impossible to provide any comprehensive look at possible strategies in the context of a chapter such as this one. Our intention is to provide the reader with a sufficient overview so that the possibilities for classroom practice can be determined. References are made within each instructional variation description so that the reader may explore each variation in more depth.

Informal Cooperative Learning

The first set of strategies we discuss are what Baloche (1998) describes as informal cooperative learning strategies. These techniques occur when teachers ask questions and then have students work cooperatively to get an answer, when teachers read stories or lecture and then ask questions, or when teachers ask the students questions and then encourage them to summarize or synthesize ideas. Often times, informal cooperative learning strategies are linked to another teaching model, such as direct instruction (see Chapter 9). When that occurs, Baloche argues that the outcome might appear as follows:

1. Teacher asks a question that serves as an anticipatory set or advance organizer for the story, video, demonstration, or lecture that is to follow. Students discuss.

2. Teacher reads story, shows video, or delivers lecture—stopping every few minutes and asking students to discuss a teacher-prepared question or problem. Questions and problems might be factual or conceptual; they might focus on the material that has just been presented or might help students bridge to a new segment of the presentation. Students discuss.

3. Teacher asks a question that helps students summarize and synthesize the material that has been presented and provides closure for the lesson. Students discuss. (pp. 100–101)

Selected informal cooperative learning approaches are outlined below. In addition Table 10-4 describes other informal approaches a teacher might use when attempting to foster team building skills among students or class building or student mastery of content. Notice how color coded co-op cards might be used to enhance student memorization of material.

TABLE 10-4   Overview of Selected Informal Cooperative Groupings

Structure	Brief Description	Functions: Academic & Social
	Team Building	
Round-Robin	Each student in turn shares something with his or her teammates.	Expressing ideas and opinion, creation of stories. Equal participation, getting acquainted with teammates.
	Class Building	
Corners	Each student moves to a corner of the room representing a teacher-determined alternative. Students discuss within corners, then listen to and paraphrase ideas from other corners.	Seeing alternative hypotheses, values, problem-solving approaches. Knowing and respecting different points of view, meeting classmates.
	Mastery	
Color-Coded Co-op Cards	Students memorize facts using a flash card game. The game is structured so that there is a maximum probability of success at each step, moving from short-term to long-term memory. Scoring is based on improvements.	Memorizing facts. Helping, praising.
Pairs Check	Students work in pairs within groups of four. Within pairs, students alternate—one solves a problem while the other coaches. After every two problems the pair checks to see if they have the same answers as the other pairs.	Practicing skills. Helping, praising.

Source: Paul J. Vermette. *Making Cooperative Learning Work* (Upper Saddle River, NJ: Prentice Hall, 1998), 23. Reprinted by permission of Prentice-Hall, Inc.

Numbered Heads Together   This technique is the one that Ms. Bernardo used in the case study provided at the beginning of this chapter. It fosters student mastery of content by having students consult with one another in response to a specific teacher question. Kagan (1989/1990) describes the following steps:

1. The teacher has students number themselves off within their groups, so that each student has a number: 1, 2, 3, or 4. (Groups can consist of three to five students.)

2. The teacher asks a question.

3. The teacher tells the students to "put their heads together" to make sure that everyone on the team knows the answer. (All students need to discuss the material relevant to the question and be able to respond.)

4. The teacher calls a number (1, 2, 3, or 4), and students with that number can raise their hands to respond. (p. 13)

Kagan (1989/1990) notes that this cooperative learning strategy is especially helpful in enhancing academic and social skills such as checking for understanding and comprehension.

Groups of Four This is a variation of Burns' (1981) group investigation model. Students work in small groups to solve problems that require both cognitive processing of information and social interactions that foster group interdependence. The following steps were followed by teachers in one study that sought to assess the efficacy of the Groups of Four strategy (see King, 1993).

1. Students work together in groups of four members.
2. Each group's membership composition is assigned randomly.
3. Each group member is assigned a particular role in the working of the group.
4. All groups work on the same problem or problem-solving activity. . . .
5. Each group works toward one product for which each member receives a group reward. (p. 403—direct quotation, but reformatted)

King attempted to empirically assess the thought processes of students who participated in a Groups of Four cooperative learning activity. He was especially interested in the reactions of low achievers who were participants in the Groups of Four strategy. King noted some of the problems confronted by low achievers in heterogeneous groups (for example, they were influenced by the dominant leadership style of selected high-ability students), but even more important was King's notion that for cooperative learning to accomplish its purposes, teachers need to carefully work with students on how to function within the group situation (see step III of the previous section).

Think-Pair-Share In Think-Pair-Share, students are required to use academic skills such as hypothesizing, inductive reasoning, and application (Kagan, 1989/1990). The social skills they utilize include group participation (learning to get along with others) and listening. The technique is intended to enable students to develop concepts and critical-thinking skills. The essential steps of the model include:

1. The teacher provides the students with a topic or idea.
2. The students then reflect independently about the meaning of the topic— the teacher should give students a short period of time for independent thinking.
3. The students pair up with other students to discuss the topic and to share respective thoughts. (This can be a random pairing.)
4. The students then share their thoughts with the class—the teacher needs to wait after each student shares (3–5 seconds) for all students to *think* about what has been *shared.*

The teacher might use Think-Pair-Share with students at the beginning of a unit when students are attempting to explore the meaning of a topic. This strategy is not difficult to implement and requires only limited practice before teachers and students feel comfortable and successful. It will require teacher patience, though. Most teachers are not used to waiting after the sharing. If teachers pair students to create questions, the technique is called Think-Pair-Question, and if they pair to create a "web," it is called Think-Pair-Web.

Groups of Three The Groups of Three strategy is effective for skill building (for example, enhanced math proficiency or vocabulary development). Typically, Groups of Three can be used on an ongoing basis (that is, the group membership would remain relatively permanent for a grading period or semester). Such permanence enables students to work together over long periods of time and to learn from one another how to develop academic and social skills. The groups are heterogeneously formed based upon academic ability. Provided below is a description of the steps and how to implement the strategy in the classroom.

1. Heterogeneous groups are formed based upon academic ability.
2. Work tasks are assigned to the group on a weekly or biweekly basis (for example, define and use vocabulary terms).
3. Opportunities are created for both group cooperation and individual accountability. (See the Jigsaw II process in the next section.)

Smith (1987) describes his use of the technique with high school English students:

> I use students' scores on a pretest to form the first-semester groups. Each group has one member from the top third of the class, one member from the middle third, and one member from the bottom third . . .
>
> The students look up the meanings of words independently. Early in the week, working in groups, they review the word meanings together. Since they have used a variety of dictionaries for their homework, the definitions they share with one another encompass a variety of shades of meaning.
>
> Late in the week, the students take two quizzes. They work with their groups to complete the first quiz (20 items involving sentence completion, analogies, and antonyms). The second (20 items involving synonyms) they complete individually.
>
> The group quizzes yield two obvious benefits. First, they give students a chance to review the week's words together. The more often students see, say, hear, and write the words, the more likely it is that these words will become part of their daily vocabularies. Second, the group quizzes give students another opportunity to strengthen their problem-solving skills. (p. 665)

Formal Cooperative Learning

Throughout the 1990s selected and more structured approaches to cooperative learning also surfaced. These strategies require a much more sustained commitment on the part of the teacher, especially if the scoring regiments are to be used. The models have in common an affirmation of each student's experiences and thoughts and, ideally, should constructively use peer pressure to enhance individual student learning. We have found that the teachers who use these models best are those who systemically received training and then mentoring on the model's usage. Whereas, informal cooperative learning strategies can be used with limited professional development, the formal approaches require more teacher training to ensure the approach is used correctly. A number of different formal approaches exist including STAD (Student Teams-Achievement Divisions) and TGT (Teams Games Tournament)—(see Devries, Edwards and Slavin, 1978; Kagan, 1992; Silver, Hanson, Strong and Schwartz, 1996). We suggest that teachers who really have an interest in the more formal approaches pursue the type of professional development work that is needed to ensure proper usage of the model. We will go into detail for one of the formal approaches (for example, Jigsaw) in sufficient depth to ensure that the reader understands the approach, but for full mastery of formal cooperative learning there is no substitute for in-depth training in the model.

One of the real virtues of formal cooperative learning approaches is the emphasis they place on improvement points. In essence, these approaches really encourage students to learn while at the same time rewarding students who continue to perform well. Clearly, one of the real reasons so many students fall into a cycle of failure is that they see few opportunities to contribute in the way a high achiever does. Jackson and Davis (2000) describe the issue poignantly:

> How schools acknowledge student achievement is another determinant of the intergroup climate on campus. As schools are increasingly able to help all students reach or exceed high academic standards, students from all backgrounds will naturally be honored for their achievement, indicating plainly to everyone that no one group is more able than another. Until this occurs routinely, and as long as gaps in achievement between groups persist, schools can supplement the practice of honoring students whose absolute level of achievement is outstanding by honoring students who have shown substantial improvement in their academic performance. (p. 176)

Jigsaw II The Jigsaw II strategy, which is based on Aronson et al.'s (1978) work, requires that students learn how to work together to enhance their total understanding of a topic. Each student is given a portion of the topic to learn well (to become an expert on that part of the topic). After the students have had some period of study with other group members who have similar responsibilities, the teacher provides all students with an opportunity to share their understanding of the topic with other group members. In this way, the students develop a more comprehensive understanding of the topic.

For a more complete understanding of Jigsaw II, the essential steps include the following:

1. Inform students that they will be working in their Jigsaw groups to achieve the lesson goals. If students have previously used Jigsaw II, the teacher's statement will be brief. If students are using it for the first time, then students need to be oriented to the size of the group (four members), the structure of the Jigsaw II activity (each person will be assigned a specific area to study within the broader topic), and the goal of the activity (to enable each "expert" to teach what is learned to the rest of the group members).

2. Create heterogeneous groups. There are a number of different ways to create the groups. Some teachers categorize all students in the class according to general groupings such as high ability, above-average ability, below-average ability, and low ability. They then select one person from each of these general groups to form the study groups. Other teachers literally rank students top to bottom with a number (1 through 28, for example) and then "renumber" the students so that seven groups of four can be formed heterogeneously (see Table 10-5).

The result would be that all the 1s form a group (that is, Fumi, Lavonne, Sarah, Tanaya). That group of students then creates a name for itself (the Fab Four, for example). At the end of this step, all students are thus assigned to a group and have a name for their group.

Bailey (1996) elaborates on the dynamics of the group assignment process:

> One technique that teachers can use to gain a picture of their classes is to develop class projects in which students serve as data collectors. Students are keen observers of the world around them. Having them keep a record of who is taking part in class can serve as a springboard for important discussions. These discussions can raise everyone's awareness of classroom dynamics, dynamics sometimes so ingrained that they have become invisible. (p. 77)

3. Present rules to govern group behavior. Once the students are in their groups, the next step is to make certain that all students know what is expected of them. Gunter, Estes, and Schwab (1995) identify the following rules to govern group behavior:

   a. No student leaves the group to meet with other class members until everyone in the original group finishes the teacher-assigned task.

   b. Each student must make certain that his or her teammates become experts in the assigned group material. Each student is, thus, responsible not only for knowing the content, but also for making sure that group members have a thorough understanding of the same material.

   c. Each student in the group is a resource. If an individual student does not understand some of the content, that student must get help from the group members before seeking help from the teacher.

4. Present content material to the whole class. There are a number of different ways this can be done. The teacher might present a lecture on the topic and then ask the students to use supplementary texts as content resources. For example, assume a teacher is preparing to have the students read a chapter in a text on communism. The textual material examines communism in the former Soviet Union and focuses on its roots, its emergence as an ideology, and its apparent demise in some industrialized countries. Students are to read 17 pages of content material concerning this concept. Four topical areas of interest are identified by the teacher: (1) persons who shaped the communist movement, (2) countries that embraced the communist ideology, (3) political structures found within communist countries, and (4) the economic consequences of communist ideology.

TABLE 10-5 Group Membership Assignment: A Sample

Student Name and Rank	Group Assignment
1. Fumi	1
2. Sue	2
3. Rodrigo	3
4. Josh	4
5. Abraham	5
6. Lori	6
7. Tonya	7
8. Nikki	7
9. Jacque	6
10. Serita	5
11. Bobby	4
12. Aurora	3
13. Nicole	2
14. Lavonne	1
15. Sarah	1
16. Julianne	2
17. Lindsay	3
18. Ramone	4
19. Latoya	5
20. Zachary	6
21. Yung Chang	7
22. Sharad	7
23. Noel	6
24. Libby	5
25. Donnelle	4
26. Jerod	3
27. Shawn	2
28. Tanaya	1

Students are ranked on left column according to ability as perceived by the teacher.

The teacher at this point has identified specific academic content for the overall topic—communism—and has four specific topical areas that become the foundation for group exploration and development.

5. Develop expert groups. The heterogeneous expert groups are then asked to study the various topic areas, and each member selects one subject within the specific topic. Hence, for our Fab Four group, Fumi selects the economic consequences of communism, Tanaya selects the political figures who shaped the communist movement, and so on. Once all the students have selected one of the four topics for study, the teacher then forms the

expert study teams. In essence, each person who selected a topic is going to become an expert in that area.

6. Organize expert groups. The teacher then has all the experts get together and study each topic. That is, all the students from all the groups who plan to study political figures in communism get together and investigate the topic as thoroughly as they can. They need to make certain that all group members thoroughly know the topic so that they can eventually teach this topical material to their original "home" team.

7. Return to study teams to teach expert knowledge. Once the students have had an opportunity to become experts, they then go back to their "home" study team and share their knowledge. Each individual shares with teammates all topical material that has been acquired. The teammates ask questions, take notes, and review the content to ensure that they understand what the expert is sharing (the expert is "teaching" the other group members). Remember everyone read all the original content material, so all team members have some understanding of each topic. The experts have more knowledge because as an "expert group" they focused on the content material in different ways: They read, watched, listened, and discussed the topic in depth.

8. Evaluate student knowledge. The teacher then tests students to assess their understanding of the topic. Students are assessed in two ways and receive points based on both their contributions to the group and their own performance. Each student receives an actual score on the test. As an example, the quiz scores of the Fab Four on the communism test are: Fumi, 96; Lavonne, 86; Sarah, 81; Tanaya, 78.

    The teacher then compares each student's actual quiz score with a base score. The teacher computes a base score by looking at previous quiz and test grades and averaging all available grades. The actual and base scores for the Fab Four are provided in Table 10-6 as well as the point differential between the two, which represents the improvement score, from which improvement points can be calculated using Table 10-7. (Incidentally, the improvement points scale can be adjusted based on the students' performance and the difficulty of the quiz.)

    The teacher then records the actual score in the grade book. The improvement points are used for team recognition, which is described in the next step.

9. Provide team recognition. Prior to the team recognition step, the teacher determines what average improvement scores the teams will need for different levels of recognition. Calculate the average improvement score by having the students add their improvement scores and divide by the number of group members. For the Fab Four the total was 80 and the average was 20.

    The teacher created three levels of recognition. Super teams are those with averages of 25+. Great teams are those with averages of 20+. And good teams are those with averages of 15+. The teacher then provides each team with a recognition certificate (or some other "reward") that acknowledges the team's level of performance. In the previous example, the Fab Four would be given a Great Team certificate.

TABLE 10-6   Scores of Fab Four Students

	Base Score	Actual Score	Improvement Score	Improvement Points
Fumi	*95*	*96*	*+1*	*20*
Lavonne	*87*	*86*	*-1*	*10*
Sarah	*80*	*81*	*+1*	*20*
Tanaya	*67*	*78*	*+11*	*30*
				Total 80
				Average 20

Source: Adapted from Cooperative Learning Series. 1990. Alexandria, VA: Association for Supervision and Curriculum Development, p. 101.

TABLE 10-7   Improvement Points Scale

Quiz Score	Improvement Points
More than 10 points below base score	*0*
10 points below to base score	*10*
Base score to 10 points above base score	*20*
More than 10 points above base score	*30*
Perfect paper (regardless of base score)	*30*

Source: Cooperative Learning Series. 1990. Alexandria, VA: Association for Supervision and Curriculum Development, p. 101.

Some teachers find that they do not like to use the team recognition after each testing situation. Instead of giving team certificates for super or great teams, the teacher has students accumulate team points and then exchange the points for some teacher defined "goods." For this to work, it is imperative that teams work together to decide how they will use their points. The "checker" in the group records the improvement points; then the team members can exchange their points when a certain level is achieved (for example, 50 improvement points can be exchanged for two answers on a quiz; 75 points can be exchanged for a homework assignment).

INSTRUCTIONAL CONNECTIONS: COMBINING TEACHING MODELS

Cooperative learning interfaces nicely with many other instructional models. Teachers would tend not to use this model in isolation; more typically, they would use it in combination with another instructional strategy. For example, in Chapter 9 we discussed how to use direct instruction when teaching skills. The authors of this book have observed numerous lessons where direct instruction

TABLE 10-8 Syntax for Concept Attainment and Cooperative Learning

Sequence of Phase	Teacher/Student Behavior	Cooperative Options
1. Present goals and establish set	Explains the goals of the lesson and gets students ready to learn	Think-Pair-Question
2. Present examples and nonexamples	Presents both examples and nonexamples	Think-Pair-Web
3. Compare and contrast	Emphasizes the comparison of examples and contrasting with nonexamples	Think-Pair-Share
4. Identify concept and agreement	Has students state the essential characteristics of the concept in pairs	Think-Pair-Share or Group Discussion
5. Test attainment and justify	Provides additional examples; students test the concept and justify their answers	Think-Pair-Share Group Discussion Numbered Heads Together
6. Analyze and evaluate	Helps students analyze their thinking processes and evaluate the effectiveness of their strategies	Think-Pair-Share Group Discussion Numbered Heads Together
7. Demonstrate understanding through independent practice of the concept	Has students independently create or find additional examples	Think-Pair-Share Group Discussion following the independent practice

Source: L. H. Mauro and L. J. Cohen. 1992. "Cooperating for Concept Development." P. 162 in N. Davidson and T. Worsham (eds.), *Enhancing Thinking Through Cooperative Learning.* New York: Teachers College Press.

and cooperative learning are combined—teachers taught a skill using direct instruction and then used cooperative groups to check (and reinforce) student understanding of the skill. Table 10-8 provides an example of how cooperative learning is combined with concept attainment, and Table 10-9 illustrates how it is used with concept formation. We also discussed how easy it is to combine informal cooperative learning with direct instruction. The important point is that as teachers develop their mastery of the models, they can begin to combine the models in ways that enhance the overall involvement of the students so that they learn requisite material.

APPLICATIONS TO DIVERSE CLASSROOMS

A great deal of attention has been given recently to the restructuring of schools in order to make American education more competitive in the world market. The school restructuring, or reinvention process, for most districts has focused

TABLE 10-9   Syntax for Concept Formation and Cooperative Learning

Sequence of Phase	Teacher/Student Behavior	Cooperative Options
1. Listing	Asks students a question that generates a list of objects or ideas	Think-Pair-Share Round Robin Roundtable Interview
2. Grouping	Asks students to group the objects into classes	Think-Pair-Share Group Discussions Team Concept Webbing Numbered Heads Together
3. Labeling	Asks students to label the various classes of objects	Think-Pair-Share Group Discussion
4. Processing	Asks students to analyze the criteria they used for listing the items	Think-Pair-Share Interview Round Robin Group Discussion Numbered Heads Together

Source: L. H. Mauro and L. J. Cohen. 1992. "Cooperating for Concept Development." P. 163 in N. Davidson and T. Worsham (eds.), *Enhancing Thinking Through Cooperative Learning*. New York: Teachers College Press.

on how to enable educators to be more accommodating to the rich human diversity found in America's schools. Reform-minded individuals, both liberals and conservatives, want schools in which all students learn, not just places that cater to the best and brightest. Of course, recommendations for how to achieve this goal vary significantly. Though many conservative educational reformers such as E. D. Hirsch suggest real reservations with cooperative learning, especially when it is used as a principal means of delivering content, there is general agreement that the model enhances student learning and motivation if it is used with other models to enhance student acquisition (Izumi and Coburn, 2001).

Cooperative learning is not a fad or a fashionable idea that suits the fancy of an intellectual elite. Cooperative learning is effective because the undergirding tenets of the strategy are good for all students. Slavin (1987) noted that "the attraction of cooperative learning for many humanistic educators probably lies not so much in accelerating student achievement as in the consistently found positive effects of cooperative learning on such variables as race relations, attitudes toward mainstream classmates, self-esteem, and other nonacademic outcomes" (p. 34). It should be of no surprise, therefore, to discover that many schools embracing the concept of character education are also espousing cooperative education (Schaps, Lewis, and Watson, 1993). The social benefits of cooperative learning represent one of its most distinguishing characteristics (Lickona, 1989).

Cooperative learning does not advantage just a few students; it should advantage all students, especially if teachers recognize that cooperative learning comes in a wide variety of forms. Indeed, some critics argue that selected forms of cooperative learning (for example, those that rely on group rewards such as Jigsaw II) may be disadvantageous for some students. Kahn (1991) asserted that group rewards diminish student motivation to learn when those rewards are tangible and extrinsic. Hence, for some students, reward-based cooperative learning may be demotivating; but for the vast majority of students, regardless of cultural background, cooperative learning (even with the reward component) represents a positive step toward enhanced self-esteem and achievement. Others argue that it may be problematic for high ability students and might limit their growth (Izumi and Coburn, 2001).

Not all cooperative learning strategies have been used with all racial and ethnic groups. Clearly, more research is needed. However, based on the studies that have been conducted to this point, the potential impact of cooperative learning for enhancing intra- and intergroup relations is significant. Where formal cooperative learning strategies such as STAD (Student Teams Achievement Division) have been used, it appears as though intergroup cooperation is enhanced (for example, European American and Asian American students developed better attitudes toward Hispanic American students) and more "close student friendships" are created (with others from different racial groups). Slavin (1995) concluded:

> The results of the studies relating cooperative learning to intergroup relations clearly indicate that when students work in ethnically mixed cooperative learning groups, they gain in cross-ethnic friendships. This research indicates that the effects of cooperative learning on intergroup relations are strong and long-lasting, and are more likely on close, reciprocated friendship choices than on distant or unreciprocated choices. There are no clear patterns indicating more consistent results for some methods than for others. All methods have had some positive effects on intergroup relations. (p. 633)

Baloche (1998) is more direct in her assessment of the benefits of cooperative learning for diverse student groups, and most particularly she discusses its implications for field-independent and field-dependent learners.

> Field-independent individuals tend to prefer situations that require analytical approaches to problem solving and to prefer material that is less imbedded in social context. Field-dependent individuals tend to prefer situations that require global approaches to problem solving and to prefer material that is more imbedded in social context. In general, European American students tend to be more field independent while Mexican American, Native American, and African American students tend to be more field dependent. Cooperative learning tends to provide a rich social context for learning, and this may explain, to some degree, why Mexican American and African American students are likely to experience greater academic success in cooperative than in competitive or individualistic learning environments. . . . It does not follow, however, that students of European descent experience greater success in environments that do not emphasize social context and cooperation. . . . [Researchers] have investigated students' self-reported preferred styles and have found that even when students do not express a preference for learning co-

operatively, they tend towards higher achievement in learning environments that are structured around substantive cooperative work. (p. 41)

PREVALENT ISSUES IN DIVERSE CLASSROOMS

Cooperative learning is not a problem-free strategy. Like all pedagogical approaches, teachers will have to deal with all varieties of student responses to a new way of organizing the classroom environment. The first two problems highlighted below are the most common of the difficult issues teachers seem to confront as they explore the efficacy of cooperative goal structures in the classroom.

Q: *What if my students just don't work well together?*

A: One of the most difficult problems for teachers new to cooperative learning is encouraging students to communicate effectively in their assigned groups. Many teachers attempt to utilize cooperative learning groups, but never consider that students need to practice working together so that they know what is expected of them in a group. This is especially true if students have functioned almost exclusively within competitive or individualistic goal structures. In order for cooperative learning to work, teachers need (1) to make certain students have opportunities to practice working together, and (2) to enable students to fully understand what it means to be in a group-participation situation.

One of the first steps in cooperative learning is providing students with practice opportunities to work together. The teacher needs to determine what skills students should practice and which norms must be operational. Cohen (1994) suggests that such "norms and skills are best taught through exercises and games, referred to as 'skillbuilders'" (p. 41). An example of a skillbuilder is provided at the end of this chapter; however, teachers should feel comfortable in using any activity that provides students with an opportunity to work together to solve a common problem (for example, have the students work in groups to put together picture puzzles; provide team-building experiences to help them build cohesiveness).

As students practice working together to solve problems, they will also need to work on how to communicate once they are in their assigned groups. For group participation to be effective, the teacher needs to make certain of the following:

1. All students in each group are talking to one another.
2. All students are making an effort to listen to the ideas of group members.
3. All students are asking questions and making contributions.
4. All students are providing reasons for their observations.
5. All students are providing constructive feedback to one another concerning participation and group cohesiveness.

Some teachers carry a clipboard around when the students are working in groups and make specific observations regarding how the students are communicating within their assigned groups. They make notes about group communication and provide feedback to members concerning social skill development. Other teachers spend a few minutes before each cooperative activity and ask the students to review how they will be expected to work with one another (for example, what words would students use to indicate they are listening to one another?). In essence, for the cooperative groups to work, students must (1) develop a sense of trust with group members, (2) work at communicating their ideas accurately, (3) support group members, and (4) work jointly to resolve academic or social conflicts within the group.

Q: *How do I deal with students who are not good at participating in groups because they lack certain academic skills?*

A: Students in classrooms possess very different academic skills. One of the real challenges confronting teachers is to create cooperative learning situations in which all students fully and equitably participate. Recently, one of the authors of this book observed a high school science teacher teaching a lesson in which the students were expected to use cooperative learning strategies. The teacher was excellent in presenting content in a cogent fashion and in guiding the students' learning—the teacher began by using a direct instruction strategy to communicate science content knowledge. However, as the lesson progressed, the observer noticed that some students were allowing others to do all the cooperative learning. (Recall that group work and cooperative learning are not the same thing.) The groups did solve the teacher-defined problem, but there was a distinct difference in the level and quality of participation by all class members in the groups.

In many cases, the nonparticipating students are what Cohen (1994) describes as "low-status" students (that is, students who do not talk as much as their peers, and who, through their nonverbal and verbal actions, communicate a message of nonparticipation). Cohen describes two different ways to solve the low-status problem. The first is what she calls the "multiple ability treatment." This strategy is especially effective when the teacher assigns a task that truly demands different skills in order for students to successfully complete the task. Teachers who use this approach, according to Cohen (1994), must

- Clearly describe the different kinds of intellectual abilities necessary for the task.
- Convince the students that the tasks they are about to do require many different intellectual abilities.
- Convince the students that no one will have all the necessary intellectual abilities, but that everyone will have some of the necessary abilities. (p. 2)

A second strategy teachers can use is described by Cohen as *"assigning competence to low-status students."* In this strategy, the teacher consciously looks for those special skills that low-status students possess, and verbally communicates about these skills to the other members of the group (for example, "I think

B. J.'s ability to draw will be invaluable to your group"; or "Si Hong's ability to understand diagrams may be useful as you try to construct the model."). With this approach the teacher makes a "public" evaluation of a real student skill. The specific steps the teacher would follow according to Cohen include:

- Assignment of competence is specific, so the student knows exactly what he or she has done well.
- Assignment is public.
- Competence is made relevant to the task. (p. 3)

With both of these strategies, the teacher's goal is to enhance the participation of all the students in the class. What better way to warrant the worth of every child (regardless of an individual's gender, racial, ethnic, or cultural background) than to find ways to ensure that each student can contribute. Catch students at what they are good at, and point out their strengths to the rest of their group members. Active students learn more than students who sit passively and allow others to do the work—teachers must find ways to make certain that all students are active learners.

Q: *How do I deal with the cooperative learning groups in Jigsaw II if I have high absenteeism rates?*

A: Student absenteeism is a major problem for many teachers, especially those in urban situations. Quite obviously, the best solution is to find a way to attract students to school—to entice them to want to be there. Still, the reality of schools is that, even with very good teachers, some students will consistently be absent. How do teachers negotiate this problem? One teacher we know uses the following strategy. On the first day (of a Jigsaw II lesson sequence) the teacher teaches the information the students need to know. Students then read the material and are responsible for knowing the answers to all the questions. When the students return the second day, the teacher forms the heterogeneous groups based on who is in attendance. Students are then assigned a number (1–4) for their expert groups, and they work in their groups to refine and extend their understandings relative to a specific question. The students return to their "home" group for that day and teach their expert material. After taking the quiz, the students calculate their team improvement points, and the teacher gives a token ("lucky bucks") to those at each level of performance (for example, three lucky bucks for super team, two for great team, and so on). The teacher distributes the lucky bucks during the team recognition time and each student must keep track of his or her own lucky bucks. Those lucky bucks can then be exchanged for "goods."

ⒺVALUATION CRITERIA ⊠

For cooperative learning to work effectively, the teacher must do much more than simply put students in groups and assign a project. Teachers need to think carefully about the composition of groups, the mechanism for ensuring full participation of students within groups, the roles that group members must play, and the nature of the task that students are expected to solve. The evaluation questions provided below focus on these dimensions as well as on the overall structure of the cooperative learning model.

Phase I: Lesson Format

1. Is the lesson content appropriate for use with cooperative learning?　　☐ Yes　　☐ No

Phase II: Organizational Structure

1. Identify the type of cooperative learning strategy to be used. Why was this strategy chosen?　　_____ _____ _____

2. Are students placed in appropriately sized groups?　　☐ Yes　　☐ No

3. Are students placed in heterogeneous groups? (Describe how the groups are organized.)　　☐ Yes　　☐ No

4. Are students provided with all the requisite materials for successfully completing the assigned task?　　☐ Yes　　☐ No

Phase III: Objectives and Roles

1. Does the teacher clearly define the academic objectives students are to achieve while in their groups?　　☐ Yes　　☐ No

2. Does the teacher clearly define the social skills students are to exhibit during the lesson?　　☐ Yes　　☐ No

3. Does the teacher define the different roles that students are to perform once they are in their groups?　　☐ Yes　　☐ No

Phase IV: Monitoring

1. Does the teacher monitor student performance in group situations?　　☐ Yes　　☐ No

2. Does the teacher provide students with feedback on how they are performing in their group?　　☐ Yes　　☐ No

3. Is there accommodation for both individual accountability and group reward
   in the defined cooperative learning
   situation?   ☐ Yes   ☐ No

4. Do the students self-monitor their
   groups?   ☐ Yes   ☐ No

SAMPLE LESSONS

The following sample lessons illustrate alternative procedures for implementing the cooperative learning instructional model. The first example is a case
study of a 5th grade lesson on Mexico. The second example is a high school
mathematics lesson using cooperative learning.

CASE STUDY I

Portia Henriques is preparing to have her 5th graders study Mexico as part
of a larger unit on Latin America. The students are going to use many supplementary texts in preparation for their "excursion" into Mexico, but the one
common text they will be using focuses on life in Latin America. Ms. Henriques spent the first class period using a concept formation activity. She had
the students generate all that they know about Mexico. The list of terms generated by the students included almost 100 items. The students then created categories for those items (for example, foods, cities), and Ms. Henriques plans to
revisit the students' work at the completion of the unit to show them how
much additional information they have learned and to expand the categories
they created during the concept formation lesson.

The students will be reading approximately 14 pages of material and focusing on four different aspects (or issues) of Mexico, including:

1. The natural environment of Mexico: Describe the landscape and climate.
2. Land use in Mexico: Describe the crops and natural resources.
3. The people of Mexico: Describe the population growth and distribution.
4. The culture of Mexico: Describe how the people live.

She asks the students to read the material on their own for homework. The
next day Ms. Henriques asks the students to get into their cooperative groups.
The assigned groups have worked together on several other occasions.

Ms. Henriques asks the students to spend a few moments in their cooperative groups and to decide which question or issue each student wants to select
for study. In the Barrio Brothers group, Teofilo (a high-ability student) selects

TABLE 10-10   Information Sheet

Issue 1

Describe the landscape and climate of Mexico.

1. There are two mountain ranges that run along Mexico's coast: the Sierra Madre West and the Sierra Madre East.

2. The Central Plateau of Mexico begins at the border of the United States and ends where the two mountain ranges meet in the southern section of Mexico.

3. Mexico City, Mexico's capital, sits at the southern end of the Central Plateau, which is also the highest elevation of the plateau.

4. Mexico has two large peninsulas: Baja and Yucatán.

5. The temperatures of Mexican cities depend on their locations. Cities at high elevations have lower year-round temperatures than cities at lower elevations. Mexico City is at a high elevation.

6. Northern Mexico is warmer than southern Mexico. The elevation of the southern section is also higher.

7. Mexico has seasonal precipitation, with the heaviest precipitation in the summer months.

issue 1, Carmelo (a middle-ability student) selects issue 2, Salvador (a middle-ability student) selects issue 3, and Ernesto (a low-ability student) selects issue 4.

Once all the students in all the groups have their assignments, Ms. Henriques asks them to get in their expert groups. All the issue 1 students get together in one corner of the room; the issue 2 students are in another corner, and so on. The students spend the rest of the class time studying together. They share information with other group members when they feel comfortable with their individual knowledge accumulation of the assigned issue. Table 10-10 is the information sheet generated by the issue 1 expert group.

The next day the students return to their cooperative groups, and each expert shares the knowledge acquired during the expert group discussion. Teofilo shares with Carmelo, Salvador, and Ernesto the information that he acquired (see Table 10-10). As he shares the information, the other students in the group take notes, ask questions, and even check the text again a couple of times to verify the accuracy of Teofilo's information. When Teofilo finishes, Carmelo begins to share his issue 2 information with his cooperative group members. The process continues until all group members have shared their ideas.

At the end of the class period, Ms. Henriques spends a few minutes reviewing some of the major ideas that she wants the students to remember. One student is from Mexico and volunteers to bring in pictures of Mexico City, where one of her aunts still lives.

Ms. Henriques informs the class that tomorrow there will be a quiz that consists of 10 true/false, 10 fill-in-the-blank, and one essay question.

The next day Ms. Henriques administers the quiz. Because of the essay section, Ms. Henriques must grade all the papers herself. She records each individual student's grade and also determines, using a process similar to that described earlier in this chapter, which groups are super, great, and good teams. The next day the individual tests are returned, and the groups are given team rewards. ∎

Follow-Up Questions

1. Identify two other cooperative learning strategies that this teacher might use.
2. What academic skills was this teacher emphasizing?
3. What social skills did this teacher emphasize?

Case Study II

Ms. Greenwald is reviewing content related to the area of a triangle with her high school geometry students. She begins by discussing the formula for computing the area of a triangle: $\frac{1}{2} b \times h$. The students spend a few minutes reviewing the formula and asking questions about calculating areas.

Ms. Greenwald then talks about the structure of the Jigsaw process. She is using the Jigsaw process to ensure that all the student know how to calculate the areas of hexagons, trapezoids, and parallelograms.

Although her class has regular heterogeneous group assignments, several students are absent, so she begins the group time by reassigning students into "new" groups.

Ms. Greenwald then distributes work sheets to students in the various groups. The sheets, distributed to students in their home groups, deal with finding the areas of the three different polygons. After all the sheets are distributed, Ms. Greenwald quiets the students and says, "Class, now I want you to rearrange yourselves. Those of you with a sheet for the area of a trapezoid are to come up here (she points to one table), and those of you with the hexagon sheet are to go there (she points to another table), and those with the parallelogram are to go back there (she points to a table in the back of the room)."

The students move from their home groups to their expert groups. She does not really tell the students what social skill she wants them to focus on during the group work. Rather, the exclusive emphasis of the lesson is on academic skills.

While the students are in their expert groups, Ms. Greenwald walks around and monitors the students' progress, answering questions and sharing more content to ensure student understanding.

The worksheets are structured to foster student thinking. For example, Worksheet #1 asks students: "Using your knowledge of the formula for the area of a triangle, find the area of a regular hexagon below"—the lengths (see Figure 10-2) are given to the students to help them with the calculations. She also asks the group to create a method (a formula) for calculating the area of the hexagon.

After students have completed their expert group work, she then asks the experts to go back to their home group and explain to the rest of their group members the content they have acquired.

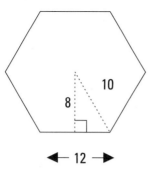

FIGURE 10-2   Measurements of a Hexagon

Once again, Ms. Greenwald walks around the class and interacts with students as they work to learn the content being taught by the respective experts. On several occasions she either reinforces or corrects the students' descriptions of how to calculate the areas of the various figures.

When the students appear to have completed their descriptions (that is, when all experts are done), Ms. Greenwald has the students return to their regular seats. She then gives them a quiz over calculating the area of a triangle, parallelogram, trapezoid, and hexagon.

Teacher Reflections

I teach three Basic Geometry classes each day. The students in these classes have a wide range of abilities, and most are not strong mathematics students. In addition, because many of the kids struggle with mathematics, it is their least favorite subject. My goal for these classes is to make the students appreciate the value of mathematics. To achieve this goal, I incorporate as many different activities into the class as possible; jigsaw is one such activity.

This lesson went very well, especially since it was a new concept for the students. I tried to develop a lesson that I knew my students would be able to accomplish with only a small amount of assistance from me. This enabled me to supervise all groups, and it gave me the opportunity to observe student interactions. I was truly amazed and impressed with how well the students worked together. They made a concerted effort to complete and to understand their specific problems, whereas, typically their only goal is to complete their work. The students were forced to become accountable for their own learning.

In my next jigsaw lesson, I will review the concepts more carefully beforehand. I briefly reviewed area formulas with my students, but I should have allotted more time for sample review problems. I think this would have made the overall lesson run more smoothly. Although the kids have used the formulas in previous lessons, they easily forget how to apply them. I had to remind several students how to use area formulas once they were in their expert groups. Their time would have been better served working with their group members. I also think it is possible to remove the quiz from future jigsaw lessons, but I would not necessarily eliminate it from the first jigsaw lesson. The slight pressure of having a quiz was invaluable; it ensured all students worked diligently as both instructor and listener. This was crucial to the success of the lesson.

When I spoke with my students after completing the jigsaw, they were fairly enthusiastic. For the most part, they enjoyed the activity, and they felt they learned from it. Few students found the activity too difficult to complete. While some students struggled more than others, they were able to receive help from their expert group members. Some students expressed a concern about the testing aspect of jigsaw. They were uneasy about being tested over material they just learned, especially because they learned it from their peers rather than from me. After a successful first jigsaw lesson, I do not feel it will be necessary to test the kids at the end of each subsequent jigsaw lesson. ∎

⑤UGGESTED LESSON DEVELOPMENT: QUESTIONS FOR REFLECTION ✔

Cooperative learning offers teachers a wide variety of options in terms of how to structure the classroom. In preparing to use the cooperative learning instructional model, the teacher should consider the following:

1. Determine what academic and social skills should be emphasized as part of the lesson.

2. Identify which cooperative learning strategy can best be used to enable students to achieve these academic and social skills.

3. Determine how to structure the heterogeneous groups. (The teams should be heterogeneously grouped by ability and by race and gender if academic and social skills are to be adequately fostered.)

4. Provide students opportunities to practice the social skills in their heterogeneous groups before having them work on specific academic skills.

5. Identify how to monitor student academic progress (that is, how will students be assessed individually and in groups?) and how to provide feedback to students about their use of selected social skills (that is, use of a social skills checklist or use of informal observations and notes using a clipboard).

ⓣECHNOLOGY ENHANCEMENT A D ① S ⓒ ◆

New workplace environments are emerging as a result of the technology advances of the past decade. These new environments are creating a demand for employees who possess the technical and interpersonal skills to work collaboratively with others in a virtual world where most communication and much work is conducted without face-to-face interaction. The technology enhancement for this chapter supports teachers in facilitating the cooperative learning model by employing a strategy specifically developed to engage students in conducting inquiry (I) on the World Wide Web while working in collaborative research teams (C).

Utilizing a WebQuest to Facilitate Cooperative Learning

As pointed out earlier in this chapter, cooperative learning strategies are many and varied. Today, new technologies offer classroom teachers an array of tools for enhancing various forms of cooperative learning. Responding to this opportunity, pioneering educators are developing instructional strategies that blend cooperative learning theory with these new technologies. One such pioneer is Bernie Dodge, a professor at San Diego State University, who in 1995 initiated the development of the WebQuest strategy. A WebQuest is an inquiry-oriented, informal cooperative learning instructional activity in which groups of students cooperate to acquire, process, and apply information acquired primarily from teacher-selected Internet resources.

A WebQuest, properly constructed to support cooperative learning, is characterized by a number of critical attributes. First, it provides students with an *introduction* that sets the stage and provides relevant background information on the question to be answered or the problem to be solved. Second, it presents students with a *clear task* that is challenging but achievable. Third, it provides *specific tasks and questions* tailored to groups of students that have been structured to work collaboratively. Fourth, it provides students with the *Web-based resources* necessary to complete the task. This is an especially important element of the WebQuest strategy because it supports students in accessing relevant and exciting sources of information, including experts available via email or synchronous conferencing, video and audio artifacts, searchable databases, as well as books and journal articles. It is particularly important here that students do not waste unnecessary time while "surfing" the web and accessing inappropriate or irrelevant sources. Fifth, a quality WebQuest describes the *process* that learners should follow in completing their assigned tasks. This process may take any number of forms, such as directing students to answer a guiding question or to recommend a solution to an ill-structured problem. Finally, the WebQuest strategy concludes by providing opportunities for students to reflect on what they have learned, what remains to be learned, and how their learning experience might be extended.

The WebQuest strategy is especially appropriate when teachers desire students to develop higher order thinking skills by tackling a complex or controversial issue that requires them to understand and mediate competing perspectives. Working in groups and exploring such problems from diverse points of view demands that students develop a range of new thinking and collaboration skills as they tackle the various tasks set forth in the WebQuest.

Teachers who engage in the process of developing their own WebQuests should be mindful that the quality of the learning experience will be a function of their attention to the fundamental elements of the cooperative learning model. For example, good WebQuest design follows the phases of the cooperative learning model as described earlier in this chapter.

Grade Level Modifications

The WebQuest strategy can be successfully employed at all grade levels, including the early elementary grades. One excellent way for teachers to get a sense of how the strategy might be applied at the grade level they teach is to explore the numerous sample WebQuests catalogued at the San Diego State University's WebQuest Web site at http://edweb.sdsu.edu/webquest/webquest.html. Clicking on the *Examples* link provides access to hundreds of WebQuests arranged by grade level categories ranging from *Kindergarten–Third Grade* through *College–Adult*. When reviewing the samples, teachers should be aware that not all of the featured WebQuests place equal emphasis on cooperative learning. In fact, reviewing selected samples in light of the critical attributes of a quality WebQuest is a good way to gain deeper insight into the important design elements.

Low Tech/High Tech Applications

The WebQuest strategy, like any other educational use of the World Wide Web, is directly affected by a variety of computer hardware and wiring factors that can combine to affect the quality of Web access experienced by teachers and their students. Obviously, the number of Internet connected computers available in a classroom is an important factor as well. Tom March, one of Bernie Dodge's collaborators, has provided teachers with a number of interesting thoughts on how to respond to these issues. Interested teachers can access this information in an online article titled *WebQuests for Learning* at http://www.ozline.com/webquests/intro.html. In addition to providing suggestions for using WebQuests in both technology-rich and technology-poor environments, March makes clear that successful use of the WebQuest strategy has less to do with bandwidth and more to do with teachers' knowledge of their students and curriculum, and the desire to create engaging and meaningful learning experiences.

Value Added for Diverse Learners

The WebQuest strategy can help meet the needs of diverse learners in the following ways: Female students, because of their generally positive disposition toward cooperative learning and peer interaction, are likely to respond positively to the strategy, especially when teachers design WebQuests that are grounded in "real world" problems and issues. Asian American students may respond favorably to the strategy because it requires students to examine specific dimensions of a problem and then search for a workable solution or answer. Native American students may appreciate the Web resources that provide strong visual stimuli and imagery. This is becoming an easier task for teachers as many Web sites now contain quality multimedia effects to help communicate information. Finally, teachers of African American and Hispanic American students may want to capitalize on the cooperative learning model because these students also have such generally positive orientations to collaborative environments for engaging ideas.

In designing WebQuests, teachers might make a special effort to connect students, via email for example, with positive role models from their respective ethnic and racial communities. Regardless, the computer represents the great equalizer in education. A student working on a computer and interacting with a Web site is not African American or Euro-American but, rather—and this is the way education should be—a learner! Computers are great equalizers, and for that reason they offer great opportunities for helping all students reach their potential.

Web-Based Resources

Teachers interested in trying the WebQuest strategy in any academic discipline, or at any grade level, will find a wealth of resources available to support their efforts. In fact, many fully developed and field-tested WebQuests are now catalogued online. In addition to the San Diego Web site mentioned earlier, teachers can access a collection of WebQuests for the elementary and secondary grades at http://www.itdc.sbcss.k12.ca.us/curriculum/webquest.html.

The following sites provide outstanding support for teachers interested in developing their own WebQuests. All of them provide a wealth of free information and resources to support the WebQuest design process. *Filamentality*, for example, is an interactive Web site at http://www.kn.pacbell.com/wired/fil/ that is sponsored by Pacific Bell and dedicated to helping teachers develop WebQuests and other Web-based teaching and learning strategies. This is an excellent site to support teachers interested in using WebQuests to facilitate cooperative learning. A wealth of information is also available at http://www.ozline.com/learning/index.htm. Finally, the San Diego State University site contains many resources in addition to its online catalogue of WebQuests. For example, teachers new to WebQuest design will find some great resources available in the *Training Materials* section at http://edweb.sdsu.edu/webquest/materials.htm.

ⓈUMMARY

Competition may be fundamental to American culture, but so, too, is cooperation! All those who work in business and industry know that they are individually accountable to produce quality work, but they must also be able to function effectively with peers and colleagues—to get along with others. Cooperation and competition do not represent an either/or dichotomy. Instead, the teacher must decide on the purposes of a lesson and the concomitant needs of the students involved in that lesson.

Effective teachers understand that students need to learn to work together just as much as they need to function independently. Living in a democratic society demands both types of skills. And learning both sets of skills requires teachers to arrange the classroom environment carefully and intentionally so that students have appropriate opportunities to learn requisite social and academic skills. For example, for some special projects, there is nothing wrong with intentionally arranging for bright students to work with other bright students. These "special" teams enable bright students to use their intellectual skills in a different way than is possible with heterogeneous groups.

Cooperative learning is not without problems. Teachers who are experimenting with the technique complain that some students dominate and others fail to participate. That is why the Cohen (1994) resources can be valuable. No technique is problem-free! The issue is whether teachers can persevere once they confront problems and can identify positive ways to resolve those issues that potentially threaten the success of this instructional model. Cooperative learning takes practice and instructional support: Teachers need to find ways of "playing with" the cooperative learning model, and they need to have available some support (administrative and curricular) to assist them as they confront difficulties endemic to the use of a new strategy such as cooperative learning.

ⓈKILLBUILDER: ALLIGATOR RIVER

Once there was a girl named Abigail who was in love with a boy named Gregory. Gregory had an unfortunate accident and broke his glasses. Abigail, being a true friend, volunteered to take them to be repaired. But the repair shop was across the river, and during a flash flood the bridge was washed away. Poor Gregory could see nothing without his glasses, so Abigail was desperate to get across the river to the repair shop. While she was standing forlornly on the bank of the river, clutching the broken glasses in her hand, a boy named Sinbad glided by in a rowboat.

She asked Sinbad if he would take her across. He agreed on the condition that while she was having the glasses repaired, she would go to a nearby store and steal a transistor radio that he had been wanting. Abigail refused to do this and went to see a friend named Ivan who had a boat.

When Abigail told Ivan her problem, he said he was too busy to help her out and didn't want to become involved. Abigail, feeling that she had no other choice, returned to Sinbad and told him she would agree to his plan.

When Abigail returned the repaired glasses to Gregory, she told him what she had had to do. Gregory was so mad at what she had done he told her that he never wanted to see her again.

Abigail, upset, turned to Slug with her tale of woe. Slug was so sorry for Abigail that he promised her he would get even with Gregory. They went to the school playground where Gregory was playing ball, and Abigail watched happily while Slug beat Gregory up and broke his new glasses.

Rank these characters from "best" to "worst": Abigail, Gregory, Sinbad, Ivan, Slug. Give reasons for your decisions.

Source: E. Cohen. 1994. *Designing Groupwork: Strategies for the Heterogeneous Classroom* (2nd ed.). New York: Teachers College Press: 178–179.

ℝEFERENCES

Aronson, E., N. Blaney, C. Stephan, J. Sikes, and M. Snapp. 1978. *The Jigsaw Classroom.* Beverly Hills, CA: Sage.

Association for Supervision and Curriculum Development. 1990. *Cooperative Learning Series: Facilitator's Manual.* Alexandria, VA: Association for Supervision and Curriculum Development.

Bailey, S. M. 1996. "Shortchanging Girls and Boys." *Educational Leadership* 53(8): 77.

Baloche, L. A. 1998. *The Cooperative Classroom.* Upper Saddle River, NJ: Prentice-Hall.

Burns, M. 1981. "Groups of Four: Solving the Management Problems." *Learning* 22(2): 46–51.

Cohen, E. 1986. *Designing Groupwork: Strategies for the Heterogeneous Classroom.* New York: Teachers' College Press.

Cohen, E. 1994. *Designing Groupwork: Strategies for the Heterogeneous Classroom* (2nd ed.). New York: Teachers' College Press.

———. 1994. *Status Treatment for the Classroom.* Videotape and manual. New York: Teachers College Press.

Crawford, M., and M. Witte. 1999. "Strategies for Mathematics: Teaching in Context." *Educational Leadership*, 57(3): 34–37.

Devries, D. L., K. J. Edwards, and R. E. Slavin. 1978. "Biracial Learning Teams and Race Relations in the Classroom: Four Field Experiments on Teams-Games-Tournaments." *Journal of Educational Psychology* 70: 356–362.

Gunter, M. A., T. H. Estes, and J. Schwab. 1995. *Instruction: A Models Approach* (2nd ed.). Boston: Allyn & Bacon.

Izumi, L. T., and K. G. Coburn. 2001. *Facing the Classroom Challenge.* San Francisco: Pacific Research Institute for Public Policy.

Jackson, A. W., and G. A. Davis. 2000. *Turning Points 2000: Educating Adolescents in the 21st Century.* New York: Teachers' College Press.

Johnson, D. W., and R. T. Johnson. 1975. *Learning Together and Alone.* Englewood Cliffs, NJ: Prentice-Hall.

———. 1987. *Learning Together and Alone* (2nd ed.). Boston: Allyn & Bacon.

———. 1989/1990. "Social Skills for Successful Group Work." *Educational Leadership* 47(4): 29–33.

———. 1998. *Learning Together and Alone* (5th ed.). Boston: Allyn & Bacon.

———, E. J. Holubec, and P. Roy. 1984. *Circles of Learning* (2nd ed.). Alexandria, VA: Association for Supervision and Curriculum Development.

Kagan, S. 1989/1990. "The Structural Approach to Cooperative Learning." *Educational Leadership* 47(4): 12–15.

———. 1992. *Cooperative Learning.* San Juan Capistrano, CA: Resources for Teachers.

Kahn, A. 1991. "Don't Spoil the Promise of Cooperative Learning." *Educational Leadership* 48(5): 93–94.

King, L. 1993. "High and Low Achievers' Perceptions and Cooperative Learning in Two Small Groups." *Elementary School Journal* 93(44): 399–416.

Lickona, T. 1989. *Educating for Character.* New York: Bantam.

Mauro, L. H., and L. J. Cohen. 1992. "Cooperating for Concept Development." Pp. 151–168 in N. Davidson and T. Worsham (eds.), *Enhancing Thinking Through Cooperative Learning.* New York: Teachers' College Press.

Schaps, E., C. C. Lewis, and M. Watson. 1993. "The Child Development Project." *Educational Leadership* 51(3): 46.

Silver, H. F., J. R. Hanson, R. W. Strong, P. B. Schwartz. 1996. *Teaching Styles and Strategies: Manual Z.* Woodbridge, NJ: Thoughtful Education Press.

Slavin, R. E. 1987. "Cooperative Learning: Where Behavioral and Humanistic Approaches to Classroom Motivation Meet." *Elementary School Journal* 88(1): 29–38.

———. 1990. "Cooperative Learning and the Cooperative School." Pp. 137–144 in R. Brandt (ed.), *Cooperative Learning Series.* Alexandria, VA: Association for Supervision and Curriculum Development.

———. 1995. "Cooperative Learning and Intergroup Relations." Pp. 628–634 in J. A. Banks and C. A. M. Banks (eds.), *Handbook of Research on Multicultural Education.* New York: Macmillan.

Smith, R. 1987. "A Teacher's Views on Cooperative Learning." *Phi Delta Kappan* 68(9): 663–665.

Vermette, P. J. 1998. *Making Cooperative Learning Work.* Upper Saddle River, NJ: Merrill Prentice Hall.

ELEVEN

• *Oral Discussion*

Chapter Objectives

At the end of this chapter, readers will be able to

1. *Describe the theoretical basis for the oral discussion model.*
2. *Identify the basic characteristics of an effective oral discussion lesson.*
3. *Identify the basic strengths and weaknesses of the model.*
4. *Identify how the model can be beneficial with diverse student populations.*
5. *Create factual, interpretive, and evaluative questions for an oral discussion lesson.*
6. *Identify ways to use technology to enhance discussion.*

❶NTRODUCTION

Who better to quote than Socrates—the master questioner? Indeed, his questions ultimately proved to be the cause for his own demise. Socrates had an ability to ask questions that disarmed those around him. In essence, he made people think by asking them questions, not by telling them truths. Indeed, Socrates, writes Strong (1997), "claimed to know only that he did not know, and achieved lasting intellectual greatness" (p. 68).

In many American classrooms, teaching consists of the teacher's talking and students' listening. Teachers want to tell truths (even half-truths at times) rather than ask questions that provoke thought. Indeed, many students listen only when the teacher is talking because their experience tells them that what the teacher says is important—teacher-disseminated information will be *on the test*. Excellent teachers understand, however, that meaningful ideas and the dialogue about those ideas are not the exclusive domain of one individual—those who have the capacity to think have the ability to help shape how others think. Young children sometimes have profound insights about old ideas; they see things in new or different ways. The "smartest" person is not necessarily the best thinker; the "dullest" individual is not without the capacity for great insight. Forrest Gump, though fictional, revealed the poignant truth that people of simple gifts have the capacity for extraordinary insights.

The teacher's challenge is to determine how to bring to the surface the gifts of all students in the classroom. Students who are expected to articulate and defend their ideas will more fully develop cognitively and socially than

Socrates: Every man is his own ruler, but perhaps you think that there is no necessity for him to rule himself; he is only required to rule others?

Callicles: What do you mean by his "ruling over himself"?

PLATO'S *GORGIAS*

those who are not expected to publicly take a position on issues of importance. For those who doubt the importance of discussions, consider the comments of the great UCLA basketball star Bill Walton. Walton described in a television interview his embarrassment with using language when speaking in front of others. He observed that it wasn't until he was an adult, and a "star," that a concerned friend helped him develop his verbal gifts. Prior to his friend's assistance, he felt awkward and inept at public speaking. Today he does public speaking (that is, motivation talks) and is an NBA broadcaster for one of the major networks.

The oral discussion model is used to help students discover their cognitive abilities through development of their own verbal gifts. It is also about trusting the educational process and allowing students to assume ownership for their learning and ideas. In a typical classroom recitation scenario, the teacher asks a question and then seeks the correct student response: "*What is the name of Nathaniel Hawthorne's female protagonist in* The Scarlet Letter, *Sung Hee?*" And then Sung Hee responds, "*Hester Prynne.*" Much of the dialogue that occurs in America's classrooms takes this shape. The teacher asks "what" questions, and the students respond with factual answers. Usually the student response mimics the specific words of a text or the specific information previously provided by the teacher. Clearly, recitations have a place in classrooms, but they must not be the dominant or exclusive form of teacher-student dialogue.

Oral discussion differs from recitation in two distinct ways. First, the students are expected to interact with others, not just with the teacher. Second, the ideas presented focus on higher cognitive outcomes, not just on the recall of factual information. Oral discussion entails several student responses following an initial teacher question. The teacher sets the stage for the interactions, but students "play off" the ideas of their peers as they explore the teacher-defined topic. They listen to and contribute to the discussion, and as they do so the conceptual complexity of the ideas is enhanced. The students and teacher have what Gall and Gillett (1980) refer to as a reciprocal influence—the "students learn not only from the teacher, but from each other" (p. 99). In essence, discussion is not a form of conversation because it is about developing knowledge and understanding and requires participants to be mutually responsive (Brookfield and Preskill, 1999).

One other characteristic of the oral discussion model makes it particularly distinctive. Memorable discussions require that students use a variety of learning modalities in order to assimilate ideas. Students need to be able to speak, observe, and listen in an oral discussion lesson. Traditional instruction puts emphasis on student listening skills, but not upon their speaking skills. A memorable discussion is intellectually demanding for both the teacher and the student. As the following example illustrates, it forces all the participants to think more deeply about ideas and to be able to defend their thoughts.

Ⓒ ASE STUDY

Ms. Sargaski's 7th grade students have been studying Middle Eastern politics and the relationship of the United States to the Middle East from 1950 to the present.

The students read pages 495–500 of a somewhat dated *World Geography* textbook (Silver Burdett Ginn, 1993) for homework. Ms. Sargaski starts the lesson by talking about some current events, such as the bombing of the World Trade Center, and then reading out loud to the class several important passages from the text. She has students read newspaper accounts of the bombing, and then she shares several ideas about the relationship between and among the Middle Eastern countries and the United States. She reviews several salient concepts related to the Islamic Revolution, the Shiites, and the theocracy that has emerged in Iran. After Ms. Sargaski is reasonably certain students understand the material well, she begins the lesson.

The students are asked to put their chairs in a large circle (whole-class roundtable) and to bring with them their books, their journals, and a copy of any notes that they have taken during their reading of the text. Once they are all situated in the group, the lesson begins.

"Class, I'm going to ask you several different types of questions. Most of these questions have several possible ways to respond, so don't look for just one correct answer. I really want to hear what you are thinking. Also, remember not to respond until I call on you."

"I'll begin with a very basic question. Why would there be such a tense relationship between the countries of Iran and the United States? Write down in your journals several explanations for the tense relationship. Don't share your ideas with anyone else at this point." The students take several minutes to jot down their ideas. The teacher then begins to ask some questions to develop the students' thinking.

"Now, class, write down one question that you have about how the United States deals with other countries when conflicts occur." She then gives the students several moments to write.

Ms. Sargaski continues, "In 1979, the Islamic Revolution occurred. As you know, the Shiite revolutionaries turned Iran into a theocracy. Jamie, define *theocracy* for me."

"It's a nation that's ruled by religious laws."

"Good. And how does that differ from a democracy, Jamie?"

"Well, in a democracy, the laws are created and passed by all the people. In a theocracy, the laws are made by religious leaders."

"That's correct. Now why do leaders in any country, regardless of whether that country is a democracy like the United States or a theocracy such as Iran, believe that their form of government should be imposed on others? Lamar?"

"I guess because they want everyone to act like they do."

"Is that the only reason? Are they concerned only with actions? Marta?"

"I think it has to do with what people believe. In a democracy we believe that all people are equal and have certain rights. In a theocracy, people are told how to act. They are told what to wear and who can vote."

"Renee, are there other reasons? Or, do you think the main issues relate to actions and beliefs?"

Renee responds, "I think it's actions and beliefs. But most people want others to act like them. We're a democracy, so we want all countries to be democracies. Iran's a theocracy, so it wants other countries to be theocracies."

"Interesting. So you think that Iran would have no problem with other countries as long as those other countries are theocracies?"

"Oh. I'm not sure."

"What aren't you sure of, Renee?"

"I don't know of other theocracies in the world."

"Well, that's a good point. There are very few theocracies. Let me give you one—the Vatican."

The class responds quizzically and almost chorally, "What?"

"That's right, the Vatican is a country, and it's also a theocracy. So, would Iran and the Vatican get along well because they are both theocracies? Jeremy?"

"No. I'm Catholic, and I don't think it's just the government. It is also what you believe. The leaders of the Vatican and Iran believe different stuff."

"And why is that 'different stuff' important, Jeremy?"

"Because what they believe begins to affect how they act and what is expected of them. I'm Catholic, but I'm not told what clothes to wear or how to behave in all circumstances."

"True, but what if you went to St. Luke's [the Catholic school down the street]? Would you then be told what to wear?"

"I never thought about that. But, yeah!"

"Class, consider this for a moment: How do you think democracies and theocracies can try to get along even when they have different beliefs and rules that determine how they govern people? One thing we might want to do is to read more about the Vatican and then use some of those ideas to help us see ways of better dealing with Iran and other theocracies. Let's turn to our books and read one more time what happened prior to and after the Islamic Revolution—turn to page 498—and then let's talk more fully about the tensions described in the book." The following text material is read:

> The new revolutionary government also changed Iran's policies toward the United States. Under the Shah, Iran and the United States had been good friends. The Ayatollah and his supporters believed that the United States helped keep the Shah in power. When he was overthrown, the new government showed its hostility toward the United States by taking Americans hostage and engaging in terrorism in the Middle East.
>
> A few years later a war broke out between Iran and its neighbor, Iraq. Hundreds of thousands of Iranians and Iraqis were killed in the fighting, and Iran's economy suffered drastically. The war ended in 1988. A year later the leader of Iran's revolution, Ayatollah Khomeini, died. The new leader of Iran has made some changes in the way the country is governed. [Source: *World Geography*. 1993, p. 498.]

After reading the material, Ms. Sargaski asked a couple of additional factual questions (for example, "Who did the Ayatollah believe helped the Shah to power?") and a series of interpretive questions (for example, "Why did Iran and Iraq go to war?" and "What types of changes might the new Iranian leader have made in how Iran is governed?"). The discussion continued for several minutes and concluded with the teacher listing some of the changes on the board. She then asked students to offer some of their questions. Some had already been answered; a couple of others were then discussed.

The teacher concluded the lesson by having the students read a pamphlet titled "Iran Today," and she asked students to compare the changes they hypothesized with what, in fact, appears to be occurring in Iran. ■

Ms. Sargaski is using oral discussion as a means of helping students more critically examine what a theocracy is and what it means for the United States to have relations with theocracies such as Afghanistan, Sudan, Iran, and even the Vatican. The students are expected to know some facts, but they are also provided an opportunity to think beyond the facts that are stated in the text or by the teacher. If the teacher had asked only factual questions, she would have fostered far less cognitive processing of information (see Chapter 3 for a discussion of taxonomical levels of thought) and, most likely, far fewer forms of student participation. Oral discussions enable students to use what they know as support for what they *think*.

THEORETICAL PERSPECTIVE

Discussions are seemingly commonplace in America's classrooms. Teachers interact with students as they attempt to explore a topic or idea. As indicated earlier, recitations and oral discussions are quite different. In recitation, the teacher is looking for a "correct" answer and the exchanges are characterized by a teacher-student-teacher-student format. In oral discussion, the teacher is working with the students to share knowledge in ways that involve more complex thinking. Gall and Gall (1976) suggest that with recitation students are recalling content, and with oral discussion the teacher is attempting to foster more critical thinking and attitude change. Given Gall and Gall's definition, it seems clear that much of what appears to be discussion in American classrooms is, in fact, recitation.

For discussions to occur, certain classroom conditions must be evidenced (Dillon, 1984). Students, for example, must feel free to express their feelings—they cannot be afraid of what others will think or how the teacher will respond—and teachers must value what students think. These conditions loom large as potential barriers to the success of a good discussion. Many students have learned to speak only when they know they are right, and to listen only when they see that the teacher is talking; students tend to ignore the contributions of their peers.

Once a teacher understands that certain preconditions must be in place in order for a discussion to occur, it then becomes possible to consider what conditions must exist in order to declare that a discussion is actually occurring. Dillon (1984), drawing on the work of a variety of other researchers, suggests three such conditions:

1. Those participating are putting forth a variety of ideas and points of view relative to a specific subject.

2. Those participating evidence a willingness to explore and examine the various ideas offered by their peers.

3. Those participating are attempting to more fully develop their understanding about the subject under discussion.

Based on these conditions, teachers, according to Gall and Gall (1976), are then in a position to achieve at least four different discussion outcomes. Understanding the outcomes is especially important for knowing when and how to use the discussion technique. Although research findings neither clearly justify nor diminish the use of discussion strategies, some evidence does suggest that if teachers want to foster enhanced subject matter mastery, attitudinal change, and problem-solving ability, then oral discussion strategies can prove to be beneficial. For instance, relative to subject matter mastery, Gall and Gall observe that it "appears that the discussion method is effective in helping students to master curriculum content, especially when cognitive outcomes beyond the level of knowledge are desired" (p. 200). In essence, discussion methods tend to foster higher cognitive achievement when the method is used in combination with other instructional models (that is, cooperative learning, synectics, inquiry). Discussion methods also tend to stimulate enhanced thinking on the part of students; students become active rather than passive participants in the learning process—they are literally constructing their own intellectual scaffolds. The consequence of this active engagement is that oral discussions can foster attitude changes in students.

For several years, researchers endeavored to determine if oral discussion strategies were more effective than other strategies such as lecture. That line of research proved to be neither especially useful nor insightful. In fact, discussion strategies have power when they are combined with other techniques, not when they are juxtaposed to them. Once again, we must emphasize that teachers really need to consider the goals of their instruction. Clearly, if the teacher is teaching a specific behavioral skill (for example, multiplying fractions), discussion may not be appropriate; the direct instruction strategy might be more useful. But if the teacher is seeking to foster enhanced mastery of content or to engender more critical thinking on the part of students, then discussion may well be useful (Bligh, 2000). As Gall and Gall (1976) note: "The nature of the intended learning outcome (for example, attitude change), rather than the curriculum content, determines the effectiveness of the discussion method" (p. 213). The academic content and process for American schools needs to focus more on awakening students' minds than in disseminating teacher-defined revelations of truth. Wiggins (1989) notes:

> What students need to experience, firsthand, is what *makes* an idea or book "great"—something hard to do well, but possible with students of all ages if teachers grasp the need for cycles of Question-Answer-Question instead of merely Question-Answer. The issue is ultimately not which great book you read but whether any book or idea is taught in a way that deadens or awakens the mind, whether the student is habituated to reading books thoughtfully, and whether the student comes to appreciate the value of warranted knowledge (as opposed to mere beliefs called "facts" by someone else).

One irony in the fuss over *Cultural Literacy* is that Hirsch (1988) has written a classic liberal argument: the point of cultural literacy is to enter the Great Conversation as a coequal. But Hirsch made a fatal (and revealing) error in his prescription of a shared base of essential information. (He also erred in his portrayal of Dewey's thinking. The caricature he presents of what he calls Dewey's "formalism" overlooks a massive corpus of writings that provide substantive guidelines on how to ensure that students truly understand academic ideas of value and substance.) The capacity to understand is only partially dependent on facts; rarely do we need to know the same things that our fellow conversants know. It is far more important for a novice to possess intellectual virtues (moral habits of mind, if you will); one must:

- know how to listen to someone who knows something one does not know,
- perceive which questions to ask for clarifying an idea's meaning or value,
- be open and respectful enough to imagine that a new and strange idea is worth attending to,
- be *inclined* to ask questions about pat statements hiding assumptions or confusions. (p. 48)

ORAL DISCUSSION: TEACHING PHASES

Phase I: Identify the Focus for Discussion

One of the first steps in oral discussion requires that the teacher identify what the focus will be for the lesson. A lot depends on whether the discussion is being used as a way of extending information covered for a lecture or if it is used as an ongoing method of helping students transform content, as one would find in Socratic Practice. If the former, the teacher might begin by asking the students to consider some topic—for example, the Mexican-American War—and then ask students to generate questions regarding that topic: Where did it occur? Why did it occur? Who were the primary military leaders? and so forth. The teacher then begins the lecture and delivers content, but then allows for discussion as each question is directly or indirectly addressed. The teacher might also add several questions that seem appropriate for students to consider, but that are not asked by the students (for example, In what ways are the Mexican War and the American Civil War connected?)

A second approach is grounded more in a "defined" curriculum of "great books." These books are, by their very nature, complex and difficult. The discussion and use of different types of questions helps students assimilate the content. Gunter, Estes, and Schwab (1995) use the "great books" approach, which requires that the teacher begin by selecting content material for the students to read (for example, the works of Tolstoy, Bacon, Chaucer, or Virgil) and then creating different types of questions (factual, interpretive, evaluative) for students to reflect upon and respond to based on those readings. Table 11-1 includes examples of questions at each of the levels for the book *Teammates* by Peter Golenbock (1990), which, incidentally, is a "good" book but certainly not

TABLE 11-1   Types of Questions for Discussions: Three-Level Approach

Factual	1.	*What one fact clearly suggests that Branch Rickey was not afraid of change?*
	2.	*What obstacles did Jackie Robinson face as a result of having made the Brooklyn Dodgers team?*
Interpretive	1.	*What did Pee Wee Reese mean by "If he's good enough to take my job, he deserves it"?*
	2.	*Why did Pee Wee Reese need to respond publicly to Jackie Robinson in front of the Cincinnati crowd?*
Evaluative	1.	*In what ways does what happened to Jackie Robinson still happen to people today?*
	2.	*Do you agree with the way in which Pee Wee Reese showed his support for Jackie Robinson?*

one of the "great" books. *Factual questions* are essentially questions derived directly from statements connected to specific textual material. These questions elicit correct or incorrect responses. Little, if any, divergent thinking occurs at this level. *Interpretive questions* focus on meaning; the reader must move beyond facts and explore the nuances of words and/or ideas. Usually these questions ask students to take information that they understand and to apply it to a new situation. These questions call for divergent thinking processes. *Evaluative* questions focus on the relationship between what the readers read and what they actually experience in their own lives. These questions are divergent in nature and ask students to make judgments about phenomena. They ask students to make decisions and draw conclusions. Some teachers reading this text will be more familiar with Bloom et al.'s (1956) taxonomy. (For a complete description, refer to Chapter 3.) Bloom orders questions hierarchically in six levels of thought processes (see Table 11-2), but like Gunter, Estes, and Schwab's question types, the lowest level focuses on factual recall of material, and the highest level demands that students pull together disparate ideas and create meaningful conceptual relationships.

We use the Gunter et al. approach in this chapter for the sake of simplicity—three levels rather than six. Actually, what is important is that teachers ask questions that foster different types of student thinking.

Once the teacher has the questions prepared—some prepared questions are essential for purposes of conducting a good discussion—the teacher should review the questions to make certain that they are clear and logically ordered so that students progress from convergent (factual) to divergent (evaluative) thinking processes. Convergent questions are not answerable in more than one way. Factual questions have "right" vs. "wrong" answers. Evaluative questions have responses that necessitate that students use facts to support their arguments, but the direction of the argument will vary according to the student making a particular point.

Teachers may find it useful to ask more factual questions at the beginning of a discussion (establishing a common understanding among students regarding

TABLE 11-2 Types of Questions for Discussion: Six-Level Approach

Knowledge	*What were the baseball leagues for blacks called in the mid-1900s?*
Comprehension	*What does the phrase "the great experiment" mean regarding Branch Rickey and Jackie Robinson?*
Application	*What do you think would have happened if that great experiment had never occurred?*
Analysis	*How important was it that Pee Wee Reese take a public stand to support Jackie Robinson?*
Synthesis	*Identify other ways that Pee Wee Reese might have shown his support for Jackie Robinson.*
Evaluation	*What additional data about Jackie Robinson or Pee Wee Reese do you need in order to better understand what happened in Cincinnati?*

the contextual facts) and then proceed to the more interpretive and evaluative questions once students have established their background knowledge.

Finally, there are some basic procedural considerations that need to be taken into account if a discussion is to be effective. Though Brookfield and Preskill (1999) outline these for use with older learners, they are equally applicable to all learners.

Don't be vague. Make certain questions are clear and unambiguous. Teachers who begin with a "What do you think?" question will be less satisfied than those who begin with a specific question, "What one reason do you think caused South Carolina to secede from the Union?"

Don't play favorites. Make certain that there is equitable student participation. Classrooms are marked by inequities. Find ways to involve all the students.

Don't fear silence. Far too many teachers fear quiet during discussion time. Let students think, reflect. Do not needlessly fill the air with words.

Don't allow students to talk over one another. Students need to learn how to respect others and listen to their comments.

Phase II: Pose the Question for Discussion

For oral discussions to be successful, the teacher must begin by posing a question that embraces the experiences of the students and is not cast at a level of abstraction that is inappropriate based upon the developmental level of youngsters or the development of the lesson and its content progression. The teacher, in essence, starts by creating, through the questioning process, some type of cognitive dissonance, but that dissonance should emerge from what the students already know and understand. Such dissonance can be facilitated in several ways: a key question, devil's advocate, student questions.

Key Question   A key question is an umbrella question that supersedes all other questions. For example, for the novel *Teammates*, the teacher might begin with the key question: "*Why was it so difficult for people in the 1950s to change their beliefs* *about who should play baseball?*" From this question, the teacher can then lead into the various factual, interpretive, and evaluative questions that have been enumerated in Tables 11-1 or 11-2. Gunter, Estes, and Schwab (1995) label key questions as "basic." For key questions to be workable, there can be no one correct response. Key questions foster dialogue, but they are not easily resolved or "correctly" answered. Good and Brophy (1997) also suggest the use of indirect questions. Such questions are less threatening and more inclusive in tone. For example, "Class, I wonder what would have happened if people like Pee Wee Reese were not willing to take a stand."

Devil's Advocate   A second way to begin classroom discussions is by taking a position that the teacher knows will be controversial. The teacher purposefully instigates a controversial (dissonant) stand on an issue. The teacher still needs to have factual, interpretive, and evaluative questions prepared, but the oral discussion begins by the teacher's posturing of a particular position: *"Nothing good happens when those who 'have' try to help those who don't 'have.'"* This statement could be made relative to the novel *Teammates*, and discussion would center around Pee Wee Reese's decision to demonstrate his support for Jackie Robinson.

The devil's advocate approach really stirs debate; it can also create big problems if the teacher is not aware of how to handle controversy. Teachers who use this technique must be aware that some students may identify the position with the teacher and subsequently either believe that the position is one that students should accept or, worse yet, share with others their perceptions of what the teacher believes (for example, "Mom, do you know that . . . really believes that African Americans should never have been allowed to play baseball?"). Anyone who has ever taught knows that this latter circumstance is a real possibility. The devil's advocate approach must be used cautiously! Quite obviously, the teacher must take special care to let students "explore" the statement, but then also make them aware that the statement does not necessarily represent a personal stance. Some teachers accomplish this by saying, "Class, some people would argue that. . . ." By couching the statements for students in this fashion, teachers are able to personally separate themselves from owning potentially inflammatory and controversial statements.

Student Question   Another approach is to ask students to generate their own questions before the content is covered. This approach builds on the natural curiosity of the students. Though some student questions may be worded poorly, a teacher can help shape them and then put them on the board for subsequent review. The teacher might then present some content and then return to the student questions as a way of extending the content.

Phase III: Foster Participation

One of the most difficult aspects associated with conducting good discussions is trying to ensure broad student involvement. Some students tend to dominate; others are reticent to participate at all. Part of the difficulty with quality oral discussions relates to room arrangement. Some teachers keep students in rows (an arrangement suitable for recitation) but forget that a primary goal of oral discussion is for students to build on the remarks of their peers. Three different classroom organizational structures enable this to occur:

Whole-Class Roundtable   With this arrangement, all the students in the class put their chairs in one large circle and/or square. The teacher becomes one of the participants within the larger configuration (circle or square), but the structure enables everyone to hear and see what is being said to and by others. Teachers must be cautious in using this technique. Because of the large size of the group, student participation can be quite limited with a few verbal students dominating the group's deliberations. Teachers should consider using the whole-class strategy as a precursor to the myriad small-group strategies—see Chapter 10, "Cooperative Learning." Other teachers can use small-group formats to "set up" the large group design—the Touchstones Project (see Zelderman, Comber, and Maistrellis, 1992) would be an example of this approach. The Touchstones Project is based on carefully selected texts that engage students at specifically designed times to discuss these texts. The texts are short (for example, an excerpt from "About Revenge" by Francis Bacon) and are assigned to be read just prior to the discussion time. Because all students read the material at the same time, they begin the discussions on "equal footing." The teacher is not an authority on the textual material, so students are required to discern their own meanings by relying on personal interpretations and interpersonal dialogue or discussion.

Buzz Group   In buzz groups the teacher divides the class into heterogeneously grouped students of four to eight. The teacher then poses a key question and asks students to identify a common response to the teacher-posed question—a response that all buzz group participants can support. One person in the group is a recorder; another serves as a reporter. The students in each group then share their ideas; the teacher has the students use factual, interpretive, and evaluative questions to refine the various concepts related to the originally posed question.

Inner Circle   In an inner circle the teacher forms students into two groups—an inner small group (those engaged in the discussion) and an outer large group (those acting as observers). McKeachie (1986) and others who advocate this strategy find that the different roles enable some students to participate effectively while others try to understand the direction of the discussion and the positions of those offering different arguments. The Touchstones Project approach (described above) relies on this type of inner-circle structure. Zelderman, Comber, and Maistrellis (1992) write,

> A typical Touchstones class has a number of segments, each designed to encourage the students to take ownership of the activity and to learn to cooperate. The class generally lasts for 40 to 45 minutes. Students enter the classroom, move the chairs into a large circle, and choose where and next to whom they sit. The books are then distributed. The text to be discussed is read aloud and then silently. Students are then given time to write down a question they feel would be interesting to discuss. Next, students work in

small groups of three to five members, either assisting one another in reformulating their individual questions, devising a group question, or discussing how to approach a text as if they were to lead the discussion. The small-group work is always composed of task-oriented activities requiring cooperation. When the class reconvenes, the groups report their results to the class. A Touchstones class occurring about 10 weeks into the year raises the cooperative task to a different level. In this meeting, the students are divided into two groups. For the first 10 to 12 minutes one of the groups will discuss a text while the other group sits in an outside circle and uses a student observation sheet. The observers keep track of the speech incidents, determine the reason for silences if these occur, and evaluate the discussion itself—giving a grade and justifying it. In the second segment of the class, the groups switch roles and go through the same process. In the last 12 minutes of the class, the entire class is reunited. The students in the outer circle present their reports, propose recommendations for class improvements, and discuss these. At this stage the students begin to cooperate, not only on specific tasks, but also on the issue of how to deal with those areas where the group is failing to cooperate. (pp. 145–146)

Before initiating any discussion, it is imperative to establish certain ground rules with the students. Discussions are intended to help students better understand their own ideas—to explore what they believe and why they believe it. For that reason, discussions require that students

1. Have a reasonable knowledge base before dialogue begins or have specific content (such as a Great Book) to discuss.

2. Listen to the contributions of their peers. No two people should speak at the same time. Discussions are not the functional equivalent of *Crossfire* (the CNN talk show) simulations; they are an opportunity for students to critically examine ideas in ways that enable them to synthesize reasonable conclusions.

3. "Play off" the ideas of other students, not just the statements or questions asked by the teacher.

4. Defend their assertions. Teachers need to ask a lot of "why" questions when students suggest ideas. Teachers should also seek out how other students feel—*"Esteban, do you agree with Tameka's observation?"* When students offer an idea that appears to lack support, the teacher should not hesitate to critically explore the idea.

Phase IV: Summarize the Students' Positions

All too often teachers conduct discussions but fail to bring closure in ways that really help students clarify their thinking. As one of our colleagues suggests, discussions can become nothing more than a sharing of collective ignorance. To avoid this, it is absolutely imperative that students start with a knowledge base and then have an opportunity to synthesize their understandings. This synthesis can occur by using one of three techniques:

Whole-Group Synthesis   The teacher writes the students' ideas on the board as they are shared and then asks the students to write in paragraph form a summary of what has been shared.

Small-Group Synthesis   The teacher asks students to work in small groups (4–8) and identify salient ideas that they all can support. They then share those ideas with the class by putting the information down on poster paper. For example, recently we observed a 6th grade lesson on owl pellets. At the completion of the lesson, the students were required to work in groups to discuss the dietary habits of owls and then write down their conclusions on poster paper. Each group then stood up and shared its conclusions with the rest of the class.

Personal Synthesis   Based on all that has been discussed concerning the concept or idea, the teacher asks each student to write a brief statement of personal belief. The writing of personal belief statements enables students to more pointedly comprehend what they understand and do not understand relative to a given situation. (Refer to Chapter 3, "Affective Domain" discussion.)

❶NSTRUCTIONAL VARIATIONS

The preceding discussion presumes that the teacher has established a content topic and identified questions that need to be explored related to that topic. Quite obviously, such a strategy is not always necessary or desirable. Three instructional variations—tutorial, inquiry group, and Socratic seminar—are described in this section. Once again, before deciding upon an instructional strategy, it is absolutely essential to determine the objective of the interactions the teacher desires among the students. The first strategy listed below is intended to enhance academic and social skills, and the second focuses more on problem-solving abilities. The first might be a complement to a direct instruction lesson; the second would be more efficacious with the inquiry model.

Tutorial

One of the most powerful instructional strategies known in education is the tutorial. Walberg (1995) observed that the tutorial achievement effects were substantial for both tutors and tutees, and especially evident in content areas such as mathematics, where skill definition is more clearly articulated. Students who work in tutoring situations get direct and immediate feedback, and they experience enhanced achievement. With the tutorial discussion, the emphasis is on ensuring that specific students exhibit task mastery. According to Orlich et al. (1985), the teacher first identifies specific students with high levels of expertise and then groups them with students who lack those same skills. The teacher then has the tutors

1. Pinpoint the learning problems of the tutored students—what don't they understand?

2. Provide the requisite knowledge that the "tutee" student lacks—the tutor teaches the information and/or helps in practicing the skills needed by the tutee.

3. Encourage the tutee students to ask their own questions and direct their own learning.

Group sizes in tutorials should be kept small—no more than four students and preferably smaller. The learning tasks must be relatively specific (for example, the tutor helps students memorize math facts or understand the steps in long division), and the tutors must truly have enhanced skill competency.

Inquiry Group

The inquiry group focuses on student problem-solving. The desired group size for inquiry is 6 to 10 students. Teachers who use this strategy should have students who are familiar with inquiry as an instructional model (see Chapter 5). According to Orlich et al. (1985), this oral discussion strategy fosters scientific thinking and the enhancement of student problem-solving skills. Either teachers or students can lead inquiry groups. Before implementing this strategy, teachers need to make certain that students know how to make thoughtful observations and how to ask questions to solve a problem.

The teacher starts by presenting a problem. The problem should be one for which there is not a readily apparent answer (a discrepant event). Once students recognize the problem, they then break into their inquiry groups and create questions for which they need a solution relative to the problem. The students should generate as many questions as they can think of. Once all the questions are listed, the students then must work together to answer those questions. Rather than relying on the teacher for the answer to a "yes" or "no" question (as occurred with inquiry—see Chapter 5), the students must rely on themselves for the information. For example, the teacher might start by stating, *"How is it possible to remove an eggshell without using your fingers?" The teacher then provides the students with the following: a 1-pint jar with a lid, 1 raw egg, 1 pint of water, 1 pint of vinegar, and 1 pint of clear pop. She tells the students that by using these materials they can remove the eggshell. The students then move into their groups and begin asking questions and forming hypotheses. They should record all of their questions and answer those to which they know the answers. Based on what they know, they then test each hypothesis.* (Incidentally, the correct solution is: vinegar in a closed jar with the egg submerged—vinegar is acetic acid; egg shells are calcium carbonate. The reaction between the acid and the calcium carbonate causes the eggshell to disappear.)

Socratic Seminar

The Socratic seminar is an outgrowth of Tredway's (1995) work to engage students in critical-thinking activities. The process for conducting a Socratic seminar is relatively simple and straightforward, but quite intellectually demanding for all involved. Tredway writes,

They [Socratic seminars] typically consist of a 50–80 minute period once a week. Students, usually in groups of 25 or fewer, read a common text prior to or during the seminar—a novel, poem, essay, or document. Or, they may study an art reproduction. They then respond to questions the teacher (or other facilitator) asks about what they've read or seen.

At Paul Junior High School in Washington, D.C., for example, a group of 7th graders were engaged recently in a series of seminars on "How to Be Kind and Forgiving in a World That Is Often Not," a compelling issue in the lives of many young people. They read excerpts from two works— "About Revenge," an essay by Francis Bacon, and *Middle Passage*, a novel by Charles Johnson in which the main character (Ngonyama) leads an uprising on a slave ship, but insists there be no revenge against his captors.

The teacher then posed this question:

To what extent would Francis Bacon agree with the ideas and actions of Ngonyama—totally, mostly, some, not at all?

The students voted on the answer, and their votes ran the gamut. To support their positions, they cited evidence from the text, disagreeing with one another's reasoning, asking one another questions, and, in a few cases, changing their minds based on classmates' ideas. Several times during the seminars, students set up comparable situations from their own experiences with friends or in the community to determine whether they agreed with the advice of Bacon or Johnson.

The question the teacher posed required students to evaluate options and make decisions. They then participated in a conversation about it. All subsequent questions in the seminar were based on the students' ideas and contributions in response to this initial question. Thus, the term *Socratic* seminar. The technique is derived from an ancient form of discourse— Socratic dialogue: Through doubt and systematic questioning of another person, one gets to ultimate truth. (p. 26)

The Socratic Seminar becomes a systematic way of helping students appreciate and understand complex content. Unfortunately, as schools become more focused on standards and the content embedded in those standards, many teachers view discussion as a waste of time. It is if the teacher is not focused on genuine inquiry. But true Socratic Seminars cause teachers and students to really challenge the thinking of one another. The following extended description of a Socratic Practice lesson is presented by Strong (1997). The example includes not only the classroom dialogue but also Strong's "reflection on action" as the dialogue occurs. This example illustrates the technique and, in abbreviated form, what happens when the technique is first tried.

Ⓢ AMPLE SOCRATIC LESSONS

It is the first day of class in a sophomore language arts classroom. Desks are arranged in a circle. After introducing myself, I specify one rule:

"The only rule we will start with is that only one person speaks at a time. This means that if I am speaking, none of you are speaking. If one of you is speaking, then none of the rest of you are speaking. Do you understand?"

They nod.

"You should take responsibility to insure that you are the only one speaking. If someone else starts to talk while you are talking, you should ask them to wait until you are finished. It is not my responsibility to insure that learning occurs here; it is your responsibility. In order to learn, we must be able to hear each other clearly. Does that make sense?"

They nod.

I pass to each student a page with the first two sentences of Immanual Kant's essay "What Is Enlightenment?":

> Enlightenment is man's emergence from his self-imposed nonage. Nonage is the inability to use one's own understanding without another's guidance.

I sit down and explain: "This year we will be using Socratic Practice to learn how to work together to understand difficult texts and their implications. Are there any questions?"

Silence. I expect that most students do not understand what I just said. That is okay. From the beginning I will speak to them as I would speak to adults. I want them to take responsibility for their own learning. That includes, most emphatically, that they ask questions when they don't understand what I am saying. Although this may seem harsh, at least it is not condescending. When they ask, I will be helpful.

Marcos: "Uhhh, what are we doing? What did you say?" . . .

"I'll try again: We, as a class, are going to take readings, like the one I just handed out, and we are going to try to learn how to work together to understand it. Am I making any sense?"

I intend to be taking responsibility for not having communicated clearly enough. The presumption is not that they are stupid for not understanding; it is that I have failed to be sufficiently clear in communication. I am modeling a willingness to take responsibility for the failure to communicate. This model will be important when students who think of themselves as more capable than others experience failure in communication; instead of accusing those who have not understood of being stupid (however kindly they make the accusation), it is important that they take responsibility for having failed to communicate clearly.

Marcos: "Uhhh, yeah, you are making a little bit of sense, maybe. I dunno. Maybe you should try again. . . ."

"Did I make sense to anyone at all? Can any of you help Marcos and me understand each other?"

Jenna: "You better say what you said again. . . ."

"Okay. We are going to take readings and try to learn how to work together to understand them. Does that make sense?"

Jenna says. "A little bit."

"What if we try for a little while and then see if what I'm saying makes sense. Is that okay? Raise your hands if that is what you want to do."

About half raise their hands. From the very beginning, I want to instill the sense that they are responsible for making educational decisions. Although I maintain final authority with respect to behavior, evaluations, and textual selection, there are many decisions where I will grant them autonomy. They must take responsibility for what occurs in the classroom in order to make progress. By granting the students authority to make certain decisions, they become responsible in a direct way for the outcomes of the decisions made. Some students are so unaccustomed to taking such responsibility that it amounts to shock treatment.

"Okay. It sounds to me that, of the people interested in doing anything here at all, a clear majority is interested in going ahead and trying Socratic Practice. Is that fair?"

Silence.

I suspect that many of them have found this a tedious process; it has just taken us five minutes to make a trivial decision. I certainly find it tedious to ask students one by one what they want to do. Later I will not. But in the beginning, I consider it very important to overcome their initial inertia by clearly and repeatedly granting them authority and holding them responsible for decisions made. Given this subtext to the conversation, it is clear that the opening text was not chosen accidentally.

"So, Marcos, do you think that we, as a class, have decided to go ahead and try it?"

"Yeah," he says dully.

"Was that really boring?"

"Yeah," he says, perking up slightly.

"Okay. Will someone please read the text?"

Silence. I let it go. One minute. Two minutes. Students stare at each other, then stare at me. I stare back at them. This does take patience in the beginning, but if I can get them to authentically take responsibility, it is all worthwhile.

Finally, Jo Anne reads: "Enlightenment is man's emergence from his self-imposed nonage. Nonage is the inability to use one's own understanding without another's guidance."

"Did that make sense to anyone?"

Marcos. "No."

"Great. That gives us something to do. Do you guys think that it is possible for you to understand those two sentences?"

Jo Anne. "Maybe."

Several mumble. "Yeah."

"Okay. Great. How can we begin working on something like this?"

Jamie, who had wanted to go home, volunteers, "Look up words."

No one seeks or asks for a dictionary; sometimes they spontaneously take action at this point.

"Any other suggestions?"

No other suggestions. Eventually we will develop and use a variety of strategies for understanding; a repertoire of strategies for understanding is crucial to learning how to learn. Cumulatively, the effects can be dramatic.

"What if we start by seeing if there is any part of this that we can understand on our own. For instance, what does it mean to 'use your own understanding?' Is that something that we can understand?"

Silence. Two minutes. On any issue where it seems reasonable to expect them capable of some reply, I try to wait them out. No progress; I'll put someone on the spot.

"Josh, what do you think it means to use your own understanding?"

"I don't know."

"Can you tell if you're using your own understanding now or not?"

"No. I don't know."

"What do the rest of you think? Is Josh using his own understanding or not right now?"

Jo Anne: "No. He's just sitting there."

Marcos: "Yes, he is. He said he doesn't know. Whatever he says is his own understanding."

Jo Anne: "So his understanding is that he doesn't know anything."

Marcos. "Yeah."

Josh, mildly indignant: "I didn't say that I didn't know anything. I said that I didn't know if I'm using my own understanding or not."

Jo Anne, mildly aggressive: "How can you not know if you're using your own understanding or not?"

A ten-minute conversation is launched in which I just sit back and listen. I'm very pleased that they are having this experience on their first day: authentic conversation among students on an issue related to the text. Most of the class seems to be enjoying it.

With five minutes left of class time, I intervene.

"That was great, but we're almost out of time. In order to improve how well we work together, we need to become aware of how we do each day. Today we'll start by rating class. On a scale of one to ten—one low, ten high—how would you rate today's conversation? Tell us why you rate it as you do. . . ."

Although there are exceptions, times when it is necessary to espouse a definite opinion, it is important that much of the time they are truly on their own with respect to understanding in contexts in which they may be expected to correct their own errors. . . .

As we go around the room, most students rate the conversation between a two and a five. As is common the first few weeks of debriefing, their reasons for rating are not very helpful with respect to improving the conversation: "It was boring." "We got out of school for the day." "I was asleep the whole hour." But that's okay. We are creating an awareness of the conversation itself as an object of reflection and judgment.

The bell rings and they leave. End of Day One.

Source: M. Strong. 1996. "Sample: Day 1." Pp. 121–127 in *The Habit of Thought: From Socratic Seminars to Socratic Practice.* Chapel Hill, NC: New View Publications.

ⒶppLicATIONS TO DIVERSE CLASSROOMS

One of the recurring themes of this book is that teachers should vary their instructional models (or teaching strategies) so that they can better accommodate the learning needs of all students. Because so many students from so many of America's diverse racial and ethnic groups tend to be field-sensitive learners, it becomes absolutely essential that teachers move beyond teacher-dominated forms of instruction and allow students to express their own ideas. Gollnick and Chinn (1994) describe this as "dialogue inquiry." In essence, with dialogue inquiry the teacher intentionally focuses on what the students know and how they are able to express it. Gollnick and Chinn write: "Too often teachers ignore students' attempts to engage in dialogue and, as a result, halt further learning by many students" (p. 302).

Part of what happens when students are encouraged to express their ideas is that they learn more about themselves and others. The wife of one of the authors of this book is an inner-city high school teacher. Her observation about urban youngsters is that many of them have verbal skills that are more developed than are their abilities in written expression. Life on the streets requires some measure of advanced verbal acumen. These same "verbal" students, however, are evaluated at school more exclusively through traditional written assessments—tests, portfolios, and so on. Teachers cannot and should not disdain traditional assessments, but instead they need to operate more bicognitively. Bicognitive teaching enables teachers to structure lessons so that students have opportunities to play to their strengths as well as to deal with their weaknesses. The concept of bicognitive development is not new. Ramirez and Castaneda (1974) described its efficacy for schools over 20 years ago. What is needed now are teachers who act on what researchers and educators now know. Teachers tend to "force" students to learn in certain ways. As we will argue in Chapter 12, teachers must operate in ways that enable students to define and refine their own abilities, not just conform to extant school structures. Subversive teachers find ways to build on students' strengths.

Teachers who use the oral discussion model effectively will find that the model accommodates both field-dependent and field-independent learners. In that regard, it is an especially important instructional model for teachers to use. It allows students to be creative and expressive, but it also demands that students be able to present ideas logically and to use factual knowledge to ground personal argument.

As readers will recall, in the previous chapters the instructional models have distinctly favored particular cognitive approaches: Cooperative learning favors students who learn best by interacting with others; direct instruction favors those who need the teacher's guidance to acquire essential skills. The oral discussion model represents, perhaps, a balance of the two and may, therefore, be an especially important bicognitive strategy for teachers to use, especially if they can deal with the types of issues described in the next section.

One of the ways in which discussions help with diverse student populations is that they bring the students' ideas more poignantly into the language of the classroom. Teachers who ask more complex questions in order to see how students can explore ideas often learn about the "limiting" of cognitive structures of the students. Such understanding helps teachers expand both the thinking and understanding of students. Ladson-Billings (1994) powerfully illustrates this in her description of Julia Devereaux:

> On one particular day, when the students had finished reading a Greek myth about a princess, Devereaux asked, "How would you describe the

princess?" Her question was designed to elicit responses about the princess's character, but the first student to respond began with a physical description. "She was beautiful, with long blond hair," said the student. Nowhere in the story was there a description that matched this response.

"What makes you say that?" Devereaux asked.

"Because that's the way princesses always are," the student replied.

"I don't have long blond hair and neither does anyone else in here. Does that mean that none of us could be a princess?" Devereaux asked. The student and several others seemed resigned to the fact that that was the case. Devereaux feigned disbelief that they were unaware of black princesses.

Slowly, without fanfare, Devereaux walked to her bookshelf and selected a book, John Steptoe's *Mufaro's Beautiful Daughters* (1987), about two African sisters, one good and one evil. After reading the fourth graders the book, Devereaux asked how many students still believed that a princess had to have long blond hair. No one raised a hand. (p. 92)

Prevalent Issues in Diverse Classrooms

Any teacher who has ever conducted a classroom discussion understands quite well some of the inherent problems associated with utilizing the oral discussion model with students. Two major questions appear particularly troublesome for teachers.

Q: *How do I deal with the differential participation of students? Some dominate; others have no desire to become involved!!*

A: There are several strategies that teachers can use to involve students in discussions. Each has power when used appropriately to foster student engagement. Some students will not participate unless the teacher intentionally calls on them. Teachers often call on nonparticipants who look distracted or who appear to be off-task—the question becomes a classroom management strategy. The effect of calling on such off-task students is to cause embarrassment. To avoid this situation, teachers should randomly call on students. Simply take a stack of 3 x 5 cards and place each student's name on a different card. When preparing to have an oral discussion with the class, shuffle the cards and select cards at random. Many teachers use this type of strategy to ensure that every student has an equitable opportunity to participate. (Incidentally, once a student's card is used, place it back in the stack so that he or she is "eligible" to be called upon again—once called upon, a student is not "free.") The side benefit of this strategy is that it also keeps some students from "stealing" all the time.

Of course, when teachers call on nonparticipants they also get more off-the-wall responses. When a student appears unresponsive or responds inappropriately, teachers have three choices:

Teacher Choice One
If the student is nonresponsive, reword the question (do not repeat it!) to ensure that it is clear. Assume "the best" of each student at first. That is, assume

that the student did not understand the question. Reword the question, and then wait for a student response. Do not move to another student until the momentum of the lesson is jeopardized—this is typically 3–5 seconds, which in some classrooms can be an eternity.

Teacher Choice Two
If the student provides a thoughtful but illogical response, call on other students to see if they agree—"*Claude, do you agree with Peg that baseball is just for boys because it requires physical strength?*" Teachers have a great deal of power in the classroom. They can accept or dismiss an idea with a nonverbal gesture or verbal utterance. Indeed, teachers may have too much power in some respects over the ideational content of a lesson. One way to limit the teachers' power is to involve students in evaluating the ideas of their peers.

Teacher Choice Three
If the student provides an illogical and unthoughtful remark, ignore the student and move on to another student. One of the main reasons students misbehave is to get attention. Often when students participate in discussions, they offer "cute" remarks in order to elicit a reaction from the class and the teacher. That teacher reaction is what the student wants! If a teacher is going to react, react privately, after the class period is over and the student no longer has an audience.

Q: *What types of questions should be avoided when conducting a discussion?*

A: All teachers fall into certain patterns when conducting discussions. Asking good questions requires thought and preparation—few teachers have the ability to create plenty of good questions spontaneously. We suggest that before a discussion begins, the teacher develop sample questions that are factual, interpretive, and evaluative. As teachers use these different types of questions, they will find that they are better able to think of questions on the spur of the moment. Researchers have found that teachers have acquired several bad habits when it comes to leading oral discussions. Good and Brophy (1997) describe a couple of these—"tugging" and "leading." "Tugging" occurs when the teacher responds to a student's statement with "What else?" Such responses seem innocuous, but they lack a clear focus for the additional thought the teacher desires. Provided below is an example of a negative "tugging" sequence; it is followed by a positive dialogue interaction:

Negative Sequence
Teacher: Why did South Carolina secede from the Union?
Student: Because they were mad at Abraham Lincoln.
Teacher: Say more!

Positive Sequence
Teacher: Why did South Carolina secede from the Union?
Student: Because they were mad at Abraham Lincoln.
Teacher: And what specifically caused them to be angry?

"Leading" occurs when the teacher makes a statement and then asks the class whether they agree, or subtly tries to co-opt them into concurring with a teacher's observation. An example follows.

Negative Example

Teacher: Class, don't you believe that Abraham Lincoln had no choice regarding his treatment of the South? Lincoln was correct in dealing harshly with the southern states, don't you agree?

Positive Example

Teacher: What choices did Lincoln have once the states in the South decided to secede from the Union?

Dillon (1984) once observed that "discussions are hard to conduct and they are hard to learn how to conduct. Contrary to common sense, questioning is a complex skill" (p. 53). Questioning is a complex skill, and for that reason teachers need to really practice developing and using different types of questions. Without such practice, teachers foster too much "tugging" and "leading" and not enough critical thinking.

Ⓔ VALUATION CRITERIA   ✖

Because oral discussion takes so many different forms, the assessment of classroom interaction patterns and processes is quite difficult. Like all of the instructional models, however, good discussions require that teachers do some preplanning of what questions they want to ask and what overall learning objectives they seek to achieve.

Phase I: Identify the Focus for Discussion

1. Identify the focus for the discussion. What major ideas are the students exploring?

   _____
   _____
   _____

2. Identify at least two questions at each of the following levels that are asked during the lesson.

   Factual:
   1. _____
   2. _____
   Interpretive:
   1. _____
   2. _____
   Evaluative:
   1. _____
   2. _____

Phase II: Pose the Question for Discussion

1. What is the first question that is asked of the students?

   _____
   _____

2. Is the initial teacher-initiated question structured to foster cognitive dissonance in the students? ☐ Yes ☐ No

3. What kind of questioning process does the teacher use to create the cognitive dissonance?
___ Key question
___ Devil's advocate
___ Student question

Phase III: Foster Participation

1. What type of classroom organizational structure does the teacher use to enable oral discussion?
___ Whole-class roundtable
___ Buzz group
___ Inner circle

2. As the discussion progresses, does one student speak at a time? ☐ Yes ☐ No

3. As the discussion progresses, do students "play off" (utilize) comments of their peers as well as respond to the questions of the teacher? ☐ Yes ☐ No

4. Does the teacher ask a lot of "why" questions in order to force students to defend their answers? ☐ Yes ☐ No

Phase IV: Summarize the Students' Positions

1. Does the teacher require students to synthesize the ideas suggested during the discussion? ☐ Yes ☐ No

2. What synthesis organizational strategy does the teacher use?
___ Whole-group synthesis
___ Small-group synthesis
___ Personal synthesis

Ⓢ AMPLE LESSONS ◆

The following lesson illustrates a teacher using the *devil's advocate* strategy. The case study presented at the beginning of this chapter was illustrative of the *key question* approach.

Ⓒ ASE STUDY I

Ms. Gwendolyn Walker has been teaching a unit on homelessness to a group of high school youngsters in Chicago. The students have read articles and books about homelessness, had guest speakers (that is, sociologists, psychologists, and justice personnel) discussed the implications of homelessness on families and society, and interviewed the homeless and those social service workers who provide services to the homeless.

The class is now ready to begin synthesizing all of these experiences through discussion and problem-solving activities. Ms. Walker begins this segment of the unit by saying, "Class, during the past couple of weeks, we have been reading books that deal with homelessness. Let's review for a couple of minutes some of the reasons why there are homeless people here in Chicago. Luis, identify some of the reasons for homelessness in our society."

"Well, some people are mentally ill. They just can't take care of themselves. Others are drug addicts. If you go down to where my mother works, you can see them on the corner, just sitting around."

"Are there any other reasons that you can think of, Julianna?"

"Well, a lot of the homeless are children."

"That's correct. Remember the one article we read estimated that between 250,000 to 750,000 school-age children are homeless. I think the stories we've read and the experiences we have encountered provide us with a good sense of what it must be like to be homeless. But I would like for us to consider what some reformers are proposing to alleviate the plight of the homeless. Specifically, they suggest people are homeless by choice, and that if we try to take care of them we only make the situation worse. We are going to use a buzz group approach today, so you'll need to get into your cooperative groups."

The students get into their assigned groups, and Ms. Walker asks for their attention. She identifies a recorder, leader, and facilitator in each group. The recorder lists the students' ideas, the leader makes certain the group stays on topic, and the facilitator makes certain everyone participates. Ms. Walker assigns several more readings to the students. Most are quite short and can be analyzed quickly.

Ms. Walker initiates the buzz group activity with, "I want you to use the material I've provided to either support or reject my statement that the homeless chose their condition, and that helping them will only make matters worse. Try to first see if your group members can agree on a response, and then look for evidence that you can use to support your ideas. Also, I would like for you to prepare some questions that you think need to be addressed."

The class begins its group work; the students discuss their ideas and prepare position statements based on the readings. The students work for almost 20 minutes before Ms. Walker tells them to wrap up their group assignment.

After the students have completed their readings and discussed their perceptions and findings from the articles, Ms. Walker begins the oral discussion phase of this lesson by asking various levels of questions. She begins by calling on Mark. "Mark, did your group decide to accept or reject my statement?"

"We rejected it."

"Why?"

"Well, first of all, kids can't help it if they're homeless, and the one article said that children are the fastest growing group of homeless people in the United States."

Most of the groups in the class reject the statement originally presented by Ms. Walker. The students offer explanations similar to that provided by Mark and his group. The teacher then asks the students for their questions. Most of the questions the students ask are factual:

- "Are more girls than boys homeless?"
- "Are more blacks than whites homeless?"

The teacher, though, adds a couple of questions of her own:

- "What does it mean in the article that new medicines will allow mentally ill people to live near-normal lives?" (interpretive)
- "In what ways might the conditions of homelessness that we've read about become worse during the next few years?" (evaluative)

Ms. Walker then lists all the questions on the board (some the students generated, while others are teacher developed) and then assigns the questions as homework for the students. She tells them to answer all the questions (she suggests some resources) and to be prepared to work in their groups the next day to see how their peers responded to the questions. ∎

Follow-Up Questions

1. Identify other ways in which Ms. Walker could have initiated the discussion. This teacher chose the devil's advocate strategy. What other strategies might have proven useful?
2. What other follow-up strategies might be used by the teacher to extend the students' thinking?

❻ASE STUDY II

Ms. Lasley teaches fine arts at an urban, Catholic high school. The day prior to this lesson her students had studied the Renaissance, especially within Italy.

On the day when this lesson occurred, she began by asking the students to review facts from the text concerning the developments and inventions that emerged during the Renaissance. Students individually made their own lists, and then Ms. Lasley put the ideas generated on an overhead. She asked them a variety of questions including, "What changes took place in Western Europe from 1450 to 1650? How were artists affected by these changes (comprehension)? . . ."

The list generated by the students was extensive (for example, development of a middle class, printing press, the Reformation and Counter Reformation), and Ms. Lasley added a few things such as the invention of gunpowder and oil paint.

Her students were put into Buzz Groups of six—she purposefully arranged them heterogeneously by ability and gender. They were then directed to write two sentences explaining why the changes occurred during the Renaissance. The group had to agree on the sentences and then share the conclusions with the rest of the class. One student acted as a recorder, and another then reported the ideas back to the whole class. Some of the students' ideas included the following:

- People became more interested in art, so that gave the artists more money.
- The artists painted and sculpted with new materials due to the trade routes that emerged.
- The printing press allowed knowledge to spread quickly around the world, allowing artists access to new ideas and ways of doing things. This influenced the way they expressed themselves.
- Artists also used realism with a combination of styles. The trade spread further and oil paint was invented.

Ms. Lasley then asked, "How have the Renaissance and the changes of that time period affected our lives today?" Students wrote a short personal synthesis in response and then handed that in at the end of the class.

Teacher Reflections

My students have studied the Renaissance three ways this year, in history class, in religion class and art history class, so they know a lot of information and have heard varied views—historical, artistic, religious.

Initially, as we were looking for facts, they were not very engaged. I talked about some of the facts, giving them a modern slant on what changes people were experiencing. I always give participation points and always call on the quiet students as much as possible. The Buzz Group approach was a good, nonthreatening way to get them involved.

When I put them into groups, it was not time consuming (that's important for me) because I had just changed their seating arrangement the week before. They are always ready to talk and work together, though I can't give too much time in groups—they get off the topic easily.

I gave them 10 minutes to come up with two sentences that explain important changes of the Renaissance in art, learning, society, trade, religion, etc.

To present their sentences, they came up front as groups to read—I had five groups of six. This class likes the limelight and takes every opportunity to be on stage.

After these, I gave them seven minutes to write a short paragraph about "how the Renaissance has affected our life today." I like the way the oral discussion expands the quality of ideas generated by the students. ■

ⓢuggested Lesson Development: Questions for Reflection

Oral discussion is an important strategy for teachers to help reinforce the learning of students. In order for oral discussion to "work," teachers need to take the following steps:

1. Determine the specific focus for the discussion. What is it that the teacher wants to accomplish?

2. Identify factual, interpretive, and evaluative questions that need to be asked.

3. Identify the strategy (*key question* or *devil's advocate*) that will be used to initiate the discussion. What specific question will then be used?

4. Identify what methods will be utilized to enhance student participation (*whole-class roundtable*, *buzz group*, or *inner circle*).

5. Identify how the students will be required to summarize their positions.

Using the same format as we use in the earlier chapters and using the above questions as prompts, develop a lesson plan that utilizes the oral discussion model. Also, once you teach the lesson, take time to reflect on ways in which you feel the approach really helped your students learn the content better.

ⓉECHNOLOGY ENHANCEMENT   A D I S ©

The technology enhancement for this chapter encourages teachers to enrich the oral discussion model by taking advantage of the exciting and expanded opportunities for communication and collaboration (C) that are afforded by the videoconferencing technology that is now being widely used in business, government and academic environments.

Videoconferencing to Extend an Oral Discussion

Each year, increasing numbers of K–12 schools are being equipped with video-conferencing technology that allows teachers and students to connect with the larger world in new and exciting ways. Many schools are currently using such interactive communication devices for a variety of purposes, including course delivery, lesson enhancement, tutoring, professional development, inter-school collaboration, virtual field-trips and accessing guest speakers and experts.

One of the most compelling benefits of videoconferencing as an oral discussion tool is the visual connection it provides and the environment it creates for discussion and interaction. Two-way videoconferencing, because it is *almost like being there*, has the power to motivate students and deepen their understanding of the content being explored.

Before discussing how videoconferencing can be used to enhance the oral discussion model, a few words about the technology itself. A two-way video-conference can be conducted using a variety of technologies that differ in several ways, including cost and quality of video transmission. For example, CU-SeeMe (pronounced "see you see me") is designed to provide low-cost, desktop videoconferencing. A computer can be equipped with a CU-SeeMe camera and the required software for between $50 and $200. The downside to this approach is that video and audio quality is low because it is limited by the capacity of the Internet, which typically offers only *4–5 frames per second*. In contrast, many schools, universities and corporations are purchasing equipment that uses multiple ISDN or T1 telephone line connections to achieve a higher quality video signal ranging from 15–30 frames per second. The cost of such systems typically ranges from \$10,000 to \$60,000 and up depending on what accessory equipment is added. Teachers interested in exploring videoconferencing should begin by checking with their building or district level technology coordinator to discuss what types of equipment are available and how they can be accessed.

There are a variety of ways to use videoconferencing to enhance the oral discussion model. In fact, virtually all of the oral discussion strategies and instructional variations discussed in this chapter can be applied in a *well-planned* videoconference. The word *well-planned* is emphasized here because thoughtful planning is critical when using this technology. Many students, when experiencing a two-way video interaction for the first time, can be somewhat intimidated and consequently reluctant to engage in the discussion. In fact, remote guest speakers or experts may react in a similar fashion if they are new to the videoconferencing experience. Teachers can overcome this problem by working with students and electronic guests prior to the *hookup* to develop questions and to discuss the format for the discussion.

One exciting feature of quality videoconferencing systems is the way in which they support users in integrating various forms of media into the videoconference. For example, document cameras can send images from photographs, printed documents, and electronic or three-dimensional objects. In addition, audio and video programs from videocassettes, compact discs, or laser discs can also be conveniently transmitted from one site to another. With this type of technology students can not only interview a laboratory scientist, but also have the opportunity to see scientific samples or data sets as well. In similar fashion, students can interact with an artist while viewing early sketches of a painting or converse with an author or poet while examining specific lines of text.

In addition to connecting with remote guest speakers or experts, teachers can also connect their students to other students for any number of compelling reasons. Imagine the power of having French language students interact with students from France, or biology students studying water quality collaborate with peers from another state who are studying environmental impacts on their local stream. Another popular use of videoconferencing that can integrate oral discussion techniques is the *electronic field trip*. Many zoos, museums, art galleries, and other public and private institutions are developing outreach programs specifically targeted at connecting with schools using teleconferencing technology.

Low Tech/High Tech Applications

As mentioned earlier, CU-SeeMe technology provides teachers working in the one-computer classroom an inexpensive method of exploring the world of videoconferencing. The fact that this technology is relatively inexpensive does not mean that it is not technically sophisticated. Most teachers will need the support of a technology coordinator or network administrator to assist with installation and operation issues. Some districts, for example, maintain network *firewalls* or security screens designed to protect users from unauthorized intrusions. Such firewalls can be configured to allow CU-SeeMe transmissions.

High-tech applications are best supported by the interactive distance learning communities (IDLCs) built by educational consortia that rely on the statewide or countywide collaboration of multiple school districts, colleges, and private sector partners. Such systems frequently employ the high-end equipment and wiring specifications that provide high quality transmissions and expanded opportunities to network with other schools and an ever-increasing number of external partners.

Value Added for Diverse Learners

Engaging students in an oral discussion via videoconference offers teachers a powerful opportunity to engage and motivate students who have a need to relate what they are studying to the real world. Female students, in particular, are likely to respond positively to the opportunity to interact with remote guest-speakers or experts. Teachers of African American and Hispanic American students should be mindful of the opportunity the technology affords to connect such students to positive role-models from the world outside of school. Finally, videoconferencing can provide Native American students with the visual stimuli and imagery that often supports their learning.

Web-Based Resources

Teachers interested in exploring videoconferencing will find a host of helpful resources on the World Wide Web. One great place to start is http://www.kn. pacbell.com/wired/vidconf/. This extensive site provides educators with a wealth of valuable information and hotlinks on a wide range of topics, including equipment and instructional ideas, as well as strategies and tools for planning, facilitating, and evaluating a videoconference. In addition, the site includes a searchable database that allows educators to quickly find other schools or content providers interested in videoconferencing. Teachers interested in enhancing the oral discussion model through the use of videoconferencing will find some excellent tips for facilitating effective interaction by clicking on the *instructional strategies* link.

SUMMARY

One of the greatest barriers for most teachers in terms of creating effective discussions is a lack of preplanning questions for focus during the lesson. Teachers are accustomed to planning lessons that have innovative components or hands-on experiences, but they are less inclined to spend a great deal of time preparing lessons involving discussions. Because of the lack of planning, many oral discussions quickly lose focus—the comments of students seem to drift among lots of different ideas, many of which are not apparently relevant to the defined topic. Teachers can mitigate the "drifting" effect by clearly understanding what questions need to be addressed and by periodically providing an internal summary of what has transpired. The teacher, in providing a summary, need not suggest conclusions, but rather can use the opportunity to make certain that all students clearly understand the major points that have been made.

Many students feel that they are not learning when they are discussing ideas. Furthermore, many teachers perceive that they are not teaching when the students are sharing their thoughts. Actually, oral discussion may be one of the most demanding of all pedagogical strategies. If the teacher just allows the students to move aimlessly around a topic, it is not a demanding instructional lesson. But if the teacher expects students to focus on a certain set of questions and to think through the nuances of an idea critically, then the intellectual demands on a teacher are substantial. Some teachers reduce the intellectual risk by asking only questions that they already have answers for—factual questions. Teachers who use interpretive and evaluative questions ensure that students involve themselves in higher-order thought processes. There are no "right" answers for interpretive and evaluative questions. Instead, what teachers must do is help students examine the efficacy of their ideas and the merits of their arguments—such exploration is not easy and requires practice and coaching, even for veteran teachers.

One additional note. The movie *Dangerous Minds* provides insights into how Louann Johnson sought to reach a group of urban high school students. The students, especially as portrayed in the movie, are racially and ethnically diverse and academically deficient. Ms. Johnson does two things to reach the students. First, she uses culturally congruent ideas (that is, the poetry of the streets). Second, she uses oral discussion as a way of involving the students in their own learning. The students discuss (and research) which Dylan Thomas poems and Bob Dylan song lyrics are similar and the meaning of their respective ideas. She especially focuses on interpretive questions—"Who is the tambourine man?"—as a way of moving the students toward an appreciation of literature. Even assuming some romanticization of Ms. Johnson's teaching, it is clear that what she did is part of what authors like Amy Tan (author of *The Joy Luck Club* and *The Hundred Secret Senses*) might call the secret senses—moving beyond direct experience and what common sense dictates. Good teachers know how to "read" students, and good teachers know that teaching is not just telling; it is also listening. No strategy demands this skill more than oral discussion.

®EFERENCES

Bligh, D. A. 2000. *What's the Use of Lectures?* San Francisco: Jossey-Bass.

Bloom, B., M. Englehart, E. Furst, W. Hill, and D. Krathwohl. 1956. *Taxonomy of Educational Objectives: The Classification of Educational Goals Handbook I: Cognitive Domain.* New York: David McKay.

Brookfield, S. D. and S. Preskill. 1999. *Discussion as a Way of Teaching.* San Francisco: Jossey Bass.

Dillon, J. T. 1984. "Research on Questioning and Discussion." *Educational Leadership* 42(3): 50–56.

Gall, M. D., and J. P. Gall. 1976. "The Discussion Method." Pp. 116–216 in N. L. Gage (ed.), *Psychology of Teaching Methods.* NSSE 75th Yearbook, Part 1. Chicago: University of Chicago Press.

Gall, M. D., and M. Gillett. 1980. "The Discussion Method in Classroom Teaching." *Theory Into Practice* 19(2): 95–103.

Golenbock, P. 1990. *Teammates*. San Diego, CA: Gulliver Books, Harcourt Brace Jovanovich.

Gollnick, D. M., and P. C. Chinn. 1994. *Multicultural Education in a Pluralistic Society* (4th ed.). New York: Macmillan.

Good, T., and J. E. Brophy. 1997. *Looking in Classrooms* (7th ed.). New York: Harper-Collins.

Gunter, M. A., T. H. Estes, and J. H. Schwab. 1995. *Instruction: A Models Approach* (2nd ed.). Boston: Allyn & Bacon.

Hirsch, E. D. 1988. *Cultural Literacy*. New York: Vintage Books.

Ladson-Billings, G. 1994. *The Dreamkeepers*. San Francisco: Jossey-Bass.

McKeachie, W. 1986. *Teaching Tips* (8th ed.). Lexington, MA: D. C. Heath.

Orlich, D. C., R. J. Harder, R. C. Callahan, C. H. Kravas, D. P. Kauchak, R. A. Pendergrass, and A. J. Keogh. 1985. *Teaching Strategies: A Guide to Better Instruction* (2nd ed.). Lexington, MA: D. C. Heath.

Ramirez, M., III, and A. Castaneda. 1974. *Cultural Democracy, Bicognitive Development, and Education*. New York: Academic Press.

Strong, M. 1997. *The Habit of Thought*. Chapel Hill, NC: New View.

Tredway, L. 1995. "Socratic Seminars: Engaging Students in Intellectual Discourse." *Educational Leadership* 53(1): 26–29.

Walberg, H. 1995. "Productive Teaching." Pp. 41–55 in A. C. Ornstein (ed.), *Teaching: Theory into Practice*. Boston: Allyn & Bacon.

Wiggins, G. 1989. "The Futility of Trying to Teach Everything of Importance." *Educational Leadership* 47(3): 44–59.

World Geography. 1993. Morristown, NJ: Silver Burdett Ginn.

Zelderman, H., G. Comber, and N. Maistrellis. 1992. "The Touchstones Project: Learning to Think Cooperatively." Pp. 138–150 in N. Davidson and T. Worsham (eds.), *Enhancing Thinking Through Cooperative Learning*. New York: Teachers' College Press.

• *Reflecting on*
Instructional Model Usage

TWELVE

• *Developing Teachers for the Culturally Diverse*

Chapter Objectives

At the end of this chapter, readers will be able to

1. *Describe inclusive versus noninclusive beliefs and behavior dispositions.*
2. *Discuss current trends in the professional development of classroom teachers.*
3. *Apply the Situational Self-Leadership framework to one's personal learning needs.*
4. *Explain the planning, acting, and reflecting phases of reflective practice.*
5. *Create an individualized professional development plan for acquiring expertise in one or more instructional models.*
6. *Value the role of teacher leadership in creating classrooms and schools where all children can learn.*

In previous chapters of *Instructional Models: Strategies for Teaching in a Diverse Society*, we emphasized the need for current and prospective teachers to be cognizant of the different ways in which students learn. These learning preferences, as we found from the literature (Cabezas, 1981; Cooper, 1987; Damico, 1983; Garcia, 1991; Hale-Benson, 1986; More, 1990; Pang, 1990, 1995; Ramirez and Castaneda, 1974; Shade and Edwards, 1987; Soldier, 1989; and Vasquez, 1991), vary from student to student primarily because of genetic predispositions and family child-rearing practices and the cultural characteristics that are a very real part of the nurturing process. We provided the reader with eight alternative instructional models that can be matched with the specific learning strengths of students; the models also enhance a teacher's instructional repertoire in order to help all students learn based upon their learning preferences. The rationale for the latter is important in order to help students acquire and apply learning skills that they have not been previously disposed to use in the classroom setting. In addition, we provided specific suggestions for how technology can be used to enhance each of the eight instructional models. In each case, the recommended technology enhancement was discussed in terms of how it can be employed to meet the learning dispositions of diverse learners. Only by developing an array of cognitive skills, both relational and analytical, and by acquiring meaningful technology skills can students truly be prepared to understand and to solve the complex problems that will surely confront them in a global society.

Coming to school every day becomes a hopeless task for some of our children unless they succeed at what they do. We teachers are the sentries against that hopelessness.

UNKNOWN

Children from different cultures process information and perceive phenomena differently. The cultural background of youngsters plays an important role in determining how students receive and communicate information. All youngsters, male and female, no matter what their cultural background, grow up in a cultural and family context that molds both their opportunities and preferences for how they learn. Just as the home is the most unequal environment for education, the school must be, in Conrath's (2001) terms, "an arena of equity" (p. 586). Conrath continues,

> Since those in corporate America, who largely shape education policy, do not accept this as a worthy agenda, alternative educators are the ones who must take the lead. When I taught Advanced Placement history, I never saw a child of poverty, and when I taught dropout prevention classes, I never saw a child of wealth. Of all the measurable differences between successful and unsuccessful students, in my experience, family income trumps all others. (p. 586)

Dealing with both reluctant and motivated learners requires that teachers take into account what students have learned. Vygotsky (1978) powerfully describes how any new learning is built upon prior knowledge and skills—what is about to be learned is based upon what has been learned. Thus, the teacher needs to consider and determine both the prior learning of each student and how to relate new learning in culturally congruent contexts. Because cultural dynamics influence learning, some youngsters learn best by taking the whole of a phenomenon and dividing it into its component parts; other youngsters learn best by taking the various components and creating new wholes. Some youngsters work best in a highly structured and teacher-directed classroom environment; other youngsters learn best in a more informal, student-initiated environment (for example, one youngster may develop cognitively through frequent and direct contact with a teacher, while another youngster may grow in a relatively independent manner). Some youngsters learn best through deductive thinking processes (reasoning from the general to the specific); other youngsters must use inductive thinking processes (reasoning from specifics to the general). In other cases, youngsters learn best in a classroom environment that helps students relate academic information to familiar (concrete) world experiences, whereas in other situations students enjoy playing with abstractions as they contemplate concrete possibilities. Some youngsters learn best visually, others learn through auditory modes, and still others learn through the use of kinesthetic/tactile activities. Finally, some youngsters learn best by working with peers in a collaborative manner (field-dependent); other youngsters prefer to learn in an isolated manner (field-independent).

As described in the cognitive style discussion of this text (Chapter 2), some students in our nation's schools have been taught at home to be involved in the issues of the family (discussions at the family meal), while in other families students have been taught to be "seen and not heard." In each case, the student will behave quite differently when interacting with teachers and fellow students, depending on the choice of alternative instructional models and strategies. In essence, to be effective, a teacher must

1. Recognize that some students, based upon gender and cultural group affiliation, learn in unique and idiosyncratic ways.

2. Recognize that students in America's classrooms vary from one another according to their cognitive style of learning.

3. Recognize that there is a positive correlation between specific student cognitive styles and the need for teachers to expand upon their instructional model repertoire.

4. Recognize the usefulness of acquiring alternative instructional models as part of a teaching repertoire.

Thus, students and even their teachers are not the same in terms of how they perceive and process phenomena; react to different situations; instruct in terms of teaching style; and communicate their thoughts, desires, and understandings. This may pose a real dilemma for schools, but to ignore its importance and use only one kind of instructional delivery system would be a disservice to those youngsters teachers are expected to serve. McDiarmid (1990) speaks against exclusive use of traditional forms of instruction when he says: "While 'all children can learn' has become the latest mantra of teacher education, the evidence is that many teachers and prospective teachers continue to believe that not all children can learn the same things" (p. 19). Only those teachers who believe in the inherent abilities of all youngsters to learn, and who utilize a variety of instructional models, will be successful in maximizing the achievement of all students. Recall (Chapter 1) that we asserted that teachers, in their pursuit of instructional change, should begin basing their instructional decisions upon three new fundamental assumptions:

New Belief 1. All youngsters can learn at significantly higher levels if teacher instructional practice changes to accommodate the diverse learning styles of students.

New Belief 2. All teachers can learn how to teach more successfully if they are provided with the proper preparation experiences.

New Belief 3. All teachers must hold considerably higher expectations for students. If students are to achieve their full academic potential, teachers must believe students can achieve more.

The previous chapters in this text have been grounded upon these "new beliefs," and the case studies, narratives, and activities presented focused on developing the teaching behaviors, values, and attitudes needed for working with youngsters in a culturally diverse society. Through the acquisition and application of a repertoire of alternative instructional models, our nation's youngsters will be able to acquire the variety of cognitive skills necessary to both strengthen and transcend their natural learning inclinations—in essence, to reach their full potential. Teachers need to utilize their students' cognitive strengths and develop in them the cognitive and affective skills necessary to maximize their learning opportunities. Why?—because students in today's schools must be prepared for a world that demands they be able to change and to solve problems in a myriad of ways.

The ideas, research findings, instructional models and technology enhancements presented in preceding chapters provide a rich set of data concerning the possible classroom environment of the future. In this final chapter, we focus specifically on three teacher roles we believe are critical to successful teaching in a culturally diverse and rapidly changing society. The first role, *Teacher as Community Builder*, will discuss the foundational need for teachers to foster, create, and manage a classroom culture characterized by *inclusiveness*. The second role, *Teacher as Learner*, will emphasize the need for teachers to take responsibility for meeting their own professional growth needs and dispositions. In addition, it will provide three specific models of professional development that can be used to enhance teacher performance in using the instructional models. The final role, *Teacher as Leader*, constitutes a call for teachers committed to teaching in a diverse society to extend their influence beyond the walls of their own classrooms to guide and support their colleagues in pursuing quality learning experiences for all children.

TEACHER AS COMMUNITY BUILDER

You cannot teach a child you do not love. You cannot teach a child you do not respect. You cannot teach a child you do not understand.

JAWANZA KUNJUFU

Because the teacher is the key player in determining the success or failure of students in the classroom, what teachers do or intend to do is of primary importance to students. As soon as students enter the classroom, they are learning from the teacher's verbal and nonverbal behaviors (that is, what the teacher does, what the teacher says, how the teacher decorates the room, and so on). The culture of the classroom community—the climate the teacher creates, the language that is used, how the teacher dresses and treats the students—all serve as strong indicators for what the teacher expects from the students. How teachers interact with their students, evaluate students' progress, communicate what they expect from them, recognize their individual needs, and demonstrate how, positively or negatively, they feel about them as individuals all provide a very clear signal about what they value in them as students and the attitudes they wish to instill.

The authors once met a teacher of urban youngsters who always dressed, day in and day out, as if she were going out to a fancy restaurant. After a few weeks of observing this 5th grade teacher, we asked her why she always dressed so well. She looked at us in astonishment and said, "Why, I'm doing the most important work of humankind. I'm teaching! And, I'm working with the most important group of people in the world. My students! They are our future! Wouldn't you communicate their importance by the way you dress for them?"

Teachers who hold youngsters dear to their hearts demonstrate their respect for their students by dressing up for them, recognizing their needs and desires in life, selecting from alternative instructional strategies, and expecting only the best from and for them in their academic pursuits. The teacher of the twenty-first century never thinks in one-dimensional terms in a multidimensional world. Teaching is not easy work! It requires much time, commitment, understanding, and knowledge in order to function effectively for the welfare of youngsters. Haberman (1995) indicates that those individuals who wish to teach urban youngsters in the twenty-first century need to exhibit specific traits in order to foster both personal and student success. These *functions* of "star teachers" are each consistent with beliefs and a set of congruent behaviors that we believe have relevance for most classroom contexts. While each function is complex and deserves in-depth exploration, the following summaries provide an overview:

1. *Persistence*—Star teachers believe that problem solving is fundamental to good teaching and that one significant problem is the challenge of meeting the individual needs of all learners.

2. *Protecting Learners and Learning*—Star teachers are highly committed to motivating and engaging students in meaningful learning activities that help students "fall in love with learning."

3. *Putting Ideas into Practice*—Star teachers can clearly articulate their beliefs about good teaching and act in congruent ways in their daily classroom practice.

4. *Approach to "At Risk" Students*—Star teachers believe that all children can learn and that it is the classroom teacher who is ultimately accountable for responding to the learning needs of diverse learners.

5. *Professional-Personal Orientation to Students*—Star teachers approach teaching with their focus on what is best for the student, not on satisfying their own emotional needs.

6. *Avoiding Burnout in the Bureaucracy*—Star teachers use the support of other teachers to counteract the burnout that so often occurs in large bureaucratic systems that seem to focus on bureaucratic needs rather than on the needs of students.

7. *Teacher Fallibility*—Star teachers recognize that students cannot learn in a classroom environment where mistakes are not accepted as part of the human condition and as a normal part of the learning process.

The teacher of the future has a very tough road to travel! The road is winding and hilly, narrow and wide, with sharp curves and sheer cliffs, but the rewards of "holding the road" are necessary to sustain the human spirit—of the teacher and the students. Teachers have to demonstrate that their students do learn, and that classroom experiences are valuable. This road of the future is also characterized by rapidly changing expectations of the teacher's role. In their pedagogical travels, teachers need to be aware of their own inclusive and noninclusive behaviors and of how these behaviors are perceived/received by those they serve. Let us first look at those pernicious teacher behaviors that exclude youngsters and potentially have a devastatingly negative affect upon them (see Table 12-1).

Understand, though, that teacher behaviors occur within a context. Teachers make a difference, but the measure of that difference is often influenced by the school. Conrath (2001) poignantly describes this phenomenon:

TABLE 12-1 Noninclusive and Inclusive Behavior Dispositions

Noninclusive Beliefs and Behavior Dispositions	*Inclusive Beliefs and Behavior Dispositions*
1. Belief in the hierarchies of power, authority, and control.	1. Ability to match the culture of the school with the culture of the home.
2. Belief that culturally diverse students are incapable of learning academically rigorous subjects.	2. Ability to utilize all types of culturally relevant materials in the instructional process.
3. Belief that cultural and linguistic diversity presents serious barriers to learning.	3. Belief that learning can take many forms through many modalities.
4. Unawareness of unique cultural characteristics of students and how these characteristics play a critical role in learning.	4. Ability to utilize cooperative and collaborative instructional activities.
5. Unawareness that public criticism of students by teachers is culturally incongruent and psychologically damaging.	5. Ability to teach youngsters how to function in different cultural and learning-style contexts.
6. Belief that learning is an individual responsibility.	6. Ability to engage students in problem-solving strategies to be used in real-life situations.
	7. Belief that one of their roles as educators is to challenge the societal status quo with students.
	8. Belief that community volunteers/aides are an integral part of the teaching-learning process.

Certainly, we should be consistent on the desired outcome for youth: successful learning. But we must be flexible on strategies to accomplish that goal. Students differ in their intellectual and emotional attributes and in their family and economic backgrounds. To treat them as if they are the same simply guarantees that some will fall by the wayside. True equity in schools calls for using different means to bring everyone to the same end. This is the splendid point of alternative education, and it is why conventional schools and alternative schools seldom understand one another. For example, if we really wish to make all students successful, competitive grading is a poor strategy. However, if we prefer that only some students succeed, a 30-to-1 student/teacher ratio, standardized testing, and the traditional six-period day are inspired strategies. (p. 586)

Noninclusive Beliefs and Behavior Dispositions

The following beliefs and behavior dispositions are typically counterproductive to the goal of creating the kind of classroom community necessary for quality teaching and learning in a diverse society. At worst, they manifest themselves as psychopathologic behaviors (Maslow, 1954) that erode motivation, deter learning, and shatter hope.

1. *Belief in the hierarchies of power, authority, and control.* Teachers who act upon this belief communicate that they are the source of learning, the source for what students must do, and the source of all permissible behavior for students. Ladson-Billings (1994) refers to this as assimilationist rather than culturally relevant teaching. Teachers who are consumed by control and authority function as if they are "the sage on the stage"; they perceive themselves in the role of taking charge, they issue nonnegotiable directives to students, and they control by overmonitoring student behavior. Teachers in such a setting view their role as that of the "authority"—one who exclusively controls and leads the teaching-learning process. Students have few decision-making rights to determine their learning regimens in such teachers' classrooms. The student role in this type of classroom is to comply with the teacher's instructions and to behave in compliant ways. Students have little opportunity to think, make decisions, and experiment through trial and error, or practice responsible behavior or democratic principles. As noted earlier from the research of Philips (1972, 1983, 1993), Ramirez and Castaneda (1974), and Soldier (1989), this type of power relationship is very contradictory to the personal and social needs of culturally diverse youngsters. There is an absence of culturally congruent instruction (Ladson-Billings, 1994) operating within power-dominated classroom environments. Marginal student empowerment occurs in such classrooms, and few opportunities to practice democratic ideals occur. In culturally congruent classrooms, teachers and students work together on tasks; teachers win over student *followership* by "proving" that they are worth following; and teachers and students explore phenomena through questioning procedures, trial and error activities, and the testing of numerous alternatives.

Some of the most innovative schools in the country are working to restructure themselves to avoid artificial hierarchies. The Hyde School (a private high school in Bath, Maine) accomplishes this by placing more responsibility on students for their own learning and on parents for supporting student learning. Such a perspective is good, not just for students of color but also for all students regardless of their color. In Western Hills High School in Cincinnati, Ohio, the school is being restructured around ideas that parallel those advocated by Leon Botstein (1997). Botstein argues that high school students disconnect because of developmental issues. Those issues demand changes in how teachers teach. Viadero (2001) describes how Western Hills and other high schools are embracing Botstein's ideas:

While Mr. Botstein's plan may be bolder than some, he is among a growing group of educators who see a need to free high schools from traditional time constraints so that all students can meet higher academic standards. Students in Rochester, NY, for example, now have the option of earning a diploma in three, four, or five years.

"We have kids coming into the 9th grade who we will look at as runners in a 1,500 meter race," Clifford B. Janey, that city's superintendent of schools, has said. "We recognize that some of our students will be running a 1,000-meter race, or a 2,000-meter race. The starting line isn't even, prior to the gun being fired."

Others advocate figuratively breaking down classroom walls so that high school students can take part in learning opportunities in real-life settings. Students might, for example, attend magnet schools run by museums, earn academic credit for workplace and volunteer experiences, work on long-term projects, take college courses, or travel.

Many school systems for years have allowed students to take part in career internships or to "dual enroll" at community colleges . . .

"If you keep kids interested in school, that makes it relevant," Ms. Brand [American Youth Policy Forum] said. "You talk to kids in middle school or high school, and the bulk of them say it's boring as all get out. They don't see any connections to real life. (p. 22)

2. *Belief that culturally diverse students are incapable of learning academically rigorous subjects.* Teachers who operationalize this belief do so from two different perspectives, both of which are equally damaging to culturally diverse students. In the first perspective, some teachers truly believe that students from culturally diverse backgrounds do not have the intellectual background, mental acuity, and academic discipline to maintain a highly rigorous schedule of courses such as algebra, geometry, chemistry, physics, and trigonometry. As a consequence, without the opportunities or encouragement to enroll in these courses, students are not adequately prepared for college or for successful participation in a global economy. With appropriate encouragement, even students from at-risk backgrounds can begin to excel. No circumstance more clearly illustrates this than does Bob Moses's work with the Algebra Project (Cambridge, Massachusetts). Jetter (1993) writes that Moses's idea was both simple and problematic:

Without algebra, the door to college and most skilled professions is locked. But many black and Hispanic students, if they take algebra at all, learn it too late to get on the college-prep mathematics track. So why not expose every child to algebra in middle school?

Moses has just begun to assess his project's long-term impact; as yet, there is insufficient data to judge its success. But anecdotal information and standardized tests from several schools appear to confirm what Algebra Project teachers have long suspected: "When these kids get the privilege of creating their own mathematics, they become independent learners," says Dorothy Strong, director of mathematics for the Chicago public schools. "And that works on the whole child." (pp. 28, 35)

Some teachers view their students as victims who are incapable of escaping the environmental conditions that prevent academic achievement; other teachers never provide students with intellectual opportunities because the students are viewed as intellectually incapable of learning. Both perspectives are racist and help maintain the negative attitude toward culturally diverse learners. Too often such teachers delude themselves that they are "helping culturally diverse students" by counseling them into "softer" subject areas in the scheduling process, or by telling students that they are either incapable of learning such subjects or will never have the opportunity to use such academically rigorous subjects anyway. The advice and behavior emanating from this belief drastically limit students in their pursuit of personal dreams.

3. *Belief that cultural and linguistic diversity presents serious barriers to learning.* Instead of believing that culturally and linguistically diverse students bring a rich background of knowledge, experience, and language proficiency to America's schools, many teachers blame poor school performance on the very diversity of students. Educators, through verbal and nonverbal behaviors, cast aspersions either by indicating that "they [the students] lack the ability, character, or motivation" (Cuban, 1989, p. 781) or by blaming the "perceived" poor home life and cultural background of the students. Students quite easily "pick up" on these negative attitudes—attitudes that subsequently have a profoundly negative impact upon them. It is interesting and at the same time discouraging to hear some educators speak so negatively about culturally diverse students. Rarely if ever do these same educators suggest that student failure may be caused by educators' own beliefs and behaviors or by the school's structural or curricular inadequacies in serving diverse populations. The very structure of the school and/or the lack of accommodation to the concept of diversity cause students to feel denigrated in terms of their needs, abilities, and experiences.

The movie *Renaissance Man*, released several years ago, provides an excellent illustration of the last two noninclusive teacher behaviors. In the movie, Bill Rago, an unemployed advertising salesman, gets a job teaching a group of new army recruits. Rago has accepted a teaching position to help a "special" group of new recruits "get ready" (that is, learn reading, writing, and the thinking skills) to become regular army. The class is composed of all males except for one female, and all students are either African American, Hispanic American, or Appalachian. This group of students has been classified by their fellow recruits on the base as "Double D's" ("Dumb as Dogshit") similar to the group "Sweat Hogs" in the 1980s television show *Welcome Back, Kotter.*

After Rago requires some initial tasks to determine the students' needs and abilities—writing a short theme and discussing a piece of writing purchased at the PX—the students ask Rago to tell them what he is reading. He responds, "*Hamlet!*" Two of the students ask him what it is about, and he responds, "It's a story about sex, murder, insanity, and incest." This piques their interest, but it is Leroy who asks Rago to tell them about the story. Rago responds, "You guys don't want to hear about *Hamlet.*" Roosevelt Hobbs then responds, "I guess you don't think we're smart enough." Rago says, "It's not that. It's very . . . complicated." To that the group moans and groans, and one hears in the background, "Here we go again"; "Oh, man"; and finally, "We're here. We're listening!" To that Rago responds by beginning to explain what the play is about. In subsequent lessons through the movie, Rago takes the students back to the historical period of the play, helps them understand figures of speech (that is, similes, metaphors, oxymorons), draws relationships to present-day figures in government and the community, and actively engages the students in the purpose and meaning of *Hamlet*. Initially, however, Rago never expected this group of students to be interested in or motivated by *Hamlet* given their backgrounds, past performances, and perceptions by others on the army base. Once he engaged the students in the subject matter and related it to real-life situations that the students could understand, their enthusiasm and interest carried them to new levels of learning and comprehension.

4. *Unawareness of unique cultural characteristics of students and how these characteristics play a critical role in learning.* Teachers described by this statement are not aware of the multicultural literature that identifies and describes some of the unique characteristics of diverse students. Unfortunately, because teacher education institutions are rarely composed of diverse faculty and rarely emphasize multicultural education, most teachers in our nation's schools are unaware of the multiplicity of cultural characteristics and dynamics. The development of multicultural concepts has major implications for how the teacher delivers instruction; how the teacher uses the curriculum to develop knowledge, skills, and attitudes in students; and what culturally relevant curricular concepts should be used in fostering the interest and motivation of students. The literature is rich with research findings as well as practical guides for working with culturally diverse student populations. That literature is not prescriptive; it is suggestive. That means that teachers cannot look for easy solutions ("OK, he's African American, so he needs concrete experiences first in order to understand abstractions"); but, rather, teachers must look at how they structure classrooms so that varied student needs are met through a variety of alternative learning experiences. The use of varied instructional strategies does not serve the interests of just African American or Hispanic American students; it enhances the quality of all students' educational experiences.

5. *Unawareness that public criticism of students by teachers is culturally incongruent and psychologically damaging.* One example of the lack of knowledge of unique cultural characteristics of diverse students relates to the use of public criticism. Many teachers regularly use public criticism and critiques to either provide feedback or "make an example" of students who exhibit unacceptable behavior. When this occurs, the child may view this as a "put-down" and either withdraw or react violently. As an example, the cultural reaction to public criticism for many Native American and African American youngsters is to put one's head down (or to lower one's eyes) as a sign of respect to the individual who is doing the criticizing (Byers and Byers, 1972). This nonverbal behavior is learned in the home and is quite common among members of both cultural groups. However, if a teacher is not knowledgeable about this natural reaction, the teacher may interpret the lowered head as disrespectful, impolite, and/or rebellious. The common response sought by most teachers would be that the youngster looks at the face of the individual speaking (for example, "Marcus, look me in the eye when I'm talking to you!"). The natural, culturally learned response by youngsters in selected ethnic and racial groups, however, is just the opposite. Only through a knowledge of and appreciation for student behaviors in

different cultural contexts can teachers more adequately respond to and interact positively with their students.

6. *Belief that learning is an individual responsibility.* In many cultures, cooperation and collaboration are highly valued processes—valued much more than individualized accomplishments. Research by Philips (1972, 1993) and Soldier (1989) with Native Americans, Au and Kawakami (1985) with Asian Americans, and Shade (1994) with African Americans has found that children from these cultural groups come to school with a disposition to value group-oriented activities. The values of cooperation and collaboration are held dearly in Native American, African American, and Hispanic American communities and are taught to youngsters through specific child-rearing practices.

The school, however, teaches personal property rights, individual responsibility and freedom, and pits children against one another through various competitive situations. The diverse cultural groups described in this text tend to emphasize the importance of large extended families whose members share property with one another and who place more value on family and how the family perceives the individual rather than on the individual desires and needs of each person within the family unit (Ramirez, 1982, 1989). Schools, however, tend to design and implement instruction through individualized processes (that is, learning alone, winning a spelling bee, having individual seating assignments by row) that are contrary to the natural learning styles of many diverse students.

Other noninclusive teacher beliefs exist that mitigate the learning of culturally diverse youngsters. The above descriptions are intended to be illustrative, not exhaustive. Indeed, complicating the situation is the fact that many school systems that work with poor and diverse students are attempting to ameliorate achievement gap and learning differences by embracing "one-size-fits-all" approaches to teaching urban youngsters. Such a circumstance creates problems for both high and low performing students and further mitigates opportunities for powerful learning. In Cuban's (2001) words,

All public schools are hardly alike. In 50 states, almost 15,000 districts with almost 90,000 schools serve almost 50 million students. The social, academic, and cultural diversity among and within districts is stunning. In the school systems of New York City, Los Angeles, and Chicago, for example, some high schools regularly send 90 percent of their graduates to college; others rarely send more than 10 percent.

Generally speaking, what exists now in the United States is a three-tiered system of schooling. Nationwide, there is a "first tier" of schools—about one in 10—that already exceeds the high academic standards and test-score thresholds set by their states. A second tier of schools—about four or five out of 10—either meet or come close to meeting their states' standards and cutoff scores on tests. The rest, the third tier of schools, don't.

Most of these latter schools are located in urban and rural districts with high concentrations of poor and minority families, where struggling learners perform in the lowest quartiles of academic achievement and often drop out.

Yet, the current reform recipe is to hammer this three-tiered system of schooling into one mold. These reforms are aimed at the large number of low-performing urban schools. Publicly admitting this is politically risky because the majority of voters who are middle-class, white, and live in sub-urbs might question such targeted use of their tax dollars. Forcing all schools to fit the same mold, however, ignores those urban and suburban students already meeting or exceeding the standards. Reformers confuse setting standards with standardization. (pp. 34–35)

We will now identify and describe selected inclusive behaviors that teachers need to focus upon in working with diverse student populations. These behaviors also emerge out of beliefs, but in this case they have a beneficial rather than a poisoning effect on the students' actions.

Inclusive Beliefs and Behavior Dispositions

The following discussion provides a description of the inclusive behaviors that teachers can employ to create an open, inclusive classroom community in which all children have the opportunity to experience acceptance, respect, and success. The list is not comprehensive. There are other behaviors that teachers should exhibit, some of which have been discussed in the previous chapters of this text. Whatever the source for inclusive behaviors, teachers of culturally diverse students need to be well versed in multicultural concepts because such a knowledge base (coupled with expanding research) will help them to become more knowledgeable and sensitive in promoting the growth and development of all of America's children.

1. *Ability to match the culture of the school with the culture of the home.* For many children in our nation's schools, the classroom environment is a mysterious and foreign place. The classroom does not look or feel like the environment or community within which children live. The pictures, bulletin boards, resource materials, structure of the desks, and teacher behaviors not only are unfamiliar to many culturally diverse youngsters, but often are in stark contrast to the messages that are communicated at home. In classrooms that seek to match the culture of the home, purposeful classroom linkages are created and sustained by both the curricular content and instructional delivery of the teacher. Students in these classrooms find it acceptable to use their past and present experiences as resources for learning (Foster, 1994; Henry, 1990; Ladson-Billings, 1990, 1991). The classroom experience builds upon acquired student experiences, which are legitimized because they become part of the formal curriculum (Ladson-Billings, 1994). In addition, students of color learn within an academic community (where cooperative learning strategies are valued) rather than in an isolated, linear-sequential manner in which one set of skills or academic content is difficult to relate to another set of skills or academic content (Ladson-Billings, 1994).

Effective teachers are those individuals who utilize community resources, topics, issues, events, and experiences in designing curriculum and delivering instruction. These teachers construct curriculum by designing community activities as examples to demonstrate the relationship between "what is worth knowing"—the curriculum—to the child's real world—the community and home life, which is familiar and knowable. Such teaching links community and home experiences. . . . "and incorporates familiar cultural and communicative patterns into the classroom practices, routines, and activities" (Foster, 1994, p. 237).

2. *Ability to utilize all types of culturally relevant materials in the instructional process.* Teachers who are interested in including culturally diverse students in the instructional process make use of instructional materials, bulletin boards, classroom decorations, and audiovisual aids that are grounded in the culture of the students. Such teachers make a commitment to link culturally familiar experiences with the abstract concepts of learning. Part of the reason for doing this is to bridge the gap between the community and the school. A number of research studies shed light upon the use of culturally relevant materials and their effect upon students.

Heath (1983), who conducted research with African American youngsters, found that using culturally related materials (that is, advertisements, street signs, food labels) had a positive effect upon student interest and motivation. Teachers could describe and demonstrate how students used the skills of reading, writing, and mathematics. Students could recognize the relationship of these skills, follow instructions on using a game or toy, price store objects and make change, and read labels and food ingredients.

Bradley (1984) found similar data in mathematics instruction conducted with Native American youngsters. Various types of geometric patterns found in Navajo Indian blankets were used to teach Euclidean geometry, number theory, coordinate geometry, and measurement processes. Such culturally familiar patterns helped students understand the study of geometry—a very complex subject area—by linking their familiarity with geometric shapes and physical objects to a very abstract academic content area.

Teachers of K–12 mathematics can use "street" math—black jack, craps, penny pitching, and/or the trading of sports cards or other items—to link the world of mathematics with the real world. Many streetwise youngsters are very skilled at mathematical processes. It is up to the teacher to bring these "street experiences" into the classroom and to use this knowledge and concomitant skills in formal ways. The various instructional models presented in Chapters 4 through 11 provide opportunities for students to connect their personal worlds with the instructional world created by the teacher. The concept formation model uses the schema of the students, while the mnemonics model can build upon the spatial intelligence of children to enable them to create visual techniques that help them remember ideas and facts. The instructional world of the teacher is one that brings together extensive content knowledge with in-depth pedagogical skill. A teacher with limited content knowledge is unable to create a vital learning atmosphere for students just as a teacher with limited pedagogical skill limits the learning possibilities for students. Ma (1999) powerfully describes the content-pedagogy nexus, a connection that emerges in the ideas as pedagogical content knowledge—the ability of a teacher to represent content in ways to make it comprehensible to students. In essence, the instructional models and even the teachers' abilities to build off of "street" experiences are maximized when they have extensive content knowledge. In Ma's words, "It seems that low-quality school mathematics and low-quality teacher knowledge of school mathematics reinforce each other" (p. 145).

Teachers who use culturally relevant materials in the classroom—whether these are origami paper, the celebration of Kwanzaa, or culturally linguistic newspapers—are bringing the familiar environment of the child into the classroom. When teachers do this, they are communicating to students that they value the youngster's cultural environment (and the youngster!), and this helps develop a culturally affirming atmosphere within the classroom.

3. *Belief that learning can take many forms through many modalities. Instructional Models: Strategies for Teaching in a Diverse Society* has been presented to affirm the inclusive behaviors of teachers. Most of the research findings in Chapter 2 describe cultural learning dispositions. By affirming students' prior experiences and the richness of the culture that they bring to the classroom, educators are able to "capture" youngsters for the learning process. Various learning modalities (that is, kinesthetic, observation of phenomena, verbal descriptions, visual-spatial relationships, auditory processes, and linear-sequential skills) are but a few ways in which youngsters process information. Jaime Escalante, the famed *Stand and Deliver* teacher, reflects this perhaps better than any other teacher. Escalante used what was familiar to the students within their homes to teach them concepts that were unfamiliar to them at school—see, once again, our illustration of this in Chapter 9.

4. *Ability to utilize cooperative and collaborative instructional activities.* One of the instructional models presented in this text is cooperative learning. Cooperative and collaborative instructional activities are another example of a culturally congruent model that teachers should use with diverse youngsters (Bradley, 1984; Gilbert and Gay, 1985). The use of cooperative activities builds upon the natural learning dispositions of a wide variety of cultural groups; educators stress group or team achievement rather than individual accomplishments. Student achievement increases for culturally diverse youngsters when learning occurs as a social activity—in a collaborative environment—rather than as an independent, competitive activity (Bishop, 1986; Philips, 1983; Ramirez, 1982, 1989; Treisman, 1985). To permit youngsters to learn in cooperative groups is a natural use of their cultural experience.

Previously, we learned that culturally diverse students favor group work over individual activities (Osborne and Bamford, 1987; Philips, 1972, 1983; Shade, 1994; Soldier, 1989). These students do not focus their attention on personal ownership, though they do value personal accomplishments. Many culturally diverse group members have highly developed social skills (that is, group activities, sharing material possessions, taking turns on tasks) because of the child-rearing practices that foster community harmony rather than individual competition. This factor may explain why Slavin and Oickle (1981) and Slavin (1987a, 1987b) found that Hispanic Americans, Native Americans, and African Americans achieve much more effectively than European Americans when cooperative learning is a major instructional strategy in classrooms.

Educators must be vigilant and cognizant of the social makeup, the political composition, and class and gender differences that children bring to the classroom. Sensitivity to these differences, and a cautious view to cultural history and variances, is necessary. However, through the process of group interaction and cooperative learning strategies, differences in class, race, and gender can be minimized over time (Cooper, Johnson, Johnson, and Wilderson, 1980; Hansell and Slavin, 1981; Johnson and Johnson, 1981; Kagan et al., 1985; Slavin, 1977, 1979, 1987a, 1987b, 1995; and Weigel, Wiser, and Cook, 1975).

Finally, teachers can vary the cooperative experiences of youngsters by periodically grouping youngsters according to similar learning styles, interests and/or needs dispositions, cultural/political groupings, homogeneous and heterogeneous groupings, role designations, and so on. Such groupings should be designed based upon specific instructional objectives. Use of cooperative learning communicates that the school values the natural cultural and learning dispositions of students as well as the use of their social and cultural patterns of communication.

5. *Ability to teach youngsters how to function in different cultural and learning-style contexts.* One of the responsibilities of educators is to extend the learning-style preferences of youngsters. As described in the research of Ramirez and Castaneda (1974), most youngsters learn how to learn through the cultural context in which they were reared. The more exposures to varying cultural child-rearing practices that a child has, the more that child can draw upon learning-style alternatives in order to understand, use, and apply phenomena.

In most classrooms across America, teachers tend to introduce new academic information and concepts through verbal instructions and directions (Appleton, 1983; Rohner, 1965). Such teacher-centered instructional styles, as examined previously, are, in many instances, in conflict with the traditional cultural patterns developed in many Native American, African American, and Hispanic American homes. As described earlier in this section, not only should educators try to connect the culture of the school and the culture of the home, but they should also help students extend their learning preferences in order to maximize their learning opportunities. Teachers need to be cognizant of which instructional behavior is appropriate for what situation, when such situations should occur, and how these situations should be assessed.

It is possible for students, given the appropriate classroom climate and skills of teachers, to alter learning-style behaviors. However, the teacher should conduct this in a conscious, deliberate, and intentional manner. We recommend that teachers spend classroom time discussing different learning-style preferences with students and providing learning-style assessments (Dunn and Griggs, 1988; Myers and McCaulley, 1985; Oxford, 1990; Weinstein, Schulte, and Cascallar, 1983) for students to determine their dominant and supporting learning styles. Although this may seem difficult to do, it is possible. We know of one teacher in an urban context who spends the first part of each semester helping students recognize their learning-style preferences and then showing them how to use those preferences as they learn the content in her class. Suggestions concerning learning-style development are provided by O'Malley and Chamot (1990), Oxford (1990), and Wenden and Rubin (1987). Oxford's text lists and describes many learning activities and teaching strategies that can be used by educators to expand student-learning styles. Her descriptions are valuable, not only because they utilize many learning domains (that is, creating mental linkages, structuring and reviewing, organizing and arranging learning, and learning study skills), but also because they provide thorough descriptions of sample lessons those teachers can use in developing learning-style skills in youngsters.

6. *Ability to engage students in problem-solving strategies to be used in real-life situations.* In order for teachers to be effective, they must not only have a thorough knowledge of their subject matter, but also know their students. This knowledge is critical in designing an instructional process that teaches youngsters problem-solving strategies that can be used in challenging the status quo. Through the use of the instructional models such as concept formation, inquiry, and synectics, student thinking is extended and problem-solving skills are introduced, practiced, and applied. By using real-life issues through case studies and by posing questions and/or problems not immediately solvable, students will be engaged in critical thinking by relating academic content, community issues, and problem-solving strategies in a meaningful manner. Students should be engaged in the process of learning as a contextualized experience that relates subject matter, problem-solving skills, personal and community issues, and a challenge to the status quo of most culturally diverse families (Ladson-Billings, 1994).

In her study of teachers of culturally diverse students, Ladson-Billings (1994) describes how some teachers challenge (through a form of subversive pedagogy) the pedagogical cycle, including the assumptions undergirding the structure of the schools.

The teachers I studied work in opposition to the school system that employs them. They are critical of the way that the school system treats employees, students, parents, and activists in the community. However, they cannot let their critique reside solely in words. They must turn it into action by challenging the system. What they do is both their lives and livelihoods. In their classrooms, they practice a subversive pedagogy. (p. 128)

Teachers who practice subversive pedagogy question the policies, procedures, and practices of those who employ them and of those institutions that prevent individual opportunity and growth. Such challenges utilize the knowledge and problem-solving skills learned through the instructional models described in this text, which can help play a large part in challenging the status quo and the low expectations ascribed to culturally diverse populations.

Though the term subversive pedagogy is a relatively recent educational term, the concept emanates from the works of Freire (1970), Giroux (1983), Herndon (1968), Holt (1967), Kohl (1967), Kozol (1967), and Postman and Weingartner (1969). Ideally, through the use of questions, posed by either the teacher or the students, a culturally congruent curriculum is constructed that engages all participants in examining the real-world problems of the community. The teacher's role in this process is not only to dictate what students need to learn, but also to facilitate and collaborate with students as mutual learners. Together teachers and students plan and design curriculum, determine how best to examine agreed-upon community issues, determine from whom to seek data and alternative solutions, and determine how to proceed in this journey of exploration and possible solution to community issues.

7. *Belief that one of their roles as educators is to challenge the societal status quo with students.* One way that students and teachers can practice their problem-solving skills is to utilize these skills in real-life situations in the community (for example, neighborhood voter registration and turnout, community environmental issues, or the elimination of drug and prostitution houses). Besides being a culturally congruent instructional behavior, challenges to the status quo are especially consistent with educators' roles as agents of societal change.

Teachers also have an important responsibility in helping students understand that society tacitly communicates low expectations regarding culturally diverse students (Ladson-Billings, 1994). Teachers must join with students to prove that these low expectations are unacceptable! Culturally diverse students must have teachers who have exceedingly high expectations for them and who consistently communicate these expectations whenever possible.

Educators who challenge the status quo also question the social and political realities that culturally diverse students face. Utilizing the problem-solving skills learned through the instructional strategies described in this text, students will develop the skills needed to better embrace the educational opportunities available to them. Educators need to become critics of society and to engage students in a transformative process. Preparing students to pursue individual opportunities for growth and development must be a major goal for teachers of diverse student populations. Teachers who engender this are individuals who are naturally curious. More importantly, they design plans to alleviate the conditions that prevent student growth.

8. *Belief that community volunteers/aides are an integral part of the teaching-learning process.* Because most of America's teachers are European American, the use of community volunteers/aides has a number of purposes:

   a. To serve as cultural role models, especially if the teacher does not share the cultural background of students.

   b. To serve as teacher aides of ESL teachers who speak primarily English.

   c. To help students make curricular connections between the academic subject matter and the local community setting.

   d. To help identify culturally familiar materials to be used in the instructional process.

Paraprofessionals, parents, community residents, and workers within the community can serve as strong role models in achieving the four purposes listed above. Heath (1983) found that parents who helped teachers link abstract curricular concepts with culturally familiar personnel and/or materials from the community reinforced what students were expected to learn. When parents participated, student achievement rose and student satisfaction toward school was positive even though the coordination of these community resources put an added burden upon teachers.

ⓉEACHER AS LEARNER

Major changes in the productivity of American schools rest on our ability to create and sustain a highly prepared teaching force for all, not just some, of our children.

LINDA DARLING-HAMMOND

The intense public scrutiny of American schools that began in the mid 1980s and continues unabated as we enter the new millennium has, in recent years, increasingly focused on the initial and continuing education of teachers. How can teacher learning be best advanced? Are new models of teacher preparation and professional development required? What are the appropriate standards by which such learning can be measured? These are just some of the central questions being asked. While debates about alternative responses have been intense, few clear answers have emerged. Two recent reviews of the literature on teacher learning (Cochran-Smith and Lytle, 1999; Wilson and Berne, 1999) describe well the complexity of the issues and the mixed results from a wide range of studies and experiments. These reviews when combined with the writings of Lieberman (1995) on teacher learning, suggest that the following trends are gaining momentum:

1. Educators are beginning to think more broadly about what types of activities and environments foster teacher learning.

2. Teacher learning can be fostered by creating new structures that value teacher expertise and provide opportunities for teachers to engage in collegial inquiry, problem solving and dialogue.

3. Teachers are being permitted or encouraged to engage in models of professional development that transcend traditional forms of teacher learning such as college coursework or inservice workshops.

4. Professional development is increasingly being viewed as an activity that takes place in a job-embedded context where the focus is on the realities of classroom life and on student learning outcomes.

5. Educational communities are placing an increasing emphasis on teachers' developing individual professional development plans that focus on their particularized needs, interests, and goals.

One important implication of the above trends is that teachers are being provided with expanded opportunities to take responsibility for planning and directing their own professional development. On the following pages, we discuss some of the various practices teachers can employ to support their professional development with specific regard to gaining skill in the effective use of the models of teaching.

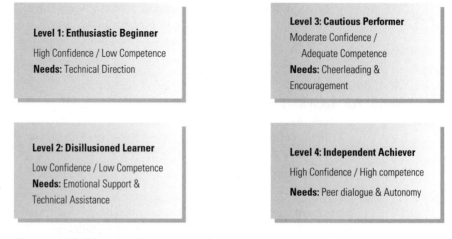

Figure 12-1 Situational Self-Leadership Framework

Source: Adapted from K. Blanchard. 1993. *Personal Excellence: Where Achievement and Fulfillment Meet* (audiocassettes). Chicago: Nightingale-Conant. Side 7

A Framework for Self-Leadership

One interesting way for teachers to reflect on their own learning critical needs is to consider *Situational Self-Leadership* theory. *Situational Self-Leadership* was adapted from the *Situational Leadership* theory developed by Hersey and Blanchard (1988). The fundamental premise of that leadership theory was that no single leadership style is best or most appropriate. Rather, it suggested that successful leaders employ leadership behaviors selected to match the maturity and motivation of their employees. The Hersey and Blanchard model was later modified (Blanchard, 1993) to support individual employees in achieving their goals in the institutional context. The *Situational Self-Leadership* framework (see Figure 12-1) is based on the theory that there are four levels of skill development that any learner (teacher or student) experiences and that those levels are influenced by two essential factors—*competence and confidence*. More specifically, competence is defined as a function of the *knowledge and experience* one brings to any given learning situation. In contrast, *confidence* is viewed as a function of the *motivation and commitment* one has for any new learning opportunity.

Importantly, the degrees of competence and confidence a teacher brings to any given learning task varies according to the learning situation itself. For example, a teacher desiring to learn more about the inquiry model might find herself at *Level Four* because she has a long history of teaching an inquiry-based science curriculum, and because she has had much success in using the approach. However, the same teacher when attempting to apply synectics could find herself at *Level Two* as she confronts her lack of technical competence and waning personal confidence.

The second important dimension of the *Situational Self-Leadership* model suggests that once a learner has assessed his or her personal level of skill development, he or she will know better what type of support is most appropriate. To illustrate how the model works in practice, consider the following examples:

Example 1. Joan Kraft, a second-year teacher at Eagle River Elementary, is unfamiliar with the use of the linkword story as a mnemonics strategy. However, having heard her sixth grade Native American students describe how they are "using stories to remember stuff in science," she is very interested in learning the technique. Joan is confident she can learn to apply the strategy in her social studies classes but realizes she can make quicker progress with the help of someone more experienced with the approach. She accepts herself as an *enthusiastic beginner* (Level 1) and approaches the science teacher for *technical direction* in creating linkword stories.

Example 2. Bill Logan is a 20-year veteran teacher who has been trying the *concept formation* model at Dunbar Intermediate School. Recently, however, he has had a series of disappointments in using the approach with his African American and Hispanic American students. His students' resistance to engage in the higher order thinking the model requires has been particularly discouraging. Having a hard time justifying the additional time the model takes, he finds himself tempted to revert to old and more directive approaches, especially when colleagues urge him to abandon his progressivist approach—just "tell the students what you want them to know." Fortunately, Bill realizes that he still needs additional technical support if he is going to master the model. Equally important, he recognizes his personal frustration. Taking responsibility for his own learning, Bill recognizes himself as a *disillusioned learner* (Level 2) and seeks out a colleague he believes can provide both *technical advice* and *emotional support*.

Example 3. Maria Ramirez, currently in her third year at Martin Luther King Elementary, left college with a commitment to using the cooperative learning model. She did her senior project on cooperative learning and successfully used the model during her student teaching. However, Maria's first year of teaching was so "hectic" that she never found the time to implement her ideas. During her second year, she tried to promote a cooperative learning workshop with colleagues but found little interest. In promoting the workshop, however, she received encouragement from Crystal, one of her team members who shared her interest in trying more cooperative learning activities. Maria is personally aware that she has been a *cautious performer* (Level 3) and decides to approach Crystal in hopes of finding the *encouragement and motivation* she needs to start, as she likes to say, "walking the talk."

Example 4. Beverly Johnson, a twelve-year veteran at John Muir High School, is an expert at oral discussion. Students, peers, and administrators respect her outstanding skill in facilitating classroom discussions. She is highly skilled at asking questions and monitoring students' oral interactions. Beverly, however, is not satisfied or motivated by the praise of her administrator. She knows she is good and recognizes that repeated praise for the same skill is no longer satisfying. What she does enjoy and learn from is the opportunity to experiment or "play" with new and creative approaches. Recognizing her *independent achiever* (Level 4) status with regard to oral discussion, Beverly has decided to stretch herself by trying her skill at facilitating an oral discussion using videoconferencing technology. She is especially excited about the opportunity to have her Asian American students interact with an Asian American author they have been reading. Beverly recognizes that she has no idea about how to make this happen and seeks the help of her district's technology coordinator. In other words, the *independent achiever*, in this learning situation, becomes an *enthusiastic beginner* in need of *technical direction*.

Models to Support Teacher Learning

Situational Self-Leadership theory suggests that the chance of a new ability or skill's being successfully integrated into a teacher's classroom practice is largely a function of the teacher's commitment and confidence with regard to that ability or skill. Importantly, these are highly related concepts. With regard to confidence, the key is not necessarily teachers' initial confidence in technical skill, but an internal sense of knowing that they can master the skill if they are *committed* to taking control of their own learning and are *motivated* enough to secure the external support needed to be successful. Like the students they teach, teachers have diverse learning dispositions as well. Consequently, it is important that teachers choose forms of staff development that best meet their own learning needs. In 1989, Dennis Sparks and Susan Loucks-Horsley proposed a conceptual framework for thinking about the professional development of classroom teachers. Their framework described the five models listed below:

1. Individually Guided Development
2. Observation & Assessment
3. Systematic School Improvement
4. Training
5. Inquiry

Using a conceptual framework such as the one used to organize the instructional models described in this text, the Sparks and Loucks-Horsley models are perhaps better viewed as five broad *categories* of staff development, each containing specific *models* to promote teacher learning (see Figure 12-2). On the following pages, we focus on three specific professional development models, each representative of a different category from the Sparks-Horsley framework. Specifically, we discuss the peer-coaching model representative of the observation and assessment category, action-research representative of the inquiry model, and the learning portfolios representative of individually guided development. First, however, a few words about the two remaining categories, *training* and *systematic school improvement*.

Teachers reading this book are most likely doing so in the context of the *training category*, reading it as a textbook in a graduate or undergraduate class, or in an inservice workshop on the models of teaching. These traditional forms of staff development continue to serve as viable methods of teacher learning. Thoughtfully designed training, provided by an expert presenter or facilitator, offers an excellent vehicle for helping teachers acquire new knowledge and skills. It becomes an increasingly powerful model when teachers are provided opportunities to see demonstrations of expert practice, receive feedback on their own trial performances, and be coached in the workplace. Teachers who

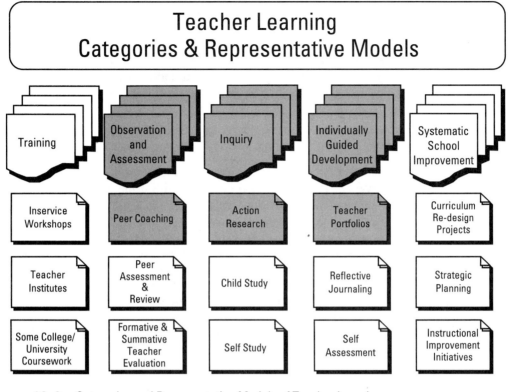

FIGURE 12-2   Categories and Representative Models of Teacher Learning

have discovered this book outside of a training environment, and who are reading it as a resource for professional improvement, might consider looking for a training opportunity at a local university or recommending a workshop on the models of teaching to their staff development committee or director.

The *systematic school improvement* category will not be discussed in detail here because it typically involves commitment to effect change at the school or district-wide level. Such efforts, however, often engage teachers and administrators in professional development activities that integrate models from the remaining four categories. A school that makes a commitment to using the models of teaching as the focus of instructional improvement could, for example, coordinate appropriate training opportunities, require teachers to prepare individualized professional development plans based on one of the models, make the models the foci of the observation and assessment process, or encourage teachers to join a collaborative action research team focused on student learning and model usage. Incidentally, in situations where the models have been used in a systemic way to enhance student performance with poor and diverse student populations, the results have been remarkably positive (Joyce, Murphy, Showers, and Murphy, 1989).

TEACHER AS REFLECTIVE PRACTITIONER

One of the most consistent themes of teacher development over the past two decades has been that of the teacher as a *reflective practitioner*. Despite the popularity of this theme, it has not always been understood or appreciated by classroom teachers who often complain that they have little or no time to be reflective. One possible reason for this reaction stems from a misunderstanding of the word *reflect*, which is often interpreted as meaning *to think after the fact*. Building on the early writings of John Dewey (1933), Donald Schön (1987) has done much to help clarify this misconception by making clear that reflective thinking is not just post-active in nature, but in fact is pre-active and interactive as well. When *reflection* is conceptualized in this manner, teachers can appreciate that the nature of their work engages them in a recursive cycle of reflective thinking that involves planning, acting, and reflecting.

Reflective thinking typically begins when teachers encounter a situation, surprise, or state of doubt that causes them to hesitate or delay in their reaction. It is this pause, as momentary as it might be, that provides the opportunity to *intellectualize* the problem and consider alternative actions and the possible consequences of those actions. This *reflective moment* can occur at any time, including while in the act of teaching itself. Take, for example, a teacher who, while monitoring group work, notices that one of her most reliable and cooperative students is distracted and off task. Her initial surprise almost summons a quick reprimand, but instead the teacher pauses long enough to make a decision to ignore the behavior and continue her observation. In this case, the selected response of no action is then monitored through continued observation, which reveals that the student in question self-corrects her behavior and returns to being a productive group member. After observing this phenomenon, the teacher momentarily reflects on the goodness of her choice, reinforcing her belief in strategically giving students opportunities to control their own behavior. In many respects, this process of confronting a problem, planning a response, taking strategic action, and then reflecting on the efficacy of the selected choice provides an appropriate way of thinking about the kind of reflection that teachers engage in when involved in professional development activity. On the following pages, we discuss peer coaching, action research, and teacher portfolios as models to promote teacher learning in the context of reflective practice. Table 12-2 provides an overview of those three models and how each can be carried out in the plan, act, and reflect phases.

Peer Coaching

Peer coaching is a professional development model representative of the *observation and assessment category* of professional development. Specifically, it is a term used to describe a relationship between two or more teachers committed to providing technical and psychological help for the improvement of instruction and the advancement of student learning. Because a peer coaching relationship can take a variety of forms, it is a professional development model that can be effectively employed to meet the needs of teachers at any of the four levels of learning from the *Situational Self-Leadership* framework.

TABLE 12-2 Three Phases of the Cycle of Reflective Practice

Phase	Peer Coaching	Action Research	Learning Portfolio
Planning	Planning the focus of the observation; selecting the observation methodology; negotiating the role of the participants	Identifying and situating the problem; framing the question; planning the method of inquiry including data collection & analysis	Selecting the purpose and theme of the portfolio; determining the desired outcomes and audience; making portfolio format and process decisions
Acting	Observation of the teaching and learning episode; making the record of evidence	Collecting the data— i.e., recording the observations, completing the interviews, etc.	Implementing planned practices; collecting and managing artifacts; making and entering personal reflections
Reflecting	Interpretation of the observational record; making meaning; planning for new action; identification of new foci	Data analysis; interpretation of results; identifying conclusions and exploring implications for practice	Processing the portfolio as it develops; making decisions to change or redirect format or process; sharing insights gained

Like any professional development activity, peer coaching takes place in institutional and interpersonal contexts that can be quite powerful. For example, many teachers believe that the words *observation, supervision,* and *evaluation* are synonymous. This misunderstanding often stems from the fact that many teachers have not experienced *observation* outside of the summative *evaluation* process conducted by their immediate *supervisor,* the principal. Consequently, it is important that peer coaches clarify their role in relation to these terms, and with regard to any program context in which the coaching occurs. Depending on that context, teachers may be in a *structured* or *formal* peer coaching relationship. For example, a beginning teacher may be assigned a formal mentor who has peer coaching as part of his or her mentoring responsibilities. Similarly, a veteran teacher may be employed in a district where peer coaching takes place in a peer assistance and review program in which coaches also have evaluation responsibilities. In contrast, peer coaching can also occur in more informal and less structured contexts. In such cases, peer-coaching relationships are typically formed in response to an individual teacher's personal need for support.

Whether in a formal or informal peer-coaching relationship, teachers committed to taking responsibility for their own professional growth must assume a proactive stance toward finding the types of support necessary to meet their personal needs. Reflecting on the Situational Self-Leadership framework is one effective way to clarify those needs. Once the learning needs are identified, it is important that they be clearly communicated to the peer coach so that appropriate coaching behaviors can be strategically employed. Effective peer coaches are comfortable adapting their coaching behaviors in a variety of ways, including the specific type of role they play in the peer-coaching process. Wolf and

Robbins (1989) identify three basic types of peer coaching roles: *coach as mirror*, *coach as collaborator*, and *coach as expert*. The following examples illustrate how each role might be applied with regard to helping a teacher develop skill in the models of teaching.

Coach as Mirror. Cybil Williams is a 4th grade teacher in her seventh year of professional practice. Last summer she attended a workshop on models of teaching provided by a veteran colleague. She left the workshop excited about several new ideas that she looked forward to trying the next school year. Cybil was especially interested in the synectics model and has been experimenting with it recently. She has planned a lesson using the strategy and would like to collect some data to help her reflect on her performance. She approaches a teammate and friend, asking her to observe her class and make a descriptive record of the lesson to serve as a *mirror* that can stimulate her personal reflections.

Coach as Collaborator. Bob Fernandez and Ed Kramer are high school social studies teachers who are both working on their Masters in Education at a local university. Last term they took a graduate course in the models of teaching. They subsequently have formed a peer-coaching team and have committed to supporting each other in implementing the models this year. Bob and Ed met in the fall and decided how they would function in their peer-coaching relationship. The first instructional model they chose to experiment with was concept attainment. Together, they have created a simple scripting form that is organized according to the five phases of the model. They agree that when conducting their observations of each other, they will simply describe what they see in each phase. They meet after each observation to discuss the script, which serves as the provocateur for their dialogue, which includes praise, suggestions, reflective questioning and a search for shared meaning.

Coach as Expert. Two years ago, Linda Rhodes, a middle school principal, formed a staff development committee. After several meetings, the committee agreed to put a school-wide focus on the models of teaching. Training was subsequently conducted, books were purchased, and peer-coaching teams were formed. The program has evolved to a place where individual teachers have been identified as having specific expertise in one or more of the models and have committed to support their colleagues interested in improving their skill. According to Linda, expert coaching happens in one of two ways in her school. In the first way, a teacher interested in a specific instructional model identifies an expert coach for that model and requests that the coach conduct a classroom observation and give specific feedback. However, more frequently teachers ask the expert coach when he or she will be using the model and ask permission to observe. After the observation, the observing teacher thanks the coach for allowing observation and may ask questions to help clarify understanding. It is understood that the only topic open for discussion is the model being observed and that comments or questions about other topics—such as student behavior, for example—are out of bounds.

As we conclude this brief discussion on coaching, closely read the description below about a coaching project at Brighton High School in Boston. To what degree do you see coach as mirror? Coach as collaborator? Or coach as expert? Which metaphor is most descriptive of the successful program as described by Guiney (2001)? Or does each metaphor work to a limited degree?

"Our coaches have played a leadership role in what we are doing," says Charles Skidmore, headmaster of Brighton High School. "When our school decided to put a real emphasis on writing and on developing key questions for students, it was our coaches who were able to come in and with some authority say, 'Here is a good way to do it . . .' They didn't say, 'This is the only way to do it' or 'We have all the answers,' but they were willing to say, 'Tell us what you are doing and let us connect you to other people and show you other practices we've seen.' So we were able to really move."

In the initial stages of their work on whole-school improvement, Brighton's teachers made progress in developing district-required "key questions"—broad, open-ended queries that provide opportunities for students to display their writing skills while testing their knowledge of what has been taught. "What the teachers weren't able to do was come to any kind of agreement about how to judge the students' writing," Skidmore says. "It was our coaches who said, 'Well, there are some protocols you can look at for this.' These were ways to look at writing that helped us see that measuring quality was not subjective."

What followed was a lengthy, collaborative process involving teachers in the development of a schoolwide objective measurement of writing now known as Brighton High's writing rubric. Coaches are training teachers in using it as a tool to gauge how well students are able to transmit ideas through written words.

"The entire process involves a buy-in by teachers," Skidmore says. "And I think that is where the coaching really worked as coaching. If our teachers had looked at the protocol and said, 'No, we're not going to do that—we don't want that,' then the coaches would have said, 'We'll find something else, something that works for you.'"

"Even though the protocols the coaches suggested for assessing student writing have worked at Brighton, along the way there has been resistance from some teachers," says Skidmore. "Teachers were saying, 'Why should I correct the same paper that somebody else corrected? And it's not even a paper that has anything to do with me. I teach history. Why should I look at English?' But the coaches were able to explain why they should do that."

Teachers' conversations about student work might, on the surface, appear to be about coming to agreement on scores. But what actually happens—when it is done well—is that teachers start talking among themselves about how they can teach so that their students can begin to achieve at higher levels. "It's this thinking about their practice that helps teachers to change their practice," says Otherine Neisler, the content coach at Brighton High. Skidmore adds, "The coaches have been able to say to our faculty members, 'Give a little bit more. Do a little bit more. Dig a little bit deeper, and see if you get something better for it.'"

"What we do is similar to what an athletic trainer does," says Roseanne Bacon Meade, Brighton's change coach. "We're like the person who says, 'You might find it easier to catch a fly ball to center if you did this or that in an exercise program.'"

"And to continue the analogy further," says Skidmore, "the suggestion comes from the coach. It is not coming from the teacher's department head or from his or her evaluator or principal. No one is saying, 'You have to do this' or 'I am going to judge you on it.' Instead, somebody is saying, 'Here is an idea. Give it a try . . .' And all of this sends a message that the focus at this school is on teaching and learning." (p. 742)

The Clinical Cycle of Support   Peer coaching is most successful when it happens in the context of a cycle of clinical support that includes three stages—planning, acting, and reflecting.

Planning—The planning conference is the critical first step in the peer-coaching process, as it provides the opportunity for participating teachers to clarify their roles. As described above, peer coaches can play one of three different roles depending on the needs and interests of the teacher they are coaching. This is an especially important part of the process as it has significant implications for the next two phases of the peer coaching cycle. The planning conference is also used to establish goals and procedures, including negotiating what observation methods will be employed and what types of data will be recorded. It also provides the interpersonal setting to begin the trust building process that is foundational to an effective peer-coaching relationship. Finally, the planning conference is especially important because it provides the opportunity for the coach to better understand the teacher's professional thinking as well as any personal issues and concerns.

Acting—In this second phase of the cycle of clinical support, the peer coach conducts an observation of the teaching and learning episode, and makes the observational record that was negotiated with the teacher being observed. There are many methods for creating a record of evidence, and experienced peer coaches develop a wide repertoire of methods over time. Such methods or tools can be organized into the five different categories described in Table 12-3. Regardless of the type of method selected, the goal is the same: to create a *descriptive, nonjudgmental* record of evidence that can be used to prompt teacher reflection and to stimulate peer dialogue focused on improved performance. Peer coaches interested in learning more about these different forms of observation will find excellent technical support from a number of writers who describe well the art and science of conducting an effective classroom observation (Borich, 1999; Good and Brophy, 1997; Peters and March, 1999).

One of the most popular methods for making the record of a classroom observation is scripting. Scripting, while it can be challenging for the beginner, has the advantage of being a relatively easy method to employ. To script a lesson, the peer coach writes a narrative description of observations that can include descriptions of teacher and student behaviors and interactions. There are two basic forms of scripting: the *open-ended narrative* method and the *focused narrative* method. In the first approach, the peer coach creates a narrative script that is linear in nature and describes the flow of the lesson as it unfolds. Some coaches use a left-hand column of the open-ended script to *time code* their entries. Others create a right-hand column, which they leave blank while scripting, and then use later to record notes, questions, or suggestions. The method is called open-ended because it is generally used to capture classroom activity in a holistic manner. In contrast, the focused-script method is designed to collect data in categories that have been strategically selected to gather data on specific

TABLE 12-3 Five Methods of Classroom Observation

Observation Method & Description	Sample Application
Videotaping or Audiotaping *Utilizes electronic media as the method for making the record of evidence to prompt teacher reflection and self-assessment.*	*A peer coach, at the request of a teacher, videotapes a direct instruction lesson so that the teacher can analyze her performance with regard to the five phases of the model.*
Visual Diagramming *Utilizes an array of visual symbols to diagram or map the story of a teaching/learning episode.*	*A peer coach and teacher create a simple classroom map based on the teacher's seating chart. The coach uses a variety of arrows and other symbols to help the teacher gain insight on student-teacher interactions during Phases II and III of the inquiry model.*
Coding *Utilizes numerical or alphabetic codes to classify or categorize teacher or student behaviors.*	*A teacher interested in diversifying her responses to student answers during oral discussion asks her peer coach to code her responses using a coding instrument selected from* Looking into Classrooms *(Good and Brophy, 1997).*
Frequency Counting *Utilizes tally marks or other counting techniques to record the frequency of teacher or student behaviors of specific interest.*	*A teacher interested in the cooperative learning model asks her peer coach to make a record of students' off task behaviors during group work. The teacher and coach brainstorm several categories of off task behaviors and the peer coach then tallies these behaviors by group.*
Scripting *Utilizes written narrative descriptions as the primary tool for capturing the story of teaching and learning situations and interactions.*	*A peer coach creates a simple focused narrative form based on the four phases of the Mnemonics model. The coach then makes a descriptive written record of teacher and student behaviors during each of the four phases of the model.*

areas of interest. This approach is particularly valuable when the teacher to be observed has a preferred focus in mind. Imagine, for example, a teacher who is particularly frustrated with his inability to manage the disruptive behaviors of one of his students. In this case, a focused script could consist of two simple categories, student and teacher. Using this approach the coach describes the behaviors of the student and the reactions of the teacher to those behaviors.

Reflecting—The final phase of the peer coaching cycle typically takes place in the context of a post-observation conference where teacher and coach meet to process the data collected during the preceding phase. Once again, the nature of the post-conference dialogue is guided by the role that the coach has agreed to play. For example, if the coach is acting as a mirror, then the main focus of the conversation might be on ensuring that the observed teacher understands the record of evidence. Comparatively, if the coach is acting in a collaborative fashion, the dialogue will likely involve two people working together

TABLE 12-4   Five Steps to Beginning a Peer Coaching Relationship

1. *Identify the specific instructional models or strategies in which you want to acquire or advance your skill.*

2. *Reflecting on the* Situational Self-Leadership *framework, determine your current level of skill development with regard to the desired learning.*

3. *Invite a colleague (mentor teacher, peer coach, team member, lead teacher) to serve as your coach.*

4. *Inform your coach of what specific types of help you desire, and confirm that he or she is willing to serve in that capacity.*

5. *Schedule an initial coaching meeting to determine the ground rules for the coaching process, including the desired role of the coach as* mirror, collaborator, *or* expert.

to make meaning of the data. Finally, if the coach has been asked to serve as an expert, it is more likely that the coach will feel free to make specific suggestions for improvement.

The post-conference is a critical time in a peer coaching relationship when serious problems can develop if the coach falls into what Glickman (1990) has described as the *interpretation trap*. This trap is sprung when a teacher feels that the peer coach is rushing to judgment or interpreting observational data without inviting and valuing the teacher's personal reflections. The interpretation trap is especially destructive when the coach violates the informal verbal contract that defined the focus of the observation, or when the feedback regarding the observation is incongruent with the role that the coach had agreed to play. For example, a coach who agreed to serve as a *mirror* for a teaching colleague but begins a post-conference with specific suggestions for how the teacher can improve his or her performance will likely create the defensiveness that almost always stifles meaningful dialogue.

An effective post-conference concludes with the coach and teacher planning the next coaching cycle or agreeing that there is no need at the current time to continue the coaching process. (See Table 12-4 for peer coaching steps.)

Action Research

Another powerful model of teacher learning is representative of the inquiry category of professional development. Known as *action research*, it engages teachers in the process of inquiring into their own practice in search of answers to personally significant questions. For many teachers, this particular approach to learning is often misunderstood and consequently underutilized as a vehicle for personal improvement. In many cases this misunderstanding stems from what Hubbard and Power (1999) describe as the problem of the "little *r* and the big *R*." They describe how many teachers associate *research* with being an "add-on" that is not congruent with their world of practice. They envision intensive library research, the statistical analysis of data, and the need to take a detached and analytic view of classroom life. While such images can and do apply to some forms of educational research, they typically do not represent the experience of teachers who have discovered that, quite to the contrary, *action research* can and should be a highly personal and highly practical endeavor.

Loucks-Horsley and colleagues (1987) describe three underlying assumptions that support the teacher as researcher as a viable and important form of teacher learning. Importantly, these assumptions are highly consistent with the current trends in professional development described earlier in this chapter:

- *The teacher is an intelligent, inquiring professional with legitimate expertise and important experience.*

- *Teachers are inclined to search for data to answer pressing questions and to reflect on the data to formulate solutions.*

- *By contributing to or formulating their own questions, and by collecting their own data to answer them, teachers will develop new understandings that will contribute to their professional growth.*

Numerous other writers have advanced definitions of action research and have discussed the implications for classroom teachers (Kemmis and McTaggert, 1988; McCutcheon and Jung, 1990; and Rapoport, 1970). Citing Grundy and Kemmis (1981), Masters (1995) points out that these diverse definitions tend to include three critical elements that must be present for inquiry to qualify as action research.

1. *The project takes as its subject matter a social practice, regarding it as a strategic action susceptible to improvement.* Simply put, teachers who engage in action research are motivated by a belief that they will gain new and valuable insights that will improve their instructional practices and positively impact student learning. Applying this element to the challenge of developing teachers for the culturally diverse, teachers engage in the action research process to explore issues involving their personal use of the instructional models and the consequent impact on student learning.

2. *The project proceeds through a spiral of cycles of planning, acting, observing and reflecting, with each of these activities being systematically and self-critically implemented and interrelated.* As this element makes clear, action research follows the same general cycle of reflective practice that guides the peer-coaching process. In this case, teachers assume responsibility for directing the research process through the various phases as they search for answers to questions of personal and practical significance.

3. *The project involves those responsible for the practice in each of the moments of the activity, widening participation in the project gradually to include others affected by the practice and maintaining collaborative control of the process.* At its best, action research has the power to effect change not only in the professional practice of the teachers involved, but also in the practice of other teachers as well. As new insights and understandings are acquired, dissemination of results becomes a logical next step in the process. Having established a conceptual understanding of the nature of action research, we now take a closer look at the phases of the research process by examining a specific case of action research focused on instructional model usage.

Planning—The first phase of the action research process involves identifying the general *landscape* the research project will explore and identifying the specific *question* it seeks to answer. Once the question has been framed, attention turns to the issue of *design*. Here the teacher crafts a plan for the project, including any possible interventions or treatments, as well as methods of data collection and analysis. Teachers considering action research for the first time are advised to think of these various steps of the planning process not as formal operations, but simply as a method of organizing the kind of thinking they do as a normal part of their professional practice. It is quite common, for example, for teachers to develop a general area of concern or interest that troubles, intrigues, or challenges them for any number of reasons. Such areas of concern or interest, once identified, provide the fertile ground from which an action research project can grow.

Consider the case of Marion Wallace who teaches in an urban middle school. Marion is responsible for teaching 150 5th and 6th grade students. Sixty-four percent of her students are African American, 21 percent are Hispanic American, and 13 percent are Caucasian American. The remaining 2 percent of Marion's students are of Asian American and Native American heritage. Recently, Marion has been particularly concerned that many of her students have difficulty making connections between the big ideas that are central to their enduring understanding of the writing process. This is particularly troubling because her analysis of the latest proficiency practice tests reveals an increasing emphasis on this cognitive skill. Marion decides to explore this area of concern through the action research process. She has had a personal interest in action research after hearing a presentation by a colleague who became involved in the process a couple of years ago. She contacts that colleague to help her get started and walks away with a loaned copy of *The Art of Classroom Inquiry: A Handbook for Teacher Researchers* (Hubbard and Power, 1993). After reading the first chapter, she decides to focus her project on the concept formation model as a tool for helping students make connections between key concepts from current and previous units of instruction. Specifically, she decides to explore the following question: How can concept formation help diverse learners identify and describe relationships between the big ideas from prior and current learning? In designing her action research project Marion decides to use a concept webbing exercise to begin her next unit. As a method for collecting baseline data, she decides to have each student, without peer or instructor support, group and label a set of key terms from the prior three units of instruction. In analyzing the students' concept webs she is especially interested in performance patterns that might be related to students' racial or ethnic heritage.

The next part of Marion's action research plan includes her decision to begin using the concept formation model, a model that allows field-dependent learners to be more engaged, throughout her upcoming units of instruction to help students develop the cognitive skills necessary for making meaningful conceptual connections. In addition, she plans to vary her use of the concept formation model in search of specific strategies that seem to work best with her diverse learners. Her initial plan calls for experimenting with teacher-generated and student-generated data in Phase I of the model. Finally, Marion chooses two forms of data collection as a way of gaining insight on student thinking. Her primary source of data, she decides, will be artifacts of student work, including student generated data lists and maps. Second, she decides to use interviews of strategically selected students as a way of deepening her insights into student thinking and approaches to learning. That is, does the model help students better "engage" the content? Remember, teachers do not use different models to be "cute" or innovative; they use them to help students learn more and better.

Acting—In the second phase of the action research process, teachers carry out the plan they devised in the preceding phase. Depending on the nature of the project, this phase may include the application of a new teacher behavior or experimentation with new student behaviors. Not every action research project, however, is focused on studying the impact of some new or different teaching or learning behavior. In contrast, a teacher may choose, for example, to engage in the action research process as a way of better understanding the existing classroom culture. The one action, however, that is always present in the acting phase is the process of collecting the data that are required to gain insight into the classroom dynamic or phenomenon of interest. In doing so, teachers may draw from a wide array of data collection tools that include various forms of structured and unstructured note-taking, interviews, artifact analysis, student observation or "kidwatching," surveys, sociograms, and audiotape or videotape transcription and analysis (Hubbard and Power, 1993).

In Marion's case, the acting phase of her research project unfolded over a six-week period during which she experimented with the use of the concept formation model, collected artifacts of student thinking, and conducted periodic student interviews. Her plan was to use the artifacts of student thinking, including independently generated concept webs, to determine if repeated exposure to the concept formation model was impacting her students' ability to make the desired conceptual connections. Interviews of purposefully selected children were used as a tool for advanced exploration of student thinking.

Reflecting—This phase of an action research project engages teachers in the process of analyzing the data they have collected in their search for an answer to their guiding question. As such, it does not always constitute the end of the action research process. In fact, it can just as easily serve as a launching pad for further exploration, as teachers are surprised or perplexed by what the data reveal and find themselves asking new questions that call for further exploration. In this fashion, the three phases of the process become self-generating as they engage teachers in an ongoing cycle of reflective practice.

In Marion's case, analysis of her students' concept webs, as well as notes taken during student interviews, led to the following conclusions. After being engaged in the concept formation model four times in a six-week period, 62 percent of 5th graders and 51 percent of 6th graders demonstrated a *marked improvement* in their ability to make defensible connections among 22 language arts concepts covering four instructional units. Marion defined marked improvement as an improvement score of 20 or more points between a student's score on the baseline concept web and the score received on the concept web produced at the end of the six-week period. While excited by these results, Marion is also curious about other aspects of the data. For example, she is especially intrigued by the fact that the class that she had previously thought of as her "weakest" made the greatest gains in the study. Stimulated by her

TABLE 12-5 Five Steps to Beginning an Action Research Project

1. *Determine what instructional model(s) are of special concern or interest at this point in your career.*

2. *Reflect on the* Situational Self-Leadership *framework, and determine your level of skill development* with regard to the action research process.

3. *If at Level 1, 2, or 3, seek the coaching support necessary to meet your action research skill development needs. If at Level 4, begin the action research planning process.*

4. *Work alone, or with the support of a coach or research collaborator, and specify what question(s) your action research project will explore.*

5. *Complete your action research plan by deciding what methods of data collection and analysis you will employ, and what methods you might use to share the results of your inquiry.*

involvement in the action research process (see Table 12-5), and encouraged by her principal, Marion has volunteered to offer a summer workshop for her district titled "Teacher as Researcher: An Introduction to Action Research."

Notice how Marion is using data to inform her teaching. The current mantra in almost all states is student achievement. Clearly, whether students learn is important. Our concern is with helping teachers better assess *how* to help students learn more effectively and to analyze the teaching act in ways that foster positive changes in teaching behaviors when the type of learning that students experience either *is* or *is not* what the teacher expects.

Teacher Portfolios

Developing a portfolio is a professional development model representative of the *individually guided development* category of teacher learning. Fundamentally, it is designed to support individual teachers in reflecting on their professional practice over a period of time. However, portfolio development at its best is carried out in collaboration with colleagues who are likewise involved in portfolio design and development. Such collaboration enriches the portfolio experience by providing opportunities for collegial dialogue and reflection and a search for shared meaning.

The word *portfolio* is an elusive one that invites multiple interpretations, and numerous writers have suggested competing definitions of the term. For the purposes of focusing on portfolios as tools to facilitate teacher learning, the authors have selected the following definition by Wolf and Dietz (1998):

> A teaching portfolio is a structured collection of teacher and student work created across diverse contexts over time, framed by reflection and enriched through collaboration, that has as its ultimate aim the advancement of teacher and student learning. (p. 13)

Before describing how teachers might use such a portfolio to enhance learning about the instructional models and their effective use with diverse learners, it is important to realize that there are many types of portfolios. In fact, there are almost as many classification schemes for types of portfolios as there are definitions of the term. In the interest of consistency, we once again refer to Wolf and Dietz (1998) who identify three types of portfolio models in use by teachers:

- Employment Portfolio
- Assessment Portfolio
- Learning Portfolio

The obvious purpose of the *employment portfolio* is to provide potential employers with insight into a candidate's qualifications for a desired position. The employment portfolio typically provides background and biographical information on the teacher including certificates or licenses held, as well as personal mission or philosophy statements. In addition, such portfolios often contain *showcase* materials designed to provide evidence of specific skills or experiences. By comparison, schools and other professional organizations use *assessment portfolios* to evaluate teachers' professional competence and performance. In such cases, teachers thoughtfully select, present, and reflect on specific pieces of evidence to demonstrate professional competence as measured against a set of specified standards. The National Board for Professional Teaching standards, for example, requires teachers to develop such portfolios as part of their application for national board certification (Wolf, 1991). Finally, in contrast with the employment or assessment portfolio, the *learning portfolio* is fundamentally focused on reflection, self-assessment, and professional growth over time.

Developing a Learning Portfolio   Before discussing the content and process of learning portfolio development, it should be pointed out that a portfolio is not a mere collection of unstructured artifacts that makes little or no sense to anyone other that the teacher who collected them. Though learning portfolios can take many forms, Dietz (1995) argues that they are based on four features that include a defined *purpose*, a focus or *theme*, an articulated *process*, and desired *outcomes*. As was the case with peer coaching and action research, we now take a closer look at the learning portfolio as it is implemented in the cycle of reflective practice.

Planning—The critical first step in the portfolio development process involves teachers in clarifying the purpose, goals, and desired outcomes for the portfolio project. Additionally, the planning stage is used make other important decisions such as how the portfolio will be structured, and how and when reflections will be made and displayed.

To illustrate the planning process in action, consider the case of Larry Wilson, a high school biology teacher who is planning a learning portfolio to support his new interest in the models of teaching. Larry works in a district that has created new policies and procedures with regard to staff development. All teachers, for example, are now required to prepare an Individualized Professional Development Plan. This plan, in addition to stating a teacher's professional development goals must also include a description of what professional development activities will be used to accomplish the stated goals. Under this new system, teachers are not limited to using graduate credit or continuing education units as evidence of professional growth. In addition, they may choose *alternate forms* of professional development.

TABLE 12-6   Portfolio Planning Questions and Exemplar Responses

Portfolio Planning Questions	*Larry Wilson's Portfolio Plan*
1. What is the purpose of the portfolio project?	*To monitor my growth and development in using the models of teaching.*
2. What is the focus, theme, or guiding question for the portfolio?	*Theme: Using diversified teaching strategies to meet the needs of diverse learners.*
3. What are the desired outcomes for this portfolio project?	*Personal competence and confidence in an expanded repertoire of teaching strategies.*
4. Who is the audience for this portfolio?	*Myself (and the district's staff development coordinator who has expressed interest in my project as a possible tool for other teachers).*
5. How will I structure my portfolio?	*A three-ring binder with eight tabs, one for each of the eight different instructional models. (Artifact entries will be limited to a maximum of 10 pieces of paper per tab.)*
6. What standards will I use for selecting portfolio artifacts?	*Artifacts, including samples of student work, instructional plans, and notes to self, will be included because they prompted a personally compelling reflection.*
7. What process will I use for making and displaying my reflections?	*Reflections will be hand written on 5 by 7 index cards and displayed with or near any related artifacts. All reflection cards will be dated.*

Larry recently completed his Masters in Education and is anxious to experiment with a couple of new ideas he found particularly intriguing during his graduate work. One of the final classes he elected to take was a course in *Models of Teaching*. Reading about and reflecting on the various instructional models caused Larry to confront the fact that he relied predominately on the lecture method, with an occasional and usually unplanned foray into oral discussion. He made a personal commitment to begin using the models as a way of diversifying his instructional practices.

The second idea that Larry found compelling was the result of a panel discussion he had observed in a graduate seminar on *New Directions in Professional Development*. One of the panelists, a high school social studies teacher, had enthusiastically shared her experience in developing what she called a *learning portfolio*. With his graduate work now behind him and a new school year just beginning, Larry has decided to develop a learning portfolio as an alternate method of professional development to achieve his goal of developing skill in the use of a wider array of models of teaching. Referring to the list of recommended readings provided by the panelist, he makes a trip to the university library and checks out books by Bullock and Hawk (2001) and Campbell, Cignetti, Melenyzer, Nettles, and Wyman (1997). After browsing these materials he identifies seven questions to guide him through the portfolio planning process (see Table 12-6).

Acting—As Larry's plan makes clear, the primary focus of his portfolio is to monitor his own professional development with regard to utilizing the models of teaching. In the acting phase of the portfolio process Larry has committed to collect and review the artifacts of interest that he identified in his portfolio plan. He quickly discovers that this process is not as time consuming as he feared it might be. For example, when grading student work, he finds himself processing the work from a second perspective that is focused on what is interesting, surprising, or informative about the work. If a particular piece strikes him as significant, he jots a quick reflection on a post-it note and sets the piece aside for duplication and further notation. Remembering the advice of the panelist, he has endeavored to be strategically selective when choosing artifacts. By the end of October, it is clear to Larry that the planning, acting, and reflecting stages of the portfolio process are not easily delineated, but occur as recurring cycles of thought. For example, he is now collecting artifacts he originally had not thought of as being significant. In addition, he has been surprised to discover how his portfolio work has led to changes in his teaching behaviors. In the middle of a lesson, he frequently finds himself thinking about a recent portfolio reflection or artifact and then making a decision to change some aspect of his teaching.

Reflecting—In contrast to *working on* his portfolio, Larry periodically feels the need to simply sit and review the work that he has done. In some respects, he finds this challenging because he seems to inevitably begin planning for some new action he would like to take. However, as previously mentioned, he has become more comfortable with this phenomenon accepting it as a normal part of the portfolio process. What has been most satisfying about these review sessions is the personal pride he feels in seeing evidence of his own learning as well as the learning of his students.

Recently, Larry has been reflecting more and more on the portfolio process itself. Some of this thinking was stimulated by a question from a colleague who wanted to know why he was spending so much time on this "portfolio thing" when it was so much easier to earn professional development credits by sitting through a summer workshop. To him, the answer was clear. After sixteen years of attending workshops and taking graduate classes, he wanted to try something new, and the portfolio idea had personal appeal. He liked the idea that it was his project, that he was doing it his way, and on his time schedule. Beyond that, he knew that he was deepening the knowledge acquired in his graduate class on the models of teaching instead of letting that knowledge "fade away."

Other thoughts have been stimulated by a rumor that the district's teacher evaluation committee is considering teacher portfolios as a method of evaluating teachers' annual performance. On this issue, Larry has mixed feelings. One of the things Larry has enjoyed most about his learning portfolio is how it has encouraged him to reflect on his professional practice in a highly personal way. He wonders about how different the experience would have been if he had known someone was going to evaluate his performance based on a review of his portfolio. For now, he is content in his own experience and in the knowledge that the director of staff development believes he can be a valuable resource to other teachers in the district who have expressed interest in the learning portfolio model of teacher development. (See Table 12-7.)

TABLE 12-7 Five Steps to Beginning a Learning Portfolio Project

1. *Determine what instructional model(s) are of special concern or interest at this point in your career.*

2. *Reflect on the* Situational Self-Leadership *framework, and determine your level of skill development* with regard to the portfolio development process.

3. *If at Level 1, 2, or 3, seek the coaching support necessary to meet your portfolio skill development needs. If at Level 4, begin the portfolio planning process.*

4. *Work alone or with the support of a coach, and specify the focus or theme of your portfolio project.*

5. *Complete your portfolio plan by answering the design questions posed in Table 12-6.*

Ⓣeacher as Leader

> *The mediocre teacher tells. The good teacher explains. The superior teacher demonstrates. The great teacher inspires.*
>
> William Arthur Ward

The teacher's work in the American classroom is more complex than ever. Teachers must respond to the needs of a diverse and changing student clientele; an increasingly changing technology; a new set of demands for both excellence and equity from all segments of society; a clamor to shrink the achievement gap between the haves and have-nots and between students of color and white students; and an array of requests to meet the social, economic, health, and educational needs of students. The global economic marketplace raises the stakes even higher in its performance demands upon schools. The role of teacher-leader is a natural and necessary outgrowth of the increased demands for excellence being placed on schools. Addressing and overcoming the problems plaguing schools require a new and dynamic form of leadership—a leadership that can come only from this nation's teachers. Teachers of the future must assume leadership positions not only in the classroom but also within the school community. Such leadership will enable teachers to utilize a repertoire of instructional models, to coach and mentor professional colleagues, to inquire about and reflect upon the various aspects of the classroom culture, to develop curricular and instructional resources for youngsters, and to strengthen the relationship between the school and home.

Max DePree (1989), the former CEO of Herman Miller (one of the country's largest producers of office furniture), described the art of leadership as "liberating people to do what is required of them in the most effective and humane way possible" (p. xx). Thus, the leader is the "servant" of the followers (students and other teachers); the leader (in this instance, the teacher) removes those obstacles that prevent others (students) from doing their work. The true teacher (leader) enables students to realize their full potential.

Much of the current literature on leadership utilizes ecclesiastical terms to delineate the qualities and characteristics of effective leaders. The notion of liberating followers and becoming a "servant of the followers" has fascinating connotations. The meaning of "liberating followers" relates to the transition from a bureaucratic, authoritarian style of leadership found in most schools today, to a postindustrial model (collaboration, team-building, problem-solving, technology-orienting, and change-producing), with the goal of educating all youngsters no matter what their cultural affiliation or gender. "Servant-leaders" learn to lead by empowering others rather than by controlling others through their line authority. They do this by building a covenant, by basing what they do on cooperation and democratic leadership, and by ministering to the needs of others rather than exerting power over their followers (Bolin, 1989; Sergiovanni, 1989, 1991). A perfect case in point that exemplifies this concept of leadership has been ably demonstrated by the South African President, Nelson Mandela. In his party's presidential and parliamentary victory rally, he addressed those in attendance not as his followers but as fellow leaders to whom he listened and from whom he learned. Mandela asserted,

> I am your servant. I don't come to you as a leader, as one above others. We are a great team. Leaders come and go, but the organization and the collective leadership that has looked after the fortunes and reversals of this organization will always be there. And the ideas I express are not ideas invented in my own mind.

Mandela exemplifies key principles of leadership: trustworthiness, respect for the dignity of all human beings, service, faithfulness, consistency, and keeping promises—all qualities that teachers as leaders will need to practice in the twenty-first century if schools are to be the vital force that Americans want for transmitting necessary cultural knowledge to students.

Given this role description of "servant-leader," writers have begun describing the need for value-based leadership (O'Toole, 1995), moral leadership (Sergiovanni, 1992), the moral purpose of schooling (Fullan, 1993), and the moral imperatives of schools (Goodlad, 1990; Goodlad, Soder, and Sirotnik, 1990). Moral leadership connotes the use of values and value judgments in the selection, extension, and day-to-day practices of educational leaders. A moral leader is consistently cognizant of the central purpose of schooling. All curricular programs, instructional delivery systems, interactions with students and colleagues, and assessment policies and procedures are intricately related to the moral purpose of schools. Such educators view their task more as a mission than a job (Murphy, 1991), and "as a meaningful calling of the highest order" (Roberts, 1990, p. 134). Moral educators are grounded in a sensitivity "to racial issues and to the goal of equal educational opportunity" (Culbertson, 1988, p. 28), responsive to the disenfranchised and undereducated youngsters rather than molding them to the outdated goals of schools (Astuto, 1990; Clark, 1990; Greenfield, 1990); and these practices call for examining current organizational structures (tracking, Carnegie units, grade levels, and so on) in order to educate all children to guarantee their future success.

The major premise used by Fullan (1993) to explain the rationale for educational change and the critical role teachers must play revolves around the idea that "the moral purpose [of teachers] is to make a difference in the lives of students regardless of background, and to help produce citizens who can live and work productively in increasingly dynamic complex societies" (p. 4). What is new about this definition, besides the use of the term moral purpose, is that it places teachers precisely at the center of continuous school improvement and change. Teachers are charged with educating critical thinkers and problem-solvers, and in making a difference in the lives of students regardless of their students' cultural backgrounds. It is a "mission" and a "calling" that teachers must embark upon in order to help youngsters reach their full potential.

To embark upon such a mission, educators (as leaders) in this nation's classrooms must be clear about their own beliefs. They must think through their assumptions about human nature and how youngsters learn, about the potential of all youngsters to learn and grow in today's society, about the role of the school and its place in the development of society, and about the measures of performance needed by their students and by themselves as teachers.

The basic requirement for change is hope. Teachers must consistently encourage students to believe that it is possible to create a better society. When this occurs, schools will be in a better position to mobilize large numbers of previously passive and hopeless youngsters and to enable them to believe in themselves and to achieve their potential. Classroom cultures need to be designed so that positive, optimistic opportunities are discovered, explored, and created. Thomas Jefferson spoke eloquently about the value of equality of opportunity—the realization that all individuals have the right to achieve their personal potential; all people should have the opportunity to exercise some considerable control over their own destiny. The classroom culture must present youngsters with these same opportunities of choice; those choices are essential for a fulfilled life. Aristotle asserted long ago that all people could achieve happiness only if they fully explored all their abilities. To fully develop their abilities, our nation's students need to believe that better living conditions can be created and that there is a role for all citizens to play in the process of fostering equitable social participation. Teachers in classrooms across this country should begin a process of pedagogical entrepreneurship—choosing from alternative value positions, seeking alternative solutions, valuing and taking risks, being advocates for their students, and acting as the best hope for the children they serve. The models of teaching described in this text are part of that "choosing" process! By making that choice, teachers are opening doors for more students to learn and explore their own potential.

ⓣEACHERS FOR TOMORROW'S WORLD

This chapter has described images of the classroom teacher as *community builder*, *learner*, and *leader*. We believe that these three images are fundamental to developing teachers for the culturally diverse. In describing the role of teacher as community builder, we emphasized the need for teachers to create a classroom culture characterized by acceptance and inclusiveness. Specifically, we argued that it is important that teachers understand the cultural backgrounds of their students, be sensitive to the uniqueness that each student brings to the classroom, be knowledgeable about how students receive and process information, be committed to seek only the best from their students, and be instructionally responsive to the educational needs of youngsters. We believe that one of the more sound ways to accomplish these ideals is through the use of the instructional models presented in this text.

In discussing the role of teacher as learner, we argued that teachers must assume responsibility for planning and facilitating their own professional development. We described the role that *Situational Self-Leadership* theory can play in that process by helping teachers identify the specific forms of help they require to meet their personal and professional needs. Additionally, we described three diverse models of teacher learning that can support teachers in developing advanced understanding of the instructional models discussed throughout this text.

Finally, in issuing a call for teacher leadership, we articulated our belief that caring, committed, and knowledgeable teachers hold the keys to creating schools where all children can learn, and where all teachers are *committed*, and *know how*, to support the learning of culturally diverse students. Consistent with current trends in the professional development of teachers, we hope that teachers will increasingly find ways to share their wisdom of practice in a community of teachers committed to meeting the learning needs and dispositions of all students. Specifically, we hope that teacher leaders can foster the understanding of colleagues with regard to the instructional models described in the preceding chapters.

Each of the eight models has a different instructional purpose (that is, helping youngsters interact effectively, taking various informational items to create a new idea, or practicing problem-solving strategies using culturally relevant organizers); focuses upon specific learning skills for youngsters (that is, questioning/thinking levels, evaluating, retaining factual information, or working cooperatively with others); and plays to the natural learning dispositions of youngsters (that is, is relationship-oriented, uses oral discussion, emphasizes the tactile or auditory, or is interested in the tangible and concrete).

One of the more important aspects of acquiring a repertoire of instructional models discussed in this text deals with the appropriateness of their use. Put another way, to identify a specific instructional model to teach a lesson (that is, synectics vs. mnemonics vs. concept formation) is of little value unless the model chosen is appropriate in teaching the lesson objectives (the purposes of the lesson and what students are expected to achieve). Further, the instructional model chosen for the lesson must also correspond to the cognitive styles and developmental levels of the youngsters who will be taught that same lesson. The basic premise of this text has been that teachers must be able to draw from a number of instructional alternatives in order to facilitate a congruent relationship between the teaching approach, student cultural background, and student-learning disposition. The teacher for tomorrow's world must be a highly skilled practitioner able to make a myriad of instructional decisions each day in order to meet the needs of students. The teacher of tomorrow is not concerned with preparing workers for the economy, though that may be a by-product of pedagogical efforts. No, the teacher is preparing learners who know how to learn, to think, to explore, and to question ideas. Without such learners, democracy is in a grave situation.

Our responsibilities as educators are not only to help youngsters learn new wonders of the world, but also to help students develop the learning skills and intellectual abilities needed for this new society. We believe that Goodlad et al. (1990) put it so well when they identified what they label as the four moral imperatives of schooling for the future. The following imperatives are Goodlad's, but the descriptions represent our analysis of the implications of these imperatives for teachers working with diverse student populations.

1. *Teachers need to be able to facilitate critical enculturation.* The role of schools is to help youngsters understand and take part in this nation's system of government—a democracy. The school's role is to help students acquire the knowledge and skills associated with this country's history and government. This is important so that students can make informed decisions concerning this nation's initiatives and future direction. The simple explanation of this imperative boils down to cultural literacy. The school has an obligation to develop in all students an understanding of our cultural heritage from a multicultural perspective; an understanding of how this nation was formed and structured—its political system and processes; an understanding of the major political, social, technological, and scientific issues that we face; and an understanding of our individual responsibilities in participating in this democracy—keeping informed, communicating with others on the issues, and the ultimate participatory act in a democracy—voting.

2. *Teachers need to provide students with access to knowledge.* The school is the only societal institution charged with providing all youngsters with access to the basic structure of each academic discipline and the concomitant skills associated with each discipline. The teacher's role is a social justice responsibility: to ensure that all youngsters have equal access to this knowledge. All students have a right to be exposed to the structure of each academic discipline (Bruner, 1960) so that they understand the concepts, generalizations, and methodological processes of inquiry unique to that discipline. The school should expect that all students be well versed in these subject areas, whether algebra, biology, American government, or a foreign language. The responsibility of educators is to provide every opportunity and experience to all students no matter what their cultural, ethnic, or gender characteristics. These educational opportunities are a basic Jeffersonian right of all youngsters in this nation.

3. *Teachers need to create an effective teacher-student connection.* The responsibility of all teachers is to ensure that pedagogy goes beyond the mechanics of teaching to a process that transcends the mere recitation of dates, details, and descriptions. Teachers must combine the principles of growth and development, alternative instructional models, disciplinary knowledge, and sensitivity to the social and political barriers that prevent learning. The teacher of the twenty-first century will need to develop partnerships with parents and community agencies in order to address the needs of students. Because many of the students in our schools today suffer a myriad of "diseases" (for example, physical and sexual abuse, neglect, substance abuse,

inconsistent value structures, and unstable home environments), the teacher and school need to take to heart the old African proverb, "It takes a whole village to raise a child." Every effort needs to be expended in developing collaborative cultures within the school and within the community.

4. *Teachers need to practice good stewardship.* If schools are to become learning organizations—institutions striving to grow and develop, seeking to help youngsters solve their dilemmas, and designing programs that better serve their communities—then they must be in the business of continual staff renewal. The responsibility of teachers is to continually seek the path of self- and organizational development during their careers. Career renewal must be of paramount concern for individual teachers and the educational organization. As teachers remain in the profession, they move through career stages. These stages serve as developmental passages because they have implications for addressing individual teacher needs and objectives. The responsibility for schools is to develop a learning environment that accommodates individual teacher renewal and, in the process, renews its own organizational culture.

The teacher for tomorrow's world will need to embody and exemplify the qualities and characteristics inherent in these moral imperatives. Each of these moral imperatives has clear implications concerning the responsibilities of teachers as educators and members of the educational profession. The question left for us is how we plan to implement these goals in a consistent fashion for all youngsters.

If schools continue to disregard the gifts, talents, and presence of culturally diverse youngsters, schools will be dangerously close to jeopardizing America's future and tomorrow's world. That future will belong only to those individuals who can function in an increasingly high-tech, internationally competitive world. The youngsters of today will be successful in tomorrow's world only if they acquire the necessary knowledge and skills from the different disciplines, exhibit and practice a willingness to continue to learn, practice problem-solving/critical-thinking skills, are willing to innovate and look for new ways of doing business, participate in cooperative, team-oriented activities, utilize various forms of technology, and respond quickly to the needs and desires of customers.

Society in general and schools in particular must create a dialogue and a sense of urgency in addressing the following questions concerning youngsters—our national treasures:

- What are the dreams of this nation with regard to its children?
- How will this nation prepare all of its youth to be full partners in these dreams?

Only those individuals who either cling to the past or have not had the opportunity to realize the possibility of their "futures" will be left behind. Regrettably, that includes far too many Americans at the present time—the large percentage of high school dropouts suggests the potential magnitude of that group. Those educators who cling to the "old ways" of teaching will limit the learning capacity of students. True, some students will thrive. Equally true, many others will disengage. Educators have a moral calling and responsibility—a mission and sense of purpose—to preserve this nation's treasures—its children—in a safe, opportunity-enhancing, and productive educational environment. This environment must be a place where all youngsters have the opportunity to realize their dreams for tomorrow's world, and part of the process of realizing that dream is to be in classrooms where teachers know what to teach and understand different ways to teach it!

ⓇEFERENCES

Appleton, N. 1983. *Cultural Pluralism in Education: Theoretical Foundations*. New York: Longman.

Astuto, T. 1990. *Reinventing School Leadership*. Working memo prepared for the Reinventing School Leadership Conference. Cambridge, MA: National Center for Educational Leadership.

Au, K., and A. Kawakami. 1985. "Research Currents: Talk Story and Learning to Read." *Language Arts 2*(4): 406–411.

Bishop, M. 1986. "Update." *Sports Illustrated 10*(February): 204–206.

Blanchard, K. 1993. *Personal Excellence: Where Achievement and Fulfillment Meet* [audiocassettes]. Chicago: Nightingale-Conant. Side 7.

Bolin, E. S. 1989. "Empowering Leadership." *Teachers College Record 91*(1): 81–96.

Borich, G. D. 1999. *Observation Skills for Effective Teaching*. Upper Saddle River, NJ: Prentice-Hall.

Botstein, L. 1997. *Jefferson's Children: Education and the Promise of American Culture*. New York: Doubleday.

Bradley, C. 1984. "Issues in Mathematics Education for Native Americans and Directions for Research." *Journal for Research in Mathematics Education 15*(2): 96–106.

Bruner, J. S. 1960. *The Process of Education*. Cambridge, MA: Harvard University Press.

Bullock, A. A., and P. Hawk. 2001. *Developing a Teaching Portfolio: A Guide for Preservice and Practicing Teachers*. Upper Saddle River, NJ: Prentice-Hall.

Byers, F., and H. Byers. 1972. "Nonverbal Communication and the Education of Children." Pp. 3–31 in C. B. Cazden, V. P. John, and D. Hymes (eds.), *Functions of Language in the Classroom*. New York: Teacher's College Press.

Cabezas, A. 1981. *Early Childhood Development in Asian and Pacific American Families: Families in Transition*. San Francisco: Asian.

Campbell, D., P. B. Cignetti, B. Melenyzer, D. H. Nettles, and R. Wyman, Jr. 1997. *How to Develop a Professional Portfolio: A Manual for Teachers*. Boston: Allyn & Bacon.

Clark, D. 1990. *Reinventing School Leadership*. Working memo prepared for the Reinventing School Leadership Conference. Cambridge, MA: National Center for Educational Leadership.

Cochran-Smith and S. Lytle. 1999. "Relationships of Knowledge and Practice: Teacher Learning in Communities." In A. I. Nejad & P. D. Pearson (eds.), *Review of Research in Education*. Washington, DC: American Educational Research Association 24: 249–305.

Conrath, J. 2001. "Changing the Odds for Young People: Next Steps for Alternative Education." *Phi Delta Kappan 82*(8): 585–587.

Cooper, G. C. 1987. "Right Hemispheric Dominance, Holistic Cognitive Style, and Black Language." In *Benjamin E. Mays Monograph Series I (I)* 61–86. Indiana University of Pennsylvania.

Cooper, L., D. Johnson, R. Johnson, and E. Wilderson. 1980. "Effects of Cooperative, Competitive, and Individualistic Experiences on Interpersonal Attraction Among Heterogeneous Peers." *Journal of Social Psychology 111*(2): 243–252.

Cuban, L. 2001. "How Systemic Reform Harms Urban Schools: And What We Can Do About It." *Education Week XX*(38).

———. 1989. "The 'At-Risk' Label and the Problem of Urban School Reform." *Phi Delta Kappan 70*(10): 781–785.

Culbertson, J. 1988. *Tomorrow's Challenges to Today's Professors of Educational Administration*. 1988 Walter Hoching lecture presented to the National Council of Professors of Educational Administration, Kalamazoo, MI.

Damico, S. B. 1983. *The Two Worlds of School: Differences in the Photographs of Black and White Adolescents*. Paper presented at annual meeting of American Educational Research Association, Montreal.

DePree, M. 1989. *Leadership Is an Art.* New York: Doubleday.

Dewey, J. 1933. *How We Think.* Chicago: Henry Regnery.

Dietz, M. 1995. "Using Portfolios as a Framework for Professional Development." *Journal of Staff Development* 16: 40–43.

Dunn, R., and S. A. Griggs. 1988. *Learning Styles: Quiet Revolution in American Schools.* Reston, VA: National Association of Secondary School Principals.

Foster, M. 1994. "Effective Black Teachers: A Literature Review." Pp. 225–242 in E. R. Hollins, J. E. King, and W. C. Hayman, (eds.), *Teaching Diverse Populations: Formulating a Knowledge Base.* Albany: State University of New York Press.

Freire, P. 1970. *Pedagogy of the Oppressed.* New York: Continuum.

Fullan, M. 1993. *Change Forces: Probing the Depth of Educational Reform.* London: Falmer Press.

Garcia, E. 1991. "Effective Instruction for Language Minority Students: The Teacher." *Journal of Education* 173(2): 130–141.

Gilbert, S., and G. Gay. 1985. "Improving the Success in School of Poor Black Children." *Phi Delta Kappan* 67(2): 133–137.

Giroux, H. A. 1983. *Theory and Resistance in Education: A Pedagogy for the Opposition.* South Hadley: Bergin and Garvey.

Glickman, C. D. 1990. *Supervision of Instruction: A Developmental Approach* (2nd ed.). Boston: Allyn & Bacon.

Good, T. L., and J. E. Brophy. 1997. *Looking into Classrooms* (7th ed.). New York: Longman.

Goodlad, J. 1990. "Studying the Education of Educators: From Conception to Findings." *Phi Delta Kappan* 71(9): 698–701.

Goodlad, J., R. Soder, and K. A. Sirotnik. (eds.). 1990. *The Moral Dimensions of Teaching.* San Francisco: Jossey-Bass.

Greenfield, W. 1990. *Reinventing School Leadership.* Working memo prepared for the Reinventing School Leadership Conference. Cambridge, MA: National Center for Educational Leadership.

Grundy, S., and S. Kemmis. 1981. *Educational Action Research in Australia: The State of the Art.* Paper presented at the Annual Meeting of the Australian Association for Research in Education, Adelaide as cited in Grundy, S. 1988. Three Modes of Action Research in S. Kemmis, and R. McTaggert (eds.). 1988. *The Action Research Reader* (3rd ed.). Geelong: Deakin University Press.

Guiney, E. 2001. "Coaching Isn't Just for Athletes: The Role of Teacher Leaders." *Phi Delta Kappan* 82(10): 740–743.

Haberman, M. 1995. *Star Teachers of Children in Poverty.* West Lafayette, IN: Kappa Delta Pi.

Hale-Benson, J. 1986. *Black Children: Their Roots, Culture, and Learning Styles* (rev. ed.). Baltimore: Johns Hopkins University Press.

Hansell, S., and R. E. Slavin. 1981. "Cooperative Learning and the Structure of Interracial Friendships." *Sociology of Education* 54: 98–106.

Heath, S.B. 1983. *Ways with Words: Language, Life, and Work in Communities and Classrooms.* Cambridge: Cambridge University Press.

Henry, A. 1990. *Black Women, Black Pedagogies: An African-Canadian Context.* Paper presented at the annual meeting of the American Educational Research Association, Boston.

Herndon, J. 1968. *The Way It Spozed to Be.* New York: Simon & Schuster.

Hersey, P., and K. H. Blanchard. 1974. "So You Want to Know Your Leadership Style?" *Training and Development Journal* 28(2): 1–15.

Hersey, P., and K. H. Blanchard. 1988. *Management of Organizational Behavior* (5th ed.). Englewood Cliffs, NJ: Prentice-Hall.

Holt, J. 1967. *How Children Fail.* New York: Pitman.

Hubbard, R. S., and B. M. Power. 1999. *Living the Questions: A Guide for Teacher-Researchers.* York, MA: Stenhouse.

———. 1993. *The Art of Classroom Inquiry: A Handbook for Teacher-Researchers.* Portsmouth, NH: Heinemann.

Jetter, A. 1993. "Mississippi Learning." *New York Times Magazine* 6(February 21): 28–72.

Johnson, D. W., and R. T. Johnson. 1981. "Effects of Cooperative and Individualistic Learning Experiences on Interethnic Interaction." *Journal of Educational Psychology* 73(3): 444–449.

Joyce, B., C. Murphy, B. Showers, and J. Murphy. 1989. "School Renewal as Cultural Change." *Educational Leadership* 47(3): 70–78.

Kagan, S., G. L. Zahn, K. E. Widaman, J. Schwarzwald, and G. Tyrell. 1985. "Classroom

Structural Bias: Impact of Cooperative and Competitive Classroom Structures on Cooperative and Competitive Individuals and Groups." Pp. 277–312 in R. E. Slavin, S. Sharan, S. Kagan, R. Hertz-Lazarowitz, C. Webb, and R. Schmuck (eds.), *Learning to Cooperate, Cooperating to Learn*. New York: Plenum.

Kemmis, S., and R. McTaggart (Eds.). 1988. *The Action Research Planner* (3rd edition). Victoria, Australia: Deakin University.

Kohl, H. 1967. *36 Children*. New York: New American Library.

Kozol, J. 1967. *Death at an Early Age: The Destruction of the Hearts and Minds of Negro Children in the Boston Public Schools*. Boston: Houghton Mifflin.

Ladson-Billings, G. 1990. "Like 'Lightning' in a Bottle: Attempting to Capture the Pedagogical Excellence of Successful Teachers of Black Students." *International Journal of Qualitative Studies in Education* 3(4): 335–344.

———. 1991. "Returning to the Source: Implications for Educating Teachers of Black Students." Pp. 227–244 in M. Foster, (ed.), *Readings on Equal Education. Volume II: Qualitative Investigations into Schools and Schooling*. New York: AMS Press.

———. 1994. *The Dreamkeepers*. San Francisco: Jossey-Bass.

Lieberman, A. 1995. "Practices that Support Teacher Development: Transforming Conceptions of Personal Learning." *Phi Delta Kappan* 76: 591–596.

Loucks-Horsley, S., C. K. Harding, M. A. Arbuckle, L. B. Murray, C. Dubea, and M. K. Williams. 1987. *Continuing to Learn*. Andover, MA: Regional Laboratory for Educational Improvement of the Northeast and Islands.

Ma, L. 1999. *Knowing and Teaching Elementary Mathematics: Teachers' Understanding of Fundamental Mathematics in China and the United States*. Mahwah, NJ: Lawrence Erlbaum.

Maslow, A. H. 1954. *Motivation and Personality*. New York: Harper and Brothers.

Masters, J. 1995. "The History of Action Research." In I. Hughes (ed.), *Action Research Electronic Reader*. The University of Sydney, online http://www.behs.cchs.usyd.edu.au/arow/Reader/rmasters.htm (download date 05.23.2001).

McCutcheon, G., and B. Jung. 1990. "Alternative Perspectives on Action Research." *Theory into Practice* 24(3).

McDiarmid, G. 1990. *What to Do About Differences? A Study of Multicultural Education for Teacher Trainees in the Los Angeles Unified School District*. Research Report 90–11. East Lansing, MI: National Center for Research on Teacher Education, Michigan State University.

More, A. J. 1990. *Learning Styles of Native Americans and Asians*. Paper presented at the annual meeting of the American Psychological Association, Boston. ERIC Document Reproduction Service No. ED 330 535.

Murphy, J. 1991. *Restructuring Schools: Capturing and Assessing the Phenomena*. New York: Teacher's College Press.

Myers, I. B., and M. McCaulley. 1985. *Manual: A Guide to the Development and Use of the Myers-Briggs Type Indicator*. Palo Alto, CA: Consulting Psychologists Press.

O'Malley, J., and A. Chamot. 1990. *Learning Strategies in Second Language Acquisition*. Cambridge: Cambridge University Press.

Osborne, B., and B. Bamford. 1987. *Torres Strait Islanders Teaching Torres Strait Islanders*. North Queensland, Townsville: Department of Pedagogics and Scientific Studies in Education, James Cook University.

O'Toole, J. 1995. *Leading Change: Overcoming the Ideology of Comfort and the Tyranny of Custom*. San Francisco: Jossey-Bass.

Oxford, R. 1990. The Strategy Inventory for Language Learning (SILL). *Appendix to Language Learning Strategies: What Every Teacher Should Know*. New York: Newbury House/Harper & Row.

Pang, V. 1990. "Asian-American Children: A Diverse Population." *Educational Forum* 55(1): 49–66.

———. 1995. "Asian Pacific American Students: A Diverse and Complex Population." Pp. 412–424 in J. Banks, and C. Banks (eds.), *Handbook of Research on Multicultural Education*. New York: Macmillan.

Peters, K. H., and J. K. March. 1999. *Collaborative Observation: Putting Classroom Instruction at the Center of School Reform*. Thousand Oaks, CA: Corwin Press.

Philips, S. 1972. "Participant Structures and Communicative Competence: Warm Springs Children in Community and Classroom." Pp. 370–394 in C. Cazden, V. John, and D. Hymes (eds.), *Functions of Language in the Classroom*. New York: Teacher's College Press.

———. 1983. *The Invisible Culture: Communication in Classroom and Community on the Warm Springs Indian Reservation.* New York: Longman.

———. 1993. *The Invisible Culture: Communication in Classroom and Community on the Warm Springs Indian Reservation.* Prospect Heights, IL: Waveland Press.

Postman, N., and C. Weingartner. 1969. *Teaching as a Subversive Activity.* New York: Delacorte.

Ramirez, M., III. 1982. *Cognitive Styles and Cultural Diversity.* Paper presented at the annual meeting of the American Educational Research Association, New York City.

———. 1989. "A Bicognitive-Multicultural Model for a Pluralistic Education." *Early Child Development and Care* 51: 129–136.

Ramirez, M., III, and A. Castaneda. 1974. *Cultural Democracy, Bicognitive Development, and Education.* New York: Academic Press.

Rapoport, R. N. 1970. "Three Dilemmas in Action Research." *Human Relations* 23(6), 499 as cited in J. McKernan. 1991. *Curriculum Action Research. A Handbook of Methods and Resources for the Reflective Practitioner.* London: Kogan Page.

Roberts, L. 1990. *Reinventing School Leadership.* Working memo prepared for the Reinventing School Leadership Conference. Cambridge, MA: National Center for Educational Leadership.

Rohner, R. 1965. "Factors Influencing the Academic Performance of Kwakiutl Children in Canada." *Comparative Education Review* 9: 331–340.

Schön, D. A. 1987. *Educating the Reflective Practitioner.* San Francisco: Jossey-Bass.

Sergiovanni, T. J. 1989. *Schooling for Tomorrow: Directing Reforms to Issues That Count.* Boston: Allyn & Bacon.

———. 1991. *The Principalship: A Reflective Practice Perspective.* Boston: Allyn & Bacon.

———. 1992. *Moral Leadership: Getting to the Heart of School Improvement.* San Francisco: Jossey-Bass.

Shade, B. J. 1994. "Understanding the African American Learner." Pp. 175–189 in E. Hollins, J. King, and W. Hayman (eds.), *Teaching Diverse Populations: Formulating a Knowledge Base.* Albany: State University of New York Press.

Shade, B. J., and P. A. Edwards. 1987. "Ecological Correlates of the Educative Style of Afro-American Children." *Journal of Negro Education* 86: 88–99.

Slavin, R. E. 1977. *Student Team Learning Techniques: Narrowing the Achievement Gap Between the Races.* Report No. 228. Baltimore: Johns Hopkins University, Center for the Study of Social Organization of Schools.

———. 1979. "Effects of Biracial Learning Teams on Cross-Racial Friendships." *Journal of Educational Psychology* 71(3): 381–387.

———. 1987a. *Cooperative Learning: Student Teams* (2nd ed.). Washington, DC: National Education Association.

———. 1987b. "Cooperative Learning: Where Behavioral and Humanistic Approaches to Classroom Motivation Meet." *Elementary School Journal* 88(l): 29–38.

———. 1995. "Cooperative Learning and Intergroup Relations." Pp. 628–634 in J. A. Banks, and C. A. M. Banks (eds.), *Handbook of Research on Multicultural Education.* New York: Macmillan.

Slavin, R. E., and E. Oickle. 1981. "Effects of Cooperative Learning Teams on Student Achievement and Race Relations: Treatment by Race Interactions." *Sociology of Education* 54: 174–180.

Soldier, L. 1989. "Cooperative Learning and the Native American Student." *Phi Delta Kappan* 71(2): 161–163.

Sparks, D., and S. L. Horsley. 1989. "Five Models of Staff Development for Teachers." *Journal of Staff Development* 10(4): 40–57.

Treisman, V. 1985. *A Study of the Mathematics Performance of Black Students at the University of California at Berkeley.* Unpublished doctoral dissertation, University of California, Berkeley.

Vasquez, J. A. 1991. "Cognitive Styles and Academic Attainment." Pp. 163–179 in J. Lynch, C. Modgil, and S. Modgil (eds.), *Cultural Diversity and the Schools: Consensus and Controversy.* London: Falconer Press.

Viadero, D. 2001. "Getting Serious About High School." *Education Week* XX(30): 1, 18, 20, 22.

Vygotsky, L. S. 1978. *Mind in Society: The Development of Higher Psychological Expectations.* Cambridge, MA: Harvard University Press.

Weigel, R. H., P. L. Wiser, and S. W. Cook. 1975. "Impact of Cooperative Learning

Experiences on Cross-Ethnic Relations and Attitudes." *Journal of Social Issues* 31(1): 219–245.

Weinstein, C. E., A. C. Schulte, and E. C. Cascallar. 1983. *The Learning and Study Strategies Inventory (LASSI): Initial Design and Development.* Manuscript, University of Texas, Austin.

Wenden, A., and J. Rubin. 1987. *Learner Strategies in Language Learning.* Englewood Cliffs, NJ: Prentice-Hall.

Wilson & Berne. 1999. "Teacher Learning and the Acquisition of Professional Knowledge: An Examination of Research on Contemporary Professional Development." In A. I. Nejad &

P. D. Pearson (eds.), *Review of Research in Education.* Washington, DC: American Educational Research Association. 24: 173–209.

Wolf, K. 1991. "The Schoolteacher's Portfolio: Issues in Design, Implementation, and Evaluation." *Phi Delta Kappan* 73: 129–136.

Wolf, K., and M. Dietz. 1998, Winter. "Teaching Portfolios: Purposes and Possibilities." *Teacher Education Quarterly*: 9–21.

Wolf, P., and P. Robbins. 1989. *Opening Doors: An Introduction to Peer Coaching* [videocassette]. Alexandria, VA: Association for Supervision and Curriculum Development.

APPENDIX

Learning Style Annotated Bibliography

Ⓛ EARNING STYLE WEB SITES

http://www.learningstyles.net/
> Definitely the place to begin . . . the site for The Center for the Study of Learning and Teaching Styles at St. John's University

http://www.learningstyle.com/
> A nice site to take the Dunn, Dunn, and Price Learning Style Inventory

http://snow.utoronto.ca/Learn2/mod3/tchstyle.html
> A nice site to take the Dunn and Dunn Teaching Style Inventory

http://www-isu.indstate.edu/ctl/styles/model2.html
> Good overview of different learning style models

http://www.Bergen.org/ETTC/courses/LearningStyles/MBTI.html
> Excellent introduction to the Myers-Briggs Personality Indicator

http://www.advisorteam.com/user/ktsintro.asp
> A good site to take the Keirsey Temperment Sorter II

http://www.snow.utoronto.ca/Learn2/mod3/tsinventory.html
> A good site to take the Sternberg/Wagner Thinking Styles Inventory

http://snow.utoronto.ca/Learn2/llreadings/debello.htm
> A review of 11 major learning style models is provided at this site

GENERAL

Learning Style Inventory by Rita Dunn, Kenneth Dunn, and Gary Price, Price Systems, Box 3271, Lawrence, KS 66044, 1978, 1981.

> A self-report, 100-item questionnaire designed to assess how students in Grades 3–12 prefer to learn. The variables that are covered are: immediate environment, emotionality, sociological needs, and physical needs.

Learning Style Inventory: Primary Version by Janet Perrin, St. John's University, Jamaica, NY 11439, 1981.

> Based upon the Dunn, Dunn, and Price instrument, this version can be used with K–2 youngsters. The questionnaire consists of pictures and questions that determine style in four areas: environment, emotional tendencies, sociological needs, and physical requirements. The questionnaire is administered individually and takes approximately 20 minutes to complete.

COGNITIVE

Gregoric Style Delineator by Anthony Gregoric, Doubleday Road, Columbia, CT 06237, 1979.

> A self-report instrument that analyzes an individual's concrete vs. abstract and random vs. sequential styles. It takes approximately 5 minutes to administer and consists of 40 words in 10 sets of 4 each. The student rank orders each set through forced-choice options.

"Cognitive Profiles" by Charles A. Letteri in C. A. Letteri, *Cognitive Profile: Basic Determinant of Academic Achievement.* Burlington, VT: Center for Cognitive Studies, 1980.

> This instrument takes seven tests of cognitive style—field independence/dependence, scanning/focusing, breadth of categorization, cognitive complexity/simplicity, reflectiveness/impulsiveness, leveling/sharpening, and tolerant/intolerant—that in combination predict student achievement level.

AFFECTIVE

"Paragraph Completion Method" by David E. Hunt in *Assessing Conceptual Level by the Paragraph Method* by D. E. Hunt et al., Toronto: Ontario Institute for Studies in Education, 1978.

> This assessment methodology measures learning styles at different conceptual levels and describes students in terms of their requirements for structure in an educational environment. It describes students in terms of their stage of development from unsocialized to dependent to independent. Grades 6–12.

SRI Student Perceiver Interview by Donald Clifton, Selection Research, Inc., 2546 South 48th Street, Lincoln, NE 68506.

> This interview process is used to assess affective styles from age 8 through adulthood. The process uses an 80-question, structured, low-stress interview as a way to identify unique characteristics of individual students. Can be administered in 30 minutes and offers information concerning the talents and interests of students.

Cognitive/Affective

Myers-Briggs Type Indicator by Isabel Briggs Myers and Katherine Briggs, Consulting Psychologists Press Inc., 577 College Avenue, Palo Alto, CA 94306, 1980.

> This instrument measures personality dispositions based upon Jung's personality types. Used for individuals from adolescence through adulthood. Categorizes individuals into 16 personality types. It provides information about the ways students prefer to perceive meaning, to express values, and to interact with the world.

"Multiple Intelligences Checklist" by Thomas Armstrong in T. Armstrong, *Multiple Intelligences in the Classroom.* Alexandria, VA: Association for Supervision and Curriculum Development, 1994.

> Provides a checklist based on Gardner's seven intelligences—linguistic, logical-mathematical, spatial, bodily-kinesthetic, musical, interpersonal, and intrapersonal—that teachers can use in conjunction with other assessment information. Each intelligence area on the checklist has a list of statements by which a teacher can assess students on their abilities based upon observations and interactions.

Bibliography

Aldrich, H. E. 1979. *Organizations and Environment.* Englewood Cliffs, NJ: Prentice Hall.

Anderson, J. A. 1988. "Cognitive Styles and Multicultural Populations." *Journal of Teacher Education* 39: 2–9.

Anderson, L. M., C. M. Evertson, and J. E. Brophy. 1979. "An Experimental Study of Effective Teaching in First Grade Reading Groups." *Elementary School Journal* 79: 193–223.

Anderson, L. W., and D. R. Krathwohl. 2001. *A Taxonomy for Learning, Teaching, and Assessing.* New York: Longman.

Appleton, N. 1983. *Cultural Pluralism in Education: Theoretical Foundations.* New York: Longman.

Arends, R. 1994. *Learning to Teach.* Boston: McGraw Hill.

Aronson, E., N. Blaney, C. Stephan, J. Sikes, and M. Snapp. 1978. *The Jigsaw Classroom.* Beverly Hills, CA: Sage.

Association for Supervision and Curriculum Development. 1990. *Cooperative Learning Series: Facilitator's Manual.* Alexandria, VA: Association for Supervision and Curriculum Development.

Astuto, T. 1990. *Reinventing School Leadership.* Working memo prepared for the Reinventing School Leadership Conference. Cambridge, MA: National Center for Educational Leadership.

Au, K., and A. Kawakami. 1985. "Research Currents: Talk Story and Learning to Read." *Language Arts* 62(4): 406–411.

Ausubel, D. P. 1960. "The Use of Advance Organizers in the Learning and Retention of Meaningful Verbal Material." *Journal of Educational Psychology* 17(3): 400–404.

Bailey, S. M. 1996. "Shortchanging Girls and Boys." *Educational Leadership* 53(8): 75–79.

Baker, Miller, J. 1986. *Toward a New Psychology of Women* (2nd ed.). Boston: Beacon.

Barker, J. A. 1992. *Future Edge: Discovering the New Paradigms of Success.* New York: William Morrow.

Baxter Magolda, M. B. 1989. "Gender Differences in Cognitive Development: An Analysis of Cognitive Complexity and Learning Styles." *Journal of College Student Development 30*(3): 213–220.

Becker, W. C. 1977. "Teaching Reading and Language to the Disadvantaged— What We Have Learned from Field Research." *Harvard Educational Review* 47: 518–543.

Belenky, M. F., B. M. Clinchy, M. R. Goldberger, and J. M. Tarule. 1986. *Women's Ways of Knowing: the Development of Self, Voice, and Mind.* New York: Basic Books.

Benjamin, D. P., S. Chambers, and G. Reiterman. 1993. "A Focus on American Indian College Persistence." *Journal of American Indian Education* 32(2): 24–40.

Bennett, C. I. 1995. *Comprehensive Multicultural Education: Theory and Practice* (3rd ed.). Boston: Allyn & Bacon.

Bereiter, C., and S. Engelmann. 1966. *Teaching Disadvantaged Children in the Preschool.* Englewood Cliffs, NJ: Prentice-Hall.

Bert, C. R. G., and M. Bert. 1992. *The Native American: An Exceptionality in Education and Counseling.* ERIC Document Reproduction Service No. ED 351 168.

Bibens, R. F. 1980. "Using Inquiry Effectively." *Theory Into Practice* 19(2): 87–92.

Bishop, M. 1986. "Update." *Sports Illustrated* 10(February): 204–206.

Blair, J. 2000. "Study Links Effective Teaching Methods and Test Score Gains." *Education Week.* October 25, 2000. pp. 24–25.

Blanchard, K. 1993. *Personal Excellence: Where Achievement and Fulfillment Meet* [audiocassettes]. Chicago: Nightingale-Conant. Side 7.

Bligh, D. A. 2000. *What's the Use of Lecture?* San Francisco: Jossey-Bass.

Bloom, B., M. Englehart, E. Furst, W. Hill, and D. Krathwohl. 1956. *Taxonomy of Educational Objectives: The Classification of Educational Goals, Handbook I: Cognitive Domain.* New York: McKay.

Bolin, E. S. 1989. "Empowering Leadership." *Teachers College Record* 91(1): 81–96.

Borich, G. D. 1988. *Effective Teaching Methods.* Columbus, OH: Merrill.

———. 1999. *Observation Skills for Effective Teaching.* Upper Saddle River, NJ: Prentice-Hall.

Borko, H., C. Brown, R. Underhill, M. Eisenhart, P. Jones, and P. Agard. 1990. *Learning to Teach Mathematics for Understanding.* College Park: University of Maryland.

Bornstein, A. 1983. *Bornstein School of Memory Training.* Los Angeles: Bornstein School of Memory Training.

Botstein, L. 1997. *Jefferson's Children: Education and the Promise of American Culture.* New York: Doubleday.

Boykin, A. W. 1994. "Harvesting Culture and Talent: African-American Children." Pp. 324–371 in J. Spencer (ed.), *Achievement and Achievement Motives.* Boston: W. H. Freeman.

Bradley, C. 1984. "Issues in Mathematics Education for Native Americans and Directions for Research." *Journal for Research in Mathematics Education* 15(2): 96–106.

Branson, R. K. 1988. "Why Schools Can't Improve: The Upper Limit Hypothesis." *Journal of Instructional Development* 10(4): 15–26.

Brewer, A. 1977. "An Indian Education." *Integrated Education* 15: 21–23.

Brookfield, S. D., and S. Preskill. 1999. *Discussion as a Way of Teaching.* San Francisco: Jossey Bass.

Brooks, J. G., and M. G. Brooks. 1993. *The Case for Constructivist Classrooms.* Washington, DC: Association for Supervision and Curriculum Development.

Brooks, M. G., and J. G. Brooks. 1999. "The Courage to be Constructivist." *Educational Leadership* 57(3): 18–24.

Brophy, J. 1982. "Successful Teaching Strategies for the Inner-City Child." *Phi Delta Kappan* 63: 527–530.

———. 1983. "Research on the Self-Fulfilling Prophecy and Teacher Expectation." *Journal of Educational Psychology* 75:631–661.

Brown, R. 1973. "Taba Rediscovered." *Science Teacher* 40(8): 30–33.

Browsher, J. E. 1993. *Why and How to Restructure Education Systems.* Paper presented at the meeting of the Association for Supervision and Curriculum Development, Washington, DC (March).

Bruner, J. S. 1960. *The Process of Education.* Cambridge, MA: Harvard University Press.

Bruner, J. S., J. J. Goodnow, and G. A. Austin. 1967. *A Study of Thinking.* New York: Science Editions.

————. 1990. *A Study of Thinking.* New Brunswick, NJ: Transaction.

Bryant, H. W. 1986. *An Investigation into the Effectiveness of Two Strategy Training Approaches on the Reading Achievement of Grade One Native Indian Children.* Unpublished doctoral dissertation. Vancouver: University of British Columbia.

Bullock, A. A., and P. Hawk. 2001. *Developing a Teaching Portfolio: A Guide for Preservice and Practicing Teachers.* Upper Saddle River, NJ: Prentice-Hall.

Burns, M. 1981. "Groups of Four: Solving the Management Problems." *Learning* 22(2): 46–51.

Byers, F., and H. Byers. 1972. "Nonverbal Communication and the Education of Children." Pp. 3–31 in C. B. Cazden, V. P. John, and D. Hymes (eds.), *Functions of Language in the Classroom.* New York: Teachers' College Press.

Cabezas, A. 1981. *Early Childhood Development in Asian and Pacific American Families: Families in Transition.* San Francisco: Asian.

Caine, R. N., and G. Caine. 1995. "Reinventing Schools Through Brain-Based Learning." *Educational Leadership* 52(7): 43–47.

Cajete, G. 1994. *Look to the Mountain: An Ecology of Indigenous Education.* Durango, CO: Kivaki Press.

Campbell, D., P. B. Cignetti, B. Melenyzer, D. H. Nettles, and R. Wyman, Jr. 1997. *How to Develop a Professional Portfolio: A Manual for Teachers.* Boston: Allyn & Bacon.

Canady, R. L., and M. D. Rettig. 1995. "The Power of Innovative Scheduling." *Educational Leadership* 54(3): 4–10.

Carnevale, A. P., and R. A. Fry. 2000. *Crossing the Great Divide: Can We Achieve Equity When Generation Y Goes to College?* Princeton, NJ: Educational Testing Service.

Carney, R. N., M. E. Levin, and J. R. Levin. 1993. "Mnemonic Strategies: Instructional Techniques Worth Remembering." *Teaching Exceptional Children* 25(4): 24–30.

Carter, K. 1990. "Teachers' Knowledge and Learning to Teach." Pp. 291–310 in W. R. Houston (ed.), *Handbook of Research on Teacher Education*. New York: Macmillan.

Center for Educational Policy. 2001: *It Takes More Than Testing: Closing the Achievement Gap*. Washington, DC: Center for Educational Policy.

Center on Educational Policy and American Youth Policy Forum. 2000. *Do You Know the Good News About American Education?* Washington, DC: Center on Educational Policy.

Chall, J. S. 2000. *The Academic Achievement Challenge*. New York: Guilford Press.

Chineworth, M. A. (ed.). 1996. *Rise 'N' Shine: Catholic Education and the African-American Community*. Washington, DC: National Catholic Educational Association.

Clark, D. 1990. *Reinventing School Leadership*. Working memo prepared for the Reinventing School Leadership Conference. Cambridge, MA: National Center for Educational Leadership.

Clayton, J. B. 1996. *Your Land, My Land: Children in the Process of Acculturation*. Portsmouth, NH: Heinemann.

Cohen, E. 1986. *Designing Groupwork: Strategies for the Heterogeneous Classroom*. New York: Teachers' College Press.

———. 1994. *Designing Groupwork: Strategies for the Heterogeneous Classroom* (2nd ed.). New York: Teachers' College Press.

———. 1994. *Status Treatment for the Classroom*. Videotape and manual. New York: Teachers' College Press.

Cohen, R. A. 1969. "Conceptual Styles, Culture Conflict, and Nonverbal Tests of Intelligence." *American Anthropologist* 71: 838–856.

Conrath, J. 2001. "Changing the Odds for Young People: Next Steps for Alternative Education." *Phi Delta Kappan* 82(8): 585–587.

Cooper, G. C. 1987. "Right Hemispheric Dominance, Holistic Cognitive Style, and Black Language." Pp. 61–86 in J. A. Anderson (ed.), *Benjamin E. Mays Monograph Series* 1(1).

Cooper, L., D. Johnson, R. Johnson, and F. Wilderson. 1980. "Effects of Cooperative, Competitive, and Individualistic Experiences of Interpersonal Attraction Among Heterogeneous Peers." *Journal of Social Psychology* 111(2): 243–252.

Cordova, F. 1983. *Filipinos: Forgotten Asian Americans*. Dubuque, IA: Kendell and Hunt.

Cox, B., and M. Ramirez III. 1981. "Cognitive Styles: Implications for Multiethnic Education." Pp. 61–71 in J. Banks et al. (eds.), *Education in the 80s: Multiethnic Education*. Washington, DC: National Education Association.

Crawford, M., and M. Witte. 1999. "Strategies for Mathematics: Teaching in Context." *Educational Leadership*, 57(3), 34–37.

Csikszentmihaly, M., and B. Schneider. 2000. *Becoming Adult*. New York: Basic Books.

Cuban, L. 1988. "Constancy and Change in Schools." Pp. 85–103 in P. W. Jackson (ed.), *Contributing to Educational Change: Perspectives on Research and Practice*. Berkeley: McCutchan.

———. 1989. "The 'At-Risk' Label and the Problem of Urban School Reform." *Phi Delta Kappan* 70(10): 784–785.

———. 2001. "How Systemic Reform Harms Urban Schools: And What We Can Do About It." *Education Week* XX(38).

Culbertson, J. 1988. *Tomorrow's Challenges to Today's Professors of Educational Administration.* 1988 Walter Hoching lecture presented to the National Council of Professors of Educational Administration, Kalamazoo, MI.

Damico, S. B. 1983. *The Two Worlds of School: Differences in the Photographs of Black and White Adolescents.* Paper presented at annual meeting of American Educational Research Association, Montreal.

Darling-Hammond, L. 1995. "Restructuring Schools for Student Success." *Daedalus* 124(4): 153–162.

Davis, J. K., and B. M. Frank. 1979. "Learning and Memory of Field Independent-Dependent Individuals." *Journal of Research in Personality* 13: 469–479.

De La Rosa, D., and C. E. Maw. 1990. *Hispanic Education: A Statistical Portrait 1990.* Washington, DC: National Council of La Rosa.

DePree, M. 1989. *Leadership Is an Art.* New York: Doubleday.

Devries, D. L., K. J. Edwards, and R. E. Slavin. 1978. "Biracial Learning Teams and Race Relations in the Classroom: Four Field Experiments on Teams-Games-Tournaments." *Journal of Educational Psychology* 70: 356–362.

Dewey, J. 1933. *How We Think.* Chicago: Henry Regnery.

Dietz, M. 1995. "Using Portfolios as a Framework for Professional Development." *Journal of Staff Development* 16: 40–43.

Dillon, J. T. 1984. "Research on Questioning and Discussion." *Educational Leadership* 42(3): 50–56.

Dinges, N.C., and A. R. Hollenbeck. 1978. "Field-Dependence-Independence in Navajo Children." *International Journal of Psychology* 13: 215–220.

Do You Know the Good News About American Education? 1997. Center on Educational Policy and American Youth Policy Forum. Washington, DC: Center on Educational Policy.

Drucker, Peter F. 1993. *Post-Capitalist Society.* New York: HarperCollins.

Dunn, R. 1993. "Learning Styles of the Multiculturally Diverse." *Emergency Librarian* 20(4): 24–30.

——, **and K. Dunn.** 1979. "Using Learning Style Data to Develop Student Prescriptions." Pp. 109–122 in National Association of Secondary School Principals, *Student Learning Styles: Diagnosing and Prescribing Programs.* Reston, VA: NASSP.

Dunn, R., and S. A. Griggs. 1988. *Learning Styles: Quiet Revolution in American Schools.* Reston, VA: National Association of Secondary School Principals.

Dunn, R., J. Gemake, F. Jalali, R. Zenhausern, P. Quinn, and J. Spiridakis. 1990. "Cross-Cultural Differences in Learning Styles of Elementary-Age Students from Four Ethnic Backgrounds." *Journal of Multicultural Counseling and Development* 18(2): 68–93.

Dusek, J. (ed.). 1985. *Teacher Expectations.* Hillsdale, NJ. Erlbaum.

Educational Testing Service. 2000. "Study Links Effective Teaching Methods and Test Score Gains." *Education Week*, 20(8): 20.

Eggen, P. D., and D. P. Kauchak. 1988. *Strategies for Teachers.* Englewood Cliffs, NJ: Prentice-Hall.

——. 2001. *Strategies for Teachers* (4th ed.). Needham Heights, MA: Allyn & Bacon.

England, D. A., and J. K. Flatley. 1985. *Homework—and Why.* Bloomington, IN: Phi Delta Kappa.

Enright, D. S. 1987. "Cognitive Style and First Language Background in Second Language Test Performance." *TESOL Quarterly* 21: 565–569.

Etzioni, A. 2001. *The Monochrome Society.* Princeton, NJ: Princeton University Press.

Finkelstein, B. 1989. *Governing the Young.* New York: Falmer Press.

Finn, C. E. Jr., M. Kanstoroom, and M. J. Petrilli. 1999. *The Quest for Better Teachers: Grading the States.* Washington, DC: Thomas B. Fordham Foundation.

Flaugher, R. L., and D. A. Roch. 1977. "Patterns of Ability Factors Among Four Ethnic Groups." Research Memorandum No. 7. Princeton, NJ: Educational Testing Service.

Foster, M. 1993. "Constancy, Change, and Constraints in the Lives of Black Women Teachers: Some Things Change, Most Stay the Same." *NWSA Journal* 3(2): 233–261.

———. 1994. "Effective Black Teachers: A Literature Review." Pp. 225–242 in E. R. Hollins, J. E. King, and W. C. Hayman (eds.), *Teaching Diverse Populations: Formulating a Knowledge Base.* Albany: State University of New York Press.

Freire, P. 1970. *Pedagogy of the Oppressed.* New York: Continuum.

Fullan, M. 1993. *Change Forces: Probing the Depth of Educational Reform.* London: Falmer Press.

Fuller, F., and O. Bown. 1975. "Becoming a teacher." Pp. 25–52 in K. Ryan (ed.), *Teacher Education* (74th Yearbook for the National Society for the Study of Education). Chicago: University of Chicago Press.

Gaardner, J. 1996. *Sophie's World.* New York: Berkeley.

Gagne, R. M. 1977. *The Conditions of Learning* (3rd ed.). New York: Holt, Rinehart and Winston.

Gall, M. D., and J. P. Gall. 1976. "The Discussion Method." Pp. 116–216 in N. L. Gage (ed.), *Psychology of Teaching Methods.* NSSE 75th Yearbook, Part 1. Chicago: University of Chicago Press.

Gall, M. D., and M. Gillett. 1980. "The Discussion Method in Classroom Teaching." *Theory Into Practice* 19(2): 95–103.

Garcia, E. 1991. "Effective Instruction for Language Minority Students: The Teacher." *Journal of Education* 173(2): 130–141.

Gardner, H. 1985. *Frames of Mind* (rev. ed.) New York: Basic Books.

———. 1991. *The Unschooled Mind: How Children Think and How Schools Should Teach.* New York: Basic Books.

———. 1985. *The Minds New Science.* New York: Basic Books.

———. 1995. "Reflections on Multiple Intelligences: Myths and Messages." *Phi Delta Kappan* 77(3): 200–209.

Gersten, R., R. Taylor, and A. Graves. 1999. In R. R. Stevens (ed.), *Teaching in American Schools.* Upper Saddle River, NJ: Merrill Prentice Hall.

Gilbert, S., and G. Gay. 1985. "Improving the Success in School of Poor Black Children." *Phi Delta Kappan* 67(2): 133–137.

Gilligan, C. 1982. *In a Different Voice: Psychological Theory and Women's Development.* Cambridge, MA: Harvard University Press.

Giroux, H. A. 1983. *Theory and Resistance in Education: A Pedagogy for the Opposition.* South Hadley: Bergin and Garvey.

————. 1992. "Educational Leadership and the Crisis of Democratic Government." *Educational Researcher* 21(4): 4–11.

Glickman, C. D. 1990. *Supervision of Instruction: A Developmental Approach* (2nd ed.). Boston: Allyn & Bacon.

Goldstein, R. 1971. *Black Life and Culture in the United States*. New York: Thomas Crowell.

Golenbock, P. 1990. *Teammates*. San Diego, CA: Gulliver Books, Harcourt Brace Jovanovich.

Gollnick, D. M., and P. C. Chinn. 1994. *Multicultural Education in a Pluralistic Society* (4th ed.). New York: Macmillan.

Good, T., and J. Brophy. 1995. *Contemporary Educational Psychology* (5th ed.) New York: Longman.

Good, T., and J. E. Brophy. 1994. *Looking in Classrooms* (6th ed.). New York: HarperCollins.

————. 1997. *Looking in Classrooms* (7th ed.). New York: Longman.

Good, T., and D. Grouws. 1979. "The Missouri Mathematics Effectiveness Project: An Experimental Study in Fourth-Grade Classrooms." *Journal of Educational Psychology* 71: 355–362.

Good, T. L., and J. E. Brophy. 1991. *Looking into Classrooms* (5th ed.). New York: HarperCollins.

Goodlad, J. 1990. "Studying the Education of Educators: From Conception to Findings." *Phi Delta Kappan* 71(9): 698–701.

Goodlad, J., R. Soder, and K. A. Sirotnik. (eds.). 1990. *The Moral Dimensions of Teaching*. San Francisco: Jossey-Bass.

Goodlad, J. I. 1990. *Teachers for Our Nation's Schools*. San Francisco: Jossey-Bass.

Gordon, W. 1961. *Synectics: The Development of Creative Capacity*. New York: Harper & Row.

Grantham-Campbell, M. 1992. *Successful Alaska Native Students: Implications 500 Years After Columbus*. Paper presented at the meeting of the American Anthropological Association, San Francisco (December).

Greenfield, W. 1990. *Reinventing School Leadership*. Working memo prepared for the Reinventing School Leadership Conference. Cambridge, MA: National Center for Educational Leadership.

Grundy, S., and S. Kemmis. 1981. *Educational Action Research in Australia: The State of the Art*. Paper presented at the Annual Meeting of the Australian Association for Research in Education, Adelaide as cited in Grundy, S. 1988. Three Modes of Action Research in S. Kemmis, and R. McTaggert (eds.). 1988. *The Action Research Reader* (3rd ed.). Geelong: Deakin University Press.

Guiney, E. 2001. "Coaching Isn't Just for Athletes: The Role of Teacher Leaders." *Phi Delta Kappan* 82(10): 740–743.

Gunter, M. A., T. H. Estes, and J. H. Schwab. 1995. *Instruction: A Models Approach* (2nd ed.). Boston: Allyn & Bacon.

Guttentag, M. 1972. "Negro-White Differences in Children's Movement." *Perceptual and Motor Skills* 35: 435–436.

Haberman, M. 1995. *Star Teachers of Children in Poverty*. West Lafayette, IN: Kappa Delta Pi.

————, **and L. Post.** 1995. "Multicultural Teaching in the Real World." Pp. 337–353 in A. C. Ornstein (ed.), *Teaching: Theory and Practice.* Boston: Allyn & Bacon.

Hale-Benson, J. 1982. *Black Children: Their Roots, Culture, and Learning Styles.* Baltimore: Johns Hopkins University Press.

————. 1986. *Black Children: Their Roots, Culture, and Learning Styles* (rev. ed.). Baltimore: Johns Hopkins University Press.

Hall, E. 1989. "Unstated Features of the Cultural Context of Learning." *Educational Forum* 54(1): 21–34.

Halverson, B. 1976. *Cognitive Style of Preschool Seminole Indian Children.* Unpublished doctoral dissertation, Florida State University, Tallahassee.

Hansell, S., and R. E. Slavin. 1981. "Cooperative Learning and the Structure of Interracial Friendships." *Sociology of Education* 54: 98–106.

Hansen, L. 1984. "Field Dependence-Independence and Language Testing: Evidence from Six Pacific Island Cultures." *TESOL Quarterly* 18: 311–324.

Hansen-Strain, L. 1987. "Cognitive Style and First Language Background in Second Language Test Performance." *TESOL Quarterly* 21: 565–569.

Hanson, H., H. Silver, and R. Strong. 1986. *Teaching Styles and Strategies.* Moorestown, NJ: Hanson, Silver, Strong and Associates.

Harrow, A. J. 1972. *A Taxonomy of the Psychomotor Domain.* New York: McKay.

Harry, B. 1992. *Cultural Diversity, Families, and the Special Education System.* New York: Teachers' College Press.

Heath, S. B. 1983. *Ways with Words: Language, Life, and Work in Communities and Classrooms.* Cambridge: Cambridge University Press.

Henry, A. 1990. *Black Women, Black Pedagogies: An African-Canadian Context.* Paper presented at the American Educational Research Association, Boston.

Henry, J. 1955. "Docility, or Giving Teacher What She Wants." *Journal of Social Issues* 11(1): 33–41.

Henson, K. T. 1986. "Inquiry Learning: A New Look." *Contemporary Education* 57(4): 181–183.

Herndon, J. 1968. *The Way It Spozed to Be.* New York: Simon & Schuster.

Herring, R. D. 1989. "Counseling Native American Children." *Implications for Elementary School Guidance and Counseling* 23(April): 272–281.

Hersey, P., and K. Blanchard. 1974. "So You Want to Know Your Leadership Style?" *Training and Development Journal* 28(2): 1–15.

Hersey, P., and K. H. Blanchard. 1988. *Management of Organizational Behavior* (5th ed.). Englewood Cliffs, NJ: Prentice-Hall.

Higbee, K. L. 1996. *Your Memory* (2nd ed.). New York: Marlowe.

Hill, D. 2001. "Rays, Rhythm, and Rhyme," *Education Week,* January 17, 2001, 32–36.

Hill, P., C. Campbell, and P. Harvey. 2000. *It Takes a City: Getting Serious About Urban Reform.* Washington, DC: Brookings Institute.

Hilliard, A. G., III. 1976. *Alternatives to IQ Testing: An Approach to the Identification of Gifted Minority Children.* Final report to the California State Department of Education.

————. 1989. "Teachers and Cultural Styles in a Pluralistic Society." *NEA Today* 1: 65–69.

———. 1992. "Behavioral Style, Culture, and Teaching and Learning." *Journal of Negro Education* 61(3): 370–373.

Hirsch, E. D., Jr. 1988. *Cultural Literacy.* New York: Vintage Books.

———. 1996. *The Schools We Need.* New York: Doubleday.

Hock, M. F., J. B. Schumaker, and D. D. Deshler. 2001. "The Case for Strategic Tutoring." *Educational Leadership* 58(7): 50–52.

Hodges, L. 1996. "Blood Ties." *New York Times* (July 19): A15.

Holt, J. 1967. *How Children Fail.* New York: Pitman.

Howard, B. C. 1987. *Learning to Persist/Persisting to Learn.* Washington, DC: Mid-Atlantic Center for Race Equity, American University.

Howe, C. 1994. "Improving the Achievement of Hispanic Students." *Educational Leadership* 51(8): 42–44.

Hubbard, R. S., and B. M. Power. 1999. *Living the Questions: A Guide for Teacher-Researchers.* York, MA: Stenhouse.

———. 1993. *The Art of Classroom Inquiry: A Handbook for Teacher-Researchers.* Portsmouth, NH: Heinemann.

Hunkins, F. P. 1972. *Questioning Strategies and Techniques.* Boston: Allyn & Bacon.

Hunter, M. 1976. *Prescription for Improved Instruction.* El Segundo, CA: TIP.

———. 1984. "Knowing, Teaching, and Supervising." Pp. 169–192 in P. L. Hosford (ed.), *Using What We Know About Teaching.* Alexandria, VA: Association for Supervision and Curriculum Development.

———. 1985. "What's Wrong with Madeline Hunter?" *Educational Leadership* 42(5): 57–60.

Hyerle, D. 1996. *Visual Tools.* Washington, DC: Association for Supervision and Curriculum Development.

Hyman, R. T. 1980. "Fielding Student Questions." *Theory Into Practice* 19(1): 38–44.

International Society for Technology in Education. 2000. Eugene, Oregon.

Investigating Solid Waste Issues. 1994. Columbus, OH: Ohio Department of Natural Resources.

Irvine, J. J., and B. J. Armento. 2001. *Culturally Responsive Teaching.* Boston: McGraw Hill.

Irvine, J. J., and D. E. York. 1995. "Learning Styles and Culturally Diverse Students: A Literature Review." Pp. 484–492 in J. H. Banks (ed.), *Handbook of Research on Multicultural Education.* New York: Macmillan.

Izumi, L. T., and K. G. Coburn. 2001. *Facing the Classroom Challenge.* San Francisco: Pacific Research Institute for Public Policy.

Jackson, A. W., and G. A. Davis. 2000. *Turning Points 2000: Educating Adolescents in the 21st Century.* New York: Teachers' College Press.

Jencks, C., and M. Phillips (eds.). 1998. *The Black and White Test Score Gap.* Washington, DC: Brookings Institution.

Jetter, A. 1993. "Mississippi Learning." *New York Times Magazine* 6(February 21): 28–72.

Johnson, D. W., and R. T. Johnson. 1975. *Learning Together and Alone.* Englewood Cliffs, NJ: Prentice-Hall.

————. 1981. "Effects of Cooperative and Individualistic Learning Experiences on Interethnic Interaction." *Journal of Educational Psychology* 73(3): 444–449.

————. 1987. *Learning Together and Alone* (2nd ed.). Boston: Allyn & Bacon.

————. 1989/1990. "Social Skills for Successful Group Work." *Educational Leadership* 47(4): 29–33.

————. 1998. *Learning Together and Alone* (5th ed.). Boston: Allyn & Bacon.

Johnson, D. W., R. T. Johnson, E. J. Holubec, and P. Roy. 1984. *Circles of Learning*. Alexandria, VA: Association for Supervision and Curriculum Development.

Joyce, B., C. Murphy, B. Showers, and J. Murphy. 1989. "School Renewal as Cultural Change." *Educational Leadership* 47(3): 70–78.

Joyce, B., and M. Weil. 1972. *Models of Teaching*. Boston: Allyn & Bacon.

————. 1986. *Models of Teaching* (3rd ed.). Englewood Cliffs, NJ: Prentice-Hall.

Joyce, B., M. Weil, and E. Calhoun. 2000. *Models of Teaching* (4th ed.). Boston: Allyn & Bacon.

Joyce, B., M. Weil, and E. Calhoun. 2000. *Models of Teaching* (5th ed.) Boston: Allyn & Bacon.

Joyce, B., M. Weil, and E. Calhoun. 2000. *Models of Teaching* (6th ed.). Boston: Allyn & Bacon.

Kagan, S. 1989/1990. "The Structural Approach to Cooperative Learning." *Educational Leadership* 47(4): 12–15.

————. 1992. *Cooperative Learning*. San Juan Capistrano, CA: Resources for Teachers.

Kagan, S., and R. Buriel. 1977. "Field Dependence-Independence and Mexican-American Culture and Education." Pp. 279–328 in J. L. Martinez Jr. (ed.), *Chicano Psychology*. Orlando, FL: Academic Press.

Kagan, S., and G. P. Knight. 1981. "Social Motives Among Anglo American and Mexican American Children: Experimental and Projective Measures." *Journal of Research in Personality* 15(1): 93–106.

Kagan, S., and M. C. Madsen. 1971. "Cooperation and Competition of Mexican, Mexican-American, and Anglo-American Children of Two Ages Under Four Instruction Sets." *Developmental Psychology* 5: 32–39.

Kagan, S., and G. L. Zahn. 1976. "Field Dependence and the School Achievement Gap Between Anglo-American and Mexican-American Children." *Journal of Educational Psychology* 67: 643–650.

Kagan, S., G. L. Zahn, K. E. Widaman, J. Schwarzwald, and G. Tyrell. 1985. "Classroom Structural Bias: Impact of Cooperative and Competitive Classroom Structures on Cooperative and Competitive Individuals and Groups." Pp. 277–312 in R. E. Slavin, S. Sharan, S. Kagan, R. Hertz-Lazarowitz, C. Webb, and R. Schmuck (eds.), *Learning to Cooperate, Cooperating to Learn*. New York: Plenum.

Kahn, A. 1991. "Don't Spoil the Promise of Cooperative Learning." *Educational Leadership* 48(5): 93–94.

Kanter, R. M. 1989. *When Giants Learn to Dance*. New York: Simon & Schuster.

Keefe, J. W. 1979. "Learning Styles: An Overview." Pp. 1–17 in *Student Learning Styles: Diagnosing and Prescribing Programs*. Reston, VA: National Association of Secondary School Principals.

Keefe, S. E., and A. M. Padilla. 1987. *Chicano Ethnicity*. Albuquerque, NM: University of New Mexico Press.

Kelly, J. A. 1984. *Influence of Culture, Gender and Academic Experience on Cognitive Style*. Unpublished dissertation, Vanderbilt University, Memphis, TN.

Kemmis, S., and R. McTaggart (eds.). 1988. *The Action Research Planner* (3rd edition). Victoria, Australia: Deakin University.

Keogh, B. K., M. F. Welles, and A. Weiss. 1972. "Field Dependence-Independence and Problem-Solving Styles of Preschool Children." Technical Report. Los Angeles: University of California.

King, L. 1993. "High and Low Achievers' Perceptions and Cooperative Learning in Two Small Groups." *Elementary School Journal* 93(44): 399–416.

Knight, G. P., and S. Kagan. 1977. "Development of Prosocial and Competitive Behaviors in Anglo-American and Mexican-American Children." *Child Development* 48(4): 1385–1394.

Kochman, T. 1972. *Rappin' and Stylin' Out: Communication in Urban Black America*. Urbana, IL: University of Illinois Press.

Kohl, H. 1967. *36 Children*. New York: New American Library.

Kolb, D. 1984. *Experiential Learning*. Englewood Cliffs, NJ: Prentice-Hall.

Kozol, J. 1967. *Death at an Early Age: The Destruction of the Hearts and Minds of Negro Children in the Boston Public Schools*. Boston: Houghton Mifflin.

Krathwohl, D., B. Bloom, and B. Masis. 1964. *Taxonomy of Educational Objectives, Handbook II: Affective Domain*. New York: McKay.

Krumboltz, J. D., and C. J. Yeh. 1996. Competitive Grading Sabotages Good Teaching. *Phi Delta Kappan*, 78(4): 324–326.

Ladson-Billings, G. 1990. "Like 'Lightning' in a Bottle: Attempting to Capture the Pedagogical Excellence of Successful Teachers of Black Students." *International Journal of Qualitative Studies in Education* 3(4): 335–344.

———. 1991. "Returning to the Source: Implications for Educating Teachers of Black Students." Pp. 227–244 in M. Foster (ed.), *Readings on Equal Education. Volume II: Qualitative Investigations into Schools and Schooling*. New York: AMS Press.

———. 1992. "Liberatory Consequences of Literacy: A Case of Culturally Relevant Instruction for African American Students." *Journal of Negro Education* 61(3): 378–391.

———. 1994. *The Dreamkeepers*. San Francisco: Jossey-Bass.

———. 2001. *Crossing Over to Canaan*. San Francisco: Jossey-Bass.

LaFrance, M., and C. Mayo. 1976. "Racial Differences in Gaze Behavior During Conversation." *Journal of Personality and Social Psychology* 33: 258–285.

Lee, V. 1997. "Catholic Lessons for Public Schools." Pp. 147–163 in D. Ravitch and J. Viteritti (eds.), *New Schools for a New Century: Redesign of Urban Education.* . New Haven, CT: Yale University Press.

Levin, J. R. 1993. "Mnemonic Strategies and Classroom Learning: A Twenty Year Report Card." *Elementary School Journal* 94(2): 235–244.

Levin, M. E., and J. R. Levin. 1990. "Scientific Mnemonomies: Methods for Maximizing More than Memory." *American Educational Research Journal* 27(2): 301–321.

Lewis, R. B., and D. H. Doorlag. 1999. *Teaching Special Students in General Education Classrooms*. Upper Saddle River, NJ: Merrill.

Lickona, T. 1989. *Educating for Character*. New York: Bantam.

Loftin, J. D. 1989. "Anglo American Jurisprudence and the Native American Tribal Quest for Religious Freedom." *American Indian Culture and Research Journal* 13(1): 1–52.

Longstreet, W. S. 1978. *Aspects of Ethnicity*. New York: Teachers College Press.

Lorayne, H., and J. Lucas. 1974. *The Memory Book*. New York: Ballantine.

Losey, K. M. 1995. "Mexican American Students and Classroom Interaction: An Overview and Critique." *American Educational Research Journal* 65(3): 283–318.

Loucks-Horsley, S., C. K. Harding, M. A. Arbuckle, L. B. Murray, C. Dubea, and M. K. Williams. 1987. *Continuing to Learn*. Andover, MA: Regional Laboratory for Educational Improvement of the Northeast and Islands.

Luria, A. R. 1968. *The Mind of a Mnemonist*. Chicago: Henry Regnery.

Ma, L. 1999. *Knowing and Teaching Elementary Mathematics: Teachers' Understanding of Fundamental Mathematics in China and the United States*. Mahwah, NJ: Lawrence Erlbaum.

Macias, C. J. 1989. "American Indian Academic Success: The Role of Indigenous Learning Strategies." *Journal of American Indian Education* (August, special issue): 43–52.

Mager, R. 1984. *Preparing Instructional Objectives* (3rd ed.). Palo Alto, CA: Fearon.

Mamchur, C. M. 1996. *A Teacher's Guide to Cognitive Type Theory and Learning Style*. Alexandria, VA: Association for Supervision and Curriculum Development.

Marshall, H., and R. Weinstein. 1984. *Classrooms Where Students Perceive High and Low Amounts of Differential Teacher Treatment*. Paper presented at the annual meeting of the American Educational Research Association, New Orleans, LA.

Maslow, A. H. 1954. *Motivation and personality*. New York: Harper and Brothers.

Masters, J. 1995. "The History of Action Research." In I. Hughes (ed.), *Action Research Electronic Reader*, The University of Sydney, online http://www.behs.cchs.usyd.edu.au/arow/Reader/rmasters.htm (download date 05.23.2001).

Mastropieri, M. A., T. E. Scruggs, and J. R. Levin. 1987. "Learning Disabled Students' Memory for Expository Prose: Mnemonic Versus Nonmnemonic Pictures." *American Educational Research Journal* 24(4): 505–519.

Mathematics Plus. 1992. Orlando, FL: Harcourt Brace Jovanovich. (See Grade 7 text, p. 169.)

Mathews, W. 1988. *Escalante: The Best Teacher in America*. New York: Henry Holt.

Mauro, L. H., and L. J. Cohen. 1992. "Cooperating for Concept Development." Pp. 151–168 in N. Davidson and T. Worsham (eds.), *Enhancing Thinking Through Cooperative Learning*. New York: Teachers' College Press.

McCaulley, M. H., G. P. MacDaid, and R. E. Kainz. 1985. "Estimated Frequencies of the MBTI Types." *Journal of Psychological Type* 9: 3–8.

McCutcheon, G., and B. Jungs. 1990. "Alternative Perspectives on Action Research." *Theory into Practice* 24(3).

McDiarmid, G. 1990. *What to Do About Differences? A Study of Multicultural Education for Teacher Trainees in the Los Angeles Unified School District*. Research Report 90–11. East Lansing, MI: National Center for Research on Teacher Education, Michigan State University.

McKeachie, W. 1986. *Teaching Tips* (8th ed.). Lexington, MA: D. C. Heath.

McKinney, C. W. 1985. "A Comparison of the Effects of a Definition, Examples, and Nonexamples on Student Acquisition of the Concept of 'Teacher Propaganda.'" *Social Education* 49: 66–70.

McShane, D. 1980. "A Review of Scores of American Indian Children on the Seschler Intelligence Scales." *White Cloud Journal* 1: 3–10.

Messick, S. 1970. "The Criterion Problem in the Evaluation of Instruction: Assessing Possible, Not Just Intended, Outcomes." Pp. 183–202 in M. C. Wittrock and G. D. E. Wiley (eds.), *The Evaluation of Instruction: Issues and Problems.* New York: Holt.

Moore, M. R. 1972. "Consideration of the Perceptual Process in the Evaluation of Musical Performance." *Journal of Research on Music Education* 20: 273–279.

More, A. J. 1990. *Learning Styles of Native Americans and Asians.* Paper presented at the annual meeting of the American Psychological Association, Boston. ERIC Document Reproduction Service No. ED 330 535.

Morgan, H. 1981. "Factors Concerning Cognitive Development and Learning Differentiation Among Black Children." Pp. 14–22 in A. E. Harrison (ed.), *Conference on Empirical Research in Black Psychology 6.*

Morse, G. 1997. "Technology Partnerships." Pp. 45–48 in A. A. Zukowski, MHSH, and R. Haney (eds.), *New Frontiers: Navigational Strategies for Integrating Technology into the School.* Washington, DC: National Catholic Educational Association.

Moss, S., and M. Fuller. 2000. "Implementing Effective Practices." *Phi Delta Kappan,* 82(4): 273–276.

Murphy, J. 1991. *Restructuring Schools: Capturing and Assessing the Phenomena.* New York: Teacher's College Press.

Myers, I. B., and M. McCaulley. 1985. *Manual: A Guide to the Development and Use of the Myers-Briggs Type Indicator.* Palo Alto, CA: Consulting Psychologists Press.

National Commission on Excellence in Education. 1983. *A Nation at Risk: The Imperative for Educational Reform.* Washington, DC: U.S. Department of Education.

National Education Goals Panel. 1999. "Progress Report on National Education Goals." *Education Week.* January 13, 1999. p. 29.

National Foundation for Women Business Owners. 1994. *Styles of Success: The Thinking and Management Styles of Women and Men Entrepreneurs.* Washington, DC: National Foundation for Women Business Owners (July).

Newman, J. W. 1998. *America's Teachers.* New York: Longman.

Newmann, F. M., and G. G. Wehlage. 1993. "Five Standards of Authentic Instruction." *Educational Leadership* 50(7): 8–12.

Nieto, S. 1996. *Affirming Diversity.* White Plains, NY: Longman.

O'Malley, J., and A. Chamot. 1990. *Learning, Strategies in Second Language Acquisition.* Cambridge: Cambridge University Press.

O'Neil, J. 1995. "Finding Time to Learn." *Educational Leadership* 53(3): 11–15.

O'Toole, J. 1995. *Leading Change: Overcoming the Ideology of Comfort and the Tyranny of Custom.* San Francisco: Jossey-Bass.

Obiakor, F. E. 1983. "Cultural Discontinuities and Schooling." *Anthropology and Education Quarterly* 13: 290–307.

———. 1987. "Variability in Minority School Performance: A Problem in Search of an Explanation." *Anthropology and Education Quarterly* 18(4): 312–334.

———. 1989. "The Individual in Collective Adaptation: A Framework for Focusing on Academic Underperformance and Dropping Out Among Involuntary Minorities." Pp. 181–204 in L. Weis, E. Farran, and H. Petrie (eds.), *Dropouts from School: Issues, Dilemmas, and Solutions.* Albany: State University of New York Press.

———. 1992. "A Cultural Ecology of Competence Among Inner-City Blacks." Pp. 45–60 in M. Spencer, G. Brookins, and W. Allen (eds.), *Beginnings: The Social and Affective Development of Black Children.* Hillsdale, NJ: Erlbaum.

Ohanian, S. 2000. "Goals 2000: What's in a Name?" *Phi Delta Kappan* 81 (5): 345–355.

Olstad, R., J. Juarez, L. Davenport, and D. Haury. 1981. *Inhibitors to Achievement in Science and Mathematics by Ethnic Minorities.* Bethesda, MD: ERIC Document Reproduction Service No. ED 223 404.

Orlich, D. C., R. J. Harder, R. C. Callahan, C. H. Kravas, D. P. Kauchak, R. A. Pendergrass, and A. J. Keogh. 1985. *Teaching Strategies: A Guide to Better Instruction* (2nd ed.). Lexington, MA: D. C. Heath.

Ornstein, A. C. 1995. *Strategies for Effective Teaching* (2nd ed.). Madison, WI: Brown and Benchmark.

———, and T. J. Lasley. 2000. *Effective Teaching* (3rd ed.). Boston, MA: McGraw-Hill.

Osborne, B., and B. Bamford. 1987. *Torres Strait Islanders Teaching Torres Strait Islanders.* North Queensland, Townsville: Department of Pedagogics and Scientific Studies in Education, James Cook University.

Osborne, D., and T. Gaebler. 1992. *Reinventing Government.* Reading, MA: Addison-Wesley.

Ovando, C. 2001. "Beyond Blaming the Victim: Successful Schools for Latino Students." *Educational Researcher* 30(3): 29–31.

Oxford, R. 1990. The Strategy Inventory for Language Learning (SILL). *Appendix to Language Learning Strategies: What Every Teacher Should Know.* New York: Newbury House/Harper & Row.

Pang, V. 1990. "Asian-American Children: A Diverse Population." *Educational Forum* 55(1): 49–66.

———. 1995. "Asian Pacific American Students: A Diverse and Complex Population." Pp. 412–424 in J. Banks, and C. Banks (eds.), *Handbook of Research on Multicultural Education.* New York: Macmillan.

Parker, W. C. 1987. "Teaching Thinking: The Pervasive Approach." *Journal of Teacher Education* 38(3): 50–56.

Pease-Alvarez, L., E. Garcia, and P. Espinoza. 1991. "Effective Instruction for Language Minority Students: An Early Childhood Case Study." *Early Childhood Research Quarterly* 6(3): 347–363.

Peters, K. H., and J. K. March. 1999. *Collaborative Observation: Putting Classroom Instruction at the Center of School Reform.* Thousand Oaks, CA: Corwin Press.

Philips, S. 1972. "Participant Structures and Communicative Competence: Warm Springs Children in Community and Classroom." Pp. 370–394 in C. Cazden, V. John, and D. Hymes (eds.), *Functions of Language in the Classroom.* New York: Teacher's College Press.

———. 1983. *The Invisible Culture: Communication in Classroom and Community on the Warm Springs Indian Reservation.* New York: Longman.

———. 1993. *The Invisible Culture: Communication in Classroom and Community on the Warm Springs Indian Reservation.* Prospect Heights, IL: Waveland Press.

Phillips, M., J. Crouse, and J. Ralph. 1998. "Does the Black and White Test Score Gap Widen after Children Enter School?" Pp. 229–272 in C. Jenks and M. Phillips (eds.), *The Black and White Test Score Gap.* Washington, DC: The Brookings Institution.

Polling, A. 1995. "Gender Balance: Lessons from Girls in Science and Mathematics." *Educational Leadership* 53(1): 30–33.

Porter, A. C. 1986. "From Research on Teaching to Staff Development: A Difficult Step." *Elementary School Journal* 87(2): 159–164.

Postman, N., and C. Weingartner. 1969. *Teaching as a Subversive Activity.* New York: Delacorte.

Pressley, M., J. R. Levin, and G. E. Miller. 1981. "How Does the Keyword Method Affect Vocabulary Comprehension and Usage?" *Reading Research Quarterly* 16: 213–226.

Pressley, M., J. R. Levin, and H. D. Delaney. 1982. "The Mnemonic Keyword Method." *Review of Educational Research* 52: 61–91.

Prom, S. E. 1982. "Salient Content and Cognitive Performance of Person- and Thing-Oriented Low Income Afro-American Children in Kindergarten and Second Grade." Doctoral dissertation, Howard University, Washington, DC.

Queen, J. A. 2000. "Block Scheduling Revisited." *Phi Delta Kappan* 82(3): 214–222.

Queen, J. A. 2000. "One School Tackles the Change to Block Scheduling." *Phi Delta Kappan* 82(3): 214–222.

Ramirez, M., III. 1973. "Cognitive Styles and Cultural Democracy in Education." *Social Science Quarterly* 53: 895–904.

———. 1982. *Cognitive Styles and Cultural Diversity.* Paper presented at the annual meeting of the American Educational Research Association, New York City (May).

———. 1989. "A Bicognitive-Multicultural Model for a Pluralistic Education." *Early Child Development and Care* 51: 129–136.

———. 1991. *Psychotherapy and Counseling with Minorities: A Cognitive Approach to Individual and Cultural Differences.* New York: Allyn & Bacon.

Ramirez, M., III, and A. Castaneda. 1974. *Cultural Democracy, Bicognitive Development and Education.* New York: Academic Press.

Ramirez, M., III, and D. R. Price-Williams. 1974. "Cognitive Style of Three Ethnic Groups in the U.S." *Journal of Cross-Cultural Psychology* 5(2): 212–219.

Rapoport, R. N. 1970. "Three Dilemmas in Action Research." *Human Relations* 23(6), 499, as cited in J. McKernan. 1991. *Curriculum Action Research. A Handbook of Methods and Resources for the Reflective Practitioner.* London: Kogan Page.

Ravitch, D. 2000. *Left Black.* New York: Simon & Schuster.

———, and C. E. Finn, Jr. 1987. *What Do Our 17-Year Olds Know?* New York: Harper & Row.

Reich, R. 2001. "Standards for What?" *Education Week* 20(41). June 20. p. 64.

Ribadeneira, D. 1990. "Educators Say School Reform Is Not Enough." Boston Globe (1) (November 13): 1.

Riche, M. F. 1991. "We're All Minorities Now." *American Demographics* (October): 26–34.

Riley, R. 1997. "Learning through Design." Pp. 1–18 in M. Davis, P. Hawley, B. McMullan, and G. Spilka (eds.) *Design as a Catalyst for Learning.* Alexandria, VA: Association for Supervision and Curriculum Development.

Robbins, P. 1986. "The Napa-Vacaville Follow-Through Project: Qualitative Outcomes, Related Procedures, and Implications for Practice." *Elementary School Journal* 87(2): 139–158.

Roberts, L. 1990. *Reinventing School Leadership.* Working memo prepared for the Reinventing School Leadership Conference. Cambridge, MA: National Center for Educational Leadership.

Roberts, S. 1993. *Who We Are*. New York: Times Books.

Robyler, M. D., and J. Edwards. 2000. *Integrating Educational Technology into Teaching* (2nd ed.). Upper Saddle River, NJ: Merrill.

Rodriguez, D., and J. Rodriguez. 1994. *Times Tables the Fun Way*. Sandy, UT: Key.

Rohner, R. 1965. "Factors Influencing the Academic Performance of Kwakiutl Children in Canada." *Comparative Education Review* 9: 331–340.

Rollman, S. A. 1978. "The Sensitivity of Black and White Americans to Nonverbal Cues of Prejudice." *Journal of Social Psychology* 105: 73–77.

Rose, C. 1985. *Accelerated Learning*. New York: Dell.

Rose, M. 1995. *Possible Lives: The Promise of Public Education in America*. New York: Houghton-Mifflin.

Rosenshine, B. 1983. "Teaching Functions in Instructional Programs." *Elementary School Journal* 83(4): 335–352.

_____. 1986. "Unsolved Issues in Teaching Content: A Critique of a Lesson on Federalist Paper No. 10." *Teaching and Teacher Education* 2(4): 301–308.

_____. 1987. "Explicit Teaching." Pp. 75–92 in D. C. Berliner and B. Rosenshine (eds.), *Talks to Teachers*. New York: Random House.

Rosenthal, R., and L. Jacobson. 1968. *Pygmalion in the Classroom: Teacher Expectation and Pupils' Intellectual Development*. New York: Holt, Rinehart, & Winston.

Rothman, R. 1995. *Measuring Up*. San Francisco: Jossey-Bass.

Sadker, D. 2001. "Confronting Curricular Bias in Teacher Education: Some Practical Ideas." *ATE Newsletter* 33(6).

Sadker, M., and D. Sadker. 1994. *Failing at Fairness*. New York: Charles Scribner's Sons.

———. 2000. *Teachers, Schools, and Society* (5th ed.). Boston: McGraw-Hill.

Sainte-Marie, B. 1999. "Beyond Autumns Stereotypes." *Education Week* October 27, 1999, pp. 37, 39.

Sanders, N. M. 1966. *Classroom Questions: What Kinds?* New York: Harper & Row.

Sanders, W. 2001. "Measurement and Analysis to Facilitate Academic Growth of Student Populations." Presentation to American Association of Colleges for Teacher Education, Dallas, Texas.

Saracho, O. N., and B. Spodek. 1984. *Cognitive Style and Children's Learning: Individual Variation in Cognitive Processes*. ERIC Document Reproduction Service No. ED 247 037.

Schaps, E., C. C. Lewis, and M. Watson. 1993. "The Child Development Project." *Educational Leadership* 51(3): 46.

Schön, D. A. 1987. *Educating the Reflective Practitioner*. San Francisco: Jossey-Bass.

Sergiovanni, T. J. 1989. *Schooling for Tomorrow: Directing Reforms to Issues That Count*. Boston: Allyn & Bacon.

———. 1991. *The Principalship: A Reflective Practice Perspective*. Boston: Allyn & Bacon.

———. 1992. *Moral Leadership: Getting to the Heart of School Improvement*. San Francisco: Jossey-Bass.

Shade, B. J. 1981. "Racial Variation in Perceptual Differentiation." *Perceptual and Motor Skills* 52: 243–248.

———. 1984. *Afro-American Patterns of Cognition: A Review of the Research*. Paper presented at the annual meeting of the American Educational Research Association, New Orleans, LA.

———. 1989. "The Influence of Perceptual Development on Cognitive Style: Cross Ethnic Comparisons." *Early Child Development and Care* 51: 137–155.

———. 1994. "Understanding the African American Learner." Pp. 175–189 in E. Hollins, J. King, and W. Hayman (eds.), *Teaching Diverse Populations: Formulating a Knowledge Base*. Albany: State University of New York Press.

———, and P. A. Edwards. 1987. "Ecological Correlates of the Educative Style of Afro-American Children." *Journal of Negro Education* 86: 88–99.

Shade, B., C. Kelly, and M. Oberg. 1997. *Creating Culturally Responsive Classrooms*. Washington, DC: American Psychological Association.

Shanker, A. 1995. "What's New?" *New Republic* (December 15): p. 15.

———. 1996. "Succeeding in School." *New Republic* (July 1): 17.

Shutiva, C. 1991. "Creativity Difference Between Reservation and Urban American Indians." *Journal of American Indian Education* 31(1): 33–52.

Silver, H. F., J. R. Hanson, R. W. Strong, P. B. Schwartz. 1996. *Teaching Styles and Strategies: Manual Z*. Woodbridge, NJ: Thoughtful Education Press.

Sizer, T. R. 1992. *Horace's School: Redesigning the American High School*. Boston: Houghton Mifflin.

Slaughter-DeFoe, D. T., K. Nakagawa, R. Takanishi, and D. J. Johnson. 1990. "Toward Cultural/Ecological Perspectives on Schooling and Achievement in African- and Asian-American Children." *Child Development* 61: 363–383.

Slavin, R. E. 1977. *Student Team Learning Techniques: Narrowing the Achievement Gap Between the Races*. Report No. 228. Baltimore: Johns Hopkins University, Center for the Study of Social Organization of Schools.

———. 1979. "Effects of Biracial Learning Teams on Cross-Racial Friendships." *Journal of Educational Psychology* 71(3): 381–387.

———. 1980. *Using Student Team Learning* (rev. ed.). Baltimore: Johns Hopkins University, Center for Social Organization of Schools.

———. 1987. *Cooperative Learning: Student Teams* (2nd ed.). Washington, DC: National Education Association.

———. 1987. "Cooperative Learning and Cooperative School." *Educational Leadership* 45(3): 7–13.

———. 1987. "Cooperative Learning: Where Behavioral and Humanistic Approaches to Classroom Motivation Meet." *Elementary School Journal* 88(1): 29–38.

———. 1990. "Cooperative Learning and the Cooperative School." Pp. 137–144 in R. Brandt (ed.), *Cooperative Learning Series*. Alexandria, VA: Association for Supervision and Curriculum Development.

———. 1995. "Cooperative Learning and Intergroup Relations." Pp. 628–634 in J. A. Banks, and C. A. M. Banks (eds.), *Handbook of Research on Multicultural Education*. New York: Macmillan.

Slavin, R. E., and E. Oickle. 1981. "Effects of Cooperative Learning Teams on Student Achievement and Race Relations: Treatment by Race Interactions." *Sociology of Education* 54: 174–180.

Smith, D. M., and D. Kolb. 1986. *Users Guide for the Learning Style Inventory: A Manual for Teachers and Trainers*. Boston: McBer.

Smith, R. 1987. "A Teacher's Views on Cooperative Learning." *Phi Delta Kappan* 68(9): 663–665.

Snow, C., M. S. Burns, and P. Griffin. (eds.). 1998. *Preventing Reading Difficulties in Young Children.* Washington, DC: National Academy Press.

Soldier, L. 1985. "To Soar with Eagles: Enculturation and Acculturation of Indian Children." *Childhood Education* 61: 185–191.

———. 1989. "Cooperative Learning and the Native American Student." *Phi Delta Kappan* 71(2): 161–163.

Sparks, D., and S. L. Horsley. 1989. "Five Models of Staff Development for Teachers." *Journal of Staff Development* 10(4): 40–57.

Sparks-Langer, G. M., M. Pasch, A. J. Starko, C. D. Moody, T. G. Gardner. 2000. *Teaching as Decisionmaking.* Upper Saddle River, NJ: Merrill Prentice Hall.

Sprenger, M. 1999. *Learning and Memory: The Brain in Action.* Washington, DC: Association for Supervision and Curriculum Development.

Stallings, J., and E. M. Krasavage. 1986. "Program Implementation and Student Achievement in a Four-Year Madeline Hunter Follow-Through Project." *Elementary School Journal* 87(2): 117–138.

Stallings, J., and P. Kaskowitz. 1974. *Follow Through Classroom Observation Evaluation, 1972–73.* Menlo Park, CA: Stanford Research Institute.

Steinberg, L. D. 1996. *Beyond the Classroom: Why School Reform Has Failed and What Parents Need to Do.* New York: Simon & Schuster.

Sternberg, R. J. 1994. "Commentary: Reforming School Reform: Comments on Multiple Intelligences: The Theory in Practice." *Teachers College Record* 95(4): 561–568.

Stevenson, H. W., and J. Stigler. 1992. *The Learning Gap.* New York: Summit.

Stevenson, H. W., C. Chen, and S. Lee. 1993. "Mathematics Achievement of Chinese, Japanese, and American Children: Ten Years Later." *Science* 259: 53–58.

Stigler, J., and J. Hiebert. 1999. *The Teaching Gap.* New York: Free Press.

Stigler, J. W., P. Gonzales, T. Kawanaka, S. Knoll, and A. Serrano. 1999. The TIMMS Videotape Classroom Study: Methods and Findings from an Exploratory Research Project on Eight Grade Mathematics Instruction in Germany, Japan, and the United States. *Education Statistics Quarterly* 1(2): 109–112.

Stipek, D. J. 1993. *Motivation to Learn* (2nd ed.). Boston: Allyn & Bacon.

Strong, M. 1997. *The Habit of Thought.* Chapel Hill, NC: New View.

Suarez, Z. E. 1993. "Cuban Americans: From Golden Exiles to Social Undesirables." Pp. 164–176 in H. P. McAdoo (ed.), *Family Ethnicity: Strength in Diversity.* Newbury Park, CA: Sage.

Suchman, R. J. 1962. *The Elementary School Training Program in Scientific Inquiry.* Report to the U.S. Office of Education, Project Title VII. Project no. 216. Project of the Illinois Studies of Inquiry. Urbana, IL: University of Illinois Press.

Suzuki, B. H. 1983. "The Education of Asian and Pacific Americans: An Introductory Overview." In D. T. Nakanishi and M. Hirano-Nakanishi (eds.), *Education of Asian and Pacific Americans: Historical Perspectives and Prescriptions for the Future.* Phoenix, AZ: Oryx Press.

Swisher, K., and D. Deyhle. 1987. "Styles of Learning and Learning Styles: Educational Conflicts for American Indian/Alaskan Native Youth." *Journal of Multilingual and Multicultural Development* 8(4): 350.

————. 1989. "The Styles of Learning Are Different, But the Teaching Is Just the Same: Suggestions for Teachers of American Indian Youth." *Journal of American Indian Education* (special issue, August): 1–14.

Taba, H. 1966. *Teaching Strategies and Cognitive Functioning in Elementary School Children.* Cooperative Research Project 2404. San Francisco: San Francisco State College.

————. 1971. *Hilda Taba Teaching Strategies Program.* Miami, FL: Institute for Staff Development.

Tafoya, T. 1982. "Coyote Eyes: Native Cognition Styles." *Journal of American Indian Education* 21(2): 21–33.

Tennyson, R. D., and M. Cocchiarella. 1986. "An Empirically Based Instructional Design Theory for Teaching Concepts." *Review of Educational Research* 56: 40–71.

Tennyson, R. D., and O. Park. 1980. "The Teaching of Concepts: A Review of Instructional Design Research Literature." *Review of Educational Research* 50(1): 55–70.

Thomas, M. D., and W. L. Bainbridge. 2001. "'All Children Can Learn': Facts and Fallacies." *ERS Spectrum* (Winter).

Thornburg, D. 1997. "2020 Visions for the Future of Education." Pp. 13–18 in A. A. Zukowski, MHSH, and R. Haney (eds.), *New Frontiers: Navigational Strategies for Integrating Technology into the School.* Washington, DC: National Catholic Educational Association.

Tienda, M. 2000. "Minorities in Higher Education: Troubling Trends and Promising Prospects." Speech presented at the Annual Convention of the University Council for Educational Administration. Albuquerque, NM.

Toffler, A. 1990. *Powershift.* New York: Bantam Books.

Tooker, E. 1983. *The Development of Political Organization in Native North America.* Washington, DC: American Ethnological Society.

Torrance, E. P. 1986. "Teaching Creative and Gifted Learners." Pp. 630–647 in M. C. Wittrock (ed.), *Handbook of Research on Teaching.* New York: Macmillan.

Traub, J. 1999. *Better By Design? A Consumer's Guide to Schoolwide Reform.* Washington, DC: Thomas B. Fordham Foundation.

Tredway, L. 1995. "Socratic Seminars: Engaging Students in Intellectual Discourse." *Educational Leadership* 53(1): 26–29.

Treisman, V. 1985. *A Study of the Mathematics Performance of Black Students at the University of California at Berkeley.* Unpublished doctoral dissertation, University of California, Berkeley.

Trueba, H. J., L. Jacobs, and E. Kirton. 1990. *Cultural Conflict and Adaptation: The Case of Hmong Children in American Society.* New York: Falmer Press.

Tuck, K., and A. Boykin. 1989. "Verve Effects: The Relationship of Task Performance to Stimulus Preference and Variability in Low-Income Black and White Children. Pp. 84–85 in A. Harrison (ed.), *The Eleventh Conference on Empirical Research in Black Psychology.* Washington, DC: NIMH.

Tyson, H. 1994. *Who Will Teach the Children? Progress and Resistance in Teacher Education.* San Francisco: Jossey-Bass.

U.S. Bureau of the Census, Economic and Statistics Administration. 1991. *1990 Census Profile: Race and Hispanic Origin.* Report No. 2.

U.S. Department of Commerce, Bureau of the Census. 1996. *Statistical Abstract of the United States.* Washington, DC: U.S. Government Printing Office.

U. S. Department of Education, National Center for Statistics, National Education Goals Report. 1994. *Building a Nation of Learners.* Washington, DC: U.S. Printing Office.

————. **The NCES Common Core of Data (CCD),** "State Nonfiscal Survey of Public Elementary/Secondary Education," 1994–95, 1997–98, and 1998–99.

U.S. Department of Education, National Center for Education Statistics. 1995. *The Condition of Education.* Washington, DC: U.S. Government Printing Office.

U.S. Department of Education, National Center for Education Statistics. 1995. *Digest of Educational Statistics.* Washington, DC: U.S. Government Printing Office.

Utley, C. A. 1983. *A Cross-Cultural Investigation of Field-Independent/Field Dependent as a Psychological Variable in Menominees Native American and Euro-American Grade School Children.* Madison, WI: Wisconsin Center for Education and Research.

Vasquez, J. A. 1991. "Cognitive Style and Academic Attainment." Pp. 163–179 in J. Lynch, C. Modgil, and S. Modgil (eds.), *Cultural Diversity and the Schools: Consensus and Controversy.* London: Falconer Press.

Vermette, P. J. 1998. *Making Cooperative Learning Work.* Upper Saddle River, NJ: Merrill Prentice Hall.

Vernon, P. A., D. N. Jackson, and S. Messick. 1988. "Cultural Influences on Patterns of Abilities in North America." Pp. 208–231 in S. H. Irvine and J. W. Berry (eds.), *Human Abilities in Cultural Context.* Cambridge, MA: Cambridge University Press.

Vernon, P. E. 1984. "Abilities and Achievements of Ethnic Groups in Canada with Special Reference to Canadian Natives and Orientals." Pp. 382–395 in R. Samuda, J. Berry, and M. Laferriere (eds.), *Multiculturalism in Canada: Social and Educational Perspectives.* Toronto: Allyn & Bacon.

Viadero, D. 1999. "A Direct Challenge." *Education Week* 18(27): 41–3.

————. 2001. "Getting Serious About High School." *Education Week* (30): 1, 18, 20, 22.

Vygotsky, L. S. 1978. *Mind in Society: The Development of Higher Psychological Expectations.* Cambridge, MA: Harvard University Press.

Walberg, H. 1995. "Productive Teaching." Pp. 41–55 in A. C. Ornstein (ed.), *Teaching: Theory into Practice.* Boston: Allyn & Bacon.

Weaver, W. T., and G. M. Prince. 1990. "Synectics: Its Potential for Education." *Phi Delta Kappan* 71(5): 378–388.

Weigel, R. H., P. L. Wiser, and S. W. Cook. 1975. "Impact of Cooperative Learning Experiences on Cross-Ethnic Relations and Attitudes." *Journal of Social Issues* 31(1): 219–245.

Weinstein, C. E., A. C. Schulte, and E. C. Cascallar. 1983. *The Learning and Study Strategies Inventory (LASSI): Initial Design and Development.* Manuscript, University of Texas, Austin.

Wenden, A., and J. Rubin. 1987. *Learner Strategies in Language Learning.* Englewood Cliffs, NJ: Prentice-Hall.

Wenglinsky, H. 2000. *How Teaching Matters: Bringing the Classroom Back into Discussions of Teacher Quality.* Princeton, NJ: Educational Testing Service.

Whimbey, A. 1977. "Teaching Sequential Thought: The Cognitive Skills Approach." *Phi Delta Kappan* 58: 255–259.

Whittington, D. 1991. "What Have 17-Year-Olds Known in the Past?" *American Educational Research Journal* 28(4): 759–780.

Wiederhold, C., and S. Kagan. 1992. "Cooperative Questioning and Critical Thinking." P. 203 in N. Davidson and T. Worsham (eds.), *Enhancing Thinking Through Cooperative Learning.* New York: Teacher's College Press.

Wiggins, G. 1989. "The Futility of Trying to Teach Everything of Importance." *Educational Leadership* 47(3): 44–59.

————, **and J. McTighte.** 2000. *Understanding by Design.* Washington DC: Association of Supervision and Curriculum Development.

Witkin, H. A., C. A. Moore, D. R. Goodenough, and P. W. Cox. 1977. "Field-Dependent and Field-Independent Cognitive Style and Their Educational Implications." *Review of Educational Research* 47: 1–64.

Witkin, H. A., R. B. Dyk, H. F. Faterson, D. R. Goodenough, and S. A. Karp. 1962. *Psychological Differentiation.* New York: Wiley.

Wlodkowski, R. J., and J. H. Jaynes. 1990. *Eager to Learn.* San Francisco: Jossey-Bass.

Wlodkowski, R. J., and M. B. Ginsberg. 1995. "A Framework for Culturally Responsive Teaching." *Educational Leadership* 53(1): 17–21.

Wolf, K. 1991. "The Schoolteacher's Portfolio: Issues in Design, Implementation, and Evaluation." *Phi Delta Kappan* 73: 129–136.

————, **and M. Dietz.** 1998, Winter. "Teaching Portfolios: Purposes and Possibilities." *Teacher Education Quarterly*: 9–21.

Wolf, P., and P. Robbins. 1989. *Opening Doors: An Introduction to Peer Coaching* [videocassette]. Alexandria, VA: Association for Supervision and Curriculum Development.

World Geography. 1993. Morristown, NJ: Silver Burdett Ginn.

Worthley, K. M. 1987. *Learning Style Factor of Field Dependence/Independence and Refugee Students.* Master's Thesis, University of Wisconsin, Stout (July).

Wright, E. L. 1981. "Fifteen Simple Discrepant Events that Teach Science Principles and Concepts." *School Science and Mathematics* 81: 575–580.

————, **and G. Govindarajan.** 1992. "Stirring the Biology Teaching Pot with Discrepant Events." *American Biology Teacher* 54(4) (April): 205–210.

Yoshiwara, F. M. 1983. "Shattering Myths: Japanese American Educational Issues." P. 23 in D. T. Nakanishi and M. Hirano-Nakanishi (eds.), *Education of Asian and Pacific Americans: Historical Perspectives and Prescriptions for the Future.* Phoenix, AZ: Oryx.

Young, V. H. 1970. "Family and Childhood in a Southern Negro Community." *American Anthropologist* 72: 269–288.

————. 1974. "A Black American Socialization Pattern." *American Ethnologist* 1: 405–413.

Yu, A., and B. Bain. 1985. *Language, Social Class and Cognitive Style: A Comparative Study of Unilingual and Bilingual Education in Hong Kong and Alberta.* Hong Kong: Hong Kong Teachers' Association.

Zehr, M. A. 2000. "Un Dia Nuevo for Schools." *Education Week* 20(10): 43–45.

Zelderman, H., G. Comber, and N. Maistrellis. 1992. "The Touchstones Project: Learning to Think Cooperatively." Pp. 138–150 in N. Davidson and T. Worsham (eds.), *Enhancing Thinking Through Cooperative Learning.* New York: Teachers' College Press.

Index

attributes, essential/nonessential, 114–115
attribute value, 115
audiotaping, 399
auditory learning styles, 373
authority, 378
automaticity, 283

B

Ball, Harriet, 233, 242–243
Banks, James, 187
barriers to learning, 380
behavior dispositions, 377–383, 383–389
beliefs/assumptions
    about learning, 374, 380
    being clear about, 410
    hierarchy of control, 378
    inclusive, 383–389
    noninclusive, 377–383
    old versus new, 11
Bennett, William, 266
blacks, achievement gap between whites and,
    21–22
block scheduling, 218
bodily-kinesthetic skills, 36
Bogardus, Emory Stephen, 50
Botstein, Leon, 378
brainstorming chart, 205
Brighton High School, 396–397
buzz groups, 349

C

case studies
    concept attainment, 111–113
    concept formation, 177–179
    cooperative learning, 303–305
    direct instruction, 268–270
    inquiry, 142–146
    mnemonics, 234–237
    single-mother families, 2–3
    synectics, 204–206
    See also sample lessons
categories of instructional models
    combining, 321–323
    reasoning skills, 76–77
    relating skills, 78
    remembering skills, 77–78
    reorganizing skills, 77
category, expanding the, 184
Census Bureau reports, 15–16
Center for Education Policy, 217
challenges to educational reform, 20–23
change, requirement for, 410
characterization by value or value complex, 96–97
child-rearing practices, 48
choosing a teaching approach, 192, 411–412
clarity of explanations, 279
class building, 314, 322

classrooms
    Art of Classroom Inquiry, The: A Handbook for
        Teacher Researchers (Hubbard and Power), 402
    observation methods, 399
    student- versus teacher-centered, 294
    See also applications of models to diverse class-
        rooms; prevalent issues in diverse classrooms
Clinical Cycle of Support peer coach, 397
closure phase
    concept attainment, 120, 130
    concept formation, 184–186, 194
    and formulating a hypothesis, 152–154, 165
Coach as Expert, 396–398
Coach as Mirror, 396
coaching roles, 394–400
coding, 399
cognition, meaning of, 33
cognitive domains of learning, 33
    analysis, 90–91
    application, 90
    comprehension, 89–90
    English literature example, 92
    evaluation, 91–93
    knowledge, 89
    synthesis, 91
cognitive objectives, 87–88
cognitive outcomes, 307
cognitive styles
    Asian American, 52
    cultural group classification by, 58
    differences in, 35
    gender differences in, 55–56
    of Hispanic Americans, 48–49
    of Native Americans, 39–43
    use of students' by teacher, 193
    See also learning/learning styles
cognitive taxonomy, 89
combining teaching models, 321–323
communication building, 322
community builders, teachers as
    noninclusive and inclusive behavior dispositions,
        377–383
    respect for students, 375
    summaries of functions of, 376
community volunteers/aides, 388–389
comparative organizers, 278
competition, 9, 49, 300
comprehension domain, 89–90
compressed conflict, 214, 220
computer-based drill and practice programs, 295–296,
    297
concept attainment, 76–77
    applications to diverse classrooms, 125–127
    case study, 111–113
    creating presentations, 136–137
    evaluation criteria, 129–130
    instructional variations, 121–125

O

objectives, 84–88
objects, characteristics of, 113
observation, 157, 159, 395, 399
oral discussion, 344
  applications to diverse classrooms, 356–358
  barriers to effective, 367–368
  evaluation criteria, 360–361
  instructional variations, 351–353
  introduction, 339–340
  lesson development suggestions, 364–365
  modes of, 43
  prevalent issues in diverse classrooms, 358–360
  sample lessons, 353–356, 361–364
  skills, 78
  skills for, 78
  technology enhancement, 365–367
  theoretical perspective, 343–345
order of performance of ethnic groups, 187
organizational structure, 310–312, 328
organization process, 96
organizers, sequential/comparative, 278

P

paradigms, 11, 24
parental involvement, 24
participation, 127, 160–161
  dealing with differential, 358–360
  fostering, 348–350
pedagogy, 387
peer coaching, 394–400
pegword strategy, 239–240, 245–246
people-oriented pictures/statues, 128–129
perceptual modalities, 34–35
performance
  of ethnic groups, 52, 187
  objectives, 84–88, 277–278
performance evaluation. See evaluation criteria
personal analogy, 210–211, 213–214, 217–218, 219–220
personalization of education, 216
personal relationships, 47, 50–51
personal synthesis, 351
person-orientation versus thing-orientation, 45
planning conference for peer coaching, 398
planning phase of action research, 405
planning step of portfolio development, 405–406
Plato, 174
populations
  Census Bureau reports, 15–16
  racial/ethnic distribution, 38–43
  states ranked by, 7, 8, 9
  See also statistics
portfolios, teacher, 404–408
positives of cooperative learning, 308
power, 378

practice
  computer-based drill and practice programs, 295–296
  guided, 280–281, 289
  independent, 283–284, 289
preconditions for oral discussion, 343–344
predicting alternatives, 158
presenting a discrepant event, 170–172
presenting new material, 136–137, 276–280, 289
prevalent issues in diverse classrooms
  concept attainment, 127–129
  concept formation, 191–193
  cooperative learning, 325–328
  direct instruction, 286–288
  inquiry, 160–164
  mnemonics, 250–253
  oral discussion, 358–360
  synectics, 217–218
private learning, 41
problem-solving, 352, 387
process feedback, 282
professional development, peer coaching, 394–400
proficiency exams, 108
Project Follow Through, 297–298
providing data, 154–157
psychological orientation of African Americans, 43–44
psychomotor domain, 33, 97
psychomotor objectives, 88
purpose (goals), 80

Q

questioning and data gathering, 151–152, 164–165
questioning strategies of teachers, 190–191
question matrix, 188
questions
  asked by students, 160
  asking, 157
  for assessment of student understanding, 280–281
  self-directed, for teachers, 79
  types of discussion, 346, 347–348
  See also inquiry

R

rationale for instructional reform. See educational/instructional reform
reasoning skills, 76–77
recall, 248, 255
receiving domain, 95
recitation, versus oral discussion, 340, 343
record data chart sample, 153
recursiveness, 279
reflecting phase of action research, 403
reflecting step of portfolio development, 407
refocusing, topic, 212, 214–215
reform. See educational/instructional reform
relating skills, 77–78
relational orientation to learning, 43

relationships, emphasis on, 56
relevancy, 285–286
remembering skills, 77–78. *See also* mnemonics
Renaissance Man (film), 380
reorganizing skills, 77
research, action, 400–404
research/studies
    African American learners, 43–47
    Asian American learners, 51–54
    comparisons of cultures, 60
    cooperative learning, 309
    direct instruction, 270–273
    on diversity, 76
    gender, 54–57
    Hispanic American learners, 47–51
    immigrant populations, 5
    impact of teachers, 13
    Native American learners, 38–43
    oral discussion, 344
    overview of, 36–38
    overview of review of literature, 36–38
    parental involvement, 24
    psychological orientation of African Americans, 43–44
    reviews of literature, 389
    on success of mnemonics, 263–264
    summary of findings, 57–58
    teacher interactions with male and female students, 54–55
    teaching-learning process, 11–12
    thinking skills, 147
    use of mnemonics, 238
    use of people-oriented pictures/statues, 128–129
    verbal interaction, 53
    See also statistics
responding, 95
retention, improved, 264
review of related literature. *See* research/studies
review process, 276, 288
Rhodes, Linda, 396
roles of teachers, 374, 375–389. *See also* teachers
"role" tasks, 312
Roman, Tracy, 134–135, 197
Rose, Mike, 62
Rosenshine, Barak, 266–267

Ⓢ

sample lessons
    concept attainment model, 130–135
    cooperative learning, 329–333
    direct instruction, 289–294
    inquiry, 166–169
    mnemonics, 255–258
    oral discussion, 361–364
    synectics, 221–225
    See also case studies
samples. *See* examples

Scholastic Achievement Test (SAT), 13, 14
schools
    competitive structure of, 305–306
    culture of, 215–216
    populations, 4
    progressive/traditional, 25–27
    restructuring of, 323–324
    schedules, 10, 100, 218
    systematic improvement of, 392–393
    three-tiered system of U.S., 382–383
school workforce, characteristics of, 62–63
scripted model of direct instruction, 270
scripting, 398–399
Sea Horse Fable, 81
selected cooperative groupings, 314
selected structures, 322
self-leadership, 390–392
sequential organizers, 278
servant leadership, 409
Simonides, 237
Situational Self-Leadership Theory, 390–392
Six-Level Approach for discussion, 347
Skidmore, Charles, 397–398
skillbuilder, Alligator River, 338
skill development, visual-spatial, 52
skills
    analytical, 53
    cooperative learning, 78
    critical thinking, 75
    Gardner's multiple intelligences, 36, 43
    global processing, 40
    oral discussion, 78
    reasoning, 76–77
    relating, 78
    remembering, 77–78
    reorganizing, 77
    thinking, 88, 124, 147
small-group synthesis, 351
Smith, Roy, 302
Socrates, 78, 146–147, 174, 339
Socratic seminars, 352–353
software
    graphic organizer, 198–199
    for presentations, 171
    programs for creating presentations, 136
spatial skills, 36
statistics
    achievement gap between blacks and whites, 21
    African Americans, 6
    Asian Americans, 8
    capacity of students to become technology-literate, 22
    changing "face" of America, 20
    children at risk, 2–3
    Hispanic Americans, 8
    Native Americans, 6
    performance levels of Asian American students, 52